THE
ENGLISH
ROCK-GARDEN

THE
ENGLISH
ROCK-GARDEN

REGINALD FARRER

Volume I

THOMAS NELSON AND SONS LTD
LONDON EDINBURGH PARIS MELBOURNE
TORONTO AND NEW YORK

THOMAS NELSON AND SONS LTD
Parkside Works Edinburgh 9
36 Park Street London W1
312 Flinders Street Melbourne C1
218 Grand Parade Centre   Cape Town

THOMAS NELSON AND SONS (CANADA) LTD
91–93 Wellington Street West   Toronto 1

THOMAS NELSON AND SONS
19 East 47th Street New York 17

SOCIÉTÉ FRANÇAISE D'EDITIONS NELSON
25 rue Henri Barbusse Paris V^e

First published June 1919
Reprinted 1922, 1925, 1928, 1930, 1938, 1948
1955

LIST OF PLATES

viii   LIST OF PLATES

FOREWORD

THIS book was written in 1913, and corrected for press at Lanchou-fu, Kansu, China, during the winter of 1914. The exigencies of war have delayed its appearance ever since, and also even now prohibit such perpetual re-settings of its type as would be necessary to bring it completely abreast of the most recent discoveries and diagnoses. And I particularly regret that the delay in its appearance has outlasted the life of Mr. R. Hooper Pearson, to whom it owes its inception. He died on June 11, 1918, and I wish here to put on record my own special expression of grief and gratitude to one who was always a good friend to me, and, in particular, shouldered the chief burden and labour of producing this book, which, alas! he has not lived to see completed.

R. F.

November 1, 1918.

INTRODUCTION

PROCLAMATIONS of purpose are often confessions of failure to achieve it. At the same time, so vast a tome as this cannot be allowed to burst upon the world unheralded by some sort of excuse for its vastness. It owes its existence then, first of all, to my own craving for guidance across the uncharted seas of catalogues. We are all rock-gardeners nowadays, and the more we grow, the more we desire to grow, and the more we want to know about the plants we are offered, no less than about the plants we possess. That this necessity for novelty may be fed we are deluged daily with successions of the most seductive catalogues, which draw the last penny from our purses with their promises. But these catalogues, by the very conditions of their being, are succinct advertisements, rather than helpful guides. Their purpose is not so much to assist as to allure : they cannot, for considerations of space, be produced upon a scale that will make them valuable documents for the cultivator. Another fault they have, to which I will return later. So what are we to do, when we are offered Heeria or Weldenia at high prices, with the brief annotation that they are pink or white in the flower as the case may be ? It is very easy to answer, " Abstain " : what gardener worthy of his garden can bear to follow a counsel so craven ? So we buy—we " plunge " courageously upon a plant of whose requirements, habits, and hardiness we are left entirely ignorant ; for the great authorities of the past are silent in the present, and the *English Flower Garden* has long been crying for an *English Rock Garden*, to supplement the errors and partialities which afflict the occasional alpines that have to take their chance in its pages among the vast mass of general herbaceous " stuff " with which it deals. And the smaller, more modern, and more special works (such as those of which I myself have been guilty) have never yet been allowed by their publishers to be on a scale competent to embrace even a tithe of the species about which information is desired. Some races, indeed, are worse offenders than others : with distraught eye one peruses long lists of Potentillas and Violas which are so many strings of naked names, without the least guidance as to which are good or bad, tall or short. But even in more distinguished races so many are our gaps of knowledge that the average ambitious gardener is either held helpless by his ignorance, or forced to become a gambler. Our possessions are vastly in excess of our information about them, in fact ; and all earnest cultivators who want to go on adding to their collections, are in urgent need of some authoritative and descriptive handbook to their hopes.

Such, at least, has been my own cry for many seasons, whenever I have taken up a seed-list, teeming with names of possible treasures unknown and undescribed. On many a specious name have I speculated, only to be rewarded with a worthless weed. And my call for help is never answered : true it is that M. Correvon has lately produced a work which claims to be just such a descriptive list. But unfortunately he has embedded this in so sumptuous a mass of old matter, in the way of republished chapters, that the description of each plant has had to be compressed into a sort of algebraical formula, which even when deciphered proves to yield a picture hardly less jejune than those offered by catalogues. Add to this that the list is far from adequate or selective, that the descriptions are often doubtful, and that M. Correvon is too famous a professor to have any slavish respect for others ; it will be seen that our prayers for help have not been answered. Accordingly at last, and for my own edification, I girt up my loins, and made the great plunge. Headlong I dived into the deep ocean of original authority ; through seas of crabbed Latin did I swim, in search of true descriptions, or suggestions of pleasant and possible plants ; Boissier became my bedfellow, and the Sargasso Seas of Ledebour emitted me at their end, barely living. In short, I ransacked all the big authorities, old and new, who have dealt with temperate and mountainous countries; and, as a result of my fishing in these deep waters, I have now come to land with a huge cargo of authentic information.

For yet another difficulty besieges the enthusiast. Even if a beautiful plant be fully described and sold to him under one name, how is he to be sure that it has a right to bear it, how is he to be sure that next year the same plant will not again be sold to him at a still higher price, and under a still stranger name? There is one way, and one way only, to resolve these doubts; and that is, to go to the original authority. But, in the first place, these learned tomes do not lie ready to the zealot's hand, but rest in the dim and dusty gloom of museum shelves; and, in the second, *experto crede*, when he has given up the time and the trouble, and has made himself a nuisance to the ever-courteous officials, this is a type of what he finds, either in polysyllabic German, or else in a cranky compilation of huge Latin epithets: that so-and-so is an acaulescent herb of circinate vernation with the leaves imparipinnatipartite or uncinate-lyrate with mucronate-crenulate lobules, setulose-papillose, decurrent, pedunculate, and persistent. After this he goes home to Robinson or Correvon—and little blame! It cannot be expected that the amateur, however keen his zeal to know his plants, is going to subjugate himself to such wearisome jargon of the professional. Yet only by this gate can the kingdom of knowledge be entered: all priests and all professionals, of every sort and time, have always fortified their gate with such frills and *chevaux-de-frises* of hideous forbiddingness. What is this?—" a peripteral Hexastyle with a pronaos and a posticum"; what but the Hephaisteion at Athens, rendered in the correct language of the architect. Of all sciences, indeed, botany has the worst name for this kind of cant, and the words " botanical description " arouse shivers in the boldest.

This, however, need not be so, once we have realised that the jargon employed really does mean something, and is, in fact, nothing more than a method of shorthand arranged to tell the initiated in quite a few words, what could otherwise only be conveyed to the profane in a great many. For instance, the fanciful description given above becomes perfectly simple and a good deal longer, when we are to imagine the plant to be " stemless with the undecaying leaves uncurling from the centre, set with bristly little warts, and cut into an uneven row of featherings, with the lobes pointed and scalloped round the edge, some having a backward, barbed, spear-headed effect, standing on footstalks down along which they continue in little wing-like flaps on either side." Therefore it seemed to me, in wading through these sloughs of uncouth epithets, that in all cases open to doubt, they ought to be translated into legible English, for the benefit of such as do really desire to know their plants, if this can be achieved without unreasonable trouble, or painful pursuit of erudition; for there is no reason why such details, if clearly and simply conveyed, should not only be helpful, but even readable and illuminating.

At the same time, in the course of my researches, I came upon the startling fact that botanists are no less sensible than other people, and as a rule are not prone to manufacture gratuitous difficulties. In other words, that nearly all species are so clear and valid that, in nine cases out of ten, it is not necessary to differentiate a plant, for the benefit of the uninstructed enthusiast, by its complete and formal description; but that, almost invariably, every species has some one or two unalterable peculiarities, leaping to the eye, or easily to be noted; and thus can immediately be recognised by any gardener to whom these peculiarities have been briefly and plainly pointed out. A very obvious instance is the punched-out hole at the base of the corolla-lobes of *Campanula excisa :* a more subtle one, the unvaryingly straight-sided calyx-segments of *Gentiana vulgaris*. This last, indeed, is more germane to my point: If cluttered up in a crowd of details, the gardener might be at a loss to diagnose this gentian : given this one, peculiar, and essential point, he confirms it at a glance, and is sure of his plant. Therefore throughout this book it has been my aim to pursue each species to its original authority, there to assimilate its description, and then, for the guidance of other enthusiasts, to boil down the diagnosis into its two or three essential and unvarying points, omitting the general cloud of symptoms in favour of the salient points, and trying to express these in the most definite and salient manner. So that, from the brief pictures that follow, cultivators may, with a minimum of trouble, be able to ascertain quite clearly, whether they have really acquired the true proprietor of the name that figures on their bill.

On the question of description much care has been spent, not only that it may be lucid, but also peptonised and easily to be assimilated. With regard to the matter of names, still more care and research are necessary. Let me point out, in the first place, to all who are inclined to throw up their hands over the vagaries of horticultural nomenclature, that the problem is far simpler than we imagine, or than catalogues allow us to believe. The specific name of a plant depends entirely on its oldest authoritative description. Find this, and you have arrived at the *ne plus ultra ;* the original name given by the first describer is the one and only name under which the plant must stand for evermore. For an instance, the name *Campanula alpestris* was imposed by Allioni on his lovely Campanula some years before Villars substituted the honorific *C. Allionii ;* therefore the plant is, only and always, *C. alpestris.* Similarly with many other species : *e.g.* the original Primulas, *hirsuta* and *viscosa* of Allioni, *Cypripedium Reginae* (*C. spectabile* of gardens), and *Campanula Bellardii* (*C. pusilla,* Haenke). Such substitutions are apt to seem tiresome and gratuitous at first to the gardener, *i.e.* very profitable to the catalogue ; yet, once the fountain-head has been reached, the matter is settled once and for all, with no possibility of appeal or further change. This book has aimed at getting back to the genuine original specific name for every species, so that these may never again appear disguised as novelties in the same list that also contains their more common superseded name. On this matter research is final ; *Primula viscosa,* All., 1785, rests on bedrock, and is for ever an unchangeable *monumentum aere perennius :*

so far as in me lies and the power of study can avail, I have done my best to ascertain these ultimate names, once and for all, and put them into the hands of all such as desire correctness and the avoidance of expensive delusions. In many of the more critical cases, indeed, the valid authority is quoted; in some, also the date at which the prevalent specific was imposed. Nor have I been at less pains to cope with synonymy : it is a very common thing in catalogues to find two or three names quoted, that all cover one species. Even such compilations as M. Correvon's are not innocent of this fault; and much care and research are accordingly necessary here, among the recognised authorities, to achieve a helpful guide as to what is a true species, what a variety, and what a mere discarded synonym.

In the matter of genera, however, the case is different. No botanist has it in his power to alter an authorised specific name : all botanists of repute have a perfect right to redistribute races at their pleasure. And this is a vagary with which it is impossible finally to cope. Silene, for instance, is now, by modern botanical fashion, made to hand over *S. Elizabethae* into the house of Melandryum, and *S. Pumilio* into that of Saponaria. All that such a book as this (or any other) can do, is to suggest the tendency of recent botany, so that the innocent may not some day be seduced by some catalogue's flaming proclamation, as a " novelty," of *Melandryum Elizabethae* or *Saponaria Pumilio.* The earnest, however, must always keep on guard, for new races are still being carved out of old, or submerged. Paoli and Fioretti, for instance, sink Oxytropis into Astragalus ; while when it comes to American botany, the brain reels before the minute and subtle class-distinctions into which patriotic pride has now mangled Aster and Oenothera. This book, like panting Time, has toiled after these eager botanists,—but not wholly, I shall hope, in vain ; for, though I have usually not recognised these transatlantic minutiae, the names of such new-made families are quoted in their place, so that the anxious inquirer after Wyomingia or Lavauxia will find, on reference, that his quest brings him to nothing newer than Aster and Oenothera. More than this cannot be done; the finality attainable in specific names is impossible in generic.

With regard to " common " names, my views are not obscure. It is perfectly absurd to pretend that there can be a common English name for Alpine species that are neither English nor common. Indeed, even if they were natives of England, it by no means follows that they would have English names, for we are not an observant race: we do not, like the Spaniards, have a distinct vernacular for our chief plants; and, when even so illustrious a native as *Gentiana verna* has no label of its own in our language, it is an idle affectation to devise one for others. Unfortunately there once arose in the past a vivid personality who had a craze for such illegitimate furbelows; and the glamour of Mr. Ruskin's fame has dazzled some of the simpler-minded whom eloquence convinces, into adopting a belief that every word he wrote was dictated verbally by an angel. This is not so. Mr. Ruskin was a man of fervid and sonorous genius; he was also a man perpetually swept by various enthusiasms of ever-increasing intensity. One of his many manias, then, was this coining of " common " names for plants that could never possess them; like all such efforts to produce an effect which is only attainable by natural evolution, the results have always an affected and pretentious air, which ultimately proves their undoing. No such artificialities can linger long in a living language, and Mr. Ruskin's Wardour Street conceits have long since perished out of our speech (if indeed they ever had a place there), and survive only on the pens of an occasional veteran, or at the heads of columns in catalogues, which then go on to speak of the plant in question by its accepted Englished name. We may well be thankful: what could possibly be easier or more beautiful than " Campanula " ? What affectation more gratuitous and silly than " Bell-flower " ? The craze reached its wildest height, however, in the unnecessary attempt to replace the simple, apt, and balanced syllables of " Saxifrage " (a good English name into the bargain!) by the regrettable brummagem mediaevalism of " Rockfoil." Such has been the work of these name-coiners; they have given no help with really difficult Latin names like Boeninghausenia, where a well-sounding English synonym might have been useful; their whole effort has been to displace good established names by strivings after a sham bric-a-brac simplicity. No more then, of such nonsense; in ninety cases out of a hundred the proper botanical names are easy and beautiful and relevant (I have often indicated the more salient meanings); in any case there are no others. And therefore I use none; though gladly recognising as I go, all those apt or beautiful old names such as Columbine or Celandine, that have been slowly coined in a nation's love, and not excogitated arduously in a library by the enthusiasm of erudition. So much for this point; my feelings upon it will also be found breaking cover again in the prefaces to Saxifraga and Soldanella.

The discretion of an author or compiler is not untrammelled. In the pursuit of final correctness over specific names I have spared no trouble to myself and no inconvenience or upset to my readers; since the right specific name, once acquired, is acquired for ever. But in dealing with races, such discretion (or indiscretion) as I may here and there have employed has been wholly in the direction of ease and convenience and simplicity. A book of this description, destined for general use, is bound to keep count indeed of botanical developments, but is not by any means bound to follow them with cumbersome fidelity. Accordingly it has seemed to me that gardeners would prefer to keep the families undivided; and I have accordingly so left them, as far as might be, quoting Heliosperma and Jovellana in their places indeed, but including their species in the original families of Silene and Calceolaria. Any attributions that I may myself have dared, will be found in due course (as, for instance, where, for the sake of convenience, I have established a definite horticultural line of cleavage between Edraianthus and Wahlenbergia). In the matter of specific names I have but very rarely allowed myself (to my knowledge) to wander from orthodox roads. I have retained the old name and rank of *Phyteuma comosum*, and have shrunk from degrading *Eritrichium nanum* into *E. tergloviense*; but suggest instead that *E. nanum* should stand as the covering-name for a very large aggregate, of which *E. tergloviense*, like *E. Chamissonis* and the rest, is but a local development. It may, however, be taken as sure that, so far as it goes, this book does mark a real and arduous stage in the progress towards correctness of name, without which our widening gardens will become ever more and more a welter of confusion. If I were to quote all the authorities I have ravaged, the volume would swell appreciably in length. Ledebour gives the foundations of knowledge for Russia and Siberia; Boissier (*Flora orientalis*) and Halaczy unveil many a treasure of the Levant; Cheeseman deals with New Zealand; Asa Gray, Nelson, and others with the various ranges of North America; the Alpine ranges of Europe need no bush, Dalla Torre, Hegi and Dunziger, Fiori and Paoletti, Bonnier, each contributing stores of knowledge (and most especially L. Marret's wonderful new series of *Icones plantarum alpinum*, with its series of photographs for each species, and full map of its distribution); Hooker affords us a remote de-spairing glimpse across the wealth of Himachal; Couttinho on Portugal, Briquet on Corsica give the very latest news; while Willkomm for Spain offers a firm foundation of knowledge. Vast gaps are still left, of course. Hope writes great notes of inter-rogation and exclamation down all the long line of the Andes, and inner China is falling uncharted into our fingers; and Tasmania confronts us with a list of possibilities that are little more than names. None the less this book has dredged the greater part of all hopeful lands, and in certain groups has been able to come to very close grips. Delphinium offers a choice of the best in Huth's monograph. By the light of Jakovatz I have tried to decipher the Acaulis group of Gentian. Phlox, Geranium, Erodium, and Polemonium represent the last words of the *Pflanzenreich*: more important still, Primula gives an even more recent recension of this vast and brilliant race, while Saxifraga, thanks to Professor Balfour's unpublished notes, holds out a number of clues in the cloudier sections of the family; to say nothing of the priceless help afforded me in Crocus and hardy Cactus, by the Crocus-king, E. A. Bowles himself.

Very soon, however, in the task of discovering truth, I came upon the knowledge that the treasures we possess are but a tithe of those that we may some day come to have. And, since catalogues each year are helping us to fill these voids, it became obvious that such a book as this, to have more than ephemeral value, must run ahead of collectors, and give authoritative notes, not only on all species that are grown, but also on all such as ought to be. In other words, I set myself to peruse my authorities, not only with a view to dealing fairly by the plants we know, but also to anticipating many catalogues as yet unborn, by discovering, through a veil of cumbrous Latin, any promise of beauty in species that we do not possess. So that in future, when confronted with the offer of a beautiful unknown, collectors may be able to refer to this volume, there to ascertain whether indeed it be beautiful or no. That such a guide is complete, or ever can be, I should, of course, be the last to claim: at the same time it cannot but be that this book will be able to make accessible a large amount of information on plants and matter hitherto unknown or buried in learned works of difficult attainment and digestion. But if you were to compile a full list of all plants possible for the rock-garden, whether good or bad, no library would hold the number of volumes to which such a work would run. Therefore (seeing that I have already exceeded the space allotted me by exactly the same amount again) my work has had to be severely selective, and my own personal taste must be held responsible for many omissions; while yet others will have been due to oversight, or to the inability of a botanical diagnosis to give any fair notion of the beauty belonging to the plant it frigidly describes.

Some authorities, indeed, are far more helpful than others: Boissier's Latin, for instance, never fails to give a picture and convey a thrill, while Ledebour's descriptions of his species are so arid and colourless that no idea can be conjured up of the species they classify. Yet when all is said and allowed for, I hope that the following pages will be found a really trustworthy guide, within their limits, not only as regards the plants we do grow, but also to those we may reasonably want to grow. Where beauties have been omitted, they will usually be found to be secondary to other and more pre-eminent beauties in the same style; where uglinesses are briefly selected for commination, it will be because, above other uglinesses, they abound in catalogues, and have the unmerited praise of the professional. In other words, if a recognised species be not quoted in these pages, I may safely promise the prospective purchaser that he will be doing most prudently if he keeps his purse-strings tight against it, unless it come before him at last with a sufficient letter of credit, in the form of a really trustworthy description.

The rigid eclecticism, however, into which this book has been forced, for fear of becoming yet vaster than it is, has endeavoured to follow certain lines of purpose, with more or less consistency, and with due allowance made for the personal predilections that in such a choice are bound to have their play. The field I have had to cover embraces not only the rock-garden, but its adjuncts, the wild garden and the bog, to say nothing of the fact that certain shrubs are especially apt for the rockwork, and cannot wholly be passed over. At the same time, if such outliers of the mountains were here to be dealt with in detail as full as the true children of the hills, not two volumes would be required, but ten. Accordingly I have been much put to it to deal compendiously and justly, yet not with excessive favouritism, by the many vague families that hover on the edge of the herbaceous border or the rubbish heap. Nor have I seen a need to deal exhaustively with yet more important races, when these have already been fully and accurately treated in cheap and easily accessible handbooks, consecrated by their own special experts to their own special claims. Accordingly, I have skated light-foot over the ocean of Iris and Lily, recommending Mr. Dykes and Mr. Groves for fully qualified pilots. In dimmer families of larger plants, I have run quickly through such races as Senecio and Spiraea, to keep the reader enlightened but not detained, while on members better qualified for the rock-garden by their size, I have paused for an ampler moment of expatiation. But it is on this debatable border-land that the question of selection has been most difficult, and the result may perhaps be found most doubtful. For, while cultivators will easily come to a rough general agreement on matters of beauty, the problem of size and admissibility will be settled differently by each gardener, according to the size of his garden. Speaking generally, my own rule has been to concentrate most of my attention on plants that do not exceed six or nine inches, and to deal more cursorily with larger subjects. To this vague rule various exceptions will be found; but I have tried to keep in the centre of my eye the needs of the rock-garden proper, rather than that of its less-exclusive fringes; and this intention, for instance, has been my chief guide in selecting from among the beauties of such large and difficult families as Pentstemon, Salvia, Digitalis, and Verbascum, that usually tend more towards the herbaceous border than the rock-garden, so far as their stature is concerned. Various omissions and brevities may thus be accounted for; while yet others may be attributed to the fact that such plants are already dealt with adequately and copiously by catalogues. Against these there is no need to compete, and readers need not be troubled with long disquisitions on Squills, when these are fully treated by every bulb-list. As for such things as Snowdrops, catalogues here again offer the best forms; the rest are differentiated by such minute frecklings as to make their deciphering rather the delight of the expert, than any matter of moment to the general gardener.

With regard to the matter of arrangement, I have usually followed a strictly alphabetical order. In certain races, however, certain very definite groups are formed, into which the species more conveniently fall. Here, accordingly, I have followed the distribution, arranging the species sometimes alphabetically in their classes (as in Draba), and sometimes botanically, as in the overcrowded race of Sempervivum; in which the members are far too subtly differentiated for each to be described at length, unless at a paralysing cost of space. Here, then, it is very much easier to have all the hairy-leaved species compendiously grouped, and then all the glabrous ones; a glance through the rapid list will at once deviate the inconvenience of the apparently disordered arrangement. For larger and more specifically important families, however, such a system would be intolerably annoying to the reader ; all the greatest races follow their due alphabetical sequence. With some of the smaller ones, however, such as Tulipa and the New Zealand Veronicas, I have taken the species in their botanical order. For this reason : that a botanically-arranged family is all in a "concatenation according," like following like, and leading on through a divergency to the next marked difference in shape or habit. So that instead of saying "*Veronica salicornioeides* differs from *V. lycopodioeides* in such and such a detail," thus necessitating either an exhaustive restatement by the writer, or a tedious cross-reference by the reader, one has the two species as links in a continuous chain, close together, and thus rapidly differentiated as members of a group, leading on from another towards the next in a clear and ordered sequence. I have tried, too, here and there, to give indications of pronunciation, in the case of the more difficult names, though I see no reason to insult my readers with suggestions as to how they shall say Geum, Gentiana, and such-like. At the same time there is nowadays really no reason why Gladiŏlus, Gladiōlus, Saxifrāga, Pentstĕmon, Androsācē, and Erĭca" should still be allowed to stand up, like dark islets of ignorance, above the pervasive widening flood of modern education. To make matters yet easier, I have invariably preserved the Greek "ei" diphthong, instead of letting it sink into "i" after the quite incomprehensible fashion of botanical spelling, which is the true "fautrix and nourrisse" (like Anne Boleyn of heresy) of such ghastly cacophonies as Erĭca for Ereica, Eye-zōōn for Aeizōön, and Eye-zoydes for Aeizoeides. Surely if they see Ereica written, and Aeizōön, even the least experienced gardeners will easily learn to say Ereica and Aeizōön. It is just as simple to say a word right as to say it wrong, nor can I see any reason why catalogues and books of botany should not, for the future, help to propagate correctness by restoring the Greek diphthong in "ei" to its proper spelling, so that no one ever again will have any excuse for pronouncing it as if it were merely a short Latin "ĭ."

But in time, yet another strand of purpose came by degrees to be woven into the fabric of this compilation, for it gradually became my wish as I went, to give (as far as I could) brief, salient, and easily recognisable pictures of the more entangled Alpines of the European ranges, — species of which enthusiastic amateurs are always falling foul, and vainly referring to the information of handbooks which are either inadequate, or else clothe their matter in such heavy fustian of technicalities that the inquirer goes away again disgusted and unenlightened, clogged with a crowd of details, instead of illuminated by one or two essential ones. Accordingly I have dealt drastically with such races as Phyteuma and Aronicum, so that the collector on the Alps may, as I hope, be able, with a glance or two, to know for certain what particular species he has found. Guidance, for instance, is especially needed among the " acaulis " Gentians ; such guidance I have tried perspicuously to give, in the hope that those who want to know, yet are saddened into indifference by a " rudis indigestaque moles " of botanical instruction and terminology, may not find it beyond their power to give the one glance which will clearly enable them at once to differentiate their species, by noting whether the calyx segments be straight-sided and the leaves pointed or blunt. In other words, embedded in the bulk of this book may be found a useful flora of the Alps, at least in so far as beautiful and interesting Alpine species are in question (for I have not troubled my readers with the identification of weeds or dullards, such as none but the botanical enthusiast will be concerned to decipher). More than this, I hope that my selection of treasures may help to keep open the eyes of those who wander yet further afield, pointing the feet of the traveller in Greece or Spain or the Levant to everything of special merit that there occurs, and enabling him to recognise the beautiful identity of *Convolvulus nitidus, Saxifraga erythrantha, Dianthus biflorus,* or *Macrotomia Cephalotes,* whenever and wherever in his travels he may have the luck or the skill to happen on them.

These, then, are the objects of this book : to help gardeners doubly by giving them information, from bed-rock, not only on all that they do grow, but on all that they may in future be offered (or ought, in any case, to long for, search out and demand) ; and also to help and inflame the traveller with true short pictures of what treasures he may expect, no less than with simple directions by which he may know them. Much may have been omitted, and much done amiss; the best that in me lay has been done, and I can no more. Nor must it be thought that this book, written as a guide and guard against catalogues, considers these with an unfriendly eye. On the contrary, to all true gardeners a new catalogue is more precious than a prayer-book; from cover to cover they are filled with kindly and seducing magic, making the rough ways plain and hard plants easy, and filling our gardens to overflowing with a thousand rich colours of hope unknown before. Yet against their seductions, their too-easy promises, their multiplication of names, the cultivator needs protection. There is, indeed, a sense in which " le catalogue, c'est l'ennemi." And therefore in these pages it will not be taken as implying any ingratitude or unfriendliness towards those luscious compilations, if I speak always as a determined critic of their protestations, plausibilities, and sweet pretences.

THE ROCK-GARDEN

It is the custom, in books of this nature, to pad the volume out with a vast amount of prefatory matter, mainly repetitive, in which the author's personal views (one's friends call them this, one's enemies, " fads ") may be fully aired, and thereby the meat of the matter, in the centre of the tome, be unduly compressed. This work of mine, however, is already, in all conscience, large enough, without being further encumbered by long disquisitions and prefaces. Nor will my personal views (or fads) be found lacking in the pages that follow; though I have indulged no undue passion for expansion, my own taste, experiences, and vagaries will be found fully set forth throughout the body of the book, in a series of personal verdicts which I hope may arouse the compliment of wrath from many a fellow-zealot who here sees his best-beloved plant dismissed as " magenta." For the shed blood of disagreeing enthusiasts is the seed of the garden, and the hostilities of gardeners seem only equalled in righteous acrimony by those of Patriarchs and Popes, Anglican Bishops, and other persons of profession presumably holy. It has been my endeavour, all through the book indeed, to preserve the vivid and personal note, at any cost to the arid grey gravity usually considered necessary to the dignity of a dictionary; not only that so the work may perhaps be found more readable and pleasant, but also that other gardeners, finding their best-beloveds, maybe, here slighted or condemned, may be able to mitigate their wrath by constant contemplation of the fact that such opinions are but the *obiter dicta* of a warm-blooded fellow-mortal, not the weighed everlasting pronouncements of some pompous and Olympian lexicographer, veiled in an awful impersonality that admits of no appeal.

Nor is there any need, again, to expatiate here on rock plants and their culture. Golden words of my own upon both these points may be purchased for sums varying from 1*s*. 6*d*. to 7*s*. 6*d*.; other people have also contributed nobly; books are both frequent and inexpensive. Why then should one go on saying at length what has already been soundly and copiously said before? Said before, indeed, so often that by this time surely one may reasonably believe that all who feel the need of this book will have so far progressed in knowledge as no longer to need the information that plants have roots, and rocks a proper system of arrangement? However, for the sake of completeness, I am informed that the good old tale must, in a measure, be told anew, and that the salubrious powder of the book itself will not prove palatable unless with a preliminary dose of jam, in the way of instructive introductions, and a foreword of information. Notoriously incapable as I am, therefore, of gauging public opinion on such matters (I have never, for my own part, been able to read the preliminary chapters of the *English Flower Garden*, which bulk so large in the volume; and have, indeed, always wished them away from that admirable book, so that one might come more immediately to the " osses," cutting the cackle), I bow my head in obedience, and submit to my editor, with the resolve none the less firmly rooted in my heart, that the oft-repeated words I now have to say shall be said so sharply, pungently, and vividly, that none shall fail to gain a prompt and clear idea of what must needs be done ; nor be suffered to wander lost in a wilderness of wise words and vague prescriptions and prefatory prettinesses.

In the first place, the site of the rock-garden must be open.

It must not be overhung by trees or bushes of any sort.

It must not be near trees or big bushes of any sort.

If there are unavoidable neighbours, a deep trench must be made between them and the rock-garden, all their roots must there be cut off, and a deep hedge of upright flagstones be sunk underground to prevent their intruding anew. Even so, the work will have to be done afresh in some five years' time.

The rock-garden should not be near a wall, a border, a formal path, a house; or within sight of any such regular and artificial construction. This, of course, is only a counsel of perfection.

The way of building a rock-garden is as follows, these being its prime necessities, no matter what its shape or scheme.

Having chosen an open aspect and conceived your plan, you must invariably excavate the soil to a foot or fifteen inches below ground level. You must then fill up this excavation with rough coarse curs, clinkers, and coke-blocks for drainage. This is the alpha and omega of success; it was never understood in the past, when we compiled our heaps of any impervious old rubbish, and then were surprised because our choice Alpines, in prepared " pockets " pecked in the mass, proved miserable and sullen. From that day dates the bad reputation of many a beautiful plant, which has now become happy and free and easy, since we have discovered that the vital secret of success in rock-gardening is to build the whole fabric soundly, on proper principles, with good soil and perfect drainage, from the very base.

Over the drainage layer (the level or slope of this will accord of course with your plan) lay a stratum of reversed turf to keep the upper soil from filtering away into the basement.

Now comes your soil : this must be a mixture both light and rich. Unmixed crude loam from field or garden should never be used in its raw state, but should be lightened, at all events, with about half its own weight of coarse sand ; if poor, enriched with a third of its own weight of sifted leaf-mould. Manure, too, is invaluable, but it *must* be old (spent stuff from a hotbed is most useful) and it must be very finely pulverised. It should only be employed, too, in the proportion of an eighth or tenth to the whole composition. Peat must be used with care, it has a sad tendency to cake and consolidate, whereas the ideal rock-garden mixture should be at once nutritious, light, and spongy, not clogging in winter rains, nor yawning under summer suns, but always cool and friable and loose in the hand, like the consistency of a rich and perfect seed-cake, crumbling yet unctuous to the touch. For this end sand is the great standby, and should be employed with freedom in every mixture, being especially necessary, and in specially large doses, wherever peat is to be employed. Whatever the mixture, it should thoroughly be dug together, compounded, and blended ; then it should be lightened by caraway seeds to taste, in the form of a liberal admixture of chips, either limestone, sandstone, or granitic. These should be about the size of the top-joint of any and all your fingers, and may be employed in different proportions to your pleasure, according as you desire merely to lighten your soil, with a sixth or tenth part of chips, or to approximate it to moraine by using an equal bulk of stones or even more. Here each garden and each taste will dictate its own composition, and each gardener will adventure for himself in the boundless land of experiment. But the general depth of soil should not be less than $2\frac{1}{2}$ feet, and need not be more than $3\frac{1}{2}$, while the central core of the mound, or foundation of the slope (no less than their base), must never be of hard and impermeable loam or dumped rubbish, but always of very coarse and perfectly open drainage rubble.

Good mixtures, generally speaking, are as follows :

$\frac{1}{2}$ loam, $\frac{1}{4}$ leaf-mould, $\frac{1}{4}$ coarse sand—an excellent compound for the common run of alpines. (Lime to taste.)

$\frac{1}{4}$ loam, $\frac{1}{4}$ old mortar-rubble, $\frac{1}{4}$ leaf-mould, $\frac{1}{4}$ sand. A mixture of at least equal merit, pre-eminent where specially calcicole plants are in question.

$\frac{1}{4}$ shredded peat, $\frac{1}{4}$ leaf-mould, $\frac{1}{2}$ coarse sand. This, with sandstone, is very useful for species of the high non-calcareous alpines, as Loiseleuria, *Trifolium alpinum*, and Meconopsis.

$\frac{1}{3}$ leaf-mould, $\frac{2}{3}$ very coarse Red Hill (or grocer's) sand makes a most luscious spongy compound, in which even *Gentiana verna* cannot help growing a foot wide in three months.

$\frac{3}{4}$ sand, $\frac{1}{4}$ blended peat and leaf-mould is a yet finer, choicer, and more exiguous mixture for very special treasures. (Lime to taste.)

$\frac{2}{3}$ ordinary good loam, $\frac{1}{3}$ blended leaf-mould and powdered old manure, makes (if sufficiently light without the addition of sand) a very good general compound for the rock-garden. (Lime to taste.)

And, of course, the changes can be indefinitely rung on all these, and more, too, according to the wish and experience of the cultivator, and his knowledge of his climate.

We now have the foundation excavated, the drainage laid in and covered, the soil mixtures prepared in special heaps at the path-side, ready to go in.

Follows the choice of stone for building. In most cases, people take the goods the gods provide them. But all artificial " stone," by whatever name described, is invariably and absolutely to be refused. Far better a rock-garden without a single rock than ill-furnished acres of Portland cement blocks or sham stalactites.

All derelict artificial rubbish, burrs, clinkers, odds and ends of Norman arches, conglomerated bricks, and such like, must be refused with equal sternness.

All granite, flint, slate, porphyry, syenite or calliard is only to be used as a resource of despair. These rocks are lifeless, arid, and unprofitable, innutritious in substance, hard and hostile of texture and outline, unfriendly to beauty, whether of conformation or plant life. They are only capable of producing chaotic gaunt piles from which a few species peer fitfully.

INTRODUCTION.

Sandstone, if not too friable, is good, but bald ; retentive of moisture and not sterile. Its bare lines, however, make it an unsympathetic building medium where better can be had.

Whinstone and millstone have the porosity of typical sandstone, with the same fault of obstinate brutality of line. They never adapt themselves to the plant or their builder, never cease, even after years of weathering, to seem crude and raw and artificial. Each block keeps a cold and barbarous isolation of its own, no matter how copiously clothed in plants ; and perpetually refuses to join hands with its neighbour in a dignified and immemorial-looking scheme. For the triumphant achievement of such a scheme, however, the rock-gardener will always and only seek for limestone.

All limestone, except the most friable and crumbling (such as some Oolites), is unparalleled in value for rock-work. By far the best of its forms, though, is the wonderful weather-worn rock of the Craven Highlands (N. Wales, Derbyshire, Westmoreland also), which has so singular a beauty, alike of colour and outline, that a rock-garden so built is well furnished in itself already, though never a plant has yet been inserted. (An instance of perfect beauty in this medium will be fresh in the minds of all those who saw Mr. Wood's exhibits at the London Shows in 1912 and 1913 —true works of art that they were, among innumerable compilations of nurserymen.) Further, it forms naturally into flutings and ribbings, bays and inlets, " moutonnements " and ripples of primeval effect, enhancing with lights and shadows the tender grey-whiteness of the stone itself, in texture soft and tender to the plants it nourishes so well, yet leonine and stark in its moulded forms, which have the rare gift of so obvious a solidarity, that block fits to block like the sections of a jigsaw puzzle, so that the merest child at work with these could hardly help compiling, without thought or effort, a rock-work that shall really look all of a piece, the creation not of man, but of the untrammelled forces of the world at work since the hills first were.

Thus our ground is dug, our soils prepared, our rock chosen.

INTRODUCTION.

Now comes the building :

Use as little rock as possible.

Better, by far, are ten large blocks than a hundred small ones.

Bury what you do use as deeply as possible in the ground.

Be sure that your stone lies always on its broadest face.

Be sure that every stone is absolutely and finally firm in its place.

Aim always at a flattened and not a spiculous effect.

No rock should overhang another.

All rock should slope deeply down into the bank behind it to convey moisture to and from the roots.

With regard to rock-garden design, learned and lovely chapters beyond end have been written, and will continue to be written.

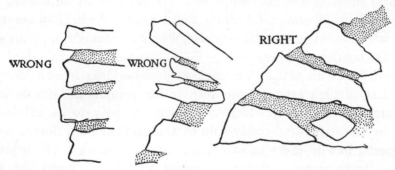

Diagram 1.

I have contributed my own abundant word to the question, and here I will only repeat that there ought to be deliberate beauty about the building itself, quite apart from the plants. When the compilation is finished it ought to look established, harmonious, and of a piece, long before a single tuft has been put in. The rock-garden ought to consist primarily for the plants, but not solely. In the old days it existed merely to show as many expensive spikes as possible, and the plants were quite a secondary consideration. Nowadays we swing towards the other extreme ; and think (and rightly) so much of our plants, that the intrinsic beauty of rocks in well-schemed arrangement often tends to be ignored. It is from a study of garden art in China and Japan that we can best recall ourselves to the lovely possibilities of rock-work in itself; and then proceed, upon this realisation, to graft our own zeal and knowledge in the cultivation of plants. Proportion, unity, restraint, are most especially to be studied. See that your rock-work, whether bank or mound or gorge, is not disjointed in effect, but so ordered that each rock looks as if it belonged to the next, and had been its bed-fellow since the foundations of the hills were laid. See that an effect of linked and unforced naturalness is achieved; see that there is no sense of ostentation or strenuous artificial violence, and above all, see that from every aspect the planes, cliffs, and slopes of your compilation give you a feeling of calm, of real inevitability and balance. Within these rules all schemes are good, and every creator must create his own. It is far better that he should do this for himself, and make errors, and learn by them, than commit the whole building to some one else, who will merely run up an expensive soulless fabric on conventional commercial lines. (Unless, indeed, he be an artist; for rock-garden building is one of the subtlest of high arts, all the subtler for seeming so simple and natural in its results, which in reality are only to be attained, not by the rough-and-ready rule of thumb that its unforced look suggests, but on those most delicate and deep-sought of all laws, that always prove to govern anything in art that looks like anarchy.) The task of learning is easy—all the important rules have been given; by contemplating garden after garden in their light, the would-be builder will soon learn the secret of that serene and placidly harmonious look that marks the well-built rock-garden, quite apart from the plants that adorn it. To talk of imitating nature, as so many vainly do, is to encourage a rank and empty delusion. To make a thing look " natural " is by no means to imitate nature. Nature often looks more artificial than the worst forms of artificial art; nature in the mountains is often chaotic, bald, dreary, and hideous in the highest degree. By making a rock-garden look natural, then, we merely mean that it must have a firm and effortless harmony of hill or vale, cliff or slope. Conventionally " natural " effects are best unaimed at—rock-gardening, like all great arts, is not imitative, but selective and adaptive. Vast congeries of rounded boulders are "natural," but neither beautiful nor helpful in the rock-garden; lowering kopjes of up-ended spikes and obelisks, ragged, vast, and gaunt, are frequent in the granitic ranges, but in the rock-garden are presumptuous, violent, and disproportionate in effect; unless the composition be on the very vastest scale, and then pyramids of chaos can close some deep and huge ravine. Even so, a mountain of stratified limestone would better suit the harmony of the whole. Of another fault beware: do not let your garden, large or small, ever lose its look of connectedness and harmony as it grows. Too many zealous and beautiful compilations have I seen that spoil themselves by adding hummock to hummock, or long potato-ridge to potato-ridge, appended each to each with no regard to harmony or unity, till the whole effect is that of a disconnected and haphazard collection of pudding-like palaeolithic barrows, or ill-conceived ramparts. Additions should always be made with a most careful eye to what has gone before. The scheme and site of the garden should always be so chosen as to admit of extensions that shall immediately fall into union with the original design, instead of hanging on to it irrelevantly like ill-judged appendages, and revealing themselves for the additions that they are.

No more advice can be given on design. Each site dictates its own, and each owner's taste must do the rest. Let but the foregoing suggestions be pondered, and, whatever the result may be, whether mountain, mound, gorge, or bank or valley, it will not prove an amorphous or disconnected huddle of stones, nor an unpropitious pyramid of spikes.

So comes the actual building, which must be firm and solid as it goes, proceeding upward from the base, burying stone by stone immovably in its place, and, as the building grows, watching from each point in turn to see that every stone you add falls inevitably into its place in the scheme, joins hands with its neighbours, and helps with all its forces in the work of harmony.

Be sure the work is firm and solid.

Be sure that the soil is firmly rammed into every crevice and hollow behind the rocks. Cavities full of air are death to roots, accumulate damp, and make homes for mice.

A very important luxury comes in at this point, if the builder can contrive or afford it. This is the underground water-pipe. All alpines respond (if their drainage is perfect) in the most marvellous way to underground waters, which remind them of the percolating snows far down in the soaked mountains into which their pertinacious toes are plunged. Not only are their roots thus kept cool and happy, but the prevalent moisture transpires through the surface soil and forms an aureole of coolness round the plants, protecting them against the arid furies of the sun. Overhead watering, on the other hand, though better than nothing, is not nearly so popular among plants in general, and even less so than usual among alpines. Therefore no pains should be spared in securing an adequate supply of water underground. A pipe should be connected with a standing water-cock, and run through the top of the mound or bank, about twelve inches down in the ground; it should then have *minute* perforations made in it alternately, on either side, at intervals of six or nine inches. The soil should then be filled in, the compilation stocked with its plants, and the water turned on. If possible, it may run steadily from April to the end of September, after which it should be turned off till the end of the following April. If, however, this full flow cannot be achieved, at least the stream should run for two half-days in the week, or one whole day. Even this, of course, is an unattainable counsel of perfection to many an earnest soul; these, however, still have it in their power to secure the underground moisture that their treasures desire. Let them sink large flower-pots along the top of their bank or mound (or drain-pipes driven straight down), and then, at intervals, fill these up with water, which will thus permeate the depths and please the plants. Smaller pots may even be sunk, behind and above special rarities, such as the Arctic Andromedas or *Androsace alpina;* and the pit shafts thus formed may easily be masked by ferns or stones.

So much, then, for the main mass of the rock-garden.

INTRODUCTION.

THE MORAINE

This is no more than an extreme extension of the chip principle, and though it bears the name, has no relation to the barren moraines of the glaciers, but rather to the upmost shingle-slopes in the highest folds of the mountains, where the loveliest and choicest of all their flowers are gathered in the fine loose slides of stone, moistened beneath by the rivers of the melting snow. And, in cultivation, the " Moraine " has often proved the answer to problems long unsolved in the management of the more difficult alpines, hitherto sadly indocile and intractable in ordinary conditions. In the moraine they flourish brightly and perennially as bay-trees, while their brilliant colours are enhanced by the lovely groundwork of soft grit shingle upon which they shine. There are very few plants to which moraine comes amiss—each garden makes a different experience of success for itself. But as the moraine spells such salvation and glory for the most difficult and glorious of plants, for these it should primarily be reserved.

It is very simply made. Let the ground—for preference in some slope between two rocks, to have a natural, shingle-slide effect—be excavated to some three feet of depth. Then let drainage rubble be laid down as before—with reversed turves atop. The remaining two feet (with a perforated water-pipe, if possible, running about twelve inches below the surface) are now to be filled up with a mixture exceeding in stoniness anything used for the banks of the rock-garden. A usual proportion is $\frac{1}{6}$ of soil ($\frac{1}{2}$ leaf-mould, $\frac{1}{2}$ sand) to $\frac{5}{6}$ of fine chips, in size from that of the thumb-nail to that of the little finger. The proportion may be varied : $\frac{1}{4}$ of soil to $\frac{3}{4}$ of chips makes a richer compound, and $\frac{1}{2}$ soil, $\frac{1}{2}$ chips results in a yet more comfortable and certain success everywhere. The chips, too, can be indefinitely varied : there may be a limestone moraine, with mortar rubble mixed, to taste, in the composition ; a granite moraine, from which all lime is excluded ; sandstone, silurian, and many another form. Other soils will, of course, be also tried : blends of peat, of leaf-mould, of loam and silver-sand, and so forth; each moraine may be divided into lockers for a different compound, for a different set of plants. The range of experiment is infinite, and such, in each, is almost invariable and triumphant. Chips and soil, then, should be thoroughly dug together, and shovelled into the excavation till all is rather over-full (stepping-stones should be sunk deep from the beginning, or even cemented on piles). Copious watering (rather than treading) will now make the mixture settle; down sinks the soil, and the surface becomes a beautiful clean sheet of shingle, on which *next day* you will write the beauty of a thousand plants. No mystery attaches to the planting of these. Brutal as it may seem, they must be riven from their pots, their roots shaken free of the encumbering earth, and then spraddled out pitilessly among the harsh stones in a scraped hole, filled in again with shingle. Water them in soundly from overhead, and they will at once take hold and prosper marvellously.

Overhead watering goes farther on the moraine than anywhere else, the chips refusing to evaporate it, while giving it also the quickest of drainage.

But underground water is better. There is no limit to the possibilities of a well-made moraine, watered from beneath. If no water can be obtained, the moraine should avoid too steep a " rake " and too torrid an aspect. The moraine should be disposed, when possible, near eye-level, as many of its loveliest treasures are of low stature, and if on the level, necessitate that a man should go upon his belly like the serpent when he wishes properly to observe them.

Hard and dice-like stones, such as flint or marble, should be as sedulously avoided in the moraine as everywhere else, roughness of surface being essential alike to pervasive moisture and the due nourishment of roots. I once saw a moraine, made by two faithful zealots, which consisted entirely of small marble squares, without the slightest admixture of soil whatever. It speaks volumes for the efficacy of the general system that even here its plants were tentatively surviving.

Some makers of moraines advocate a cemented trough or

bed to hold the whole. There is no doubt that brilliant results are thus obtained (especially in climates where damp is more desiderated than drainage); but then no less brilliant ones are obtained without it, so why go to the expense of so unnecessary and elaborate a luxury? At the same time there may be thirsty climates and gardens, or defective water supplies, where it may be thought advisable to retain such moisture as flows through. For their benefit, then, I append a description and diagram of the cement-bound moraine, while at the same time preferring to advise all such as are allowed, by their convictions and their climate, to abstain from such unnecessary expense.

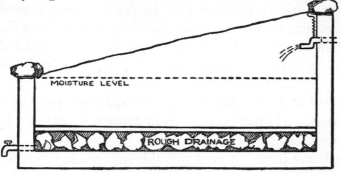

MOISTURE LEVEL

ROUGH DRAINAGE

Diagram 2.

The cement should be some six inches thick. At the bottom of the lowest barrier must be a drain to let off the moisture. Over the cement floor must be a foot of rough drainage, with reversed turves in a floor over this to keep the shingle from sifting down.

The ordinary moraine may be imagined from this diagram, by omitting the cement walls and floor.

Special Beds.—These are fully suggested in the general preface to Gentiana (*q.v.*). Their composition, of course, may be endlessly varied to suit different orders of plants. Their general principles remain the same. Experiments in all directions lie ready to the hand of growing experience. In hot, dry places a special mixture of very poor and pebbly gravel with about one-fifth of leaf-mould will prove invaluable for drought-loving Southerners, which in damper climates and richer soils are apt to prove rank and impermanent.

The Bog-Garden needs only the good underlying drainage of all other beds, filled with a stodgy, fat, and heavy mixture of loam, leaf-mould, manure, sand, and peat. More and meatier manure may well be used here, as the intention is to produce a compound of extreme and luscious richness. Through this water must incessantly percolate. Different climates have different needs, and in damp ones a cement bottom or trough for the bog-garden is not only unnecessary but even dangerous, as here the object is to ensure the quickest of drainage. In hot counties and countries, however, moisture may be precious or evanescent; and then the bog, no less than the moraine, may be contained in a cemented trough, so long as there be an ample outlet drain at the bottom of its lower end, as well as a thoroughly sufficient bed of drainage-rubble between soil and cement. Different mixtures of soil will of course be arranged for different parts of the bog at pleasure, and different degrees of humidity achieved by slopes and depressions.

The Water-Garden is an invaluable adjunct to the rock-garden, if the outlines of the pool can be so schemed as to make it look harmonious and inevitable there. The cultivation of its inmates is of the simplest; they either will not thrive at all, or else, in ninety-nine cases out of a hundred, thrive you out of house and home. First of all, the lines of the pool and stream should be mapped out; they must be neither straight nor gratuitously wobbly, but as far as the eye and taste of the designer can achieve, should represent the real thrust and flux of naturally flowing water into bay and inlet. A nurseryman's usual idea of a pond is a thing shaped like a kidney-bean, or a figure of eight. But cape should answer to bay, not to brother cape, and bay must answer headland. At the same time the strictest economy should be observed in such flourishes, lest the outline of the pool become artificially undulating and diverse, like the soul of man. One good point should be made, and emphasised once for all, in a headland with a beautiful out-standing boulder; but good points never bear repetition, and the finer the dominant feature, the quieter should be the lines of the rest.

The ground for the pool should now be dug out for some $4\frac{1}{2}$ to 5 feet, and the basin lined with a thoroughly well-founded coating of cement some six or seven inches thick. No lesser measures are of any avail, and always, in the long run, cost more to make good and set right than would have been the original cost of the job if done properly from the beginning. (This is an invariable and inexorable law in all gardening.) The depth allowed should be graded from some 4 to $4\frac{1}{2}$ feet at one end, for the larger and more stalwart-growing Nymphæas, to $2\frac{1}{2}$ and less at the other

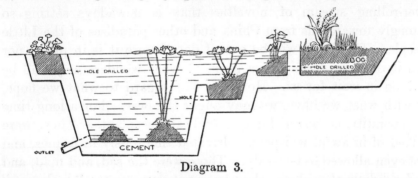

Diagram 3.

for smaller ones, and such delights as *Richardia africana*. It is a very good idea, too, to arrange a series of secondary overflow-shallows, shoaling off into mere bog, for daintier and less aquatic subjects. Indeed, it should always be arranged that there be a second trough all round the pond, to serve as a marsh-border, of varying widths, and quickly obliterate the pool's thick and uncomely lips of cement. And finally, as the pool will require cleaning and weeding at least once in every two years, a drain should always be arranged at the bottom, by which the water may be let off.

With regard to the soil and the planting;—in a small pool it is probably best to plant the main water-lilies on widely separated hillocks of very stiff and rich soil, composed of blended clay, heavy loam, leaf-mould, and manure. This should be well-blended, and compacted into a neat dumpling. Then the fat white roots should be splayed out in the spongy mass and covered over. Turn on the water now, and fill the pool; no matter how small may be the inserted fragments of your expensive Nymphaeas, and how great the apparently hopeless depth of water covering them, the summer will not be old before they have reached the surface and expanded a few glowing crowns, in earnest of the abundance which they will thenceforth never fail to produce through all succeeding seasons.

Its Plants.—Our plants, unlike patronage, come to us from the South, East, and West, as well as the North. There is no limit to their beauty and variety, nor any keeping abreast with the ever-rolling stream of novelties that is nowadays setting so strongly towards us from China and other paradises of the Little People. This book will be out of date before it is in proof, nor can it do more than give a guess at what wonders may still be lurking in wait for us. However, with regard to what we hope, as with what we have, we may augur the best. For a long time a superstitious terror hung round alpine plants. They were talked of in awful whispers, cultivated timorously in frames, and not even allowed to be hardy. Those were the sad, and mad, and bad old days of pockets, which were not even sweet; " rockeries " were clayey mounds, or dogs' graves, or almond puddings of spikes, or rooteries, or dank depressions in the woodland. The plants invariably died; and alpines, like orchids, acquired a name for difficulty and danger that neither race deserves. These clouds, however, have long since rolled away, and now, granted the absolute essentials of a free soil, perfect drainage, and an open aspect, the enormous majority of mountain plants prove more satisfactory in our hands, more promptly and abundantly repaying, than any other class of garden delights; for now we cultivate our species, we no longer " cover our rockeries." Now we study the nature, character, temper, and digestion of each plant, as if we recognised in it, indeed, a near relation. Erudite physicians gather in conclave over this or that valetudinarian, and excogitate

INTRODUCTION.

treatments and compare notes on diet, and bicker over the merits of their respective diagnoses. Very sound work is now being done in studying the chemistry of soils, and the precise conditions of moisture and nutrition. We are no longer empirical; scientific experiments are made in even the sacred corpus—by no means " vile "—of *Campanula alpestris ;* and at least one brilliantly successful cultivator achieved his gardening by going round with a barrowful of medicine bottles, administering to each difficult plant in turn a teaspoonful three times a day of its own especial dose ; while yet another, in a series of back yards, led all the highest alpines by the nose, with a succession of scientifically compounded and drifted rubbish-heaps.

Such high flights are not as yet within reach of the beginner. But there is no doubt that along these lines the triumphs of the future lie. Our successes will no longer be haphazard, at the end of a long line of failures, but will be assured and certain from the beginning, on a basis of sound knowledge. For instance, the long-vexed question of lime-loving versus lime-hating plants has caused as much ink to flow as any holy dogma of Christendom. Nature confronts us with endless and suggestive inconsistencies ; there are species absolutely faithful to the limestone, such as *Phyteuma comosum,* others indifferent, as the Flannel Flower (Edelweiss) ; many are constant to the granite in nature, abhorring limestone, yet in the average garden seem careless on the point ; while yet other granite-lovers appear irreconcilable to lime in cultivation. But now we know the complete answer to the riddle : all plants of every sort require lime, to a greater or less degree. The gardener's quest is to discover what dose of lime is helpful, and what harmful, to each particular species. This quest, again, is further complicated by the clear fact that each garden has an effect of its own upon the plant's disposition in the matter, and that the degree of tolerance engendered by different cultural conditions depends upon deep laws to which science is only beginning to dig down. All naturally lime-loving plants give no trouble ; they can hardly have too much of their native element, yet sometimes (as *Saxifraga cochlearis*) seem to contain, like Mrs. Elton, such abundant resources in themselves as to be indifferent whether there be much or little lime in their soil. On either hand, then, they are safe. With confessed or apparent lime-haters, however, the problems offered are very nice. *Campanula alpestris* is their type; yet even this species, so apparently calcifuge in nature, accepts a certain amount of lime in the garden. The amount tolerated, indeed, is infinitesimal, but seems to be increasing as the plant develops a new cultural constitution; while varying conditions in varying gardens will certainly cause the tolerated amount to vary, in accordance with hygrographic and other laws as yet unmapped. At the same time, many are the naturally calcifuge species, which in the changed circumstances of the garden are quite indifferent as to whether there be lime—and abundant lime too—in their soil; and, indeed, it is only the most difficult even of granitic plants that give the cultivator any trouble in the matter. Hints of this capacity for tolerance, in altered ways of life, may readily be found in nature; typical, and notoriously inexorable lime-haters on the Alps are Eritrichium and *Primula hirsuta*, yet Eritrichium certainly seems to have a lime-loving form, while *Primula hirsuta*, though frail and pinched in habit, may be seen (in sites significantly more saxatile than usual), wedged fast into the white limestone cliffs of the Grigna. Variations in the other direction are, I think, much rarer: plants that have the habit of lime seem to develop a more incurable craving. Yet even in nature I have once (and only once) seen a non-calcicole tuft (very pale and sickly) of the universally calcareous *Potentilla nitida*, on the dark granitic rocks of Torsoleto, while in cultivation the plant seems easily pleased with itself, no matter what its soil. Therefore, if one says such and such a species is never found on lime or on granite, one must use " never " most carefully, in Mary Crawford's sense of " hardly ever." A rule is none the less valid, however, for having its rare exceptions; and cultivators will take no harm by following nature's indications as far as lime-hating plants are concerned. The taming of such to lime, and the ascertaining how much of it in each garden each may bear, offers many problems of the very greatest interest, but of little immediate concern to the average cultivator. Such plants as *Primula viscosa* or *Saponaria pumilio* it will always be easiest to treat, at least at first, as irreconcilable or unreconciled lime-haters; while others, such as Flannel Flower, are amphibious, and yet others (the large majority), like *Potentilla nitida*, *Phyteuma comosum*, and *Primula Allionii*, may safely be regarded as positively longing for almost any amount of lime, even if, in the garden, they sometimes appear to be doing without it.

These points are dealt with in the following pages as occasion offers, or knowledge and experience afford. With absolute rules for success in cultivation no book can claim to deal, the gift of prophecy having perished from among us. We can only give, repeat, reiterate, insist upon, the great fundamental laws of light, rich soil, *perfect* drainage, and open situation. The degree of success after this depends on the climatic conditions, the soil conditions, the care of the cultivator, and last, but by no means least, the idiosyncrasy of each plant. This last point is far too little recognised as a dominant factor in joy. As in a family of babies or kittens, one or two are usually unexplicably pre-eminent in size and strength, so in a family of seedlings there will be found exceptions in amplitude and force of development, showing already characteristics of vigour which will persist through life, and make them, in maturity, the easy delight of their owner; while his neighbour, in a similar soil and garden, is wrestling miserably with the sad changelings that have resulted from the inferior children of the batch. For this intervention of mere chance there is no remedy; but just as I urge on all cultivators the advisability of always choosing and collecting their plants in flower, so as to secure the forms that best please them, so, in doing this, let me further press them to look out for broadness of leaf. Not only is this usually a symptom of fine form, but it is also a pretty certain indication of a robust idiosyncrasy as well. This being said and allowed for, the rest depends on cultivation and experiment. The plant must be inducted properly into its place.   (The best months are March and April, when it awakes, or August and early September (if well watered), when the roots for next year can push forth at once and take hold of the warm, sun-ripened soil before the winter.)   It must not be packed or poked into a case-hardened hole in the ground, but be delicately placed in well-broken earth, planted well down to its neck, with its roots not wadded or condensed, but spread abroad distinctly, so that each may start on a journey of its own.   Then more broken soil must be poured on them, the hole filled up, the soil pressed down firmly and tightly round the plant, but not violently.   Then the level must be made flat with more soil, and the work is done. After this it only remains to top-dress the plant thoroughly in spring, with a mixture of $\frac{1}{3}$ leaf-mould to $\frac{2}{3}$ of very coarse grit and sand, to make good the denudations of the winter rains; first being sure to press it back firmly into the soil, from which the frosts have probably lifted it.   This top-dressing is, indeed, a most valuable help to triumph, representing in the garden the silt of detritus left by molten snows and snow-torrents in the alpine spring, which often bury the plants almost wholly from sight, and always cause them to rejoice with doubled vigour.

But in coping with alpine vegetation (all that follows applies much more feebly to lowland plants, and hardly at all to those of the bog) the essential point, when site and drainage and soil are safe, is that of moisture.   The conditions of plant-life, indeed, between 5 to 10,000 feet are so peculiar in this matter that, setting aside all differences of altitude, it remains a miracle that the children of the high hills should be, generically, so strangely easy and vigorous in cultivation.   For some six months of the year, more or less, they lie beneath a bed of snow, perfectly dry and warm and comfortable in an unchanging temperature, not wholly dormant indeed, but in a state of almost suspended animation; to this period of complete rest succeeds a brief and crowded hour of glorious life.   Soldanella makes her flower-buds beneath the snow-field, and generates warmth (they say) to melt a passage at last up into the daylight.   Thus life on the hills begins to pulse about the end of May; by mid-June the alps are open and all the hills are a sponge of moisture, through which the melting snowfields up above are percolating rapidly away towards the swelling rivers in the valleys far beneath. At once the flowers leap to life, in a serried riot of splendour, springing from the unbound earth, now uniformly cool and damp, transpiring eagerly in the crystalline rays of the alpine sun. So, as the summer proceeds, continues the procession of loveliness; by July and August the lower alps are drier, and vegetation, having achieved its end, is coming gradually to a pause, reposing on its laurels. But now at last awake the highest crests and shingles, the last of the winter's impermanent snow weeps itself away from the stone-banks and ledges, full noontide is come for *Ranunculus glacialis*, and Eritrichium mocks the heaven in its dark precipice. Here, as below a month or two before, a state of acute but violently drained humidity is set up; yet the high alpines have no such period of comparative drought as follows through July and August on the always well-watered alp below, for in September the snows once more begin to descend, and by October the crags are held firm once more in the unchanging bondage of the frost. Through that short space, however, the high alpines have made the most of their freedom: as the plants of the alp exceed those of the plains and woodlands in brilliancy, so are they themselves in turn outshone by the population of the upmost rocks, where the conditions are so strenuous and yet propitious, that there the plants lose thought of growth, and concentrate all their energies on getting as much size and glow as possible, as rapidly as possible, into their compacted clumps of almost stemless flowers. They are well nourished in their gaunt crests and shingles with rich grit and decayed vegetable matter of their own dead selves for twenty thousand years; they are well watered all through their growing period, not only by the melting snow, but also by frequent alpine rains and the transpirations of the soil that wrap them in a crystal halo, intensifying and clarifying and filtering the glories of the alpine sun, which here descends through the thin diamond air with an intensity unknown below, engendering a correspondingly increased intensity of colour in the flowers that it so encourages, elicits, and ripens. The high alpines have to face a keener competition for insect favour, too, than prevails in the bee- and butterfly-crowded Alps beneath; fewer are the winged visitors of the upper shingles, each plant has to cry shrilly against its rivals " come here, come here "; colour is their call, and so their whole surrounding chain of circumstances combines to press them into brilliance and inspire them; scent is but rarely used, though some of the highest Crucifers and Valerians excel in it, and even Eritrichium has a little haunting honeyed breath of its own.

Consider, then, the change to conditions of cultivation in our gardens. Different parts of the country vary in the matter of humidity, but, for a general rule, the English winter is one long succession of clogging damps, while the English summer, even when hot and bright, is apt to be arid and choking with thirst. But thirst is a state unknown to the children of the hills, and even more abhorrent and strange to them are our long, wet, open winters, dank and corrupting. Many of them, too, in their high clear places, have developed a fine coat of fur to garner all the damps of the air in the summer sunlight of the Alps, secured as they are against excess of moisture while they sleep, by the complete dryness and uniform temperature of the packed pure coverlid of snow beneath which they sit at rest in the unrelaxing grasp of the alpine winter. But in our lachrymose midnight of the season they are alternately rained upon and snowed upon, tugged out of the ground, soaked and sodden again, till the downy cushion becomes a dead sponge of decay, and the bare straggled roots across the sloughy ground have nothing but a rotten corpse to sustain. From all this preface as to their habits, then, springs one absolute and vital rule in the cultivation of mountain plants :

No well-drained alpine can easily be kept too damp in summer; no alpine can ever possibly be kept too dry in winter.

The devising of means towards these ends is the test of the cultivator's zeal and ingenuity. At the same time it must be understood that though this rule is general and absolute, it is only stringent in the case of the most difficult and downy high alpines, such as Eritrichium and the Aretian Androsaces. To these a special quarter might be assigned in a special cliff, and the whole covered in winter with a light from a frame. Panes of glass poised singly over each specimen have their use, but they do not keep out the contagious wet from the soaked surrounding soil, nor is there any precaution that can prevent the whole air from being charged with humidity to an extent unbearable by the fluffy cushion.

The problem of moisture has already been dealt with, that of aspect remains, and depends upon it closely. No *alpine* plant is a genuine lover of shade, and in gardens where the water-supply is sufficient they may all safely be trusted in the most sunny positions. If, however, the water-supply be poor or precarious and the climate especially torrid, then the more delicate and capricious of the higher alpines may profitably be given a site under the lee of some large rock, or on some ledge where the sun falls only for half the day. The danger from sunshine, however, is not really urgent, unless the soil be hard and bad, or the climate of an Arabian aridity; given good drainage, and light rich open ground, almost every alpine plant prefers an open and exposed position, with all the light and air it can get. In much hotter and drier countries than our own, success is attained by despising drainage and mixing a liberal proportion of Sphagnum-moss in the soil, as to make it a moisture-holding sponge. To English conditions, however, this method is quite unsuited, and inevitably proves fatal to its victims—as has, indeed, been pointed out by M. Correvon, the discoverer of this medium, who has had such triumphs by its means in the blazing heats of Geneva, where the winters are of a correspondingly ice-bound intensity. Nor must any word of such well-favoured cultivators ever induce an English gardener to underrate the paramount, absolute, and vital importance of perfect drainage.

Yet another precaution may be suggested, though, like many others here noted, it will also be found occasionally insisted upon in the following pages. Do not plant your treasures in stately and cherished isolation. Root loves to wrestle in the ground with root, and out of the rivalry each develops especial happiness and vigour in the company of the other. From the point of view that concerns the health of the plants, an interwoven carpet of colours is the effect to be aimed at ; and to attain this by wise and well-balanced juxtapositions will always be the aim of the wise gardener, and the triumph of the successful and experienced one. A well-cultivated stretch of rock-work should look as if it were not cultivated at all, sheeted carpets of colour succeeding each other through the year automatically, spontaneous and apparently untended. Many associations are suggested in the course of this book, alike for health and for colour-contrasts, but they are only a tithe of those that enthusiasts may well think out, appreciating, as they must, the importance of the point, no less than the nice adjustment and knowledge required, if one of the species imprudently chosen is not to swamp and overgrow its neighbour. Yet even here it is possible to be too cautious—some alpines will stand a surprisingly high strain of rivalry, as any one will know who has seen radiant carpets of *Gentiana verna* in meadows that in two months' time will be a dense hayfield two feet deep, with the Gentian maturing its seed in deep drought, far down beneath the close forest of stems that roof it in. But note, the overgrowing must only come with the maturing period of the germ ; in flower, the Gentian would not tolerate such a liberty.

From yet another point of view, too, the natural interwoven carpet is wanted. For what can be uglier and less harmonious than the large unbroken stretches in which you sometimes see alpines laid out, each species in a broad irregular space to itself, with each plant inserted at a neat distance from the next, quite regularly, like bedded-out stocks, and with the bare ground between picked sedulously clean of weeds, and raked as tidy as a tablecloth ? This is nothing more than the despised carpet bedding of our ancestors, only with Saxifrage and Alyssum instead of Alternanthera and Perilla, and with the slabs of colour laid down in deliberately irregular and shapeless blotches instead of regular lines and rings.

INTRODUCTION.

It is impossible to codify cast-iron rules for the successful cultivation of each plant. Only the fool or the tiro dogmatises; the further one progresses in knowledge, the more certain one grows of one's ignorance. The small, faint, illuminated patch of our experience only shows up the vast darkness by which our little islet of light is surrounded, and makes it seem yet smaller by comparison. General rules for cultivation have already been abundantly propounded; and it must never be forgotten that the enormous majority of alpine plants require no more. At the same time I have also given a general sketch of the conditions under which they grow in nature, not because it is by any means desirable to copy these with slavish precision, but because, from the native circumstances of its success, the enthusiast will soon be able to divine the riddle of each plant's personality and act accordingly. It would be idle waste of labour to attempt any precise imitation of the natural conditions under which a given species thrives; silly, because impossible adequately to do so— idle, because very probably it will thrive quite as well, if not indeed much better, under quite different ones. Sea-sand plants, for instance, are often luxuriant in common loam, and many an alpine is fat and happy in the ordinary border. It is only as a resource of despair and a confession of failure, after all other experiments have failed, that one tries to achieve some empirical reproduction of its native circumstances, in the case of an especially difficult and recalcitrant treasure. Otherwise, though study of a plant's normal surroundings is of acute interest and value, it should be undertaken chiefly as a means of detecting the plant's own character; and estimated, like the Apocrypha, as an ensample of right living, but not as in any way essential to horticultural salvation.

For the same reasons I have also given, in most cases, the fatherland of each plant, and, wherever possible, the actual rocks and circumstances in which it may be seen, not necessarily, of course, all of them, but enough to give a general notion of its range. To learn that a given species is to be found at low elevations on cool limestone rocks of Dalmatia, for instance, may often

INTRODUCTION.

be of some help, where unassisted inexperience might otherwise plant it high and hot on sun-flogged granite. Here, then, though these generalities are subject, of course, to the greatest caution, and to many an exception—usually noted in its place—in the case of special plants, I may also suggest the following hints as being offered by the names of the various countries from which the several species are sent. The European Alps, first of all, from the Pyrenees to Transylvania, offer climatic conditions curiously sympathetic to our own, so that the plants of these, our comparatively neighbouring ranges, will always be the beloved and abundant staple of our rock gardens. From South and Central Spain, North Africa, and South Italy come many species of surprising adaptability and hardiness here, but requiring especially perfect drainage, and a specially warm situation, in hot soil. Very much less exacting, but still lovers of sunshine and warmth, are the great bulk of species from the coasts of Dalmatia, Greece, and the northern ranges of Asia Minor. Caucasus, Epirus, Thessaly, and the Balkans provide races usually as simple as those of our own alps, but often yet more tolerant of a good baking in summer. Going further south and advancing into Palestine and Syria, conditions are reached with which most of our gardens cannot cope, being unable to provide the blazing and bone-dry summer required. The Alps of Persia and India have been as yet too sparingly tapped : on the Roof of the World an awful cold prevails in winter, but the profound valleys send up such steaming emanations that there ten thousand feet counts less in a prognosis of hardiness than would two hundred on the shores of the Mediterranean. Notoriously miffy, therefore, and uncertain, are some of the Himalayan alpines ; and the same reproach, in very ample measure, is falling on the new glories that float down upon us from time to time out of the high but too southerly ranges of China, north of the Himalaya, in Yunnan and Szechuan. Tibet, however, with its Polar cold, is still almost a blank in our experience, and so are the great northerly ranges along its topmost Chinese frontier, to say nothing of the Altai. Northern Europe, Russia, and Northern Asia have a hot summer and a long bitter winter; little trouble is given us, however, by their general run of plants. Going yet further north again, onto the fringes of the everlasting ice, we meet disappointment in a race of flowers that run towards stem, unlike the alpines, thanks to their longer summer; and show a corresponding diminution alike in the size and the brilliancy of their blossoms. The beauties among them, however, require conditions of especial coolness and constant humidity for their success. Now we cross towards the Americas. Japan, it must never be forgotten, stretches far down towards the tropics, from regions verging on the Arctic circle; therefore, to claim Japan for its origin is no testimonial to a plant's hardiness, unless it can add that it hails from regions ranging northward from Yokohama. The alpines of Central and Northern Japan are as safe with us, as they are usually beautiful; there the summer is very hot, and the winter intensely cold, and the atmosphere, except during the frozen reign of winter, always surcharged with moisture, assisted by inconveniently frequent and abundant rains.

The Alps of the New World, at least in Canada and the northern States, offer no very marked difference from the climatic conditions in those of the Old, but from the mid Rockies southwards the plants develop, in English conditions, a great impatience of wet, a great craving for sun and perfect drainage, and a general tendency to be a little miffish and uncertain on cold soils and in damp winters. The more southerly ranges, indeed, have races of alpine treasures as yet unguessed at in gardens, where however they will usually be found, most probably, a trifle capricious. As to the Andes, this vast and gorgeous range of giants is crested all along with wonders, but these are as yet to us bare names and wizened phantoms of themselves in herbaria, so that of their usual habits we have as yet no chance to speak. Continuing further south still, we come towards a mountainous land of awful winds and rains and chilliness. Species of the Chilean Andes are, on the whole, very comfortable in a cool English climate, while more and more coolness, more and more moisture, seem to be the usual needs of such rare treasures as have yet come to us from Tierra del Fuego and the Falklands. Australia is, of course, a hopeless country for the rock-gardener; nor is South Africa much better, owing to its fierce and ripening summer; but New Zealand, at least from the mountains of the South Island, offers us a number of lovely things, as yet mostly untried, that seem to enjoy much the same humid alpine conditions as prevail in the ranges of Central Japan. As for the Auckland and the Campbell Islands, there lurk some coy nymphs of most especial loveliness, which from their circumstances and home ought by no means to prove impracticable in our gardens.

I have already advised the really earnest-minded to buy or collect their plants in flower. This is not to say that one's taste in alpines develops into a cast-iron florist's standard, but the best alone is good enough for the gardener, and almost all plants show some variation into finer and less fine forms. This rule has hardly an exception: a type is never rigid as a railway line, and in a hundred of its representatives will surely be found a percentage of exceptions to the rule in amplitude of petal, size or colour of flower, or shortness of stem. Even a botanical and fixed diagnostic may vary in degree; and a species distinct by a hairy leaf may, in some specimens, have more or less hairiness than the description indicates. But it must be noted that while a botanical type is combined from the presence in greater or less degree of a certain number of invariable characteristics, no specific difference can ever be built on any one irrelevant and personal variation, such as large flower, or difference of colour. At the same time, though all these picked forms are nothing more than varieties, the gardener has the satisfaction of knowing them quite constant. A true albino is always an albino, a vivid-coloured development never loses its fire, and from a big-blossomed clump will never spring a flower of inferior design. Therefore I lay stress yet again on the necessity of selecting your plants in flower; there must be no uniform standard of perfection, yet in beauty there are always many and diverse degrees. A typical case in point is that of *Dianthus neglectus*. This is always beautiful indeed, but the type has an inclination to be a trifle lanky in the leg, and starry in the petal; whereas one day upon the high lawns of its alps it will yield you a dozen special forms pre-eminent in different ways—especially free and unanimous in bloom, perhaps, or massed in a compact and nearly stemless clump of colour, or blazing with a special incandescence of pink, or notably round and solid and comely in the amplified flower. And all these will "to their own selves prove true" in the garden for evermore, so that the eye of discernment is indeed necessary to their selection. For the average nurseryman cannot be expected to go out and make a choice among the living plants ; he commissions a Continental collector to send him so many hundreds of *Dianthus neglectus*, and the collector, anxious only to make up his quantity without regard to quality, simply goes up in August and rakes out at haphazard all the clumps he comes across, until the required number is fulfilled. Most of these, then, will be more or less typical, but there will also, with luck, be a certain number of variations for the better (and also for the worse) ; the enthusiast who is unable to go and make his own choice on the wild hills will do well, therefore, to see that collected stock in flower next year, that he may be sure of getting its most beautiful forms.

More nonsense is talked about collecting alpines, perhaps, than about any other subject in the garden. Even about myself, I have been told, are spread a number of legends, always ignorant, and occasionally malicious. Those who love and know the flowers of the alps as only those of long and arduous experience can hope to do,—those, of all people, are not to be accused of "devastating" the ranges and exterminating rare plants. Such an accusation can only be brought by envy or ignorance. For there is no such thing in the Alps as a "rare" plant ; there are many plants, indeed, that are extremely rare in distribution, and it is this sense of the word that has misled the uninformed. But when once the distribution of a "rare" plant is reached, it will there be found in such abundant millions that not all the collectors of the world (and there are perhaps ten serious ones now on earth) could make any mark upon its meadows in ten hundred years. Very "rare," for instance, is *Primula spectabilis ;* yet, in its own tiny territory, all the hill-tops are crested for miles with the blush of its roseate ripples. This is the typical "rarity" of an alpine ; I know of no species that is rare in number as well as in distribution. If a collector happens on one station where its specimens are few and far between, he will, of course, leave them alone and go on to the next ridge, where he will probably find it abounding. Hybrids, however, are often rare in the true sense, and here the true collector will take half a clump, or one out of three, respecting the rest. Even here, however, arises an arguable point : What is the precise value of all this cant about original stations ? What value, other than a purely sentimental one, has a tuft of *Primula Kellereri* sitting alone on a rocky bank of Kraxenträger, unvisited from aeon's end to aeon's end, and giving no pleasure to anybody, except a barren delight to professors in being able to quote it as living there. How incomparably greater a value has it in a chosen place on the rock garden, giving not less pleasure to itself but more, growing twice the size in a season, and delighting endless crowds, alike of the simple and the learned, with its health, its prestige, its rarity, and its incomparable flowers, that otherwise, to gratify a sterile fad, would have been doomed for ever to waste their sweetness on mountain mice and marmots. Parkinson has a very sensible remark on the wild tulips ; he says that, being removed to our gardens, they give more delight than ever to their own naturals. Now this appears to me the gist of the whole matter. If there be in all the world only one specimen of a species or variety, is it not better that it should be where it can give joy to man, rather than remain where it can do good to nobody, and merely feed the pride of a few people who know its whereabouts, and hug a half-sentimental and wholly selfish satisfaction in the monopoly of that knowledge ? At the same time I myself turn to scorn with prudent lips, the falsehood of extremes ; and, in any case where it was possible, would leave a portion of the original clump ; yet at an extreme pinch, if no other choice offered, I should carry my principles to their conclusion, and bring home the single crown without scruple, confident of merit in doing so, by rendering fruitful to many what was heretofore an unseen and barren beauty.

INTRODUCTION.

For I admit no question as to the survival of the collected plant. Properly collected, it runs no risk at all. There are, of course, many species that should never be touched, as their full-grown roots defy dynamite. Such are the Columbines and the great Anemones; of these you must either seek out seedlings, or return for seed; though all, and especially the Anemones, will speedily root again in sand from a mutilated stock. Entrenched in stark cliffs, too, many an alpine derides the trowel; and here its conquest is a matter of hunting for some more rotten piece of rock, and there bringing the persuasion of hammer and chisels to bear. In all these cases there is risk of failure or damage to the plant; the true-hearted collector will go very cautiously, and if he fails, as fail he sometimes must, to get his plant unhurt, he will feel pangs of manslaughterer's conscience that will impel him to greater care and delicacy than ever. The remaining children of the hills, however, lend themselves lovingly to the trowel, whether they be dug from the alpine turf or lifted from the stony screes and arêtes of the summits (or, as can be done with all cushion Saxifrages, merely torn off rootless in the wad, then pulled to pieces, and every rosette grown on as a cutting). The essentials are due reverence, and a straight downward drive, about five inches away from the plant, with a long and narrow flat fern-trowel, made all in one piece.

The whole sod should thus be dug all round, and levered up, when it will be found that the perfect root has usually been secured entire. Now, the plant should be enucleated from the sod, and every particle of earth removed. For besides adding to the weight of the package, earth is harmful to the roots in transit, breeding stagnation and decay. Then the plant goes into the collecting-box at once; and this should always be of tin. If ever an accident should happen, and a too difficult plant be badly dug, or an inferior form collected and then discarded in favour of a better, these sad victims must never be cast out rootless to perish by the wayside, but should reverently be planted again in some propitious place of the hills. No true collector marks his track with *disjecta membra*.

INTRODUCTION.

The despatch offers no difficulty. Tins or wooden boxes should be procured (the Italians eat biscuits, so their alps abound in tin boxes ; the Austrians don't, so in the Dolomites and Eastern ranges the quest is often arduous), the earthless plants packed firmly in, without wrappings, moss, or other precaution, except where some especially precious bale may be wrapped in stiff newspaper, with about a dozen drops of water poured down to the roots inside. Special care must be taken with the downy cushions of Eritrichium and the high Androsaces ; they must have their heads perfectly dry, while they appreciate a good supply of water at their feet. Otherwise humidity is wholly to be avoided ; the plants provide their own, and the tin preserves it. At most, if plants and weather be very dry, a very few drops should be sprinkled now and then in the packing ; this should be perfectly tight, without possibility of shaking ; but the plants, however closely pressed, should not be bruised or broken. So arranged, a very handsome number will be contained in one square biscuit box; and this will give promise, of course, by propagation, of at least twice again the amount. The postal weight allowed is up to 5 kilos (10 lbs.), and, sent by parcel post, there is no difficulty or embargo anywhere of any sort, though the filling up of the three postal certificates to each package is a nuisance. The transit takes from seven days, on a main line such as the Brenner, to a fortnight or so in places remote from the beaten track. In all cases, however, the plants on arrival will be found very nearly as fresh and lively as when they started. There is, however, a protected district in south-east Switzerland—a large "park" reserved in the heart of the Bernina district, behind, but not including the Heuthal ; while the Alps of the Valais have recently been rendered sacrosanct. M. Correvon has been the prime mover in these excellent works. Otherwise the Alps from end to end are open to the enthusiast.*

The collector is not unlucky in the moment at which he has

---

* Since this was written the Swiss Government has forbidden the uprooting of alpine plants without a licence.

perforce to work. At least I hold a strong belief that the height of flower-time is, in reality, the safest moment to move all plants. This, of course, does not apply to specimens already established in the garden; but is certainly a good and solid rule for all those that have to undertake a long journey, with, at its end, no demand for immediate display. For thus the plant is taken at the top of its crescendo of energy, and the reason for that crescendo is also cut off, so that the accumulated energy remains free to divert into another channel. With the first pulsations of the hills their plants, awakened to new life, begin passionately working up their force towards the maturing of their seed; this, and not the bearing of flowers, being the real strain and apex of their existence, upon which all their efforts converge. If, then, they are taken up in full bloom, you are secure of their highest degree of activity; but the shock of removal, and the travail of the journey, cut off the hope (and stress) of subsequent seed; so that the plant's full vitality (hardly, if at all, diminished by the change) is switched off from the toil of pregnancy and is able to devote its undistracted attention to the work of making fresh roots and re-establishing itself. There is no other moment, indeed, at which the plant's personality is at such high tension, and capable of such doughty deeds; there is no close time for collecting, yet the best of all possible moments is that in which the plant is at the full pitch of its force, with nothing now to do with that force except prepare fresh roots. Spring collecting loses the flowers; autumn collecting often finds the seed already forming, and the plant's vitality thereby diminished to an extent corresponding with the germ's state of advancement in the pod. Furthermore, at this point it is at full flower-time the roots of the current season cease to rove, and the plant is at poise, awaiting the moment when, about the end of August, the new fibres fare forth, to anchor the tuft securely in the ground against the storms and ground-swell of the winter. Therefore it is that I not only believe, above all, in collecting the plant in flower, but also especially favour late August as a replanting time, that it may promptly take hold with its new roots of the warmed and comfortable soil.

INTRODUCTION.

On arrival at home all collected alpine plants should be cleaned of dead, bruised, and rotting foliage, and their broken or crushed ends of root should be cut cleanly away. They should then have a period of not less than six weeks or two months of recuperation in a frame bed of pure sand about two feet deep to its drainage ; left moist beneath, either by pipes, or by drains driven perpendicularly in at the top, flush with the sand, and then periodically filled up with water. This bed may be in any aspect, but a sunny one is usually preferable ; and, if the heat at any time becomes excessive, bass matting should be cast over the frame, on which the light, as a rule, remains, but is so lifted up as to admit abundance of air. Thus treated, collected plants prodigiously root again and re-establish themselves ; a naked little carrot of *Campanula alpina,* put out in sand, comes up at the end of three weeks, the nucleus of a solid ball held together by a web of new white fibres. The cool and innutritious fine roughness of the sand stimulates the stock immediately into forming fresh rootage ; while, if the plant be left there too long, the same conditions ultimately tend to starve the abundant new growth it has engendered—though no harm is taken by leaving a July collected plant to re-establish itself in sand through the summer, and there sit dormant on until next spring ; indeed, in the case of woody plants, this treatment is almost essential.

Thus it is that certainty of success can be obtained with some cent. per cent. of alpine plants so collected, so despatched, and so treated in convalescence. Their planting has been already discussed ; the question of their propagation now remains for consideration. By far the most rapidly profitable method is by division. Almost all alpine plants form clumps, and almost any detached rosette will root immediately if removed at any time during the summer and inserted in sand. Indeed, with a large number, such as the mossy and silver Saxifrages, any shoot pulled off will be found already to have little fibres of its own, and merely requires to be stuck into the ground wherever a fresh plant be desired for nook or ledge. With many others, again, as, for instance, the race of Dianthus, cuttings usually offer a very easy and ready way of increasing our stocks. These should be taken in July or August, and struck in the sand bed, bottom heat being here of special use in making them root quickly and grow sturdily. Division, on the other hand, though possible in any open weather at any time of year, is usually undertaken in spring or the end of summer. With very precious varieties these are the only methods of securing really trustworthy reproductions of the original. In the case of rare shrubs and woody plants, grafting is often the best or only means of multiplication; but this is work for a specialist, and is best left to such.

The raising of seeds, however, is the most copious way of adding to our stock, to say nothing of the fact that a home-raised seedling is, *ipso facto*, bound to have a longer life in front of it than a mature collected clump, besides having the adventurous constitution of youth untarnished by maturity or the shock of separation from its native hills. At the same time a young seedling, with its long thread-like fibre, is by no means so easy to insert into a crevice as is a healthy cutting with the new roots just pushing, and about half an inch in length, or even less. The seedling, however, if successfully ensconced, is quicker in growth than the cutting, though I cannot conceal my own preference for dealing with the latter. Alpine seed, as a rule, is either very prompt and profuse in coming up, as in all Columbines, Pinks, and Poppies, or else partial, spasmodic, slow, or difficult, as often in Primulas, Gentians, and mountain Pansies. A most vital point is to obtain quite fresh mature seeds and to sow them as soon as possible. Spring sowing, indeed, is the general horticultural fashion, and has this much to say for it, that seed sown between January and March can germinate at once, under the immediate impulsion of the spring, without lying dormant through the deadness of the year in the unpropitious conditions that, in spite of all our care, replace in gardens the generative bed of snow beneath which they impatiently await, in perfect tranquillity, the release of the mountains in spring. It must not, however, be forgotten that the seed is already a living plant, but with only itself to subsist on until sown; therefore, if kept out of the ground for too long, it will so far have devoured itself and consumed its own albumen, as to have no vigour left for germination, when the moment at last arrives. This principle is true of all seeds, though those of different families differ widely in longevity; Primula, for instance, being specially short-lived, if not given a chance of springing promptly from mother-earth.

Shallow pots or pans are best for sowing, and it is important to pick out only such as, in the burning, have achieved just the right point of porosity. These can be told from the fact that their outside is smooth and fine to the finger, this indicating that they have a proper susceptibility to moisture, instead of forcing too rapid evaporation and consequent dust-dryness of soil no matter how well watered, as do those pots that have been baked to a crust in the kiln, and consequently are coarse, rough, and crust-like to the touch, dry and hollow-sounding, too, to the tap, as an ancient bone in the desert. The chosen pans should have a generous layer of drainage, and must then be filled with finely mixed fine soil, pressed firm and even about half an inch below the rim. It is very important that this soil should first of all be thoroughly sterilised by heat, so as to kill out all germ life that would otherwise develop into slime and weeds and fungus. The seed should then be sown sparingly over the surface, and covered with a very thin sifting of still finer soil, except in the case of especially small seeds, such as those of Saxifraga, which should be sprinkled over the pressed level of the compost, and not covered at all. Such odd things are sometimes done that these instructions are not unnecessary. I have known of whole-hearted enthusiasts who sowed their seed at the bottom of two feet of soil, and then sat waiting piously for years in the hope of seeing it come up. The sown seed may perhaps then be surfaced with a peppering of coarse grit, and then should be kept both close and dark, with brown paper laid over the top of the pot, and glass put over that again to keep a uniform moist atmosphere. The full pots should never be watered overhead, but stood in saucers containing water, and, on first sowing, be thoroughly soaked, by being left for some hours in a bucket, just so full of water that it does not overflow the brim. Every other day glass and paper should be removed, and any speck of Marchantia or slime removed on the point of a pin, before it has had time to overgrow the surface and clog the soil. So treated, and especially if a little heat can be supplied, most seed should have germinated in a month or so; the seedlings may be pricked out about three months after that, and in another three will be quite ripe for their permanent place in the garden.

Some, however, are much smaller and more deliberate in growth than others; and, above all, some seed, even when quite happy and sound, is very much slower to germinate than others. The pot, therefore, should not be despaired of in such cases, until it has stood barren for more than two years. Conspicuously slow of germination are many a Ranunculus, Paeonia, Hellebore, and Aconite. Primulas, too, have a capricious way of lying low until their second season. On the other hand, a Dianthus, Poppy, or Columbine that does not spring up within six months of sowing, at the very outside, may well be looked on as beyond hope. The biology of seeds is indeed a profound and subtle mystery, involving chemical changes and correlations of the utmost delicacy. The use of heat is evident, whether engendered by pipes or assisted by the pervasive radiance of the sun; the uses of cold are equally certain and far more striking, but unfortunately snow is not so easy to command as warmth. At the same time, even a few hours of driven snow on a seed-pot will have an almost magical effect in eliciting seedlings. Up spring the little plants immediately it has melted, and if only we could secure an artificial supply of permanent snow for our pots, there is no doubt that all germination would be far more prompt, sure, general, and unanimous. As it is, we have to be content with serving every opportunity of opening our frames to snow, and heaping it upon the pans of seed; the rest is a matter of experiment, and lies as yet behind unlifted veils of science. We only know that alternations of cold and heat, drought and damp, act like charms upon the seed. If pots can be kept dry for a time, and then damp; kept piled with snow for a period, with alternative sojourns in a dry cellar, dark and hot, germination becomes eager and profuse. Unfortunately, almost every species differs in the period of drought or damp that it requires. At present we are all groping, through countless experiences, after clear general laws, and the specific application of each. Yet one or two more points may be added to help the zealot. Many seeds are greatly stimulated to burst their prison by being soaked in hot water for some twenty-four hours before sowing. This applies not only to obviously hard-shelled seeds like that of Paeonia, but to many alpines, and most especially to Gentiana. And again, if delay be protracted, and hope in the gardener's heart be fainting low, an application of camphor to the surface will often elicit life, even at the eleventh hour, from sluggish and recalcitrant seeds, while in the case of extra-precious ones they may be lured into germination between sheets of blotting-paper, laid in a warm place, and kept moist one day and dry the next. When their life is started, however, they require pricking off at once on to a very fine humid surface of soil in a pot, and the job is one of such exquisite delicacy as to call for the fingers of a fairy.

The Alpine House

Mention has often here been made of frame and glass house. These, if designed solely for the cultivation of alpines, should have no heat at all, and be always as light, airy, and well-drained as possible. Thus contrived, an alpine house is the richest joy of January, besides offering us our only chance of getting full satisfaction out of such precocious loveliness as *Saxifraga Burseriana* and the little bulbous Irises of Asia Minor, that otherwise spring so prematurely from the dead and sodden world, that they are almost certain, in the open garden, to be flogged to pieces by rain and battered out of their beauty, splashed with mud and obliterated, pecked asunder by birds, and nibbled into rags by the early rising slug. No pleasure, on the contrary, is greater than a clean little house, airy and sweet, filled with clean, undamaged potfuls of Saxifrage, Iris, Adonis, and so forth, all shining in untarnished radiance, and developing under protection of the

INTRODUCTION.

glass such unsuspected charms as the delicate fragrance exhaled, under these undisturbed conditions, by *Saxifraga Burseriana.* The cultivation of such plants is of the simplest; their pots (keep these on the small side) must be quite clean, their soil quite wholesome, their drainage open and abundant, their water supply constant but never excessive. They should be stood in saucers of water when thirsty, instead of receiving their dose from over-head. Their drink, too, should be the stored gift of the clouds, in the case of all convicted or suspected anti-lime fanatics, rather than that of lake or river, in which lime is probably present, in proportions, however minute, quite capable of poisoning a pot. It must also be remembered incessantly that soil soon becomes exhausted; no plant should be left for more than a year without repotting. Primulas, it is to be noted, are especially impatient of too long a sojourn in the same soil and pot. On the whole, then, while the alpine house demands its pots, and the supply-frames necessitate yet more, I am wholly opposed to the systematic frame-culture of alpines. They are neither appropriate, pleasant, nor permanently happy in such confined and unnatural circumstances, and always seem like pining birds in cruel and grotesque imprisonment. So much for the uses and delights of the cold alpine house, and the undesirability of that cold frame cultivation which was our forefathers' only notion of dealing with alpines, and that only in a spirit of prayerful despair. The moment, however, that artificial heat, in any form or degree, is added to either house or frame, then its whole purpose changes completely. It becomes a luxuriant centre of propagation and germination; it ceases to be a healthy medium for the permanent cultivation of alpines. Heat, therefore, may only be admitted when your frame or house is meant for the rapid increase of your stock by seeds and cuttings, rather than as a settled habitation for grown-up plants in pots.

And now my tale of annotations is as full as I dare make it. I will stand no longer between my readers and the stored ocean of knowledge in which the following pages will salubriously merge him. Against trusting too exclusively to my experiences

INTRODUCTION.

I need not warn my foes, and will not warn my friends. All good gardeners know that knowledge is a first-hand article; all good gardeners know that each must buy it for himself, and that the utmost any fellow-enthusiast can do is to use his own observation as a basement for suggestions and recommendations of special applications under invariable general rules as well possessed by one as by another; while their particular applications vary so from one garden to the next, that the advice of even the most veteran expert, in any special case (being drawn from what he himself has undergone, or seen other people undergo), can only be taken by its recipients as a well-meant suggestion, deserving some consideration. Therefore I give you my plant notes for what they are worth; good or bad, they represent my apex of effort on your behalf. To err, again, is human: who will pretend that such a pile of pages is virgin of error, inconsistency, or loose end? But let not the learned be ungenerously extreme to mark what is done amiss: whose pages are not sometimes speckled with a lapse or two? As to completeness, why, if absolute correctness is a sheer inaccessibility, completeness is not by any means less so. I dare not even begin to think of all the essentials I have probably left out; the very mention of completeness chills my soul with an impotent despair. Hastily I bring my apologies to a close, feeling words inadequate. So here is a book of reference for the rock-gardener. If it serves for even a decade to keep him tolerably safe in the mazes of catalogues, and abreast of some rare treasures that still look upon us from the land of hope, then I shall consider that my work has not been done in vain. And speaking for myself, I can only say that of all my garden-books this one will chiefly be my constant companion, guide, and solace. To me at least it is already a dictionary of real succour. It contains at least a thousand times as much knowledge as I myself possess, or can ever hope to attain.

REGINALD FARRER.

INGLEBOROUGH, 1914.

THE

ENGLISH ROCK-GARDEN

A

Abronia, a race of very attractive little plants from California, of prostrate habit, with heads of flower suggesting a Verbena, though in reality they claim no relationship. In cultivation are *A. arenaria, A. latifolia* (yellow), *A. fragrans,* and *A. umbellata* (which has sometimes been called *A. rosea*). All four, being Californians, require consideration of that fact, and, though not necessarily tender, are best adapted for covering some warm and open slope on the sunny side of the rock-work in light and sandy soil. They are easily to be raised from seed, and are most to be recommended for climates warmer and drier than those of the Northerly and Westerly mountain-regions of England and Scotland.

Acaena forms a curious small group among Rosaceae, having some affinities with Poterium. The race belongs almost entirely to New Zealand, Chile, and the Antarctic Islands, being peculiarly abundant in New Zealand. None the less the Acaenas are thoroughly hardy, and deserve to be freely used as foliage plants, for tucking into any soil, to cover any unconsidered or useless tract of the rock-garden in sheets of most beautiful foliage, from which, in due course, spring spinous or inconspicuous heads of blossom, quite unattractive except in the case of *A. microphylla*. Their value for furnishing is their special merit, and they serve admirably for carpets to Crocus and Colchicum, delicately enhancing the flawless cups that spring through their carpet of roseate or blue-grey ferny foliage. They can be raised from seed, or multiplied with almost excessive ease by bits pulled off and stuck in somewhere else. Many species now appear in lists, but often without specific description. Here, then, is an account of what may be expected from the best of them :

ACAENA.

A. adscendens is far from the prostrate condition so valuable in the family, and is a large coarse thing of straggling and weedy habit, with stout 4 to 8 inch stems, short stout bristles, and leaves rounded, grey, glabrous, glaucous, and coarsely toothed.

A. ageratifolia is a larger ascendent plant with very fine green foliage like a neatly condensed fern.

A. argentea, a most lovely species from Chile, forms a mat of grey soft foliage.

A. Buchananii is closely prostrate and branchy. The little pale grey leaves are made up of three to six pairs of small round or oval folioles, with minute deep toothing at their edge. The bristles of the flower-head are yellow, and the species is a New Zealander.

A. digitata is a Chilean species, of no very special charm in my eyes.

A. glabra may be known among its kin by being perfectly smooth, without hairs or bristles of any kind. Nor does it ever produce bristles even in the flower-heads; but these, though quite unarmed, are hedgehoggy with stamens, in the case of the male flowers. (New Zealand.)

A. glauca is singularly beautiful—a prostrate plant with little silky rosaceous leaves, of a soft grey-blue tone.

A. lucida, from the Antarctic Islands, is a less carpeting mass, whose foliage suggests that of *Anthemis montana*, though narrower in form.

A. lyrata, if the name have authority, is an attractive species, with the leaflets broad, and rounded along the leaf, suggesting the effect of a Ceterach-fern, but grey and thick, with the final lobe of the leaf larger than the rest, which diminish towards the base of the stem. Each lobe is prettily scalloped, and the whole growth has great attraction, though the flowers, borne in minute rounded heads, are not so much inconspicuous as hideous.

A. microphylla, on the contrary, is certainly the reigning favourite in our gardens, not only on account of its charming smooth rose-like foliage, varying from rosy-bronze to a beautiful blue-grey tone, but also, and no less, for the innumerable little round balls of flower that sit about all over the carpet, shock-headed with long spines of bright crimson. This species hails from New Zealand, and sometimes appears under the synonyms of *A. depressa* and *A. inermis*.

A. Novae Zelandiae, whose provenance is thus left in no doubt, is a marked improvement on the larger species, and well known in gardens. Here the stock is stout and woody and creeping, with uprising stems, clothed in silky leaves made up of four to seven rounded leaflets coarsely toothed at their edge. The flower-heads are large and coarse and purplish.

A. sanguisorbae has much the same habit, but is smoother and less silky, with smaller rounder heads of purplish blossom.

A. sericea is yet another of the creepers, having fine narrow leaflets, silver-grey with a coat of down, set with deep toothings, especially at their ends.

A. splendens, from Chile, luxuriates yet more in a glistering armour of silver. (Among other members of the race worth growing are *A. laevigata*, *A. pinnatifida*, *A. ovalifolia*, and *A. magellanica*. *A. pumila* is a quaint break in its family, upright, fine, and graceful, exactly suggesting an intrigue between *Thalictrum alpinum* and *Poterium sanguisorba*.)

Acantholeimon brings us now to a race of incomparably higher rank in the rock-garden. The Thornyfields are a curious and beautiful race of vindictive little vegetable hedgehogs, fierce spiny cushions from which spring, in late summer, abundant graceful plumes of blossom, pink or white, each flower enclosed in a contrasting chaffy cup. The race is most nearly allied to the Sea-lavenders, but has more reminiscence of some strange saxifrage gone spiteful-mad but unusually graceful; it is entirely confined to the upper mountain rocks in the Alps of Asia Minor, extending across Persia to the borders of India. In cultivation the whole family is grateful for a very warm dry corner, in a light and perfectly well-drained soil, enriched with lime, and diversified by abundance of chips and grit. Here they will all prove perfectly hardy and vigorous, but have a tiresome habit of unexpectedly passing away in full flood-tide of prosperity without any assignable reason. Nor is it possible to propagate them easily, except by seed ; with the one honourable exception of the best-known of all, the indestructible and delightful *A. glumaceum*, which will strike fresh roots from its branches, if soil be worked down in the mass, and the several shoots either firmly inserted or layered like a carnation. In such an important and beautiful family we have need to know more, not only about such species as we possess, but also about the many others, no less beautiful, of which at present we only live in hopes.

A. acerosum, another of whose names has been *A. Pinardii*, forms wide bushlings of 6 to 10 inches, the spiny leaves being about 2 or 3 inches long, bright blue-grey, with lime-pits stamped upon them. They are very specially long, fat and thorny. The undivided flower-sprays rise up to 6 or 8 inches, carrying many spikelets of white flowers. (Anatolia, &c.)

3

A. androsaceum, a false name for *A. Echinus, q.v.*

A. araxanthum, though beautiful with long leaves and lax long plumes of white flower, is not likely to be of much help to our gardens, belonging, as it does, to the hot fields of Araxes.

A. armenum has shorter leaves than the last, denser spikes and smaller flowers. *A. Balansae* is a variety of this, and sometimes is offered under the name of *A. Haussknechtii.*

A. avenaceum, from Khorassan, earns its name with a long fine single purple blossom-shower, as it were an oat's, rising some foot or so above the clump.

A. Balansae belongs to *A. armenum, q.v.*

A. Bodeanum forms a very dense close tuft of green spiny foliage (with velvety varieties, *pictum, cappadocicum, cataonicum*), and the flower-spike is tight and dense too, dividing into two branches, with flowers overlapping each other, in chaffy bracts of bright purple.

A. Calvertii, on the contrary, is much closer in look and habit to our well-known *A. glumaceum*, but is of a disposition so much milder as hardly to be prickly at all. Its flowers, too, are of a richer purple. (Armenia.)

A. caryophyllaceum, from Kurdistan, has a strong general resemblance in fatness and length of intensely spiny leaf to *A. acerosum*, but its foliage is so wholly devoid of lime as to be of a pale green. The bloom-spikes are undivided, and the chaffy calyx veined outside with violet.

A. diapensioeides must indeed be longed for : in its habit and size of leaf it exactly resembles a close tuffet of *Saxifraga caesia*. So far this delight of Kok-i-Baba mountain in Afghanistan has never, I think, rejoiced our gardens with a sight of its short fat leaves. But to call a thing Diapensioeides is to make it even more desirable than if one called it Allionii (and perhaps less difficult) ; so that after unresting efforts we must surely one day possess this.

A. Echīnus, wrongfully dethroned from its specific rank in some lists, is in reality the plant that lurks in others under the name of *A. androsaceum*. It forms a perfectly tight mass of green spines from which the velvety glandular few-flowered spikes hardly rise at all ; the flowers are white, but their enclosing chaffy star is veined with purple.

A. Fominii belongs to *A. lepturoeides, q.v.*

A. glumaceum is the best known of its race, forming wide rather lax cushions, of green and rather lax spiny leaves, from which spray freely abroad its delicate flowers of pink all through the summer. This species, so far the most amenable—perhaps because the longest

known—has quite acclimatised itself in all our gardens, though its
native places are the torrid cliffs and slopes of Ararat, and thence
away into Russian Armenia.

A. Haussknechtii. See under *A. armenum.*

A. Hohenackeri.—This species has also been wronged by inclusion
under the last. In point of fact, it is a much denser and more tufted,
smaller plant, with thick overlapping, two-branched spikes that hardly
rise more than 2 or 3 inches from the tuft, with about an inch of
blossom. The leaves, too, are glaucous-blue, and stamped with lime-
pits or even scales. The leaves are short, spiny, keeled so as to be
triangular in section, and pointed like little awls ; and the trunks are
clothed densely in the recurving relics of their dead. (Eastern
Caucasus, &c.)

A. Karelinii, from the salt plains of South Russia, is a looser thing
altogether, forming lax, almost shrubby masses of limy, blue-grey
foliage, which in spring is fat and fleshy, but develops into thorniness
with the summer as a young life grows spiky with experience. The
blossom-shower, about 4 inches long, is scattered and delicate.

A. Kotschyi is a quite blue dense tuft, with little unbranching
spikes very short indeed, erect, with bracts and flowers closely overlapping. The blossoms are pink and few ; the leaves extremely
short and unusually broad. The whole aspect of the mass suggests
the charm of *Saxifraga diapensioeides ;* its native hills are those of
the Cilician Taurus, and that notable mountain of Berytagh.

A. latifolium, from Kurdistan, forms a tight blue tuffet of spines,
from which rise arching graceful spikes of 8 or 10 inches, above the
3-inch cushion, and shower forth a fine display of handsome rosy
stars.

A. laxiflorum forms a 3-inch mass almost like a small shrub, with
not so many leaves as usual to the rosette, and those fat and frail.
This species dwells in river-shingles, and the erect 6-inch spike is
furnished with poor little pallid flowers.

A. lepturoeides is a very fine species with which our acquaintance
is but recent. Its habit is rather large-rosetted, the short boughs
being densely set with recurved dead leaves. The living ones are
glaucous-blue, pitted with lime and perfectly smooth. The spike of
whitish blossoms is quite lax, either single, or dividing into two equal
branches, with many minor branchlings of blossom.

A. libanóticum makes a little mound of more or less glaucous
leaves, the boughs being clothed with dead ones. The flower-scape is
also adorned with leaves, but fewer and shorter, the spike itself being
single and undivided, with from four to seven spicules of large white

flowers, whose enveloping cup is nerved outside with purple. (Heights of Lebanon, Hermon, &c.)

A. lycopódioeides carries us far from the Levant, into the high mountains of Kashmir, where, at some 11,000 to 14,000 feet, it forms very minute tight masses like a Lycopodium, hardly an inch in height, of narrow tiny foliage. The scapes rise up to 2 inches or so, divide into two sprays, and carry large rosy flowers in a white cup. This should indeed be a specially lovely thing—like a thorny pink Eritrichium, but with larger flowers, and every promise of a temper more affable, and a habit more resistent. One derives yet further hope from learning that on its own high places this beauty is common.

A. melananthum, from the Kuh Daena range above Shiraz in Persia, has short broad leaves, densely overlapping, forming blue-grey cushions whose invitingness is lessened by their being horrid with short dense thorny twigs similar to its cousin *A. genistoeides*. The flowers appear almost to sit upon the tuft; they are worthy of the clump, pink or white, set off by a starry cup of dark purple, which gives the plant its ill-fitting name—ill-fitting, seeing that here it is the calyx, not the flower, that is dark in colour.

A. Perroninii is a Cilician species, improving on the beauty of even *A. Echinus* in having larger flowers, coupled with the same hillocky habit and glaucous-blue colouring. (Cilician Alps.)

A. petraeum bears a promising name that always inspires the gardener with hope. Nor does it disgrace the epithet—a little tight dense grey tuffet from the rocks of Kurdistan, producing a short scape ending in a loose spike of soft pink blooms.

A. Pinardii. See under *A. acerosum*.

A. sahendicum, when it exchanges for our gardens the hot mountains of Sahend in Persia, will prove a twin to *A. glumaceum*, but is much more closely tufty, glabrous and grey, with rusty-coloured flower-spikes.

A. ulicinum occupies the same rocks as *A. libanoticum*, from which it differs in being dark green, and not glaucous, with shorter foliage and a very brief congested spike, with three, four, or five spicules of blossom. In fact, by its piny habit and green colouring it seems to earn its epithet of " gorse-like."

A. venustum is by now a name well known to catalogues. Its true owner should form masses of rather loose tufts, the leaves being rather broad, blue-grey, scaled with lime, and the lowest on the shoot less prickly than the rest (though not the more, on that account, to be by any means recommended as bedding). The spike is loose and usually undivided, though sometimes branching into twin sprays;

the flowers are large and beautiful, of a bright clear rose-pink or purple. There are varieties of this, as of many others (*A. tenuifolium* is sent as a form of *A. lepturoeides*), and the range of the species is through the Cilician Taurus.

A. Wiedemannii, from Galatia, is, in all its habit, a twin to *A. Echinus*, but is perfectly glabrous and smooth, without any glands or velvetiness anywhere ; and the flower-spike is less tight and serried. Nor need it be supposed that this list precludes us from further hope in the race. For here follows a list of other names, some of which may prove—though there do exist various ugly and insignificant Acantholeimons—to cover species as good as (if not perhaps better than) several of those already named : *Acantholeimon aspadanum, festucaceum, flexuosum, oliganthum* (often 10 inches high), *brachystachyum* (handsome with dark bracts, purple-bordered, and flowers boldly veined with red), *scabrellum, subulatum, quinquelobum, curviflorum, tragacanthinum, truncatum, viscidulum, roseum, aristulatum,* and others. However, even without these additions, the foregoing list already contains sufficient to whet our appetites and keep our gardens subsisting for some time to come, on enlarged hopes in the family of Acantholeimon.

Acanthophyllum, though often similar to the last in habit and looks, in reality is a little group in the cousinhood of Dianthus, haunting high hot rocks from the Caucasus to Persia. Its members are but little known in gardens, nor is there any very solid hope that they will really prove trustworthy ornaments there. *A. spinosum* is a Caucasian species, but the especial beauty of the family is *A. grandiflorum*, of which, alas, it is hardly fair to expect courage against our climate, seeing that it is in the cliffs above Quetta that it forms its lovely wide flat tufts of silvery foliage, upon which sit tight the beautiful big flowers of glowing purple.

Acanthosonchus. See under **Sonchus spinosus.**

Acanthus does not, of course, belong by rights to the rock-garden. Yet decorative value is always decorative value, and a thing beautiful in itself is hardly ever out of place. There are many big gardens accordingly where, in rich and very deep soil, in a situation calculated to shelter and enhance the tropical splendour of their foliage, the cultivator may live to be grateful (if he leaves them ample verge and marge) to such enormous and glistering splendours as *A. Candelabrum, longifolius, mollis* (with its variety *latifolius*), *rigidus,* and *spinosus.* Not only are they superb in dark and hearty sheen of their great divided corinthian foliage, but above this come towering columns of immortal flowers, emerging from their bracts, hooded and lipped in streaks of violet or pink on a ground of dim white. Though plants of the South, they prove resistent to our climate without fuss or protection. There are, however, two species whose stature fits them, no less than their charm, for a more choice and prominent place in the rock-garden.

A. *Dioscoridis var. Perringii* (*A. Perringii* or *Caroli-Alexandri* of catalogues) is a most beautiful alpine from Cappadocian Antitaurus, where in nature it is said to dislike lime. It is quite dwarf, the broad grey-green thorny leaves lying out almost flat upon the ground, while from their heart rise up stocky stems of 9 or 10 inches, crowded with handsome noble rosy flowers, almost, in suggestion, like some pink Brunella glorified unimaginably, and taught to look well-bred. No difficulty waits upon the culture of this treasure in free warm soil, light and well drained. It can, like all its kin, be easily raised from seed, or else multiplied by division, or by root-cuttings, in spring or autumn.

A. *hirsutus* is yet another dwarf, from the mountains of Lydia and Caria. It spreads and ramifies freely through its bed, instead of remaining a tuffet of crowns like the last ; and in autumn the leaf-buds for the next season may be seen heartfully emerging from the bare soil. These leaves are gentler than is the rule in the race—tender, and of tender green, armed with tender thorns that do not even threaten, and accordingly run the risk of being called mere bristles. The flower-columns do not exceed some 9 or 10 inches, and the flowers are yellow.

Aceranthus is a curious small race of woodlanders from Japan, closely allied to Epimedium. Of these A. *sagittifolius* has the foliage, but its flowers are small and insignificant. On the other hand, A. *diphyllus* is a most charming thing, only about 4 or 5 inches high, with two little leaves like pointed shields, with teeth so sharp as to look almost bristly, and a small loose spike of blossoms which are large and conspicuous for the size of the plant. Not generally known in cultivation, this delicate fine beauty should prove a treasure for any cool woodland corner where Epimedium and Vancouveria are happy.

Achilléa is a vast race of the temperate zone, most common in the Old World, and rising, from the meadows, to considerable heights in the alpine region. Unfortunately the curse of Compositae lies hard on Achillea, and the family is painfully prolific in frightful weeds, many of which are also coarse and rampant in growth as well as being dim and dirty in flower. Much danger attaches to the mention of any undescribed Achillea in a catalogue ; for the sake, however, of the rare good species in this race, it is fair that the whole should not be condemned, but the sheep be duly shepherded away from the goats.

A. abrotanoeides, from Dalmatia and the far Eastern Alps, has a close resemblance to the Western *A. Clavennae*, whose habit, and divided leaves, and clusters of fairly large white flowers on stalks of 6 to 9 inches, it possesses; but the leaves are ashy-grey with a felted down, and the whole plant smells of wormwood.

A. ageratifolia is simply a false name for *Anthemis aeizoon, q.v.*

A. ambrosiaca is a 6-inch plant with very ferny foliage and the rays of the flower rather short.

A. argentea, a most beautiful mass of silver-white mounded leaves, emitting white marguerites.

A. atrata is an abundant and well-known alpine, with many children, sub-species, and varieties all along the ranges. It has the carriage of a Camomile, and a clustered head—on a stem of 6 inches or so—of large flowers which are, unfortunately, of a grubby and world-soiled white, indescribably unalluring, with a sad bad eye of dirty darkness. In the same condemnation and of much the same type is *A. nana* (like a woolly little Milfoil), as well as *A. Clusiana, A. moochata* (tho formor moro finely ferny, the latter greyer and smaller-flowered than Atrata, with an eye that is always yellow), together with *A. Herba-rota*, which has oblong leaves, only scalloped, and intensely aromatic; otherwise resembling ugly little rare *A. moschata* of the granitic heights. All these from the European ranges—with hybrids so many that there is no safety in undescribed Achilleas, all these being dismal weeds; while from the Levantine mountains we have similar dinginesses in *A. armenorum* and *A. Aucheri*. And Switzerland also produces *A. Huteri*, another species of quite secondary rank; as is also *A. Fraasii*.

A. aurea makes flat mounds of compacted feathery foliage, from which through the summer rises a great number of erect stems about 5 inches high, with flattened heads of yellow flower.

A. Barbeyana, however, shows the silver lining to the cloud of the race, so brilliantly does the whole plant shine with silver sheen—a neat dense little gleaming tuft, very rare on the mountain-tops of Aetolia, with white flowers in a dense simple head, at the top of stems from 2 to 6 inches.

A. cartilaginea, a species from Taurus and East Caucasus, brings us into the clearly defined group of which our native *A. Ptarmica*, though so lank for the garden, is a real ornament, with its tall aspiring *élancé* habit, and loose few-flowered heads of large and handsome white stars. *A. cartilaginea*, however, is shorter, its leaves are broader

9

than the narrow-toothed foliage of Ptarmica, and it is clothed, beside, in a fine down, whereas Ptarmica is smooth. To the same useful group belong *A. lingulata* (*A. buglossis* of catalogues, a big, rather coarse affair), *A. grandiflora* from alpine Caucasus, Armenia, &c., a fine species, though tall, with flowers equalling or surpassing Ptarmica's in size, the whole growth being more or less without down, and the narrow leaves merely saw-edged instead of toothed. Incomparably the best of this group, however, is *A. sibirica* (*A. mongolica* of catalogues), which is not only in all respects an improved Ptarmica, neater in habit and much larger in bloom, but has also produced an improved version of even itself under the name of Perry's White, a really beautiful thing, better fitted of course for the border than for the rock-garden, unless indeed the rock-garden be big enough to admit of wide stretches, one of which might gloriously be planted with this in combination with *Delphinium Belladonna* or *Delphinium grandiflorum*. (Similar but more straggling, and inferior, is the North-American *A. borealis*.)

A. Clavennae, from the high region of the eastern European Alps, is also a beautiful species, forming wide tufts of long, oval, irregularly lobed leaves, which are hoary white with down, while high above them rise the 6-inch stems, carrying clear white flowers of fair size in a loose head. In the rock-garden ideal associations for this plant would be *Campanula rotundifolia* and *Senecio abrotanifolius* or *S. tyrolensis*.

A. clypeolata heads a group which all in habit resemble our common Yarrow, magnified or in miniature, with dense wide flattish heads of white, pink, or golden yellow. Among the best of these weeds is *A. holosericea*, from rocky places in pinewoods and higher regions in Greece and the Levant, with oval leaves cut into oval leaflets of which the end one is the biggest, and all clothed most beautifully in a robe of shining silver. Another good one should be *A. pseudopectinata*, from fields at the foot of the Balkans, whose flowers are of a rich orange gold. Others in this clan, of little or no merit, being too often gawky and dull, are *tomentosa*, *ligustica*, *setacea*, *odorata*, *crithmifolia*, *nobilis*, *filipendulina*, *pectinata*, and such a large army of others that, rather than run through the whole dismal roll-call, I will merely repeat with emphasis my warning against ever buying any Achillea from garden or catalogue unless you have either seen it for yourself and liked it, or else feel yourself enlightened with a really reassuring description. But undescribed Achilleas in catalogues are best avoided, and the confusion in the race is terrible.

ACHILLEA.

A. x *Kellereri*, however, is a really beautiful creation, one of the few fine hybrids of a race in which the species, especially in the high-alpine groups, interbreed with a freedom that results in a confusion of strains as dingy as their parents. *A. Kellereri* may well be an ornament to the choicest rock-garden—a mass of long, finely-cut leaves that suggest an *Asplenium viride* that has gone grey in a frost, and fine white flowers, ample and clear, an improvement on Clavennae's, carried on loose heads at the top of 6-inch stems. Of much the same attractiveness are *A. Jaborneggii*, of similar habit, but with leaves perfectly green ; *A. macedonica* of gardens, a doubtful species, in habit like *Parrya Menziesii*, in neat rosettes, but possibly belonging to *A. serbica*, which is really a false name of *Anthemis aeizoon ; A. Morisii*, like a tiny, depressed child of *A. Jaborneggii ; A. Obristii*, after the style of Huteri, rambling about the face of the ground on long weak trunks, each tipped with a rosette of oval leaves, deeply gashed into six or eight rather pointed lobes.

A. pyrenaica, from the highest grass-banks and earth-pans in the Pyrenees of Catalonia, is a fine species, with pitted leaves deeply saw-toothed, and uprising stems, from 6 to 10 inches, clad in a few leaves, and carrying flowers larger than those of Ptarmica in a loose scant cluster.

A. rupestris, however, though reduced unfairly to a mere variety of comparatively dingy *A. Herba-rota* by Fiori and Paoletti, remains far and away the most beautiful and valuable of the Achilleas for the rock-garden, now that the race has been stripped of the brilliant plume which it long unjustly claimed for its own clan, and which has now at last, though not in catalogues, been allowed to rejoin its own family as *Anthemis aeizoon*. *A. rupestris* belongs to South Europe, and is quite dwarf, with tiny leafy rosettes, perfectly green, more or less glandular, and perfectly smooth at the hem, without toothing or gash or scallop—at least in the lowest leaves of the rosette, for the inner ones often have a little irregular gashing at their base. The plant spreads readily into a neat mat, and sends up numerous 6-inch stems, carrying loose heads of ample pure white flowers with whitish eye.

A. serbica is simply yet another false name by which Achillea still tries to claim the beauty of *Anthemis aeizoon, q.v.*

A. sericea is a rank Milfoil after the style of our own Yarrow, but with wide heads of mustardy yellow, from the Balkans.

A. tomentosa is, however, the best of this section, a comparatively neat little thing, with the usual fine foliage, densely downy to the point of being woolly. The habit is that of a dwarf and tidy Yarrow —such a Yarrow as would not dishonour an edging—but the broad

11

flat flower-heads are of a golden yellow so bright as to make quite a brilliant effect in a generous mass. The plant has a very wide distribution, through all Southern Europe to Siberia ; and as such Southerly Yarrows are lovers of dry places, and as *A. tomentosa* has the special danger-signal of down, it is safer to put it in a warmish, dryish exposure in well-drained poor soil. In such circumstances it grows and spreads as easily as the rest of its easy kin, though it must be remembered that the hybrids which owe a share in their existence to *A. Clavennae* are apt to prove, anyhow, a trifle impermanent in the garden. All, however, can be pulled to pieces and multiplied at pleasure.

A. umbellata is not far from Moschata, but of a much more pleasing style, approaching rather to Clavennae in its beauty, but dwarfer, with tiny oval leaves, cut into half a dozen pointed little lobes, and all densely white with wool laid on in a coat. Up, then, come the flower-stems, some 5 or 6 inches, carrying loose heads of good white blossom. *A. umbellata* frequents the rocky places of alpine and sub-alpine Greece—more especially the alpine. Romance may be quarried from the thought that J. S. Mill once found a one-headed form between Megaspelaion and Styx, in Arcadia. (Perhaps the romance clings less to the finder than to the names of the places where he found it.) There is also, in gardens, another variety, often appearing as a species, under the name of *A. argentata ;* it does not differ from the type, except in the added charm of being much more refulgent in its silvery whiteness.

A. Wilczekii, finally, forms lush handsome stretches of great grey rosettes curiously suggestive of masses of *Saxifraga Cotyledon* gone limp and ashen, and with a fine saw-edge to each leaf. The flower-stems, however, are gawky, and the flowers of a coarse dinginess unpardonable.

Achlys triphylla is a neat and unassuming little Berberidaceous stranger from North America, with a trefoil of clear green leaves. It is best left to fill up some unconsidered corner under shrubs at its own free will.

Aciphylla is a race of Umbellifers from New Zealand, much more resembling in their habit very fine fierce, needle-leaved Agaves. A stiff mass or tuft of Aciphylla makes a brave effect in the garden, but in England their culture can hardly be generally recommended ; nor need it be pressed ; for, though in warm corners and in good, perfectly-drained soil they may be caused to thrive, their beauty is not so compelling as to make them worth any excess of care. The larger species, making spiny masses from 2 to 5 feet high, are *Colensoi,*

Traversii, squarrosa, and *Hookeri :* much smaller and better fitted for the rock-garden are *Lyallii, Traillii, Kirkii, Monroi, polita,* attaining from 4 to 18 inches. Quite tiny bundles of cruel needles are *Dobsonii* and *simplex,* wee species, intensely spiny and glaucous-grey. The flowers of all are negligible.

Though **Aconitum** need not necessarily have any place in the rock-garden, on however large a scale it may be built, and though the race is sinister and evil in its poisonous sombre splendour almost beyond any other that we have, yet, for the guidance of those who find nothing but nude names in lists, I may briefly go through the best species that may be used to adorn remoter corners of the large rock-garden, in any soil that is deep and rich and cool, whether in sun or shade, though shade best fits the gloomy tone of their magnificence.

HERBACEOUS ACONITES USUALLY WITH BLUE FLOWERS

Some among very many : by no means all, or most, of distinct garden value

album, large pure white and splendid flowers, very freely borne in August. A specially noble Levantine, grievously rare.

autumnale, a variety of *japonicum,* medium height, with stumpy wide helmets of blue, appearing in September to October.

biflorum, a real rock-garden plant of the choicest. Only 6 inches high, with one pair of big pale-blue helmets in June. (Siberia.)

californicum, more properly *oregonense* or *columbianum,* has deeply divided leaves and conical pale-blue helmets in September ; the true plant is extremely rare in cultivation, forms of Napellus being sent out instead.

Delavayi, new in from China, about 4 feet high, hairy, dark blue. October.

elatum, immense flowers in loose spikes of 3 or 4 feet, in June.

japonicum, 3 feet, not very stout spikes of blue-violet helmets, very woolly and large, in July and August.

Kusnetzowii is a smooth 3-foot species, with tripartite leaves and close spikes of clear blue, with almost semicircular hood.

Napellus, our own dismal Monkshood, now wild, or at all events now widely established along the stream sides of the West, and so persistent in its malign attendance upon man that it even climbs high into the Alps, and there forms dense jungles round the highest chalets, in the hope that some day somebody may eat of its poisoned root and die. Napellus has innumerable forms, not necessarily to be named, unless it be to single out the varieties *carneum* and *roseum* for special warning, these alluring epithets covering, in reality, colours of a dim and unwholesome dinginess. The blue and white bicolor form is good, however, and so is the dark-blue form called Spark's variety. *Eminens* is a much taller development. All forms bloom in high summer, through July and August.

paniculatum, another European species, with loose heads of rather handsome big blossoms, variegated from blue to white.

pyramidale (*Stoerkeanum*), silken violet flowers with woolly helm. July.

tauricum, a form quite near Napellus, dark rich blue. July to August.

variegatum, with leaves very finely and deeply slit, and flowers in spires of deep-blue to white, with a woolly helm remarkably incurving. July.

Wilsonii, incomparably the most magnificent of all. A giant from China, attaining 6 feet or so, with very handsome dark foliage, and great loose towers through late summer and autumn, of enormous ample flowers, imperial in their deep violet, carried on long stalks, so that the aspiring column has a rare delicacy in all its splendour.

HERBACEOUS ACONITES WITH YELLOW FLOWERS

Ánthŏra, a really handsome but uncommon species from the European Alps, with habit and flowers not unlike those of Napellus, but that the helmets are gathered into a much shorter spike, are fewer in number, and of a clear yellow.

Lycoctŏnum is *A. Vulparia*, *q.v.*

orientale (*ochroleucum*) has a narrow cylindrical helm of yellowy-white, and does not exceed 3 feet in height.

pyrenaicum, very nearly a form of Vulparia, and sometimes called *neapolitanum*. It is close to its type but better worth growing, having leaves more finely divided, and long close spikes of flowers, but of a clearer yellow.

Vulpária (*Lycoctonum*) is the common universal Aconite of the alpine woods—a tall species, with long thin close spikes of long thin narrow flowers of pale yellow.

(*A. aureum*, about 18 inches high, with flowers not golden by any means, but of a greenish yellow, is a species of obscure place and provenance and name.)

ACTAEA.

CLIMBING ACONITES.

albo-violaceum, a straggly species from Manchuria, with very broad divisions to the hairy leaves, and long spikes of blue and white helmets, exceedingly long and high in the cap. The plant is a very handsome one for damp and shady places, to ramble over other things.

Barrii, dark violet flowers, earlier than those of Vilmorinianum; and a hardier habit, if that be necessary.

Hemsleyanum, a variety of the Japanese *A. Szukinii*, broad leaves, hardly divided to the middle, and rambling spikes of dark violet flowers, usually some ten to the spike.

villosum, from the Altai, an immense ramper, attaining 12 feet, one of the most robust and the handsomest, with clear blue flowers in July, well before all the others of this late-blooming group. The plant is thickly hairy, and the leaves more finely cut than in the next.

Vilmorinianum is even longer than the last; it produces deep violet flowers in September.

volubile, with two forms, broad- or narrow-lobed as to the leaf-divisions, and flowers slightly hanging, from dark bronze violet to a more sombre note, tinged with green. All these species are easy to raise from seed, though germination is sometimes slow; and all can be multiplied at pleasure by division. Their place is, with the gorgeous exception of *Wilsonii*, rather in the wild garden, or away in savage and shady moist reaches of the great rock-garden, than in the general border. At the same time even there they may have a place; while in situations more natural they have a special value either as columns of blue and ominous darkness in rough places, or rambling wildly about over shrubs and among them, running up at last to outrival *Vicia cracca* in the embraces of *Lilium auratum*, and supersede the violet fires of the vetch with a more profound note of blue as the season draws on.

Actaea.—All the many catalogue-names in this race—*rubra*, *nigra*, and so forth—boil themselves down at last into the names of two sound species. *A. alba* is the North-American version, a taller thing than ours, of less ample foliage, with leaves more sharply divided; while our own *A. spicata* is dwarfer, with very handsome spreading leaves, suggesting a smooth and lax little *Spiraea Aruncus*. *Actaea spicata* is a universal plant of European mountain-woods, and strays into the alpine region of England. There are high level wastes of stone under Ingleborough where, far down in the dark crevasses between the blocks of limestone, wave plumy jungles of Herb-Christopher, the fluffy little white spikes, like those of some Spiraea, shining

ACTINELLA.

pure above the lush green of the beautiful expanded leafage. The flowers appear in June, and the ensuing fruit is a bitterly poisonous berry of shining black—the Baneberry of the Actaea's second popular name. The colour of this, however, varies, and catalogues, according to the white or scarlet berry, send out as species *A. rubra, A. erythrosticta, A. leucocarpa*, all being little if anything more than local variations on our own *A. spicata*, a rarity of real beauty and interest for any cool shady corner of the garden, where on a miniature scale of 18 inches or so it will imitate the grace and charm of *Spiraea Aruncus*, with the bonus of a handsome perilous fruit thrown in.

Actinella form a little race of not very interesting American Composites with golden flowers. They do not ask for special treatment, but lie under suspicion of biennial habits. Among those in cultivation are *A. acaulis, A. grandiflora*, and *A. scaposa*.

Actinoměris is yet another of the same kin and country. A 3-foot herbaceous plant is *A. squarrosa*, with the needs and manner of Helianthus, and golden flowers in radiating clusters in autumn.

Adēnóphora, on the other hand, is a very important race, coming so close under the shadow of Campanula as only by minute botanical differences in the customs of the seed-capsule to be distinguished. Perhaps on account of this cousinship, too close and too august, Adenophora is strangely neglected in gardens, the idea being, it seems, that the large Campanulas have spoken the last word in their kind, and that nothing further remains to be said. None the less, the Adenophoras are, many of them, most exquisite and graceful beauties, often adding a delicacy of habit that the great Campanulas lack. They are, too, of quite easy culture in light well-drained soil, and can be raised profusely from seed. New species in this race are now coming yearly in from China, which makes it premature as yet to canvass the culture and the merits of *A. Baileyana* and *A. Bulleyana*. But among the best of older species are :

A. coronopifolia, which is in habit almost exactly suggestive of *C. rhomboidalis*, growing to about a foot, with very narrow toothed leaves and loose spires of pendent purple harebells.

A. coronata, on the other hand, has root-leaves and stem-leaves after the fashion of *C. rotundifolia*. Its stems rise up to the same height as the last, and its flowers are large and bulging bells, constricted at the mouth.

A. denticulata is larger and coarser, with more bells.

A. Gmelinii, from Siberia, has narrow foliage, with the flowers in clusters at the top of the 12-inch stem.

A. Lamarckii is a species from Transylvania, and in all its parts

PLATE 1.

ACANTHOLEIMON VENUSTUM.
(Photo. R. A. Malby.)

ACHILLEA ARGENTEA.
(Photo. R.B.G., Kew.)

PLATE 2.

ADONIS VOLGENSIS.
(Photo. R.B.G., Kew.)

AETHIONEMA ARMENUM.
(Photo. R. A. Malby.)

imitates *C. rhomboidalis* with a slavish fidelity rare even among the Adenophoras, where imitation of their noble cousins has become a craze.

A. liliiflora (*A. liliifolia* of catalogues), on the contrary, strikes out for itself a new and original line of beauty. For though the big root leaves, toothed and spoon-shaped, are inclined to be rank, the tall flower-stems carry a gracious loose fountain of blossom, little branches standing out horizontally from the stem, and each carrying a carillon of charming blue-violet bells. The plant belongs to European coppices in the mountainous regions, and deserves cultivation in any place likely to be affected by its cousin, *C. latifolia.*

A. megalantha is a new species of the Chinese mountains, a very free grower and flowerer about 18 inches high, and yet again like a much more graceful and nude-stemmed *C. rhomboidalis*, with flowers of a pale and tender blue.

A. polymorpha, from China, breaks Chinese tradition by once more being merely imitative. The copy this time is of *C. rapunculoeides*, but here the spike is leafier, and stands more erect ; the rampant habit, however, is faithfully adhered to.

A. Potaninii, however, follows more along the lines of *A. liliiflora*, a much taller grower than the last, and much more branchy—the last, indeed, is more or less of a mere spire—with Liliiflora's delightful sprays of blossom, soft lilac-blue. *A. Potaninii* comes to us from Turkestan, and is the one Adenophora that appears with any regularity in catalogues.

A. stylosa belongs to the woods of Northern Asia, and is a narrow-leaved plant attaining to 18 inches, and closely reminiscent of *C. rhomboidalis*, but that the style sticks far out of the flower, like the horn of a unicorn.

A. verticillata grows to some 3 or 4 feet, and has its narrow egg-shaped pointed leaves arranged upon its stem in whorls of four at a time. The hanging bluebells are crowded towards the top of the spire.

Nor does this, of course, by any means exhaust the list of Adenophoras. But from these scant hints an idea may be gained of their general appearance and generic resemblances ; so that, in buying any new Adenophora from a list, it will be well to get so full a description as to guarantee you against merely getting something very like what you already have. It must not be forgotten, too, that the Adenophoras, though perfectly easy and even rampant, are lovers of wood and copse in cool mountainous regions, so that they will be less happy in Southerly gardens if the site chosen for them be dusty and torrid and dry. They bloom with the tall Campanulas.

ADENOSTYLIS.

Adenóstÿlis forms a small family of Composites which no one in the Alps can see without admiration. In the higher pastures, especially near chalets, as in the lower lush meadows, *A. albifrons* makes a magnificent spectacle, with its huge coarsely-toothed kidney-shaped leaves, more or less grey below with down, and then, on stems of 18 inches or 2 feet, wide conspicuous great heads of mauve-pink foam. Much less notable is *A. alpina*, a smaller growth in all its parts, much smoother, white-stemmed, and with toothed leaves like a big pointed-winged heart ; and the flowers are rather laxer in the head, though not at all dimmer in the tone of their soft lilac-pink. The Tyrolese *A. crassifolia*, however, returns more towards the splendour of Albifrons, but the leaves are leathery, almost like those of some Bergenia-Saxifrage (though not glossy), and woolly beneath ; the plant is much dwarfer in habit, and the branching flower-heads are much looser, though each radiating stem is crowned with a generous tuft of pinky-mauve. Other species are *A. viridis* and *A. leucophylla* (in which the leaves are white with down, usually on both sides, but certainly on the upper) ; and all the species are lovers of moist cool soil in mountain-woods, open lush places, damp rocks, mossy gorges, and so forth. Similar conditions will best suit them in the garden ; but it must be remembered that they are not choice treasures so much as magnificent and ramping weeds that need to be planted in wide stretches for their full decorative value to be seen. In such a spacious and suitable situation they would associate brilliantly with *Geranium sylvaticum* or *G. ibericum*, especially if Trollius were added to complete the character of the picture.

Adonis is a race largely composed of annual cornfield weeds, of which the best is the brilliant *A. flammea*. But there is an alpine section, comprising some half a dozen species, so very closely allied that it would seem as if they were all developments of one original form. These bloom early in the year, and some very early, almost before the leaves appear (like *Anemone alpina* by the melting snow-patches) ; all have large yellow flowers, quite close to the ground when they flower, but with stems afterwards elongating till the plant grows stout and rank and leafy with its expanded foliage. These species thrive readily in any deep rich soil in an open and sunny position, deserving, however, a little protection for their flowers against the inclemencies of early spring, in the case of the most pre-cocious species. They are not easy of propagation, seed being slow and untrustworthy, while the clumps are inclined to resent being moved or divided.

A. amurensis, the earliest of all (March), has my own warmest affection in a group of plants spoiled for me by the hint of green in the gold of their yellows. This is a species of farthest Asia, of which the Japanese make constant use in their exquisite toy-gardens that compress a dozen miles of mountain or shore into the compass of a salver. Here the forest may be represented by three little plum-trees of as many inches high, so many balls of white and rosy blossom, while on the foreshore lie scattered two or three buds of *A. amurensis*, neat globes of gold on the dark surface. Ultimately, however, the charming kitten grows into an unattractive cat, and *A. amurensis* follows the coarsening ways of its family. None the less, it is a beautiful thing, especially in its earlier stages; and varies, not only into a double form, but into varieties reported as white and pink.

A. chrysocyathus, the Golden-cup, is the Adonis of the Indian Alps, where it precisely echoes *A. pyrenaica*, and ranges Eastward towards the rising sun in Japan.

A. dahurica (March to April) is a Siberian version of *A. vernalis*, but earlier, more golden, and better worth possessing; while *A. distorta* is yet another form from Italy that blooms later.

A. pyrenaica (June to July) is the best of the Europeans, with the most brilliant golden suns of blossom. It is distinct from *A. vernalis* in that its lowest leaves are not reduced to scales, but have regular long stalks, and are like the rest. Its bundles of seed-heads too are much larger, and it grows more strongly and branching. *A. pyrenaica* belongs to the mountain-fields of Catalonia and Aragon.

A. vernalis (April to May) is the most generally cultivated, a species from warm limy exposures of Europe and away to the Caucasus, with unbranched stems, and the lowest leaves like over-lapping scales, and bright yellow many-rayed suns of blossom on stems that develop to about 10 inches. This is always the better for lime in a warm corner.

A. volgensis has the leaf-habit of *A. vernalis*, but the blossoms are more those of Pyrenaica, though produced much earlier, in April.

A. Walziana, from Eastern Europe, is a supposed hybrid between Vernalis and Volgensis; hardly sufficiently distinct to be craved for.

Aegopodium Podagraria is more coarsely known as the Goutweed, and, if a friend should dare offer you the variegated form, regard him for ever afterwards with suspicion.

Aethionēma takes us back into the sunny limestones of the Levant, where dwells this lovely race of tiny bushlings set with spires of blossom, pink or yellow or white—among the most well-bred plants, alike in habit, leafage, and blossom, in the whole vast race of Cruciferae, whose highest ambition is to provide the world with salubrious but uninteresting vegetables, whereas the Aethionemas—even if they have not the whole-hearted ostentatiousness of Aubrietia—stand high among the most precious and exquisite queens of the rock-garden. They all, it must be remembered, are Levantines and Southerners; all, therefore, appreciate full sunshine, and a light, rich, well-drained soil in chinks or on ledges (or in moraines), admixed, as a rule, with lime. But, given so much preliminary consideration, it is amazing that these gaieties should prove so perfectly hardy and happy and persistent in our gardens, where they are long since established in high favour, and can quite easily be multiplied either from seed or cuttings. Indeed, they even interbreed. In gardens and catalogues reigns the direst confusion with regard to Aethionema, and though, for instance, *Ae. grandiflorum* appears in every list, it is at least very doubtful if or where the genuine species is to be found in cultivation at all. The following list comprises the finest species : anything not here included should have an honest and remarkably alluring description, if enthusiasts are to be safe in buying it.

Ae. armenum, which carries its provenance clearly written in its name, is a tiny thing of 3 or 4 inches, with many crowded blue-grey leaves, short and pointed. The charming veined pinky flowers are in close elongated domes, and smaller than in *Ae. pulchellum*, which otherwise the growth resembles.

Ae. Bourgaei, sometimes transferred into another race as *Eunomia*, is a dwarf and most attractive tuft, exactly like beloved *Thlaspi rotundifolium*, from the highest screes and summits of Cappadocia, with leaves opposite to each other on the little creeping stems, large pink flowers, and fruit in flattened heads.

Ae. caespitosum, from the Armenian Alps, forms a wee dense tuffet, with minute finely narrow leaves, densely huddled, and domes of medium-sized pink blossom.

Ae. capitatum is close twin to *Ae. coridifolium*, but may be distinguished by its tight flower-heads, the size and shape of a hazel-nut. (Alps of Cappadocia.)

Ae. cappadocicum is a worthless annual weed, also known as *Ae. Buxbaumii*.

Ae. cardiophyllum inhabits Pisidia, Cappadocia, and Armenia. It is a 6-inch, leafy plant, with heart-shaped leaves, and rather small flowers.

Ae. chloraefolium (Eunomia) is a dwarf tuft of trailing frail floppy twigs beset with fleshy little round foliage, giving the stem-embracing effect of *Chlora perfoliata*. The flowers are large and pink ; the fruit is carried in a flat head or umbel.

AETHIONEMA.

Ae. cordatum (Eunomia) is a copy of *Ae. cardiophyllum*, but here the clear yellow crosses are larger, at the ends of the few straggling stems, whose lower leafage of heart-shaped grey leaves tends to fall away at last, but while they linger, make the shoots look almost like those of some very much diminished Kalanchoe. (Armenia, Lycia, Lebanon, &c.)

Ae. coridifolium is the most abused name in the race. Every other Aethionema in catalogues turns out to be *Ae. coridifolium*. In point of fact, the most fashionable wearer of this name in gardens is probablv *Ae. pulchellum*. And the *Iberis jucunda* of lists is *Ae. coridifolium*, which too often also does duty for the half-mythical *Ae. grandiflorum*. *Aethionema coridifolium* is a many-stemmed bushling, the twigs all being *undivided and unbranching from the base*, rather succulent and fat, thick-set with short oblong or narrow blue-grey leaves, either pointed or blunt at the tip. The large flowers are borne in short dense heads of pink, and in freedom the plant compares with *Ae. pulchellum*, but the leaves are shorter, and the seed-pods are boat-shaped (*not heart-shaped*), edged with only a narrow wing of membrane. (Limestone Alps of Lebanon.)

Ae. diastrophis, from Russian Armenia, is very close to *Ae. pulchellum*, but may be known by its much smaller seed-pods, and the membranous wings that surround them, which are cut to the middle, sharply. In beauty and charm, however, it rivals *Ae. pulchellum*.

Ae. grandiflorum is the glory of the race, and if it be so much a myth to-day in gardens and catalogues, this may be only because it begets its own confusion by interbreeding with Coridifolium. The true *Aethionema grandiflorum* has *long boughs undivided and unbranching from the base*, forming a loose bush of 12 inches or more, either erect or more or less flopping. The leaves are long, blue-grey, drawn-out and rather blunt. The *fruit-heads are short and dense, each pod being nearly round* (boat-shaped in *Ae. coridifolium*, heart-shaped in *Ae. pulchellum*), but a little broader than long. The flower-spikes are loose and lovely, the flowers being pink and very beautiful, the largest in the race, as big as those of *Arabis alpina*, each petal being four times the length of each sepal. This glory of the garden hails from the Schirder Ghyll on Elburs in Persia, and is the biggest of the family.

Ae. heterophyllum is a queer and most desirable treasure from Talysch, exactly like *Petrocallis pyrenaica* in looks and habit, with prostrate naked minute branches, emitting little leafy shoots of angular narrow leaves, with short spikes of pink blossom—the whole thing being like a tuft of close moss to see.

21

Ae. iberideum makes a neat, compact, and characteristic leafy clump often seen in gardens, with many erect stems of 6 inches or so, thickly set with glaucous-grey foliage, broadly egg-shaped and pointed, tapering to the stem. The flowers are largish and white, sitting in scant clusters at the tips of the leafy shoots. *Ae. iberideum* is generally distributed in the Levantine Alps, and has had the alternative name of *Ae. brachystachyum*. Its blooms hardly balance its leafage.

Ae. lacerum is found in the rocks of Pylae in Cilicia, a beautiful little species of some 6 inches, with largish egg-shaped leaves, rather pointed, the lowest alone having a minute stalk. The flowers are big, with long petals, and stamens standing free. The seed-pods, too, are attenuated.

Ae. lignosum (Eunomia) is a prostrate woody twisted plant, with short 4-inch boughs beset with short broadish blunt foliage, and ending in a tight head of large pink blossoms exactly as in *Ae. capitatum*. The sepals in this species are rimmed with pink, and the charmer is found at some 8000 to 9000 feet on Berytagh in Cataonia.

Ae. membranaceum (Eunomia) is a 6- or 9-inch bush of erect unbranching stems, from Elvend in Persia. The leaves are narrowly oblong, and stand up rather stiffly along the shoots; the pink flowers are large, and the fruit is carried in a rather dense head of overlapping flat round pods.

Ae. Moricandianum (Eunomia), from the mountains of Caria, is a splendid species very near *Ae. cordatum*, but the yellow blooms are still larger, and the leaves are all opposite to each other, blunt, and hardly heart-shaped at the base. The plant forms few, low, leafy twigs, the leaves sitting close to the stem, without a stalk, or nearly. The handsome flowers rival those of *Ae. grandiflorum*, with a long projecting style.

Ae. oppositifolium (Eunomia) is a reproduction in style and beauty of *Ae. chloraefolium*.

Ae. persicum of gardens is an obscure name, the true species being of little value, as it dies after flowering.

Ae. pulchellum is *Ae. coridifolium* of too many gardens, but not of De Candolle; being his variety β of *Ae. grandiflorum*. From this it may at once be known by its diminished size, and petals only two and a half times as long as the sepals; and from both *Ae. grandiflorum* and *Ae. coridifolium* by the fact that its erect or *flopping boughs are branched* into many minor shoots. The fruit spikes are longer than in these last, and the *seed-pods are obovate, deeply heart-lobed* at the end, with rather broad, nibbled-looking wings of membrane. The species ranges from Elburs to Armenian Pontus, where it is common.

It is one of our most treasured beauties, alike for habit and loveliness of flower.

Ae. rotundifolium (Eunomia) is a most dainty and charming little jewel of neat habit, from the screes of Elburs. It forms a minute neat tuft of 3 or 4 inches, each shoot being clothed in small round leaves of a most beautiful glaucous-blue metallic note, deepening sometimes to bronze, and cunningly enhancing the already sufficient attraction of the big pink flowers nestling in clusters at the tip of each spray.

Ae. rubescens (Eunomia) is a most lovely high-alpine from the summits of the Cappadocian mountains, where it makes a tight and dense neat tuffet exactly like that of *Thlaspi rotundifolium*, with fine creeping stems and flattened fruit-heads. The blossoms are large, of clear pink, and the fat obovate leaves are arranged alternately to each other upon the stem, this being the chief particular in which the plant differs from the no less lovely *Ae. Bourgaei*. (There is, unfortunately, no convenient periphrasis for the term "obovate," which is often very important as a diagnostic, and cannot be evaded. Let me then explain that it merely means egg-shaped, but with the *broad end of the egg uppermost*.)

Ae. salmasium (Eunomia).—Here again we have the dainty habit of the high-alpine Thlaspi, and the whole growth resembles *Ae. cordatum*, but that the leaves are of different shapes; the lower ones are oblong, either rounded at the base or a little drawn out, while the upper ones are broadly egg-shaped, pointed, and deeply heart-shaped at the base; the flowers are yellow. From Aderbidjan in Persia.

Ae. saxatile is a worthless and impermanent weed with minute flowers. There is, however, a variety sub-species from Crete, called *Ae. gracile*, and another, *Aethionema graecum*, with flowers twice the size. Not one of these, however, is to be recommended, any more than the ugly and tiny-blossomed *Ae. Thomasianum* from the South of Europe, of which a fuss is sometimes delusively made in catalogues.

Ae. schistosum sounds as if it broke away from the lime-loving tradition of its family. It belongs to the Cilician Taurus, forming a neat mass of many erect little undivided stems without branches, densely leafy to the tips with very narrow leaves, rather long for the plant and rather pointed. The pink flowers are large, and the fruit-head remarkably short, with big overlapping round flat pods, sometimes broader than their length.

Ae. speciosum is in the same range of charm—a 3- or 4-inch tuft of many rather erect unbranching stems, clothed in oblong egg-shaped blunt little leaves, of brilliant blue-grey tone. The blooms are fine and pink, in clusters; the fruit-heads rather lax, each pod standing away on a small stalk that sometimes curves downwards. General in the Alps of Cappadocia, Cilicia, and Armenia.

Ae. stylosum is a treasure of Lebanon, with few short stems only 2 or 3 inches high, clothed in rather large narrow egg-shaped foliage more or less pointed, and the lowest with a quite short foot-stalk. The big rose-pink blossoms are gathered in a head, and from each protrudes a long style.

Ae. subulatum, a bushling so minute as to be only a tight tuft of very short very leafy stems, the leaves fat, almost cylindrical in section, and the flowers rather small. This species has a likeness to *Ae. schistosum*, and comes from Argaeus in Cappadocia.

There are, of course, many others in this race, including a large supply of weeds and annuals unworthy of comment. The above choice, however, covers most of the more valuable alpine species, which, for sunny moraine or rock-work, are all delights of the very first rank.

Aethiopappus pulcherrimus deserves its name (but sometimes has that of Centaurea), for this hardy Caucasian perennial is a very handsome herbaceous plant with fine deep-cut dark foliage, grey beneath, and ample glowing Sweet-Sultans carried aloft on stiff stems throughout the later summer. As the stem attains some 3 feet in height, it is not indicated for the choicer corners of the rock-garden, but makes a fine show in wilder places, thriving readily in free light soil, and easily divided. *Ae. Balansae*, however, lives on the granitic high Alps of Lazic Pontus, at some 9000 feet, a tuft of undivided pointed leaves, all white with wool, and its 6-inch stems carry great starry blooms of yellow.

Agapanthus.—Though these glorious blue Amaryllids are justly beloved as tub-plants to stand on terraces in summer, it is not sufficiently realised that three species of the race at least are perfectly hardy and extremely valuable in the large rock-garden, where, if planted in good very deep loam, in a sheltered and exalted position, they increase from year to year their sheaves of glossy strap-shaped foliage, and glorify the duller days of late summer with their loose heads of clear and lovely blue. The best of all is *A. intermedius*, the most beautiful alike in habit and clarity of tone ; then comes *A. Mooreanus minor*, quite sufficiently attractive itself, with tall graceful 2-foot stems and loose showers of china-blue trumpets. Taller, and with a specially delightful head of blossoms splaying out and down, each blue flower on a longer finer footstalk, is *A. Weillighii*, which, though as hardy as the rest, is so rare and noble as to deserve being indulged with an eiderdown of cinders in climates where the winter is wet or inclement. The especial association of all these should be of course with the glowing spires of the earliest and smallest Kniphofias, so precious even by themselves, in little groups of delicate aspiring flames, on bold high places of the rock-work in August and September.

Agāvē applanata *var.* **Parryi** is a splendid neat-rosetted huge Agave from stations so high in the mountains of Arizona that it proves hardy in Europe if duly considered in the matter of a dry, well-drained, and sheltered position, with, perhaps, in districts especially raw, a little protection of bracken or yew-boughs in winter.

Agrimonia.—Not one of the species of Agrimonia is worth the trouble of planting in the garden.

Ainsliaea, a quaint race of Japanese Composites, of most graceful appearance, suggestive of Prenanthes, but often more dwarf and fountain-like in effect. The best species are *A. acerifolia, dissecta, uniflora,* and *cordata.*

Ajuga, a robust and not very interesting group of Labiates, most useful for covering tracts of ground in unconsidered corners. *A. genevensis,* however, with a specially fine deep blue-flowered variety *Brockbankii,* throws out no runners, but sends up in May and June loose shaggy spikes of 6 inches or so, revealing flowers of blue or rose, and suitable for dry sunny places. *A. pyramidalis* is much the same, but only short-haired, with thicker columns of clear blue blossom. A form of this is *A. metallica crispa,* a very favourite catalogue-plant, with smooth curled leaves of a dark and splendid metallic sheen, admirably setting off the sapphire blue flowers that peer out from the thick-leaved column of the spike. The most useful coverer of dishonourable ground, however, is our own smooth and glossy *A. reptans,* which throws out runners in every direction with feverish rapidity, and is profuse, in spring, with its shining leafy columns a-twinkle with blue dragons. The type varies indefinitely in colour, and there are many named forms, besides a metallic-leafed one, and another of dense compact habit. Much less attractive is the Bulgarian *A. Laxmannii,* with small striped blossoms of blue and white.

Alchemilla alpina, the alpine Ladies Mantle, about the most interesting alpine plant produced by the jejune mountains of the English Lake-district, is often admitted to the rock-garden on that account, no less than because of the beautiful silver sheen on the under side of its five- to nine-fingered leaves, gathered into spreading mats. However, the spreading mats so freely spread, and the insignificant flowers so pitilessly seed, that the garden is likely to be happier in the end without *Alchemilla alpina.* And there is no other of its large race that at present has any claim to enter there.

Alĕtrís farinosa is a North-American species, not unlike a larger Tofieldia in habit ; it is not very easy to grow, is by no means worth the effort, and is, altogether, the kind of thing described by the wisest catalogues as "interesting."

Alfredia, worthless Composites in the Thistle section.

Alisma contains two good things for the water garden—our native graceful water-plantain, *A. Plantago,* with its tall loose sheaves of innumerable small stars, all throughout the summer in any depth of water not exceeding 2 feet, but best in the shallows. Unfortunately the plant is so profuse a seeder that the whole garden soon grows full of nothing else. Far choicer is wee *A. natans,* whose small oval leaves lie dark on the face of the waters, and show up the beauty of its dainty three-petalled flowers of pure white floating among them. This plant may be trusted not to be troublesome, and is an extremely rare native of a few British pools in the West.

Alkanna makes up a race of South-European and Levantine Borages, sometimes coarse and biennial, but sometimes really splendid. In cultivation are *A. lutea,* and the handsome *A. tinctoria,* like a golden foot-high Lithospermum ; and even better things may be expected of *A. incana,* which is another nobly beautiful rock plant from alpine fissures in the cliffs of Caria and Pisidia, graceful in habit, all softly grey with down, and carrying blue flowers as fine as those of *Lithospermum purpureo-coeruleum. A. areolata,* from shady places on Cadmus, is rough, not downy. *A. primulaefolia* attains only to 4 or 6 inches, with sticky little narrow leaves and yellow flowers ; and *A. scardica,* from alpine regions between 5000 to 7000 feet, is only half a foot high with blue flowers, while *A. rostellata* is a yellow counterpart of *A. incana.* For all these the treatment appropriate to sun-loving Anchusa is suggested.

Allectorūrus yedoensis, though very rare in cultivation, is a lovely little fairy that ought to offer no problem of delicacy considering its specific name. From among arching glossy strap-shaped leaves, like those of some tiny Imantophyllum, shoot up loose graceful plumes of rosy-lilac stars, suggesting those of an Anthericum, to which, indeed, the plant is closely related, and to whose simple treatment we all hope it may respond (*Anthericum yedoense*).

Allium.—The vast family of the Garlics, ranging all across the northern and southern regions of the temperate zone, is disqualified in the garden on account of its prevalent and odious stink, which, combined with the predominance in the family of inconspicuous weeds, sheds a disability on even the beautiful species that here and there occur. Almost all Garlics, however, are of the easiest and most unnoticeable culture, if poked deep into good light soil in an open place ; and their beauty is such as to win admittance for the following (among such others, too, as shall in future sound worthy, with clear detailed promise of beauty), notwithstanding the unnegotiable evils of their savour : *A. Moly*, from shady woods of Spain, is very handsome, with broad glaucous leaves and loose heads of large golden flowers on stems of some 8 inches or more. This species spreads rapidly and is indestructible. *A. coeruleum* (*A. azureum*) has erect fine stems a foot high or more, with delicate narrow foliage, and erect globes of bright blue in May and June. *A. cyaneum* is similar, but dwarfer and altogether more refined, with hanging little heads ; while its cousin *A. kansuense* (July) has flowers of a lovely bluebell tone (see Appendix). *A. giganteum*, from Central Asia, bears huge broad leaves, and then very tall stems, rising far above them, each crowned with a great ball of bright lilac-coloured flowers. *A. Aschersonii* is sometimes offered as *A. orientale* and *A. Erdellii*, under both of which names it proves a coarse and dowdy ugliness. *A. haemanthoeides*, from snow-level at 10,000 to 13,000 feet in the Alps of Persia and Kurdistan, is a treasure still to be desired, for it is near in style to our own *A. triquetrum*, but only 3 or 4 inches high, and with flowers twice the size, of gleaming white ; while not unworthy of comparison with this in beauty is the rose-coloured, round-headed *A. Akaka*, from meadows and earth-pans on the Alps of Turkish Armenia. On the other hand, *A. Libani*, though dwarfer, is as ugly as *A. Aschersonii;* but *A. Schubertii* (May, June) is one of the marvels of the family, with broad glaucous leaves, and rather short stout stems on which appear enormous heads of small pink flowers, with countless other flowers springing far out from the tight globe on every side. Unfortunately this shock-headed Garlic inhabits the fields of Palestine and Damascus ; accordingly it requires a warm dry soil, and is not very trustworthy in our climate. Our own native *A. schoenoprason*, the Chives of more domestic language, is not without its value, too, in the garden ; nor will any one be ungrateful to its countless heads of rich violet purple when once they have seen it staining all the bogs of the upper Alps in an imperial splendour, growing specially fine, and with the most lavish jungles, in the wettest places. Into Cornwall also strays its improved variety, an even finer thing in size and colour of flower, which has sometimes been raised to specific rank as *A. sibiricum* (July to August). *A. neapolitanum* (June), from South Europe, is most favourably known in the race because it abhors the usual fashion and does not stink, while its loose heads of fine white flowers are gathered in stacks and exported to England for decoration. In cultivation *A. neapolitanum* is hardy, but requires a sheltered place and soil light and perfectly drained. Akin to this is *A. calyptratum* from Asia Minor, while *A. cilicicum* and *A. gomphrenoeides* are cousins to Schoenoprason, the latter being a rare plant from rock-faces of Vitylos in Laconia, only attaining 6 or 10 inches, with heads of large and brilliant bloom (this is *A. ascalonicum* of some authorities but not of Linnaeus). Returning to larger subjects, we are often offered *A. karataviense*, which proves a rather coarse plant with stolid globes of pinky white nestling amid broad glaucous foliage, two leaves to each bulb. Much taller is *A. Rosenbachianum* from Central Asia, which has exactly the habit of *A. giganteum*, but here the flowers are of pale and not resplendent pinkish tone (besides, in *A. giganteum* the leaves hug the ground). And tall, rather delicate and graceful *A. fragrans*, of South-west Europe and North America, goes one better than even *A. neapolitanum* in its avoidance of the family smell. For, though its flowers, carried loosely on tall-stemmed heads in late summer, are nothing much to look at, they have the astonishing charm of a really delicious scent. No wonder that its eccentricity has decided some authorities to regard it as a by-blow of the family, and to put it in a house and race apart, as *Nothoscordon fragrans*. One wishes as much could be said for pretty little *A. triquetrum* (May), which, from shady cool banks and moist places in Spain and Liguria, has established its claim to be an English native in Cornwall. However, *A. triquetrum* may plead other utilities ; for now it promises to develop into a popular vegetable. The plant has great attraction, and is always to be known by its fat, three-sided stems of some 6 inches or so, each carrying perhaps six large pendulous flowers of a diaphanous white, looking like the ghost of a dead white flower drowned long ago in deep water. As for our common *A. ursinum*, no one will ever say such sweet things for that ; *A. ursinum*, though as charming as a Garlic can be, has a most pestilential smell, and a most invasive habit. Let no one admit it to the garden ; its only place is the wild wood, where it amuses itself by making the unwary mistake it for Lily of the Valley—until they have picked it. By far the most beautiful, however, of all the race are the three alpines, *A. Ostrowskyanum*, *A. oreophilum*, and *A. narcissiflorum*. *A. Ostrowskyanum* comes to us from the Alps of Turkestan, with stems that rise to a foot or so, hanging out large flowers of rich dark-red violet. *A. oreophilum*, with two flat narrow recurving little leaves, sends up a stem of only 3 inches or so, with clustered domes of big purple blossoms. This beautiful mountain-jewel comes from the screes of alpine Caucasus and Daghestan at some 7800 to 9000 feet. It has been figured in the *Gartenflora*, i. 775, and yet remains persistently confused in catalogues and made synonymous with the next. (Indeed, some lists appear to treat *A. Ostrowskyanum, narcissiflorum,* and *oreophilum* as if they were all one species, and even, by a superfluity of naughtiness, turn *A. oreophilum* into *A.* "*oreophyllum,*" which is mere nonsense. "Mountain-leaf" has no meaning; "Mountain-lover" is no less apt a description of this Allium than of me.)

A. narcissiflorum (*A. grandiflorum* and *A. pedemontanum*) is the glory of its race, not only in our own European mountains but in all the ranges of all the world. Let no one be deluded by catalogues into buying in place of this, as an alpine Allium, the large and dowdy *A. Victorialis* (which apparently, in defiance of grammar, we must follow the original authority's fantasy in calling *A. Victorialis*); nor is there much hope or profit in attempting neat and tiny *A. alpestre* from the upmost meadows of the Alps—occurring in scattered clumps, for instance, on the gypsum-dunes in front of the Hotel de la Poste on the Mont Cenis, as *A. Victorialis* luxuriates rankly on the hummocks of the upper Heuthal. In places far more august dwells *A. narcissiflorum,* in the steep earth-pans and stony screes high up in the most awesome shelves of the limestone Alps of Piedmont (and far away into the Caucasus). Here it runs underground, forming a huge ramifying mass of root-stocks below in the unnegotiable stony hard earth, and the surface of that barren place is covered with a waving green jungle of upstanding strap-shaped leaves, up among which come shooting, in August, springy stems of 8 or 10 inches, each hanging out a loose head of some six or eight flowers, very large and lovely indeed, great pendent bells of glowing vinous red. Unfortunately an evil godmother has dowered this beauty with a commensurate drawback, in the form of an exaggerated stench—a stench so horrible that one can hardly bear to collect it, to say nothing of the fact that its soil is like rock, and one's own foothold slithering and insecure upon the lip of abysmal precipices. None the less, *A. narcissiflorum* responds easily to culture in warm dry places of the rock-garden, and should surely appreciate the moraine; as also should *A. Balansae,* a near relation in beauty and brilliance to *A. oreophilum,* but differing in pink flowers rather narrower, and their segments blunt, not sharp. (Lazic Pontus.) Nor, to finish, need we grudge a welcome to pretty little *A. pulchellum* from Southern Europe, with quite slight graceful aspiring stems, and heads of pink flowers standing airily out this way and that, irregularly, from a small head composed chiefly of buds and bulbils. The plant blooms in high summer, and has special charm if planted among similar graceful things, such as fine grasses, *Campanula rotundifolia,* and white Linums.

ALSINE.

Alsine, a typical race of minute—as a rule—tufted rock-plants nearly related to the Pinks, with flowers usually minute and almost invariably white. Only the most subtle differences separate Alsine from Arenaria, in which family all the most brilliant members of Alsine have at times been allowed to take refuge, but are now most usually reclaimed. At the same time, a certain amount of confusion still subsists, and the same species may be found twice in the same catalogue, both under Alsine and again under Arenaria. It is as well to remember this. The essential generic difference between Arenaria and Alsine ought to be that in Alsine the seed-capsule has as many divisions as the flower has styles, while in Arenaria it has *twice* as many divisions as the flower has styles. Botanists, however, are never weary of playing games ; and the following lists of both races must be read as containing many species in each that may well be, and often are, referred to the other.

The best species of Alsine—the race containing many minute-flowered dowdy little high alpine weeds—are probably the following :

A. Bauhinorum heads the list—one of the most beautiful plants that the rock-garden can desire. It is often called *Arenaria* or *Alsine liniflora,* and is the lime-loving counterpart of the hardly less beautiful *A. laricifolia.* It is by no means uncommon in sunny rocks and stony exposures of the Southern limestones (Col de Pesio, &c.), and in the garden, under similar conditions of a sunny slope in light soil, still further lightened with limestone chips, it has no scruple about growing on quite normally into its natural woody trunked masses, forming loose mats of fine green fur, from which rise such an abundance of very large pure-white flowers on waving airy stems that the whole cushion becomes an undulating 8-inch mound of snowy cups and stars, till one greatly regrets the loss of a name so descriptive and apt as Liniflora. July to August ; seed.

A. erythrosepala, from alpine Anatolia, forms tight dense masses, from which emerge the almost stemless heads of blossom, the sepals having a rim of red. This, like all other of the dwarf mats, should have a choice and handy position, in light rocky soil, in a chink or in the moraine. Like all the rest of its race, it comes easily from seed.

A. eurytanica is a neat little species from the Alps of Greece, not unlike our own *A. verna,* but very much handsomer, forming a loose green tuffet of moss from which rise 6-inch stems, each carrying a loose shower of from five to thirteen flowers, as large and brilliant as in *Arenaria montana.* The whole plant is quite hairless and green, most particularly to be desired, it seems.

A. gracilis (or *Arenaria gracilis*) is a form or species allied to *A.*

30

pinifolia, but taller, making tight dark cushion-masses, from which rise 6-inch stems of white blossom. The leaves are longer and stiffer than the closer fur of Pinifolia.

A. groenlandica makes a minute green scab of moss, bestarred with white flowers, the petals being twice the length of the sepals.

A. imbricata (Caucasus) has much the same habit, but the stems lie about and attain to 2 or 3 inches, with white flowers of fine size, more than twice as large as in *A. macrocarpa*.

A. juniperina belongs to *A. Villarsii, q.v.*

A. laricifolia is the granitic twin to *A. Bauhinorum*, and a plant of no less beauty and identical habit. The two types are clearly close together, and possibly are merely different soil-developments of one original. But in *A. laricifolia*, among other points, the seed-capsule should equal the calyx, instead of surpassing it as in Bauhinorum. *A. laricifolia* is common all over the granitic Alps in stony sunny places, from the far Western ranges away into the Carpathians ; neither this species nor the equally lovely Bauhinorum has ever quite come to its own in the garden, although so choice, easy, and vigorous. Carpets of either species would make, before they themselves are glorious in bloom, the most perfect cover for choice Crocus in spring or autumn, and for the tinier Narcissi.

A. leucocephala makes neat little tidy cushions of grey velvet in the high-alpine fields of Caria and Pisidia. The flowers are small, carried in a little head on stems of 2 or 3 inches.

A. macrocarpa forms a dense or flopping tuft along the ground. The closely clustered blunt leaves, very narrow, are edged with teeth, and eyelashed with minute bristles, though the surface of the leaf itself is smooth. The blossoms are large and handsome. (Arctic Siberia.)

A. montana must here be mentioned as a dreadful warning. For *Arenaria montana*, with which the name is sometimes confused, is one of the rock-garden's greatest and most universal prides, whereas the true *Alsine montana* is a worthless annual weed.

A. parnassica is a rare species, with quite short leaves overlapping on the stems, and the old ones remaining. It forms into specially wide dwarf mats like a stunted form of *Arenaria graminifolia*, but that the leaves are shorter, and the grass of the turf accordingly finer.

A. pinifolia, another dense tuffet, with close rosettes of narrow foliage on the barren shoots, and loose stems of 5 inches or more, with white flowers.

A. procumbens is a curious small species from the sea-sands of

Aegina, lying splayed out flat upon the shore in the shape of a star, with roseate blossoms. Whether it would prove permanent or hardy with us its habitat would lead us to doubt, were not such unlikely things perpetually happening.

A. recurva ranges right across the Alps from the Eastern chains, far away into Asia—a most variable little high alpine closely akin to *A. verna*, forming dense tufts of emerald fur, with fine-forked stems, more or less downy. *A. nivalis* and *A. condensata* are varieties. The plant gets its name from the sidelong twist of its narrow blunt leaves like the finest grass.

A. rimarum is a desirable small tuffet, neat and tight, from rock crevices in the Cilician Taurus. In general habit it resembles *A. imbricata*, but that it is all downy with glands, with the petals two and a half times as long as the calyx.

A. robusta is a form or synonym of *A. gracilis, q.v.*

A. Rosani. See under *Arenaria graminifolia.*

A. rupestris, however, is the jewel of jewels, most especially to be longed for. In all respects it is the counterpart of *A. verna*, but that it breaks bravely away from the stainless traditions of the family by erupting into a profusion of delicate pink stars. It comes from high cliffs of Lebanon and the Levantine Alps.

A. umbellulifera, from the Cilician Alps, is a beauty of which we are still in want. It has the leaves overlapping in four regular rows up the stem, as in *A. setacea* (a thing of no great merit), but otherwise has the neat tufted habit of *A. verna*, except that the larger and more brilliant flowers are carried in a flat head or umbel on a 5-inch stem, and have their petals narrowing to the base.

A. verna has served as the standard of comparison for many of the foregoing species. It is one of the most charming of our native alpines, abundant on the limestone at high altitudes, as for instance on the Western face of Ingleborough. Here it forms tidy masses of fine and dainty emerald fur, finer and closer and greener than the finest grass, the little leaves being more or less downy with glands. The frail and dainty flower-stems rise up in early summer, and spray or flop to the length of some 3 inches, carrying loosely, on forked sprays, clear white stars about half an inch across, whose dimensions do not widely vary, though the plant itself differs much in size of development, attaining extraordinary exaggeration if it can indulge itself on a diet of lead in the neighbourhood of old mines.

A. Villarsii has little fine greyish leaves in a tuft, with taller stems of 7 inches or so, and rather inferior flowers after the style of *A. recurva*, disproportionate to the promising tufts and mats of green foliage. In

PLATE 3.

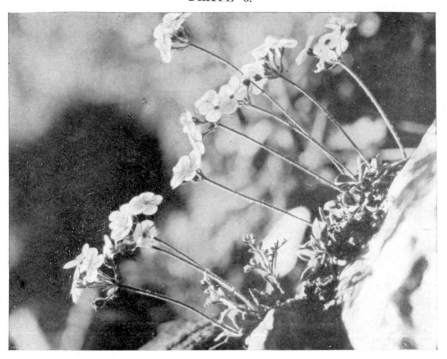

ANDROSACE TIBETICA.
(Photo. W. Purdom.)

VOL. I.   ALLIUM CYANEUM MACROSTEMON.
(Photo. W. Purdom.)

A. austriaca, from the limestones of the Eastern Alps, the foliage is yet longer and furrier, but the flower is also a trifle larger.

Alyssopsis Kotschyi is a small hoary-grey tufted Crucifer from the crevices of Lebanon, with the yellow flowers of Alyssum and the general habit of Draba.

Alyssum, an immense race of rather low-growing annual or perennial Crucifers, especially abundant in the warmer climates of Europe, and abounding across the temperate zone of the Old World. Many are weeds, but many, again, are of the highest value in the rock-garden, where all grow readily in light soil or moraine, in a sunny exposure, and may be profusely multiplied by seed. The blooming season is usually in spring and early summer; and the unvarying colour of the flowers in every true Alyssum is always and only *yellow,* plants with white or pink flowers having now been banished into races of their own. Here follows a list of some of the best species—all those mentioned being perennials.

A. alpestre is a most common and most variable species of universal distribution in all the Alps to Western Asia and North Africa. It is a prostrate, almost shrubby, diffuse plant, hoary grey all over with starry hairs. The little leaves are oblong, *the petals rounded,* the flowers in unbranched heads, the pods small, more or less obovate. *A. serpyllifolium,* from Spain, Mont Cenis, &c., is a well-marked form, with minute leaves like a Thyme, indeed, much more densely grey, and flowers small and pale. Quite near *A. alpestre,* too, is *A. bracteatum* from the Persian Alps, but here the flowers are of a softer yellow, and the petals are scalloped instead of being smooth at the edge. The flower-head, again, is looser and more divided, the leaves more rounded, silvery with white scales.

A. argenteum is a useful thing, but in quite a different style—the type of the tall-growing species, attaining 18 inches or so, and then expanding a wide flattish loose head of very small deep golden blossoms that make a fine effect when appearing in a mass, the more so that they open in later summer, and would associate worthily with *Campanula rotundifolia.* Others in this non-alpine group are *A. constellatum, A. masmenaeum, A. elatum* (really fine, from the pine-woods of Lycia and Caria, with flowers as large as in *A. saxatile*); *A. crenulatum* (from Mount Cassius in North Syria), after the same kind, almost shrubby; *A. floribundum,* a close copy; *A. peltarioeides, A. samariferum,* and, most curious of all, that strange and rare plant *A. corsicum,* which is only found in one small district near Bastia, where it fills all the fields with the glow of its wide golden heads, a species akin to *A. argenteum,* but twice the height, and in its

3-foot stature exceeding every other of its race. However, great as may be the utility of this handsome group, its members cannot compare in brilliancy and charm with the neater-habited dwarf alpine species. The real heart of the rock-gardener can hardly hold anything beyond 6 inches, or a foot at the most.

A. aeizoeides, accordingly, takes us back to that precious clan. For this is a beautiful little species from Armenia and Olympus, very tufty and as brilliantly silvery with scales as *A. lepidotum*, but in *A. aeizoeides* the tiny leaves that thickly clothe the boughs are quite narrow and linear, while the petals are narrowly wedge-shaped.

A. argyrophyllum is another silver-scaly tuffet, with weak prostrate boughs, rather frail, and naked at the base. The leaves are obovate and the flowers pale yellow, larger than those of *A. montanum*, in clustering heads, and as attractive as the whole plant, which chiefly differs from *A. idaeum* in having narrower scaly pods of half the size.

A. armenum, from the alpine meadows of Turkish Cilicia, is most like *A. montanum*, but hoary with long stiff starry hairs lying low along the growths. The flowers are straw-coloured and the ovary felted.

A. atlanticum, a dwarf plant all silver-grey, with dense starry hairs as beautiful under the microscope as frost-crystals (a speciality of this family). The spatulate or spoon-shaped little leaves are huddled along the branches, and at their end arise big golden blossoms in a dense mound. The species ranges from Atlas to the warm limy cliffs of Granada between 1000 to 4000 feet, and thence away across South Russia. (It is to be noted that the epithet refers to Atlas the mountain, and has nothing to do with the Atlantic Ocean or regions, which so much more readily come to mind.)

A. aurantiacum decorates the high mountains of Lycia, and is a tufted, silver-scaled beauty, with short prostrate undivided shoots, oblong narrow foliage, and flowers large and of a goodly rich orange.

A. Bilimekii, from rocks near Granada, should prove very attractive indeed. For it is mere *A. saxatile*, but reduced to a tidy habit and the height of 3 or 4 inches at the outside.

A. bracteatum is a near cousin of *A. alpestre*, with twisty flopping stems, much rounder, silvery-scaly leaves, and pale yellow blooms with notched petals (not entire) in a looser, larger head. (Persian Alps.)

A. callichroum forms a nest of upstanding, short shoots, thick set with rounded slightly incurving leaves, large for the plant, beautifully hoary-silver, with a conspicuously brighter rim.

A. condensatum has hard uprising stems of some 6 inches, with hoary scaly little obovate leaves, each with a small stalk of its own, all up the stem, and large lemon-pale flowers with obovate petals, in a head that often widens till it seems almost to form an umbel. The pod, too, is longer than is usual. (High Alps of North Syria and Lycia.)

A. creticum is a sub-shrub after the invaluable habit of *A. saxatile*, twisted and woody, attaining a foot or so high, with leaves often an inch long, and heads of golden flowers twice the size of Montanum's. Its leafage has the further advantage, so fashionable in this family, of being scaled with silver; and it inhabits the cliffs of Lassiti in Crete, at the height of some 6000 feet.

A. cuneifolium is a pretty but rare species from high up in the Sierra Nevada and Eastern Pyrenees, Dauphiné and the Abruzzi. It has specially twisted stems, with all its silvery leaves obovate, and soft yellow flowers. Quite near, but with shoots much straighter, lying splayed along the ground, is *A. diffusum*, an extremely rare weakling from high-alpine earth-slides at about 9000 feet in the Sierra Nevada.

A. cyclocarpum = Ptilotrichum cyclocarpum, q.v.

A. edentulum is the correct name for a most beautiful saxatiloid Alyssum often offered as *A. gemonense*, and as such one of the most valuable in the family, being in appearance a rather neater and smaller *A. saxatile*, with rather larger flowers, of a flaming golden fire, with petals cleft almost to the base. (Eastern Alps to the Banat.)

A. erosulum is a false name for *A. suffruticosum, q.v.*

A. Fischerianum is a species from North Russia, herbaceous at first and then becoming almost shrubby. The blossoms are in undivided heads at the end of the shoots, and the leaves are narrowly oblong, hoary, and rather rough.

A. gemonense, a false name for *A. edentulum, q.v.*

A. Haussknechtii, from Berytagh in Cataonia, forms a small tidy tuft of 3 inches or so in nature, freely branching, and all clothed in silver scales, with obovate yellow petals. (A twin to this is *A. lanigerum*, from North Persia.)

A. idaeum is a plant well beloved in the rock-garden, with frail, prostrate, and slender shoots. In appearance it is not at all unlike *A. Wulfenianum* of the Eastern Alps, but the leaves are longer and more pointed, narrower, and less flat and few upon the flopping stems; they are oblong-rounded at first, then oval-acute, finely fringed, and shimmering silver-green with their minute scales. The soft yellow petals are oblong wedge-shaped, and the pods are very nearly round and quite smooth but densely hoary. From the stony summit of

Cretan Ida ; and a treasure in the rock-garden, especially to flop and fall with its long flattish shoots from some sunny ledge or crevice.

A. Lagascae = Ptilotrichum purpureum, q.v.

A. lepidotum, a tight close tuft all glorious with silver glitter, made up of short dense leafy little shoots of tiny oval-elliptic foliage, from which the heads of yellow blossom hardly emerge, but cover the whole tuft. A specially charming plant (not unlike *A. aeizoeides*), from the high Alps of Lycia.

A. montanum, though not the most attractive of its group, serves admirably for an illustration, as being the common alpine Alyssum of the main European ranges, and universally known in cultivation. It is a tufted plant, greyish-green, attaining about 8 inches at the most, with closely congested boughs, mounding themselves up, and lying out along the ground, unbranching, and rising at their ends, beset with small rough oval-oblong leaves covered with a dense ashy-grey felt. The flowers are particularly numerous, rather small, arranged in a lax long head, bright yellow, *with notched petals*. (The species is variable : *A. ochroleucum* and *A. Hymettium* are varieties.) Closely akin is *A. Mulleri* from Turkish Armenia and North Persia, but with leaves much narrower and the whole growth more hoary. Also *A. mouradicum*, from Phrygia, at alpine elevations—a small sub-shrubby thing, with fruit perfectly smooth, and boughs flopping and uprising in the same way. While from the mountains of Ispahan comes *A. persicum*, an erect-growing stalwart of 6 inches or a foot, sub-shrubby and branching, silver-scaly, with leaves half an inch long, and flowers larger than in *A. montanum*, with unnotched obovate petals, and seed-pods with a wide margin ; and *A. Moellendorffianum* from Bosnia is yet another closely allied species, most attractive, with foliage densely silvery.

A. ovirense is a false name for *A. Wulfenianum, q.v.*

A. oxycarpum, with its variety *A. kurdicum*, is like a miniature of *A. alpestre*.

A. praecox, from the Cilician Taurus, has broader leaves and bigger seeds, deeper flowers, and much baggier seed-pods than in any form of *A. montanum*. The plant is sub-shrubby and scaled with silver.

A. purpureum = Ptilotrichum purpureum, q.v.

A. repens, with a variety known as *A. Rochellii*, is a creeping yellowish plant, covered in a soft short pelt. The flowers are unusually large. (Mountains of Achaia, Central Arcadia, and Transylvania.)

A. Robertianum is an extremely rare species peculiar to great elevations in Corsica and Sardinia. It is quite close to *A. alpestre*, and the deep pod is not six times the size of Alpestre's, as has been misleadingly stated by Godron and Grenier. Another version, yet distinct, is a new species, *A. Tavolarae*, discovered on limy rocks there, down by the sea. This rises to the height of 15 inches, and is branchy, erect, and larger in all its parts.

A. rostratum is in reality a worthless biennial. The plant which figures under this name in gardens and catalogues is simply *A. alpestre*.

A. saxatile needs no description, standing high among the twelve most popular cheap and cherished splendours of the rock-garden in spring, when its hoary grey, lax-leaved foot-high bushes are smothered in their loose wide hillocks of gold. The double variety is even richer of effect : there is a compacta-form ; and the variety *A. citrinum*, with flowers of a refulgent moony citron-yellow, is by far the most beautiful of all, and cries aloud for such a contrast as that of Aubrietia Lavender. This *A. saxatile* type ranges from South Europe to the East.

A. serpyllifolium. See under *A. alpestre*.

A. sphacioticum, from the mountain-tops of Crete, from 6500 to 7000 feet, forms a dense and minute little tufty 3-inch shrubling, with undivided stems rising from a vertical root, all clothed in small ovate leaves, silvery-scaly, diminishing up the stem till they dwindle to being narrow oblong. The flowers are lemon-yellow, larger than those of Montanum.

A. spinosum = Ptilotrichum spinosum, q.v.

A. suffruticosum is woody and sub-shrubby, with short, twisting prostrate shoots, clothed in oblong narrow leaves, scaly and with silver hairs. There is a smaller and more condensed variety, *A. olympicum*. The range of the type is among the mountains of Syria.

A. Wiersbickii is a species from Eastern Europe in the relationship of *A. montanum*, but no more specially alluring.

A. Wulfenianum is another species mistreated by catalogues, which know it not, although they freely offer it, sending out forms of Montanum instead. True *A. Wulfenianum* is a really beautiful plant, in habit akin to *A. idaeum*, but much larger, and flopping handsomely down the face of a rock in sheets of many brittle fleshy tortuous shoots, set with rounded leaves very fat and thick, and shimmering with silver as delightfully as those of *A. idaeum*, but noticeably rounder, less elongate, and fewer. The flower-heads are ample and loose enough to show the shape of each large blossom, of a refulgent clear pale yellow with broad petals notched at the end. This is *A. ovirense* of some foreign collectors—a name drawn from the Hoch Obir in the

Karawanken, that gaunt peak looking out over Klagenfurt and its lake ; for there in the topmost screes and silt-pans of the summit-ridge may *A. Wulfenianum* be found gleaming pale through the mists that wrap the mountain, their lemony gleam well served by the silvery foliage on which they lie. (In the garden it turns greener.)

Most of the remaining members of this family, as often reckoned, will be found restored to their convenient places, under the names Koeniga, Schivereckia, Ptilotrichum, Berteroa, and Vesicaria.

Amphicŏmē is a small Indian race, nearly allied to Incarvillea. *A. arguta* forms a very little bush, throwing up branching stems of a foot or two from a creeping root-stock. The fine ferny leaves, quite smooth, make an attractive feathery mass, and at the end of the sprays hang dainty rosy trumpets. In the same range is *A. Emodi*, but with hairy foliage and flowers rather larger, about 2 inches in length. Both these plants ought to be trustworthy, for the first is found at 7000 feet in Kumaon, and the second has a range between 2000 to 9000 feet in the mountains of India to Afghanistan. None the less they are far too rarely seen in gardens, a sufficient symptom that they require a warm and sheltered position in good light soil, with protection against excessive damp in winter. See Appendix for a problem.

Amphoricarpus Neumeyeri, which sometimes appears in catalogues, is a Dalmatian Composite of some attraction, like a dwarf 6-inch Centaurea, forming a tuft of lanceolate-leaved rosettes, with flowers of a purplish red. It thrives in any sunny place in poor soil on the rock-work, perhaps among grasses, but has no special charm.

Amsonia is a race of North-American plants, tall and leafy, with blue flowers, allied to Vincetoxicum. They are, however, coarse and rank, most fitted for wild places, open and dampish, in the wood garden. *A. salicifolia* sometimes flaunts in catalogues.

Anacyclus, a race of Composites, most closely allied to Pyrethrum, often confused with it and often merged into it. There are several species in cultivation, but none of value ; but see Pyrethrum and Leucocyclus, as all genuine species of Anacyclus are worthless annuals.

Anagallis.—Besides many splendid annuals of upright or flopping habit, such as *A. linifolia* (*A. grandiflora*), this genus might offer the rock- and bog-garden several delightful trailing treasures, of which not one could be more precious than our own native *A. tenella*, from heaths and marshes all over England, covering the earth with its freely-rooting flat branches, set with roundish pairs of shining leaves as in some of the New Zealand Epilobiums, and powdered over, all the summer through, with countless little wide cups of a delicate pale pink, rising on delicate fine stems from the sprays. *A. tenella* is of easy culture in any congruous place in the garden, low and damp ; but labours under strong suspicion of being no better than an annual. And the remaining creepers of the race are unfortunately natives of Africa and South America ; but there ought surely to be hope of success in *A. Meyeri-johannis*, seeing that it grows by the verge of eternal snows on Kilimanjaro, from 9000 to 13,000 feet—a most beautiful thing, quite prostrate and rooting all along, with little leaves so fat and crowded against each other on the shoots that they have to stand up in two packed rows, upon which, here and there, sits a single pearly cup, staring straight into the mists that perpetually wrap the mountain.

Anaphalis, close relations of Antennaria, and for the same use and treatment in hot dry places, though taller and less ornamental as a rule.

Anarrhīnum bellidifolium and *A. laxiflorum* are close cousins to Antirrhinum, of which the first species belongs to the Mediterranean region, and the second is a glabrous plant from the high Spanish mountains, with rosettes of narrow, then widening leaves, and small white snapdragons in one-sided bunches. A speciality for rather cool corners of the rock-work.

Anchonium, a small race of Crucifers from the Levant, of which *A. Billiardieri* sounds rather like the sphinx sent out by nurseries as *Arabis Billiardieri*. Much more important, however, is *A. Tournefortii*, sometimes found in cultivation under the name of *A. helichrysifolium*, with narrow, hoary-grey foliage, quite smooth-edged, sending up 6-inch stems, either simple or branching, of big fragrant yellow flowers. From the stony alpine region of Armenian Taurus and Cappadocia, and excellently fitted for the sunny moraine, or poor-soiled warm bank. Like all Crucifers, it should multiply readily from seed.

Anchusa, though a family of vast and Boragineous weeds, including some truly glorious border-plants, offers us one or two smaller species that might be of use in the sunny, dry places of the rock-garden, if we could get them. Such are *A. caespitosa*, from the highest summits of Crete, forming a dense bristly tuft, with the leaves pressed flat to the ground, and perhaps half a dozen fine flowers almost sitting upon the tuft. *A. myosotidiflora*, from copses of Caucasus and the Altai, has lately come into cultivation, and is now proclaimed by catalogues with their usual candid air of ecstasy. In point of fact, it is rather a coarse thing, with large triangular heart-shaped leaves like greenish flannel, on long stalks ; and foot-high showers of blossoms which, though of a true dazzling blue, are far too small for the lush development of the plant. However, it may have its place in cool, shady, and undesirable corners, though even there it is not more attractive than our own *A. sempervirens* of similar situations, with flowers larger, and of the same brilliancy, even if the growth have a tight leafy habit, not like the airy and spraying grace of *A. myosotidiflora's*. Raised from seed. *A. affinis*, too, from the waysides of the Southern Alps, is very handsome with its long crosiers of blossom, of a rich and true imperial violet at their best stage ; but we have little hope of another dark purple species, *A. limbata*, which is a dwarf and beautiful biennial, of painfully rare occurrence on the hot limestones near Aleppo.

Andromeda. See **Cassiope**.

Andrósăcē.—Perhaps of all mountain-races this name is engraved most deeply on the rock-gardener's heart, like Calais on Queen Mary's, standing as well for his highest hope and pride as for his bitterest disappointments. The huge clan, so intimately allied to Primula that in days past they have been confused one with another, divides into many marked sections. In the first place, there is the more or less worthless race of annuals, headed by the deceptively-named *A. maxima*, which has the smallest flowers of any on record. This section is called Andraspis, and belongs to dry warm and barren places, at comparatively low elevations, in the Old and the New World alike. Such of these as may be thought worth growing are easily to be raised from seed ; but hitherto our gardens have found them nearly all to be useless and unrewarding weeds. Next comes the section Pseudo-Primula—the connecting link between Primula and Androsace, and therefore confined to the local centre of both, the highlands between India and China. The plants in this group are usually large and soft and leafy, lax alike in texture and constitution ; they are, in appearance, suggestive of *Cortusa* or *Primula obconica*, and are chiefly met with in the lower mountain region. Only one of them has yet publicly appeared in cultivation ; and, though of perennial and often stoloniferous habit, they are not likely to be very resistent to our climate, nor long-lived in the outdoor garden. With the third section, however, we ascend to the alpine heights in the company of *A. Chamaejasme*, whose name it bears. In distribution this famous group is wholly arctic and alpine, ranging from the Old World across into the most northerly regions of the New, representing a transition from the section Andraspis to that of Aretia, the last and the highest of all, a race perverse and precious, dear to the gardener's heart and purse, a set of impenetrable tiny domes in the hard rock of summit-cliffs in the Alps, of which the type is *A. helvetica*. This august group is entirely confined to the most terrible elevations of the Old World.

With regard to cultivation, Andraspis needs little and is worthy of less ; Pseudo-Primula, loose and soft, should be tried in a light soil, cool and rich, not exposed to excess of sun or wind, nor allowed to suffer from extremes of cold in winter, or stagnant moisture. Chamaejasme offers least difficulty of the lot, and gives the most abounding reward—most of the species responding freely to treatment in any light sandy soil, well-drained and enriched with chips. They answer, too, especially to the conditions of the moraine. Rather more sand and a warmer exposure is perhaps indicated for the Indian species in climates of especial rigour, though in most districts they tend to ramp even excessively. As to the Aretias, vain is any hope that we shall ever desist from the effort to grow them—they are so incomparably charming ; and one well-flowered clump of *A. helvetica* or *A. × Heeri* is well worth its long line of dead and vanished predecessors. This section is undoubtedly very difficult, with the precise difficulties that attended the cultivation of Eritrichium ; for the high-alpine Aretias, especially the woolly ones (the smooth-leaved species are infinitely less troublesome), require a long period of dead and absolute rest if they are to tide over the winter and harden their souls to a properly generous display of flower again in spring. And such conditions of firm drought from November to April are just those most difficult of attainment in cultivation ; even in the best built garden it is not possible to avoid the circumambient miasma of wet that winter brings, even by roofing over the plants with glass, which may avert immediate rain-drops indeed, but cannot dry the corroding damp of the atmosphere, so keenly resented by those dense fluffy tufts that are longing to go to rest, instead of which they have to remain awake and act reluctantly as living sponges. And to make a high-alpine Androsace do anything reluctantly, is to make it retire as firmly and promptly from the world as a cat retires from a chair in which it has been placed against its will. However, love and care never go eternally unrewarded ; overhanging dry stations can be found in the garden, and some of the Aretias are more easily grateful than the others. No one need ever despair, so long as the clumps have their perfect drainage, their firm and immovable position in a sunny crevice of rock (or in good moraine, perhaps), and their due protection against damp in winter. And the more complete the plant's winter rest, the more prone will it be to show its alpine generosity and brilliancy of blossom when summer wakes it again to life. With too many alpines, imperfect rest, as with too many human beings, leads to a scanty and pallid efflorescence in the next morning of their life.

With regard to propagation, nearly all the species of the Chamaejasme section throw runners readily and can be endlessly multiplied ;

so, very often, do the Pseudo-Primulas, which can also be raised easily from seeds (like the last). Seed-raising, however, of the Aretias is apt to prove a chancy and precarious pleasure ; if the question of multiplying them occurs, it is best most carefully to remove some of the outer trunks from the main cushion in August and insert them into sand-beds, which should then be made reasonably damp—*i.e.* not allowed to get frizzled and dusty, but kept firm and cool.

Androsace aeizoon, a widely variable species in the section of Chamaejasme and sarmentosa, with handsome rosettes of broad spoon-shaped leaves, neatly overlapping, leathery, bluish-grey, rough-edged, eyelashed, sprinkled (especially at the tips) with microscopic white globules. The bare stems are rather tall for the plant, and rise to some 6 or 12 inches, carrying a loose head of flowers in varying shades of pink. The species belongs to the main chains of Central Asia, and is quite protean ; the form *A. himalaica* being comparatively poor, while *A. integra* and *A. coccinea* (intense red), both from China, are much desired. Its habit is to form a mass of tufts, without offsets.

A. albana, often catalogued, lies under suspicion. The true *A. albana* is an Andraspid from alpine regions of Transcaucasia, forming downy rosettes of spoon-shaped leaves, which send up three- or four-finger-high stems, each carrying a close cluster of white flowers, almost sitting in a bunch. (Annual.) *A. albana*, of lists, may be anything.

A. alpina takes us into very different country and kindred. For this is *A. glacialis* of later authorities—the royal rose-pink splendour of the highest alpine shingles that makes *Silene acaulis* appear by comparison so shrill a vulgarian in colour and habit. *A. alpina*, though an Aretia, is not a rock-plant, nor a dense tight tuft. It inhabits the whole alpine chain of Central Europe at great elevations, and always upon non-calcareous rock (this seems to be an absolute rule) ; here, in fine detritus of the topmost slopes, moist with the melting snows percolating beneath, the Androsace achieves in pink what Eritrichium achieves in blue, but forming much wider looser mats, often a foot across, of softly downy, leafy shoots, ending in tiny rosettes, which are hidden from sight in summer by an unbroken sheet of colour so pure and soft and soothing in the gentle yet startling clarity of its pink that I know of no other alpine colour or show to equal it. Nor is it any anguish to collect, like its kin, but comes up from its loose shingles with a tidy wet wad of roots that seems to promise success in cultivation. And, in point of fact, *A. alpina* is by no means hard to grow, in a loose rich mixture of sandy peat and chips and leaf-mould and grit. If water can be arranged to trickle through the bed about 12 inches below the surface, all through the summer, so much the better for the vigour of the Androsace, though it must, of course, be turned off at the end of October and the plant kept dry. If such care be too elaborate, a flower-pot or drain-pipe, driven deep into the earth near the plant, and periodically filled with water, will have the desired effect. But in flower it is too rarely that *A. alpina* remembers its splendour of the hills; a dozen pallid pink stars, if you are lucky, sprinkle the surface of the mat, instead of concealing it with a dense overlapping crowd of ample glowing rosy beauties, radiant and golden-eyed in the alpine air. It is curious, however, that in the Dolomites, where the plant is found on volcanic outcrops, it develops into a strangely different form, usually inhabiting hard rock, and with flowers invariably of pure white, which very, very rarely seem to fade into a pale pink. Nor are they so free and large, nor the cushion so wide and hearty, as in the glacial regions of Switzerland, where *A. alpina* is one of the few species that there reach their most brilliant development.

A. arachnoidea. See under *A. villosa.*

A. arctica, from the Behring Straits, is a most minute and densely-tufted Aretia, densely downy, not yet introduced into cultivation.

A. × aretioeides, known to but few, is a natural hybrid between *A. alpina* and *A. obtusifolia.* At the same time it is not uncommon in districts affected by its parents, and should be looked out for by travellers in the Oberland and Valais, as for instance on the Riffel, on the Albula, and behind the hotel on the Torrenthorn. It is a very pretty little plant, forming neat tufts of two or three clustered rosettes of bluntish leaves, downy with tiny starry hairs. These tufts send up a number of neat bare stems, hardly an inch or two high, carrying sometimes one pink flower, but more often a rayed head. *A. Brüggeri* is probably another name for this charming cross.

A. brigantiaca. See under *A. carnea.*

A. bryomorpha is an Aretia from the Pamir, suggesting *A. helvetica,* but with looser and more columnar tuffets, and narrower leaves quite smooth except for a fine fringe of hairs. The flowers are pale pink, and the clump's baldness offers us good hope that it may prove tolerant of our conditions. It has the short corolla of Androsace, but otherwise suggests the habit of the nearly allied Dionysias, an almost unknown race of alpine Aretias, particularly beautiful, from the high Alps of Persia.

A. caespitosa is the one true Androsace we could have from Persia, if indeed the plant be truly reported thence; which is doubtful, seeing that its only other stations are far away in the cliffs of Eastern Siberia. It is a true and tight Aretia, with very narrow little leaves, not closely overlapping, with a long point, and set with a few whitish hairs, especially towards their tip. *A. caespitosa* forms wide masses, from which the rather large flowers—bigger than in *A. helvetica*—just emerge and stand aloof. Quite similar, again, is *A. Vegae* from Arctic Eastern Siberia, but the leaves here broaden a little towards their blunted tip.

A. carnea is one of the best known and best grown of our alpine species. It belongs to the group of Chamaejasme, but is practically smooth and without down, forming larger or smaller tufts or mats of emerald-green foliage, broader or narrower, almost wholly hairless and downless, with only a few small hairs at the edge. The flowers are lovely, of a brighter or paler or very pale pink, carried in loose heads at the top of 2- or 3-inch stems more or less downy. This species has a most abundant distribution, if not a specially wide range, from the Pyrenees through the Alps, only as far as the Stelvio. In these limits, however, it varies indefinitely in size and length and breadth of leaf, in strength and width of tuffet, in size and colour of blossom. Its varieties and synonyms are, accordingly, the despair of gardeners and the happy chance of catalogues. These are now proclaiming *A. Reverchonii* with shouts of glee as a "novelty." Now, anything that has not been in cultivation more than twelve years is a "novelty," we know; but even this pleasant definition will not serve to save *A. Reverchonii*, which is merely a later and discarded synonym of *A. carnea*-type. As for *A. Halleri*, now announced with yet more poignant trumpet-blasts, this is *A. carnea var. Halleri* from the Cevennes, with leaves much longer, eyelashed, always recurved at the tip, and glossy-green. Yet another form is *A. carnea var. brigantiaca*, from grassy places on the Mont Cenis and other heights, with narrow spreading leaves, recurving, with the edges more or less toothed towards their tip (Mont Cenis also yields a frail weak and narrow-leaved small form, with almost annual-looking tufts of two or three rosettes, and flowers of a diaphanous pearly pink). There is also a hoary, lax-tufted downy form, *A. puberula*, and gardens know a very broad-leaved variety, with large and few rosettes in the mat, and full-faced blooms of glowing pink, under the name of *A. carnea eximia*, now become regrettably rare in cultivation. But the finest of all forms, far exceeding *A. carnea*-type itself in merit, is that form from the Pyrenees which has almost earned the specific rank conferred on it by catalogues and gardens as *A. Laggeri*. *A. carnea var. Laggeri* is a development restricted to the Pyrenees—a most lovely plant, forming wider but much smaller tuffets than the type, of dark emerald-green leaves much shorter and narrower and finer and more hypnum-like, never recurving. From these rise more frequent heads in spring, of flowers a trifle larger perhaps, and of a much more glowing note of pink with a golden eye. All these forms of *A. carnea*, being smooth, and not affecting such great elevations as their rock-haunting cousins, are perfectly easy and permanent and hardy in English gardens without any trouble at all, in any kindly mixture of peat, leaf-mould, and gritty loam, with good drainage and an admixture of chips, to give them a reminder of the scantily furnished places that they love on the upper alpine pastures, in the loose peat of the mountain turf, with all the waters of the world draining sharply away far down beneath them, in the heart of the steep slopes on which they live.

A. Chamaejasme, which has the privilege of giving its name to the group, is quite common in all the alpine turf, straggling threadily far and wide in the grass, with its little fluffy rosettes of rather silvery pointed leaves appearing here and there ; and here and there its heads of blossom that, beginning by being as white and ample as pearls, fade by degrees, through tones of cream from the yellow eye as it begins to run, to a soft and delicate blurred rose with a crimson central ring. Nor does any difficulty attend the culture of *A. Chamaejasme* in any cool open soil or moraine, in treatment suited to *A. carnea ;* and it is specially fitted to be associated with *Gentiana verna*. The species is one of the very few that overflow into the Northern regions of the New World, crossing from the extremities of Arctic Siberia. In the course of these wanderings, accordingly, it has diverged into many well-marked forms or varieties, some of which may some day be offered as unexplained new species. These are *A. Chamaejasme var. carinata*, a denser-rosetted development, with leaves so much fatter as to seem keeled beneath—(this is a form from the Cascade Mountains in the Rockies, and American national pride has differentiated it absurdly as a species, under the name of *Drosace carinata*); *A. Chamaejasme var. arctica*, still denser, and thickly shrouded in long yellowish hairs ; *capitata*, a very good form from the Kurile Islands, with broader leaves and rosettes almost globular, and fine large flowers, two to five in a tight head, on little stems not an inch high ; *ciliata*, a smooth, glabrous variety, the leaves having a fringe of hair and no more ; *triflora*, robust and fleshy, clothed in transparent hairs ; *coronata*, also fleshy, but quite tight and tiny, with densely overlapping leaves almost forming into columns (and *uniflora* is a yet tighter and minuter form with hardly any stem at all, and one or two flowers at the most): both these last from grim altitudes in Kumaon and Western Tibet, and probably best suited, like the condensed arctic forms, for cultivation in the select moraine, with water flowing beneath.

ANDROSACE.

A. Charpentieri is a very rare and beautiful Aretia, confined to a few summits above Como and Lugano, where, in the topmost ridges, often in grass, it forms wide and rather lax masses of shoots, bare below, with rosettes at the end, of rather *broad, blunt leaves narrowing a little to the base*, and *quite downy all over with fine hairs*, but especially at the edge (thus clearly remote from *A. Wulfeniana* and *A. ciliata*, which both *have bald leaves*). Up from these come the little downy flower-stalks, standing erect, twice as long as the leaves, and each carrying one rose-pink flower, with the petals oval, hardly notched at all at the end. In cultivation, in light free well-drained soil, this treasure is by no means difficult, and generously repaying, being much less insistent on rest and resentful of winter damp than its much tighter and woollier cousins from the much greater elevations of the Central Alps.

A. Chumbyi. See under *A. sarmentosa*.

A. ciliata, apart from its localities, may be known from *A. Charpentieri*, which it resembles in rose-pink blossom and possession of a little stem to each bloom, by having larger flowers (the largest and finest in this group—about one-third of an inch) on stems scarcely rising above the leaves (in downy *A. Charpentieri* and smooth *A. Wulfeniana* these stems are *twice* the length of the leaves in height), which are narrower and shorter in proportion, quite *smooth and hairless* except for a fringe at their edge, and not growing narrower at the base. They are nearly a quarter of an inch long, oblong-spoon-shaped, arranged in a neat rosette at the top of the lax branches, from which they die away below each year, not forming a column of dead relics. This beautiful Aretia is very rare in the highest limestone rocks of the Pyrenees (Port d'Oo, Pic de Salettes, and Maladetta, at 9000 feet). In cultivation it is not by any means intractable under careful treatment in choice crevices, not having the down that spells death to so many of its kindred and neighbours from those heights.

A. cylindrica is yet another extremely rare prize, occurring on the limestone at upmost elevations in the Western Pyrenees (Oule de Marboré, Maladetta) here and there. This curious small species rises on stepping-stones of its dead leaves, till every shoot has become a dense aged column of dead foliage, crowned with thick fat downy leaves, longish, very broad and blunt, hoary grey, from which appear lonely, on fine little stems of some half an inch, the milk-white stars. This plant, being downy, requires the same care as is exacted by the much tinier Helvetica, but has successfully weathered winters even here in crevices of the Cliff above the Ingleborough Lake (N. Yorkshire).

A. Duthieana will prove a pleasant companion to its close relations,

ANDROSACE.

A. primuloeides and *A. sarmentosa.* It is a high-alpine from Hazara, with a dense rosette of oblong rather pointed leaves, all the same length, and shaggy at first with long snow-white hairs, but then going bald. This rosette sends out runners, and the stalks are hardly 2 inches high, carrying three to six flowers in a head.

A. × *Escheri* marks a dim and doubtful record of a hybrid between *A. obtusifolia* and *A. Chamaejasme.*

A. flavescens stands far away from the rest of its group in the matter of colour. For this species closely resembles *A. primuloeides* (the true species), forming a mat, bright green, of neat rosettes, emitting stolons. The leaves are nearly an inch long, and the graceful 2- to 7-inch stems are as green as they. But the whole clump is clad in a fine silk ; and the flowers, about the same size as those of Primuloeides, are carried in heads of about ten or more on graceful stalks, and are of a pale yellow. (Keria Pass, North-west Tibet.)

A. foliosa, Duby, seems not to be in general cultivation, despite the incessant offer of it by catalogues, which invariably, by foliosa, mean the true *A. strigillosa,* Franch. (*A. foliosa,* Klatt), which usually occurs a little lower down in the same column. The genuine species is much smaller in habit than strigillosa, and with flowers finer and larger ; it is a rosette-plant of the sarmentosa group, with *perfectly smooth foliage,* and at the top of an 8-inch stem a bunch of lilac-coloured flowers about half an inch across. At their base the leaves, hardly forming a proper rosette, draw down to a sort of prolonged semi-leaf of a foot-stalk, which enfolds or sheaths the stock. The stems and pedicles are downy, while the *smooth* leaves have a fringe of hair and are oval, about 1½ inch long, ending in a point. The crown emits runners, from fat bare dark stems. (North-west Himalaya.)

A. glacialis. See *A. alpina.*

A. globifera is a curious tiny member of the Aretia group from Kumaon, which perhaps belongs more nearly to the Chamaejasmes, and should prosper with care in the select moraine. It forms a loose branchy mat of many little rosettes exactly like wee balls, not more than one-sixth of an inch through, smooth outside, but woolly inside, with a dense mass of leaves, of which the outer ones, when young, end in a tuft of white hair and are sharp, but follow the fashion of human life in becoming blunted and bald as they grow older. The small stems are twice the length of the leaves, each carrying one pink flower, almost, if not quite, as large as the green pilule from which it just arises. However, sometimes two flowers are found, and thus threaten to transfer *A. globifera* to the Chamaejasme group.

A. Halleri. See under *A. carnea.*

ANDROSACE.

A. Harrissii, from Chitral, differs from all the other Asiatic Chamae-jasmes in having an almost lignescent stock and leaves *entirely smooth*. It branches about with twisting half-woody shoots like a Dionysia. The little leaves are fleshy, pale green, hairless, and rosetted so tightly as to pile up into a column of dead ones beneath the minute rosette of the current year, each leaf being about one-sixth of an inch long. The stems, again, are some half an inch high, from the end of each shoot, carrying a loose head of two to five white flowers, this many-flowered habit alone distinguishing it from the Aretias, *which never have a stalk at all, or a bunch of flowers*, but only single blooms, springing each by itself straight from the cushion, on a stem or peduncle of its own.

A. Haussmannii is the special Aretia of the Dolomites, a very distinct rare thing, forming larger or smaller tufts of loose and rather large flat rosettes, the leaves being comparatively long and narrow and splayed-out, almost hoar-frosted with glandular and starry microscopic hairs, till they take a note half metallic and half glaucous. In the middle of each tiny rosette lies a round bud like a dreaming pearl at dawn, just flushed with life ; and this in due time develops a stem of about one-fifth of an inch, and opens into a rather thin and squinny white star, no proper fulfilment of the promises held out by that rosette and that bud. Pale pink is the official description of the blossoms, by the way, but they have invariably been whitish in my experience of the plant in its native places, where it haunts the walls and highest peaks of the Dolomites, especially in the Fassa district, descending upon the Antermoja Pass, and even seeding down into the shingles behind the Grasleiten Hut, where it grows into patches of rosettes far more ample than the wizen little clumps of one or two crowns that it makes in its native precipices. And on the other side, beyond the Antermoja Lake, there is a scree-slope where it grows like the commonest cruciferous weed, among jungles of *Papaver rhaeticum*. In cultural needs *A. Haussmannii* follows *A. helvetica*, but clearly ought to require far less care, and should thrive freely in moraine, where its lovely leafage alone will make it welcome.

A. hedraeantha is a beautiful Chamaejasme, coming between *Duthieana* and *obtusifolia*. It hails from the ranges of Rilo in the Balkans, and answers quite happily to cultivation either in the choice bed or in the moraine—a neat mass of bright green rosettes, with leathery blunt small leaves, perfectly smooth except for a most faint and minute fringe. The stems are notably short in stature, barely half an inch in height, each carrying from five to ten violet-rose flowers in a tight head.

A. × Heeri takes us back into the Swiss Alps, where at one point in

PLATE 4.

ALYSSUM ALPESTRE.
(Photo. R. A. Malby.)

ANDROSACE ALPINA.
(Photo. R. A. Malby.)

PLATE 5.

ANDROSACE CARNEA HALLERI.
(Photo. R.B.G., Edinburgh.)

ANDROSACE LACTEA.
(Photo. R.B.G., Edinburgh.)

ANDROSACE.

Glarus, not far from that strange hole in the wall of mountains which is called the Martinsloch, may very sparingly be found on the stark rosy cliffs this delicate hybrid between *A. helvetica* and *A. alpina*. The plant, together with Helvetica's saxatile proclivities, has Helvetica's tight tufted habit, though a little softer and looser (under the influence of Alpina); while from Alpina it inherits its blossoms of glowing pink. *A. Heeri* is sometimes introduced to cultivation, but always proves miffy and difficult. It should be looked for in all districts where the parents occur. I myself once found a single specimen at the top of the old Breitenboden glacier-bed, close under the shadow of the Schwarz-horn in the Oberland; and no doubt many more await discovery.

A. helvetica, when all is said and done, remains the gardener's type and darling among the high-alpine Androsaces, so cosy look its rounded hummocks in their rock, so beautiful its generous eruption of pearly rounded stars. Through all the European Alps it ranges, sporadic but abundant at great elevations, hugging the hard limestone cliffs and topmost wind-swept ridges of stone. Here, close in their cracks, are ensconced the plants, forming fat little ash-green domes of minutely-rosetted leaves, glistering with microscopic hairs and giving the effect of so many soft velvet pincushions, until with the melting of the snow and the unbinding of the mountains from their sleep the fountains of life are loosed, and the hoary tuft conceals itself beneath an overlay of milky-white flowers, flat on the cushion, laughing out across the gulfs of the world with their bright gold eyes. So lives *A. helvetica*, till in winter the iron once more descends, and the Beauty is held in her long magic sleep, or put to bed beneath a warm grey coverlid of snow. And yet, in cultivation, where all are homesick for their native air, *A. helvetica* is unquestionably the easiest of the high-alpine section; and even in the damp chill Cliff above the lake at Ingleborough has weathered five successive winters of wet and darkness, never ceasing to increase the number of its rosettes each year. In the Alps the plant can be confused with none; the great height at which it is found, the hard limy rock (limestone as a rule), reveal its identity. *A. imbricata* is white as wool; and of its other kindred none has the very short, thick, fat, inward-curving little downy leaves, dusty-green rather than grey, and giving a globular look to each microscopic rosette. It is most abundant in the Oberland, and I have often seen it in other regions, as on the actual summit of Piz Padella in the Engadine. In the Dolomites, which do not run high enough to please it, *A. helvetica* seems to be replaced by *A. Hauss-mannii;* but in one point, at the comparatively low elevations of the Schlern, there are cliffs and gullies full of it; while its green sponges hang out from the sheer 6000-foot precipice with which the Southern face of the Marmolata drops to earth ; and I have even seen it lingering sadly in exile on the black volcanic range across the valley of the Fedaja Pass, where it reluctantly intrudes on cliffs that belong to *A. alpina* and *Eritrichium nanum*.

A. Henryi is the only Pseudo-Primula as yet verging upon cultivation. Its general look might be described as that of a stouter, shorter, neater, fatter, fleshier *Primula obconica*, with rounded scalloped downy leaves on long stalks, and stiff upstanding stems that can attain a foot, and carry a neat domed head of pale lilac flowers rather small for the foliage, but very concise-looking and tidy and respectable. *A. Henryi* comes from South Shensi, and has, indeed, altogether a prim and luscious look, suggesting that it may be either biennial or tender or both.

A. hirtella is a most interesting Aretia, which has developed in times long past out of *A. pubescens*, and even now is quite close to it—forming a perfectly dense dome of rosettes, with narrow tiny leaves, splayed-out and upstanding and bright grey with a thick felt of down. The flowers are white and rather small; and the plant, to the casual eye, has still a first cousin's resemblance to *A. pubescens*, though the leaves are shorter, blunter, fatter, much whiter-grey, less upstanding, and so forming into a flatter cushion. *A. hirtella* occurs extremely rarely in the West Central Pyrenees, only on the Pic de Gabizos and the Sum d'Aucubat above Eaux-Bonnes ; and, if it be considered as a recent and special local development from *A. pubescens*, this means that the separation has occurred in ages remote indeed, but comparatively modern as compared with the dim and dizzy antiquity that shrouds species which are true palaeogenic specialities, such as, for instance, *Borderea pyrenaica* in these same Pyrenees, an inconspicuous tiny Bryony, not climbing, which is yet, in temperate Europe, the one and remotely exiled member of the great tropical family of the Yams, and a reminder, across the unfathomable abyss of aeons, of hotter ages when the configuration of the continents was different. By comparison with this, *A. hirtella* is the merest parvenu, though its portrait might perhaps have been painted in the caves of Altamira.

A. × *hybrida* is a reputed intermediate between *A. helvetica* and *A. pubescens*, reported from Mount Javernaz above Bex.

A. imbricata stands for the extreme type of the Aretias. This tight rock-tuft goes beyond all its kindred in exaction ; for, while these are content to arrange for their supplies of atmospheric moisture in summer by donning a transpiring Jaeger felt of down, *A. imbricata* is such a *malade imaginaire* that it spends its life in a dense white

woollen blanket, taking sun-cures in the hardest and hottest black
granite precipices of the Southern Alps, where along the adamantine
walls its minute masses look as if someone had poked in lines of cotton
wool in pads, so dense is the silver-whiteness of its close wads,
recalling otherwise those of Helvetica, but that its blunt little leaves,
even if not longer, are much less fat, and so have not the incurved
effect. *A. imbricata* is invariably faithful to the granite, in its hardest
cliffs and in its very hottest and driest aspects. It is, accordingly,
not only a most difficult plant to collect, but also the most difficult
of its section to grow, requiring rather the treatment of a tropical
Opuntia than that of a high-alpine Androsace. It is one of the species
confined to the central and seaward Alps—Graians, Valais, Oberland
(rare), Cottians, and Maritimes (common)—descending through the
Pyrenees to the Sierra Nevada ; it seems to grow more and more
abundant as it comes South, and in the Cottian ranges drops to quite
low elevations, in very torrid exposures above Bobbio ; and may be
seen abounding on the Southern face of Monte Moro, or above Arolla
towards the Col de Bertol, or in the high places of the Maritimes
sharing the iron cliffs of the Ciriegia and the Boréon with *Saxifraga
florulenta*, though the Saxifrage is still far down in bud when the
Androsace is covering its snow-white cushions with a profusion of
rather small stars which there, though always by courtesy described
as white, seem in reality to be of so impure a tone as to verge upon
a pale and rather dirty yellow.

A. lactea takes us back to the section of *A. carnea* and *A. Chamaejasme*,
and is a welcome change from the perversities of the Aretia group.
For *A. lactea* is only alpine and sub-alpine, its glossy spiny-looking
bright dark-green mats of glossy rosettes (each more than an inch
across, and the whole mass often about 8 inches) being found in the
upper grass-land of the mountain region through the limestone Alps
from the Jura away to Transylvania. From the flattened towzle of
glossy narrow little foliage about ¾- to 1¼-inch long there spring gracious 8-inch stems, often less in nature and often more in the garden,
which break quite soon into a head of blossom—if one can so describe
the long delicate stems that spray about this way and that—each one
supporting a single lovely large white flower with a golden eye, the
effect being that of a loose and scattering rocket of blossom. The
whole plant, besides being of vigorous constitution, is entirely smooth
and hairless, consequently it is as much more vigorous even than
Carnea as its habit is larger and laxer ; in the garden it runs freely
about, shooting up fresh rosettes from underground, and taking
happy possession of any light and pleasant strip of well-drained alpine

ANDROSACE.

soil which may have abundance of water in early summer, or moisture flowing beneath. There is no necessity to indulge *A. lactea* with shade, so long as its ground is well watered ; this I learned to my cost when I thought I sighted it on cool copsy rocks half-way up the Wiener Schneeberg, and came all the way down again only to find that the object had been *Silene alpestris*, which, from a distance, it certainly does superficially resemble in manner and habit. But then, toiling in torrid midday up that mountain again, I suddenly found the genuine Androsace abundant in the hot and stony turf at the top, close beneath the Empress Elizabeth's chapel, among *Dianthus alpinus* and the Primulas Auricula and *P. Clusiana*.

A. lactiflora, however, lest any one should fall into confusion, is that pretty annual or biennial species which gardeners often know as *A. coronopifolia* (*A. Chaixii* is another smaller and inferior Andraspid). Nor is this so very unlike the style of the last, though quite inferior in size and grace of blossom. For from the large and ample rosette of toothed leaves spring many stems of many white flowers in a graceful fountain. It is of the easiest culture, of course, in dryish open poor soil, and seeds like cress. But *A. armeniaca*, from alpine Armenia, is still prettier, a neat little dwarf thing, with tidy rosettes, and heads of white flowers twice the size of Albana's.

A. Laggeri. See *A. carnea.*

A. lanuginosa is among our most precious and universal rock-garden ornaments, loving a light sandy soil in a warm exposure, and thence trailing far and wide its prostrate shoots of pure silver, from which through all the later summer—so precious an advantage—arise the Verbena-like heads of soft rose-lilac, beautifully adapted for contrast with the violet and lavender autumn crocuses upspringing through the slack tissue of its gleaming sprays, but not really fitted, so rampant is its scale, for any companionship but those of bulbs. *A. lanuginosa* comes from medium elevations in the North-western Himalayas, but is perfectly hardy and vigorous anywhere in our islands. It can easily be struck from cuttings, and there is a variety *A. Leichtlinii* in which the flowers are whitish, with distinct eyes of crimson or yellow, appearing in the same umbel.

A. longifolia. See under *A. sempervivoeides*, and Appendix.

A. macrantha is one of the best among the annual Andraspids. It is like an enlarged Armeniaca, with big rosettes of toothed leaves, and bare stems of some 5 inches or so, carrying a profusion of white flowers rather more than half an inch across. (Alpine Turkish Armenia.)

A. Matildae, a most curious and precious Aretia, confined to the summit rocks of Amaro and the Gran Sasso d'Italia in the Abruzzi, where, snuggled securely into the crevices, it masses its rosettes of rather broad, pointed foliage, perfectly smooth and of the glossiest green. The rosettes are oddly large for this group, and might suggest those of *A. hedraeantha*, but that the leaves are longer, about one-half to two-thirds of an inch, stiffer, more pointed, grooved, recurving, and of so brilliant a polish. The flowers are carried, of course, lonely on each quite short stemling; they are white, and almost unduly small for the plant (no bigger than those of wee-rosetted Helvetica), which, though so choice, is perfectly easy of cultivation in any choice crevice or moraine.

A. mucronifolia (highest grassy crests of Tibet, R.F. 1914) is a compact glorified Chamaejasme, forming a lax low mass, without runners, each shoot being thickly set with minute bud-like globules of leaves, which are wee, overlapping, incurved, and fleshy, each globule only being about a third of an inch through. The little stems are half an inch high, carrying from three to six blossoms in round heads, covering the whole cushion in domed snowdrifts, fragrant of hawthorn and exquisitely beautiful. (See Appendix.)

A. muscoeides is a delicious remote Aretia from the high inhospitable cliffs of Ladak, most curious in habit, forming rambling mossy masses of frail naked branches, set at intervals with bunches of tiny leaves, and branching again and yet again, each time with poodle-tuffets of foliage at intervals, till each shoot ends with a pair of flowers, large and sturdy for the size of the moss-mass—which may readily be known, by those fortunate enough to see it, not only by its habit, and its rufous or ochreous stems, but by the grey-green tone of its foliage, unique among the Asiatic Aretias, but recalling that of *Douglasia Vitaliana*.

A. obtusifolia is a species closely allied to *A. Chamaejasme*, from the European Alps, but considerably less attractive. It forms a clump of rosettes, the leaves being long and blunt, not silky at all, and much greener than in Chamaejasme, while the stems are also much taller and the tuft not at all rambling, throwing no runners. So much taller are the scapes, indeed, attaining some 6 inches at their tallest, that the flowers, already rather small for the size of their calyces (and smaller than those of *A. Chamaejasme*), look a little mean by comparison with the plant's stature, and are of a rather impure white. In Switzerland this is not a common species, but is found on the granites above Arolla (and indeed, throughout the rest of its distribution through the Eastern Alps to Transylvania, seems to prefer the granitic formations at least as markedly as *A. Chamaejasme* prefers the calcareous). It varies, however, greatly in stature and form, and one of its most marked varieties, the dwarfed, one- or two-flowered *A.*

obtusifolia var. aretioeides, occurs on dolomitic limestone in the Vajolon valley under the wall of King Laurin's Rose-garden.

A. Pacheri. See *A. Wulfeniana*, of which it is a later synonym.

A. × pedemontana is a natural hybrid between *A. carnea* and *A. obtusifolia*, which has occurred in gardens and been recorded from the Alps of Piedmont. It resembles a small *A. obtusifolia*, but the leaves are vaguely toothed (instead of being *perfectly entire*, as in *all Androsaces of the villosa-sarmentosa group*) and keeled underneath, while the calyx is smooth and not hairy. The flowers appear to be white, and differ also from those of *A. carnea* in projecting upon their little foot-stalks even in the blossoming stage, instead of forming a closer head.

A. Poissonii forms loose mats of shoots very short, not more than 1 to 1½ inch, each ending in globules of foliage, piled one above another, standing supported on columns of withered remains, the outer leaves having the transparent hairs of *A. Chamaejasme*, and the inner ones, at least those in the uppermost globule, being bluish green. All the leaves are rounded and eyelashed, thus differing from *A. globifera* (with which it has been confused), as well as in having no wool anywhere, but only hairs upon its leaves, which are not smooth outside ; the flowers also have no scape and seem to be almost sitting upon the pilules of foliage, as in *A. helvetica*. (Jurkia Pass in the Sikkim-Himalaya, &c.)

A. Prattiana, when at last it arrives, should prove perhaps the most beautiful of all species in the group of sarmentosa and Chamaejasme. It throws no stolons, and has rosettes of pointed hairy foliage, bristly and narrow, 3 to 4½ inches in length. The stiff and equally bristly hairy stem is about twice or three times as high as the leaves are long, and the flowers are of intense purple-rose, notably handsome, and carried in a loose head. (Szechuan.)

A. primuloeides.—Round this name clings much obscurity ; catalogues announce it freely, but the result is always either *A. sarmentosa* or *A. sempervivoeides*. Perhaps this may be due in part to the fact that Hooker's names, of grandifolia, foliosa, and primuloeides, are all of obscure application, with no reference to the species that now rightly bear them. The true *A. primuloeides*, which may most likely not be in cultivation, is a lax stoloniferous plant closely akin to *A. sarmentosa*, with the same bald runners from 2 to 4 inches long, hairy at first and then smooth. The leaves of the *rosettes are all clothed in very long white fluff*, the lower ones lying pressed to the ground, being half an inch long, the rest, standing up in the usual way, much longer, sometimes 6 inches, often with short stalks, and always *blunt*. The erect hairy 4-inch scapes come up at the sides in the axils of the shoots, and the flesh-pink blossoms, nearly half an inch across, are carried in heads, the length of each flower's stem varying considerably in different specimens; and a sure means of telling this species from *A. sarmentosa* in any form is that the little leaves or bracts that spread out below the flower-head are of *unequal size*, some very small and others much larger, instead of all being equal as in sarmentosa. (Kumaon, Kashmir, Hazara, &c.)

A. pubescens carries us back again far up into the alpine mountains cold, for this is a beautiful and rather rare Aretia of the highest primary rocks, often mistaken for *A. helvetica* (which it exactly resembles in habit and pearly flowers), but easily to be known by the fact that its downy leaves are quite longer and narrower and more pointed, and *stand up instead of curving inwards*, so that the tuft has not the dense pincushiony effect of *A. helvetica*. It occurs, very sporadically, at great elevations, from the Pyrenees to the Glockner, and may be seen, among other high-alpines, in the gaunt topmost schistose and sandstone ridges of the Nunda and the Mont Lamet of the Mont Cenis, in situations exactly such as those in which on other hills you would expect *A. helvetica*. In cultivation *A. pubescens* runs neck to neck with *A. helvetica* for comparative ease and happiness of temper; it is even thriving on the limestone Cliff at Ingleborough, and actually developing heartily from a chance seedling strayed into a most improbable mossy crevice on a shady rock, overhung with bushes of *Daphne Laureola*.

A. pyrenaica is a most special small Aretia confined to the non-calcareous cliffs of the Central Pyrenees. It is a most distinct plant, forming very minute dense star-fishes of splayed-out foliage, in rosettes not crowded together, though forming a uniform cushion. The wee leaves of the rosette, blunt, longish, and narrow, are conspicuously curved and flattened *outwards;* and, though downy all over, have a characteristic special fringe of little glandular hairs. The flower-stems are long for the size of the tiny mass, coming up by ones or twos from each nucleus, and rising to the height of nearly half an inch, usually bending and curving, each carrying one white flower the same size as Helvetica's, though a trifle starrier in outline. The look of the plant is unmistakable, the rosettes being so individual and the cushion so shallow-domed, even if you have not the luck to see it for yourself in the highest cliffs of the Port d'Oo, the Pic Campviel, or the Pic de Salettes. In cultivation *A. pyrenaica* offers no special difficulty, under the conditions of care exacted by all high-alpine Aretias. In such circumstances it lives successfully and flowers well, not having by any means the dangerous temper of *A. imbricata* and *A. Heeri*.

ANDROSACE.

A. Reverchonii. See *A. carnea*, of which it is a later and inadmissible synonym.

A. sarmentosa needs no description, for every warm sandy loam and every decent moraine rejoices in its widely-ramifying masses of ample tidy tufts, silvery at first, and then smoothly green ; no less than in those numerous heads of soft pinky Verbenas that come so stalwartly and freely up on 6-inch hairy stems in early summer. The type, in the course of its distribution through all the ranges from Himalaya to Szechuan, takes occasion to vary greatly, and among the varieties three have been named and are sometimes offered as separate species. *A. sarmentosa var. Watkinsii* is a much smaller condensed form, with tighter rosettes about a fifth of sarmentosa's ; another diminished version, but not so distinct or small, is *A. s. yunnanensis ;* while the best known and most beautiful of all holds a median place between these two, and is *A. sarmentosa var. Chumbyi (A. Chumbyi* of catalogues)—a neat compact and dainty thing, densely silky, and with flowers much more glowing than those of the type, and of the same size, but carried more freely and on stems of only 3 or 4 inches. This treasure is as perfectly easy as the rest, but its beauty well repays choice places and the select moraine, or other chosen corners too fine for the robustious and invasive cheeriness of *A. sarmentosa,* which is such that there are rumours of a garden on the warm coast of Lancashire, where the plant (being then little known) was ignorantly tucked into a rose-bed many years ago, and liked that inauspicious situation so well that for many years this noble Himalayan alpine has gone on acting as a covert to those succulent and sybaritic growths, as if it were the commonest of weeds in the way of Viola or Cerastium.

A. selago is a charming Aretia from great elevations in mid-Himalaya. It forms especially tight dense tufts of very minute triangular blunt leaves fluffed at the edge and green when young (before age darkens them all), packed and squeezed together into impenetrable globules not an eighth of an inch through. The handsome big blossoms are bright rose-purple, carried aloft singly on fluffy stems of varying length, hardly ever exceeding an inch or so, and often almost imperceptible. We pine as yet in vain for *A. selago.*

A. sempervivoeides (often offered too as *A. primuloeides,* from which it is wholly distinct) is a lovely member of the same sarmentosa group, running all over the surface of warm light soil or a moist moraine, with many beautiful and neat rosettes of fleshy oval leaves, densely overlapping, green, and perfectly smooth, except for a longish fringe of hair at their edge, which is frequently tinged with russet-red. Little bud-like promises of new rosettes come out upon the naked fat runners, and the roseate flowers are carried in the characteristic Verbena-heads of the section, on scapes of 3 or 4 inches. This species ranges through all the North-western Himalaya. A thing called *A. sempervivoeides var. tibetica exscapa*, from quite low, poor, hot ground in Kansu, is in reality the glorious *A. longifolia*, which, though it belongs to this section and carries its white flowers (one to four) in a head, yet imitates the habit of the Aretias in forming a dense low mat of leaves and almost stemless blossoms, the leaves of the rosettes being greenish-grey, about an inch long, perfectly hairless and smooth, narrow, and ending in a fat horny spine. It is perfectly beautiful, like a glorified white *A. alpina* in effect, making great carpets in the most improbable torrid banks. (See Appendix.)

A. spinulifera is a most curious species of this same section, which came into cultivation some seasons since from Sündermann under the label " species from Tibet." Or so at least it would seem, though the official range for *A. spinulifera* is from the mountains of Yunnan up to Central China. At first all that is to be perceived is a tight over-lapping little cone of greyish-green, spiny-looking bracts, with a strayed old leaf or so of *A. sarmentosa* emerging mysteriously from the tip. But in time the whole unfolds into a rosette of narrow obovate foliage, dense with rough silvery hairs, pointed and even ending in a thorny tip (though this character is not very constant), and, when young, positively spiny. The rosette forms no runners, but develops by de-grees into a clump, from which shoot up tall stems, very hairy, about 6 or 8 inches in height, at the top of which unfold tight heads of a few large and lovely flowers, softly rose-pink with a golden eye. *A. spinulifera* has a wide range up and down its native mountains, but attains its finest development at about 8000 or 12,000 feet, growing especially magnificent on the stony grassy edges of pine-woods facing north. The thorny character here almost wholly disappears, and the mass of plants, all shimmering silver with their crystalline stems and heads of golden-eyed rosy blossom, make a rare effect of beauty and splendour against the sombre woods behind. In cultivation *A. spinulifera* has all the cheeriness that distinguishes this group ; but, though any reasonably open rich cool soils should suit it, we might as well at first pursue the natural lead, and avoid giving it such torrid situations as would by no means come amiss to *A. lanuginosa*.

A. strigillosa is really what always passes not only for itself, but also, in the same page of the same catalogue, for the rarer and more worthless *A. foliosa*. (This is *A. foliosa*, Klatt, not *A. foliosa*, Duby.) The leaves of this Anak are large and loose, about 3½ inches ; it has a running trunk as thick as a goose-quill, many-headed, and set with the remains of many seasons' dead foliage ; various lax irregular untidy leafy rosettes are thrown up here and there, the whole clump being rough with coarse brief bristles. The leaves are oblong, more or less blunt, upstanding, and drawing gradually out below to a petiole or leaf-stalk as long as themselves, the blade, instead of being smooth, set all over with short transparent bristles, and having a callous tip. The flowers are rather few to a head, widely bell-shaped, lilac-mauve, about a quarter of an inch across, carried loosely, each on a longish foot-stalk. The species is of stout habit and the easiest culture in any cool, rich soil, though it has not any brilliancy or charm.

A. *tibetica* is yet another cousin of sarmentosa that has just lately come into cultivation and promises to stay. It can either throw out stolons or compile its new rosette-buds so as to form a tuffet. The foliage of the rosettes is lengthily spoon-shaped, almost an inch long or more, fleshy, pointed, perfectly smooth, with a fringe round the edge, which sometimes has a cartilaginous rim. Among the neat leaves the stems rise up or recline a little ; they are about 2 or 4 inches high ; then open the rather broad and conspicuous bracts that have shielded the blossom-head—a spraying umbel of delicate pink or rich pink flowers, faintly fragrant. The type varies greatly in dimension of bracts and other particulars ; named forms are *A. t. himalaica* and *A. t. Mariae*, the first emitting runners, and the second forming a dense tuft. In the plant shown at the R.H.S. in 1913 the bracts were too broad and evident, the whole effect rather leafy. There should be no doubt that *A. tibetica* will answer to hotter treatment than *A. spinulifera*, and closely copies the charm of *A. Chamaejasme*. (See Appendix.)

A. *Vegae*. See under *A. caespitosa*.

A. *villosa* is a yet more important and beloved species than *A. Chamaejasme*, which it closely resembles in size and charm of pearly flower-heads ; but the whole plant is smaller, and very neat rather than straggling, with compact masses of rosettes most glorious in a vesture of shimmering silver silk, and heads of blossom large and ample, on many little stems of 2 to 3 inches. *A. penicillata*, often offered by catalogues, is merely a synonym of *A. villosa*-type ; but in the course of its enormous distribution over the mountains of the world, throughout all the alpine chains of Europe, Asia, and Northern America, *A. villosa* falls into as many diversities of form as *A. Chamaejasme ;* and, since many of these are now listed as separate species, it will be as well to make note here that they *are* mere varieties. First and foremost comes lovely little *A. v. arachnoidea* (*A. arachnoidea* of catalogues), which is a smaller, neater, compacter thing even than the type, and even more fluffily silver; its sheeny tidy clumps may be seen in the open stony ground along the limestone ridges of the Karawanken summits, in company with *Ranunculus Traunfellneri*, *Alyssum ovirense* (*Wulfenianum*), and *Gentiana Froelichii*. *A. v. villosissima*, from Afghanistan, has runners almost woody, very short stems, very dense, very woolly rosettes of leaves which, from being bright green and heavily vested in white hairs, ultimately lose them all and turn a sad grey; *A. v. robusta* and *A. v. Jacquemontiana* are two variable Indian forms, of which *A. v. Jacquemontiana* has rose-pink flowers, and a clothing of long hairs, not silvery so much as russety-white; others more or less remote, variable and obscure, are *bisulca* and *incana* from China, and minute *dasyphylla* from the whole distribution of the species, dividing again into sub-varieties of its own, *glabrata* being a smoother form from Bithynian Olympus, and *globiferoeides* a stronger plant from Lebanon, with fat rosettes, smoothish outside and woolly within, and stemless flowers very fine and large. In all its range *A. villosa* belongs not so much to the alpine turf, like *A. Chamaejasme*, as to higher levels in the open screes and stony places on the necks of the mountains, always most especially, if not invariably, on the limestone mountains. It is a local plant, but like many local plants abundant where found; the limestone **Alps** of Styria are as thick with the type as are those of the Karawanken with its variety arachnoidea. Like most species of world-wide distribution, inured to every sort of difficulty and triumphant over all, *A. villosa* has a most robust and hearty nature. In all light good soils, well-drained, in every garden it will readily thrive, and is most especially suited to glorify the fine moraine, where its silvers associate delicately with the violets of *Viola cenisia* and *V. Dubyana*. However, in climates where the winter is very wet, it will be as well to look on that silver with a protecting eye when November begins her sullen weeping. A pane of glass over the tuft will keep it gleaming and fresh, preserving it from the clogging wet. It is only for its silk that *A. villosa* requires even so much care, not for any fault in its temper and constitution.

A. Watkinsii. See under *A. sarmentosa.*

A. Wulfeniana is a very rare species from the non-calcareous mountains of the Eastern Alps, where it forms mats not unlike those of *Silene acaulis* in general effect, the leaves of the rosettes being *narrow, pointed, sharp, bright green, and perfectly smooth* but for a few stellar hairs at the edge and tip. Even if not collected from high slate and granite ridges—as on the Eisenhut—it can easily be told from the other rose-flowered Aretias with which it might be confused: from *A. Charpentieri* by the utter lack of down upon its bright green leaves, from *A. ciliata* by their being stiffer, much narrower, pointed, and more shining. The flowers stand up each on a little stem of nearly half an inch, twice as long as the leaves, and are bright pink, nearly as big again as those of *A. Charpentieri*, and almost as big as those of *A. ciliata*. This treasure is easy of culture for a high-alpine Aretian Androsace, not fearing damp on its bald leaves, and thriving in cool and light moraine mixture, especially, like all the rest of the less saxatile species, if water percolate far beneath throughout the summer, and the drainage be sharp and perfect. Catalogues now often try to sell this as a novelty, under the name of *A. Pacheri*, which is a later and invalid synonym.

ANDROSACES REMAINING UNNOTICED, AS BEING REMOTE, IMPOSSIBLE, INFERIOR, OR UNOBTAINED

PSEUDO-PRIMULA	CHAMAEJASME	ARETIA	ANDRASPIS
A. geraniifolia	A. mirabilis	A. alaschanica	A. multiscapa
A. Paxiana	A. Hookeriana	A. Tschuktschorum	A. erecta
A. cuscutiformis	A. akbaitalensis	A. Delavayi	A. Raddeana
A. rotundifolia	A. arguta	A. Lehmannii	A. maxima
A. axillaris		A. squarrosula	A. Engleri
A. dissecta		A. tapete	A. Chaixii
A. sutchuenensis		A. Apus	A. elongata
A. saxifragaefolia		A. ferruginea	A. septentrionalis
A. Gmelinii			A. filiformis
A. cordifolia			A. asprella
A. alchemilloeides			A. Gormanii

Andryala is a race of woolly-leaved Composites very close to Hieracium, and indeed so close that *A. lanata*, the one popular member of the family, has now been transferred to Hieracium. Still remains, however, *A. Achardii* from hot mountain cliffs of Spain, an almost woody rock-plant for a very hot dry crevice, with silky-silvery whity-yellow leaves, and golden flowers each by itself on a 4-inch glandular stem. It should not be allowed to suffer from winter-wet.

Anemone.—This glorious family meets us on the threshold of its house with the problem of its name. Is it Anémone or is it Anemône ? Linnaeus called it Anémŏne, twisting the word out of ἄνεμος, to mean wind-flower, a significance, in spite of rhapsodists, singularly inappropriate, and one which the Greek word ἀνεμώνη is hardly capable of carrying. But before him Tournefort, with prior authority, had called the race Anemône, from the Syrian Na-ma'an, the cry of lament for dead Adonis, whose blood flames yearly back again to light in the pulsing scarlets of *A. fulgens* and *A. coronaria*. Therefore it seems that Adonis has indeed the weight of age, appropriateness, and romance ; and that we *ought* now to twist our tongues to the profounder music of Anemône. But who will ?

Very few of the Anemones are rock-plants, the race being subalpine and alpine, descending also to the fields at much lower elevations, and abundant in the New World as in the Old, though there for the most part vastly inferior. Yet so important is the family, in the rock-garden especially, and so many are the dingy new species now creeping into commerce undescribed, on their way through our purses straight to the rubbish-heap, that the species must surely be dealt with in detail. And in so dealing let us include Pulsatilla and Hepatica, two groups of Anemone nowadays by some botanists removed each into a race of its own. All the Anemones but a few are temperate in their tastes, and in cultivation only the woodland section likes coppice and shade and moist cool soil. The alpine section, on the contrary, enjoys a soil that is very deep and rich and cool indeed, but with full exposure to sun and air ; the meadow group is happy in the same conditions, but, being dwarfer, needs a position more in the foreground. The blooming season opens with *A. blanda* in February, ranges right through the summer, with *A. rivularis* taking up the mantle of its predecessors that have filled the earlier months, and closes at last with the late frosts that massacre the profuse remaining buds of *A. japonica* and *A. vitifolia*. Nearly all Anemones come readily and generously from seed, but it is essential that the seed should be sown as fresh as possible, for in the seed of Anemone the living germ has but little surrounding nourishment to keep it alive, and soon, if not sown, has devoured all its envelope and dies of inanition, impatient and frustrate. The running species can also be pulled to pieces, or their offsets removed at pleasure ; but all the clump-forming kinds acutely resent division (they do not even readily condone removal), and take a season or two to recover.

A. acutiloba is a North American of no merit.

A. albana may merely be a high-alpine form of *A. pratensis*, but here the divisions of the root-leaves are shorter and blunter, their lobes being oblong rather than sharp-pointed, while the leaf-frill that envelops the bloom is also much less slit and gashed. The leaves appear with the buds in early spring ; and the single-flowered stems are some 4 or 5 inches high, with large blossoms varying in colour from milky white through yellows to pale-blue, rather nodding and bell-shaped, and never violet as in Pratensis. (Alpine meadows of Eastern Caucasus, and away to India.) Cultivation is quite easy in any deep soil and open bank.

ANEMONE.

A. alpina is the Great King of Glory in the race, as none will ever deny who has seen him at his best, for instance, on the Mont Cenis at the alpine levels, covering all the farthest hills with blobs of snow, as up come the huge ferny masses of foliage, and the royal snowy flowers on their 2-foot stems ; while where the snows have but recently departed, there, from the dank brown earth, danced over with the fringy little violet bells of Soldanella and pierced by the long fluted opalescent chalices of *Crocus albiflorus*, sit close to the ground those tight clumps of bronzy, pearly globes, just beginning to unfold their golden tassels to the daylight, not by any means to be foretold for the stalwart splendours that they will ultimately become, as the stems develop and slowly the leaves unfold ; only to attain their maximum of wide-spread majesty when the blossoms are gone, and have given place in due time to wildly whirling strüwelpeter balls of twisting silver-fluffy seeds, hardly less beautiful in their way than the flowers whose radiant youth is thus worthily represented by reverend age. The plant is one that loves the upper alpine fields, where it grows in long lush grass and makes it unfit for hay ; but it does not climb to the highest alpine lawns where *A. vernalis* principally reigns, and it dies before the onslaughts of culture and manure. This species is purely Eurasiatic, but is replaced in the Rockies by *A. occidentalis*, while *A. alpina* occupies almost all the alpine chains of the Old World, and develops into many different forms, some of which have received separate names, and few of which attain the splendour of the Graian grandeur. The most interesting and famous of these varieties is the sulphur one which is known to gardens and catalogues as *A. sulfurea*. This plant possesses the public imagination almost exclusively, because it possesses the Swiss Alps almost to the exclusion of the type, which, there indeed, is often small and poor (though fine forms have come from seed gathered high above Rosenlaui). *A. a. sulfurea* at its best is certainly most magnificent, though never quite attaining the dimensions of the best Alpinas ; in the Engadine it is specially fine, as on the passes going over to Chamonix. It has been said that this form belongs to the granite, while the type adheres to the limestone. In gardens the distinction is valueless, and in nature quite untrustworthy, though acceptable as a very rough general proposition. For, in the granites, for instance, of the Madonna della Finestra above Saint Martin Vésubie, the alpine Anemone is an ample and splendid form of pure *A. alpina* (in similar or more rocky conditions at the head of the Boréon in the next valley it is *A. a. sulfurea*), while all over the limestone meadows at the top of the Pordoi Pass, the lawn is full of typical *A. a. sulfurea*, though here, indeed, in a poor and wizen guise. On

the Mont Cenis, again, Alpina itself varies, and in a waving drift of
snow there will be seen creamy flowers, and pale-yellow flowers, and
here and there a citron-coloured beauty only by the minutest eye of
doubt to be distinguished from *A. a. sulfurea.* In the Alps of the far
South, in Piedmont and Lombardy, *A. alpina* itself becomes so small
and mean as hardly to be known ; it is already growing inferior in the
copse-edges of the Cottians, while on the Grigna or the Forcella
Lungieres it is such a single-stalked puny little 5-inch affair that one
often takes it at first or second sight for something quite distinct.
So protean is the species, in fact, that botanists have recognised the
impossibility of naming fixed varieties ; the only one, after Sulfurea,
that has any existence in catalogues is *A. a. Burseriana*, which is a
secondary name for *A. a. myrrhidifolia*, a form differing from the
type in being of rather smaller habit, and in having leaves so much
more deeply, finely, and closely cut that they do indeed resemble
those of some small Sweet Cicely. Yet another in the same kind is
A. a. millefoliata, while the minutest development is *A. a. alpicola.* It
only remains to be added that *A. alpina* sometimes has flowers of
different sexes—one possessing only a golden tassel of anthers, and
its neighbour only a naked greenish bunch of carpels.

All these Anemones have huge wooden roots of a length, stoutness,
and toughness that makes them perfectly impregnable except by a
pickaxe or mattock. At the same time, the difficulty of collecting
living specimens has been greatly exaggerated ; for, if some 6 inches
or more of the woody stock be broken and torn away, it will readily
emit new fibres if sent home and carefully treated in the sand-bed.
However, of course the plant's development is thus retarded, and
this method is only recommended in the case of very special varieties,
such as a most beautiful windmill-whirling double form from the
Mont Cenis, which flowered happily and in full character the second
season in England, and now is a large thriving clump. In general
it is best to collect fresh seed in autumn, and sow it as soon as possible
in good rich cool loam, perhaps with a dash of peat ; if snow can be
induced to lie on the bed or pan, so much the better for the seed,
whose germination will thus be mysteriously accelerated. But in
any case the seedlings should appear profusely in spring, and after a
season's growth the young plants may be put out in the place where
they are to remain—some very deep well-drained bed of light rich
soil, perfectly open to sun and air. Here they should flower the
next year, and in another summer or two have formed big crowns,
which will then increase in size and splendour for ever and for
ever without further attention, till one big bush will show as many

as sixty great pearly radiant moons simultaneously at their full in June.

A. altaica is a beautiful thing, almost unknown in cultivation hitherto. It is like a glorified wood Anemone, with leaves suggesting a small Anemonopsis. Its large flowers are many-rayed, most like a big Celandine, white and delicately veined with soft blue. Its cultural needs will be those of *A. nemorosa*, and its constitution is undoubted, as it comes from the far mountain-woods of Northern Asia.

A. amoena is a synonym of *A. pulsatilla.*

A. angulosa. See under *A. Hepatica.*

A. antucensis comes from Chile, and should be an interesting little Anemone, akin to *A. nemorosa* and requiring similar treatment.

A. apennina needs neither praise nor description. Its exquisite ragged many-rayed stars of clear blue are among the first joys of spring, twinkling among grass or in forgotten corners of the garden. For no matter into what odd corners you may cast out your superfluous tuber-mats of *A. apennina*, they will promptly root and establish themselves, and reward you one day with an unexpected flash of heaven as you go round the garden. There are white and pink and dark-blue forms, but nothing can surpass the loveliness of the common Apennina, which is such a lover of our country and climate that it has tried hard to take out naturalisation-papers, establishing itself here and there in English woods till botanists were once inclined to recognise it as a native. But, if you want to establish the plant quickly, it is best, if possible, to buy your clumps in full activity, when the leaves are just dying down ; for, if you wait till autumn, as catalogues prescribe, you receive the dried tubers only, which are sometimes apt to be chary about sending up life again above ground next year.

A. baikalensis of our nurserymen and gardens is wholly a fraud, being nothing more than a variety or synonym of *A. silvestris.* The true *A. baikalensis* is hairy, with only one root-leaf, which has a long stalk and is more or less rounded in outline and cut into three divisions. The white blossoms are about an inch and a half across, one or two, carried each on its stem, larger than those of *A. nemorosa*, and very like those of *A. blanda. A. baikalensis*, in similar treatment, throws out white runners, and soon forms a neat and thick but not invasive clump.

A. baldensis is, with *A. vernalis*, the one really alpine Anemone of the European ranges. It is essentially a Southern species and avoids the central chains, being found always in austere stony places, screes, and higher earth-pans : usually abundant where it occurs : in Spain,

PLATE 6.

ANDROSACE LANUGINOSA.
(Photo. R. A. Malby.)

ANDROSACE SARMENTOSA CHUMBYI.
(Photo. R. A. Malby.)

PLATE 7*a*.

ANEMONE PULSATILLA.
(Photo. R. A. Malby.)

ANEMONE NEMOROSA (var. ALLENII).
(Photo. R. A. Malby.)

ANEMONE   RUPICOLA.
(Photo. R.B.G , Edinburgh.)

along the Pyrenees; the Alps of Provence, Dauphiné, and Savoy;
Bex, Oberland, and Fribourg ; Salzburg, Great Glockner, and through
the Dolomites away to Herzegovina and Transylvania. It seems indifferent as to its rock and soil (though specially common and hearty
in the Dolomites), and never descends from its high elevations. It is
a most characteristic and recognisable prize, running about profusely
underground among the stones, and sending up, every here and
there, dainty barren tufts of fine dark curly leaves rather like those of
Pig-nut. Much more sparsely from these come up the graceful stems
of 5 or 6 inches, the frill a long way below the solitary beautiful white
flower (often bluish at the back), which has many oval sepals and an
eye of gold, looking almost like a broad-rayed single Chrysanthemum.
When this is over the stem grows taller, and the seed forms into close
and oval woolly heads not unlike a strawberry in general effect, with
the points of the carpels just coming through to finish off the picture
by suggesting the seeds.   Unfortunately *A. baldensis* is often paradoxically difficult and unsatisfactory in cultivation, for a habit that seems
to promise such weedlike readiness and vigour. Its best chance will
probably be in a very earthy moraine, with a few large coarse blocks
buried in it and water flowing below. In America its place is taken
by *A. Drummondii*.

A. barbulata, from China, is a half-sized version of the pleasant
and useful *A. pennsylvanica, q.v.*

A. Berlandieri. See under *A. caroliniana.*

A. biflora is a hairless thing from Kashmir, attaining some 8 inches,
with two flowers of a dull red.

A. blanda decks all the islands and coasts of the Eastern Mediterranean in a sheet of colour with the first breath of returning spring.
It is a small bulbous plant, like a neater, dwarfer, fleshier-leaved
A. apennina, with flowers much larger, tidier and more brilliant (like
huge single daisies, neat-rayed, with a minute golden centre), and
ranging through every lovely colour from the normal brilliant soft
blue (often with a clear white eye), through the blandest pinks and
richest purples, to pure white. And all forms will spring up in the
garden from a single importation out of the Levant. There is also
a striking variety called *A. blanda var. scythinica*, in which the stalwart
flowers are blue outside and white within. *A. blanda* is a very much
compacter grower than *A. apennina*, and never forms into wide and
crowded clumps ; therefore, being so small and so early, and so
quickly dying down out of the way as soon as it has finished taking
the winds of March with beauty, it should be promoted to the very
choicest and sunniest places (for so do its stars most readily open), at

the edge of little shrubs, or among such things as will spring up later, and never mind its evanescent lovely company, with which it indulges them freely by seeding copiously all over the place.

A. borealis. See under *A. parviflora.*

A. Bungeana comes from Siberia, and is rather like a smaller version of *A. albana,* with shorter stem and nearly erect purple flowers, appearing at the same time as the leaves, woolly with a pressed-down coat of white hairs, and narrow shorter jags.

A. caerulea is so called because it is hardly ever blue. None the less it is a charming woodland delicacy from Siberia, almost exactly like our yellow *A. ranunculoeides,* but that its blossoms are of a tender and opalescent pinky colour.

A. canadensis is a synonym for *A. pennsylvanica, q.v.*

A. caroliniana is a delicate frail tuft also, akin to *A. decapetala,* with each division of the leaves always having a little stalk to itself. The stem is weak, about 6 inches high, with the frill far down, and then a single flower, of eight to ten purply-white sepals, large and attractive. This is a North-American woodlander, soothing in its silkiness ; *A. Berlandieri* is dwarfer and stouter and hairier, with the jags of the foliage oval and not sharply narrow.

A. cernua, from Japan, is a member of the Pulsatilla group, but quite unattractive as I have seen it—a leafy dulness, with tall stems each carrying one nodding flower, much too small, narrow in outline, and of a sombre dirty-claret colour.

A. coronaria, on the contrary, gives very nearly the finest scarlet in the whole range of hardy plants. It is the great fiery Anemone of the Mediterranean coast, with the comparatively few broad oval sepals, looking like some enriched and well-bred Poppy. It diverges into innumerable other colour-forms, however, in cultivation, to say nothing of its much smaller and dwarfer violet variety which is so much commoner nowadays in the fields behind Cannes. And of the vast hybrid race of Coronarias the rock-garden may hold itself excused ; even though splendid, they are galumphing and inappropriate there. With regard to the gorgeous wild type, no rules beyond those of full sun and light loam can be given. For if *A. coronaria* approves your soil and climate it will make itself a weed ; if for some unknown reason it dislikes your neighbour's similar garden next door, nothing will induce it to do anything but dwindle and mimp away year by year and die. It exacts full value for its astounding beauty in the way of a regal beauty's conceded capriciousness.

A. cylindrica turns out to be a really worthless weed, with flowers of a feeble yellowish-green, carried singly on long naked foot-stalks.

ANEMONE.

A. dahurica is quite close to *A. pratensis*, if not indeed a pink-flowered form.

A. decapetala, from North America, has three-lobed root-leaves, rather hairy, each of them heart-shaped-oval in outline, and deeply cut into three divisions. The flowers are bluey-white, on foot-stalks of varying length. (Woods.)

A. demissa, a Chinese form of *A. narcissiflora*, *q.v.*

A. Drummondii replaces *A. baldensis* at great elevations in the Rockies. It is a lovely little stranger, suggesting a glorified and snow-white Winter-aconite; and should be grown in the select moraine, or in rich peaty soil very full of chips, with water flowing beneath.

A. elongata is much to be desired. It dwells in Nepal and Garwhal at 16,000 feet, and attains a height itself of 2 or 3 feet, being, exactly, a diminished and more dainty version of beautiful *A. rivularis*, with large soft foliage, and tall loose showers of small bluey-white stars. These both require cool rich soil, and specially love the bog, where they throw up their radiating heads (the flower-stems more drawn out in *A. elongata*) towards later summer, when flowers altogether are far and few in the rock-garden, and Anemones still further and fewer.

A. Falconeri, from the Himalaya, is a Hepatica with a genuine stalk.

A. Fanninii is the giant of the family, a vast and leafy six-footer from Africa, with enormous leafage, and whity-blue flowers quite insignificant in comparison with the size of the plant. Up to a certain point *A. Fanninii* is fairly hardy, in a rich sheltered border; but, though interesting, it is hardly worth the pains of purchase or care.

A. flaccida does not at all deserve its name. In point of fact, it is a stout and stalwart small beauty of much charm from the mountain woods of Japan. Its little leaves are thick and almost fleshy, not unlike miniatures of a common buttercup's, with characteristic pale touches at the base of the shallowish lobes into which they are cut. The stems, it is true, decline a little, but they are quite sound, not more than 3 or 4 inches long, with a beautiful pure-white flower, fine and ample for the proportions of the clump.

A. flavescens comes very near to *A. patens*, from which it chiefly differs in having the leaves (which appear after the *erect* yellow blossoms) much more divided, but none of the divisions with any sort of stalk to itself.

A. formosa is a name from Asia Minor, which seems to be the most attractive part of the obscurity it shelters.

67

A. fulgens we shall never see in its real fulness. For this is the Red of all red Anemones from the Levant, which ousts even Coronaria from the throne of King of the Scarlets. The species is most variable : we grow its pretty dwarf lilac-starred variety called *A. fulgens stellata* (often simply *A. stellata* in catalogues) with ease and success in warm dry borders and rock-gardens ; we cope successfully with the other varieties, *A. hortensis* and *A. pavonina ;* but *A. fulgens*-type, as its ardent many-rayed suns of scarlet dazzle the wide fields of Greece and Asia Minor, is too hot and blazing and intemperate a glory for climates so mild and respectable as ours. But when we see the many-rayed tuber-rooted red or pink Anemones of the South offered for sale or in our gardens, we may remember to what species it is they belong, and of what resplendence they are the comparatively feeble representatives.

A. globosa, from North America, frequently advertised, has quite small miserable-looking blooms of a dull and dirty red, carried at the end of tall, stiff, erect stalks. It is really *A. multifida, q.v. ;* should be thrown to the dust-bin.

A. Griffithii is a little Himalayan Wood-anemone very closely akin to *A. nemorosa.*

A. Halleri need never be mistaken for any other of the Pulsatilla group to which it belongs. It is an outstanding species, all shaggy-silky grey with long fine hairs, and the divisions of the leaves, so far from being fine and ferny as in the Pulsatillas, are *thick, few, broad, flat,* and *sharp.* The flowers stand nearly erect, on stems of 5 or 6 inches (or more at last), and are large and ample, of a goodly rich violet, sheeny outside with silk (very rarely varying to white or pink). *A. Halleri* is not a common find, occurring on rough grassy hills of the mountains at alpine elevations, but sporadic and oddly local. In Switzerland it is only found above Zermatt, in Savoy only in one strictly limited station on the Mont Cenis, in rough turf, with *Dianthus neglectus, Aster alpinus, and Orchis sambucina*, among stunted bushes of *Rosa alpina* and *R. pimpinellifolia*, and so on, here and there through the eastern and western ranges, occupying a quite narrow strip, from the Maritimes, through the Cottians to the Southern edge of the Pennines, always abhorring the limestone. After flowering, the splendid leaves develop and stand up, forming a tuft, 5 inches high or so, round the yet further elongated fruiting-stem. The root is deep and tough ; the plant is best raised from seed, and grown in deep and perhaps non-calcareous loam with perfect drainage and full sun. It comes a good second to *A. sinensis* in its group.

A. helleborifolia, from Chile, has been confused with *A. decapetala*, but is a really distinct and pretty thing, about 6 inches or a foot high, with heads of white flowers branching into other heads again with three or four flowers to each. The root-leaves are not nearly so numerous as in *A. decapetala*, and are not leathery. It is called "Centella" at home, and is used to raise blisters.

A. Hepatica is an invaluable, stemless little woodlander of all the alpine woods that our gardens know hardly less well. It luxuriates in damp rich woodland soil, and forms, in time, huge clumps; and it acutely resents being divided and disturbed. It has countless coloured forms, and a very miffy and expensive double white. In the Southern Alps (especially) it seems to develop white marblings and blotchings most becoming to the dark-green leather of its smooth trilobed leaves (*A. triloba* is nothing else). From Eastern Europe comes a glorified form, much larger, much greener, much leafier, and with leaves inclining to pucker into three hollows and then have scalloped edges. This is now raised to specific rank as *A. angulosa*, a recognition to which it is clearly entitled, though here it is more convenient to treat it under *A. Hepatica*, of which it has the habits, uses, and needs, though so much bigger in all its parts. The big beautiful blossoms are of Hepatica's clear blue, but vary to named forms of darker or paler. They both flower with *A. blanda*, or even earlier; though *A. angulosa* tends to be a little later than Hepatica.

A. hepaticaefolia, the Estrella of Valdivia (where it grows), has all its foliage at the base, and then a hairy stem of a foot or two, carrying a wide umbrella-shaped head of large pale yellow flowers.

A. Hudsoniana is a synonym of *A. multifida, q.v.*

A. hupehensis. See under *A. japonica.*

A. japonica is the latest and one of the loveliest of our Anemones, and, though beautiful in all borders, has a grace so well-bred and oriental as to be perfectly harmonious also in deep damp sweeps of the large rock-garden. There are countless named forms, and lilac-pink tones are much in favour. But those who best love *A. japonica* prefer the dazzling innocence of the pure whites; of these, old Honorine Jobert still keeps a high place, but has now been dethroned by Géante Blanche, the most broad-leaved, tall-stemmed, stalwart, and magnificent of all, with the largest and the most noble snow-white flowers. This does not as yet seem to establish quite so readily or ramp so vigorously as the rest; but it has not long been on its trial. *A. j. Lady Gilmour*, or *crispifolia*, is a curious pink-flowered variety with leaves all curled and twisted like parsley. Of other border varieties no more need be mentioned, but two acknowledged species have recently come to hand from China, *A. mupinensis* and *A.*

hupehensis, which to a more moderate estimate seem more like mere local developments of *A. japonica*; they both have rosy-mauve flowers, and have no outstanding value in the garden, but still less in the rock-garden, except for the interest of their provenance and relationship. But a genuine species in close kinship to *A. japonica* is beautiful *A. vitifolia* from the temperate regions of the Himalaya. This is, to all intents and purposes of the garden, a gracious and non-spreading *A. japonica* with handsome flowers of pure white. It blooms extremely late, and has been suspected of tenderness; which seems, however, a false alarm, as it lived here quite happily for several years in a corner not particularly sheltered. (See Appendix.)

A. lithophila is a species close to *A. parviflora*, with stout little stems from 4 to 6 inches high, and charming stars of whity-blue standing erect from a fat stock. (Damp North-American rocks.)

A. Lyallii is so far a mere blind name, the seed-boxes in which its labels stand being blank, and no authority discoverable.

A. magellanica of catalogues is a valueless thing : it looks so North-American in ugliness that one can hardly trust its name.

A. mandschuriensis. See *A. sinensis*.

A. mexicana, a most beautiful novelty, not unlike a much magnified upright Nemorosa, of some 8 inches in habit, with wide hairy stems, a creeping and increasing rhizome, and lovely pink flowers held up to catch such light as filters through the alpine coppice on the Mexican mountains. It will enjoy damp boggy places in limy woodland, but should have a sheltered place and winter-care until we learn its degree of hardiness.

A. montana belongs to the Pulsatilla group in which there is so much puzzlement (to say nothing of variations and interbreedings that justly bewilder even the trained botanist). It should, however, be easily known ; its leaves are fine and ferny, but not so much so as in Pulsatilla, *and they are not grey, but dark green ;* the flower-stalk is taller, and the flowers are deep purply black or reddish purple, obviously *nodding*, especially when clouds are about. They are usually tucked far into their leaf-frill, and narrowly bell-shaped, until at last they open out into a star. Finally, it is a species confined to the South, on sunny grassy hills at low elevations, as, for instance, above Bozen, reaching its limit no further away than at Brixen, and nowhere northward of that point to be seen.

A. multifida is the correct name of the worthless weed so often offered under the names of *A. globosa* and *A. Hudsoniana*. It produces a number of tall erect foot-stalks, each carrying a single dingy little bloom of dull greenish red.

ANEMONE.

A. mupinensis. See under *A. japonica.*

A. narcissiflora is always and everywhere a well-beloved friend, easily adorning cool or sunny copsy corners in the rock-garden, with its soft fan-shaped, deep-cut leaves, and its foot-high heads of six to ten lovely flowers exactly like so many Apple-blossoms. Occasionally it may damp off in winter if the soil be too heavy, nor does its life appear to exceed six or seven years; but during that time it goes on from season to season in ever-increasing splendour, and looks specially characteristic if small ferns share its home, and the alpine Columbines among which it is so often found. It is a generally abundant species (apparently quite indifferent—*pace* other authorities, who call it a lime-lover—as to the soil or rock it grows on), not only in the Alps, where it has its centre in the main chains, but also all over the great mountain ranges of the Old World and across the Behring Straits into America, creeping down to South Park in the Colorado Rockies, and in Yunnan attaining actually to the tropic of Cancer. It is a lover of open places in sub-alpine and alpine woods, or in the meadows just above, where it often makes the turf a dense waving Narcissus-field of fallen Apple-blossoms, as on one open copsy shoulder, I remember, of the Cottian Alps, looking far out over the Plain of Lombardy. Being so widely-travelled, *A. narcissiflora* takes many marked forms as it goes, especially in the Caucasus and the high mountains of Asia, whence two of them have lately come to us, clothed in the solemn preciousness attaching to "new species." These are *A. narcissiflora var. demissa*, in Eastern Asia from Tibet to Kamschatka, a fluffy form, with softer and less divided foliage and weaker stems, and *A. n. var. polyanthes*, ranging the other way from Tibet to Kashmir, with abundant heads of blossom. There is also a one-flowered variety, *A. n. monantha;* and yet another is already to hand from Russia as *A. villosissima* (sometimes *A. villosa*), an extra-specially fluffy form of an already fluffy type. All these are beautiful, but must be guarded against when they ask seven and sixpence for themselves as "new species," being in reality only local varieties of a type, almost more beautiful and charming still, that sells at eighteenpence. (See Appendix.)

A. nemorosa, though only the common Wood-anemone, need not be ashamed to uphold its swinging delicate head among the proudest beauties of the race. It has by this time developed many lovely forms, and it is especially curious how in the far West of Wales, England, and Ireland, its colour tends to change into the most beautiful blues that even reach the clear soft brilliancy of *A. apennina.* Many of these have names; especially beautiful is *A. n. Allenii,* late-flowering and very large indeed, of the most exquisitely clear and subtle tone of lavender-blue. *Blue Bonnet*, however, is the biggest and latest of all, a plant not so tall, but strangely fat and solid in growth, with imposing solid, stolid flowers of a rich clear blue. Frailer than these two rarities, and much commoner, but inspired with an unparalleled exquisiteness of grace, is loose-flowered fragile-seeming *A. n. Robinsoniana*, in habit a delicately-waving Wood-anemone, forming rapidly into handsome stretches, and tossing up into the winds of March its large and gracious rounded stars of a pale powder-blue, softly yellowish or creamy outside. And any Cornish wood will provide you with as many Blue Kings and Lavender Queens as any list could want—to say nothing of the more ordinary rosy and mauve forms—*atropurpurea, rosea*, and so forth. The best I ever saw of these was one I found myself in a Cornish wood and called *Adonis*—especially stalwart and sturdy, with burnished mahogany-coloured buds, glossy and varnished, the splendid flowers being held perfectly straight up into the day, of a brilliant warm vinous lilac. As for white varieties, there is, of course, the double form, and a very pretty one called *bracteata*, with all the carpels gone into a neat little rosette of whiteness at the centre of each flower, giving a charming effect of dead and glacial purity. But the finest form of these is the too-rare *A. n. Leedsii*, which is simply *A. nemorosa* of enormous size and the most stainless snowiness. But in regions fertile of *A. nemorosa* the gardener should incessantly keep a skinned eye for such special forms. As for the hybrids of *A. nemorosa*, they will be found at the end of this list among the other children of their parents.

A. nikoensis is a Nemorosa from the woods of mountainous Japan, with sharper leaves, more sharply toothed and divided.

A. Nuttaliana is an American form or synonym of *A. patens, q.v.*

A. obtusiloba should be a really delightful species of the temperate and alpine Himalaya, forming large tufts of soft smooth or hairy leaves, broad and round and unmercifully cut ; from these rise up the stems, six inches to a foot high, each carrying, on pedicles of varying lengths, handsome blossoms of gold or white or purple.

A. occidentalis.—This species has the honour of replacing *A. alpina* in the New World. And not inadequately does it do so—a handsome plant of nearly the same stature, with foliage so much more minutely divided as to be like the very finest Anthriscus or Cicely. It occurs at alpine elevations, down the Rockies (it may be seen by the Lakes in the Clouds above Laggan) ; a diminished version of *A. alpina* with the same flowers, rather starrier, but no less white.

A. palmata is a curious-minded African stranger which just strays

ANEMONE.

into South Europe, and may here and there be found in dry hot places in the Department of Var, forming wide low mats and patches of short-stemmed leafage, dark and glossy and round in outline, with three to five blunt lobes, from which, on bare stems of some 6 inches (and often more in cultivation), are carried the big flowers of glittering golden yellow, exactly like those of a Celandine glorified out of knowledge. Contrary to expectation, *A. palmata* is perfectly hardy in England, and though in nature a drought-loving species, it even makes happy shining masses in weeping Westmorland. It is a plant, accordingly, of conspicuous value for the garden, where room can be allowed for it to spread, in some sunny bank of deep rich soil, assisted with a little sandy peat, and perfectly drained. But indeed, even in Lancashire, one sees it growing freely as a border-plant on warm exposures. There is also a good variety *alba*, with white flowers; but the essential glory of *A. palmata* is, after all, its glowing glittering gold, so rare a beauty in this race.

A. parviflora, whose synonym is *A. borealis*, turns out a most charming little thing, from damp limestone rocks in Labrador and Alaska and Siberia. It suggests the habit and snowy loveliness of *Ranunculus alpester*, from four inches to a foot high, the leaves being divided into three wedge-shaped leaflets with scalloped lobes. The white blossoms stand lonely on the stems, and are more or less tinged with blue toward their base.

A. patens, a Field-anemone allied to Pulsatilla, from mid-Germany and Russia. The leaves unfold *after* the bloom, and *are cut into three lobes, these three lobes being again cut into two or three jags*, and each foliole or leaflet having more or less of a minute foot-stalk. These leaves are often longer than the stem, and their general outline is roundish; on the upper surface they are comparatively smooth and green, but woolly underneath. The flower-frill is much less gashed than in Pulsatilla, pratensis, and montana. The purple goblet (widely variable, from violet to yellow and white) is carried *rather erect*, and the three outer segments of it are silky, with a little silky imperial at their tip; the whole tuft is quite dwarf at flowering-time. Open soil in sun. (*A. Nuttaliana* from America is a form of this.)

A. pavonina. See under *A. fulgens*.

A. pavoniana must be most carefully distinguished from the last. This is a Spanish species, with the habit of *A. baldensis*, with three-lobed leaves again gashed and cut; and stems of 6 or 10 inches, carrying one, two, or three white flowers. The root is cylindric.

A. pennsylvanica, sometimes offered under the synonym of *A. dichotoma* or *A. canadensis*, though not by any means admissible to a choice place, has its value for effect. It ramifies vehemently through any light soil, and sends up, on long upstanding stems, soft hairy foliage rather like that of *Ranunculus bulbosus*, but larger, softer, duller, greener, and much taller, on stems of 4 or 5 inches. Up among these and well above the leaves, to a foot or more, spring the dainty and divergently-branching stems, each of which sends up, on a graceful foot-stalk, one creamy-white star, which, though not remarkably large for the plant, yet gives a pleasant result of charm and gladness, glorifying early summer and lingering on. There is no question about propagating *A. pennsylvanica*, but rather of keeping it in check, if happy. Yet, if it does not fancy its soil, it will not grow, and proves as capricious as its more showy betters.

A. polyanthes. See under *A. narcissiflora.*

A. pratensis, another very wide-spread and very variable Field-anemone of the Pulsatilla group. The leaves are here pretty much as in *A. Pulsatilla*, not lobed, but gashed to the middle, and then cut and slit again and again. The flowers never really open properly; they are always long and *narrow* and cylindric and *hanging*, of a dull purple, with their sepals hardly any longer than the yellow anthers and the carpels inside, by which the bloom accordingly looks rather uncomfortably cramped and crowded. It is a thing of no special beauty, but of enormous distribution, occupying practically the whole of Europe and nearer Asia, whereas *A. patens* belongs chiefly to mid-Germany (ranging into Russia as far as the Lena), and *A. montana* is confined wholly to ranges much further South. There is a variety of *A. pratensis*, *A. p. montana*, on Monte Baldo; but *A. pratensis* itself has often interbred and been entangled in the more Southerly parts of its distribution with the true species *A. montana* where they both occur. The mountains of Auvergne produce a form with blooms so dark as to be almost chocolate black.

A. Pulsatilla is, in need and habit, the type of these Field-anemones, which all are found at low elevations in hard dry soil on hot and grassy hills. *A. Pulsatilla* is by far the best known of its European cousins, and by far the most beautiful, with the exception of *A. Halleri*. Its range does not run so far North as that of Pratensis, but in Europe itself is almost equally wide (in the Alps of Central Europe it comes no further South than Hal in the Tyrol, but descends far down into Italy, upon Rome itself); the Romans probably brought it into England in their train, and it produces a beautiful green dye, which has earned the plant its English name of Pasque-flower, because it was used for staining the Easter eggs. And now on Roman works, such as the Devil's Dyke near Newmarket, its lovely great violet

starry cups with the golden tassel at their heart lie thick upon the
sere ground under the wild skies of March, before the little silky
ferny foliage on which they sit so close at flower-time has fully
developed its leaflets. As time goes by both leaves and stem grow up,
and in the garden *A. Pulsatilla* forms a waving mass of foliage and tall
seed-heads, totally different from the neatness that its starvation diet
enforces in nature. The tuft at first is silky-grey, but ultimately
becomes less silky, though hardly less grey ; the leaves are not lobed,
but gashed to the stem on either side, each strip being then itself cut
and cut again into narrow pointed little thongs, the whole effect being
like that of a grey carrot to a casual glance. The blossoms are held
erect, are densely silky outside, and of a rich purple. As they grow
old, indeed, and the stem gets tall (ultimately attaining to a foot or
more), they tend to droop, but their first inclination is to be audacious
and confront the sky, especially when wild and in their stemless stage.
The sepals also are *notably full and outspread and longer than the
stamens*, a clear note to distinguish it from *A. pratensis ;* while its
distribution separates it from *A. montana*, whose leaves *are green not
grey*, and whose flower is *bell-shaped and nodding.* From *A. patens*,
among other points, it differs in having the *leaves not lobed into three
finely cut and re-cut segments*, but gashed down the stem into no less
finely feathered divisions. In gardens the species has sometimes been
confused with *A. Halleri*, an unintelligible error when we remember
Halleri's taller stalk, and much broader simpler leaf-lobings shaggy
with silver wool. In cultivation the only complaint against *A. Pulsatilla* is that it grows too well and gets a little rank, losing something
of its brilliancy and neat and gem-like beauty as you see it constella-
ting the green downs of Château-Gaillard with its gold-eyed stars of
violet, or reminding the sere Campagna of the days when Rome wore
purple. There are many paler and darker forms of *A. Pulsatilla*, and
a pretty albino called *White Swan.* But by far its loveliest development has just been introduced to cultivation under the barbarous and
intolerable name of *Mrs. van der Elst*—no doubt a most admirable
person, but this pernicious habit of giving ugly human names to
beautiful flowers ought to be rigidly confined to artificial products
like roses and carnations, without being inflicted on the wild children
of the hills, on which they sit so cumbrously and with so much more
grotesque an air. In any case this form of Pulsatilla is of extraordinary charm (which makes the name so much the worse)—being
indistinguishable from the type, except that its chalices are of a soft
rosy shell-pink, absolutely clean and true, without the slightest taint
of mauve or magenta. This seems less healthy than the type in

cultivation, and no doubt will not come true from the seed in which all Pulsatillas are so profuse, and from which they yield so interesting a range of colour-forms. Finally, though the species be so easy and repaying in any sunny place and good soil—but better in rather poor if the habit is not to be coarsened—remember that *A. Pulsatilla* is essentially lime-craving, and that a large part of its consistent attachment to the Romans and their works is owing to cupboard-love for the superior quality of their mortar-rubble.

A. quinquefolia is a smaller and frailer *A. nemorosa* from America.

A. Raddeana is a very frail, fine woodland species from Japan, lying along the ground, and looking like a delicate small Trientalis.

A. ranunculoeides, which like *A. apennina* has established itself in English woods, is a small Wood-anemone with fewer broader rays, of a shrill canary-yellow. It is a common sub-alpine species, and in the woods of Ferrara, under the long slope of Monte Baldo, it develops into a finer and fuller form than the type.

A. reflexa, from Siberia, so curiously does indeed reflex the segments of its white flowers that they form globes, as it were, the wrong side out.

A. Richardsonii is a synonym of *A. multifida, q.v.*

A. riparia is a repetition of *A. cylindrica*, but not so worthless, having (together with thinner, greener, less downy foliage) flowers of better size, and of a reddish-white.

A. rivularis may be magnified from the earlier description of *A. elongata*. This is one of our most precious Anemones, showering up its rich loose heads of blossoms, with their blue reverse, in summer, and thriving heartily in any cool, moist, or boggy corner. This species, so perfectly trustworthy and hardy, is yet almost tropical at one end of its distribution through the ranges of temperate India, where it is found at last in the hill-woods of Ceylon.

A. rupestris, again, is a small rock-haunting golden treasure from the Himalaya, close to the last.

A. rupicola is a softly silky thing about a foot high, with two or three largish flowers to a scape (or more), white, and silky outside. The leaves are three-lobed and then gashed again. The plant has a vague suggestion of a fine *A. narcissiflora*, if the cultivated specimens are true, which is not by any means to be taken for granted.

A. silvestris, from the woods of Germany and Austria, is one of the most valuable and lovely of all, especially for any cool moist corner of the rock-garden, where it may be allowed to run at its own wild will. For run it does, with an irrepressible zeal, if suited in its soil, which should be a light rich loam. Here its tufts of dark and

handsome leaves come up all over the place, and from many of the
tufts ascend the tall bare stems, about 8 inches high, each carrying
a single very large flower, slightly nodding and fragrant, rather like
those of a smaller and much tidier five-sepalled *A. japonica*, of a soft
and warmer white, perfectly pure, yet creamy in tone. There is
also a double form, and a variety called *major* or *grandiflora* which
is freer in bloom than the type, and slightly larger.

A. sinensis, to adopt the proper spelling, rather than the old
"chinensis," is the Purple Emperor of the Pulsatilla group, having
leaves and blooms after the style of Halleri, but the flower very much
larger and very much more brilliant, with many more sepals to its
radiance. It is *A. sinensis* that blooms in spring between the flagstones
of dead emperors' graves so gloriously in Asia ; in March the only
sign of life in that silent mountain-valley of death where the ancient
sovereigns of China rest are the wide imperial purple stars of the
Anemone, sitting stemless on their silken clumps of leaves (already
unfolding with the flowers) in the crevices between the immemorial
flagstones. This most splendid beauty has at last come into cultivation, though under the false name of *A. mandschuriensis ;* it is
hard to raise from seed, the seedlings having a way of miffing off
disconsolately ; it has even proved so unsatisfactory to grow that
gardeners have come to suspect the plant of being a vampire, drawing
the blood of its imperial glory only from the dust of dead emperors,
and contemptuously unable to subsist on any nutrition less august.
However, this must surely be a libel, for it is not true that the Anemone
never blows so violet as where some buried Asiatic Caesar may have
bled ; on the contrary, the shimmering silver and purple clumps of
the Anemone may be seen quite as profuse and splendid in perfectly
plebeian ordinary ground, rough and stony, by the highwaysides,
where, if ever anybody died or laid their dust, it assuredly was no
emperor, but only common clay of the men who made that road : the
immortal road by which the departed godheads were carried to
those last palaces, each lonely in its square forest of Arbor-vitae, along
the slopes of that vast and lonely valley of the hills where no sound of
man or his works has since been suffered to break the calm of those
undying dead. In point of actual fact, however, *A. sinensis* is
not so rigidly confined to the neighbourhood of courts extinct, but
ranges all across North China and Mongolia and the sad barren hills
of Korea, growing always in places open and stony and severe. Therefore I believe that, in cultivation, regard must be had to this austere
nature of the plant, and that it should be planted in deep but very
hard soil, rocky and perfectly well-drained, in the fullest exposure to

sun and wind, and there wedged in immovably between blocks of stone rammed down on either side. And, in any case, no trouble would be too great for the successful culture of this treasure—no, not even if we each had to murder an emperor for ourselves, and bury him deep in stony ground beneath big flagstones. But, for the moment, the Anemone is almost as rare in our gardens as the emperors of which it is the apt and imperial symbol.

A. stylosa is a worthless and extremely rare species from Utah, and *A. sphenophylla* from Chile follows closely the ways of *A. decapetala*.

A. tetonensis is an American, like a dwarf and rather improved and more purple *A. globosa*.

A. tetrasepala, on the contrary, comes from the Western Himalaya, and is a fine handsome cousin of *A. narcissiflora*, but with only four divisions to the flower instead of five.

A. trifolia brings us back to the European Alps and the relationship of *A. nemorosa*. Of this *A. trifolia* is a rather larger, stouter, more firm-leafed version, of the liveliest beauty. Its range is through the woods of South Tyrol and Carinthia, and all along the Ligurian Riviera. It often, as on the Cima Tombea, shares the upper slopes, just about the last copse-growths, with *A. nemorosa*, which it makes to look rather wizen and dowdy by comparison. And in the woods round Misurina it varies unexplainably into the most lovely tones of soft clear blue, sometimes looking at last as if a large Hepatica had got hung by mistake above the leaves of a fine and solid *A. nemorosa*. This species takes the treatment of its cousinhood, but is far too rarely seen—though of course it is fair to say that, unless you desire a full collection of the various groups, *A. nemorosa* itself fairly fills the bill as regards all the essential charms of its own section.

A. triternata is an American species, with specially thin and ferny leaves at the base.

A. trulliifolia, from the upper Himalaya, is a beautiful small alpine, a reduced version of *A. obtusiloba*, with golden flowers.

A. vernalis takes us high, high into the Alps again, and is the boldest climber of all its race, at least in Europe. It is on the highest alpine grasses that you will come upon the Lady of the Snow. Spread out flat upon the ground, still sere and bare with the passing of winter, lie pressed the two or three carroty leaves, more coarsely and sparingly cut than in any Pulsatilla ; next, an inch or two of stem, shaggy with fur of bronzy gold, a fluffy frill of the same, and then, almost sitting upon the moor, like some mystic water-lily, a great goblet-shaped flower, staring up to the sun, white as an opalescent pearl within, and tasselled with fire, while the outside of the pearl is a-shimmer with gold and violet silk, iridescent as it catches the sun in countless shifting shades of lilac and fawn and milk. Let no one persuade you that the Lady of the Snow is not beautiful, as you see her floating on the darkness of the earth, so dead and cold in the first moment of the dawn, and offering to the drowsy creatures of the air the new wine from her opening white chalice, brimmed over with its foam of gold. At the same time truth must be told ; in lower stations, and in later stages, the stem is longer, and the blossom looks correspondingly smaller ; worst of all, the Lady of the Snow clings so desperately to her departing beauties that she will not let them go, nor confess to growing old. The blossom fades but never falls, the pearly skin turns into a withered hag's, till in the end that once peerless loveliness takes a blowzy and disreputable look, like some raddled and unreverend dowager in a chestnut wig ; while all the while her cousin Alpina, more wise, is advancing honestly into the full beauty of old age, and reaping the reward of its honourable silver heads. *A. vernalis*, however, though apparently so pure-bred an alpine, has a most curious distribution, and is only accidentally alpine at all. For its most abundant distribution is in the Scandinavian Peninsula ; from thence it ranges into Russia and straggles away South towards the Caucasus, but never gets there. It next makes a few astonishing appearances in North Germany and France, in situations not by any means alpine, but like those preferred by the Pratensis group. Then come the Alpine chains ; and here the Anemone is abundant again, this time as a plant of the upmost short alpine turf, but diminishing so markedly as you go sunwards that it is quite hard to come upon it in the Cottians and Maritimes. It now, however, breaks out again to right and left in Transylvania and the Pyrenees, occurring after that sporadically all down the hills of Spain to the Sierra Nevada. In cultivation it is perfectly easy and pleasant, offering no difficulty at all, but actually preferring, contrary to intuition and experience, the fattest and richest of soil (in full sun, of course) if its flowers are to be as opulent and splendid as they are on the Alps. It is not hard to collect ; it is readily re-established ; and it comes abundantly from seed.

A. virginiana is not a good plant—from 2 to 3 feet high, with soft, veined, ample foliage, and small yellowish stars, carried each by itself on a long foot-stalk, from the main stem that branches into a head of three or four.

A. Wallichiana is a member of the Pulsatilla group, with six wide sepals very woolly outside, leaves half the stalk's length, and the neck-stem above the frill twice the length of the frill itself.

A. Wolfgangiana is *A. Nuttaliana*, an American form or synonym of *A. montana*.

A. zephyra, from the central Rockies, in sub-alpine woods, should be a lovely thing, being described as a large-flowered, lemon-coloured version of *A. narcissiflora*.

HYBRIDS OF ANEMONE

A. × *Seemannii*, nemorosa × ranunculoeides, a pretty little straw-yellow Wood-anemone which many gardeners have raised and others have found occurring.

A. × *Pittonii*, nemorosa × trifolia.

A. × *Haeckellii*, patens × pratensis.

A. × *intermedia*, patens × vernalis.

A. × *affinis*, Pulsatilla × pratensis.

A. × *mixta*, Pulsatilla grandis × pratensis nigricans.

A. × *propinqua*, Pulsatilla × vernalis.

A. × *bolzanensis*, montana × vernalis (on the Klobenstein above Bozen).

A. × *spuria*, pratensis × vernalis.

A. × *vernalpina*, vernalis × alpina (in cultivation).

A. × *Wilczekii*, alpina sulfurea × vernalis.

A. × *Emiliana*, Halleri × vernalis.

A. × *ochroleuca*, alpina × alpina sulfurea (a very doubtful cross).

Any or all of these hybrids may from time to time be offered ; meanwhile there would be few more interesting tasks than to raise the best of them over again in gardens.

Anemonella thalictrifolia was long known as *Anemone thalictroeides*, or *Thalictrum anemonoeides*. It is, none the less, a very distinct little American woodland beauty, frail and early, like a single-flowered Isopyrum with one pearly and comely blossom.

Anemonopsis macrophylla is a most stately Japanese plant, akin to Ranunculus and Aquilegia. From a fleshy creeping stock it sends up glossy foliage, suggesting that of Cimicifuga or Actaea, but darker and thicker and more lucent. The hanging flowers are carried in summer after the style of *Anemone japonica*, and their effect is rather that of big belated Columbines, spurless and very waxy, white-centred, and of a rich lavender-blue. Anemonopsis is not always easy to deal with, but succeeds best in deep woodland soil, cool and rich, in a warm and sheltered corner. In such a place it may be remembered at Edge in Cheshire, growing stalwartly,

PLATE 8.

VOL. I.   AQUILEGIA JUCUNDA [A. GLANDULOSA of gardens].

(Photo. R. A. Malby.)

thicker and taller than its usual height, which is about 14 inches, rather more or rather less.

Anemopsis comes here not because its name is really Anemopsis (for it is, in fact, *Houttuynia californica*, and there is another one, *H. cordata*, in Japan), but because catalogues always call it " Anemiopsis," and more usually still endeavour to go one better yet, and impose it on an ardent world as a new *Anemonopsis*. The Houttuynias, however, though utterly unworthy of any such kinship, have their value ; *H. californica*, from a tuft of fleshy-oval leaves, sends up flowers with a tall central cone, surrounded by six expanded leaf-bracts that have the look of pure white petals dotted with red ; *H. cordata* is a smaller thing, and runs about in and out of the garden walls in Japan, with heart-shaped leaves, not fleshy, and a profusion all the summer through of four-petalled-looking snow-white stars, with a cone at their centre. In gardens both species like cool moist and rather shady corners, where *H. cordata* at least may run at will. The fault of this, however, is the peculiarly nauseating smell of its blossoms.

Antennaria.—The race of Cat's Ears is large and confused. Except when lured by very special descriptions, the rock-gardener has no need to travel beyond our native *A. dioica*, with its neat spreading masses of silver-grey rosettes (excellently well-adapted for a crocus-carpet), and chaffy Composite heads of small everlastings, white or pink, on stems of 2 or 3 inches. This is a matting-plant for any rather worthless situation ; but one of the most beautiful associations I have ever seen was on the Mont Cenis, where raged a large mass of the Antennaria, with flowers in tangles of the most clear and tender pink above their silver floor, into which were thrusting up thick azure clumps of *Gentiana aestiva*. Among the myriad other confused Cat's Ears are *A. arctica*, with browner heads ; *A. hyperborea*, with rose-pink flowers ; *A. nivale*, proclaimed as being something special ; and *A. plantaginifolia* from North-east America, with broader leaves still whiter with down. *A. tomentosa* is a form of *A. dioica*.

Anthĕmis.—The Camomiles are very often annuals, very often annual weeds, very often half-hardy annual weeds. However, there are several that ascend to alpine elevations, and several that are handsome and useful perennials whether they ascend there or not. Their rule is light well-drained soil in full sun, and all can be raised from seed, and freely struck as cuttings. For the rock-garden let us try to mention only the best of the dwarf-growing, perennial, decumbent species that bloom in full and later summer.

A. aciphylla, from Caria, has the leaves cut into specially long, specially fine strips, each delicately pointed. *A. taygetea* is rather smaller.

A. aeizoon is the beautiful thing that masquerades in lists (even of Kew) as *Achillea serbica*, or *Achillea ageratifolia*, or *Achillea aeizoon* —all these names being but the Betsy, Bessy, and Bet to the one and original Elizabeth of *Anthemis aeizoon*. It is, anyhow, a most attractive species, forming masses of low silver-grey rosettes, with very narrow leaves, finely saw-edged; and an abundance of snow-pure daisies on 5-inch stems, with brilliant broad white rays and a whitish eye; it is quite easy and permanent in a dry well-drained sunny place in good light soil or moraine—the treatment, indeed, indicated for all the choice species, of which this is perhaps the queen.

A. aetnensis. See under *A. montana*.

A. alpina has the usual single Marguerite to a stem. *A. mucronulata* is quite near, but much looser in habit, with a few particularly broad short rays to the flower.

A. anatolica is like a diminished version of *A. montana*, with the cup into which the florets are gathered conical instead of rounded.

A. Barbeyana, a beautiful species from the Alps of Aetolia, forms a dense cushion of notably finely-cut, silky-grey foliage, cut combwise along the stems; while the white daisies of the family are carried in *close heads of from four to seven in number*.

A. Biebersteinii is often seen in gardens, but is a rather coarse weed like a Camomile, with profusion of bright golden Marguerites lonely on longish stalks. It is all silky-hairy, and comes from the mountains of the Levant. *A. B. Marshalliana, pectinata, Rudolphiana*, are different varieties of this.

A. carpatica, from the whole range of the Southerly Alps from the Pyrenees to the Carpathians in the upmost stony places, is often confused with *A. montana*, from which, however, it may be known by having its leaves cut into irregular and much broader jags, much fewer than in *A. montana*. Its flowers also—big single Chrysanthemums—are always lonely on their stems; its habit is much neater, and its inclinations much more ambitiously higher-alpine.

A. cassia is a dense close silver-silky tuft; the leaves being slit on either side into long, quite narrow sharp strips, continuing down the leaf-stalk; the stems are tall, about 12 or 15 inches high, often branching, and carrying, at the end of each, one nobly large flower, as big as in *Chrysanthemum maximum*. From alpine elevations of Mount Cassius in Northern Syria, and greatly to be desired.

A. cinerea, from the Balkan range of Rilo, has a hard stock and forms a mass of ash-grey downy leaves, which are cut into short oblong jags, these again being slit into featherings. The stems are a foot high, all the upper part being bare, as usual, and the white flowers are particularly fine.

A. Cupaniana is a treasure from Italy, perfectly hardy and of the greatest value, though not by any means small or dainty. It forms a vast decumbent mass often a yard or more across, and perhaps 6 inches deep, of fat shoots embedded in masses of neat ferny foliage, rather plump and grey, and pleasantly aromatic. From these all the summer through, and far on into December if allowed, springs an unceasing profusion of large and brilliant snowy Marguerites carried well aloft, some 6 inches or more above the mass. This beauty seems indifferent to sun or shade, heavy soil or light ; it came under a suspicion of tenderness, which has by now been utterly dispelled. Nor is *A. Cupaniana* anything but soundly perennial ; though, for increase rather than for any guarantee, it may be remembered that every shoot will make a goodly specimen if struck in sand.

A. fruticulosa belongs to the lower alpine region of Caucasus. It makes almost a little dwarf bush, with big flowers and leaves all closely white-silked, cut into strips of varying length, breadth, and sharpness.

A. graveolens is a larger version of *A. anatolica*, not at all silky, but green, odorous, and with longer rays to the flower.

A. Grisebachii has especial charm in its fine accumulations of grey foliage, but should be starved in the moraine lest full soil corrupt its vigour and cause it to die back.

A. iberica, from Levantine mountains, is near to *A. carpatica*, but here the leaf-slits are so short that the whole leaf looks narrow-oblong instead of amply egg-shaped in general outline. The stems are from 6 to 12 inches high, and the blossoms very large and fine. And there is a still better variety, *A. i. minor*, being a quite neat, specially dwarf tuffet with stems of not more than 3 or 4 inches, from the high-alpine stony places of Kasbek at about 8000 feet.

A. Kotschyi, not unknown in gardens, differs from all forms of *A. montana* in having short, yellow rays to the flower. The silky leaves each have a little foot-stalk, and are shortly oval in outline, cut into a few lobes, which again are gashed into three to five short, blunt, and narrow strips. (Alps of Taurus.)

A. montana, that recurrent name, has innumerable synonyms and varieties. It is also *A. macedonica* Griseb., and as such sometimes appears in the same list as *A. montana*. A typical cushion-forming, fine-leaved mountain Camomile, often with branching shoots and several daisies, it occupies rocky places all along the Northern borders of the Mediterranean from Spain to the Levant. Countless local developments, varieties, or kindred species (some with no rays to the flowers) have been differentiated; among these are *A. Linnaeana*, *cronia* (dwarf), *tenuiloba*, *pentelica* (sometimes rayless), *incana* and *anatolica* (not to be confused with *A. anatolica* the species). *Blancheana* is a sub-species from Lebanon, but the jags of the leaves are here shorter, and start away from each other. More important than these, and often offered as species, are: *Anthemis montana var. aetnensis*, a beautiful closer tuffet, with Marguerites that break the family tradition by diverging from white to pink; *A. m. Columnae*, all silvery-silky; *A. m. petraea*, quite smooth and green and silkless, but sweetly scented; and *A. m. saxatilis*, all white with silky wool. A very kindred thing is *A. leucanthemifolia*, from hills above Smyrna, differing in its long, fine sharply-pointed segments and strips to its leaves; not very distinct, again, are *A. sterilis* and *A. candicans*.

A. ptarmicaefolia, from the mountains of the Levant, is a quite different species, forming minute running carpets, rooting as they go. The little leaves are more or less slit on either side into a few huddled blunt jags, and the rays of the flower are unfortunately not usually as long as the disk—though in this there is variation.

A. rigescens is like a pale smooth version of the common Camomile.

A. tricolor, though really beautiful, offers scant hope of being hardy, but is well worth the trial—a silky flopping plant, of no more than some 3 to 5 inches, from the sea-rocks of Cyprus; the small leaves are oblong, feathered into lobes which are again feathered into a few short oblong narrow little jags; and the flowers are larger than those of *A. montana*, white, but going rose-red at the base.

Anthericum is a family of delicate alpine Asphodels with fine loose sprays of lovely white stars. Unfortunately the best of the species has now been banished into a race to itself, and *Anthericum Liliastrum* is Anthericum no longer, while *A. baeticum*, from the damp alpine fields of Spain (with quite dwarf forms, one- or two-flowered, from still higher up), is so far unknown in our gardens. There yet remain, however, *A. Liliago* and *A. ramosum* (sometimes *A. graminifolium*). This last is very familiar and grateful in the garden—a haunter of sub-alpine rocks, forming an ever-widening tuft of long and frail grassy leaves, from which in later summer spring increasing multitudes of light graceful stems, gracefully branching, and set with small white stars. Any reasonable conditions of cool soil suit *A. ramosum* perfectly, and it may be fancied that its one objection would be to being parched and grilled. Much more uncommon in cultivation is *A. Liliago*, because it holds the middle position between the fine starriness of *A. ramosum* and the sumptuous ecclesiastical splendour of what is now *Anthericum Liliastrum* no longer. *A. Liliago* has shorter stems than *A. ramosum*, and flowers much larger and longer, though barely half the size of Liliastrum's. It does not form into a wide mass, but keeps a single crown, like Liliastrum (of which, indeed, it is a precise miniature), from which rise dainty foot-high stems, laxly set with very shallow wide, six-rayed trumpets. It is quite easy of culture, and especially abundant at low elevations in the Southern Alps. In cleared open grassy slopes among the chestnut-groves above Bobbio, its airy spires rise pure and brilliant against the bright green background of the lawn ; while on hotter sunnier banks it stands profuse in the rough sparse flowering grasses among the waving pinks of *Dianthus inodorus*, the gold-and-violet of *Aster alpinus*, and the stocky ruby-red catherine-wheels of *Sempervivum arachnoideum*. Here, indeed, is a hint for the gardener who has hot banks to plant in poorish soil. As for *A. yedoense*, this is surely *Allectorurus yedoensis*.

Anthyllis is a family of Southerly and tropical Pea-flowers, all essentially rock-plants, one of them being locally abundant on the limestones and serpentine rocks of England. Many of the species are woolly-haired, and all of them require, or prefer, a hot dry and well-drained corner in sunny rocks. (Seed.)

A. alpestris is a variety, rather finer, of our own *A. Vulneraria.*

A. aurea is a lovely thing—a tiny bushling from the mountain-tops above Ragusa, with feathered foliage, perfectly smooth but bright silver with close-pressed hairs, most beautiful to see. On this mass appear the flowers, bright golden yellow, in dense fat heads.

A. Barba-Jovis comes from the Mediterranean region—a handsome woolly shrub of much larger habit, with yellow blossoms. It could not be called really trustworthy in England, any more than *A. sericea, A. rupestris*, or any others of the sun-craving sea-level section.

A. illyrica should be a beautiful violet Anthyllis akin to Vulneraria, and indeed accepted as a mere variety.

A. montana is not uncommon in gardens, nor in hot rocky places in the Southern Alps—as, for instance, on the sunny limestones opposite Saint Martin Vésubie. It makes a prostrate mat of densely woolly feathered leaves, ashy-grey in effect, on which lie largish heads of flowers, pink indeed, but like so many Pea-flowers—a race most strong in yellows, but rather weak in good pinks (with all due reserves for *Lathyrus odoratus*)—lacking just that final touch required to give clearness and brilliance : in short, a very useful pretty little cushion for sunny dry corners, with flowers of a rather sullen shade of sunlit claret in high summer.

A. podocephala, quite common in the limestone and dolomite cliffs (especially on Northern exposures), between 2000 and 3000 feet, in the mountains of Malaga, forms a bush of a foot or two of fluffy foliage, with really splendid, many-headed big clusters of golden blooms emerging on long stems from the axils of the leaves.

A. rosea is yet another Spanish beauty—a dense tight tuffet of gleaming silver, with big hemispherical heads, on short stems, of large flowers, pink in the wing and violet in the keel. This belongs to limestone precipices about 3000 feet up in the Sierra de Mallorca.

A. tejedensis is akin to *A. podocephala*, but cosily neat and close and dwarf and declining, and perfectly snowy-white in its foliage. The stems of the flower-heads are shorter, and the flowers themselves range from bright gold to rich violet, looking incomparably charming upon the wide low mats of light silver that the plant achieves in the same rocky soils and situations as those affected by *A. podocephala*, but much higher up, at about 7000 feet in the mountains of Granada and the Sierra Nevada. In cultivation there should be little doubt as to the hardiness, with luck, of *A. rosea* and *A. podocephala*, in warm dry rock-work, but none at all about that of the alpine *A. tejedensis*.

A. Vulneraria, the English Ladies'-fingers, is an ornamental enough thing from grassy rocks, locally abundant all over the country. It has further forms, however, that vary from the yellow of the type. Not very notable is the rather lymphatic white, but *A. illyrica* is a goodly violet development. Then there is a rose or red variety, called *rubriflora* or *Dillenii*, which may be seen on the rocks of Cornwall. Finally there is a little completely prostrate form of this last, called *minor*, with smaller red flowers on longer stems. But *A. Vulneraria* is a vast and tangled name, its many developments requiring systematic treatment.

Antirrhinum.—The common Snapdragon is gorgeous enough in its home-bred forms of cream or salmon, or scarlet or crimson; but for those who prefer unsophisticated pure species, there are the following—omitting annuals and weeds :

A. Asarina should more rightly now be called *Asarrhina Loebelii*, this being the name that has prior authority. However, it is so near Antirrhinum, and as *A. Asarina* has rooted itself so deep in our lists and walls, that perhaps the more convenient later name may be allowed to stand. It makes a mass of frail and fleshy stems, twisting and depending from the rocks in which it must be put. The leaves are opposite to each other, ivy-shaped and with scalloped edge, large and soft and sticky-grey like the whole fat and brittle plant. The flowers are big, borne by themselves in the axils of the leaves, pale citron yellow, and the lip striped with red. It blooms, like the others, all the summer through, and is so saxatile that some of the happiest and oldest specimens seen in our gardens spring and wax huge from some seed strayed into a microscopic crack of cliff or ancient wall where there appears not to be any sustenance.

A. Barrelieri grows straight and stiff and rather graceful, attaining 2 or 3 feet, with rather few and sparse narrow dark leaves, and long loose spikes of rather smaller variable Snapdragons. (Eastern border of Spain, and so Westward in South Europe.) It is hardy, like the rest, yet cultivators must remember where the Snapdragons come from. They demand full sun and drought; they hate shade and damp, more especially in winter.

A. Charidemii should be a pretty rock-plant, from crevices of Almeria, attaining 2 or 3 feet, with rather narrow alternate leaves, oval and more or less downy. The pink, crimson-striped dragons are carried in specially lax spires.

A. glutinosum, a frail cliff-lover, *very glandular and sticky*, almost woody at the base, densely branchy and twisting and flopping and leafy, the uprising shoots at the end being quite short, and the whole spray thickly clothed in short expanded, little egg-shaped leaves. The flowers are as in the last, but a trifle smaller. There is also a variety, *A. g. rupestre*, which has a much tighter habit, and rose-pink Snapdragons. *A. glutinosum* is found on walls and rocks at low levels in Castille and Nevada, scarcely attaining even to the sub-alpine region. Yet it will happily stand our climate, if it has the advantage of a well-drained sheltered corner that is dry in winter. Seed or cuttings.

A. hispanicum is offered in cultivation, but looks doubtful. The true typical species is close akin to *A. Barrelieri* (but with foliage broader, though no less pointed), from which it is easily known by being *sticky*, especially near the tops of the shoots. It is a twisting branchy thing, attaining to 2 or 3 feet, with flowers nearly the size of Majus, ample and pale yellow with orange lip. The species abounds in the walls of Spain, and varies into broader-leaved and less viscid forms. No doubt the colour may vary also.

A. latifolium is the common Snapdragon of the Riviera. Its blossoms are yellow, but it may at once be known from *A. majus* by its broader leaves, which are clothed in a fine down instead of being bald as those of the common Snapdragon. Akin to this is the rare *A. meonanthum* (with a bigger variety *A. Huettii*), with flowers half the size.

A. molle is a most frail grower, not glandular, but white with soft hairs. It haunts the warm crevices of Catalonia, from which it weakly flops with long stems, and their boughs are beset with very small roundish hoary-white foliage. The blooms are large, thickly fluffy outside, white also, with a yellow palate and the upper lip streaked with red. They are carried in short lax spikes, or are sometimes almost solitary.

A. sempervirens is yet another frail and prostrate species, with intricate branches not more than 8 inches or so in length, minutely downy. The leaves are opposite to each other, *evergreen*, narrow-oval and downy as the sprays. The flowers are produced from the upper axils on laxish shoots opposite like the leaves. In size they are only half those of *A. molle*, whitish and lilac-striped, with a yellow palate. (Rocks of the Pyrenees.) It may be quite easily told from *A. glutinosum*, which, *inter alia*, is almost a woody wiry mass, densely *sticky, and not evergreen*. Both are in cultivation, and succeed well; there seems to be no reason why we should go on lacking *A. molle* and *A. Charidemii*.

Aphyllanthes monspeliensis forms a clan all to its lone self among the Lilies. It makes wide semicircular masses—for so it goes on spreading fanwise from its start—of tapering stems exactly like those of a glaucous-grey Rush. There is nothing more by way of foliage than these waving or flopping tangles of Rush-like stems. And then, in early summer, a certain number of these erupt at the tip into a small brown sheath, still more like that of a wizened Rush. But from this unpromising chaff there suddenly emerges a beautiful six-rayed star of delicate blue. Aphyllanthes is a most interesting monotype; it crosses from North Africa and occurs in Spain, then ranges all along most of the Franco-Italian Riviera, appearing quite sporadically but in generous abundance. It is curiously local, and its wide colonies cease abruptly and unexpectedly. It may be seen here and there throughout the heathery tract between Cannes and Grasse; and, beyond Turbia, may be found profuse in a very hard, close and clammy yellow loam. It makes wide inextricable mats of specially long tough roots, anchoring itself a thousand times to its soil; from which accordingly it is only extracted with great difficulty, a spade or a mattock being wanted to get up even a fragment of those vast and aged masses. This disturbance the plant resents; for it hates division, and in the garden should never be disturbed. However, when once re-established it is thoroughly easy and hardy, enjoying a deep, light, and rich soil. In nature it does not seem to like the full Mediterranean sun, but affects the shadier and cooler slopes;

therefore while in the North of England it will take all the pale sun-rays it can get, in the more torrid South it may prefer to live on the outskirts of some small light bush, even as the finest specimen I know anywhere is luxuriating near London close by an over-shadowing Cytisus—and wholly for years refused to luxuriate until there so placed. In the market Aphyllanthes is too often sold in over-divided, tiny pieces which have thus been drained of the will to live ; yet this can hardly be wondered at, seeing that the rarity is not of readily-handled increase, spreading indeed, but disliking removal, and not by any means free or prompt in seed.

Apocȳnum, a race of tall, rank and running Vincaetoxicum-like rampers, mostly from America, for the cool sheltered wild-garden in dampish, half-shady places ; but taller and leafier than Vincaetoxicum, with branching stems of honey-sweet flower-heads, pink or white.

Aponogēton distachyon, the Water Hawthorn of the Cape, is quite hardy and a well-known grateful adornment for still waters of 2 or 3 feet in depth, on whose surface its dark leaves lie like those of some Potamogeton all the year, while through the winter appear in profusion its two-branched heads of deliciously scented whiteness.

Aquilegia.—What race has so delicate and desirable a charm as this ? The Columbines, however, are not alpines so much as sub-alpines, not often ascending to great elevations, but preferring, as a rule, the more open places of the mountain woods and coppices, among such things as the dwarf pines, the *narcissiflora* Anemones, and the Woodland-lilies. Though many of the more ordinary sorts are per-fectly easy and perennial, it is sadly notorious that in droughty parts of England some of the most lovely queens of this race are corre-spondingly difficult and miffy in temper—as short-lived as a Mid-Victorian heroine, and as resentful of all parched peas or crumpled rose-leaves in their beds as Hans Andersen's Princess. In point of fact, the prime requirement—a hard one, but by no means impossible of attainment—is a very rich soil that shall always be perfectly porous and sweet and light, crumbling and never caking, spongy with vege-table matter, freely loosened with an admixture of chips, and sharply drained with the most unfailing and absolute precision. Let such a bed be made then in a sheltered corner, where its inhabitants will fear no more the summer sun nor the furious winter's rages, in a place not overshadowed nor dank ; shielded from wind, yet open to a certain amount of sunshine, never for too long together at its full strength ; and there, in the lee of *Pinus montana*, or some such light sufficient weather-guard, there need be no difficulty about making at least a temporary success of even *A. Stuartii*. But while the plants require the sharpest and most rough drainage below their roots, they have a corresponding dislike to being left parched and torrid. Therefore, as an ideal, water ought to be flowing away beneath them all the summer through ; and, failing that, a sunk pot in the soil, periodically filled, should give them what they want. It will, however, be understood by anyone who has seen nearly a hundred square yards of ordinary rich kitchen-garden, open to all the winds and sunshine that descend, a wild and waving blue-and-white jungle of *A. jucunda*, that these minutiae are recommended only for the most miffy of the species, in districts not sub-alpine, where Columbines are not naturally at home. As for propagation, it is not wise to move or touch any Columbine that is well established. They can best be raised from seed, which is produced with lavish generosity and germinates with no less. Unfortunately the species so lavishly inter-breed that the offspring are hardly ever true, except in the case of a few species such as *A. jucunda*, which never seems to mar its purity with any other strain, or to influence the blood of its kindred.

Aquilegia alpina is the glory and the despair of all who have ever seen its huge celestial crowns of loveliness waving delicately amid the herbage of the Mont Cenis, the Vorder Wellhorn, or the Combes de Barant. There can be nothing more beautiful in all nature. But those who have not there so seen it have no notion of the plant, its true habit and refulgence ; for not only do nurserymen always sub-stitute for it some smaller and dingier Columbine of common blood, but the true *A. alpina* has never yet, by a curious fatality, been ade-quately figured. In all plates of it, either the drawing, or the colour, or both, have been misleading, wrong, and unfair. It is a stately and superb thing indeed, with leaves much ampler, greener, and cut into far longer, more numerous and finer lobes than those of *A. vulgaris*. One may almost, when sought and seeker both are young, mistake them for those of *Thalictrum aquilegifolium* (how just a name !). The stems can attain to 18 inches, carrying, each on its long stem, several enormous wide flowers of the most velvety deep clear-blue throughout, rather slack in texture, and with a brilliant golden heart of stamens. (It is quite a heresy to think there is a blue-and-white *A. alpina ;* the plant such heretics no doubt mean is *A. jucunda—A. alpina* being invariably and altogether of its own peculiar melting powder-blue.) This glorious wonder of the lower alpine copse is very rare indeed in the main mass of the Swiss Alps, beginning to be more common in the Engadine, and becoming inordinately abundant through the Cottian ranges down into the Maritimes, where its profusion is such that, above La Maddalena, for instance, close to San Dalmazzo de Tenda, all the rolling woods are waving-blue with the acres of its blossom, floating down the distances in a haze of dreamy peat-reek like bluebells in an English May. To take the roots of *A. alpina* is hardly possible; and seed can never be obtained true unless you can get it with your own hands, or from some trustworthy authority on the spot. It may be owing to all these uncertainties, or to some inherent vice in the plant itself, but the Alpine Columbine, though not hard, it seems, of culture, has always been a disappointment in our gardens, and has earned for itself a bad name. It is murmured that it loses the size of its blossom in captivity, and fades with home-sickness into a sad flat indigo, lifeless and uninteresting.

A. Amaliae, a glandular Columbine from Thessaly, like a smaller *A. vulgaris*, with flowers of blue and white.

A. aragonensis does not exceed some 6 inches, with all the foliage coming from the base, and then a bare stem, carrying one nodding blue blossom with golden anthers. The leaves are simply lobed in threes and finely downy. (Mountain woods of Aragon.)

A. arctica. See *A. formosa.*

A. atrata. See under *A. vulgaris.* (This form is also called *A. nigricans.*)

A. atropurpurea is a Russian species of no particular merit. In gardens the name is sometimes used for the dark purple variety of *A. vulgaris.*

A. aurea is a species from the sub-alpine woods of Macedonia, forming cushions of foliage, from which rise up the 18-inch stems with large yellow flowers.

A. Bauhinii. See under *A. pyrenaica.*

A. Bernardii is a most beautiful and rare Columbine peculiar to Corsica, where it is found in the higher copses on Monte Rotondo and Renoso. It has, often, taller and less leafy stems than those of *A. alpina,* and the leaves (which are smooth underneath) are larger and less divided than in *A. glandulosa.* The flowers are enormous, wide open, and full, with particularly broad petals and the spur very nearly straight. They are larger than those of *A. Reuteri* and *A. Kitaibelii,* of a most splendid and penetrating soft clear blue.

A. Bertolonii. See under *A. pyrenaica.*

A. brevistyla. See *A. saximontana.*

A. californica. See *A. truncata.*

A. canadensis. See *A. elegantula.*

A. caucasica is a specially fine form of *A. vulgaris.*

A. chrysantha (*A. thalictrifolia,* Rydb.) needs no introduction—an extremely beautiful species like a pale-golden version of the next, from the South-west States ; it can attain more than 3 feet in height, and holds its golden great flowers erect ; they have ostentatious long spurs, and there is also an exquisite dream-like variety *alba*, with blossoms of a faint creamy white, close to one's ideal of *A. coerulea leptocera*. This species, too, has interbred most successfully with *A. coerulea*, its sister in beauty, and produced noble long-spurred delicate Columbines of the highest value, beauty, and good nature.

A. coerulea, which is the State Flower of Colorado, is a most beautiful thing. It is smaller and slighter in habit than the rest, with foliage fine and frail and comparatively scant, ferny and delicate, gathered at the foot of the slim foot-high stems, that seem so slight to sustain the enormous blossoms staring straight up at the passer-by. These are of the most refulgent soft lavender-blue, with creamy centre of petals, and long, long spurs standing out from each other. Hardly any other of our Columbines except *A. chrysantha* has quite this erect-flower habit ; and, indeed, for diaphanous glamour and elfin grace it might easily be maintained that *A. coerulea* is queen of the family. She is also, however, of a temper aptly typified by her evanescent loveliness ; and is almost more satisfactory in many gardens if treated as a biennial (if pure seed can be got), seeing that thus every year one can arrange for the bewildering show of loveliness that the tuft always achieves in its second season, too often after that to disappear pitilessly from a distasteful world. In cultivation, however, there is an endless range of hybrids between *A. coerulea* and the other North-American Columbines of the elegantula-chrysantha-flavescens kindred; and the result is a garden race of superb and vigorous stalwarts, forming high mounds of leafage, surmounted all through the season by ample sheaves of long-spurred blossoms in richest constellations of rose, mauve, purple, and crimson, with immense spurred petals of cream or white or gold. But these perhaps are illegitimate developments, too huge and artificial for the rock-garden, with flowers fine indeed, but never having the uncanny size and magic of *A. coerulea*. There yet remains, however, a wild form of *A. coerulea* for which the choicest hole in our hearts and gardens is gaping. For in the high ravines of Utah and Colorado there is also found a plant of lower and neater stature than typical *A. coerulea*, with the same enormous upright flowers—but this time of a very soft uniform cream-colour verging towards white, and having the look of strange Eucharis-lilies gone astray upon the mountains. This is *A. coerulea var. leptocera*—a treasure long desired, but so far unobtained, for nurserymen always confuse it with the doubtful *species*, *A. leptoceras*, Fisch. and Meyer, which seems to be a long-spurred thing near *A. vulgaris* with rather the habit of *A. elegantula.* In any case, whenever *A. coerulea leptocera* is ordered, it often arrives, indeed, but always proves a more or less uninteresting form of what apparently is the ordinary Columbine.

A. dichroa is a small species from damp woods of Portugal. Its stems are from 8 to 20 inches high, its leaves divided into largish lobes, and glaucous-green above. The flower is not remarkably big, pink and white, or blue and white. *A. dichroa var. Moelleriana* is a minute form.

A. ecalcarata is one of the oddest of the race. It comes from the Far East and has the subtle charm of Japan—a small plant about 8 inches or barely a foot high, with pendulous flowers, full-faced and large, without any spurs at all, and of a burnt-sienna brown which, though at first sight unattractive, soon impresses you with your own barbarousness in having thought it so. For indeed it is a rich and sympathetic shade, taking hot tones of claret and chocolate against the light. The species is quite easy to grow in any open soil, and comes unvaryingly true from seed. (See Appendix.)

A. Einseleana. See under *A. pyrenaica.*

A. elegantula must stand as the prior name of the graceful summer-blooming American Columbine which often appears in lists as *A. canadensis.* It earns its name, indeed—a dainty tall grower with abundance of hanging flowers, long and narrow, with conspicuous spidery spurs of scarlet behind the yellow of the blossom. It is common and easy.

A. eximia. See under *A. truncata.*

A. flabellata, from Japan, is another plant that conveys the mystic fascination of the East. It is a stout and stocky little species, not of tall habit, but variable in this respect, for there is a specially dwarf form called *nana* by gardeners; as a rule, the typical growth is about 8 inches or a foot, with a mass of specially fat foliage, rather glaucous-grey, in ample lobules. The flowers are many and large for the clump, wide and shallow in outline, with hooky spurs. They are very thick and waxy in texture, and their plump star of lilac sepals is rounded in outline, while the inner cup of their petals tends to be a bowl rather than a trumpet; and in colour they are of a lovely waxy lavender, with the spurs and their petals of a creamy white. In cultivation *A. flabellata* is perfectly easy, sure and permanent and true—a neat and tidy species, early-blooming, and of special loveliness.

A. formosa is a finer, dwarfer, and more vivid form of *A. elegantula,* and is sometimes also sent out under the name of *A. arctica.*

A glandulosa, one must conclude, is not in cultivation, the pretender which so gloriously bears aloft the name in lucky gardens being the true *A. jucunda* of Fisch. and Meyer. *A. glandulosa* should be a much dwarfer thing, much more miffy and shy-flowering, though with big splendid blossoms of *uniform dark blue*. The labellum again, or blade of the petals at the centre of the flower, which is rounded in *A. jucunda*, is pointed in *A. glandulosa*, and the outspread sepals are oblong, not egg-shaped, and the stamens spray out in a bushy tassel instead of keeping more or less parallel with the opening bloom; while the lips of the hook-spurred petals—the labella—do not touch all round as in *A. jucunda*, but the petals are wholly separate all the way down—thus giving a starry-eyed effect—and are pointed at the end, dark blue, and tipped with darker colour still. In any case, whether hard or easy, shy or bold, it is much to be wished that we could make acquaintance with the true-blue, star-faced *A. glandulosa*.

A. Haenkeana is a fine alpine form of *A. vulgaris*, with leaves especially deeply cleft, and few flowers (on naked stems), especially large and ample and limpidly cœrulean. Another marked form is *A. salvatorensis*, from the mountain of San Salvatore above Lugano; this is like a small version of *A. Einseleana*, so fine are the flowers of deep purple with hooked spurs.

A. haylodgensis. See under *A. Stuartii*.

A. × Helenae is a noble, solid, and robust-natured garden hybrid whose parents are *A. flabellata nana* and *A. coerulea*. The result is a really beautiful thing, of admirable constitution, erect and stiff, about 15 inches high, with fine blooms of blue and white, large and firm.

A. × Jaeschkanii is another garden hybrid of no special value.

A. Jonesii takes us into altogether different regions, for this is a rare and very tiny treasure of the central Rockies, with all the little leaves at the base, their lobules gathered in close clusters; and then a naked stem, not more than an inch and a half to three inches high, carrying a single large blossom. This is a true alpine, and it is much to be hoped that Mr. Jones will now hasten up there again to procure us his Columbine.

A. jucunda, Fisch. and Meyer, is the glorious "*A. glandulosa*" of our gardens—a most vigorous and long-lived stalwart, forming increasing masses from year to year, and breaking up into mounds and clumps of vivid green foliage, high above which shoot the copious 18-inch or 2-foot stems, each carrying on long graceful foot-stalks several enormous flowers, very ample and splendid in outline, whose star of broad sepals is richly blue, while the no less broad petals, in a wide five-lobed-looking cup at the centre, are of a clear and conspicuous white. Enough has already been said as to the distinctions between this and the almost unknown *A. glandulosa ;* but, apart from its blue-and-whiteness, and its far greater strength, height, and brilliancy, will be noticed the amplitude of the petals, so full as to touch all round, and the notable breadth of the deep-blue sepals. The royal flowers are not really horizontally borne, but seem just a little to nod with their own grandeur; and a dense field-like patch of the *A. jucunda*, one foaming sea of green, high over which wave and waver the countless wide stars of blue and white, is one of the most beautiful things that the garden can ever show, either in early June or at any other time. Originally introduced from Forres, where it was long a speciality, *A. jucunda* proves a glory of magnificent constitution, in any soil that is duly deep and rich and cool. Clumps should be moved only when they are first beginning to show signs of life in the dawn of spring, in which case the crown sustains no check, and shows no resentment ; and, as for seed, *A. jucunda*, the unquestionable sovereign of the race, annihilating even *A. coerulea* and *A. alpina*, still further earns our gratitude by always breeding absolutely true. Not only does no other strain ever appear in seedlings of *A. jucunda*, but *A. jucunda* itself never seems to contribute any of its blood or beauty to any of the blooming rivals by which it is surrounded at flowering-time. This in itself would be sufficient disproof, if disproof were needed, of an unlucky theory lately broached, that our so-called *A. glandulosa* of gardens was, in reality, the hybrid *A. Stuartii.* Not only is *A.×Stuartii* a well-known miff, altogether smaller and feebler (though with the same immense flowers), but no hybrid ever yet succeeded in breeding true to itself always and only and absolutely, refusing all temptations to belong to other nations. Finally, if anything be worthy of association with *A. jucunda*, what could be more noble and suitable company than pale lemony *Trollius* and *Anemone narcissiflora ?*

A. Kitaibelii. See under *A. pyrenaica.*

A. lactiflora is a white-flowered species, akin to *A. leptoceras,* Fisch. and Meyer, but softly downy all over—a North-Eurasian Columbine of grace and beauty, with long spurs either straight or just incurving at the tip.

A. laramiensis, together with *A. flavescens* and *A. Eastwoodiae*, are somewhat dim Americans of no special interest.

A. leptocera. See under *A. coerulea.*

A. leptoceras, Fisch. and Meyer, is an obscure Siberian, suggestive of a big *A. vulgaris*, with fine blue flowers and long straight spurs.

A. Litardieri has almost passed beyond reach even of aspiration.

For this jewel has only been once or twice sighted, and then only in mossy rocks high on the slope of one mountain in Corsica, whence surely some devoted gardener will seek us seed. *A. Litardieri* is a quite minute, low clump-forming species, a weak little tuffet whose small and dainty leaf-lobules rather suggest those of a solider *Isopyrum thalictroeides*. These leaves are all springing from the many root-stocks that make the clump ; the naked stem rises well above them, not more than 5 inches high, and the bright blue flower, large indeed for the plant, has a special beauty of its own. For here the out-standing petals of the cup and the wide-spread sepals of the star are of exactly the same length, with the result that the broad bloom has the look of a perfectly balanced and graceful rosette. Whereas in all other Columbines the sepals are more or less longer than the petals, or the petals than the sepals—thus diverting towards different beauties in either direction, like the Pagoda and the Dâgaba ; but only here is the precise and perfect mean achieved. I need hardly say that on any collector who touches the roots of a rare Columbine the curses of the world will hang (no less than those of the Columbine, which is nearly certain to die, and has already offered to buy off his rapacity with seed, if he will only wait) ; but on him who touches the last remaining tufts of *A. Litardieri*, if any such exist, hang curses of quite especial vehemence and weight and heat.

A. lutea, from Bulgaria, is a short-spurred species with yellow flowers.

A. nevadensis, from the hill-woods of Granada, is like a hook-spurred, pale-blue *A. vulgaris*, with styles and stamens sticking well out of the flower.

A. nivalis is reported a small and special beauty.

A. olympica, which is also *A. Wittmanniana* of gardens (and also probably *A. Ottonis*), is a tall handsome species from the Levant, in the kindred of *A. vulgaris*, but rather viscid with glands, and with larger leaf-lobes, and larger flowers of blue and white or pale blue, rather waxy, and with spurs incurved, indeed, but not knobbed. This Columbine, as I have had it, comes true from seed of its own, though its potency is very evident in the offspring of its neighbours.

A. oreophila carries us back into the dreamlands of hope. It should be a beautiful American species, not more than 8 inches high at the most, with blossoms cream-coloured and blue.

A. Ottonis. See *A. olympica*.

A. oxysepala, from Northern Asia, is a close cousin of *A. glandulosa*, but far more vigorous, attaining 2 feet, very free-flowering and very early, one of the best of all, large-flowered, with pointed wide stars

of blue sepals, and a clear yellow cup of petals. It has a name for
seeding true, yet is but rarely seen.

A. pyrenaica is a most important charmer which brings us on to
debatable land strewn with the corpses of botanists dead in mutual
war over its varieties and sub-species. First of all, for the sake of
clearness, let us see *A. pyrenaica* itself. This is, to speak roughly, a
miniature of great *A. alpina*, about half the size, but far more refined.
The leaves are small and neat, springing round the base, comparatively few and lacy; the stems stand up nearly naked, to the height
of about a foot, and the plant is almost wholly smooth, except that
the upper part of the stalk tends to be sticky, and that there is fine
down on the outside of the petals and sepals, which are evenly balanced
against each other, though not precisely so as in *A. Litardieri*. The
flowers are large and royally handsome, of a richer, deeper blue than
those of *A. alpina*, with a gorgeously contrasting central tassel of gold.
The genuine typical *A. pyrenaica* is *only* met with in the Pyrenees;
but all along the Southern chains of the Alps there stretches a string
of forms and sub-species which are cruelly difficult to disentangle and
have bred endless confusion, different botanists having given the same
names at different times to different varieties. With these it would
not be necessary here to cope, but that several of them are often
offered as species; while, in the mountains themselves, it is satisfactory to get some idea of what Columbine one is seeing. Therefore
I will follow the lead of Paoli and Fioretti, drastic though it be, in
treating all these forms (sub-species though some of them may be, if not
actually true species) as members of the aggregate *A. pyrenaica*—of
which, let it be remembered, they all have the same general configuration : more or less the same habit, more or less the big and lovely
dark-blue flower, invariably glorified by its central fluff of golden
stamens. *A. Bertolonii*, Schott, ranges from the Pyrenees to the
Herzegovina. It has large blossoms, rich blue, *downy outside*, and
with a *fine fringe of hairs to the flower-segments*. The spur is large,
incurved and hooked; the lobes of the root-leaves long and rather
pointed, standing well away from each other; and the leaves themselves *are almost entirely smooth, hairless and downless and glandless*.
A. Kitaibelii, on the contrary, has *downy foliage, densely downy at the
base*. The flower is no less fine and ample, but here the spur is *bald*,
only a *little curved*, and rather shorter than the blade of the petal it
belongs to, the blade again being a trifle shorter than the expanded
ray of the sepal. *A. Kitaibelii* may be found in the Dolomite district,
as for instance near Agordo, and so forth. *A. Einseleana* is a plant
downy at the base, but perfectly smooth above; the petals are rather

shorter than the sepals, and the spur is either straight or just *slightly incurved*, the whole *bloom being considerably smaller* than those of the two last (and of *A. pyrenaica*), about an inch across, *and purple*. It ranges all along the Maritime Alps and down through the Apennines. *A. alpina*, Sternb. (*A. Bauhinii*, Schott ; *A. Portae*, Huter ; *A. viscosa*, Rchb.) has the *diminished purple* flowers of the last, *but is densely viscid all over*, the petals being a trifle shorter than the sepals, and the spur (which is smooth and straight, or a little incurving) equal in length to the blade of the petal. *A. thalictrifolia* seems to be yet another synonym of this, described as being "pilose," with *leaves taller and wider and more splayed about* than in any form of Einseleana or Pyrenaica. At least the distribution precisely tallies with that of *A. alpina* (Sternb.), which, if not by any means extensive, is certainly peculiar. For the form covered by these names is entirely confined to the Val Ampola, the neighbourhood of Storo, and the Cima Tombea above it. Here, and nowhere else, it may freely be found, growing graceful and charming in the limestone rocks and stony places, a prettier thing than Einseleana, full of a grace and beauty of its own, though not having the noble sapphirine splendour of the nevertheless more dainty-habited Pyrenaica, Kitaibelii, and Bertolonii. All these Columbines, however, are of the easiest culture, and should be tried also in the moraine, or in some such stony light and open limy ground, in situations sunny (in the North) but not too torrid.

A. Reuteri, hovering on the edge of cultivation, will prove a most beautiful addition to our Columbines. It is a very rare species, confined to the Western and Maritime Alps, where it sometimes seems to take the place of *A. alpina* at rather lower elevations ; as round the Miniera de Tenda, some hundreds of feet below the woods which Alpina is occupying in myriad strength. Of *A. alpina*, *A. Reuteri* is a most dainty diminished and paler replica ; but the flowers, though smaller than those of *A. alpina*, are magnificent and numerous on the graceful foot-high stems, and of a quite peculiar and entrancing soft clear refulgence, like a jewel which, at twilight, as the blossoms dance in the gathering dusk against the obscurity of the rough grass, seems to glow and burn with a cold electric flame of blue. It is a lovely thing, indeed, growing in poor soil, in the most desperately hard and stony places—often hovering in and out of light *Pinus montana* scrub, where its vivid cerulean stars shine cool in company with the flaming scarlet Turks'-caps of *Lilium pomponium*, waxed and glossy. In England, therefore, sunnier, stonier sites might be generally prescribed for this species than for such as *A. alpina* and *A. pyrenaica*.

A. saximontana is still a hope and nothing more. High, high in the

AQUILEGIA.

Central Rockies dwells *A. saximontana,* so rare and so little known that it seems hard on the plant already to be burdened with a synonym, and called also *A. brevistyla.* It is a small treasure, quite hairless, throwing up several stems not more than 5 or 6 inches high, and displaying flowers three-quarters of an inch across, bluish or pale blue.

A. sibirica is a bicolor Columbine, perfectly smooth and with the spur longer than the blade of the petal.

A. Skinneri, from Guatemala, likes a sheltered warm place in light soil. It rises to 2 feet or so, and its gracefully hanging blooms are greenish yellow, with long spurs of burnished red in August.

A. x *Stuartii* has for its parents *A.* "*glandulosa*" (possibly *A. jucunda*), and *A. olympica.* One would not own the parentage, in this case, of so rare and unknown a plant as the *true* Glandulosa, unless the offspring's habit be held to prove it. For surely from two species so hearty as Jucunda and Olympica an equally hearty child might have been expected to result ; whereas the influence of just such a miff as the true Glandulosa is exactly what might have been expected to produce an invalid. For *A. Stuartii* has no constitution at all, wants the coolest and most careful treatment, and often will not respond even to that, and in no case for very long. None the less it is a most wonderfully beautiful thing, a diminished, much less leafy, and more delicate version of *A. jucunda,* but with flowers in no way lessened, though carried rather more definitely horizontally, and rather frailer in texture, looking extraordinarily large and rich as they balance on the fine stems of 6 inches or so. There are also other remarkable hybrids in this group, of sounder constitution, coming under the names of *A.* x *haylodgensis,* and all with their due inheritance of loveliness.

A. thalictrifolia. See *A. pyrenaica var. alpina.*

A. truncata (which has been *A. eximia* and *A. californica*) is a generally popular common garden Columbine of 2 feet or so, with pendent flowers, long-spurred, of yellow, orange, and scarlet ; but especially valuable as a parent.

A. viridiflora is an unshowy but pretty little blackish-flowered fragrant species from N. Asia, which has never made good its hold in English gardens, though it is often being introduced, and cherished as a rarity. (Da-Tung Alps, hot low rocks, 1915 : most attractive.)

A. viscosa, Rchb. See under *A. pyrenaica.*

A. viscosa, Ten. See under *A. vulgaris.*

A. vulgaris, the common wild English Columbine, is by no means to be despised in copsy corners of the garden ; the genuine wild form, with its big flowers of pure true blue, being incomparably more attractive than the garden-mules that diverge into every dingy shade of claret and purple, even attaining to many horrible reduplications. There is, however, a beautiful and large white variety, sometimes offered as *nivea grandiflora*, or as *Munstead White*; and a variegated-leaved variety *Vervaeneana*. But the alpine wild variations are much more appropriate and interesting; the common type in many of the Alps has smaller flowers of a dense chocolate darkness, which is then called *A. v. atrata*. More remarkable than this, and with better blossoms, larger and not so sombre, is a form found on the way up to the Malga Valbona, above Daone in the Alps of Judicaria. This is a slenderer grower altogether, one-stemmed, with few large, large-lobed leaves of a conspicuous deep bronze, which remains constant in cultivation. Yet another rare natural form is sometimes talked of with enthusiasm, and is a special treasure in the district of the Cima Tombea (whence another Columbine, as we have seen, is called *A. (pyrenaica) viscosa*, Rchb.). But *A. viscosa*, Ten., is nothing more nor less (if indeed there be no confusion in this matter) than a form of *A. vulgaris*; you may know it from the fact that it is *densely sticky* all over, *and sweetly fragrant*, with blooms which are described (by one who has collected it, going down from the Tombea district to Garda) in terms of unqualified rapture. It has been suggested that this *A. viscosa* may have some affinity with the rather misty *A. Ottonis*, which, however, is better left at present lurking in decent obscurity under the wing of *A. Wittmanniana*, which seems but a synonym of *A. olympica*.

Arăbis, as a rule, is a race neither elegant in appearance nor pleasing in smell—a large family of cruciferous coarse weeds, among which *A. albida* is a well-known ramping loose Wall-cress, with toothed grey-flannelly leaves, and countless spikes of large white flowers almost all the year through, but especially in spring; the double form is curiously beautiful and recommendable, giving an unanalysable suggestion of Lily-of-the-valley spires, especially when cut. (The whole plant has a coarse smell if bruised.)

A. alpina is really by no means to be confused with this, for it does not flop or ramp, but grows more upright (about 8 to 10 inches), with smaller toothed leaves *deeply heart-shaped at the base*, so as to embrace the stem; these leaves are greener, set with fewer grey hairs, the flowers are smaller, white, though improved in the variety *A. alpina superba*, a rather pretentious differentiation for what is, after all, no such wonderful acquisition, though its Verbena-like heads of white have a certain effect.

ARABIS.

A. ambigua, with *incarnata*, *sinuata*, and others, are tufted perennials from the far north of Asia, that may or may not prove worth the growing.

A. androsacea is a lovely little plant from Taurus, forming clumps of neat rosettes, reminiscent of those of *Androsace villosa*, and the more so that these also are silver-silky with hairs.

A. aubrietioeides bears an ambitious name, which it earns by forming close, grey-hairy or green tufts of blunt obovate leaves, with a few blunt teeth. These leaves are gathered at the base, while the upper ones embrace the stem of the flower-spike, which carries a few purple flowers, fine and large. (Cilician Alps.)

A. Billiardieri, from Lebanon, is a form of *A. albida*, rather weakly, but more pleasant in its *rosea* variety, which has typical blossoms of a soft rosy lilac, the spikes not being quite so much over-weighted by the mass of coarse leafage below, as in most forms of *A. albida*.

A. blepharophylla, from California, grows from 4 to 8 inches high. All the leaves have an eyelash of soft hairs, and the large flowers are purplish pink. It is not particularly permanent unless in warm sandy soil, perfectly drained, in a sunny place.

A. bryoeides is a very neat wee cushion, all hoary, from high places on Athos.

A. Carduchorum is the same thing as *Draba gigas*, Stur.—a plant with mats of loose rosettes made up of stiff narrow green leaves, rather blunt. The flowers and the whole growth are indeed like those of a lax Draba, but the fine white blossoms are but shyly produced as a rule in England.

A. cilicica comes under *A. ionocalyx* from the woods of Caria—a species not by any means valuable, a foot high, big-leaved and bristlish, with red calyx.

A. coerulea has a most alluring name, which it earns very easily. For though the flowers are certainly quite bluish, they are so microscopically small as to be nearly invisible, gathered on a miserable spike above a biennial rosette. This is a quite common weed of the highest alpine shingles, and perfectly worthless.

A. dacica is a tidy little tuffet with large attractive flowers of white or pink, for the moraine or choice place, such as is demanded by all Arabids that are not rank weeds.

A. drabaefolia is also *Draba hirta*, *Arabis Boissieri*, Griseb., or *Draba saxicola* or *setulosa*. It is a choice species close to *A. androsacea*, but green instead of silver, though with the same fringe of hair to the foliage ; it comes from the Bithynian Olympus.

A. exilis contains a part of *A. Hoelboellii, q.v.*, as does also *A. rhodantha*, a thing of little merit.

A. Ferdinandi-Coburgi, cumbrously named after that enlightened monarch of Bulgaria, is a close kinsman to *A. procurrens*, but is smaller in growth, lower in height, and with leaves greyish instead of lucent emerald. It comes from Macedonia.

A. flagellosa makes runners all over the place, after the style of *Nepeta hederacea*, with very dainty little nodding loose clusters of large white blossoms rising 2 or 3 inches above the neat obovate upstanding leaves. It is a Japanese species, and should have great charm in some cool and shady bed where it can run.

A. formosa has fine flesh-pink flowers, some inch and a half across, on erect stiff twigs of from 8 to 16 inches. It belongs to North America, and the leaves are never toothed.

A. Halleri is yet another runner, for cool, damp, shady places. It belongs to Mid-Europe, and has feathered leaves, and white flowers of good size, even prettier in the form called *rosea*.

A. Hoelboellii, sometimes offered, should be avoided if there is any danger of getting the true plant. For it is a biennial, attaining to 3 feet in height, with leafy stems, pink stars, leaves downy only at the base, and pods deflexing when in fruit. It is a North-American species, and contains within its range of variation many names into which it is often divided — as *A. rhodantha, exilis, brachycarpa*, and *Drummondii*.

A. Kellereri.—A massed silvery clump, emitting white flowers, and altogether of much charm for chink or moraine.

A. Lemmonii, another from North America, is much prettier than its compatriots—a perennial, green and smooth above, with all the leaves devoid of toothings. The basal ones are fat and thick ; the stem rises to 6 or 8 inches, and the blossoms are purple.

A. lucida only needs mention on account of its variegated forms, which, for those who like such things, are just the sort of things they like, making clumps of largish rosettes, brightly lucent-green, with a yellow or whitish border. The flowers are worthless, in a lank spike, and the plant of the easiest culture.

A. oblanceolata forms sound perennial tufts, from which shoot up many stems of about a foot, all leafy with foliage that amply embraces the stalk and even overlaps into pointed wings on either side beyond it. They are not specially hairy, and the flowers are red-purple.

A. pedemontana has the interest of its remarkable rarity. It is a neat rosetted species, sending up stems of 6 inches or so, with graceful heads of quite large and conspicuous white bloom. It may be seen here and there in the lighter copses and brushwood in the alpine elevations of the Cottians and Maritimes.

A. perelegans is a magnificent biennial like a great wild Stock, from the Yellowstone Park, with stems of 2 or 3 feet, and big violet blossoms.

A. petraea, a very rare native plant of our high mountains, is not worth growing except for its interest, being like a much diminished and not running or specially procumbent version of *A. albida*, never more than about 6 inches long or high.

A. procurrens is a useful species in common use for cool banks; it forms mats, emitting leafy runners of shining green foliage, while the flowers are large and white on stems of nearly a foot. (South-east Europe.)

A. purpurea, from the Cyprian Olympus, is much like *A. aubrietioeides*, but only half the size, a neat small thing.

A. recondita, from North America, has pretty much the look and habit of *A. Lemmonii*, but here the basal leaves are thin in texture, with a toothed edge.

A. rugocarpa, a compatriot, is purple all over, flowers and leaves and all—the leaves being bristly and downy, and the whole growth not more than 2 or 4 inches high.

A. Sturii is a prized rock-plant for sunny places, forming little cushions of neat and glossy dark-green leafage, with copious heads of pleasant and rather large white blossoms on stems of 2 or 3 inches.

A. sulfurea, a minute hoary grey species with oblong leaves, has yellow flowers, and may be seen on the high Alps of Persia (*Draba Aucheri*).

A. verna belongs to great elevations in the mountains of Granada. It has rather small purple blooms, and grows to about 8 or 10 inches, with the green or hoary leaves almost embracing the stems.

A. Wilczekiana, a novelty which forms thick clumps of very stiffly hairy rosettes.

Aralia.—The only Aralia for which the rock-garden need cry is *A. polaris* from the Campbell and Auckland Islands, which has a horrid smell indeed, but forms splendid domed masses (some 2 to 4 feet high) of bright-green foliage among rocks down there by the sea, and then proceeds to hide these balls of verdure with noble flat heads, a foot across, of wax-white flowers.

Arctostaphÿlos.—The Bearberries form a very large family, especially in America, of low-growing, mat-forming or trailing bushes, with glossy leaves and flowers like those of a small pink Arbutus, to be followed by berries. None so far are of any specially valuable conspicuousness or beauty in the garden, though our own *A. Uva-ursi*, and the much rarer and neater Arctic species, *A. alpina*, may be planted, for their interest, in heathy open peat-beds, to serve as a cover for daffodils or other bulbs.

Arenaria. See also under **Alsine**.

A. acerosa is a most lovely treasure, neat and tiny, with rosettes like those of *A. Ledebouriana*, which it closely resembles, but the stems do not branch, and the snowy stars are twice as big, on shorter foot-stalks. Its home is in the Alps of Lycia and Anatolia; it should prove a jewel of the first water for choice banks or moraines.

A. aequicaulis is very near *Alsine verna*, but here the leaves are sticky.

A. armeniaca makes a mass of 6-inch shoots, above a mass of longish grassy leaves, and with flowers gathered into tight round heads like a nut. As a rule these cluster-headed Arenarias are rather dull and dowdy, therefore let us deal with them here compendiously, and be done. Of similar persuasion, then—fitted, at pleasure, to make mats of fine grassy turf, but inconsiderable in bloom —are *A. dianthoeides, A. graminea, A. graminifolia, A. scariosa, A. Steveniana, A. rigida, A. blepharophylla, A. pungens, A. capitata, A. holostea* (with flowers twice the size, however, of those of *A. rigida*), *A. caricifolia* (with grassy leaves often 12 inches long, and short many-flowered heads of blossom twice as big as usual), *A. festucoeides, A. Griffithii, A. gypsophiloeides, A. polycnemifolia, A. Hookeri*, and *A. isaurica*.

A. Armeriastrum, a most variable species, from high elevations in the limiest mountains of Granada. It forms a close tuffet, with dense terminal heads of flower. Some of its varieties are *A. A. elongata, A. A. frigida* (a very much condensed form), and *A. A. caesia*, which is loose and grey.

A. balearica, the indestructible rock-sheeting Arenaria of the Balearic Islands, which in any cool place and in many sunny ones becomes the most beautiful of terrible weeds, wrapping everything in its minute but undivorceable embrace, and covering the yards it has occupied with countless galaxies of clear white stars on tiny stems of half an inch or so. It should *never* be admitted even within seeding distance of anything choice or precious, otherwise the gardener's time is taken up for evermore with clearing the latter anew every day from the octopus-like attentions of the Arenaria. But for wild rocks, walks, walls, and cliffs there is nothing more precious and beautiful.

A. caespitosa. See under **Sagina**.

A. ciliata is the type from which diverges *A. gothica, q.v.*

A. ciliolata, a high-alpine from Sikkim, is a lax and hairy little plant with fine fringed leaves, oblong egg-shaped, and large flowers sitting almost huddled upon them on stems of half an inch.

A. confusa (*A. congesta* of some authors) belongs to the American group of Cluster-heads ; under which lead here follow *A. Fendleri* (with pallid yellowy flowers), *A. Tweedyi*, *A. Hookeri*, and *A. uintahensis.*

A. cretica makes dense tufts, akin to those of *A. gracilis*, but with *larger flowers*, one to three on their stems, above the stiff little oblong egg-shaped minute leaves, blunt and hairless. (From the rocks of Crete.)

A. cucubaloeides is a grassy mat of great value, from Turkish Armenia, even if it did not send up flowers so fine and ample, like those of *Linum tenuifolium*, carried in loose showers of from five to thirteen, on stems of a foot or 18 inches in height.

A. drypidea makes a 3-inch tuffet of glaucous-grey fine foliage smooth and pointed, but not prickly. It emits no leafy barren shoots, but sends up a spray of 6 inches carrying several blooms.

A. erinacea forms minute blue-grey scabs upon the high limestones of Leon and Granada, the tiny little leaves being packed as it were into four rows on the shoots, quite minute and pointed, with the white blossoms sitting close on the lichen-like mass.

A. foliosa, from India, is a close copy of *Alsine juniperina.* See under *Alsine Villarsii* for the picture of both.

A. formosa has very handsome flowers, loosely carried on thread-like erect stems above a freely branching mass of shoots, clothed in fleshy foliage perfectly smooth and hairless. (Altai.)

A. glandulifera is a diminished and densely glandular version of *A. ciliolata*, with Ciliolata's long flexing hairs, and with flowers much smaller.

A. gothica, a form or sub-species emerging from *A. ciliata*, but much more charming, and differing in its prostrate habit from the kindred *A. norvegica* (also, like both these last, an extremely rare native of Great Britain). *A. gothica* is a quite tiny plant, with shoots not more than an inch long or so, lying upon the ground, and set with pairs of glossy little oval leaves, dark-green and fat-looking. The flowers are borne all through the summer, lying here and there on the tuft, and are large for so minute a thing, of a clear and solid white. It is so that *A. gothica*, one of our rarest species (if truly English indeed it be), can be seen in a few places of limestone débris and very fine sparse grass, at intervals along the upper limestone level on the eastern slope of Ingleborough. But in cultivation, though always more or less perennial, the stems may grow more erect, and its blossoms seem to dwindle and turn inconspicuous if subjected to the Capuan influences of the ordinary garden soil, rather than kept slim in the Spartan diet of the moraine.

A. gracilis is in the same style of charm as *A. grandiflora*—a diffuse prostrate tuffet, but with elliptic-narrow leaves, which are almost finely saw-edged, and meeting each other at their bases. The gracious flower-stems stand erect with two handsome snowy stars.

A. graminifolia is also *Alsine Rosanii* of gardens. It is not at all important, but for its turfy masses of grass-like foliage, shaggy with glandular hair, green and glossy. The dowdy blooms are of little attraction, carried in clusters and comparatively inconspicuous.

A. grandiflora.—If flowers so splendid only earn the name of *A. montana*, what will one not expect from an Arenaria called Grandiflora ? In point of fact one only gets something like a conspicuously glorified *A. verna*. It is a pity, however, that the name should lead to such disappointment as to discredit its bearer, for *A. grandiflora* is really very beautiful, forming a loose and small mass of prostrate dense shoots, scattered about over the ground, and clothed in fine-pointed little narrow green leaves of the brightest and glossiest green, like those of a Sagina grown out of knowledge, not stiff or prickly, but often recurring, and with a fine faint fringe of hairs just at their base. From these come rather frail stems of a few inches, carrying a few large and handsome blossoms of purest white. *A. grandiflora*—which is also *A. triflora* (L.) and *A. juniperifolia* (Vill.) [nothing to do with *Alsine juniperina*]—dwells in high rocky places from Spain to Moravia, and gives the rule for all the choice alpine Arenarias of the garden, enjoying a sunny well-drained place in light loose soil or in the moraine.

A. Huteri is much in the same style as *A. Saxifraga*, but distinctly finer, with leaves and tufts recalling those of *Lychnis pyrenaica*, but fringed with hairs. This is peculiar to the Alps of Venetia, as *A. Saxifraga* to the Maritimes and Corsica.

A. incrassata is a very much looser, prostrate, fatter-textured *A. grandiflora* from the mountains of North-Central Spain.

A. kashmirica resembles *Alsine juniperina*, but here the leaves are stiffer, and clothed in glandular down.

A. Ledebouriana is a most charming tiny gem, forming clumps of neat rosettes, microscopic and dainty, like those of *Armeria caespitosa*, but only a quarter of the size, wholly smooth and of a blue-grey tone. The flowers, on delicate branching sprays, are worthy of the plant, though quite outclassed by those of the kindred *A. acerosa*. *A. Ledebouriana* is common in the Levantine Alps, and in our gardens, though so wee and choice, is quite satisfactory to deal with.

ARENARIA.

A. Lessertiana makes a densely spiny mass of spreading prickly leaves, from which the stems rise erect, with large white blossoms carried often on specially long foot-stalks. There is a variety *minor*, much dwarfer, from greater elevations on the Persian Alps, where the type has its home.

A. libanotica copies *A. cretica*, but is barely an inch high.

A. lychnidea has short erect narrow leaves, and forms a dense tuffet on the cliffs of Ararat and Caucasus. The frail stems are some 3 or 4 inches high, carrying from one to five large white flowers rather close together, as in *Saxifraga Vandellii*.

A. macrantha, from the mountains of Colorado, likewise makes tuffets and has similar stems with fine white flowers according to its name. But here the tuffet is much laxer and more spreading; the plant is perfectly hairless and the leaves very narrow.

A. melandryoeides may be found at about 15,000 feet in Sikkim. It is a loose species, not more than 2 or 4 inches high, with foliage almost fleshy, glandular on both sides, dull green or purplish. The blooms can be as much as an inch and a half across, really magnificent for the dwarf tuft.

A. montana, with its huge sheets of egg-shaped greyish pointed leaves, falling so happily over any sunny rock in the garden, and covering itself in June with profusion of white flowers as big as a florin, is a species from rocky places all over the lower mountain region of Spain. It does not seed freely, as a rule, although so vast and robust and indispensable in cultivation.

A. monticola forms beautiful glossy mats of bright green shining little stiff leaves with a stiff midrib, on the highest mountains of Sikkim and Tibet. And on these mats come sitting noble white blossoms of nearly an inch across. (Similar, but not so good, are *A. pulvinaris*, *A. oreophila*, *A. globifera*, and *A. densissima*.)

A. musciformis, from the same region, answers to its name, and is like a wee moss-cushion, on which appear the narrow-petalled white flowers about a third of an inch in width. Quite similar is *A. polytrichoeides*, with very dense stiff overlapping little leaves, forming bright green domes.

A. Nuttallii (*A. pungens* of some authorities, but not of commerce or Willkomm.) is glandular-downy, with sharp leaves and many flowers in a loose scattering shower, on stems of some 3 to 6 inches. (From the La Plata mountains of Colorado.)

A. picta, from Asia Minor, is a dainty little plant, looking like *Tunica Saxifraga*, and producing sprays of similar pink stars.

A. pinifolia. See under *Alsine pinifolia*.

ARENARIA.

A. pungens, Willkomm., is a Spanish species, from 8000 or 9000 feet up in the Sierra Nevada, where it forms wide and cruelly prickly mounds of thorny leaves, some 6 to 9 inches across. The blooms, which do not seem to have any especial merit, are solitary, or as many as three, carried on long stiff foot-stalks, the stem being clothed at intervals with pairs of long, spiny, very narrow leaves. It sounds as if, of the two pretenders to the name of Pungens, gardeners would most wisely choose *A. Nuttallii*—though indeed the glossy spiny masses of *A. pungens* have attraction in their place, forming a lucent but forbidding mat in the sun.

A. purpurascens stands quite alone in the race, one of the most cherished of plants in the garden, where it loves rather cooler exposures than the rest, as well may be, seeing that it comes from moist earthpans and chinks of the mountains in Aragon and Catalonia. It forms, with us, dwarf, neat, loose masses of shoots, clothed in broadly-oval, pointed little foliage, dark-green and rather glossy. The blossoms sit close and cover the mats in July and August ; they are handsome and ample for the wide mass, and of a lovely delicate rose-lilac, seeming deeper at the centres. (Division or seed.)

A. racemosa is a loose grower from Spain, about 2 or 3 inches high, with flowers not only from the ends of the shoots but also from the axils of the leaves that clothe them.

A. sajanensis comes near the European *A. biflora*. It is densely glandular and hairy, with flopping leafy stems, the foliage being narrow and rather stiff, the flowers one to three on stems of an inch to two and a half. (North America.)

A. Saxifraga is a very handsome but very variable species from the hills of Southern Europe. Its leaves are broadly ovate or rounded, and the stems carry, in many-blossomed showers, big white blooms as fine as an alpine Cerastium's, with wide petals. This is *A. Bertolonii* of Paoli and Fioretti, varying into forms distinguished as *A. italica*, *Salisii*, *Burnatii*, and *Morisii*.

A. saxosa, from Colorado, is glaucous-green and rather fleshy in its tufts, with flowers of no remarkable value in loose array on stems of 5 inches or so.

A. Stracheyi makes a perfectly bald and hairless minute tuft on the high stony places of Tibet, and the stars that cover it are about three-quarters of an inch across.

A. tetraquetra is well known in our gardens. It is a species of South Europe. It is akin to *A. erinacea*, with leaves arranged in the same dense pairs, first one way and then the other, so as to look like four regular rows. But the tuffet is larger, and the leaves are rounded-ovate. It forms a neat tuft, but produces no very startling effect.

A. tetrasticha has the same curious leaf-arrangement—a dwarf prostrate mat of weak shoots about 2 or 3 inches long, from the Alps of Persia, sending up its flowers on little erect delicate stems. The whole plant is smooth and glaucous blue-grey.

A. tmolea.—A dwarf cushion, with the one-to-three-flowered sprays hardly rising above it, the shoots being packed with stiff minute leaves, ovate-oblong. (This species also includes *A. Kotschyana.*) (Anatolian Alps, &c.)

A. valentina makes almost a small dense bush, sub-shrubby, of stiff foliage rather sharp, from which emerge the flowers, on long foot-stalks, either lonely or in sprays. (Limestone crags of Valentia.)

Arisaema, a race of picturesque Aroids from Japan and North America, best fitted for moist deep soil by the bog-garden, where their large handsome foliage waves impressively, and among them are seen the dingy great Arum-flowers, often hooded over and ending in a long rat-tail wisp. Among the best are *A. triphyllum, A. ringens, A. amurense,* and *A. japonicum.*

Arisarum offers yet more Aroids, of which *A. europaeum* is the universal little dark-striped Arum of the South, while *A. proboscideum* may often be seen running in and out of walls on the Ligurian Riviera— a thing of most eccentric charm, forming in the garden masses of small arrow-shaped leaves, very green and dark and lucent, among which you will see the wild brown tails and hind-quarters of many mice disappearing and diving in June. But these mice are the tips of the flowers—sombre wee Arums with the tip of the hood prolonged into that agitated tail, quite unlike the more ordinary flower of *A. europaeum.* Not only is *A. proboscideum* of the easiest culture in the garden, forming neat thick tufts, but, in defiance of its Ligurian memories, it even revels in the deep and soaking bog no less.

Armeria.—The Thrifts are a confusing family of the seashores in Southern Europe, some of them abounding in England. Not only, however, do they abound on the seashore, but those same species, besides others, are often found at alpine elevations. In the garden the race is not of conspicuous importance, the species not all being very markedly distinct, and many of them rather sickly or impure in the tone of their pink, especially furious, indeed, in the intensified versions that gardeners call splendens and coccinea. The cultivation of almost all, however, is quite easy in light well-drained soil in full sun, where the commoner species will even swell into edgings. In the following list only the more valuable will be found, without compiling a complete and tangled catalogue from all the many species that fill the shores of the South.

A. alpina, from the Alps and Pyrenees, is a good low-growing clump; so is our own Sea-pink *A. maritima*, with its improved garden form *A. Laucheana*, and yet another called *A. bracteata rubra*, with flowers of specially virulent colour—for the curse of Armeria is to be either pallid or aniline in tone. *A. vulgaris*, *A. labradorica*, and *A. plantaginea* (perhaps only a broader-leaved form of *A. maritima*) are others of the same persuasion ; and *A. Boissieriana*, with hard stiff glaucous leaves and a profusion of pink flower-heads on stems of 6 or 12 inches, is an improvement on these ; while *A. pungens* forms dense intricate but repellent cushions of very stiff blue-grey foliage incurving and pitilessly spiny, with flowers above it of palest pink on 12-inch stems.

Of the taller-growing species incomparably the finest is *A. latifolia*, which is also *A. cephalotes*, *A. formosa*, and *A. pseudo-armeria* of gardens —a really superb thing, in tufts of flaccid leaves, broad and mild and bright green, with stems of 2 feet or so, carrying very large heads of very large flowers in a clear and striking tone of glowing pink. This beauty belongs to the mountains of Valentia, and should have a rather poor soil and a warm well-drained position in the sun if it is to prove a safe and enduring perennial (but like all the rest it can be easily raised from seed ; even as, like the rest, it blooms through summer to autumn). In our gardens it is as affable as well-known.

Other tall-growing species are : *A. macrocephala*, only less fine, with erect leaves, elongate and narrow and incurved and prickly, and big pink heads on stems of 2 to 3 feet ; *A. baetica*, with hard glaucous foliage and stout stalks ; *A. pinifolia*, more graceful, a downy and densely-tufted species from the coasts of Spain ; and *A. magellensis*, quite elegant and charming, with rather greyish narrow-leaved tufts, bending stems, and rather small heads of pretty anæmic blossoms. The jewels, however, of the race—though *A. setacea* and *A. juncea* may be admitted—are the rock species, with *A. splendens* at their head.

A. caespitosa is a most lovely plant, forming tight dense clumps of splayed-out narrow-leaved and tiny rosettes, suggesting those of some strange Androsace, and on these are crowded the almost stemless chaffy heads of large palest pink flowers, whose only possible reproach is that they are a trifle washy and diaphanous and undecided in colour. None the less this species is a little alpine treasure for close crevices in rock-work, in light and well-drained soil ; it may be seen especially luxuriant at Edinburgh, though its home is at some 6000 or 8000 feet in the Sierra de Guadarrama.

A. filicaulis haunts the same rocky and alpine positions in the

Pyrenees of Aragon. Here the leaves are broader, and outspread in a dense and tidy series of rosettes, the inner ones being flatter and narrower, keeled, very daintily dotted with lime—most graceful in effect. The stems are as fat as the foliage, the flowers are pink or white, about half an inch across, in round heads at the top of 12-inch stems. Closely similar is *A. Duriaei*, but here the leaves are green and neither limy nor stiff, while the flowers are rather larger.

A. splendens—not to be confused with horticultural varieties called "Splendens" of the commoner Thrifts—is a magnificent high-alpine species from the bare earth-pans and screes and muddy places of the Sierra Nevada, &c., where it abounds between 8000 to 10,000 feet. This forms very dense tufts of rosettes, with many frail and delicate little stems of 2 or 3 inches emerging from them, and each carrying a large head of large and rosy flowers, together with bracts that turn a brilliant purple. There are, of course, countless other Thrifts, but the above list should cover, I hope, the most distinct species in a large and often rather indistinguishable family.

Arnebia has now lost all its loveliest members, which will be found in the fold of **Macrotomia.**

Arnica.—Gay, handsome Composites of the high-alpine turf in the Old and the New World. Every traveller well knows the gorgeous golden suns of the one species in the European Alps, *A. montana*, with its basal rosettes of large oval foliage, flannelly and soft and puckered as it lies in a rosette on the ground, and then sends up the stalwart stem, wearing a pair or so of leaves opposite to each other—a very rare peculiarity in Composites. The flower-stem often splits in two equal erect stalks, each carrying a flower, with a third on the much shorter original stem in the middle. *A. montana* is extremely abundant in the high turf of the Alpine chain, more often on the granitic ranges, though not especially. In some parts of the Dolomites it makes a show of extraordinary golden glory among the filmy flowering grasses, in contrast with the no less abundant great china-blue bearded bells of *Campanula barbata ;* while on the Col de Pesio, in early August, you look down upon a solid firmament of its suns, through which come shooting in myriads the long sweet lilac spires of *Gymnadenia odoratissima*. Nothing of all this does Arnica seem to achieve in cultivation, where it often seems a rather unsatisfactory mimp, no matter how carefully you may plant it in full sun in beds of well-drained stony peat. There are, however, beside this, other Arnicas of the New World, in no way approaching *A. montana* in gorgeousness, but often with a charm of their own, though more in the style of some daintier *Crepis* or *Hieracium*. These should be tried in the same stony cool peat that sometimes fails to inspire heart into *A. montana*. Of these probably the best will prove *A. chionopappa*, about 12 inches high, with graceful stems, and about three large flowers ; its basal leaves are on fine long stalks, and it comes from cold limy cliffs in East Quebec ; *A. mollis*, often called *A. Chamissonis* (Man.), or *A. lanceolata* (Nutt.), twice as tall, crisply hairy with soft hairs, with many flowers, each perhaps 3 inches across ; *A. cordifolia*, a 2-foot plant with coarsely-toothed leaves, and 2- or 3-inch blossom-heads on fine foot-stalks ; *A. acaulis*, very handsome, and suggesting *A. montana*, forming a basal rosette of thick leaves, from which comes up a scape carrying one large and brilliantly showy golden-orange flower ; *A. fulgens* has sharp oblong leaves and golden blooms on long stalks, attaining in all a foot or so ; while *A. Louisiana* is the gem of the lot—a rare little beauty from the neighbourhood of Lake Louise, only about 8 inches high, with elliptic glandular foliage, and a number of beautiful nodding flowers of a very pale yellow and with rays so few and broad and pointed as to give the effect of a citron-coloured star.

Aronicum; a race so closely akin to **Doronicum** that there is no real telling them finally apart. There are, however, three species (or more or less species) that bear this name in the main chains of the Alps, and it may therefore be useful to precisify them a little. These are all native to considerable elevations, found often in damp water-courses, in stony places and in the highest shingles, where their lush and leafy habit always seems out of place, and as if they must certainly be half-hardy things planted there by some faddist who perhaps had taken a dislike to them.

A. Clusii has its hairy leaves narrow-oblong on a foot-stalk. They are widened, indeed, so as to be broadly oval, but not to the point of making lobes like a heart—or, rather, more obviously triangular. The stem-leaves sit straight to the stalk, and almost clasp it, but without flowing out into rounded lobes on the other side. The hollow hairy stem is never branched, about 6 or 9 inches high, with rather smaller flowers than in the others, only some inch and a half across.

A. glaciale (if the species be recognised) is shorter still, hardly more than half a foot high, from a spreading scaly dark root-stock ; the basal leaves are blunt and oblong, diminishing to their petiole and widened at the base ; the lower stem-leaves are narrow, embracing the stem and overflowing on the other side in short broad wings ; the upper ones have leaf-stalks, and all widely coarsely toothed with open teeth. The pale suns are about an inch or an inch and a half across. Not everyone, however, admits the existence of *A. glaciale*.

A. scorpioeides has a fat pale horizontal root-stock, from which come up fat hollow stems half a foot to 18 inches high (often with only one flower-head), hairy all the way up, and leafy with oval leaves, which embrace the stem and overflow on the other side into short wings, while the upper ones sit tight to the stalk and are heart-shaped oval. The lower basal leaves are on long stalks, large, lax, and in shape like a heart with lobes flattened across, all the leaves both above and below being wavy with irregular toothing. The flowers are very large, about 2 or 3 inches across, and, like those of the others, brilliant golden-yellow. Apart from the limp and slack-textured Doronicoid appearance of all these plants, they would really be gladly accepted for the high-alpines they certainly are, although they do not look it. In culture they offer no more difficulty than Doronicum, and appreciate deep cool and stony ground in sun.

Artemisia.—The huge family of the Wormwoods is essentially addicted to low places, deserts, woody wastes and hedgerows, offering, in its usual style, nothing for the rock-garden except tall *A. lactiflora*, if room can be found for it in some deep remote corner of the wilder parts, where its fine dark-feathered foliage, white beneath, will fill the summer, and its heavy spraying plumes of silver-whiteness glorify the autumn. But the family in the course of its roamings wanders high upon the mountains, and has there developed a most lovely and complicated race of quite dwarf silvery tuffets of aromatic foliage most ferny and beautiful, though true it is that the flower-spikes or heads do not amount to much ; none the less the white or frosted-looking fine ferniness of the alpine Wormwoods is of unequalled charm and value in the rock-garden, most especially in the moraine, where their exquisite silveriness looks especially in place upon the grey chips, and acts as a perfect foil to the pink of *Dianthus alpinus*, or the rich purple of *Viola Dubyana*. In such conditions all are of the same perfect ease of culture and permanence, needing only to be divided when a given tuft has grown too large for its own safety. As for the flower-spikes, they may as well in most cases be nipped off, for it is but rarely that they add to the lovely charm of the mass, and they are certainly not wanted unless to help in identifying the species. As all the following are mat-forming, carpet-forming silvery or woolly-leaved dwarfs, all requiring the same stony conditions in the same soil or the lack of it, there is no need to worry the reader with specific descriptions, except in the case of those species from the European Alps, which it may prove helpful to be able to distinguish.

A. assoana : is very beautiful and silvery. A creeping branching thing from high sandy places in the limestone mountains of South-east and Central Spain, forming compact tufts of densely silky little leaves, each cut into three lobes, and then those lobes feathered again into forked strips.

A. caespitosa, a plant of the Siberian and Altaic deserts, forming mats of small leaves, of which the lower ones are either uncut or divided only into threes. It sends up many stems, and the whole growth is silky-white.

A. camphorata, from rocks in Castille, is more sub-shrubby, without down or silk, with fattish foliage in very narrow jags. Even among its cousins *A. camphorata* stands out in its intense aromatic fragrance.

A. caucasica (*A. alpina*, Pall.), a diminished *A. splendens*, all clothed in close sheets of silver down, with finely fringy leaves and flower-heads in a spike, with individual foot-stalks not so long as in *A. splendens*. (Sunny rocks of Taurus and Caucasus.)

A. eriantha is a European species from great elevations in the Southern and Central Alps. It is possibly a variety of *A. Genipii*, but has fernier foliage, the silver leaves being small and hand-shaped, gashed into irregular fat jags. The plant has the same close spike, with flowers set close upon it as in the much narrower-leaved *A. spicata*, and each capitule, sitting crowded to the stem, has a big bract-like leaflet below to protect it. The "blossoms," however, are larger and narrower, more crowded at the tip on a taller spire, and the cup that holds the florets is *perfectly bald and smooth at the base inside*, though outside all woolly and fluffy. And the leaves on the stems are almost as large, if not quite, as those at the base, and the spike can diverge into sprays.

A. frigida, from sandy hills in Saskatchewan, is a woodyish stalwart of 4 to 20 inches with narrow sharp strips to the silky-white leafage.

A. Genipi is an enlarged version of *A. eriantha*, with flowers in a spike and leaves less finely cut. It bears a significant name, which might be shared by any other of the alpine Wormwoods, for the special chemical principle of their race is particularly strong in these condensed and concentrated high-alpine species ; which are not only strongly sweet and aromatic, but almost redeem the sinister fame of *A. Absinthium* by the countervailing benefits they offer to exhausted humanity in the hills. Not only are they the base of all delicious and wholesome liqueurs, so that Carthusians and Benedictines cannot distil their marvels unless they are working high on the Alps, with the mountain Artemisias sitting round to help them, but even when Benedictine and Chartreuse are far-off hopeless names, the strayed reveller may still pluck help from Artemisia at need. For a few of these leaves, bruised and nibbled, will bring back vigour to the most weary ; and no traveller or climber, if he only knew it, need feel his sinews or his heart give out, in even the most awful stony wildernesses of the upmost Alps, so long as the silver lace of any mountain Wormwood is heaped about on the shingles beneath his aching feet.

A. glacialis is a much tinier, compacter, fatter, more matted plant, fluffy, with tiny much more hand-shaped leaves on foot-stalks, all velvety with the softest and most shimmering silver-whiteness. The foliage at the base continues up the stems (cut into threes and then cut and cut again—less cut on the stems). The stems are many, erect, and about 4 or 5 inches high, carrying the little flowers of quite attractive bright golden yellow, not in a spike but *in a dense head at the tip*, and the inner base of the cup has hairs. (Very high granitic ranges of the main Southern and Central chains.)

A. Globularia is a Russian, closely akin to *A. glacialis*, but here the blossoms are purple, the heads stand apart from each other on more definite stems, and the inside of the cup that holds the florets is quite smooth at the base and without hairs.

A. glomerata, from Northern Asia, still pursues its family craving for sufficient moisture in the places it chooses, by donning the usual vesture of silky whiteness. The leaves are palm-shaped and fingered, the dense head of flower-heads enclosed as it were in a frill of foliage all feathered and slit.

A. granatensis, abundant in the highest schistose ridges of the Sierra Nevada, between 7000 to 11,000 feet, runs along the ground in dense mats of very tiny fan-shaped leaves very densely silvery, and each with a stem of its own. The flower-stems are few, and carry only a few leaves, the lower flower-heads have a marked long foot-stalk, and the whole exquisite sheet smells intensely of Camomile.

A. Haussknechtii is a perfectly snow-white dwarf from crevices at gaunt altitudes in Turkestan.

A. lanata (Willd.) is a synonym of *A. pedemontana*, Balb., *q.v.*

A. leontopodioeides is a silver-silky little oddity from Kamchatka which really does imitate the Flannel-flower, though its leaves are slit and gashed, for it has a simple rounded head of blossoms, enclosed in spreading bract-like leafage.

A. melanolepis is like a minutely stunted form of *A. splendens*, entrancingly neat, with stems of only a couple of inches, and the microscopic leaves all brilliant-silver with close-pressed silk. (Rocks of Elburs, 10,000 feet.)

A. minor dwells far aloft on the austere and stony places of Tibet—a deliciously-scented tuft of small stemless foliage closely overlapping and fan-shaped, feathered into double strips.

A. Mutellina is one of the most important and beloved species of the European Alps. It may easily be known by its especially beautiful leafage, which is very long and fine, cut into the most delicately thread-like strips, and refulgently silvery, lying limply about in shocks upon the shingle. Its spikes, too, are quite distinct ; they are about 6 or 8 inches high, with a few filmy leaves here and there, *finely slashed and on drawn-out stems* of marked length. And the flower-heads are not carried in a cluster at the top, nor in the spike all the way up, but in a *series of small bunches*, here and there on the stems. *Towards their apex the inner base of the cup is markedly full of fluff.* (Great elevations in all the main ranges, more especially on granite.)

A. nana is an impostor in this section of dwarfs. Its name leads one to believe it the dwarfest of all, whereas in point of fact it is a comparatively large and coarse species, sending up loose weedy-looking spires of scattered reddish flower-heads, held erect in little clusters, on stems of 7 or 8 inches. The leaves, too, though very finely cut indeed, are wholly green and nearly scentless, and rather suggest those of Caraway or Fennel. It is only quoted as a warning.

A. nitida better deserves its name (it is also *A. lanata*, Koch). For this is another most lovely high-alpine, forming tufted mats, and closely allied to *A. Mutellina*. But here the leaves are much smaller, more compact, and not so lacy ; they do not lie about, but tend to gather together and stand erect on their notably long foot-stalks (much more like tiny hands reaching aloft a number of delicate fingers). The whole plant is much tighter and tuftier in effect accordingly, and the stems are much slighter, with smaller, fewer leaflets sitting more closely to them, and they carry many more little bunches of flower-heads (*which are smooth outside, not hairy or woolly*), scattered loosely nearly all the way up, and with fewer flower-heads to a bunch, smaller, and inclined to droop a little instead of being erect as in *A. Mutellina*. (Screes and limestone cliffs of the Southern Alps and Tyrol.) Not far remote is *A. norica*, from the ranges of the Hohe Tauern.

A. Parryi and *A. Pattersonii* are Americans from the high Alps of Colorado, of which *A. Pattersonii* is the whiter with tomentum, though tending to grow more naked as it gets on in months.

A. pedatifida, from dry places in Wyoming, is a tightly-matted species, hoary with close down, and with foliage cleft once or twice into divisions, cut again into three narrow strips. The few-headed flower-spike is only about 3 inches high at the most, whereas in its silky compatriot, *A. scopulorum*, they rise from 4 to 8 inches.

A. pedemontana (*A. lanata*, Willd.), another important European species, is very near to *A. caucasica* and *A. Genipi*, and is almost a larger version of *A. assoana*, but bigger and laxer in tuft, with the flower-heads on short stalks, horizontal or inclined to nod ; *the inner base of the cup has no hairs or fluff;* while in *A. caucasica* the leaves are feathered all along to the base on either side, in *A. pedemontana* they expand like a flattened hand, and are then cut into three fat lobes, which again are slashed into several more, those of the middle segment being fewest. From *A. Genipi* it differs chiefly in being finer of effect, with a laxer habit, and flower-heads gathered in *a loose and interrupted spike,* rather after the style of *A. Mutellina.*

A. spicata recalls the picture of *A. eriantha.* But here the conspicuous spike is a little stocky column, with each flower-head nestling by a long oval leaf standing out from the stem as in an Ajuga. The plant is smaller and tighter and a dense tuft, the spike dwarfer, the lower heads tending to have a foot-stalk, and the stem always without branches. The leaves at the base are on long foot-stalks too, divided into three segments and then re-gashed. They are smallish for their stems, and, like all the mass, are densely silvery, most pungently aromatic, and bitterly stimulating to the taste. If by nothing else this may be known from *A. Mutellina* by the many incised leaflets that sit stemless all the way up the stalk, fat, almost oblong, with only a gash or two at their base, instead of *very* finely slit, fewer, and on drawn-out foot-stalks ; also the inside base of the cup that holds the florets is quite smooth and without hairs. But indeed there is very little likeness between the two.

A. splendens is a truly superb species from Argaeus and Caucasus, at 9000 to 10,000 feet. It makes a stout fat stock, from which it throws up many tufts of brilliantly silvery fine foliage cut into the most delicate and gleaming strips. And it must be noted that the outside of the flower-heads is *not* woolly, as in nearly all the others except *A. nitida.*

A. Steveniana is a silky-woolly Russian, and so are *A. senjavinensis, Meyeriana, Triniana,* and *Lagopus. A. trifurcata* and *A. heterophylla* come from Baikal, and have nodding flowers ; while *A. Villarsii* is a European alpine species, near akin to *A. pedemontana* and *A. eriantha.*

A. subspinescens is a variety of *A. persica,* and they both form almost spiny mounds of silver at very great heights on the Alps of Persia towards the snow-level (12,000 to 13,000 feet).

Arthropodium cirrhatum is a New Zealander, for deep sheltered nooks and deep rich soil in warm climates. It forms masses of glossy lax strap-shaped leaves like Imantophyllum (which hates wind), and sends up multitudes of tall stems carrying showers of white stars.

Arum.—No Arum is by any means indispensable to the rock-garden, nor is any one of them really desirable or appropriate there, though in large territories the finely-cut tropical-looking foliage of *A. crinitum* at least is grateful in a hot deep corner ; though the same cannot be said for its big flowers of sombre violet, which stink so excessively as to make the garden unapproachable to anyone except the crowding flies that are allured by its promise of corruption. *A. Dioscoridis* pokes naked, almost stemless, weird flowers up through the bare earth of the Levant, and follows on with foliage as an after-thought ; but the whole race is Southern, demanding hot dry seasons and perfect drainage. They are not fitted for general culture in England, least of all in the rock-garden. (The same applies to sub-ordinate races, *Biarum* and *Ischarum*.)

Asarum is a family of meek little tuft-forming Aristolochiads, far removed from the ramping huge traditions of their grand tropical cousins. They are little edging-plants, with more or less kidney-shaped leaves, often marbled in fantastic patterns that have enabled the enthusiasm of Japan to name some seventy varieties in *A. Sieboldii* alone. But for the rock-garden these glossy dwarfs have no charm but that of their evergreen quaintness, the flowers being not only of no value, but decently concealed beneath the foliage like those of Aspidistra, which they somewhat suggest. Some of them, however, *A. caudatum*, *A. europaeum*, *A. Sieboldii*, and so forth, may find an undisturbed place in some cool and worthless corner on the shady side of the garden, where their mottled sombre masses have a value.

Asparagus.—Few things could possibly be more noble than the common Asparagus, but especially desirable for the rock-work is trailing *A. tenuifolius* from Southern Europe, which is quite hardy in a well-drained fairly sheltered place, and has not only the charm of its trail-ing branches of fine emerald fur, but the profuse creamy stars of blossom diffuse the most penetrating and enrapturing scent of violets. There is also a pretty and hardy *A. filicinus* from the Himalaya.

Asperula brings us back into the land of rocks. For though many of the Woodruffs are woodlanders indeed, like our own *A. odorata*, there is a large section of beautiful small-tufted plants from the high cliffs of the South, that want nothing better than to be happy with us in light well-drained loam, or in the moraine, always asking for full sun and the proper precaution of sharp drainage against winter-wet.

A. arcadiensis is incomparably the most important of all, and is always by nurserymen made a synonym of *A. Athoa* and *A. suberosa*, two names of one quite inferior (though lovely) species, with which it has nothing whatever to do. The genuine *A. arcadiensis* comes from the alpine rocks of the Peloponnesus ; it sends up a multitude of short, frail, very leafy stems each year, not more than 3 or 4 inches long, forming a close mass all fluffy with the profuse grey wool that clothes the whole growth, stem, and narrow little leaves and all, until at last the flowers come forth, six to eight in a bunch at the tip of the shoots, appearing to sit almost upon the cobwebby grey tuffet. And these are the most exquisite and astonishing long trumpets of pure and delicate rose-pink, quite waxy and smooth in texture, especially notable too on their misty ash-grey ground. Beautiful as is *A. arcadiensis*, it needs the care that its appearance earns and suggests. For it detests excessive damp in winter, as nearly all alpine fluffers do ; and should, besides its perfect drainage and its light soil in a sunny corner of the rock-work or choice moraine, have the protection of a pane of glass over it after October, as if it were indeed one of the precious Aretian Androsaces with which its glory not unsuccessfully competes. It is a hard plant to propagate, rather miffy and dangerous to touch, not setting seed, and difficult to strike from cuttings.

A. Boissieri is another tufty species with yellow flowers.

A. cynanchica is the English Squinancy Wort—a spidery thing from hot banks, with clusters of long, pink trumpets, pretty in themselves but not well balanced against the splaying bare stems, along which lie whorled leaves at rare intervals, so long and thin themselves as merely to emphasize the gaunt nakedness of the stems. However, on the Mont Cenis there lives a form of this which is worth cultivation in even the choicest dry hot place of the most choice garden. *A. c. Jordanii* makes a dear little neat clump with spraying stalks on all sides, not more than 3 or 4 inches long, carrying larger bunches of larger brighter blossoms, waxy and pink with tips of rose, most delicate and charming in effect, and forming quite a bouquet of bloom.

A. Gussonii has been falsely figured by its author as *A. nitida*. It is, none the less, an Italian species of beauty and charm, after the same kind.

A. hexaphylla, a rare plant from the Maritime Alps, is very pretty indeed, but much laxer and looser, not forming any sort of a cushion, but flopping here and there with fine fragile 6-inch stems, set at intervals with little narrow leaves in whorls of six, and then ending in bunches of charming pearly-pink starry trumpets. In cultivation it needs no attention ; one of the best pieces I know developed from a chance seedling in a collected clump of *Saxifraga diapensioeides* from the rocks of Tenda. The Asperula killed the Saxifrage in no time, and has completely occupied its bishopric ever since, in yearly increasing vigour. Rather larger and stouter than this, again, is

ASPERULA.

A. longiflora, from the limestone Alps of the eastern ranges, and very much less rare.

A. hirta is a smooth-leaved small species from the Pyrenees, forming beautiful soft fine mats of rather lax and graceful shoots, with the leaves narrow and smooth and green, arranged in whorls of from four to seven. The shoots are not more than 3 or 4 inches high or so, square and leafy, and end in clusters of beautiful rosy stars almost concealing the cushion, which has the further merit of emitting runners underground. It is a common beauty in its native Alps and has looser or more condensed forms, named accordingly.

A. nitida, from the Bithynian Olympus, is yet another tuffet-plant, rather close, 3 or 4 inches high, with flopping twisting stems more or less well-clad in hairless leaves. Here again the flowers are pink.

A. pendula depends in a very dense minutely downy mass from the crevices and alpine grottoes of Granada—a huddle of tiny round stems half an inch or two inches long, closely beset with foliage arranged in whorls of eight or ten, green above and hoary below. The blossoms are borne in quite narrow heads and are hairy outside, produced not from the end of the shoot only, but all the way up from the base.

A. pontica is much the same, but the leaves of this are longer, so that the flower-tubes look correspondingly shorter.

A. pulvinaris, from hill-tops of Attica at about 4000 feet, makes specially dense tufts, 4 and 5 inches across, clothed in the fur, and furnished with the lovely long corollas, of Sibthorb's *A. suberosa*, with sharp little leaves, seeming double-grooved because of the salient median nerve, and with a flattened edge, arranged in whorls of four.

A. suberosa, or *A. Athoa*, has the too-frequent honour of lending its name to *A. arcadiensis*. Of this honour it is so amply worthy as well to deserve its own rightful name to itself. For it makes a beautiful close cushion, from a fat woody-barked stock, of short fine undivided stems, leafy, especially towards the base, with sharp and short upstanding narrow leaves arranged in whorls of four, the whole thing forming a densely hoary fluffet of grey velvet. The flowers are produced not from the ends of the shoots alone, but also from the axils of the upper leaves, thus producing a loose spike of blossom about 2 inches long ; and are of a lovely glowing pinkness, delicate trumpets, but almost exactly *half the length of those of arcadiensis;* in addition to which they are *not waxy-smooth outside*, but roughened with a very minute soft bristliness. This plant, were it not for the remote and too rarely realised supremacy of the *A. arcadiensis* whose place it so often usurps, would certainly be the queen of the race. It comes from the high and holy summit of Athos, whence it draws its invalid

PLATE 9.

ASTER FARRERI.
(Photo. W. Purdom.)

ASPERULA HIRTA.
(Photo. R. A. Malby.)

VOL. I.

PLATE 10.

ASTRAGALUS MONSPESSULANUS.
(Photo. R.B.G., Edinburgh.)

VOL. I

later name of *A. Athoa*. And such is the beauty of this, and such is the obscurity of modern horticulture, darkened with a multitude of counsel, that we must even confess to a secret doubt as to whether the genuine *A. arcadiensis* is now anywhere in cultivation at all, or whether it is in all gardens represented by the beautiful *A. Athoa* (or *A. suberosa*), under whose name it purports to be sent out.

Aster.—This vast race has given some superb species to the rock-garden, and offers at least as many more. But at the same time the race also abounds in the most dim, dismal, and gawky weeds, one of the worst weaknesses in the big wild Asters being the tendency of their purples to degenerate into a faint dead shade that from a little distance looks as if they were of an inferior grey. This fault has been to a certain extent remedied in the case of the gorgeous garden-race of Michaelmas Daisies, which rank among the most precious of herbaceous stuff. These, however, can at will be chosen from catalogues, or, even better, picked out for oneself at shows. Their place, too, is in the border only. But in the big rock-garden there are many big Asters to be hankered for, even of the larger habit ; and many enthusiasts who would there like to grow the best of the wild true species, if they could make sure what these were. In this attempt, however, catalogues give no help, but merely quote the several names of species almost without comment, or with the one word " Blue," which in the case of Aster merely illuminates darkness, seeing the enormous range of pallid tones which that charitably all-embracing word is made to cover. Therefore, though it would be excessive labour ill spent, botanically to describe the wild Asters of the Northern and Central United States, my aim will be, as soon as I have dealt in more ample detail with the lovely rock species that deserve such honour, cursorily to indicate the strength or weakness of some of the rest ; though it will of course be found that in the select list there will occur some species that have no right there, but ought to go into the second class ; while in the second there are obviously several magnificent or well-known treasures that should be moved up into the first. And, with regard to the culture of all these, indeed, and propagation, there is as a rule only excessive easiness, Asters turning into weeds on the very smallest provocation. (See Appendix for Asters of Kansu-Tibet.)

A. acris, like good wine, needs no bush, but forms the loveliest of all for itself, of stems about 3 feet high, with fine narrow leaves and glorious thick showers of countless small few-rayed flowers, bright violet-blue, of an elegance and airy charm quite irresistible anywhere— a universal August-joy in the garden, from the South of Europe.

A. alpinus, abundant at alpine elevations of all the European chains in the highest fine turf of the mountains, and often in company with similar tuffets and wide clumps of the Flannel-flower, is one of the loveliest of all, and one of the best known. (Division or seed.) In any light soil, enriched at need with chips of lime, it succeeds indefatigably in full sun, and glorifies June with its abundant flowers of richest violet, with a solid eye of bright gold. In the moraine, too, it looks especially beautiful, particularly mixed with masses of Edelweiss as on the Alps, the silver and purple making a noble contrast which requires no further addition (unless it be the sheeny silvers of *Artemisia Mutellina*), though it does not suffer if the loose spires of the best Aeizoon Saxifrages come showering up among them as they do on the high shoulder below the Laemmern glacier. Single-stemmed and purple though the species is, there are many variations, some of which carry distinctive names, though the gardener could pick out a couple of dozen quite as good or better for himself in half an hour among its tuffets on the Alps. But *A. a. baldensis* is a form which has the peculiarity of branching stems that carry several bright flowers of rosier note ; and, as for the endless pinks, dark violets (very beautiful), and whites, these there is no need to describe, any more than the forms of greater or lesser height, or congestion of habit. Slugs do not despise this plant, which also inspires a fatal passion in mice.

A. Amellus, though in a much less choice style, has a degree of beauty that fits it as well for the rock-garden or the border. It is a common sub-alpine of the copses and wood-edges in the South of Europe, growing 2 feet or more in height, with leafy stems carrying several large heads of splendid blue-purple in late summer and autumn. In habit it is neat but of rapid increase ; there are innumerable varieties which may be found offered in catalogues of Michaelmas Daisies, seeing that *A. Amellus* is quite fitted to hold its head high among the most choice and beautiful of cultivated forms. Among the most splendid of these, however, is the form *A. A. bessarabicus*, especially profuse with flowers of special size and especially rich violet-blue ; and in the same kinship is another beautiful Aster by the name of *A. cassubicus*, to say nothing of the closely allied species *A. amelloeides*. But not one of these has the cloudy loveliness of *A. acris*.

A. altaicus may have the benefit of the doubt and be admitted to this select fold. For though by one authority it sounds but poor, by another it is favourably painted as being about 6 or 8 inches high with leafy stems, rather hoary, and flower-heads of " blue " in a loose cluster. (Alps of North Persia to Siberia and Tibet.)

A. andinus admits of no doubt to have the benefit of. It is a species from the high Alps of America, in the style of *A. alpinus*, with large glories of violet and gold, carried solitary on their short stems.

A. apricus, from the highest Alps of Wyoming, is another plant that offers us joy, being only some 4 inches high, and forming a fine tuft of oblong spoon-shaped leaves, thick and ample, whose stalks are winged at the base ; the stems are rather few, erect or weak, about 4 inches high, each carrying a noble blossom whose rays are blended with purple and red in a manner characteristic and sumptuous.

A. brachytrichus, though meeker and milder, deserves a place in the gallery of charm. It forms a compact tuft, very free in producing its single-flowered stems, about a foot or 9 inches high, which are set with rather narrow foliage. Narrow, too, are the rays of the blossoms, and of a soft, rather than striking, pale lilac. (Alps of Asia.)

A. campestris, which ranges through the Rockies from Colorado to Montana and Wyoming, is a specially beautiful alpine. It runs freely underground, and then sends up erect slender stems usually undivided and carrying only one flower, or else branching so as to produce several. These stems are stickyish with glands above, and purplish in colour, the leaves being rather narrow, sharp, and fringed with hair. The flowers are resplendent, some 2 inches across, of a lovely dark azure.

A. catalaunicus, from the mountain-tops of Catalonia, is a diminished, creeping *A. Amellus* with narrower stiff foliage and blossoms of half the size.

A. caucasicus is a foot or two high, with leafy stems each ending in a single Amellus-looking flower.

A. conspicuus is the finest species of the Central Rockies. It rises from 1 to more than 3 feet high, with stiff, saw-toothed veiny leaves, and abundant domed clusters of flowers, rich violet, and each about an inch and a half across.

A. culminis is yet another unknown beauty of a high-alpine American Aster in the way of *A. alpinus* and *A. andinus*.

A. diplostephioeides appears in all gardens and catalogues, yet seems to be totally unknown in any, the name being everywhere assumed by the no less splendid *A. subcoeruleus, q.v. A. diplostephioeides* is a stranger from high altitudes up to 16,000 feet in Kashmir and Sikkim. Its basal leaves are *perfectly smooth* at the edge, and diminish to a long slender foot-stalk. From the assembled tufts of these spring stems of about a foot or more, with *a few leaves* upon their lower part, but *none approaching the great flower-head*, of which the containing green scales are in *only one row*. The blossom itself is very large and splendid, with many spreading rays of clear pale blue-violet, and the eye or disk is *never yellow* and *always purple*.

A. Falconeri, a variety of this, even more newly come into cultivation, is even more magnificent. It seems to form a rather simple and biennial-looking basal rosette; the foliage is toothed, and narrows quickly to a *quite short but definite foot-stalk;* the toothed leaves continue freely up the foot-high stem, and some three or four of them even envelop the cup of the flower-head, which is composed of green scales in *two or three rows*, and *densely* (not slightly) hairy at their edge. The flower is enormous, with countless very long and rather narrow rays of clear blue-violet, tending, many of the inner ones, to incurve a little at their tip, so that the erect bloom has the look of a huge expanded Sea-anemone; and the eye of the disk is *bright golden yellow*. This glorious thing has hardly yet come into general cultivation; it haunts the high mountains of Kashmir as far west as the Kamri Pass, and is well raised from seed. There seems no reason to suppose that it will not prove a sound perennial, though, being as yet so rare and precious, it will be treated to a specially good sunny place in light soil or moraine-mixture, watered from below.

A. Fendleri, from the plains of Texas, attains some 6 or 12 inches, with firm and rather bristly leaves, and flowers three-quarters of an inch across.

A. flaccidus is a much hairier and longer-haired version of *A. alpinus* from the Altai.

A. fulcratus is found in the mountains of South Colorado. It is a beautiful half-prostrate species, emitting subterranean runners, and the leaves are perfectly hairless and untoothed, spoon-shaped or egg-shaped in outline, and very small upon the whitely downy purple stems, which usually carry only one large Aster nearly 2 inches across, of a rich rose or hot lilac; but, if longer, they occasionally branch and produce more.

A. Geyeri is like a dwarf form of the common *A. laevis*, only about a foot or a foot and a half high, with the smooth leaves all more or less stem-embracing, while the lower ones have a leaf-stalk, with a leafy prolongation on either side. The large and handsome flowers are in clusters, clear pale violet-blue. (Wyoming.)

A. griseus has a weakly branching habit; the plant is rough with short bristles till it has a glaucous-grey hoar-frosted look; and the big blossoms are of a pale violet which is said to be attractive.

A. heterochaeta is found at great altitudes in Western Tibet and the Altai, from 16,000 to 18,000 feet. It is a glorified Alpinus, practically stemless, the enormous violet flower seeming to sit tight on the smooth-edged, pointed foliage. The whole tuft is densely woolly.

A. himalaicus is from 6 to 18 inches high, closely fluffy, and with leafy stems and blossoms of about an inch and a half across, with very narrow rays, and the scales of the very leafy flower-cup curving outward.

A. integrifolius belongs to moist open places in the sub-alpine woods of the central Rockies. It is more or less fluffy-downy, with oval stem-embracing leaves, and clustered bluish-purple flowers about an inch and a half across on stems of some 8 to 16 inches.

A. inulaefolius (Calimeris) has flowers as fine as Amellus in panicles on leafy stems. (Pine-woods of Lazic Pontus.)

A. Kingii, from the high alps of the Rockies, is near *A. alpinus* and *A. andinus*.

A. laetevirens grows about 2 feet high at the most, and has bright-green, willow-like foliage, and ample clusters of fine large rose-pink blossoms. (From the central Rockies.)

A. Laka carries solitary large purple flowers on uprising stems of some 6 or 8 inches, leafy with broad leafage, oval heart-shaped, pointed and toothed, with the foot-stalks sheathing the stems. (Laka, 10,000 to 11,000 feet.)

A. lichiangensis is a bonus of the gods. It was never consciously collected, but in a seed-pan filled with germs of some Chinese Primula or other there appeared one day two seedlings, which ultimately developed into the most exquisite high-alpine Aster ever seen. From a neat and tiny basal rosette of bright-green oval leaves there rises a little stem of about 3 inches, bearing erect a single flower of the most glorious imperial purple, of a most special elegance and charm. When this jewel comes out into the public hands it should have the very choicest of positions, in rich well-watered stony soil, with peat and sand admixed ; or else in the moraine-bed of chips and soil, where water flows perpetually beneath.

A. Pattersonii has thick tongue-shaped leaves, clad in a certain amount of wool, from which rises up a stem branching at the top, and carrying large brilliant violet blooms about an inch and a half across. (From the high mountains of Colorado.) American botanists, never tired of having fun with their own native species, have had great times with Aster, Erigeron, Townsendia, and the other overlapping, interfading families, redistributing them, and turning one into another as Harlequin does at the pantomime. Accordingly *A. Pattersonii* now often appears as *Machaeranthera Pattersonii*. For people in the Old World it may be sufficient to retain Aster and Erigeron, uncomplicated by Wyomingia and Ionactis; at the same time it should be remembered that such strange new names, if offered in catalogues, may very likely here be found described under their older and more familiar styles. It is possible enough, with hard labour, to get at the original specific name of a plant ; but the generic can always be subsequently altered at any time by any botanist, according to some scheme of rearrangement that he may want to make. Therefore, though there is finality in the one case, and correctness may be both sought, found, and insisted on, in the other one has nothing to go on but the shifting bog of critical re-dispositions, which, in such subtly differentiated families as Aster and many another, offers us a footing so insecure and impermanent that no generic name can be regarded as finally established.

A. peregrinus, with *A. foliaceus* and *A. salsuginosus*, grows erect, sometimes branching, with one to three flower-heads. The leaves are oblong and smooth, the stem only villous-downy above.

A. pulchellus is another case in point. American authorities now call it *Oreastrum alpigenum*. None the less it may be gratefully remembered and asked for as *Aster pulchellus*—for so indeed it is, a charming tuft of narrow tongue-shaped leaves from the high mountains of Wyoming, with radiating scapes of some 3 to 6 inches, each carrying one large purple flower about an inch and a half across.

A. proximus is a twin to *A. laetevirens*, but here the leaves are dark green, and without any toothing at the edge.

A. pseudo-amellus repeats the beauty of *A. Amellus*, but here the bracts that enclose the cup are specially large and leafy. (Alps of Kumaon, 800 to 900 feet.)

A. Purdomii is a very lovely novelty from damp rich soil, high on the mountains of Shensi, in the kinship of *A. alpinus*, and a dangerous rival. (Purdom, 1910.)

A. Richardsonii, from the Altai and moist places in North America, is, like *A. Amellus*, not more than a foot high, downy-woolly above and hairy below, with branching stems, each carrying a large purple flower an inch and a half across.

A. roseus (Calimeris) is a generous dwarf tuft, with very many stems from a woody base, and abundant showers of fine pink blossoms. (Eastern Caucasus.)

A. scapigerus, also from Siberian Altai, is an ennobled cousin of *A. alpinus*. Here there are no leaves at all on the stems, but they are gathered into a basal tuft, oblong, hispid, and without any toothing at their edge. The stems are only about 4 inches high, and the flowers glorious as in *A. alpinus.*

A. scopulorum has now, by American botany, been driven out of the family, and ordered for the time being to set up house for itself as *Ionactis alpina.* It forms a single clump of short, stiff, very narrow foliage all ashy-grey with soft hairs. The splendid light-violet blooms, some inch and a half wide, are carried lonely on stems half a foot tall at the most. (High Alps of Wyoming, &c.)

A. sibiricus is in the group of *A. Amellus*, with leaves rounded and more or less stem-embracing, toothed, saw-edged or entire. (Altai.)

A. silenifolius, from Eastern Siberia, is yet another beautiful *A. alpinus.* The leaves are narrow oblong, rather pointed, and clothed in a certain amount of spreading hair ; while the suns of violet and gold are borne lonely on short stems, the rays being twice as long as the disk is broad.

A. Stracheyi is a quite small and charming little rambling species, with runners. The basal leaves are oval spoon-shaped, with a few coarse teeth here and there, softly downy. There are one or two small leaves on the dwarf scapes, each of which carries a flower-head about three-quarters of an inch across, the rays themselves being half an inch. (From the alps of Kumaon, at about 12,000 feet.)

A. subcoeruleus is the beautiful impostor which in all gardens has borne the name of *A. diplostephioeides*—from which at the outset it may be always and absolutely known by the eye of the blossom, which is yellow (whereas in *A. diplostephioeides* it is *purple*). This is a most precious species, forming wide mats of soft oval green foliage, from which in June rise a profusion of tall almost naked stems, perhaps some 15 inches high, each of which carries a magnificent *Aster-alpinus* flower with a golden eye. This beauty is only known in cultivation, its origin being unknown, but suspected to lie somewhere away in the mountains of Hazara, about the Western borders of Kashmir. The variety *A. s. Leichtlinii* is one of special size and vigour and brilliant splendour—though the type itself hardly admits of being improved in any of these respects.

A. tataricus is not a specially interesting Amelloid species, with erect hispid stems, freely branching, with elongated sprays.

A. tibeticus follows the excellent fashion of *A. alpinus* in only pro-ducing one flower to a stem. In this species the stems are specially numerous, standing erect in a dense little forest not exceeding a foot at the outside, and more usually about 6 inches. The abundant flowers are conspicuous, too, in the abundance of their bright-blue rays, about a couple of inches across. There are but few leaves on the stems, which have a slight coat of downy hairiness ; the foliage at the base is narrow-oblong, without any toothing, blunt, with a little foot-stalk, and altogether small. The lovely plant belongs to all the Western Himalaya and Tibet, at highest Alpine elevations, 15,000 to 16,000 feet.

A. tricephalus is a taller version of *A. himalaicus*, with narrower bracts, and occasionally earning its name by diverging into branches, each with a flower-head at the end. (Sikkim, 10,000 to 14,000 feet.)

A. yunnanensis, quite a new novelty (no common quality in " Novelties "), with a bright-leaved form called *A. y. atroviridis*, pro-mises to be a delight. It forms a compact tuft with abundance of erect stems some 9 inches high or so, each flaunting a fine flower of bright clear blue, with very broad rays. In habit it recalls *A. brachytrichus*, though said to be incomparably more brilliant.

Aster species of less merit. The following species are taller, ranker, or of less use and place in the rock-garden (including a few of special merit ; many more will also be found in Nicholson's *Dictionary of Gardening*, but Nicholson is inclined to use his star of recommendation a little too generously).

A. acuminatus, tall coarse-toothed leaves, flowers large and few, pale whitish purple.

A. adscendens, valueless.

A. amethystinus is possibly a hybrid between *A. Novae-Angliae* and *A. multiflorus*. It is a rare plant of moist places, 3 feet high, soft-leaved, very branchy, with flowers of clear blue. In gardens the name often stands for *A. grandiflorus*.

A. anomalus, 3 feet, frail ; violet blossoms. Limestone cliffs in woods.

A. asperulus, quite near the beautiful *A. Thompsonii*, but with the leaves prolonging themselves in little wing-like flaps along the leaf-stalk.

A. azureus, leaves long, heart-shaped, rough ; bright blue flowers in racemes.

A. Canbyi, stout and leafy, and without value.

A. coerulescens. See *A. salicifolius*.

A. commutatus, a stiff, leafy, branchy 2- to 3-foot plant, with large whitish flowers.

A. concinnus, leaves rather serrate, smallish violet flowers. Woods, rare.

A. concolor, wandlike fine stems, about 2 feet high, with many crowded heads of small violet stars.

A. cordifolius, a coarse leafy thing with pallid flowers.

ASTER SPECIES.

A. Cordineri, leaves a most spinulous, dark-green ; large but pale in blossom.

A. depauperatus, a crowded-blossomed species, akin to *A. ericoeides*.

A. divaricatus, slender ; heart-shaped toothy foliage, and thin poor blooms.

A. dumosus, a well-known and beautiful Aster about 2 feet high, the parent of many garden forms, even more beautiful and clear-flowered.

A. ericoeides, not less well-known and beautiful, with some no less lovely forms and improvements. See any catalogue. Three feet and more.

A. frondeus, a dim and unprofitable species.

A. furcatus, a leafy slender plant with starved-looking stars.

A. glaucus, 1 to 2 feet, smooth and glaucous ; bright violet panicles.

A. glomeratus, stout, coarse and leafy, with short poor flower-rays.

A. gracilis, few diminished stars. A little over a foot in height ; violet.

A. grandiflorus, one of the most sumptuous of late-flowering border beauties—tall and leafy, with magnificent, many-rayed flowers of dark rich violet, very late. Dry places of Virginia, but perfectly hardy and thanking you for a sunny aspect. (The "Christmas" Aster.)

A. hebeclados, a poor and pallid weakly thing.

A. Herveyi, rather coarse, about 2 feet high ; purple.

A. infirmus is a slender flaccid plant with creamy-white flowers.

A. junceus, a species from cold boggy lands, with slender upright undivided stems, and large flowers ranging from purple to pink and white ; the leaves particularly narrow and rushlike in effect.

A. laevis, rather excessively ample and leafy ; dullish violet blooms of deadened tone.

A. lateriflorus (*A. diffusus*, Aitch.), sharp-toothed leaves ; bluish white.

A. linarifolius, narrow-leaved and graceful, from 6 inches to 2 feet, with many stems, and big violet flowers either alone at the top of each, or at the ends of undividing branches.

A. Lindleyanus, a big, leafy stalwart, with big blue-violet flowers in ample panicles, of handsome effect. From 1 to more than 3 feet.

A. longifolius, about 2 or 3 feet, with leaves more or less embracing the stems, and big branching panicles of big flowers in that rather flat tone described euphemistically as "purplish violet."

(1,919) 129 I

A. macrophyllus, a very coarse and very variable great weed.

A. major, a big purple-flowered species from moist woods in the Selkirks, attaining 6 feet, with coarsely toothed stem-embracing leaves.

A. meritus forms a wide mat and has inferior scanty-rayed stars.

A. modestus has an undivided stem, notably narrow foliage, and a few large flowers of rich dark violet. It prefers rich soils in nature.

A. multiflorus, a very branching bush-Aster, roughish, with small white flowers.

A. Nelsonii, a slender grower from moist rocks, with feeble starved florets.

A. nemoralis, from bogs and cool places far up the Hudson and in Newfoundland, is a better species, with an even better form called *A. n. Blakei*. It is about 2 feet high, with stiff untoothed leaves curling over at the edge ; the flowers are large and lilac, several to the head.

A. Novae-Angliae, " mater pulchra filiarum pulcherrimarum," is in nature rare, especially affecting damp calcareous places in East Quebec. This and its seedlings are never so tall as the next.

A. Novi-Belgii, on the contrary, is very common all along the Atlantic border of the States, where it takes many forms. It may be separated easily from the last by its much greater stature, with leaves more or less embracing the stem. They are more or less toothed, and thinnish in texture. It attains nearly 4 feet at home, and has flowers of bright violet, while in the garden it doubles its height, and diverges into almost every gorgeous colour of the rainbow—the last and richest glory of the herbaceous border.

A. paniculatus, a leafy, very variable and branching 6-footer, with large flowers of a rather lifeless pale purple.

A. patens is a bigger form of *A. gracilis*, some 2 or 3 feet high, with oblong petioled leaves and panicles of lax-rayed violet stars of bright violet.

A. polyphyllus is quite close to *A. ericoeides*, but larger in the blossom.

A. Porteri is a most beautiful plant abundant in Colorado, with 2- or 3-foot stems, and ample graceful heads, showery and sprayed, of delicate and well-built white flowers. Though in reality hardy, *A. Porteri* should have well-drained light dryish soil, lest it depart from heavier ground in winter, as its habit sometimes is.

A. prenanthoeides has leaves embracing the stem and overlapping it ; the height is 2 or 3 feet, and the blossoms purply. Streams and rich woods.

A. ptarmicoeides makes a really dainty and delightful little clump, graceful and of fine habit, sending up stems of some 18 inches from a tuft of narrow foliage, and carrying loose flattish heads of creamy-white, with yellow eye—the whole habit being indeed suggestive of a refined *Achillea Ptarmica.*

A. puniceus is especially remarkable for its power of growing no less happily in 3 or 4 inches of water as it does almost anywhere on land. It forms masses of stalwart stems about 4 feet high, clothed in leafage of ample cheerful green, rather smooth and limp in look, but more or less hairy; the flowers are produced in August, in very ample panicles, and are themselves very ample and of bright clear blue, well furnished with a quantity of narrowish rays. It is a splendid beauty, extremely variable in its native haunts in bogs and damp places in the northernmost States.

A. pyrenaeus is yet another Aster deserving capitals. It belongs to the hills of Catalonia, and from the central tuft it sends up a number of stiff undivided stems about 3 feet high, clothed in oval-pointed toothed foliage, grey with soft down, and almost embracing the stem. The large and brilliant purple flowers are carried at the top in a loosely branching head. (July to August.)

A. radula, specially rough-leaved with stars of pale poor violet.

A. salicifolius recalls *A. paniculatus,* but the leaves are stiffer, and the heads are carried in broad heads like a thyrsus. (*A. caerulescens* is a form of this.)

A. Schreberi has much the same faults as *A. glomeratus.*

A. sericeus is beautiful but a little uncertain. It is a slender branching thing, about 2 feet high, with narrow leaves all shining with a coat of silver silk, and large flowers of a brilliant violet-purple. It belongs to the prairies, and especially desires very light soil in a warm position, with perfect drainage.

A. Shortii is a good species—slender and spreading, with full-faced flowers in well-furnished racemes.

A. sikkimensis attains 3 or 4 feet and is lavishly branchy, with soft narrowish stem-embracing leaves, and abundance of flowers, blue, not large, upon the twisting sprays.

A. spectabilis grows some 2 feet high, with oval, long-pointed foliage, all sharply toothed, and no great abundance of fine big flowers of clear violet.

A. surculosus has the flowers of *A. spectabilis,* but here the leaves are stiff and without any toothing. It comes from bogs and running water about New Jersey.

A. tardiflorus (*A. patulus,* Lam.) has stem-clasping leaves and panicles of pale lightish-blue stars.

ASTER SPECIES.

A. tenuifolius, from the salt-marshes of Massachusetts, has perfectly smooth stems and leaves; the stem goes zigzagging this way and that, attaining perhaps to 2 feet of height, or to 4 inches. The leaves are long and fleshy and quite untoothed at the edge, while the flowers, though fine and large, are of a pale purple.

A. Thompsonii is one of the most beautiful of all—an Indian species, coming to us from the highlands of Nepal and Kashmir. It is a frail and slight grower, deplorably difficult of increase, as it neither seeds nor runs nor forms a clump. The leafy stems rise to some 3 feet, set thickly with their oval-pointed toothed, roughly hairy, green-grey foliage; the flowers are borne separately, in summer, and are very large and graceful, of a clear lilac-blue. It should have good soil, well drained, and in the sun. There is also a lower-growing form, called in lists *A. T. nana*, yet more especially fitted for the rock-garden.

A. Tradescantii, from low grounds, is from half a foot to 3 feet high, with slender panicles of pale purple blossoms, flattened with that grey tone which " pale purple " so often connotes in Aster. These wild species, however, have their place, where this colour is no drawback. Let them be turned out into rough ground of heath and grass and sedge, then their sad pale orbs take a strangely delicate and tragic beauty, shining clear and pale with a still and cool lucidity in the dim and dying herbage. And so may be seen at Wisley.

A. turbinellus, however, keeps its grace and astonishing delicacy of beauty high among modern rivals in the border—a tall and quite spiderly elegant plant with large purple flowers on very long sprays, waving this way and that from the wiry, narrow-leaved and bare-looking branches.

A. umbellatus is more than a six-footer, excessively leafy, with flat heads of many whitish flowers.

A. undulatus is another weedy gawk of no use.

A. Vahlii should be a precious rarity, and comes from the Antarctic Islands; it cannot be the worthless thing sent out under these names, one hopes, for in that case it is a pity it ever took the trouble to come so far—a densely, ineradicably-spreading mass, with ragged spindly stars of pallid dull blue in summer, carried on stems of some 18 inches high, above the tufts of long narrow smooth foliage.

A. vimineus is like a six-foot *A. dumosus*, with lesser flowers, but still very attractive in its habit of bending sprays with innumerable little daisies. *A. v. saxatilis* is a dwarfer, neater form.

A. virgatus has the flowers of *A. laevis*, but the leaves are narrower, the growth more slender, and its whole effect more graceful and neat.

132

ASTILBE.

A. Willkommii, in the sands of Eastern Spain, makes a grey-green leafy plant, with heads of flowers, one to eight, each being about an inch across.

Asterolinosy̌ris Willmottiae should more rightly be called Linosyris. It is an interesting hybrid between *Linosyris* and *Aster acris*, which has succeeded in losing all the beauty of both its parents—arriving at a weak and muddy compromise between the clear lavender-blue loveliness of the Aster and the rayless gold of Linosyris.

Astilbe has nowadays innumerable hybrids, contributed by the violent magenta-crimson of *A. Davidii* (itself as beautiful as any for cool moist places, beyond possibility of attacking other colours). Such are Solferino, Crépuscule, Princess Juliana, Lachskönigin (or the inevitable " Salmon Queen "), and, finally, the most lovely of all these tall and fluffily beautiful pink Spiraeas for cool borders of the bog, the deceptively named *A.* × **Magenta**, which the prudent avoided for some years on account of its unfortunate name, until they discovered at last that it was called (almost as irrelevantly) after the battle and not the colour ; but it is, in point of fact, a most noble fountain of long loose fluffy spikes in rich and tender shades of pink. *A. grandis* and *A. rivularis* are huge tropical splendours for the large bog, the former, however, not being a ramper like the latter, but resting content to grow into a massive clump from which arise its stiff six-foot spires, the more stately perhaps, though not so beautiful as the spouting foaming plumes of *A. rivularis* and its improved variety *A. r. Moerheimii*. Known beyond need of mention are the Chinese and Japanese Spiraeas of our forcing-houses, *A. japonica* and *A. sinensis*, which are not only beautiful and hardy themselves by the water-side, but have given us also delicate pink forms in Peach-blossom and the looser-plumed Queen Alexandra ; these, with countless more names not here in place to record (since every catalogue contains them and describes them—with new ones every season)—all resulting from marriages between *A. Davidii* and one or other of the more gracious-spiked white species, or with the stately *A. Thunbergii*, with stems of a yard in height and its spires of whity pink. Their generic name is *A.* × *Arendsii ;* and though more and more imposing fancy titles perpetually appear, from a packet of seed everyone who wishes could get some equally nameable forms for himself, to glorify the water-side in the comparatively empty hours of August. Most specially within the scope of our present subject, however, is *A. simplicifolia*, a gift of the gods from Japan, which turned up " unbeknownst " one day in an imported mass of Schizocodon, and ere long revealed itself as the most lovely little Astilbe imaginable, for any cool moist and shady corner on the most

133

select of rock-works. For this is a neat tuft of glossy dark leaves like long pointed shields with toothed edges, but quite undivided and unfeathered as are the leaves of the rest. Up above these in summer come shooting gracious airy 8-inch plumes of white blossom, sometimes so copiously produced indeed that the clump gives the only trouble it ever occasions cultivators by blooming itself into its grave. However, it can easily be raised from seed, though it shares the general weakness of Astilbe as regards the inviolability of the family taboo, and clearly interbreeds ; for, among my seedlings here, one of the best plants has feathered foliage, and altogether suggests a very minute form of *A. sinensis.*

A. Tacquetii, again, now on the Austrian horizon of our hopes, will prove a rock-garden treasure of the first rank. For this is yet another dwarf—a 6-inch version of *A. sinensis,* but with drooping plumes. It will prosper and emit runners in any cool choice place, and its force of character is guaranteed by the fact that it comes from Korea.

Astragǎlus is a name that breaks the rock-gardener's heart. There are many large families of Pea-flowers, but Astragalus beats them nearly all ; a race of vast distribution alike in the Old World and in the New, frequenting, as a rule, deserts and dry terrible places, where it often develops into masses of thorns ; but, on the other hand, descending into lush fields and woods and there waxing fat, and ascending high also into the warmer mountain chains, and offering the rock-garden a large choice.   Yet the choice is hard to make ; there are some thousand-odd species of Astragalus in the world, and the fact that there are only half a dozen of them or so (if that) in general cultivation sheds a lurid light on the unattractiveness of the race.   In point of fact, dense over Astragalus lies that curse of the family's ineffectualness (outside yellows).   Their colour so often lacks just the touch that gives value and brilliancy ; they are, not to put too fine a point upon it, for the large part a cousinhood of forbidding weeds, often difficult and nearly always worthless.   Here and there, however, we know of deserving species ; and this fact has caused me with a jealous and unwearied eye to sift the enormous lists of Astragali that come in from almost every country, to see whether here and there, through the mists of a Latin diagnosis, it may prove possible to discern a promise of prettiness.   So much being ascertained, it only remains to get seed of the Astragalus in question ; it will germinate readily, and beyond all reasonable doubt will thrive in some sunny place in very light and stony soil—stony almost to the pitch of being moraine, but rather on the hard side, so long as it be hot and perfectly drained. (No Astragalus should ever be lifted, moved, divided, or otherwise propagated than by seed.) I propose, then, first of all to take such European species as we have, and deal with them ; then cursorily to suggest the names of such foreigners as have sounded to me as if they might perhaps be beautiful. It cannot be promised that all such species will fulfil that promise, nor that the mesh of this net shall not have let some worthy species slip through ; in any case it should feed up the amateur of Astragalus with hopes for some little time to come ; and, in the meantime, as with Aster or any large race prolific in rubbish, the enthusiast may well find it a help and a saving to purchase no species unmentioned in this book, unless with the fullest and most alluring credentials and description.

But few of our own alpine species are worth attention, and the very name *A. alpina,* that accepted promise of good things, belongs to a rather feeble little pallor, whose cluster-bunches of small blue-and-white flowers we all know, in the upper turf of the mountain pastures. (This is also *Phaca astragalina* (DC.), the other alpine Phacas being yet inferior things, often weedy, with yellow blossoms.) *A. danicus,* however, is really a most dainty small beauty for the sunny rock or moraine, forming neat and perfectly dwarf mats of little leaves, arranged in pairs of tiny greyish rounded leaflets, among which nestle the heads of comparatively fine Pea-flowers, which in the variety *albus* are especially pretty.

A. alopecuroeides, on the other hand, is a type of the rank and tall-growing development of the family from lusher places—a branch which this list, seeking choice alpines only, has not touched. *A. alopecuroeides* rises from 18 inches to 3 feet, standing erect, with leaves of a fine green, very long and narrow and delicate, like a big *Asplenium viride's,* but with the pinnae narrower and pointed, composed of twenty-five or thirty oval leaflets ; the flowers, in dense cylindric fox-brush bunches, are of a golden yellow. This plant is a rarity, from sub-alpine regions in the valley of Cogne, &c.

A. aristatus deserves mention as being the type, in the European southern Alps, of the spiny desert-section of the family. In the Graians, Cottians, and Maritimes especially, on high and barren hot slopes, it forms mounds and mats of spiny branches, in which nestle the dowdy little heads of yellow flower, in the wings of the minute leaves.

A. hypoglottis is an alpine species often seen in cultivation, much finer than *A. alpinus,* but of the same prostrate habit, hairy and diffuse upon the ground. The bunch of bloom stands erect, about an inch long or more, made up of handsome violet blossoms in an almost globular head. The leaves are composed of some eight or twelve pairs of oval leaflets. There is a white form of this also, no less worthy of cultivation than the species, which is a genuinely pretty thing.

A. monspessulanus, however, is the jewel of the family, as we now have it in our gardens, of which it is an unquestionable ornament. It grows into wide but graceful masses of quite dwarf tufts of prostrate habit, running underground ; the leaves are quite long and narrow, made up of the most delicate small pairs of leaflets, rather distant, so as to give the effect of a drawn out and etiolate frond of *Asplenium trichomanes*, darkened, weak, dulled, and magnified ; while among these on dwarfish stems rise up the long loose spikes of big nodding flowers, of a vinous red-purple.

A. Onobrychis, again, is not unworthy of a place. It forms lax downy tufts, as much as 18 inches across ; the leaflets are rather narrow, and much more distant than in the last ; and the large bluish-purple flowers stand up in heads well above the foliage.

A. Tragacantha is the most illustrious of the group, as its name says that it produces tragacanth-gum—which it doesn't !

OTHER SUGGESTED ASTRAGALI OUT OF A THOUSAND

A. apollineus, a 4-inch tuffet of grey with short ascending stems and most attractive flowers of red-violet. Rare : on Parnassus.

A. argyrothamnus, a silver-sheeny mound of fine thorns from Lebanon, making a round densely-branching bush, with violet blossoms at the base of microscopic leaves, whose place the thorns have taken in the plant's development—dry desert-ground species tending to develop thorns at the expense of foliage, so as not to tempt browsers with the one, and so as to avert them with the other.

A. cadmicus, a silky crevice-plant, 2 to 6 inches high, with violet-keeled blooms. (High regions of Lycia and Cappadocia.)

A. Chamaeleuke, densely silky prostrate and almost stemless, with many 2-inch foot-stalks, carrying from three to eight large flowers of light violet, more than an inch long. (From the Alps of Wyoming, Montana, and Idaho.)

A. chionophilus duly loves the snow, as its name tells us. For it is found at great elevations in stony places beside the melting snow in the mountains of Isauria and Cappadocia—a densely silky thing again, with fine thread-like shoots, leaves an inch long, and big violet blossoms.

ASTRAGALUS.

A. chrysanthus, attaining a foot and a half or more on Elburs, with golden flowers and larger development.

A. crassicarpus is a prostrate species from dry plains of America, with purple spikes of bloom, followed by swollen seed-pods like little plums.

A. cruentiflorus is another thorn-bush from high on Hermon, very dense, and shimmering-silver, with tiny flowers tightly gathered in heads of scarlet, not projecting beyond such leaves as the plant possesses.

A. Eastwoodiae.—A branched American species, about 4 or 5 inches high, with narrow hairless foliage, and flower-stems as long, carrying a few stout violet blossoms about three-quarters of an inch in length.

A. flavescens makes an interesting little bush of 6 inches or a foot, all clothed in fulvous-yellow felt, with yellow thorns. (Alps of Lydia above Sardis, &c.)

A. glareosus (*A. argophyllus*) grows into a dense depressed mat of silver-silky foliage, up among which come the slight stems, bearing a few narrow blossoms of bright violet. (Central Rockies.)

A. hololeucus, from the sub-alpine region of Elburs, has flowers of pale blue, above a cushion all closely hoary with silver. (*A. alyssoeides* is a replica of this reduced in all its parts.)

A. hypoglottioeides, with *A. striatus, tibetanus, oxyodon, rigidulus, confertus, Lessertianus*, &c., makes up a race of silvery high-alpine tuffets from India and Tibet in the line of *A. hypoglottis*, which might, some of them, prove worthy of introduction.

A. incanus, a European species from desert places of Southern France, Italy, &c., tufted, all closely silvery-white, with racemes or loose spikes of bloom that range from white to purple.

A. kadscharensis belongs to the ruins of an old castle above Tiflis. It has short, ascending stems, green and not silky, with large flowers of a beautiful bright blue-violet, the stems of the plant being about 2 or 3 inches long, while the foot-stalk that carries the blossoms is some 3 or 4.

A. lilacinus, from the base of Demavend, is all hoary with close silver, very dwarf, not more than 1 or 2 inches, with the stems of the flower-heads six or twelve.

A. macrorrhizus is a humble dense thing, silky at first, and then growing greener, perfectly dwarf, with yellow flowers, from hills of Eastern Spain.

A. missouriensis, closely silky, few blossoms, half an inch long, violet, in spiky heads.

A. nummularioeides may be found in dry barren places close to the snows of the Sierra Nevada. This, like *A. macrorrhizus*, is a humble dense mat, only silky at first. The flowers range from pale pink to purple, carried in globular heads, on stems of not more than 4 inches.

A. Ruprechtii suggests an Oxytropis. It is hoary and almost stemless, with leaves 5 inches long and the foot-stalks of the blossom-heads half a foot. The flowers are of violet and yellow. (East Caucasus.) Still smaller than this in all its parts is *A. hyalolepis*.

A. sanguinolentus has flower-stems rather shorter than the leaves, lying weakly down, the flowers being white, but with a blood-red keel. (Stony places of Caucasus and Georgia.)

A. sericophyllus, from the pine-region of Kithairon, is woody at the base, with graceful long peduncles, and Pea-blossoms of blue and white, contrasting well with the hoary vesture of silk that gives the plant its name.

A. Shortianus (*A. cyaneus*) is almost stemless, very closely silver-silky, the foot-stalks of the heads not being as long as the leaves, while the flowers themselves are fine and large, of bright violet-blue. It is found in Wyoming and Montana.

A. simplicifolius occurs in the dry plains and barrens of the central Rockies, forming a close mat of silk, into which nestle heads of two or three violet blossoms.

A. striatus, from the American plains, has flowers of yellow, tipped with purple (a special leguminous trick that usually results in dowdiness of effect), followed by pods like little plums.

A. utahensis is prostrate and woolly, with dark purple blooms.

A. zerdanus forms a dense hoary-grey tuft, matted with many short shoots in the stony places of South Persia, at 12,000 or 13,000 feet. It is a lovely sight, especially when the heads of brilliant blue-violet blossom just stand up above the mass on their stems of 2 inches or so.

Astrantia makes an oasis of attractiveness in the family of Umbelliferae ; not that, to the casual eye, their charm suggests any connection with that usually most uncharming (except for their foliage and culinary or veneficent properties) family of inconspicuous-flowered tiresome weeds.

A. Biebersteiniana is in all respects *A. major* divided by half. The radical leaves are three-cleft with the two side-lobes cleft in two, and deep-toothed, while the middle one remains a simple oblong. It occupies all the Caucasus, and like *A. major* deepens into more or less pinkish forms, which in this species are apt to be specially pure and bright. It grows eagerly in cool open soil, and blooms in summer.

A. carniolica is yet another pretty species, which I suspect of being confused in some gardens with *A. gracilis*, and in others with the larger and stouter *A. helleborifolia*. And there are various other species still, in this kind, from various parts of the Alps, all pretty and easy, but not especially distinct in value for the garden that already rejoices in major, minor, gracilis, and helleborifolia—major and helleborifolia being plants for open and crowded meadowy places, while gracilis and minor will grace the choicest bank in cool soil and shade.

A. gracilis, very abundant in similar places, even down to the roadsides, in the Karawanken, is a trifle larger and more solid than *A. minor*, but inspired with no less striking an air of breeding and grace. In cultivation it answers to the same treatment ; and, indeed, all the Astrantias are of the easiest culture in any open cool loam.

A. helleborifolia, with *A. maxima*, *A. heterophylla*, and *A. caucasica*, are others from Eastern regions ; *A. helleborifolia* having the lower leaves cut finger-wise, into three fat broad lobes which are not cleft again. These are found in grassy places all through the Caucasus.

A. major is abundant in the sub-alpine fields of the main European ranges. Inclining to be large, its best place in cultivation is in some sub-alpine piece of herbage, with Trollius, *Geranium sylvaticum*, *Campanula rotundifolia*, *Paradisea Liliastrum*, and others of its old friends and neighbours. Here it thrives happily for ever, and looks at home with its comely green ranunculoid foliage and stems of big greenish-pink bracty stars.

A. minor is quite a different little beauty, which does not seem to attract the general eye, though to my own it is especially delightful. For it is of very delicate habit—a slight tuft of dark-green finely-cleft leaves, well above which, all the summer through, aspire loose dainty sheaves of fairy-like ivory stars, filled with the spidery whiteness of the genuine flowers. This dainty forest elf dwells in the mossy rocks and woodland places of the alpine chains, alike on lime (in the Bernese Oberland) or on granite (in the Maritime Alps). In any case it makes no difficulty about growing finely in England, in any cool, deep, moist soil, whether calcareous or not, in a sheltered and shady position.

Atraphaxis form a small group of bushling Polygonads, tufted or ramping, with flowers of bright or paler pink in little bunches. But the race is purely Southern, and demands intense heat and drought on the rock-work, so that it cannot really be called suitable to our more temperate climate.

Aubrietia makes almost the only exception to the rule that prescribes true species for the rock-garden, rather than their improved or hybridised garden forms. And so complete an exception does it make, that there is now in cultivation really no room, except in the gardens of the most curious, for the original species out of which the gorgeous Aubrietias of general cultivation have developed, without losing an iota of their native grace and charm, but supplementing it with a splendour, hearty yet well-bred, far outshining anything that can be shown by most of their parents.

The species are : *A. canescens*, lilac ; *A. croatica*, violet blue ; *A. deltoidea*, violet (with variegated-leaved forms, green and "gold," green and "silver"—otherwise margined with white or with yellow ; *A. erubescens*, whitish ; *A. Hendersonii*, violet-reddish ; *A. Leichtlinii*, which still holds its head high even in these days of marvellous hybrids, for its flowers are very large and of a rich crimson-rose (it has been one of the most potent and valuable parents) ; *A. libanotica*, lilac ; *A. olympica*, dark purple ; *A. Pinardii*, reddish ; *A. tauricola*, lilac-violet to white, with an albino. And it must not be forgotten what a debt of gratitude we owe to these, not only for their glorious children, but also for their own beauty, even though it now be overshadowed, except in the case of *A. Leichtlinii* (perhaps itself a hybrid).

Of the hybrids there is no end ; every garden has its own named forms, and there is no expense more unprofitable than that of giving comparatively large sums for some newly-raised Aubrietia seedling, when in your own frame, from a packet of seed from some good garden strain, you could raise for yourself a whole stock containing several plants (at least), which will be quite as good as any pom-pously-named novelty. Of these the best are *A. Moerheimii*, a really lovely form, with nobly large and ample flowers of soft rose, which yields again the most beautiful big-flowered seedlings in tender shades of pink and lavender and rich violet ; *A.* Lavender itself, one of the very best, rather tufty and compact, with big well-filled crosses of the serenest moonlit lilac-lavender ; Fire King, a result of Leichtlinii, of brilliant colour, but sometimes a little thin and straggling in growth, inheriting that one fault of *A. Leichtlini's* ; Craven Gem, a good purple, always in bloom ; and, of other imperial violets, a long and ever-increasing strain—Pritchard's A 1, Mrs. Lloyd-Edwards', Wallace's, Doctor Mules, H. Marshall's, Potter's—in fact a named form for almost everybody who ever set eyes upon an Aubrietia. Not that one would disparage the splendour of the plants themselves, but they are dis-honoured by this reckless multiplicity of names. They glorify the garden in spring, in sheets of unimaginable violet and rose and lavender, such as will make *Pinardii* or *tauricola* give up the ghost and die ; but really it is not worth while to go on so lavishly naming every other seedling, where all are so good. One wants a special box of new adjectives to differentiate between the various purples named above, and ever-new ones go on arriving without end ; yet all are glorious, and the newest is always said to be the best, and proclaimed with loudest applause. It is indeed a wonder with how greedy a zeal this Levantine race, from Lebanon and Olympus and Asia, has adopted the English climate, when nothing, *a priori*, would have seemed so improbable as that they should prove hardy at all. In point of fact, they so little seem to crave for torrid sun-heat that they can hardly, if at all, be grown upon the Riviera ; while in our gardens —every back-yard seen from the train in spring bears witness to the ways of Aubrietia, of which every shoot stuck into the border will root, if it be a case of multiplying some special form ; while from a threepenny packet of seed hundreds of feet of desert rock-work may be made to blossom like the rose.

Azolla caroliniana is a minute water-weed, consisting of small, crowded crimpy leaves, like frizzled-up Marchantia fronds gone red ; they float upon the face of the waters, and look extremely pretty, especially after a shower, when the water-jewels lie sparkling among their crimpiness. But they also multiply at such an inordinate rate, every broken-off fragment forming a new plant in a day, and a new mat in a week, after the importunate habit of aquatics when they thrive at all, that there is very soon no coping with it, and the pond becomes one unbroken sheet of curly russet-red Marchantia, on to which misguided cats take jumps after their prey, supposing it to be solid ground. Fortunately, though ineradicable by man, it is more amenable to the displeasure of Heaven ; and, not being particularly hardy, is ultimately swept away by a winter of especial severity.

B

Ballota spinosa, the only member of the Horehound family to make any claim for admittance to the rock-garden, does not make that claim very effectually. It is a rare and rather ugly little spiny rarity with white flowers, which demands especial conditions of sun and drought and drainage, when, in point of fact, it is not worthy of a place in the garden at all, except for curiosity.

Banffya petraea. See under **Gypsophila transylvanica.**

Baptisia is a rather second-class rank group of North-American Leguminosae, not unlike upstanding glabrous Lupines. In cool soil

141

room may be found in the wild garden for *B. australis.* Spikes of blue, with a form *alba,* blooming in summer.

Barbaraea, the common yellow Winter-cress (*B. vulgaris*), is valued in borders on account of a deeply brilliant-yellow double form ; but there are some species more legitimately admissible to the choice rock-garden.

B. brachycarpa, though it only has the flowers of *B. vulgaris,* makes a neat and tiny clump not more than 2 or 3 inches high, about damp places and water-courses high in Phrygia and on the Bithynian Olympus.

B. rupicola is more important. It is a tidy and low-growing thing (though attaining to a foot, if drawn up in shade), forming a tap-root the first year, and then running from a knotty stock. It is an almost stemless plant, with very large golden-yellow flowers, and the leaves at the base of the tuft heart-shaped or egg-shaped. (From the mountains of Corsica—Incudine, Ciarnente, Fourche de Bavella, &c.)

Bartsia alpina, much as one may appreciate its stiff little spikes of dull metallic purple leaves and flowers, in the wetter, finer fields of the Alps or in favoured corners of English alpine meadows, especially when its spires of darkness are associated with the roseate sheets of *Primula farinosa,* is nevertheless not a friend to the garden. Like many of its close cousins in Scrophularineae—Gerardia, Castilleja, and Euphrasia, for instance—there is about it the taint of the parasitic, and the best, if not the only way, to have the Bartsia in cultivation will be to bring it down in a great sod from the mountain, with all its companions included ; and even in this case next year will probably find the Bartsia gone, and the whole garden possessed by some terrible weed imported in the Bartsia's clump.

Bellévália, a dainty little race, so close to Múscări and Hyacinthus as to be often submerged in one or the other. There are many species in the Levant of these small Hyacinths, and among these (choice for any wholesome sunny place, especially in company with equally select Daffodils, such as *N. triandrus calathinus* and *N. Bulbocodium monophyllus*) are : *B. leucophaea,* of pale colour, from Servia and South-east Russia ; *B. nervosa* (also *B. aleppica*), from 2 to 5 inches high, with azure bells, from the hot limestone hills of Aleppo ; *B. Heldreichii,* from the orchards of Pamphylia, about 3 inches tall, with flowers of intense violet-blue, packed in a close head on minute erect stems ; *B. azurea,* very like *Muscari pallens,* but with the characteristic bell of brilliant blue, wide and *unconstricted at the mouth* (the diagnosis of Bellevalia from Muscari), a treasure found especially near the lead-mines of the Cilician Taurus ; and *B. nivalis,* whose tight heads of blossom may be seen on their 3-inch stems, high up beside the snows of Tröodos and Hermon.

Bellidiastrum Michelii has hovered for a long time on the edge of Aster, and has even been accorded the name of *Aster Bellidiastrum*. Bellidiastrum, however, is by far the better name, for it holds much more of Bellis than of Aster. For this is the giant Daisy of moist places, rocks, and banks, in all the alpine woods—exactly, to the gardener's eye, like an exaggerated, lax, and tall version of *Bellis perennis*, with slack limp leaves and stems of often a foot high, with fine white flowers. It has no especial loveliness, but for memory's sake it may be given a happy place in some cool shady part of the rock-work.

Bellis.—Some rock-gardens entertain a large fat pink double Daisy called Alice, but when this and all its kind are gone to their own place, there will be room for the graceful *B. silvestris* of the Riviera— an exaggerated version of the common Daisy, with looser leaves, more toothed and upstanding, much taller and more gracious stems, often nearly a foot high, and much larger flowers, inclining to nod, and tinged and tipped with vivid crimson. Sandy soil and a cool place.

B. rotundifolia comes from Atlas and is a most delicate lovely little jewel, of minute tidy leafage, grey and soft and downy ; the flowers are dainty round daisies on upright stems. More generally cultivated is its variety *B. r. coerulescens*, in which the daisies are of a most subtle and diaphanous shade of pale lilac-blue, often almost evanescent into white. *B. rotundifolia* must have a very sheltered, warm, and perfectly-drained corner in the rock-garden if it is to prove permanent there ; but in any moraine it tends to become as much of a self-sowing weed as *B. perennis* itself.

Bellium rotundifolium seems also to be *B. minutum* (Urv.), under which name it is most usually offered and cultivated. It is a microscopic Daisyling with flowers white within and darkish purple without, and makes a lovely mass in some choice place. It comes from Greece and the Levant, *e.g.* rocks of Therasia and Euboea.

B. bellidioeides inhabits sandy sunny places of South France and Italy, and a patch of it may perhaps still be seen by one roadside mounting out of Cannes. It is exactly a miniature of *B. perennis*, throwing little runners, and spreading into a very pretty patch in open poor soil, well-drained and in full sun. (It is also called *B. droseraefolium*, Gou., and *B. nivale*, Regui.)

B. crassifolium is a most charming rarity from Corsica, making a wide sheet in some sheltered warm and well-drained place, with minute fat leaves, waxy and glossy, above which on stems of a couple of inches, appear the profuse and delightful little daisies.

Berardia subacaulis, a very rare and very frightful Composite, only found in wild and wholly stony places on the Alps of Dauphiné, with large round leaves, woolly and fat, and hardly any stem to the heads of inconspicuous flower.

Bérbĕris.—Though here be no place to deal critically with shrubs, it must yet be pointed out that many of the new Chinese Barberries are neat things, of the greatest possible beauty and charm for the right places of the bold rock-garden, and especially as centres of shelter for choice bulbs or woodland plants. Among these, of the larger and smaller sorts, are *B. concinna, B. dulcis, B. empetrifolia, B. Gaignepainii, B. Hookeri compacta, B. Jamesonii, B. sanguinea* (larger), *B. dictyophylla* (larger), all the dwarfer forms of *B. stenophylla* (as *B. s. diversifolia, gracilis,* and *Irwinii*), *B. subcaulialata* (larger), *B. Thunbergii minor, B. verruculosa, B. Wallichiana hypoleuca* (of gardens), *B. concinna,* and the most fine and lovely *B. Wilsonae.* These all are of the easiest culture in any soil ; they should have generous room for further development, especially such as *Wilsonae, sanguinea,* and the varieties of *stenophylla.* Their flowers, as a rule, are not less beautiful than the incandescent little scarlet plums that follow on *Wilsonae,* after blossoms like minute and delicate Maréchal Niel roses, delicately sweet.

Bergenia. See under **Saxifraga.**

Berkheya. See, if it is worth the trouble, under **Stobaea.**

Berteróa, a small cruciferous group, not to be included in Alyssum, because here the petals are cleft to the base, which never happens in true Alyssum. They are, however, the same in habit and look, for garden purposes, but a more or less biennial race, of scant value. The one most usual in cultivation is *A. incana,* a hoary plant, differing from true Alyssum also in having white flowers.

Betonica.—The Betonies are coarse kitchen-garden-looking herbs, of which even the best, such as *B. grandiflora* (with varieties *superba, alba,* and the dwarfer *rosea*) and *B. nivea,* are all best avoided in the rock-garden, where the silvered flannel leaves of some species may make a pretty mat, but the whorled spikes of labiate flowers in clumps near the top of a tallish stem have no attraction of elegance, and often, if "crimson," are crimson only by the horticultural courtesy which thus avoids crude mention of the magenta therein too often predominating.

Betula nana, the dwarf birch of the northern and Arctic regions, makes a fine and lacy little bush for the rock-garden, not more than a yard high at the most, and rather more across, extremely dainty with its long straightish sprays, and small oval scalloped foliage.

Bidens, in a race of Composites almost uniformly coarse and without charm, supplies us with one lovely species in *B. dahlioeides*, from the Mexican highlands, which must be planted in warm, sheltered places, not too dry, in particularly poor starvation-soil, in full sun. Thus it will prove hardy, and show its full grace, without becoming lush and soft, or attaining unpleasing elevations of 2 feet or so. Properly used and kept strung up by Spartan treatment, it makes only a basal tuft of unevenly-gashed leaves, from which in profusion spring the perfectly naked stems, each carrying a single large pink or mauve-pale flower like that of a Cosmos. Except in specially warm gardens it would be better, at all events while the plant is rare, to store its tubers in winter like a Dahlia's, taking care that they are not allowed to get parched or shrivelled. It should be a most beautiful thing if starved.

Biebersteinia forms a beautiful little family of Geraniads, in many ways more suggestive in look of the finest cluster-headed Polemoniums. They need careful culture in well-drained sunny poor soil, or in the moraine. They make almost bulbiform many-headed stocks, with leaves like those of a closely packed and fine Erodium, and the flowers, of pink or cream or yellow, are gathered into bunches at the top of stems that vary from one foot to two and a half in *B. Orphánĭdis*, to a bare 6 inches in *B. odora*. This last should, indeed, besides its sweetness, be one of the most useful as well as the most charming of the lot, for it occurs by springs in the Altai, and ranges away thence into Tibet, so that its hardiness ought not to admit of doubt. *B. Orphanĭdis* is the only species ever seen in cultivation, and that too rarely. It is found in stony glens of Greece and the Levant, especially in the alpine region of Kyllene, the foliage being particularly like that of an Erodium, and the rose-pink flowers in a dense cluster. *B. heterostēmon*, from China, has smaller blossoms, and *B. multifida* is yet another species that we await.

Biscutella is a race of biennial Crucifers, of which the only one here fit for comment is the common *B. laevigata* of the upper alpine turf and stony places—a graceful thing about a foot high, with hoary-grey leaves and very loose spraying showers of pale golden yellow. This, however, is no less biennial than the rest, even if old intimacy induce the gardener to give it a place. *B. lucida*, from the Southern ranges, differs chiefly in having the foliage dark-green and glossy.

Bletia. See under **Orchidaceae,** where all of the race are gathered together, with the exception of Cypripedium.

Boenninghausenia albiflora offers perhaps the finest example of what a plant's name should not be. They who imposed this dismal cacophony on the " White Rue " have incurred a heavy responsibility in having so long kept out of the garden one of its most daintily beautiful beauties. For who is going to show off Boenninghausenia, or run the risk of having to masticate such a mouthful, in case some enthusiastic inquirer asks what that delicate shower of whiteness may be called ? We justly burke the word as being an indecency ; and with the word we have also submitted to the loss of the plant. But the White Rue can be omitted no longer ; it is a thing so fantastically charming, very dainty in habit, and in its glaucous-grey leafage and fat leaflets almost suggesting some of the Coronillas. It grows about a foot or 18 inches high, with sprays of the most ravishing small flowers, pure snow-white, all through the later summer. Its range is from moderate elevations of 4000 to 8000 feet, from Marri to Sikkim, and thence through those marvellous mountains of Asia across into Japan. In cultivation it is accordingly perfectly hardy, and needs no more special treatment than the Thalictrum on whose habit it so refines.

Boltonia, big border plants like very floriferous Asters, of which *B. asteroeides*, or *B. glastifolia*, has flowers white with tinges of pink and purple, while *B. latisquama*, of the same habit, is more purplish ; it is often confused, however, with *Diplostephium amygdalinum*, whose other name is *Aster umbellatus*.

Bongardia Rauwolfii is a curious small Berberidead from the clayey heavy hot fields of the Levant, with a knubbly flattened sort of bulb, and finely-feathered basal leaves, often reddened as they lie on the ground. Then from the bulb there springs a naked stem of 8 or 10 inches, with hanging blossoms of golden yellow. This pretty curiosity must have light and sandy soil, perfectly drained, yet with sufficiency of water in spring, in some corner of sun and shelter. The same treatment should be followed for such of the closely-related **Leontice** as come from the Levant—*L. leontopetalum, L. Smirnowii, Eversmannii, minor, Vesicaria,* &c.—all of the same interesting habit, with flowers of varying colour, *L. altaica* being taken by some as a synonym of *Bongardia*, and **Caulophyllum** being of the same kind.

Borrāgo.—The Borrages, as a rule, are coarse and inadmissible, and for *B. orientalis*, this must now be looked for under **Psilostēmon ;** but *B. laxiflora* is a valuable species from Corsica, forming the usual basal tuft, indeed, of coarse and bristly leaves, but then emitting long prostrate stems that are set, the whole summer through, with large upturned stars of a delicate and very pale clear azure. This plant should have, however, only the poorest soil, in the fullest sun ; as rich feeding dulls the edge of its brilliance, and turns its thoughts rather to leaf than to flower. It is not a long-lived plant, but sows itself profusely.

Bottionaea thysantoeides is a Liliaceous thing from Chile, not specially hardy or attractive. When well-grown it attains to nearly 2 feet, with quite narrow blue-green leaves, and loose showers of hairy narrow-rayed nodding stars of greenish-white. (*Trichopetalum gracile.*)

Boykinia, a useful rather than choice race, for cool damp shady places by water, very closely allied to Saxifraga. They form masses of handsome leafage, roundish kidney-shaped, and fingered into five to seven fat lobes; well above these in the summer shoot the many leafy stems some 2 feet in height, carrying wide heads of cream-white flowers, which, though described by various authorities rather contemptuously as "small," are yet by no means without a certain amplitude and solidity of effect, and make quite a handsome show upon good clumps. The species to be reckoned with, all being pretty much alike, are *B. aconitifolia, major, occidentalis*, and *minor*.

Brasenia peltata is a North-American Aquatic of accepted hardiness for shallow waters, on the surface of which float its shield-like leaves, with fringed brown-purple blooms in July and August.

Brassica, though in their large clan there are some striking huge weeds, offer the rock-garden no comely or congruous Cabbage, unless it be the dwarf and golden-flowered *B. repanda* from Southern Europe, which is only some 8 inches in stature; while *B. Richeri* from the Eastern ranges has paler blossoms, and leaves of a glaucous blue-green.

Braya, a race of worthless little alpine cruciferous weeds, some of them of the most merciful rarity.

Brickellia grandiflora, sometimes offered from America in terms of the most passionate laudation, proves a thoroughly coarse and ugly Composite, in the line of Eupatorium, with showers of hanging tasselled heads in dim and dowdy greenish colours.

Brodiaea, a beautiful race of American bulbs, many of them summer-blooming, some of them quite dwarf and choice and brilliant, with ample cups of intense violet, some of them tall and splendid, with wide sprayed heads of blue, and at least one of them, if allowed to remain in the family, a scarlet-belled climber. They all repay culture in light soil in sun; on heavy ground and in wet-wintered climates they have a tendency to die out in a year or two, but in more favoured and home-like districts they make themselves correspondingly at home, and even seed themselves. Full lists and adequate descriptions of the best and most generally useful species will be found in any good and adequate catalogue of bulbs, such as that of Van Tubergen.

Bruckenthalia spiculifolia is, to all gardening intents and purposes, a most dainty and charming miniature of the common Ling. It is a plant of central Europe, rejoicing in the usual heathy conditions, and sheeting the mountains of Bulgaria in its mats of close brilliant green fur. It should make a fine subject among which to poke choice bulbs of medium growth.

Brunella is now the accepted spelling for what used to be Prunella, our own native Self-heal, of which *B. grandiflora* and *B. pyrenaica* are immensely glorified versions, and yet still possess that readiness of *B. vulgaris* to sow tiny seedlings among the choicest treasures, out of which their long tenacious roots can only be tugged with the utmost difficulty and disturbance. Others are *B. incisa*, and a form *Webbiana*, with flowers of blue-violet, varying to a pink development called *rosea ;* with a variety *alba*, also, to every form or species.

Bryanthus has now gone wholly into **Menziesia,** *q.v.* We may, however, keep under this name that beautiful small heath called *B. erectus*, which is traditionally a hybrid between Rhodothamnus and Kalmia. It is in habit a neat Bryanthus, with erect shoots well clothed in fine green yew-like foliage ; and then large salver-shaped flowers of pink in clusters at the top of the 6- or 8-inch shoots. It answers to any fair heathy treatment, but is not invariably prone to Methusaleh's longevity.

B. Breweri. See under **Menziesia.**

Bulbinella Hookeri is a stout little asphodeloid species for the bog, which has long been in cultivation under the name of *Chrysobactron*—forming tufts of lax green foliage, with spikes in summer, about a foot high, or more, of golden-yellow stars. But we shall have an infinitely finer thing when we have acquired *B. Rossii* from the Antarctic Islands, whose slopes it gilds with its enormous masses, and its stalwart 4-foot spikes of dense blossom, like some more serried and brilliant Eremurus. The climate in the Auckland and Campbell group being more odious and inclement by far than ours, many of the plants that come from thence should certainly appreciate the change, and prove robust and hardy. The only delay about their introduction is that the islands are so far away that no one ever goes there.

Bulbocodium vernum is a pleasant cousin to autumn Crocus that is not a Crocus, nor even a Colchicum, and does not bloom in autumn. It is in earliest spring, high on the flanks of the Alps, that you will see its narrow strap-rayed stars of magenta-lilac peering up through the bare earth in long ragged cups round the patches of melting snow. It is not till afterwards that the leaves appear ; and, indeed, the whole growth is quite close in habit to Colchicum, and answers moderately well to the same cultivation.

Buphthalmum, with **Telekia,** form a group of golden-sunned Composites near Erigeron. Of these *B. grandiflorum* and *B. speciosum* (Telekia) are handsome rank upstanding things of merit for show in rough border or wild places. *B. speciosissimum* (Telekia), so alluringly named, is a rare plant from limestone crevices high up in the sheer cliffs of the Lombard mountains far above the Lakes. But, though a fine stout species, it is not worthy either of its name or of its habitat—a rather coarse thing, very leafy with long soft oval leaves, that dwarf and dim the glory of the enormous golden-rayed flowers that crown its foot-high stems. None the less it is a notable beauty, only to call it "the extremely beautiful" is to overload the market, and provoke a reaction of disappointment against its charm, which thus undergoes an unmerited slump. It is of the easiest culture in any sunny rock-garden.

Bupleurum, a curious and large family of Umbelliferae, not remote (in their unlikeness to the rest) from Astrantia ; but here the clumps are of much neater habit and oval-oblong leafage, with the star-forming bracts of the flowers in shades of greeny gold. There are several pretty alpine species, none of them appearing really robust in cultivation. They should all be tried in light sunny soil or stony peat-mixture, in crevices and in the moraine. Among the best are *B. graminifolium*, a branching grower, with very narrow smooth grassy foliage and golden showers of stars all through the summer ; *B. stellatum* has fewer flowers with broader bracts ; *A. ranunculoeides* is a variable type, which ought more properly to be called *B. baldense*, with a variety *olympicum*. This, at its best, is the prettiest of all, and the only one worth cosseting ; a neat small thing, with many stems and loose heads of greeny-gold stars, not more than 2 or 3 inches high, in hearty clustered tufts, with short narrow foliage. There are many other species, none of conspicuous merit.

Butŏmus umbellatus, the common Flowering-rush of our canal-banks, is a valuable Aquatic for the wet places or shallows of the water garden, with its jungles of lax keeled leaves about 2 feet high, and its yet taller stems carrying a loose erect head of pale mauve-pink starry cups. Like most aquatics, it will grow almost too well.

C

Cacalia makes up a group of American Composites which as a rule are singularly useless and unpleasing weeds. The one interesting species of which we hear is *C. calva*, a most curious plant having exactly the port and foliage of a very finely-cut-leaved *Anemone narcissiflora*, and producing also white flowers in umbels of pretty much the same appearance. *C. calva* is an alpine from the high mountains of Mexico, and should be hardy in a warm, well-drained, and sheltered place, with perhaps a little protection if the winter proves especially raw and cold. The rest of the Cacalias come indistinguishably close under Senecio, in which they are often included; and have all the faults of that huge and often hideous race.

Caccinia, a race of Borrages from the mountains of Persia, delighting in hot sandy soil. *C. glauca* has notably attractive blue-grey oval foliage, fat and metallic, set with bristles; and long flopping stems beset with stars of violet blue flowers that make a fine harmony with the leaves, as they pass through their different shades of purple towards pink. Even more beautiful, and perhaps more certainly hardy, might prove *C. strigosa*, which has the same habit, but longer flowers of a very intense azure; while *C. Rauwolfii* has narrower foliage, and blossoms of a purer blue. All the species have the same alluring fat glaucous foliage, and all are to be raised from seed. *C. Kotschyi* is yet another.

Cachrys, an uninteresting fine-leaved family of small Umbellifers, after the fashion and with the needs of Athamanta.

Calamintha now shows a tendency to retreat under the shadow of Satureja, but the gardener may still have occasion, under its older name, to order the great alpine Calaminth, which makes so splendid a show in July and August, in a weakly ascending mass of 6- or 8-inch stems, each ending in violet and white-lipped flowers. Very much more choice and delightful, however, is *C. grandiflora*, a variety of the last, far more splendid in size and colour of blossom, and rather more decumbent in habit; it may be seen in violet sheets on the roadside rocks at the top of the Mont Cenis Pass, and answers easily to the same quite ordinary treatment that suits its type.

Calandrinia, a family of North-American Portulacas, of which only about two hover on the edge of being satisfactory in the rock-gardens of England, and those only if kept in very poor soil, dry and pebbly, in the fullest exposure to sun and nothing else. These are:

C. pygmaea, by far the more valuable species—a minute rock plant, with a rosette of narrow fleshy leaves hugging the ground, and purplish-crimson silky flowers, usually by themselves on a naked stem of some 2 inches. This is also the hardier, but unfortunately also the rarer. (The family stands close akin to Lewisia.)

C. umbellata is common in cultivation, growing about 6 inches high, with a loose umbel of repulsively aniline crimson blossoms, satiny and rich. These both are best raised from seed.

Calceolaria has hardly yet begun to arrive. This gorgeous family belongs to South America, and occupies all the mountainous backbone of the Andes, extending into the Antarctic Islands far down in the inclement South. And so many are the alpine members of the race, too, that it is impossible but that many of them shall prove as hardy as they are beautiful. But at present the average garden thinks itself rather advanced and adventurous if it admits the two well-known species—though these two are both as hearty and vigorous as dandelions. (See also *Jovellana*.)

C. Darwinii has the habit of *C. polyrrhiza*—that is, it forms a rampant spreading mat, from which spring fine stems, branching from a pair of leaves near its base, into twin peduncles long and delicate of 5 inches or so, each carrying one solitary flower, with an enormous flattened triangular bag of a yellow lip, spotted with chestnut just by the rim. This is an Antarctic plant, almost wholly smooth, which should prove a glorious treasure when at last introduced successfully.

C. Fothergillii is a creeping species with hairy little leaves, rounded, spoon-shaped, and opposite each other at the base of the stems, which rise to some 3 or 4 inches, each carrying one flat-bagged yellow flower spotted with red or violet. This inhabits cold exposed places in the cold exposed Falkland Islands, and ought to find an English garden a Capua. It is impossible to say more for the treatment of these almost untried treasures, than that they will probably enjoy a deep, cool, and rather moist soil, preferentially of a peaty complexion, perfectly well-drained, and with so ample an allowance of sharp stones that the bed will almost take on the aspect of a moraine—which precise conditions, indeed, some of the species affect in nature. But very likely none of these precautions will prove necessary, any more than for *C. plantaginea*.

C. falklandica is like a woodier *C. uniflora*, but has a more diffuse habit, longer foliage, and flowers dotted with purple.

C. glacialis, by its mere name, makes the heart of the gardener leap up in anticipation. It is found in exactly the preferred situations of *Ranunculus glacialis*, beside the mountain-lakes of Potosi at snow-level of Quebrada in the Bolivian Andes. Here it forms the most charming of neat tufts, emitting a profuse display of brilliant golden bags on fine single stems from amid the nest of leafage.

C. Mathewsii haunts the Andes of Ayacucho, between 10,000 to 11,000 feet, and is a leafy minutely small tuffet barely half an inch high, with stems of some 2 to 5 inches, each carrying one noble golden flower, spotted with purple.

C. mendocina makes fleshy rosettes of almost round fleshy leaves, pointed, hairy, and as broad as they are long, in the Alps of Chile. The naked stems are about 3 inches tall, and on each unfolds an ample round-bellied blossom of golden yellow.

C. plantaginea, from the cold wet lands of Tierra del Fuego and arid Patagonia, is now revelling in our kindlier conditions—a plant of hearty splendour and very leafy, with broad shining corrugated foliage, and loose branching showers of bloom in the later summer on stems about a foot or 18 inches tall. It is absolutely hardy in any decent garden soil or situation, as might be expected, and, though not so exquisite for the rock-garden as the one-flowered species, is a most notable addition, whose only fault is that slugs sometimes spoil the contour of its rich foliage, by nibbling it into untidiness.

C. polyrrhiza is much neater, and quite invaluable for low damp soil on the edge of the bog. Here it runs densely, forming in no time enormous mats of low serried leafage, increasing with insatiable vigour; and then sends up its fine single stems, rather earlier than the last, in most generous profusion. Each stem is about 6 or 8 inches high, naked, and carrying one, or a very few, fine round-bagged yellow slippers—an indispensable and indestructible charmer.

C. scapiflora has the whole habit of *C. mendocina*, with bare stems of greater length attaining some 6 inches, and each carrying a yellow purple-dotted pouch much smaller than in *C. Mathewsii*. It is found in the rocks of high-alpine regions, at some 13,000 to 14,000 feet, in the Andes of Lima, &c.

C. umbellata will rejoice us in a new style, for this is a Peruvian alpine for hot and sunny faces, producing heads of slippers that are not yellow as in the others, but rosy-red.

C. uniflora is found at the height of 3000 feet in the moraines or shingle-slopes of South Patagonia. It forms almost cushiony masses and sends up fine stems of 2 or 4 inches, each carrying one or two large flowers of pure yellow, unspotted and undefiled.

Nor need it be thought that this list even begins to tap the promised strength of Calceolaria, from the highest alpine regions of South America. Even of the neat and appropriate low-growing species, with single flowers and cushioned habit, these are only a little foretaste to whet the appetite—are there not also *C. lepidota, C. Pritchardii, C. nudicaulis,* with many another ; to say nothing of the larger and stouter species after the decorative habit of *C. plantaginea ?*

Calla Aethiopica, the famous Arum Lily of the Cape, is perfectly hardy in rich soil at the bottom of some 18 inches to 2 feet of water. If its blossoms lose a little in size, they gain incalculably in effect, from thus being seen in lavish profusion out of doors from August onwards. *C. palustris* is a tiny species, not by any means akin to the last in splendid elegance and purity—a little ramper for mud-flats and submerged edges of the bog, with small fat heart-shaped leaves along the runners, and small flowers of a greening white.

Callianthemum, with one exception, brings us back into our own Alps. For this is the race of Ranunculads with fat and ferny foliage, which so long has been included in Ranunculus itself. They are plants of the middle alpine regions, in moist places or in alpine turf ; and in cultivation enjoy any good and open soil with sufficiency of well-drained moisture in flowering time—that is, from spring into the early days of summer. In due course of time they can be divided, if any one be sacrilegious enough to spoil an old-established tuft ; but are best collected straight from their hills, or raised from seed, if such can be got, which is rare ; or raised, which is rarer still.

C. anemonoeides (*Ranunculus anemonoeides*) is confined entirely to the Eastern Alps of upper and lower Austria, where it is found usually among damp rocks in the zone of the pine-woods, at about 3000 feet at the most, but usually lower. It is a beautiful thing of easy culture and increase ; in early spring, before the leaves, and almost stemless, appear a number of very large flowers of pearly or pinky white, like many-rayed single Chrysanthemums. Then the stems elongate, and the long leaves, finely divided into fattish lobes, fattish in texture, and of a soft grey-green, begin to develop into ample low-lying masses, as the fruiting stems shoot out or up.

C. cashmirianum is the representative of Callianthemum in the former cradle of the race. For the family is of enormous antiquity, and, like the Perfect Law, has had its cradle in the mountains of Asia ; and, like the Perfect Law again, has died from the centre of its distribution, and is now found scattered over the world, in patches remote from each other, each species occupying some range quite locally, and removed by hundreds or thousands of miles from the nearest realm of its next relation. *C. cashmirianum,* then, still dwells at upper elevations in the damp places of Sikkim, a cousin to the last, with the same blue-grey foliage, with the lobules fat and almost rounded.

C. coriandrifolium is *Callianthemum rutaefolium* or *Ranunculus rutaefolius*, by far the commonest, but also the least attractive of its race, having a wide but very scattered distribution from the Pyrenees (where it is extremely rare) away, at intervals through all the alpine chains, as far as Transylvania and Bosnia, having three special bunches of abundance—on the Graians and Swiss-Italian borders about the lower Engadine ; then, all along the Hohe Tauern and Ziller-thaler ranges and down into the Dolomites ; and now a big bare space is left on the map, until the plant reappears at last in a long caterpillar-curve of distribution, from the Hungarian Carpathians through Roumania and Transylvania down to Bosnia. It is a species of the alpine turf, and may be seen very abundant in places on the Mont Cenis, on the Pasterze moor above Heiligenblut, on the Schlern, and on many other beautiful and trodden slopes—a tuft of rather rank development, with most ample coriandrous foliage, handsome, fat and ferny, and flower-stems unfolded at the same time, rather low, and branching into one or two foot-stalks, each carrying a typical daisy of the family (rather inadequate to the lush foliage), though here the resemblance is rather to Camomile than to Chrysanthemum, the rays being fewer, broader, and shorter, of a cold dead white, still further chilled by the eye of the blossom, which has a greenish-yellow note. To keep it starved, however, so that at home this dispro-portion of leaf to blossom should not be felt, it is better to grow *C. coriandrifolium* not in the fat kitchen-garden soil that it loves, but in a poor stony mixture akin to moraine.

C. Kernerianum, Freyn, is the strangest and loneliest of the race—a remote thrown-off colony from *C. anemonoeides*, which in the whole world is only to be seen in the grassy turf along the summit ridges of Monte Baldo (with here and there a rare occurrence in Judicaria), where, however, it makes a lavish carpet in company with *Geranium argenteum, Gentiana vulgaris, Ranunculus alpester,* Edelweiss, and the Primulas *spectabilis* and *Auricula*. It was long held a mere variety of *C. ane-monoeides*, which it greatly resembles, but is a much finer, frailer, smaller thing altogether, not forming into a clump, and hugging the ground closely not only with the very beautiful, fringier, blue-grey fern-fronds of its foliage, but also with the large single flowers of lilac-white. In cultivation it is as easy as the rest, though far more select and exquisite, even if no more beautiful ; and for a select place accordingly in the underground-watered bed or well-soiled moraine mixture, among the choicest treasures. A particularly fine photo-graph from Edinburgh, figured in 1913, and claiming to represent *C. anemonoeides*, was clearly in reality a remarkable specimen of this much rarer species. (See also Appendix.)

Callirrhoë, a group of trailing Mallows, of indifferently hardy temper, even in hot and sandy soils, with rapidly evanescent flowers of rather aniline tone. The best and most generally known is *C. involucrata*, with long loose branches, five-fingered foliage, and silky cups of a purplish lilac ; rather better, because more compact, is its variety, *C. lineariloba*, with roots that plunge to a great depth, and flowers of purplish colours and a white base.

Callixĕnē (including *Luzuriaga*). *C. polyphylla* (*Luzuriaga radicans*) is the best of a small group of almost shrubby Liliaceous plants from the far Southern hemisphere, where, in the woodland, *C. polyphylla* forms neat mats of glossy foliage not unlike that of some quite minute and broad-leaved creeping Box or Ruscus, from which in time emerge white flowers like Lilies of the Valley, hanging from the axils. It can twine and attain to a couple of feet, but in gardens is more usually seen small and nestling to the ground. This species belongs to Chile, and is soundly hardy, though not specially easy to grow, liking damp woodland soil in the protection of dense shade. Others among the lesser species are *C. drymophylla* from Tasmania, *C. parviflora* from New Zealand, and *C. marginata*, which is very abundant and deliciously sweet-scented in the Falklands ; all, if acquired, for the same treatment. The last might be the easiest.

Calochortus ?—No ! They are not fitted for general outdoor culture in England ; and those bold heroes who must needs decorate their rock-gardens with the exquisite but precarious beauty of the Mariposas, will find them fully set forth and described in catalogues, which even have so lively a sense of their difficulty that they actually give directions for their culture, though in terms of hope more warm than experience warrants. The race is vast and lovely, and apparently in nature fitted for every unpleasant diversity of soil, whether in bog-land, heavy and hard, or in the lightest of hot sands. None the less the utmost they will do in England (except in the gardens of the specially favoured) is to arise just once from their elaborate beds, wave at the world their painted waxen heads and delicate fringes, and then go on to join the Oncocyclus Irids in a better land.

Caltha.—Besides our native Marsh Marigold, the Water-buttercups offer some other pleasant species for the decoration of the bog.

C. dioneaefolia makes deep and dense tuffets of minute oval leaves, fat and dark green, deeply shining, clustered on a thick trunk. They exactly resemble those of Dionaea in miniature, with the fringed overlapping lobes at the end. This most curious attractive rarity is abundant in Tierra del Fuego, where it carpets the cold ground and illuminates the darkness with its small pale stars of yellow.

C. leptosepala. See *C. rotundifolia.*

C. natans is a pretty delicate North-American species, which floats upon the surface of shallow ponds, with little flowers of pinky-white.

C. Novae Zelandiae grows in the same sods with *Ranunculus Lyallii*, and often arrives unexpectedly in the masses of its neighbour, and in better condition. It is a small delightful plant, in growth at present as light as a Ficaria, with heart-shaped glossy leaves very deeply lobed and with the lobes turned up against the stems, on stalks of 6 inches or so. The blossoms are borne each by itself ; they are about an inch and a half across, pale yellow, and sweetly scented. It should have a choice cool place, being a dainty neat thing of tuberous habit.

C. polypetala is by far the best, despite the absurdity of this ignorant name for a race that has no petals at all, but only those gleaming golden sepals that take their place. *C. polypetala* is a vast ramping Aquatic, preferring to grow in shallow water, across which it sends its flopping branches to root again, while the main tuft is tossing high its sprays of enormous blossoms that leave poor *C. palustris* utterly eclipsed. None the less, it is a ramper that can soon become a weed ; and modest gardens will always have place for *C. palustris* (which, when all is said and done, has bigger flowers in proportion, and of a more brilliant golden flame, especially in the variety called Tyerman's, which is much neater than the type in its tuft, and with larger blooms in an even brighter colour). *C. polypetala* comes from the Alps of Armenia, Pontus, North Persia, &c. ; there is a romantic legend that it was for long only known in Europe in the ponds of the Vatican, whence the old Pope refused to let it go forth from that sacred seclusion into an heretic though horticultural world ; but that one day some hero adventured thither on the high quest, enshrouded in a bevy of aunts, whom he discharged upon the custodians to hold them in talk, while he himself hooked out some fragments of the Caltha with his umbrella. However this may be (and tales of heroism are too rare to die, their essential truth being found in their quality rather than in any cold historic accuracy they may happen to possess) —the Caltha is a noble plant, well worthy of a papal pool, but by no means distinguishing between the waters of truth and those of any humbler and heretical horticulturist.

C. rotundifolia (*C. leptosepala*) is a North-American species, also for a cool place, rather wet. It makes a tidy tuft of upspringing dark foliage, amid which in summer appear the flowers, like bluish-white celandines, each borne on a single stem.

C. sagittata carpets the wide moors of the Falklands, forming very dense mats of its clumps, with yellow fragrant flowers, whose yellow is edged with purple, and their segments protracted into a long tail, which has earned it its secondary name of *C. appendiculata*. It should, when acquired, have the treatment of *C. dioneaefolia*, in a choice corner of moist ground.

Campanŭla.—This august race is so vast and complicated that the best thing is to plunge into it at once and go through its serried ranks with care, seeing the huge confusion that there reigns, and the necessity of weeding the many beautiful sheep from the many goats in the family. Treatment must be understood, in all cases without special note, to imply perfectly ordinary soil for the large-growing species : for the choicer alpines choose crevices or banks of well-made light limy (almost invariably) soil in the rock-work or in the moraine in open positions ; while for the white woolly-leaved Levantines hot dry chinks and moraines and sheltered sunny places in deep and light and stony soil are indicated, with protection in raw climates against winter wet. All can be profusely raised from seed, though many can, with equal precision and far greater rapidity, be multiplied by division. And all have the very special advantage (not by any means generally realised or acted on with sufficient liveliness of gratitude) of blooming in late summer, when the rock-garden is too often lamenting its early show in a green desolation. The *R.H.S. Journal* for June 1907 contains a valuable paper on this race by the late Col. Beddome, though naturally it allows of amplification, and in some cases of correction, and in others the suggestion of a different verdict. In the following list I name none but perennials or beautiful biennials and monocarpics, with exceptions made in the case of a few specially meritorious annuals. And for the future it may be taken that almost any Campanula not included in this résumé may prove a weed or an annual or both, unless a special description guarantees its novelty and its beauty.

C. abietina, a well-known plant in gardens by now, is found in the stony summit-ridges of Peristeri, about Janina, and so forth. It forms wide mats, made up of narrow-leaved brilliant green rosettes packed together, from which rise very fine stems of a foot or so, carrying wide-open solid stars of violet, closely resembling those of *C. patula*, with which this much dwarfer and perennial species has been confused. But though perennial, indeed, it requires frequent division in the garden if its wide mats are not to exhaust themselves and die out. It is a beautiful species, and thrives in light and stony ground.

C. acuminata = *C. americana*.

CAMPANULA.

C. acutangula = *C. arvatica*, *q.v.*

C. Adamii (Willd.) = *C. lasiocarpa*.

C. Adamii (Bieb.) = *C. bellidifolia*.

C. adscendens is a rather misty Siberian Campanula, akin to *C. uniflora*, or possibly only a variety of *C. rotundifolia*.

C. adsurgens, from heathy places in Galicia, throws up a number of fine, finely downy stems, flopping or trying to stand as erect as their frailness will allow. They are about a foot high, nearly without branches and rather leafy, carrying a number of nodding pale-blue flowers, downy outside and with a protruding style. The lower leaves are heart-shaped, on long foot-stalks, the upper ones smaller and narrower. The root is annual or biennial.

C. aeizoon also is but a biennial, but truly strange and striking. High in the sheer cliff-crevices of Parnassus it makes great smooth-leaved rosettes exactly like those of *Saxifraga longifolia*, from which comes a dense thyrsus of wide pale-blue flowers like those of our own harebell, large and lovely. And then—death ; but abundant seed.

C. affinis may possibly be only a variety of *C. speciosa*, from which it differs in carrying its blooms erect, in many undivided stems that spring to as much as nearly 4 feet in height ; the leaves are much more finely scalloped than in the other, and the erect bells are cleft to the middle, *with a projecting style*, carried in long cylindrical racemes and with *broad segments to the calyx, half the length of the flower*. This beautiful ample plant is found in the rocky mountain-woods of Eastern Spain, but its claim to be a species truly distinct from *C. speciosa* is not admitted by all, though on the description undeniable. Like the other it is probably monocarpous rather than perennial.

C. aggregata, a coarse and worthless form of *C. glomerata*.

C. "alaskana." See under *C. rotundifolia*.

C. alata, a large and handsome leafy thing from Algiers, in the way of *C. peregrina*.

C. alliariaefolia, another handsome but large and leafy species from the Caucasus, often seeding itself into a nuisance. It has big heart-shaped flannelly leaves, and tall branching stems producing a profusion of comparatively small cream-white bells.

C. Allionii (Vill.) is *C. alpestris*, All., *q.v.*

C. alpestris is an old friend, now restored to a yet older name. For this is *C. Allionii* of all our gardens and lists. (*C. Allionii*, Vill., 1779, but swept out by the prior name *C. alpestris* of Allioni himself, 1755.) This glorious species, running about everywhere among the stones, and sending up in August, above its tufts of very narrow grey or greying hairy leaves, those immense flowers like Canterbury bells, scattered haphazard across the arid expanses of the lower alpine shingles, where it is at home, is one of the garden problems completely solved by the moraine. Before that invention *C. alpestris* was one of the hardest of alpine Campanulas, and got a notorious name ; but now, in the moraine, it has turned one of the easiest, and even begins to think about becoming a weed. In cultivation it blooms, too, much earlier than on its own hills, and is usually over by mid-June. In nature it ranges through the Graian, Cottian, and Maritime districts, occurring always in rocky stony ground, and often among rough grasses and weeds, at elevations not necessarily high-alpine. Indeed, the plant does not usually climb to the upmost shingles where *Viola cenisia* is at home with the white buttercups ; its favoured places are in lower and harder, more earth-bound slopes of stone, where its huge tap goes plunging deep, and its branches wander round far and wide, sending up tufts of leafage at their end when the fancy takes them. It is by no means true that *C. alpestris* says "all or nothing" when you go to collect it ; for the smallest runner, if inserted carefully into the sand-bed, and kept reasonably moist, will make a sound-rooted youngling in about a month's time. On various hills the type varies greatly, unlike the others of the high-alpine group (to which indeed it does not belong, but is much more closely akin to some of the noble dwarf single-flowered Bells of the Levant). On the Mont Cenis the prevalent form, for instance, has very narrow foliage, almost silvery-grey in effect, and the flowers are usually rather small and pinched and pale. Broad foliage as a rule spells amplitude of bell ; in the Cottians and the Maritimes occur forms with much wider softer foliage of bright green, often waved and curly, whose stemless stems carry immense solid ample flowers of the most gorgeous satiny purple. These forms, too, are as a rule of much freer habit and more rapid increase. All alike are in common cultivation, but the broad-leaved splendour was that sent out by Backhouse in former days, which has sometimes, therefore, seemed to dispossess the narrow-leaved grey squin of later collectors. Finally, though *C. alpestris* is in nature so passionate a cleaver to the non-calcareous ranges, it is by no means certain that in cultivation this fact is not more of a general hint than a rigid prescription. In many gardens it is already beginning to develop something not unlike a fancy for lime ; and though such guidances of nature give good general help at starting with a new species, it never does to adopt and insist upon them as laws of the Medes and Persians. "Souvent plante varie, bien fol est qui s'y fie" to the absolute dogmatic rules laid down by those in whom experience has not bred a knowledge of the facts.

CAMPANULA.

C. alpina in a different style is quite as beautiful as *C. alpestris*. It is a small taprooting species from the high turf of the Styrian lime-stones, where in the miles of moorland filled with *Primula Clusiana* and sheeted in the carpets of *P. minima*, may everywhere be seen its neat single rosette of narrow bright-green glossy leaves, delicately scalloped at the edge. From this, in June, the plant sends up at the side of the clump a stout short spike, on which the big hairy bells of a very clear pale or dark electric blue are carried on foot-stalks so long as to give the effect of a graceful fountain of blossom. The plant varies most curiously, though not so much, like *C. alpestris*, in its flower. For while the typical form is almost wholly hairless, lucent, glossy, and bright-green, with only a fringe of hair, at times, to the leaf, yet in many cases the whole growth is so wrapped in wool as to have a grey and almost fluffy look. In cultivation *C. alpina* is as easy as possible, but, being only a taproot and never spreading from the one rosette or tuft of rosettes, it must have only the choicest place, in light rich loam, very deep, with plenty of sun, plenty of water, and plenty of stone. It is not by any means a biennial, as is some-times said ; but occasionally flowers so profusely as to exhaust the resources of its taproot and die. Slugs, again, are a yet more frequent cause of death, nibbling away the entire rosette in a night till nothing but the naked stump is left. Like most of these species, it appreciates abundance of lime.

C. altaica (L. and DC.) = *C. pilosa.*

C. altaica (Led.) = *C. Stevenii.*

C. amabilis = *C. phyctidocalyx.*

C. americana (*C. obliqua*) is coarse, rank, and worthless.

C. anchusiflora is a smallish thing akin to *C. orphanidea*, softly grey-hairy, from the sea-rocks of the Aegean ; it has leafy stems, and the lower leaves are lyrate with all their lobes scalloped, the end one large and oval-heart-shaped, while the lowest prolong themselves in flaps down the leaf-stalk. The flowers, though not very large, are wide open, blue, softly downy, and borne with lovely profusion in a tall oval dome of blossom about a foot high at the most.

C. Andrewsii is the correct name of what used to be called *C. tomen-tosa*—an ashy-grey downy rock-plant of monocarpic habit, with a great number of twisting stems that sometimes branch a little, and tend to hug the cliff-face ; and so carry a one-sided spray of tubular blue-velvet bells, sitting tight to the bough. The root-leaves are oblong spoon-shaped, and toothed or scalloped, diminishing down to a leaf-stalk, or cut and feathered at times, or else gashed into lobes all the way up, of which by far the largest is the top one, fat and rounded,

PLATE 11.

CAMPANULA ALPESTRIS [C. ALLIONII, Vill., and of gardens].

(Photo. R. A. Malby.)

VOL. I.   CAMPANULA BELLARDII [C. PUSILLA, Haenke, and of gardens].

(Photo. R. A. Malby.)

PLATE 12.

CAMPANULA CARPATICA.
(Photo. R.B.G., Kew.)

CAMPANULA CENISIA.
(Photo. R.B.G., Edinburgh.)

and the rest quite minute. In fact it is a most polymorphic type, and there is still much obscurity as to its synonyms, sub-species, forms, and varieties. It is found in all the crevices of Greece, and its development *C. A. brachyantha*, with shorter flowers, is *C. rupestris* of the Flora Graeca, yet another complicated and crowded name. Yet more conflicting and overshadowing names are *C. Celsii, C. eriantha, C. lyrata.*

C. arcuata. See *C. rotundifolia.*

C. ardonensis is a precious tufted beauty of almost grassy look, perfectly smooth and hairless, in a dense matted tuft of many fine narrow leaves, almost entirely smooth at the edges, and diminishing downwards to very long petioles. Up among these, and hardly rising above them, come delicate stems, each one carrying a single magnificent bell of intense violet-blue, rather narrow and quite hairless. This beautiful thing has the habits, root, and precise cultural needs and values of *C. alpestris;* it has come into cultivation from the district of the Ardon River in Central Caucasus, where it occupies, like *C. alpestris,* stony, grassy places in the alpine region; by the glacier-lake of Zei may be found its variety *C. A. kryophila,* compressed and stunted. Slugs and mice adore it no less than I.

C. argaea is an inferior *C. spicata,* with smaller flowers.

C. argentea is vainly longed for at present. It dwells in the high alpine crevices of Turkish Armenia, forming flat minute masses of rosettes, with narrow spoon-shaped foliage untoothed at the edge, and richly sheeny with a close coat of silver. The flowers are tubes of blue-velvet, borne either alone or just a few at the ends of stems not more than 2 or 3 inches high.

C. aristata is an Indian species of not much hope or merit, though perhaps a trifle more blue and less black than usually painted. (See under *C. foliosa, seq.*)

C. arvatica is a most exquisite little thing, whose character lay at first under suspicion. It is, roughly speaking, like a boneless and frail-branched *C. cenisia,* with the lovely violet stars of *C. Waldsteiniana* or *C. Elatines*—a most delicate alpine, from the limiest crevices and screes of the Picos de Europa, by Aliva, in Spain, where it lies out upon the stones in spreading spokes of those weak, few-inched branches, each turning up to heaven a row or spray of wide-rayed open purple stars. The leaves from the central tuft are many and rounded, each carried on a long foot-stalk, and, at first, rather suggesting those of a small *C. rotundifolia.* In cultivation this new rare jewel takes a prominent place in the very choicest moraine, but it does not always survive the winter, though its claim to be a sound spreading perennial is now admitted. In any case it can freely be raised from seed. It was introduced under the false name of *C. acutangula*, which may still be found in some catalogues, while others obscure it yet further by calling the plant *C. acutangulare*. (*Sic!*)

C. Athoa, an inferior Clot-head in the kinship of *C. glomerata*.

C. attica, the false name of the beautiful large-flowered annual, whose proper name is *C. ramosissima*, but which is also called *C. drabaefolia* and *C. Loreyi*.

C. Aucheri restores us to the charms of *C. alpestris* and *C. ardonensis*. *C. Aucheri* can always be known from all forms of *C. tridentata* and *C. Saxifraga* by the *outside of the great violet bell, which is downy* instead of being waxy-smooth ; also, its foliage is scalloped *all* the way round the edge. The same downiness of the flower distinguishes it from the bald-belled *C. bellidifolia* in its smaller forms. *C. Aucheri* has the utmost neatness and beauty, a tuft of rosettes, as in *C. alpestris*, and exactly in similar places, abundant in the alpine region of Eastern Caucasus to North Persia, with small oval leaves, scalloped at the edge, and diminishing to a foot-stalk ; and the usual glorious bells of purple, in which this section is so profuse. For choice bed or moraine. A darling of slugs, always keen to discern the best.

C. Autraniana, a fine big leafy Caucasian stalwart, with toothed leaves and goodly flowers.

C. axillaris, a large and stalwart border plant, with toothed leafage, and flowers in their axils almost stemless. (And some other more or less valueless things in this letter are *C. Alphonsii*, *C. alsinoeides*, *C. aparinoeides*, *C. argyrotricha*, *C. asperrima*, *C. atlantica*, *C. aurita*.)

C. Balchiniana, a garden hybrid of *C. isophylla, q.v.*

C. Balfourii. See under *C. pulla*.

C. barbata is the noble bearded Bell of the Alps, and one of their most lovely glories, when its stout campanili of fluffy china-blue wave amid golden Arnica in the showering grasses. It can be 2 feet high ; it can be 2 inches ; it can have more than twenty flowers, and it can only have one (a delicious dwarf-habited form called *C. b. uniflora*, and thus often confused with the true species *C. uniflora*, but unfortunately not constant). It can also branch and hold out lateral arms with flowers held upwards instead of hanging. But there is never anything more beautiful than the type *C. barbata*, with its not uncommon and exquisite pure-white forms ; in gardens it should have quite sharp drainage and quite poor soil, or be established in crevices or the moraine, if it is to prove a permanent perennial. For, like *C. alpina*, which is like a minute cousin, of wholly different effect, it forms but one long taproot, easily exhausted by the generosity of its bloom, and so left without strength against winter wets and rottenness. It seeds, of course, profusely.

C. Barrelieri, a garden name for *C. fragilis*.

C. Baumgartenii. See under *C. rotundifolia*.

C. bavarica, a synonym of *C. Portenschlagiana*, q.v.

C. Bayerniana, about 2 inches high, from alpine rocks of Trans-caucasia and North Persia, makes a very dense tuft of very minute toothed leaves on long petioles, round or oval, with a stem of tubular blue flowers, almost wholly smooth outside or only quite minutely downy.

C. Beauverdiana, a rather thready and straggling, but elegant Caucasian, with scalloped oval foliage at the base, and then stems of a foot or so, nude-looking and fine, with branches carrying large open shallow stars of purple on particularly long foot-stalks. Ordinary beds.

C. Bellardii, Ten.—It is indeed a comfort that after all these years of confusion it has now been ascertained that this name of 1785 takes the precedence over Haenke's "*C. Hals Pusilla*" of 1788, which has bred among us such an unutterable tangle—and the more deplorable that there is not a garden in England that does not revel in this most delicate of common little alpine weeds. But in all catalogues Haenke's name has got so entangled with *C. caespitosa*, Scop., and *C. modesta* (which are both absolutely distinct species, one of them uncommon in cultivation and the other almost unknown), that now the three are spoken of as one, and, what is worse, *C. pusilla* of Haenke almost always in catalogues appears by a double error under the name of *C. caespitosa*. Therefore it is providential that we can now quite simply get rid of all this trouble by letting the invalid name of *C. pusilla* (Haenke) drop altogether. And we make a fresh start and revive the only correct name of *C. Bellardii*, thus leaving the true *C. caespitosa* and the true *C. modesta* to take once more their long-usurped places in lists. *C. Bellardii* needs no praise; all the mountain shingles from July onwards blush blue with the countless myriads of its dancing bells. Nor do our gardens blush any more scantily; and *C. Bellardii* again and again earns sighs of gratitude as it fills the stray corners in August, and the niches by the steps, and the pathside itself with a riot of dainty colour and quivering fairy-bells—the most indestructible and amiable of hearty rampers. Nor is the white form less lovely—the " religieuse des prés," the quiet pure little nun of so many an old cottage edging. The species, indeed, varies abundantly; there are many softer tones, from a true silver-blue to more pallid notes : only perhaps allowed to stand as " silver " by the hospitable enthusiasm of catalogues, or with the names of prominent female enthusiasts to enhance their value. But such varieties are often to be found in such goodly percentage that one day above the Mont Cenis will produce you as many, quite as good, blooming nameless and unnoted amid their kindred crowds. And among the best where all are good is the extra-blue and extra-rampant dolomitic form called *C. B. tyrolensis*—a better name than most, for what heart could be so hard as to pile discordant human honorifics and Misses and Misters upon such fairies as these, that ask at least for the music of an old forgotten tongue—even though *C. B. cochlearifolia* and *C. B. Kladniana* are not happy notions in the same line, but lead the unwary to suppose that these pompous names cover something much more interesting than rather indistinct forms of *C. Bellardii*, by no means worthy of special expense. Not only the colour but the shape of bell varies, too, in *C. Bellardii*, and sometimes one finds wide-trumpet forms, narrow at the base, instead of the usual ample and regular bell ; one such, of purest white, I found in 1913, and yet another day its sister, a modest person of gentle grey-blue. These, not having read the works of Mrs. Florence Barclay, my mind is safe in setting aside as " Little Lady " and " little White Lady," for such indeed they are. The most wonderful form, however, has been long in coming to its own. It was some eight years since that under the slopes of the Vorder Wellhorn I came upon a really astonishing *C. Bellardii*, very dwarf, with flowers of enormous size, and of a delicate pallor which might almost deserve the name of silvery, were it not more feelingly to be painted as a diaphanous and pale china-blue, like a fine cloud at night with the moon behind it. This treasure was despatched with due care to England, enwrapped in many exhortations to special attention in dealing with it. And it was never heard of again. All that boxful was potted carefully, according to instructions. But nothing was heard of the Campanula again ; and all hope of its survival had been lost, when, three seasons ago, it suddenly took away the garden's breath by blooming in the pot where it had lain " perdue " for so long. And, having taken the first costly step, it went ahead with leaps and bounds—grows and spreads now with the rapidity of gout-weed, and takes the winds of August with a profusion of soft and delicate beauty far beyond that of all its sisters. *C. Bellardii Miranda* is going to be one of the greatest of our rock-garden plants, as those few to whom she has been rigidly entrusted from their several gardens and soils independently proclaim—prodigiously free in growth, and prodigiously free, from

CAMPANULA.

summer right away through autumn, with those comely pale bells, no longer carried, however, on such dwarf stems, but in taller spraying showers, even when all the other Bellardiis are over and done. Her Ariel has been later in appearing, but was recognised last season, above the Glocknerhaus—almost her twin in size, and of a rich clear powder-blue, markedly deeper at the rim, and pale inside, which gives the pendent flowers on a high ledge something of the charm of C. G. F. Wilson to look up at.

C. bellidifolia, approaching in its smaller forms to *C. Aucheri*, is yet another rock plant from the cliffs of central Caucasus (as, for instance, from about 3000 to 6000 feet round Vladikafkas), forming tufts of rosettes, with round scallop-toothed leaves, diminishing into a stalk so much longer than themselves as to have a truly spoon-like (or daisyish) effect. These rosettes are thrown up in masses from a many-headed stock, and each emits a profuse display of violet bells, purple and splendid as those of *Wahlenbergia serpyllifolia* in its best form (and very much of a size), on stems of not more than about 2 or 3 inches or so. The flowers *are perfectly smooth outside*, instead of being downy as in *C. Aucheri*, and the *leaves are quite hairless*, except for a little fringe of down sometimes at their edge. It is an entrancingly attractive treasure, alike to slugs and gardeners, and thrives happily in rich perfectly light limy loam, with abundance of stone-chips. The moraine sometimes seems too arid for it.

C. bellidifolia (Friv. ex Nyman)=*C. orphanidea.*

C. bellidifolia (Lapeyr.)=*C. patula.*

C. betonicaefolia, small tubular flowers; large downy leafage and coarse habit.

C. betulaefolia, if the true species be obtained, is a lovely thing, fragile, with a great number of weak stems from the central neck, erect or declining, often branching and twisting at the top, so as to bear on each 6-inch stem a loose fountain of bright narrow bells as big as those of *C. alpestris*, on erect pedicels. The whole mass is bright green and hairless too—always a good sign—except perhaps for a faint occasional trace of down. The leaves of the rosette are almost fleshy, rounded, wedge-shaped, sharply toothed, and diminishing to long foot-stalks. From rock crevices at some 6000 feet in Turkish Armenia, &c. Monocarpic.

C. Biebersteiniana=*C. tridentata*, q.v.

C. Billardieri is not ungraceful, though the flowers are not large. The leaves are toothed, rounded, heart-shaped, and the whole effect is like a fine frail Harebell. Caucasus and Levant.

C. bithynica=*C. oreadum*, q.v.

CAMPANULA.

C. bononiensis is a species common in Southern Europe, but of no special interest or value, forming a tall erect leafy spike, set thickly with rather small rather tubular blooms of a rather dim and uncertain lilac-purple, stiff and sessile. There is a variety *ruthenica* which might offer itself to the unwary as a species, and, though usually rather ugly, *C. bononiensis* itself can sometimes be seen in prettier, and sometimes in quite attractive forms. Near San Dalmazzo de Tenda it is not at its best.

C. Burghaltii, a splendid but doubtful garden development. See under *C. punctata*, of which it is most probably a form or hybrid.

C. caespitosa (Scop.) has nothing whatever to do with *C. Bellardii*, *C. pusilla* (Haenke), *C. modesta*, *C. tyrolensis*, *C. pumila*, or any other of the distinct species which have been shoved under its wing in gardens until all trace of the genuine species has been lost. *C. caespitosa* is not a runner, but from one central tap throws up a dense cushion of many serried shoots, thick-set with little narrow toothed leaves in no way distinct from those of *C. Bellardii*, except by their number and density on the far more dense tuft, made up of far more, and more close-packed, barren shoots devoid of runners. But above this mat come shooting wholly different flowers on wholly different stems— tall, very thin, and bare and wiry, attaining as much as a foot, and arching and bending out this way and that, with all the airy grace of *Dierama pulcherrimum*, beneath the burden of a long rather one-sided loose shower of the most lovely hanging bells, delicately strongly ribbed outside, and so pulled-in at the mouth that they look like elongated globules of exquisite clear-blue water, as they waver and sway and tinkle to the lightest wind. It is one of the daintiest of Campanulas, and in the garden answers as perfectly to any ordinary treatment as *C. Bellardii* itself. In nature it begins far away, so that perhaps the long obscurity that has wrapped it may be explained. It can first be seen rather feebly beginning, in the Dolomites, occurring by the roadside between Toblach and Cortina in stony poor places ; but in the Karawanken it is the reigning Bell, shaking tall sheaves at the passer-by, from every sandy barren road-cutting as he crosses the Seeland Pass. In the Dolomites it has to share its home with *C. Bellardii*, but has not so deep a belt of distribution. In the Karawanken, *C. Bellardii* is comparatively rarely seen, and then often only at the higher elevations, while *C. caespitosa* wholly takes its place and never seems to ascend. It blooms with the other through July to September, and should be best multiplied from seed. It is truly figured, though vilely coloured, and from a specimen of poor stature, in the *Ic. Flo. Germ.*, t. xciv. ; and quite lately, in the notice of some correspondent as to some form of the delusive *C. "valdensis,"* the description sounded suspiciously, as if it really covered the genuine *C. caespitosa,* so long lost in the weltering chaos of *C. "pusilla."*

C. calaminthifolia can hardly be a synonym of *C. orphanidea.* This pious Harebell clings to the ruins of the temple of Zeus on Delos. It is a rather luscious rock-plant, monocarpic, with many weak decumbent leafy stems, the leaves being fattish, narrow-oblong, and toothed at their edge, drawing to a foot-stalk; while those on the stem sit tight to it and are round. Unlike the quite smooth *C. heterophylla,* which this Levantine closely resembles, it is softly downy. The flowers are rather small blue tubes, with the tips of the lobes recurving.

C. calycina (Roem. and Sch.)=*C. rapunculus, q.v.*

C. candida, from limestone crevices of Turkestan and Western Persia, is quite close to *C. argentea* in all its habit and its silver-sheen, but the small ovate leaves are coarsely and sharply toothed, the stem is a little longer—some 5 inches or so—and the tubular bluebells are narrowly funnel-shaped, fluffyish outside, and rather larger, though still not big.

C. canescens (Biel.)=*C. sibirica, q.v.*

C. cantabrica is a pretty thing from Leon, with a radishy root, and rounded basal foliage, dim green, curling down at the edge; all the stem-leaves are crowded quite at the base of the stems, which rise to some 2 or 4 inches only, set with a few narrow leaflings, and each carrying one erect flower, which is a narrow blue trumpet, with the lobes short and spread out.

C. carnica. See under *C. rotundifolia.*

C. carpatica, from a threepenny pinch of seed, will fill the roughest desert with its jungles of gaping open cups, blue, or pallid, or white. This lovely wild plant, which actually does come from the Carpathians, is now almost wild in every garden, where, indeed, it is of habit and freedom too lavish and robust for admission into choice places. It has also yielded the following forms or hybrids, of which more appear under new names each season : *alba, caelestina* (merely a good blue, which it is quite absurd to call *caelestine,* such a note never being found in Campanula, except in old coloured illustrations, which remind one of Gentians) ; *Fergusonii,* a hybrid with *C. pyramidalis,* giving an ample pyramidal habit, thick-set with very noble wide-open stars of violet-blue, a superb cross of good constitution ; *Hendersonii,* another hybrid, but of inferior character and rather miffy temper—as often happens when the two parents are too distantly related in their race (this should also be *C. Tymonsii* of lists, but what comes out under that name is a different thing, suggesting other parentage, not so far from *C. haylodgensis*—a good doer, but of no special merit); *Isabel*, with fine flat flowers ; *White Star*, pretty much the same, but pure white and very fine and free ; *pelviformis*, flat ; *Riverslea*, a form or hybrid with larger flowers still, and also flat ; *Little Gem*, a dwarf ; and last of all the glorious *C. turbinata*, which is so wholly distinct (and so rare) that we will continue to preserve its specific rank.

C. cashmiriana is found between 6000 to 11,000 feet in the mountains of its name-country. It is a stiff, zigzagging grower, hoary with almost woolly down, and with oblong woolly foliage entire or a little toothed, about an inch long ; and most noble large flowers of brilliant blue (*C. cana* of some authorities). It is a slender straggler ; and yet slenderer yet, in the same style, is *C. evolvulacea*. These both sound, as described, admirable ; it is only fair to add that this favourable opinion is not universally endorsed.

C. caucasica MB. is quite near *C. sibirica*, with small tubular flowers which hardly spoil the effect, as the whole growth is so small, not more than 2 or 4 inches high, running about with frail and almost naked rooting shoots in the screes of sub-alpine Caucasus, and then sending up short branching downy leaves and stems, bearing three to five blossoms in a lax spray. Probably biennial, and possibly a mere stunted form of *C. sibirica*.

C. Cavolinii (Ten.)=*C. fragilis*, q.v.

C. Celsii is the prepotent name of *C. lyrata*, a monocarpic species of waste places in Asia Minor. *C. Celsii* is altogether bristly with minute short hairs, the stems ascend, frail, branching and elastic, to some 2 feet, clothed in leaves of which the lower ones have leaf-stalks and are lyrate—that is, are cut into fat small lobes all the way up, with a conspicuously big fat and rounded one at the end (what resemblance this may have to a lyre nobody knows), while the upper ones are pointed, narrow, oblong, hugging the stems. The crown throws up a spike which begins to flower on erect stiff branches from the very base, so that it builds a portly mound of tubular blue blossoms, sitting solitary almost tight to their boughs, and bristlish on the outside.

C. celtidifolia=*C. lactiflora*, q.v.

C. cenisia is sometimes found sharing a stone-slide with *C. alpestris*, but never descends, like *C. alpestris*, to humbler elevations. In the gaunt screes of the highest Alps it forms sheer masses of colour—a huddled sheet of wide-open stars, pale and clear electric grey-blue in tone, so densely crowded each on its single shoot of an inch or so that nothing can be seen of the matted wee rosettes hugging the stones beneath, and made up of soft, bright-green leaves, wee and rounded, with a delicate eyelash of hairs at their edge (which is perfectly free of toothing or scallop). *C. cenisia*, though indifferent as to what rock it lives on, is a local species, though always most abundant where found—as, for instance, at great elevations in the Oberland and Valais, very massive on the Mont Cenis, from which it has its name, and scattered through Tyrol and the Western ranges. There is also a most lovely pure-white form, no less easy and floriferous than the type. For, all things considered, it is not unfair to call *C. cenisia* an easy doer. Inhabiting as it does, however, always and only, the highest and barest of shingle-slopes, where it makes its widest masses tucked in between rough blocks more or less superimposed and tilting back into the slope, so that the rootage is packed into a sort of sandwich, where its central tap may dive deep and far into the moist and worthless grit, while its fine white-cotton runners squeeze out and along this way and that, and appear as fresh tuffets round the corner or along the edge of the next stone—growing thus, I say, it is obvious that in cultivation this exacting plant will usually die in any but shingly conditions. And so it does, but in those conditions, in deep and roughly gritty moraine, with water flowing beneath it all through the growing season, it not only makes itself at home and spreads almost as it does in its own austere places, but also flowers with an almost equal generosity all the summer through—a very rare concession in a high-alpine. It even, in favouring climates, seeds itself ; a beautiful tuft of the albino, which flowered copiously from June to October, has now at least three promising olive-branches in its bed. On the Alps *C. cenisia* dies down to rest like *C. alpestris*, but in the softer conditions of the garden tends not to do this, and then regrets its lack of winter rest and is grateful if a pane of glass will keep off the rain from its green rosettes, while those of *C. alpestris* are long ago lost memories.

C. cephallenica is a rock plant quite close to *C. garganica*, but even more desirable, because its flowers are carried on longer stems, and are more numerous, larger, and at once taller and wider.

C. Cervicaria, a quite useless and ugly cluster-headed biennial.

C. cichoracea (Sibth. and Sm.)=*C. lingulata*.

C. ciliata is a very precious beauty so nearly akin to *C. tridentata* as even by some authorities to have been confused and submerged. It may, however, be clearly known by its much lesser degree of hairiness. For its oval scalloped leaves, narrowing to their base, are *perfectly smooth but for a little fringe of backward pointing hairs at their edge.* The calyx, too, instead of being woollyish, is merely *fringed with rather stiff hairs.* Otherwise the plant is the same in habit and charm—a running, tuft-emitting *C. alpestris*, with royal violet bells, solitary on stems of 4 to 6 inches; from rocky places and barren shingles on Elburs and Shahdagh.

C. cissophylla has narrow blue-velvet tubes, and is not far removed from *C. Billardieri*, though with smaller flowers. Rocks of Persian Kurdistan, 4000 to 6000 feet.

C. cochlearifolia. See under *C. Bellardii* and also under *C. versicolor.*

C. collina colours the sub-alpine fields of Lazic Pontus about Trebizond, and up to some 5000 feet in central and eastern Caucasus. It is one of the most gorgeous Campanulas we have, with tufts of downy foliage scallop-edged and oblong heart-shaped on longish foot-stalks, and then the graceful foot-high stems, gracefully carrying magnificent big bells of imperial purple, satiny and brilliant, whose only fault is that they pass over almost as quickly as the roseate hues of early dawn, so that, when June is by, nothing is left but a memory. *C. collina* thrives admirably and runs freely, in any good and open loam. In its higher range, too, it turns into a 2- to 3-inch dwarf, and thus trenches boldly on the splendour of *C. Saxifraga.* Division and seed.

C. colorata is a worthless Indian, not only ugly but tender. It has been indiscreetly praised by some who cannot have seen it—a rambling inconspicuous weed, neither new, nor fine, nor hardy.

C. compacta, from the high region of Davrosdagh in Pisidia, forms hard and dense tuffets, all hoary-grey, of densely-rosetted basal leaves, quite narrow spoon-shaped, blunted at the tip. The stiff stems are only some 2 to 5 inches high, with fluffy calyces emitting large smooth erect stars of blossom with erect and spreading lobes and a deeply-cleft corolla.

C. conferta is of the same value.

C. corymbosa is a big border species, in the way of *C. Medium*, handsome and impressive, with lordly pyramids of bells.

C. Costae may be described as a robuster and more branching version of *C. patula*, with much narrower calyx-segments. (Spain. Biennial.)

C. crispa is found in the rock-crevices of Turkish Armenia. It is a fine monocarpic species with tufts of shining green leafage, oblong heart-shaped, on foot-stalks, and at the edge all scalloped and crimped. The flower-stems are about a foot high, clothed in a close raceme of large handsome blossoms, blue or white.

C. cristallocalyx, a stiff and comparatively ugly form of *C. persicifolia*, which wears a full set of crystal bristles on its calyx.

C. Cymbalaria (Sibth. and Sm.)=*C. Billardieri, q.v.*

CAMPANULA.

C. dahurica is a Campanula like *C. glomerata*, with clusters of purple cups, possibly no more than a variety of *C. glomerata* itself, though later in flower, and a good deal more brilliant, making quite a noble show of violet heads in September.

C. damascena, not from Damascus but from Hermon, is a rather impossible and perhaps undesirable mass of dense, hispid and fragile leafy stems, about 3 to 6 inches high, each carrying some half a dozen smallish flowers (possibly this = *C. dulcis*).

C. dasyantha = *C. pilosa*.

C. dasycarpa is said to be a 4-inch, blue-flowering species of the Eastern Alps. A most obscure name, perhaps covering yet another in the group of *C. rotundifolia*, unless it be a slip for *C. dasyantha*.

C. denticulata, with egg-shaped toothed leaves, makes a really handsome sight, with branches from the axils, and large, pinkish flowers. (Armenia.) It scarcely sounds identical with Boissier's *C. betulae-folia* (*q.v.*), as sometimes claimed.

C. desertorum. Close to *C. glomerata*.

C. dichotoma, a tolerable little annual.

C. divergens. See under *C. sibirica*.

C. drabaefolia = *C. ramosissima*, *q.v.*

C. dulcis is suggestive of a finer and more graceful *C. mollis*—with blossoms which are whitish and funnel-shaped, but do not offer us much hopes of seeing them, as they are produced in the chinks of Sinai. It is only a mercy the plant is not prettier.

C. Elatines belongs, like so many rare Campanulas of its section, to a quite small district, in which, however, it abounds, and at no great elevations. It comes nearer home than any others of its group, abounding on the hot black cliffs low down in the Cottian Alps, where it looks extremely beautiful with its long brittle arms running out from the fat stock, from amid the tuft of small ivy-shaped pointed leaves, scalloped and crimped, and either grey with down or perfectly smooth and glossy. The branches hug the rock, and are set all over with a profusion of big flat stars in a very rich deep tone of clear violet-blue. It is much lovelier than *C. garganica*, of which it is indeed so much the mother that now *C. garganica* in all its forms has been reduced by many authorities to a mere variety of *C. Elatines*. This species, however, is far more elegant in growth and less leafy, with flowers comparatively larger, and of a much more brilliant colour, carried on sprays more fine and dainty. *C. Elatines* is perfectly easy of culture in any warm well-drained crevice in light loam, though, like all the saxatile southerners, such a crevice it should have, not only for its health but also to show its full character. It is much sought by slugs, and is curiously rare in cultivation, considering alike its beauty and its happy temper. It has no objection with us to the lime it avoids in nature, and there seems no difference of constitution between the grey and the glabrous forms.

C. elatinoeides, similar in habit, is a larger coarser thing, with stems upstanding and thick, with flannelly heart-shaped foliage amid which the smaller flowers make less of an effect. It comes from the limestone cliffs and grottoes in the Bergamask group, as above Edolo in the Val Camonica, and about Bormio, constant, like the last, to lower elevations, though on different rock.

C. elegans, as sent out, has always proved a suspiciously faithful copy of *C. rapunculoeides*. And even the species *C. elegans*, R. and Sch., is obscure and doubtful. It should have a downy tallish stem, set with very narrow leaves, perfectly untoothed at the edge, and sitting close to the stem. The flowers are produced from the axils, developing at last into a spike ; and the calyx-segments stick out abruptly in five sharp points so stiff as to be almost prickly. (Siberia.)

C. ephesia takes us back to the monocarpics of the Levant. For this is so close to *C. Andrewsii* as now to be often reckoned only a variety or sub-species. But it is an even better thing, sacred to Artemis of Ephesus as *C. calaminthifolia* to Zeus on Delos. On the ruins of the great temple it makes mounds of one or two feet, hidden in blossoms which are larger than those of *C. Andrewsii*, and not tubular in shape, but broad and frank-mouthed bells of blue.

C. erinoeides, an annual weed.

C. Ērīnus, no less an annual, and still more a weed, though this name is falsely applied instead to a jewel. See under *C. garganica*.

C. eriocarpa is merely a variety of *C. latifolia* with a rather neater smaller habit, and flowers of a much deeper and more brilliant purple. See under *C. latifolia*.

C. esculenta, a rare Abyssinian, with a thick taproot ; rosettes of oblong hairy leaves, and large flowers lonely on their stems.

C. euclasta is no use, as it forms its wide tufts of grey velvet in the blazing rocks of Damascus.

C. excisa sets our feet once more on the Alps. For this delicate and dainty little thing is very rare and also very abundant, being only found in the upper stone-slides on the Northern and the Southern slopes of Monte Rosa—with one remote and unexpected appearance in the Engadine. In its own home it begins almost immediately outside Macugnaga, and climbs all the way to the Belvedere glacier, running about in the grassy edges of the path and in the scant rough soil round the rocks and pine-tree roots, frail and thready in growth, and in flower, too, so narrow and starved-looking that one recognises the plant at once, as one has sometimes seen it in gardens. But at the glacier-level, suddenly what a change! For there, beside the stream beds, the plant makes masses of hazy violet-blue, some hundreds of yards across, growing in nothing but perfectly pure granite dust among the rounded boulders. Here it is indeed in character—developing into a glorified mimic of *C. Bellardii*, in deeper tones of blue, with finer, more wiry, more abundant stems, each carrying one flower, of much the same size and shape, but with five-folded lobes, and the curious punched-out hole at the base of each segment, that has given the plant its name. It should be seen in full bloom to be believed; and also to be collected, for the long, narrow-tubed bells that are seen in cultivation by no means represent the best of *C. excisa*, which can develop into splendid full expanding bells, amazing in their profusion and delicate loveliness of form and colour, varying to paler tones, and sometimes to pure white. *C. excisa* has long been a great difficulty in culture—half that difficulty arising from the fact that attempts can only be made with nursery stuff, over-propagated for the market, and thereby weakened beyond much hope of recovery. But experiment with a hearty wad from the moraines of the Belvedere, and stick it into sand to begin with, and there should be no subsequent trouble. Sometimes one has heard of the plant thriving in the moss on shady rocks in the North; this suggests a piece collected from the lower woodlands, and reminiscent of its former habit, straggling and frail, coming up in a new corner every year. The glacial forms are of a far more ample splendour, forming compact mats from a central fine white tap, rather as is the way of *C. caespitosa*. Such should be planted in a very loose mixture of one part leaf-mould to two of the very coarsest Redhill sand, such as is used to cover the floor of a canary's cage, and then, in a few months' time—especially if that bed be watered underground—you will be hewing up stout clumps of it as a weed, and casting it out upon your friends. It can also be well grown in fine and gritty moraine, if well supplied with water; the question as to its absolute or only partial antipathy to lime has not been settled; all one can say is that by the light of nature it is easier to follow nature's hints and treat the plant, at all events at first, as resolutely calciphobe.

C. expansa, an annual in the kinship of *C. rapunculus;* as are also *C. phrygia, Kotschyana, ghilanea, sindjarensis, fastigiata, stellaris, dichotoma, Reuteriana* (big blue flowers), *rimarum, Balansae, dimorphantha, Raveyi, propinqua,* and *delicatula.*

C. farinulenta. See under *C. rotundifolia.*

CAMPANULA.

C. *fastigiata* is a rare pretty annual from Algiers and Central Spain, like a very neat and densely-tufted Specularia, making a small mound of an inch or two, all covered with open stars of brightest violet.

C. *fenestrellata* is a Croatian species or form intimately connected with C. *garganica;* of the same beauty and for the same uses. Its present forms in cultivation seem to be wholly smooth and hairless, but of course no certain character can be built on that.

C. *Fergusonii.* See under C. *carpatica.*

C. *ficarioeides.* See under C. *rotundifolia.*

C. *floribunda* = C. *isophylla, q.v.*

C. *foliosa,* a large cluster-head from Thessalian wood-edges, with many blossoms to the bunch; worthless species are C. *fastigiata, filicaulis, floridana,* and the deceitfully named C. *fulgens.* But C. *aristata,* from 11,000 feet in Kashmir and Tibet, is not so bad as sometimes represented—a graceful smooth plant with a number of 12-inch stems, each carrying one flower.

C. *fragilis* has another name that is misapplied. For this is sometimes confused with the yet grander C. *isophylla.* It is also called sometimes C. *Cavolinii* and C. *Barrelieri.* It is a beautiful Italian rock-plant forming tufts in the cliffs of long-stemmed fleshy little foliage not unlike that of C. *Bellardii,* either quite glossy-smooth or else hairy (sporting greatly in this respect, as they all do), from which depend or flop a lavish number of unbranched stems from 4 to 16 inches long, heaped and piled with beautiful ample open starry cups of blue, twice the size of C. *garganica's,* but barely half that of *isophylla's* or *Raineri's,* but fuller and deeper-lobed than in C. *garganica.* In cultivation it is far too rarely seen, its name having become obscure; but is an easy and delightful thing for sunny rocks, and the general treatment of C. *Elatines.* It has been also divided into many named varieties, of which there are C. *f. hirsuta, diffusa,* and another, *cochlearifolia,* which is already breeding confusion with a form of C. *Bellardii* that bears the same epithet.

C. *garganica,* from the rocks of Italy and all the Adriatic, has become a generally-prized rock-garden ornament, though not perhaps quite equal in beauty to either C. *Elatines* or C. *fragilis,* the growth, though heartier, being much lusher and leafier than in the first, and the blossoms flatter and thinner than in the second, so that altogether they seem rather less impressive than in either of the others—perfectly expanded starfishes of blue or slate-blue or electric blue or white, scattered abundantly along the rock-hugging branches that spread away from the thick central tuft of little pointed heart-shaped leaves, and splay tightly along the face of the cliff like the suckers of an octopus. There are many forms in cultivation, all delightfully easy and valuable and perpetual-flowering, for sunny chinks on the rock-work ; some are smooth and hairless, others densely ashen-grey with down ; some have white flowers and some have blue, but all have names accordingly. The only form that has no name is the finest of all—that very beautiful thing which nurseries used to call *C. Erinus*, and which is no more than a neat and glossy-green variety of *C. garganica*, forming a refined small rosette, from which spread raying stems, not too leafy, set with a graceful profusion of most beautiful flat flowers that look much larger for the plant, and are of a rich china-blue with an eye of white. It is of compact habit and the easiest growth. Yet another form has recently been sent out under the false and cloudy name of *C. rupestris*. This has longer, more scattered and straggling branches, comparatively bare also, and with the leafage of the rosette all crimped and glossy-smooth as in the last ; but the stars are not so flat, and thinner in outline, of quite a spidery effect, violet, with a white eye.

C. glomerata may be found quite commonly on many English downs. It is almost the finest of the Cluster-heads, and ranges in many forms across the world to Manchuria. Among its countless named local developments, the best is *C. g. dahurica* (sometimes confusingly advertised as *C. speciosa*), with flowers of a really superb violet, very late in the season. The bells of *C. stenosiphon*, from the sub-alpine beech-woods of Thessaly, are rather narrower ; those of *C. foliosa* are larger and more numerous ; so also are those of *C. machrochlamys*, wrapped in an envelope of leafage, and this has the advantage, too, of being not more than 6 inches high, but is unfortunately a biennial, as is also *C. involucrata*. But *C. glomerata* in all its forms is soundly perennial, and really useful in any ordinary place in any ordinary soil. Associated with the sulphur-yellow of *Cephalaria alpina*, its clustering heads of violet on their stems of a foot or 18 inches make a delicately splendid contrast (and another is the same Cephalaria, with the tenderer violet of *C. latifolia eriocarpa*). But *C. glomerata*, besides white forms, and a double one of little merit, also achieves a strikingly beautiful dwarf variety called *C. g. compacta*, a mound of imperial purple not more than 3 or 4 inches high, and nearly twice as much across; while *C. g. pusilla* is yet smaller and of daintier style.

C. grandis=*C. latiloba*.

C. Grossekii is coarse as its name seems to promise ; it is in the way of *C. alliariaefolia*, but not a plant worth growing.

C. gumbetica is a microscopic reproduction of *C. Bayerniana*, minutely downy-grey; and with very much larger blossoms, wide-open and star-cut as in *C. cenisia*, produced one or two at the end, from the axils of the innumerable tiny erect or flopping stems that spring a couple of inches or so from the tuft of minute rounded leaves like a Nummularia's, nestling into the sheer limestones of Gumbet in the Caucasus, and driving its delicate roots far down into the heart of the rock.

C. gummifera (Willd.)=*C. sarmatica*, *q.v.*

C. hagielia fades into *C. Andrewsii* and can no more be held distinct. Its only interest lies in its being a Christian Campanula, which asks the protection of Holy Elias (as its name declares) instead of clinging, like *C. ephesia* and *C. calaminthifolia*, heathen plants, to the ruins of Zeus and Artemis.

C. Hawkinsiana is a species of incomparable beauty from cliffs of serpentine and silex in the sub-alpine regions of Thessaly and Epirus. It forms a tuft of fleshy rounded little hairless leaves, diminishing to quite a short foot-stalk, and almost entire at the edge, or perhaps a trifle toothed. Then from this there floats out a cloud of 12- or 18-inch stems, airy and almost naked, but for a few minute narrow leaves here and there, each carrying at the end a single flower, large and rich and wide, of the most refulgent purple. Colonel Beddome cannot have got this true, or grown it well (or else its original describer must have overflowed with excessive zeal). For he declares it of botanical interest only.

C. × *haylodgensis*, a really beautiful small garden hybrid, between (probably) *C. Bellardii* and *C. isophylla*, with neat vigorous low growth of glossy foliage of a bright pale-green verging on a yellowish tone; and covered in later summer and autumn with a profusion of large, wide erect flowers of clear bright blue. It is of the easiest culture, and there is a double form that is not ugly.

C. hederacea. See under *Wahlenbergia*.

C. hemschinica, a beautiful biennial in the section of *C. patula*, which it closely resembles, but that it is only some 12 inches high, with larger star-cups in a less lax shower. (Alpine fields of Pontus and Bulgaria, &c.) Sometimes in this species, too, the leaves continue down the stem in a leafy flap or wing.

C. Hendersonii. See under *C. carpatica*.

C. Herminii the Colonel admits to be pretty as it claims—though it should be much more nearly akin to *C. Bellardii* than to *C. rotundifolia*, as well as being far too beautiful to be damned with such a faintly praising word as "pretty," for it forms lax and spreading masses and mats of perfectly glabrous smooth green leaves, long-

PLATE 13.

CAMPANULA EXCISA.
(Photo. R. A. Malby.)

CAMPANULA   FRAGILIS.
(Photo. R.B.G., Edinburgh.)

PLATE 14.

CAMPANULA GARGANICA.
(Photo. R. A. Malby.)

CAMPANULA HOSTII.
(Photo. R.B.G., Edinburgh.)

PLATE 15.

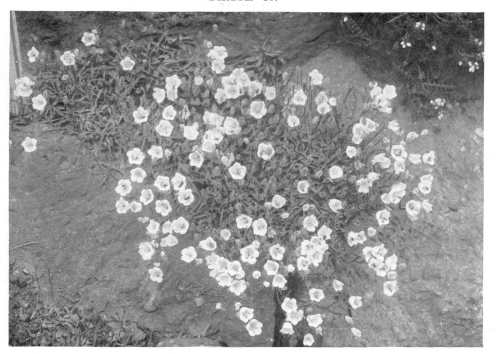

CAMPANULA MACRORRHIZA.
(Photo. R.B.G., Edinburgh.)

CAMPANULA PORTENSCHLAGIANA.
(Photo. R. A. Malby.)

PLATE 16.

CAMPANULA LATIFOLIA.

CAMPANULA LACTIFLORA.

stemmed, rounded, either entire or dimly scalloped ; the stems are nearly naked, and usually unbranching ; they rise to 8 inches or more, each carrying a single large and ravishing bell of pale clear blue, erect or slightly nodding, quite wide open, and deeply cleft into five lobes. It fills the alpine pastures and the stream-sides in damp grassy places of the Sierra Nevada, the Guadarrama, &c., between 6500 to 10,000 feet, and should prosper well among the Rotundifolias accordingly.

C. heterophylla is quite close to *C. calaminthifolia*, differing only in being *perfectly smooth and without down.* (Cliffs of the Aegean.)

C. hirsuta, an obscure but surely beautiful species from the valley of Virma Dol, Crna Planina. In habit and leafage it rather recalls a small and graceful *C. barbata ;* but here the flowers are in a loose cluster of only a few at the bending top of the 6- to 8-inch stems, and are very large, open bells, more in the style of *C. Raineri's*, but rather more swelling in outline, more deeply cloven, and almost pendulous. The record, however, is old and unrenewed.

C. hispanica is so closely allied to *C. rotundifolia*, and perhaps, like *C. carnica, Hostii, Scheuchzeri, stenocodon, Baumgartenii, Marchesettii*, and a host of other too subtly differentiated fading forms, it ought to be included in the huge polymorphic aggregate for which the name of *C. rotundifolia* is the most convenient. *C. hispanica* is a running grower, occupying the grassy limy hills of Central and Eastern Spain. In appearance it is less like a Harebell, however, than some dwarfed form of *C. rhomboidalis*, with short, finely bristling stems of not more than a foot, carrying bells of a dark deep blue.

C. Hostii. See under *C. rotundifolia.*

C. hypopolia has but newly arrived in our midst from the Ossetian Caucasus, and its whole habit suggests rather a frail Cerastium than a Campanula. It runs about with very fine subterranean stems, quite happily in light stony soil or moraine, throwing up, here and there, now a barren tuft of foliage, and now an erect stem of 5 or 6 inches, extremely dainty, delicate, and rarely set with narrow foliage, diminishing to the stem, faintly and remotely scalloped, smooth above or nearly so, but hoary grey-white on the under side. The stems do not branch, so much as develop sometimes a number of equal stemlings standing erect so as to form a flat loose head of large wide-open beautiful flowers, soft with down outside, and of the noblest effect upon their threadlike support ; in this, and their whole beauty, not far removed from that of *C. Waldsteiniana*, but lax and running in habit, instead of staying at home in an increasing tuft.

C. imeretina, from crevices in the lower region of Imeretia in the

CAMPANULA.

Caucasus (where it blooms from mid-November onwards), makes a woody base, and sends out ascendent flexuous and rather bristlish stems that divide higher up into two forks and do not exceed some 9 inches or so. The leaves are obovate, diminishing to a foot-stalk, along which they continue in a leafy flap; and the abundant blossoms are fine and large and blue. It ought to be perennial, but is near akin to the confessedly biennial *C. sibirica divergens;* and, indeed, in all this indiscreetly free-flowering section, it is as well to make sure of them, by sowing annually some of the abundant seed, for fear the parent, no matter how perennial, should prove to have exhausted itself with its generosity.

C. incanescens, a hopeless and worthless weed from Persia akin to *C. damascena.*

C. inconcessa. See under *C. rotundifolia.*

C. incurva is the correct name of the plant too often sent out as *C. Leutweinii.* This is a monocarpic from the sheer rocks of Euboea and the face of Olympus that fronts the Gulf of Thessaly (where it grows at between 500 and 1500 feet); it forms a fat neck with a rosette of hoary heart-shaped or kidney-shaped leafage, bluntly scalloped, on foot-stalks; from this there rises a magnificent panicle a foot high, of pale-blue flowers as large as a Canterbury Bell. Seed should be raised and saved of this, as, though not annual, it merely continues until it has flowered, and then irremediably dies—like the Canterbury Bell itself.

C. infundibulum is said to be synonymous with *C. Stevenii.* As figured, it is a finer thing, with one immense trumpet lonely on a frail stem thin-set with specially narrow leaves.

C. Intybus=C. trachyphylla, q.v.

C. involucrata attains 6 or 10 inches, and is a glomerate species, with fine large violet bells in heads, set off by a spreading frill of foliage. (Cappadocia.)

C. Isabel. See under *C. carpatica.*

C. isophylla is that glorious Beauty which makes such sheets of wide blue or white saucers, dependent from baskets in cottage-windows. This strange and lonely species, like a loose cataract of *C. carpatica,* snowed over with the more exquisite flowers of *C. Raineri,* has only one dwelling-place in the world—in a few hundred yards of limy conglomerate cliff on the Capo di Noli, between Savona and Genoa, with the Mediterranean lapping at its feet, and the great expresses thundering hourly by to Rome. None the less *C. isophylla* bids us never despair of our plants, be they from climates never so warm, or themselves so improbable of success in our land of cold and wet; for it is perfectly vigorous and hardy even in the coldest and rawest parts of England, where it scarcely even needs the protecting pane of glass that is put over it in winter, hardly so much for the actual needs of the Campanula as in pious and wistful memory of the sunshine far away on the Capo di Noli. So, in any light soil, *C. isophylla* is superb to enthrone on the top of some sunny sheer rock, falling over it and down in a cascade of colour hardly less rich than those it forms in the protection of a cottage living-room. It is also sold under the name of *C. floribunda*. *C. Mayi* is a form with variegated leaves, treated as a synonym of *C. × Balchiniana*, and often sent out as its variegated form; but the genuine *C. Balchiniana* has no variations, and is, in point of fact, a beautiful and free-blooming intermediate between *C. isophylla alba* and *C. fragilis*, for the same uses as its parents, between which it stands about midway.

C. istriaca is a prostrate Campanula close to *C. garganica*, with hairy leaves, egg-shaped or heart-shaped, and big wide-open blossoms, notably deeply cleft and freely produced.

C. janisensis (Rch.)=*C. rapunculoeides*, q.v.

C. Jaubertiana is a Spanish species from alpine limestone cliffs in the Aragonian Pyrenees on the south side. In its first year it makes a tuft of ten or twenty barren shoots, clothed in tiny oval-rounded leatherish leaves on longish stalks, quite smooth and unevenly toothed. Then, from the middle of this, there spring four or five flower-stems next year, each carrying two or four large narrow tubular bells of blue, with spreading lobes, and yellowish at the base, nodding at first on their long foot-stalks and then standing erect.

C. × Justiniana will be but rarely met with. It is a natural hybrid between the variety *cochleariifolia* of *C. Bellardii* and *C. rotundifolia linifolia*. In habit and beauty it holds of both its parents—a very dainty lovely spreading little Ariel, with gracious bare stems fine and frail and branching, each producing several nodding bells of deep and misty powder-blue, on long thread-like pedicels. When got, it thrives as heartily as either of its parents, between whom it is clearly intermediate in habit, size, and colour—much smaller than *C. linifolia* in growth and blossom, much larger and more graceful than *C. Bellardii*, with barer, finer sprays, and flowers in shape a compromise between those of its parents, but in colour leaning more towards the violets of *C. linifolia*, counteracted by the china-tone of *C. Bellardii*; and all invested in a soft bloom of down. (Tre Croce di Rimbianco, in stones at the path-side.)

C. kamtchatica. Not specially valuable, a frail thing, creeping underground, with stalked foliage and calyx-segments as long as the corolla or longer.

C. Kerneri. See under *C. rotundifolia.*

C. Kladniana=C. Bellardii (var.).

C. Kolenatiana is, alas! but biennial or monocarpic; but a most lovely species none the less, from rocky places in the Southern Caucasus: and in our gardens fitted for light and rocky places also; where, from the fat stock, ascend innumerable stiff scantily-branching stalks, with the basal leaves blunt and heart-shaped or oval, on stems of 2 or 3 inches, and scalloped at the edge. Then, when the plant is ready, every shoot breaks into flower, and the whole thing becomes a round bush of a foot or more in height, one loose ball of innumerable big nodding flowers of violet-blue, ample shallow cups with ample recurving lobes, and the anthers standing free as in Symphyandra.

C. Lacei carries large bluebells in terminal clusters, on stems set with very narrow leaves, while those at the base are saw-edged, still narrow, but not quite so fine—a pretty thing from Kumaon.

C. laciniata, on the sea-rocks of Pholegandros in the Aegean, makes rosettes of narrow oval foliage, continuing down the leaf-stalk in wings which are cut and jagged into oblong-toothed strips or lobes, the whole growth being minutely downy and of a pale green. Then, from the rosette, up rises a branching trunk of 1 or 2 feet high, becoming an immense crowded pyramid of large blue flowers quite shallow and with a long protruding style. After flowering the plant sets abundance of seed and dies, being not so much monocarpic as frankly biennial.

C. lactiflora, also sold as *C. celtidifolia,* is a superb species that sows itself all over the place, even if individual crowns do not always live for more than a couple of years or so. Its stems, several from the tuft, and set with many largish sharply-toothed rhomboidal leaves all the way up, tower to the height of 5 feet or more, breaking at the top into a great spreading dome of countless erect shallow-cupped stars of soft greyish-blue or white. Not, of course, for a choice place.

C. Lambertiana=C. rapunculus.

C. lamiifolia (Bieb.)=*C. alliariaefolia.*

C. lanata (*C. velutina,* Vel.), a stately noble plant from the cliffs of Rilo and Rhodope, making a wide basal tuft of big heart-shaped pointed grey-flannel leafage, and then breaking into a 3-foot pyramidal candelabrum of Canterbury Bells which, in the original description, should be blue, but in actual fact are of a waxy pale-yellow verging upon a peachy pink, to many eyes of the rarest subtlety and charm. And, lover of hot dry cliffs though *C. lanata* may be in nature, in the damp warmth of the South of Ireland it actually towers to 3 feet and more of splendour, and actually in the open border, having a curious way of sending out long stiff straight branches at the base of the pyramid, thus making a tray of blossom on which the loose and stalwart central cone is carried. But, after such a display, seed should be sedulously collected. For such a growth cannot stand many shows of such a kind. And again, in countries where the winter-wet is not warm and genial, it will usually be best to treat it as a rock-plant for rich sunny crevices, and have regard perhaps to the woolliness of its leaves when winter is at her most lachrymose.

C. lanceolata (Lap.)=*C. rhomboidalis.*

C. lanceolata (DC.)=*C. Stevenii.*

C. lancifolia (Schrb.)=*C. rotundifolia.*

C. Langgsdorffiana=*C. rotundifolia.*

C. lasiocarpa, on the contrary (*C. algida*), is one of the choicest treasures that the choicest or most ambitious rock-garden could desire. It comes from the high rocky summits of Kamchatka and Arctic America. The lower leaves are spoon-shaped, oblong and pointed, and all are clearly toothed or even gashed with long and definite sharp teeth. And then this tuft sends up a stem of 6 inches or so, each carrying one enormous erect bluebell, wide and opulent. The root is perennial, but *C. lasiocarpa* should have the care we lavish on *C. excisa*, which, indeed, it should even more lavishly repay.

C. latifolia, our own native woodlander of the North, is superbly handsome, with its stalwart leafy spikes and erectish trumpets of palest lilac. But the seed is so profuse, and the ramping habit so excessive, that *C. latifolia* is best kept for the wild garden, where in cool moist soil it will occupy a hundred square yards with fire-like rapidity. Its variety *C. l. eriocarpa*, from the far North, is much neater and less invasive, not so tall or leafy, not nearly so rampant, and with flowers of equal size, but of a much deeper and richer violet-purple, satiny and splendid. This is well fitted for good places on the upper banks, attaining some 3 feet only, instead of the 4 or 5 feet of *C. latifolia*. There is also another magnificent form called *C. l. macrantha*, which has goblets of rather less depth, indeed, but very large ; together with the habit, but not the spreading tendencies of *C. latifolia*. And one might suspect *C. latifolia* to have had some share in producing that sumptuous mystery *C. Burghaltii*, for which see under *C. punctata*.

C. latiloba is the correct name of the fine border plant usually called in gardens *C. grandis*. This, though useful and free with its large blue saucers, may be described as a spoiled *C. persicifolia*, for here the blue saucers stick stiffly all the way up the stiff three-foot stems, instead of having the detached and delicate grace of *C. persicifolia's*.

C. Ledebouriana makes a splash of colour in the cliffs of Ararat—a tuft of 2-inch leaves about an inch and a half in length (with their stalk), and on the upper side coated with backward-lying close-pressed stiff hairs ; otherwise like a diminished copy of *C. Saxifraga*, with a quantity of rather smaller violet bells, appearing solitary on 2-inch stems all round each rosette.

C. Lehmanniana ; very pretty, in the cliffs of Karatau only about 2 inches high, but in cultivation sometimes attaining to 8 or 10 inches. The leaves are narrow, saw-edged and grey ; while the flowers are fine blue tubular bells, carried in a shower on delicate foot-stalks.

C. leucoclada, a hopeless ugly little rock-tuft from cliffs above Quetta.

C. leucosiphon, not much better ; narrow white funnel-shaped tubes of no good size, above masses of soft and woolly leaves, only fitted for the sheltered grottoes where it lives in the Isaurian Taurus.

C. Leutweinii=C. incurva, q.v.

C. libanotica, a variety of *C. stricta, q.v.* But the garden plant of this name is extremely doubtful. See under *C. stricta*.

C. lingulata, a worthless Cluster-head.

C. linifolia. See under *C. rotundifolia*, where all these shadowy species will be found gathered together.

C. Loefflingii, a pretty annual Spanish species, but very variable, usually with a generous abundance of flowers, suggesting those of *C. rhomboidalis.* Its correct name is *C. lusitanica*.

C. longistyla ; a most beautiful thing, though only biennial at the best ; but its great violet bells, with their long protruding style, are carried so gracefully on spikes of a foot or 18 inches, that in charm they recall those of *C. collina*, and in size surpass them.

C. Loreyi=C. ramosissima, q.v.

C. lourica, a minute hoary dense tuft with purple bells solitary on stems of a couple of inches or so, the leaves being narrowly oblong and closely packed, while the plant in other respects is a reduced condensed version of *C. trichopoda* from the cliffs of Elburs.

C. lusitanica is the correct name of *C. Loefflingii.* See above.

C. lyrata=C. Celsii.

C. macrantha. See under *C. latifolia*.

C. macrochlamys carries its flowers in a crowd, enclosed in a frill of foliage—a curious but not lovely Cluster-head.

C. macrorrhiza, that beautiful Harebell which fills all the walls and rocks of all the Riviera, even at midwinter, with waving clouds of violet bells on wiry fine stems of a foot and more, is in reality so close to *C. rotundifolia* as perhaps hardly with propriety to be kept apart. Yet it does unquestionably differ far more widely than most of the other so-called species—filling the crevices where it lives with *a fat and swelling stock*, from which pour out its *freely-branching sprays* in countless profusion, while its scalloped basal leaves are egg-shaped in outline, rather than round as in *C. rotundifolia*. Also the flowers and capsules tend to stand erect, though in this matter they seem to vary; and one form has even been distinguished as *C. m. sardoa*, while yet another tries to claim specific rank as *C. sabatia, q.v.* To the gardener's eye, however, no species could be more distinct from the Harebell; the innumerable blossoms, if rather smaller, being also shallower and of a warm vinous violet and more vase-shaped, and much more numerous, displayed in a riotous cloud throughout the season. By degrees, however, it loses this habit of winter-blooming, daunted by the inclemency of our climate, and takes to more ordinary hours; at which it is far more generous and beautiful anywhere on the rock-work, in chink or ledge, than even *C. rotundifolia* itself.

C. macrostachya is *C. multiflora*, an inferior minuter biennial *C. glomerata*.

C. macrostyla, though only an annual, is none the less well worth sowing—being quite small, with an enormous gaping flower of pink or white or purple, with an enormous style sticking far out of it.

C. Marchesettii. See under *C. rotundifolia.*

C. Mayi. See under *C. isophylla.*

C. Medium.—Few things could be more beautiful on the higher and wilder banks of the rock-garden than the various single forms of the Canterbury Bell, which in no border ever looks quite as noble as when its violet chimes ring out from the more barren road-cuttings going up to Saint Martin Vésubie, or tower in every shade of white and pink and violet in the chalky railway cuttings going down to Dover. But, glorious as the Canterbury Bell may be, and old-established in our hearts and gardens, it is but one in a section of Campanulas of which some will surely prove quite its equal in beauty, though for all these years the glory of *C. Medium* has closed our eyes to the possibility of anything else as good in the same line.

C. michauxioeides is not, however, one of these. For this is an interesting but rather ugly biennial, from the mountain region of Cadmus in Caria, stalwart, but with little inferior flowers, reflexed and starry as those of a Michauxia. Those who declare them to be as fine as those of *C. rapunculoeides* must have been giving way to enthusiasm.

CAMPANULA.

C. microphylla (Cav.)=*C. mollis, q.v.*

C. mirabilis, justly acclaimed with shouts of rapture when it was discovered and introduced from the one ripe capsule on the one specimen found first by Alboff in the Caucasus, has not by any means answered to general expectations. It seems to require imperatively a very poor, pebbly, and worthless barren place in sun or shade, such as no gardener would dream *a priori* of inflicting upon a plant so rare, expensive, and precious. But if happy in such—and it is a pre-destined glory of the moraine—it will go on from year to year making an increasing flat rosette of smooth glossy-green saw-toothed leaves not unlike those of a verdant *Saxifraga Cotyledon*, from which in the fullness of days there arises a spouting fountain of fine pale-blue bells some half the size of those in *C. Medium*. After which the foot-high spike lays down its head, and *C. mirabilis* passes utterly away, leaving seed behind to keep its memory green in the moraine that knows it no more.

C. modesta has nothing to do with either *C. caespitosa* or *C. Bellardii,* but is a perfectly distinct high-alpine from some 12,000 or 14,000 feet in Sikkim, where it throws up solitary dark-blue flowers of conical outline, cut into lobes half the length of the whole bell (which is only about a third of an inch). The leaves are oval on long stems, and the bloom-stalks about 6 or 7 inches ; and the species, closely akin to *C. aristata,* has no special value, except to remind gardeners and catalogues that there is such a thing.

C. Moerheimii. See under *C. persicifolia.*

C. moesiaca is a biennial species from Bulgaria ; but pretty, in the way of a pale-belled *C. glomerata.*

C. mollis is a small rock-species of the limestones of Southern Europe, etc., with tiny oval leaves of white velvet, those of the rosettes being spoon-shaped, while the rest nestle close to the stems, and are very much smaller, fragile, and quite smooth-edged, unless perhaps they sometimes have a wavy scallop. The flower-stems are frail too, flopping or trying to stand up, branching. The flowers are un-grudgingly produced about the ends of the 3- to 12-inch sprays, standing rather erect, each on its own foot-stalk, in clusters or showers of wide open blue cups about half an inch across. For careful culture in choice hot chinks or moraine.

C. monanthos, an obscure species from Crna Planina, with the leaves and general habit of *C. bellidifolia,* but the single stem is much taller, about 6 inches or so, carrying a nodding folded narrow little blossom, rather suggesting that of a *C. excisa* without the punched hole. (An old and unconfirmed record.)

CAMPANULA.

C. Morettiana calls us back into the Dolomites, where, here and there in their most merciless walls of limestone, you may be fortunate enough to see its minute tuffets of foliage, of which the tiny lower leaves are heart-shaped, saw-edged, and stalked, while the rather numerous stem-leaves are tinier still, and oval, sitting close to the stalk. And the whole growth is grey with rather coarse and crystalline bristling hair. And each stem, about 2 or 3 inches high, carries, as a rule, only one flower—a splendid large bell of violet blue, erect and sturdy and astonishing. Though very hard to collect from those stark and adamantine walls far up above the Fassathal (we should all be glad to know how Mr. Stuart Thompson found it growing in "stony pastures"—one of the most incurably saxatile of its whole race), *C. Morettiana* is by no means hard to grow in well-drained chink or moraine. But, being so minute, and being usually sent out in collected pieces, which of necessity are fragmentary, it is as well to give it a season of re-establishment in a small pot, a consideration which it heartily requites. Like so many of the best rock-garden Campanulas, this beauty has a sadly small and local distribution; in South Tyrol and the adjoining hills of Lombardy, between the no less limited range of *C. Raineri* in the limestones of Bergamo to the West, and a long way from the domain of *C. Zoysii* in the high limestones of the Karawanken to the East. In the grim fastnesses of the Schlernklamm above Salegg it may be seen sharing the unassailable cliffs with *Saxifraga Burseriana tridentina*, *Phyteuma comosum*, and *Asplenium Seelosii*—each one more impregnable than the other—but the Campanula perhaps the most. Beware of impostors in nurseries.

C. multiflora is also the thing called *C. macrostachya*—a worthless Macedonian and Bulgarian biennial, with flowers like those of a small and inferior *C. glomerata*.

C. muralis (Port.)=*C. Portenschlagiana*, q.v.

C. naesica, an ugly Bosnian biennial in the way of *C. thyrsoidea*.

C. nitida (Ait.)=*C. planiflora*, q.v.

C. nobilis=*C. punctata*, q.v.

C. numidica (Desf.)=*C. mollis*, q.v.

C. odontosepala, a large coarse and leafy weed, after the style of *C. americana*.

C. Olivieri (DC.)=*C. calaminthifolia*, q.v.

C. olympica, from the lower mountain region of the Bithynian Olympus, is a handsome biennial species after the manner of *C. patula*, but with looser showers of more numerous large erect violet stars.

C. orbelica, however, is a welcome contribution from the Balkans—

an easy and lovely jewel from bare open spaces on the mountains of Bulgaria, very closely resembling beloved *C. alpina*, but that here the pedicels of the flowers are much longer (though in this Alpina itself is variable). Colonel Beddome, however, allies it rather with *C. linifolia*, though not at all thereby denying its charms and claims.

C. oreadum, also, is no less a treasure, from the cliffs 9000 feet on the Thessalian Olympus. It is not unlike *C. tridentata*, but here the narrow-oblong foliage, grey with close hairs, is *without any toothing*, while the twisting stems can carry as many as five flowers, instead of invariably only one. The tuft is neat and charming, and the big violet-purple bells, of rather narrow outline, are superb upon their long foot-stalks, almost in a little candelabrum from the base, a loose pyramid of 4 or 5 inches high. It differs from the kindred *C. rupicola* in *having calyx-segments narrow-pointed and without any toothing at the edge*; and the Oreads alone, as yet, rejoice in it.

C. orphanidea dwells in the summit-rocks of Athos, which it shares with the monks and with *Saxifraga juniperina*. It is a delightful small species, akin to *C. Andrewsii* but much finer, with downy-white heart-shaped leaves on flattened foot-stalks, forming a rosette from which splay out the 4- to 6-inch branches set with rounded minuter leaflings, faintly waved and scalloped, on a yet longer foot-stalk. The blossoms are large for the plant, carried in sprays of six or nine, rather narrow bells of intense violet. This, like all the flannel-leaved Levantine Campanulas, will probably be glad of a close hot crevice and protection from rain in wet winters. But we have our experience with *C. isophylla* to warn us against being too chicken-hearted with Aegean and Mediterranean delicacies; and our experience with *C. lanata* to show that even the dangers of wool and grey-flannel foliage can sometimes be overrated.

C. Pallasiana = *C. pilosa, q.v.*

C. parnassica. See *Edraianthus Parnassi, q.v.*

C. Parryi comes from Georgetown in America, around which favoured spot it sends its creeping roots and runners; the spoon-shaped basal leaves are fringed with hairs and very veiny, smooth-edged, or else a little toothed; among these come up the undivided—or sometimes branching—stems, slender and erect, some 3 to 10 inches tall, each one carrying a single shallow bowl of a wide blue blossom, most beautiful to see. It is a great improvement on *C. Steveni*, which in some ways it recalls, and in others will follow.

C. patula is a brightly handsome biennial, occurring in England, and sometimes filling the alpine meadows—as below Heiligenblut—with a tossing sea of hot lilac-lavender. Its stems can attain to 2 or 3 feet, wirily slight and slender in growth, set all up with oval-toothed leafage, veiny and flimsyish ; then crowning the stems in a loose shower are several, or many, wide, erect, and particularly full-rayed stars, or shallow bells, of a luminous rose-purple, varying to palest tones and a stainless white.

C. pelia, yet another form coming close under *C. Andrewsii*, and with no special worth of its own.

C. pelviformis (Hort.) is a form of *C. carpatica.*

C. pelviformis (Lam.)=*C. corymbosa* (Desf.), *q.v.* (also *C. tubulosa*, Lam.).

C. peregrina is a large border plant, in the way of a yet further coarsened *C. latiloba.*

C. persicifolia.—The Peach-leaved Bell is far too well known for description. It is so beautiful a thing, so graceful in spite of its immense bowls of blue and white on those tall and dainty stems, that England may well feel a thrill of pride in the knowledge that at last, after having vainly established itself in many places and been detected as a mere denizen or desirable alien, *C. persicifolia* has now made good its many attempts at citizenship by being found genuinely wild in the West. Its varieties are of every degree of value, nor do they need a better description as a rule than their names ; but, in the rock-garden, *Moerheimii* and *Pfitzeri* must be guarded against as being doubles or half doubles, as are also *Coupe d'Azur* and *Vineta. La Fée*, however, is a white of exquisite purity.

C. petraea is a species of great rarity and great ugliness, from the rocks of Tyrol, &c., where it forms big fat trunks, crowned with tufts of flannelly grey foliage, long-oblong and scalloped, on foot-stalks, the flower-stems carrying at the top a cluster of dirty-yellow small tubular bells. It is not a biennial, but the gardener sometimes wishes it were, the plant's rarity otherwise protecting it from removal by any reverent hand.

C. petrophila abounds on damp rocks and in cool places on the Northern slopes of Caucasus, from 6000 to 9500 feet—a diffuse slack mat with fine thready stems, dwarf and leafy, set with minute and rounded stalked leaves scalloped just at the tip. The sprays are set with a certain number of yet smaller leaves, and the flowers (often as many as five, carried on long and leafy foot-stalks) are wide bells of pale blue, often bearded, and graceful on their stems. It is said to recall *C. rhomboidalis*, but sounds absolutely distinct in most respects.

C. Pfitzeri. See under *C. persicifolia.*

C. phyctidocalyx is the unpleasing name by which we must now know that handsome species which once was much more appropriately called *C. amabilis*. It is a very pleasant border-plant, not unlike *C. persicifolia*, but the leaves of the basal rosettes are spoon-shaped and most prettily crimped, while the large blossoms are a little smaller and much flatter, purple, with a paling eye. Unfortunately it comes from South Armenia, and, though not at all tender, cannot yet be always called a really satisfactory species in the open.

C. pilosa, also known as *C. dasyantha* (Bieb.), *Pallasiana* (Roehm. and Schl.), and *altaica* (DC.), is not properly revealed by this multiplicity of names to be one of the most desirable of the whole race. All across high Siberia, through the Arctic Islands to Japan, it forms single tufts exactly like those of *C. alpestris*, but that the long narrow leaves are sharply toothed. Among these rises one stalwart little stem of about 6 inches (with only here and there one minute suggestion of a bract-like leaf), woolly-hairy at first and then bald, standing unbowed beneath the burden of one enormous broad bell of blue, large and solid as in *C. Raineri*, but bearded outside with a fluff of fine hairs.

C. pinifolia. See under *C. rotundifolia*.

C. planiflora, an interesting and valuable thing from North America, rather obscure in its history and confused in catalogues, which sometimes call it *C. nitida*, and have at other times even placed it doubtfully as a dwarf form of *C. pyramidalis*. But this last is not an American plant at all ; nor has *C. planiflora* any resemblance to it, being much more approximate to a stunted development of *C. latiloba*. It has a marked personality, being stiff and stocky, about 9 inches or a foot in height, with smooth hard and leathery foliage, narrow-oblong and scalloped ; while on the stem sit tight the big fat flowers, round and flat and rather stolid-looking, of cool powder-blue (or white). It is quite easy of culture in any ordinary place, suggesting most of all, perhaps, a much condensed and blank-faced form of *C. persicifolia*. It has a look of Spartan sturdiness and character, and might justly be described in the words of an eminent authority as " a very dressy little alpine."

C. podanthoeides, as its name implies, is a quaint small plant hardly like a Campanula, as it nestles into the cliffs of Berytagh, forming a minute tuffet of fleshy, pointed oblong leaves ; the stems are only some inch or so high, packed with leaves so diminutive as to look like mere scales ; the flowers are in a head of two or three, the blue corolla cloven into lobes three-quarters of its depth. (It is also *C. rimarum* of some.)

C. Portenschlagiana (Roehm. and Schl.), often called *C. muralis*

(Post. Herb.), or *C. bavarica,* is, in point of fact, a species of the South. *C. garganica* goes no further than the Western side of Dalmatia, at which point the tale is taken up by *C. Portenschlagiana,* abounding through Eastern Dalmatia, in all the walls and fissures—as in the cliffs by Almissa and Macarska and throughout the province. Yet here again this Southern species has become, with *C. Bellardii,* perhaps the most indispensable, indestructible, and generally magnificent of Campanulas for all gardens great or small. True it is that we might have hoped good things of those smooth and hairless leaves, but who could ever have foretold the generosity of their abounding masses, and the way in which they are hidden beneath that inordinate profusion of starry violet cups ? As is natural in a wild Campanula made so tame, the type has developed into various forms, indulged by gardeners with names ; there is *major* and there is *minor,* and there is the ordinary species under its name of *bavarica* (no doubt because it must have struck the imagination in some Bavarian garden). Yet none of these is sufficiently marked to oust the august proper name of *C. Portenschlagiana,* which, cumbrous though it be, has the advantage, not only of being correct, but also of covering one of the most precious of garden Bells, which grows profusely, and pulls to pieces and propagates with the utmost ease.

C. praesignis. See under *C. rotundifolia.*

C. primulaefolia (Brot.)=*C. peregrina, q.v.*

C. × *Profusion* is a garden-hybrid of great merit, of which the parentage is obscure. It is certain that the seed-parent was *C. pyramidalis,* but whether the father was *C. carpatica* or *C. isophylla* does not seem so sure. In any case it is a pretty thing, adopting the dwarf stature of the father, without the slightest reminiscence of its stalwart and enormous mother. Two forms are said to be in existence ; one with blue flowers, and the other with mauvish grey, less attractive.

C. pseudocarnica. See under *C. rotundifolia.*

C. pseudo-Raineri. See under *C. turbinata.*

C. ptarmicaefolia, an ugly thing from Erzeroum, with very narrow basal leaves, and long crowded spikes or heads of little bugles.

C. pubescens (Schl.)=*C. Bellardii.*

C. pubiflora (Rupr.)=*C. Aucheri.*

C. pulcherrima is merely the brazen name adopted by that lovely but terrible weed *C. rapunculoeides,* when it wants to delude us into admitting it to our gardens. Never was such a wolf in such a woolly sheep's coat of a seductive (and indeed in itself not mendacious) name.

C. pulla is the imperial glory of the alpine section, where, in dark humus or in ordinary poor yellow loam among the blocks of mountain limestone on the Styrian Alps, its fine thready rootlets run about along the edges of the stones, outlining their rims with emerald, or expanding into broad masses of bright-green glossy leaves, oval-pointed and toothed, from which come up those daintiest of stems, each hanging out one sheeny bell of violet satin. In old days it was the tradition that *C. pulla* hated lime, and all sorts of precautions were taken to avoid it, with the result that the victim was usually a mimp. Now, however, we have realized the truth at last—that no good limy loam, especially if clammy or rather moist, can ever come amiss to the essentially calcareous *C. pulla ;* and it is rapidly becoming a weed accordingly, either on the banks of the rock-work, or (most especially) in the moraine-mixture, where it is neither to hold nor to bind. In nature there occurs here and there a strange form suggesting a hybrid of *C. pulla* × *C. rhomboidalis*—a leafy thing intermediate in height, but rather resembling a specially tall and stout *C. pulla*, with flowers which, instead of being dark purple, as one would have expected, are of a delicate whitish violet, large and satiny as in *C. pulla* itself. Like *C. pulla*, this is of the heartiest habit. These two, again, are remarkable among the alpine Campanulas, for their tolerance of a shaded cool exposure, even if they are also quite happy in full sun ; though *C. Morettiana* has not their appreciation of damp soil by any means, this also may sometimes be found on cool dank cliffs, though certainly more robust when more fully exposed to light and air.

C. × *pulloeides* is a garden-hybrid of extreme beauty, a magnified version of *C. pulla*, nearly twice the height, softer, hairier, and with flowers of twice the size, much shorter and wider in the bell, but of the same dazzling violet, and sheeny texture. It suggests the influence of *C. turbinata* on *C. pulla*, and is no less hearty of habit in good conditions. Yet another important garden-plant is the hybrid called almost always *C. G. F. Wilson*, but sometimes *C. Balfourii*, and still more often, in foreign lists, trying to delude one into hope of a new species by calling itself *C. Wilsonii*. It is a remarkably massive small treasure, with a remarkable profusion of flowers which are half-erect, open, wide bells of violet, paler at the base, the whole development and vigour and hairiness and greyness of it suggesting that here the other parent must have been *C. turbinata*. Of this again there is a form called Aurea, because the foliage tends to turn of an unwholesome yellowish green ; this should be avoided, as being far more weakly than the other, which is among the most vigorous glories of high summer in any open place.

C. pulvinaris, however, from Cappadocia, is one of the choicest, forming a neat tuft, small and dense, with minute narrow leaves and well-built lovely blossoms.

C. punctata is a slight noble species from Northern Asia, where you may often see it by the pathside in the Alps of Japan. It runs freely here and there, here and there sending up its soft oval heart-shaped leaves on their long stalks ; then come the flower-spikes, about a foot high or more, from which hang out a few of the most beautiful long bells, waxy-creamy pink, peppered inside with red dots. This campanula looks as if it should become a real weed with us, yet comparatively rarely proves a success out of doors in England unless in very light and sandy soils, and in full sun. Two most notable garden plants, however, clearly derive from *C. punctata*. These are *C. van Houttei* and *C. Burghaltii*, the one with long purple bells. and the other much nearer to *C. punctata*, but both thriving with the utmost heartiness, and proving of the utmost preciousness alike in rock-garden or border ; uniting to the grace of *C. punctata* a much more leafy, free and energetic habit suggesting the influence of *C. latifolia*. Of the two the smaller seems to be *C. van Houttei*, forming tufts and colonies of narrowish-leaved stems of about a foot, from which depend those long and delicate bells. The origin of both these is unknown, and it is even quite possible that *C. van Houttei* at least may be merely a garden development of some specially vigorous form of *C. punctata* itself ; they both take after that species, anyhow, in blooming rather early for their race—towards mid-June.

C. pusilla (Haenke)=*C. Bellardii*, Ten., *q.v.*

C. pyramidalis is too tall and stout and graceless for the rock-garden, with its gaunt stiff spires, so closely stuck with a mass of large flowers that will not open properly in a unanimous spike of splendour, but only here and there a stray saucer of white or blue at a time, most ill-furnished and untidy in effect.

C. Raddeana comes from the Alps of Transcaucasia, and is a useful and charming new arrival, in aspect suggestive of *Symphyandra armena*, but with larger blossoms. These are of a most glorious violet, in design like those of a Harebell, but longer and fuller, gracefully carried on stems of 9 inches or so, while the basal leaves of the tuft are specially attractive—round, glossy, heart-shaped, delicately scalloped and toothed at the edge, and spraying about this way and that on their long fine stems. *C. Raddeana* grows well and increases rapidly in any good open soil and place.

C. radicosa (*C. Boissieri*, Sprun.) sends out an unstinted supply of weak flopping stems, which carry one-sided leafy sprigs or spikes of flowers smaller than in *C. Elatines*, but of a good rich purple, and after the same star-pattern with the style more or less sticking out. They are often bunched in clusters of from one to three on each branchlet. These stalks are hardly longer than the central rosettes, which are made up of long oblong blunt leaves, saw-edged or scalloped, diminishing down to a long petiole, and about an inch and a half in all. The whole growth is smooth or else clothed in spreading down. (Mountain-tops, as on the summit-rocks of Taygetos.)

C. radula attains a foot or so in the rocks of higher Kurdistan, where it forms a fat stock, and so emits rosettes of firm ovate leaves, crimped and sharply toothed, with a foot-stalk of half their length (which is about a couple of inches or less or more). From this rise many rather weak, almost unbranching sprays, erect, pale green, bristly and leafy, developing each into a fine fountain of rather narrow bright violet-blue goblets, which, however, are bigger and broader than in that handsome biennial, *C. sibirica*. Probably this also is monocarpic. There is a minor form, *C. r. coriacea*, only about half a foot high, from the limestone cliffs of Van in Armenia at elevations of some 5000 feet.

C. Raineri occupies but an infinitesimal space of the world's wide expanse. For this, the most sensational perhaps of our European Alpine Bells, is confined to the upper limestones of the Bergamask mountains about the Italian Lakes, where it shares the untraversable precipices with *Saxifraga Vandellii*, the Saxifrage always being found on the sunny exposure, and the Campanula very often, and apparently by choice, most abundant in the cooler, where it fills every chink and cranny with its long fine runners, outlining each crack in the precipice with its tufts of ash-grey little leafage, rhomboidal-pointed and toothed; or, in nooks where it has more room, develops into a hoary tufted mass hidden in August by a close crowd of immense china-blue cups of a delicate swelling outline, a waxy-smooth texture, and a radiant charm of serene and unconquerable beauty impossible to express, there in those gaunt places making splashes of blueness up and down the impregnable walls. In cultivation, however, *C. Raineri* is of no less unconquerable temper; the least fragment will form a plant, if inserted in sand; and, in any good moraine, chipful limy bed of soil, or even ordinary crevice, it will accumulate tufts of foliage actually more hearty than at home, and at least as lavish of their blossoms; but here they develop their stems to some 3 or 4 inches to produce their saintly chalices, instead of bearing them close upon a tight mass after the condensed habit of the Alps. The only enemy before whom *C. Raineri* goes down is the slug; against which the only

PLATE 17.

CAMPANULA RADDEANA.
(Photo. R.B.G., Edinburgh.)

CAMPANULA RAINERI.
(Photo. R.B.G.. Edinburgh.)

PLATE 18.

CAMPANULA SPECIOSA.
(Photo. R. A. Malby.)

CAMPANULA SARMATICA.
(Photo. R.B.G., Edinburgh.)

VOL. I.

sure remedy is nothing more or less than an orange—which, if cut across and eaten out with a spoon, then leaves you the squeezed drained halves to put about in the rock-garden, where they will at once attract every slug from miles around, which can thus be captured by the hundred each morning and consigned to their just doom. It is true that this may make your garden look a little as if a beanfeast had there lately raged ; however, even this is better than rings of zinc or bran, and incomparably better than finding your *C. Raineri* in the morning a bare ruined choir where late the sweet buds sang—to say nothing of the economical fact that you have already had the felicity of eating your orange. For *C. pseudo-Raineri*, see under *C. turbinata*.

C. ramosissima, the brilliant annual often called *attica, Loreyi*, or *drabaefolia*.

C. rapunculoeides, the most insatiable and irrepressible of beautiful weeds. If once its tall and arching spires of violet bells prevail on you to admit it to your garden, neither you nor its choice inmates will ever know peace again.

C. Rapunculus, an English biennial, not in the least like Rapunculoeides, whose name says that it has taken *C. Rapunculus* for a model. For this is rather more in the style of *C. patula*, but with uglyish narrower cups sitting more stiffly to the spike, and in all ways vastly inferior, though variable.

C. Regina (Alboff)=*C. mirabilis, q.v.*

C. Reiseri is a handsome rock-species, in the cousinship of *C. anchusaeflora*, but an improvement in having much larger wider blossoms, on stiff stout stems. There is a variety too, *C. R. Leonis*, with sprays that never branch. Both are weak floppets, and both have the style sticking far out of the expanded flower.

C. retrorsa, a Levantine annual in the way of *C. Loefflingi*.

C. Reuteriana, from Asia Minor, comes very near to *C. strigosa, q.v.*

C. rhomboidalis is well known to all who have seen the alpine fields one undulating sea of sapphire waves beneath its sheaves of noble deep-blue Harebells gathered loosely towards the top of those stalwart stems, clothed in rhomboidal toothy foliage all the way up. In cultivation this beautiful thing is no less stalwart and splendid in any border, but its 2 feet or 18 inches fit it chiefly for bolder sweeps in the rock-garden, among such old friends and neighbours as *Anemone alpina*. Especially lovely, too, are its varieties, which have so far been almost all spared the indignity of names. These are of every tone, from dark midnight-blue, through lilacs and delicate china-blues, deeper or paler, to clear silvery tones, and at last to virgin white.

CAMPANULA.

These you must get for yourself. An hour in any alpine hayfield in August will bring you in half a dozen things for whose match in beauty you might easily range a Vincent Square Show in vain. And, finally, a "novelty" sent out recently as Little Gem is surely nothing else but one of these forms of *C. rhomboidalis*, but not a favourable sample, nor deserving its distinction, being neither little, nor a gem, but a rather leafy *C. rhomboidalis* of sombre colour, differing chiefly from the type in a slightly dwarfer habit and yellowish-green foliage.

C. Riverslea. See under *C. carpatica.*

C. Rosani (Ten.)=*C. versicolor, q.v.*

C. rotundifolia is best considered as a huge aggregate, of which our common Harebell, that specially bears that name, is only one. Every country and almost every alp produces a slightly different-seeming Harebell, and on the most subtle and minute and evanescent peculiarities of each have botanists built up an imposing list of species ; which, however, all tend to fade into Rotundifolia again after a year or two of cultivation, losing that precise hairiness of calyx or deflexion of lobe, on the strength of which they had been promoted to specific rank, and published to the world as, let us say, *C. Marchesettii*, thus cruelly to delude innocent purchasers who, under that name, had thought to be buying some new and thrilling Campanula. These, then, are the sub-species into which *C. rotundifolia* offers itself to purchasers by a dozen specifics, all meaning pretty much the same thing ; though some, indeed, of the forms are well-marked and valuable. *C. rotundifolia* of the North is always lovely with its pale-blue flowers loose and abundant ; it has a beautiful white form, a ragged-robin development like a blue whirlwind called *C. r. soldanellaeflora*, a double pale-blue rosette which is paradoxically pretty, and the rather ambitiously named *C. r. Warleyi*, which appears to be another semi-double form or garden hybrid of extra-free growth. Then follow a crowd of dim and unmarked plants whose claim to recognition are of the slightest, as indeed is most properly conceded by *C. inconcessa*, if not by *C. Marchesettii, C. solstitialis*, and *C. praesignis*, all depending upon some slight differentiation that the change from one side of the hill to the other would probably wipe away. More marked, though not easily distinguishable in the eye of the garden, are *C. carnica*, *C. pseudo-carnica, C. Langsdorffii, C. arcuata*, and *C. linifolia*—these being forms replacing typical *C. rotundifolia* in the Alps—handsome ordinary Harebells, but with flowers of much more violet tone than ours, and varying widely alike in size of bloom and depth of colour. There are pure whites, and delicate silver-pales, and from one pinch of seed a dozen different nameable forms. The thing called *Cam-*

194

panula alaskana, again, is nothing more than a specially ample and splendid development of the English Harebell; while more alpine meadow-kinds of misty and evanescent personality are *C. Baumgartenii, C. pinifolia, C. ficarioeides, C. farinulenta,* and the form sent out wrongly as *C. subpyrenaica.* A quite different affair, however, is that most distinct treasure called by catalogues *C. Hostii;* this is a solid-flowered *C. rotundifolia* of dwarfer, stiffer, stockier habit, with rather larger and wider bells rather more rigidly arranged in a tighter raceme. This is chiefly known in its beautiful white variety, very common and useful in gardens, but I have once collected a single clump of the purple type in the river-bed by Rosenlaui, a most striking and sturdy Campanula of 8 inches. But now we go back to the land of vagueness with magnificent frail-stemmed *C. Scheuchzeri,* whose startlingly big bells of richest violet are the joy of everyone who sees them nodding in damp places on the Alps. Nothing could well appear a more definite species. Yet in cultivation it always slips back in a year or two into something indistinguishable from the aggregate species *C. rotundifolia.* There is an albino of this, too, and a variety *C. S. Kerneri,* both of which lie under the same condemnation. *C. valdensis,* however, escapes—one of the most marked of the group, quite constant and very beautiful. It has a graceful habit, erect but not stiff, about 9 inches high; and is notably lavish, especially in the garden, with flowers of large size and the most enthralling bishop's purple, which contrasts nobly with the dense silver down in which the whole plant is vested, and which it never loses. This was long sent out from a famous nursery under the name of *C. alpina*—too high a presumption for even so glorious a mere form as this. Last of the group comes the strangest of all, *C. stenocodon,* a rarity occurring in dry stony places of the Maritime Alps, as for instance on the way up to the Miniera di Tenda above San Dalmazzo. This is not in any way really and permanently to be distinguished from the group of *C. rotundifolia* except—and most markedly—by its extraordinary and unvarying flowers, which, instead of being bells, are long narrow tubes of violet-blue, in shape not unlike those of *C. Tommasiniana.* It is a fine thing, vigorous and elegant, having all the heartiness of the family, and delighting in moraine.

C. ruderalis is yet another species with narrow bells of deep blue. But this removes our gaze to the high and arid places of Afghanistan, where, at some 9000 to 12,000 feet, will be found this tuffet, all rough and bristlish, of minute oblong-elliptic foliage, from which rise delicate stems of 6 inches or so, carrying either one flower or a loose flight of two or three.

C. rupestris is a vague and invalid name. Beautiful things and ugly have alike been sent out under it. The true *C. rupestris* makes a silver-haired rosette of lyrate leaves, after the kind of *C. Andrewsii*; as indeed it should be, for it is only the variety *brachyantha* of *C. Andrewsii* itself, producing shorter velvety bells of pale beautiful colour and a waxy crystalline texture. Beware of sham *C. rupestris* in catalogues.

C. rupicola is a very lovely little rock-plant from the crevices of Parnassus. In habit it is near *C. oreadum*, but here the small ash-grey oval leaves of the tuft, wedge-shaped at the base, *are toothed instead of being smooth* at the edge. The crown throws out a number of flopping stems of about 6 inches, delicate and branching, with sprays each bearing two or three flowers; and these are handsome long bells of violet-blue. But in this species the segments of the calyx are short, broad, blunt, and gashed into teeth; instead of being narrow-pointed, velvety, and perfectly entire at the edge, as in *C. oreadum*. There is no reason why *C. rupicola* should not prove a sound perennial, in well-drained crevice or moraine.

C. Ruprechtii, from the Alps of North Persia, is not unlike *C. Saxifraga*, but here the stalks are finer and more twisting, about 2 or 3 inches in length, and softly downy; it also spreads from the branching rhizome, which here is thick and fattish. The blossoms, borne lonely on their delicate stems, are large purple bells as in *C. Saxifraga*.

C. ruthenica (MB.)=*C. bononiensis, q.v.*

C. sabatia is a form of *C. macrorrhiza* from the Capo di Noli, which only differs from the type in having crystalline bristles on the calyx.

C. sardoa (Levier). See under *C. macrorrhiza*.

C. sarmatica inhabits the rocky places and stony slopes of Central Caucasus, up to about 4000 feet or rather more. It is a vigorous and coarse stalwart of medium size, with long oval-oblong scalloped foliage, grey and downy, on long stalks; the flower-spikes are several from the same clump, about a foot or so in height, and densely laden with goodly hanging bells of pale grey-blue. It is of the easiest culture in any open place, and seeds profusely. But it cannot, as has sometimes been claimed, enter into comparison with *C. barbata*, having no such grace in its magnificence. It blooms quite early in the summer, and is soon over.

C. Sartorii dwells in the high rocky summits and grottoes of Andros. It is a velvety frail thing, with procumbent leafy boughs carrying scattered sprays of violet stars above the minute rounded leaves, cut at the end into five or seven teeth, with a stem as long as themselves (which is not saying much). The whole beautiful and most desirable mass recalls *C. Portenschlagiana*, of which it is an almost precise repetition, except that the entire tuft is clothed in down instead of being perfectly green and smooth; while the leafage is smaller, the habit more decumbent, and the flowers, which are very nearly if not quite as large as in its bigger rival, are not so deeply cleft, forming more perfect cups, from which the stigma slightly projects.

C. saxatilis was long the disconcertingly doubtful name of a species disconcertingly rare, seen once or twice on the North coast of Crete, and then for many a season despaired of, until the same thing, or a form intimately allied to it, was found in the Carpathians. *C. saxatilis* is a species of quite pre-eminent beauty (even after the last)—a rock-plant, imitating *C. Raineri* in all its habit and beauty, and perhaps actually threatening the supremacy of its almost unsurpassable model; for here, though the leaves, tuffets, and so forth are nearly interchangeable (but the leaves are more oblong-spoon-shaped), and the shoots upon their stems of an inch or two carry likewise as many as five flowers, these flowers themselves strike out a different line of grandeur, *tubular* deep bells of the richest sapphire velvet and amplest size. There is also a variety *C. s. Simonellii*, with only one bloom to a shoot, which must be a treasure; but meanwhile we have yet got to acquire the type, which must be more of a treasure still.

C. Saxifraga, however, we already possess, to our delight, though the most unnecessary confusion prevails between this species and the allied *C. tridentata;* till, in the weakness of despair, many lists throw up their hands, and make the two synonymous. *C. Saxifraga*, like the other, makes a series of tufts, composed of low-lying narrow leafage, tapering by degrees to a stalk; and above this, on single stems of 2 or 3 inches, appear magnificent violet bells, suggesting those of *C. alpestris*, but more abundant, thrown out from the rosette in numbers instead of standing solitary and horizontal-belled, one in the middle of each. The differences between this and the closely-allied *C. tridentata* are marked and simple. The habit is the same; but in *C. Saxifraga* the narrow leaves are *quite untoothed at the edge*, or else, *if* toothed, are *toothed from the middle of the leaf* along to its tip, instead of merely having some three or five marked notches across their very end, as in *C. tridentata;* the calyx-segments, too, are longer here in proportion to the corolla. This royal Amethyst replaces *C. alpestris* in steep rocky places between 4000 and 5000 feet in the Northern Caucasus and away to Russian Armenia, while *C. tridentata* occupies the same rough stony grounds, and fulfils the same high function, in Pontus and Cappadocia at much greater altitudes, between 6500 and 10,000 feet. They both have the needs and respond heartily to the treatment of *C. alpestris*, even as they follow it in the same line of loveliness.

CAMPANULA.

CC. scabrella, Scouleri, sindjarensis, specularioeides, stellaris, sub-alpina, and *sylvatica* are all useless for the garden, or unworthy.

C. Scheuchzeri. See under *C. rotundifolia.*

C. sclerotricha, a worthless biennial coarse thing like *C. Grossekii,* from shady gardens of Persia.

C. scutellata is only an annual, but worth admission, being a fine species from the Balkan regions and Greece, suggesting *C. linifolia,* but with more splendid bells of violet.

C. serotina has little claim to recognition, for it is hardly more than a late-blooming form of *C. glomerata,* and biennial, it seems, at that.

C. sibirica, however, is far from worthless, though equally biennial. It is general in Central Europe, of erect growth, with panicles of purple blossoms narrowly arranged on their sprays. There is a more diffuse form called *C. s. divergens,* which is really very beautiful. They can both be sown in waste poor places in the sun.

C. sidoniensis is another admissible annual, like a magnified *C. abietina,* but of straggling loose habit—or, in other words, like a large form of *C. patula.*

C. silenifolia comes from the Baikal, and at its worst is leafy and rather coarse, while at its best it earns praise, being after the way of an improved *C. Steveni,* with minutely-toothed leaves, faintly fringed with hair, but otherwise wholly green and smooth. These continue up the rather tall stems, that display as many as eight large shallow starry cups of violet, carried in a loose shower, each by itself.

C. × Smithii is now probably lost. It was a little Come-by-chance with small hairy leaves and 6-inch hairy stems, producing a profusion of half-erect flowers of grey-blue. It is said to have sprung to birth spontaneously in a frame containing *C. fragilis* and *C. "caespitosa"* —the *C. caespitosa* here meaning, not the genuine species, but *C. Bellardii.*

C. solstitialis. See under *C. rotundifolia.*

C. spathulata (WK.)=*C. sibirica divergens.*

C. spathulata. See under *C. Spruneri,* of which it is a variety.

C. speciosa is a superb species, chiefly Pyrenean, which is either biennial or monocarpic. It is found in rocky places of Catalonia, and again in the Cevennes, records of it from the South of France being most suspicious. It forms great flat rosettes sometimes 18 inches across or so, of narrow bristly greyish foliage, scalloped at the edge all along, and coarsely toothed at the tip. This, at flowering time, lies even flatter than ever, as up comes one stocky spike of a foot or more, liberally set with enormous violet Canterbury bells; after which the plant seeds and dies. In cultivation it can do magnificently in very hard, hot, and deep stony ground in fullest sun. *C. affinis, q.v.,* *may* be only a variety of this, but differs profoundly in many points, and is not so certainly not perennial. In *C. speciosa* the spike is about a foot high. (It can be only about 4 inches, furnished with only two or three bells, and the rosette about three in diameter; in which case the neat clump suggests some absurd hybrid between *C. alpestris* and *C. alpina.*) The flowers hang, the segments of the calyx are quite narrow and not more than a third of the bell's total length, and the style is no longer than the corolla and does not protrude; in *C. affinis* the stems from the rosettes are numerous instead of only single, they are never less than a foot, and rise usually to much greater heights, often attaining nearly 4 feet; the flowers are held *erect* in a long cylindrical raceme, the calyx-lobes are *broadly egg-shaped* and *half the length* of the bell, which is lobed to the middle, far more deeply than in *C. speciosa,* and with the *style projecting far out of its mouth.*

C. " speciosa " of some lists is merely a big-flowered form of *C. glomerata,* usually the one called *C. g. dahurica. C. glomerata* varies distractingly, and there is even a tiny 2-inch dainty form called *C. g. pusilla.*

C. sphaerothrix (Griseb.)=*C. expansa.*

C. spicata is not uncommon in dry hot places at low elevations in the Alps. It is a rather ugly biennial, with tall rat-tail spikes of small purple bells sitting tight and close and erect along the stiff stalk. It has produced a hybrid at Kew, with *C. thyrsoidea,* which is said to stand precisely between its parents, and should therefore double the ugliness of both, with the added ugliness of yellow blent with purple.

C. Spruneri is a feeble thing but very beautiful, tangled up with oaks and brooms in the coppices of Argolis beside the echoing sea; and thence ascends to the sub-alpine regions of Olenos, Kyllene, and Parnassus. It throws out a number of weak stems from a central tuft of pale-green foliage, exactly as in *C. Stevenii,* but with a few minute warty hairs. The shoots spread here and there through the ground, emerging at last in sprays that lie weakly down and then rise up at the end, each carrying from three to half a dozen very large and lovely pale-blue flowers as big as Persicifolia's, on fine dainty branches. It has borrowed many names of other species in its time, and has been in turn *C. ramosissima, C. Herminii,* and *C. patula;* in its highest reaches on the upper slopes of Parnassus it develops an alpine variety called *C. S. spathulata,* quite dwarf, with spatulate leaves and one large flower.

C. × *Stansfieldii* is a gift of Heaven, and its history is wrapped in cloud. It was, and sometimes still is, imported with the Dalmatian

Bells that seem to be its parents. For the plant appears an obvious intermediate, if natural distribution will admit such a thing (as it does at one point, on Monte Maggiore), between *C. Tommasiniana* and *C. Waldsteiniana*, or possibly *C. pulla*. For it has a quickly-rambling habit unlike either *C. Tommasiniana's* or *C. Waldsteiniana's*, forming rapidly into ever-widening colonies of delicate 4- or 5-inch stems, not densely set, but spreading easily about, and leafy with rhomboidal pale-green leaves, rather hairy. Each of these shoots ends in a single pendent bell, shallow and wide, of soft warm violet, suggesting the influence rather of *C. pulla* upon the narrow china-blue tubes of *C. Tommasiniana*, to which in all other points it stands quite close, though the leafage, borne in the same way, is broader and makes more effect. *C. × Stansfieldii* is a treasure of the highest claims, and is of the easiest culture in open limy soil.

C. Stelleri is an even better variety of *C. pilosa*, q.v.

C. stenocodon. See under *C. rotundifolia*.

C. stenosiphon; a form or sub-species of *C. glomerata*,=*C. Boissieri* (Sprun.), and handsome with large flower-clusters, in the beech-woods of Thessaly.

C. Stevenii has lately come into general cultivation amid plaudits, from some point of its enormous range from the dry upper alpine grasses of Demavend, through all Asia Minor, Armenia, Cappadocia, Caucasus, and away into the Altai and Siberia. It forms mats of fine green foliage rather like those of *C. abietina*, smooth at the edge, or faintly scalloped, and wholly bald and green but for a minute fringe of hair sometimes at their base. Up come tall straggling and very weakly stems that cry for pea-sticks; and, at the height of 6 or 9 inches, these produce flowers in Abietina's tone of warm vinous lilac, but much paler, longer, deeply cleft and recurving, rather shallow bells instead of still shallower open stars. Much more attractive is the dwarf variety, *C. S. nana*, which is really charming, having all the vigorous matting habit of the type, but carrying its blossoms on stems so short that they have not time to think of flopping or straggling beneath their burden. This must be a high-alpine development, and has a marked preference for quite *damp places* in the garden, and rather cool though always open exposures.

C. stricta is a big species in the way of *C. Trachelium*, tall and handsome, from elevations of some 5000 feet in Asia Minor, it has narrow foliage and rather large flowers. There is some confusion in gardens as to a problem now (1913) being sent out as *C. "libanotica."* The thing so called is said to be pre-eminent in flower. But it is plainly a mere form or sub-species of *C. persicifolia*, of much reduced size, and

PLATE 19.

CAMPANULA × STANSFIELDII.
(Photo. R. A. Malby.)

CAMPANULA TURBINATA.
(Photo. R. A. Malby.)

PLATE 20.

CAMPANULA ZOYSII.
(Photo. R. A. Malby.)

CARLINA ACANTHIFOLIA.
(Photo. R. A. Malby.)

PLATE 21.

CELMISIA MONROI.

CAMPANULA THYRSOEIDES.

with leaves picturesquely curled and crimped along their edge at first, and coarsely sharply toothed with a mark of white in each dentation. The spikes, too, are those of *C. persicifolia*, about a foot or less in height, and tending, it seems, to appear in late autumn. But what authority can the name possess ? For the one recorded *C. libanotica* (DC.) is a variety of *C. stricta ;* and *C. stricta* is not only a species in the group of Trachelium, not of Persicifolia, but *C. s. libanotica* should be a *decumbent* variety even of that. So that there must be arrest of judgment with regard to the name of gardeners' *C. "libanotica,"* though it may fairly be said that this pleasant Persicifolia-plant has promise.

C. strigosa, a pretty hairy annual of small growth and large blossom ; common in the fields of Palestine.

C. suanetica, from near Muri in the Suanetian Caucasus, is much to be looked for. It is an improvement on *C. radula,* but has larger, long-pointed leaves, perfectly smooth and deeply heart-shaped, about 2 or 3 inches long, carried on graceful foot-stalks of 3 or 4 inches, with many erect unbranching leafy stems, breaking each into a great fountain, a foot high or more, of violet-blue bells, bigger and broader than in *C. radula.*

C. subpyrenaica, of too many lists, is merely yet another form or sub-species in the group of *C. rotundifolia.*

C. subpyrenaica, Timb., the true species, from Montserrat, stands closest to *C. persicifolia,* of which it might only prove a form. It has very long narrow outward-curving leaves, and flowers few and extremely large, at the top of the stem, even surpassing Persicifolia's in size, and with a bigger calyx, covered with broad bent hairs. Its description suggests some affinities with the stiff ugly thing sent out sometimes as *C. cristallocalyx ;* but it is plain that whatever the hairiness of the calyx, *C. subpyrenaica* should be a valuable species, if species indeed it be.

C. sulfurea, a really charming annual for a group, with bright yellow flowers.

C. telephioeides is reminiscent of *C. radicosa, q.v.;* a frail and feeble floppet from damp alpine grass-slopes on Berytagh at about 8000 to 9000 feet. They both suggest *C. Elatines,* alike in habit and in flower-star, staring upwards from the prostrate sprays. But *C. telephioeides* has a difference from *C. radicosa* in wearing the bracts quite narrow instead of broadly egg-shaped, and the style invariably sticks up far out of the flowers.

C. tenella (Jord.)=*C. Bellardii.*

C. Tenorii (Mor.)=*C. versicolor,* Sibth., *q.v.*

CAMPANULA.

C. teucrioeides rambles about in the stone shingles on the Western face of Tmolos, above Bozdagh in Lydia, near the summit. It makes fine little downy leafy stems, with extremely minute leaves, wedge-shaped-oval, and almost feathered into five or seven deep triangular teeth, the lower ones with a very short stalk, and the rest sitting straight to the shoots, which attain 3 inches, rather less than more, and there end, in one (or occasionally two) nodding bells of blue, most delicate and charming. A typical and precious moraine jewel.

C. thyrsoeides is a common alpine of the upper meadows, which is not by any means without its uses, though only monocarpic. It forms a wide rosette of many very long and narrow leaves, hoary-grey, like the whole growth, with rough bristles. From this comes up a stout trunk of 9 or even 18 inches, packed close and tight with rather large erectish bells of pale straw-yellow. In the right places, as in the grass and among more showy meadow-plants, *C. thyrsoeides* can give a good account of itself, and is not even devoid of magnificence in a choicer spot, on some high ledge. It seeds profusely and even automatically.

C. tomentella = *C. versicolor*, q.v.

C. tomentosa = *C. Andrewsii*, q.v.

C. Tommasiniana gives a welcome instance of an endemic species which has perfectly established itself in cultivation. This lovely treasure is confined to the district about Istria, and even there is local. But in cultivation it is the delight of any open soil, in a select corner, sending up sheaves and bushes from its increasing tuft, of fine single stems, often 6 or 9 inches high, set with thick and narrowish saw-edged foliage, and then in summer and on into August hanging out a little steepleful of long pale-blue bells beneath which the elastic leafy shoots must bend and sway and decline. It never runs, but adds yearly to the size of its clumps, and can best be multiplied by their outer developments carefully taken off in August and propagated on. There also dwells on Monte Maggiore, one of Tommasiniana's homes, a form of *C. Waldsteiniana* called *C. W. Freyeri*, which not only for a long time bred a quite unnecessary confusion between the two remarkably distinct species, but may also have provided the opportunity for the production of *C. Stansfieldii*.

C. Trachelium, the Nettle-bell, is not uncommon in England, but a fine thing none the less, trying, not unsuccessfully, to hit a mean between the respective beauties of *C. glomerata* and *C. latifolia*. Though too coarse for choice places, it is handsome in the grass of the wild garden, and the alpine meadows have yielded a beautiful albino, as well as some delicate shades of grey and very pale blue.

C. trachyphylla, also called *C. Intybus*, is a quite inferior and coarse-leaved small-flowered weed in the section of *C. Trachelium*, and is no more worth culture than another coarsened version, *C. trachelioeides*.

C. trichopoda (*C. spathulata*, Ehrenb.), not appreciated by all authorities at its face-value, is a rock-plant, daintily grey with down, and with very very many, very very fine stems springing out to some 5 inches from the central rosette, which is made up of oval little leaves, perfectly smooth-edged, and drawing down to a thread-like petiole rather thin and membranous in texture. This may be seen about 5000 feet up, on the shady cliffs and cool places of Lebanon, its lax and almost fleshy branchlings splaying flat against the face of the cliff, and breaking out in a galaxy of small pale-blue flowers.

C. tridentata is the beautiful delight of all our gardens, so often confused with *C. Saxifraga*. From this it differs principally and obviously in the long narrow-oval leaves. These are the same, to start with, in both species, and have the same fringe of almost woolly hair. But in *C. Saxifraga they are perfectly smooth all round their edge*, or, if toothed at all, *toothed from the middle of the leaf-blade along up to its tip*. But in *C. tridentata* they are perfectly *smooth-edged up to the end*, and then *there*, and there *only*, and there *always*, notched into three definite nicks (very rarely into five or six). Otherwise these cousins of *C. alpestris* form a trinity of beauty with *C. ciliata*, from which, among other points, *C. Saxifraga* differs finally in having a *woollyish calyx*, not set with any stiffish hairs as in *C. ciliata*. They are all of them most resplendent tuft-forming species of the stony rough places and alpine barrens, profusely radiating from their rosettes those single stalks, each carrying one voluminous bell of violet. *C. tridentata* lives in Pontus, Armenia, and Cappadocia, from 6500 to 10,000 feet, and in its higher reaches develops a stemless form called *C. stenophylla*. The type itself has had many names, besides the illegitimate one that belongs to *C. Saxifraga*, for it has been *C. tridens* (Rupr., Bieb., R. and Schl.) and also *C. rupestris* (MB.). And there has even been a despairing movement by Trautvetter to sweep into the one name of *C. tridentata* all the following diverse and distinct Campanulas : *CC. ciliata, Saxifraga, Ruprechtii, bellidifolia, Aucheri, ardonensis*, and *petrophila*—a confession of weakness in no way justified by the clearly separable characters of the different species as described. The culture of *C. tridentata* is, of course, the same as that of the others in its group ; and, like all the rest, and *C. alpestris* also, it is an ornament of mid summer, profusely blooming and then quickly passing over, with no more glory to fill the remaining months, when the Elatinoids, Garganicas, Rotundifolias, Bellardiis, Isophyllas, and *C. Zoysii* appear, to take up the torch and carry it gloriously forward into the last hours of autumn.

C. tubulosa (Lam.)=*C. corymbosa*, Desf. (*C. pelviformis*, Lam.). The other *C. tubulosa* is not nearly so well worthy of consideration, being close to *C. hagielia*, but with shorter stems and fewer smaller flowers, and narrower tubes.

C. turbinata can hardly be claimed as a species apart from *C. carpatica*, but it is so rare in gardens that one may give it a corner of choice ; Carpaticas of every shape and size being sent out under this name indeed, but hardly ever the true *C. turbinata*, that flat mass of grey-hairy foliage, almost close upon which stand up those huge saucer-cups of china-blue, each by itself, and giving at last almost the effect of a coarsened and profuser and more unanimously-flowering *C. Raineri*. Indeed, if ever there really has been a superior form of *C. Raineri*, or any basis for that mysterious name, *C. pseudo-Raineri*, one might suspect in it the influence of *C. turbinata*, if in point of fact it were anything more than a slightly diverse form of *C. Raineri* itself, or perhaps sometimes no other than pure *C. turbinata*. (*C.* × *turbinata* × *Raineri* is a good thing.)

C. tymphaea is so close to Edraianthus that it ought perhaps to be removed from Campanula, like the ci-devant *C. Parnassi*. *C. tymphaea* is also a very rare species, peculiar to Pindus, where the sheep usually eat it down to the rosette of long narrow spidery leaves, minutely scalloped ; perhaps because they dislike, except as food, these un-beautiful purple funnels gathered into a tight head at the top of the 12-inch stem.

C. tyrolensis is a form of *C. Bellardii*, q.v.

C.uniflora, from Norway, through all the Arctic Circle and down into the Colorado Rockies, is a rare and precious species, running about in the high and stony places after the manner of *C. Bellardii*, with thick little smooth-edged leafage at the base, spoon-shaped or oblong. The stems rise to about 4 inches or less, set here and there with quite narrow leaflings, and ending each in a single beautiful bell of deep-blue, swinging rather horizontal, and about half an inch in length. This is a most lovely delicate jewel, asking for the moist moraine or grit-bed, where it should be sedulously watched and cherished.

C. urticaefolia (Sch.)=*C. Trachelium.*

C. valdensis. See under *C. rotundifolia ;* but so beautiful a plant with its silver-hoary foliage and its unalterable big violet bells, that it clamours unappeasably for rank of its own.

C. van Houttei. See under *C. punctata.*

C. Velenowskyi, a magnificent Bell, close to *C. rotundifolia*, but very large ; the lower leaves being oval and long-stalked, while the upper ones are quite narrow and hug the stem.

C. velutina (Desf.)=*C. mollis.*

C. velutina (Vel.)=*C. lanata.*

C. verruculosa (Link.)=*C. Rapunculus.*

C. versicolor, a most stalwart beauty, but hardly ever seen, all kinds of hispid and horrid gawky weeds having been sent out under this name, which in reality belongs to a perfectly *smooth-leaved* species, rather like a smaller and neater *C. pyramidalis,* but a more certain perennial. It has curving stems, fat and frail and leafy, breaking into a dense pyramid or thyrsus (not a close unbranched stiff spike as in the other) of magnified flowers, wide and saucer-shaped, cleft about three-quarters of their depth into spreading lobes, and dark-violet at their centre, fading outwards to a paler rim. The leaves of the rosette are fattish too, oval or oblong heart-shaped, scalloped or saw-edged, and on long leaf-stalks. *C. versicolor,* still out of reach, is found in Greece in crevices and cliffs of the lower wood-region. There is a downy variety, *C. v. tomentella,* and another, *C. v. thessala,* with smaller flowers, from the Thessalian Olympus.

C. vesula (All.)=*C. persicifolia.*

C. Waldsteiniana inhabits the summit-chinks in some of the Dalmatian mountains—an entrancing and well-beloved joy of the rock-garden, where, in any happy limy rich loam, light and well drained, it forms, like *C. Tommasiniana,* ever-increasing tufty bushes of upright stems ; but here the stems are shorter and stiffer, only about 6 inches or so, and too vigorous ever to give way beneath the flower ; and these, again, are not bells, but the most beautiful wide stars of violet like those of *C. Elatines,* with a paler eye, staring straight up into the eye of day from the top of each little wiry stalk, covering the 4-inch mass in August and September, after which the plant does not die down, but life goes out of the shoots and they are still standing in November, sere and withered skeletons. The leaves are oval, small, and rather dark ; and the whole lovely clump, so delicate and yet so sturdy and male, is quite beyond possibility of mistake or confusion with any other in the garden.

C. Warleyi. See under *C. rotundifolia.*

C. White Star. See under *C. carpatica.*

C. Younghii Brandii, a pubescent form of *C. Lacei, q.v.*

C. Zoysii is the last and strangest of the race—that minute exquisite rock-jewel which you may see filling the crevices and high chinks of the Karawanken, in just such limestone cliffs and crannies as those beloved by *C. Raineri* further West. But *C. Zoysii* is far smaller, making rosettes of quite tiny spoon-shaped foliage, perfectly smooth and glossy and bright green, among which come shoots of several inches carrying a number of long pale-blue bells so oddly bulging and puckered at the mouth as to resemble nothing on earth so much as a tiny soda-water bottle with a ham-frill on the end. And these, in nature, are produced so late in bud that one wonders how they can ever manage to bloom, seeing that hardly any are open even when September is already settling down upon the hills ; just as one wonders, indeed, for what attraction or what defence its wisdom has developed that extraordinary five-lobed pucker of the mouth, which is thus tightly closed, forming a five-rayed star of straight lines, and still further protected by a fluff of fine white inside the lips if you force them apart. In cultivation *C. Zoysii* is always spoken of with a dread and awe, attributable surely to its weird loveliness rather than to any trouble-someness in the plant's own nature ; the idea being that a thing so odd and crotchety in appearance must needs have a temper to match. This is not so ; if *C. Zoysii* " dies on " any gardener it will either be by slugs, or by that excessive care and loving-kindness which de-stroys so many precious alpine gems. Let *C. Zoysii* be put into a bed of rich limy loam, abounding in chips and rubble, perfectly drained, and watered perhaps from underground : then that fantastic little elf will there increase like *C. Bellardii*, and form almost rank tufts, bending about this way and that beneath the profuse weight of its pale and pinched fairy-phials, produced from July till the end of September (and in the moraine it simply grows a yard across and there is no holding it). In fact, under any good treatment in stony ground, sufficiently watered, drained and open, *C. Zoysii* may always be relied on to do its ample little best for you, if trusted so to do, and not incessantly cosseted and worried with attentions it does not want. But it must be safeguarded night and day from slugs, to whom it seems to be caviare and truffles and oysters all combined, attracting them even away from the rich feasts of *C. Raineri* and *C. Elatines*. There was once said to be—as indeed there ought to be, and must— a ravishing variety of virgin white ; this was accordingly purchased for the vast sums commensurate to its worth. And the blossoms that ensued were of a finer blue than in any of the others.

Cardámïne, with one or two honourable exceptions, might be said to be a negligible race. *CC. alpina, carnosa, resedifolia* are poor straggling little alpine Crucifers, weedy and of no charm. *C. asari-folia* is equally undesirable in a large coarse style ; and there are many more of such, all the handsomer Cardamines having now gone away into Dentaria. The common Cuckoo-pint, or Lady's-smock, remains one of the best, and its double form is a really decorative plant for a cool border, amazingly profuse and effective in flower, and no less generous with self-sown seedlings which come true to their parent. The rock-garden, however, has no need to look beyond *C. trifolia*, a beautiful woodland species from the South of Europe, which thrives robustly anywhere in our islands in cool soil, on the shady side of the rock-work at its foot, but in the warmer parts of the South and West becomes at last a weed of almost tropical exuberance. It forms dense low mats of fat trefoil leaves almost fleshy, leathery, and of a very dark sullen green, purple underneath ; and the conspicuous and graceful heads of large white flowers are produced on 3- or 4-inch stems all over the mass in March and April—a most pure and cheering sight, even as the dark heartiness of the little leaves is a potent consolation in winter. Of the larger sorts, again, *C. macrophylla* is a fine and lavish thing for a cool, damp corner by the water, with ample foliage and large pale-purple flowers on graceful stems ; but as a race the Cardamines need not long detain our doubts or our desires.

Carduncellus.—A group of Composites of quite tertiary claims. The best is *C. monspeliensium*, which makes a rosette of pale-green leathery-feathered foliage, amid which sits in summer, almost stemless, a spidery thistly-looking blue flower, about an inch or rather more across. *C. minimus* is sometimes offered also, and is a smaller species of simpler leaf. Their place is on hot, poor, and worthless banks.

Carduus.—No Thistle is ever anything but a weed and a ramper, though few things are more magnificent in wild places than our own *C. eriophorus*, and the Melancholy Thistle of the North—melancholy, poor thing, because it has no spines. This has portly elegance and smooth charm and a clean fragrance (and so has its Albino), but soon proves so grisly an invader in the garden that it has to be discarded, a work which takes some seasons of unremitting toil.

Carex is known for a pest, but *C. baldensis* is small and pretty, if you can dare admit it—a fine wee running Sedge, with little fluffs of white in summer on stems of 3 or 4 inches.

Carlina acanthifolia is the huge stemless Thistle of the Alps, where over the dry green slopes you may see outspread upon the ground its glittering star of intensely spiny handsome leaves, while in the middle sits flat upon it an immense Everlasting-flower, suggesting some wild water-lily invented for an evil sea by Aubrey Beardsley, shimmering and silvery and immortal. It thrives in any deep sunny loam, which should be kept poor, to preserve the stature of the starfish, lest it show any tendency to wax fat and taller and coarser, after the fashion of the handsome but lyingly-named *C. acaulis*, which, together with our own much smaller but still silvery and everlasting *C. vulgaris,* lacks the special charm of unique *C. acanthifolia.*

Carpesium macrocephalum is a large leafy Composite from Japan, with big heads of yellow blossom that are nodding at first. It is not a matter for praise.

Cassandra calyculata.—Another little heath-cousin, closely akin to Cassiope and Andromeda, and asking for the choice treatment of these. It is a bushling of 18 inches, hanging out small white bells upon the lower part of the shoots. Though pleasant, it has no special force of attraction.

Cassíŏpē, a specially fascinating little group of very high alpine or arctic heaths, of more or less minute habit, with the look, as a rule, of a Selaginella or a scaly New-Zealand Veronica, and with the flowers of Lily of the valley. With one exception they are miffy and mimpish jewels, requiring perfect drainage, yet abundance of moisture, not only through their soil (which should consist of half-shredded peat and leaf-mould mixed, and half of very coarse gritty sand, with liberal admixture of chips), but also all around them in the circumambient air. They will prosper best in the underground-watered bed, and their exquisite charm well repays the loving-kindness that it exacts. Among the species are : *C. fastigiata,* a precious and envied plant in gardens, from the great heights of Himalaya, like a wee Cypress-bush of 5 inches or so, in a neat tuft, with its queenly pure little bells hanging out here and there at the side of its four-square column of overlapping green scales, between each of which it shows a *silver lining of chaffy membrane,* which helps, no less than its erecter, tighter, smaller habit and larger flower, to distinguish it from the well-known *C. tetragona,* which is quite an easy and most profitable species to deal with in any open peaty place, nor by any means impatient of a reasonable amount of drought—in fact the one Cassiope thoroughly well adapted for cultivation, in the same style as the last, but larger and much laxer in growth, making Lycopodium bushlings a foot across, liberally hung with wax-drops that seem a trifle smaller and less brilliant than in *C. fastigiata,* but are, nevertheless, of the purest Lily-of-the-valley beauty all through the summer. It covers North America and Arctic Russia, and may be seen by the Lakes in the Clouds above Laggan in the Rockies. In *C. ericoeides* (Arctic Russia, &c.), whose name describes its non-scaly, fine foliage like a heath's, finally fringed and bristly, the flowers have only three lobes to the bell ; while in *C. Mertensiana,* from the Central Rockies, there are four, and the bells themselves are pinkish, and the plant returns to the smooth Lycopodium habit of *C. tetragona*, but with three-sided columns. Not so in the case of the most precious and fine of all, *C. hypnoeides*, from Norway and the chills of the Arctic North, which is the most minute and filmy mass of fine green fur, with large ravishing white bells, preposterously big for the tuft, emerging and swinging on thread-like stems from the ends of the shoots, instead of sprouting from the sides. This is worth any pains to keep in health ; which is almost as hard to do, say the disappointed, as to get hold of it at all. But in a certain Banbury garden, hot and open, there is a specimen of it daring successfully the arid or mouldy extremes of the English climate ; and the plant need never be despaired of, if only sound roots can be acquired. From the neighbourhood of London it departs indignant, and, having no suburban leanings, is as rebellious as a suffragette at Kew. *C. Redowskyi* in East Siberia makes shining masses of dark foliage with a darker margin, and four-lobed flower-bells ; and *C. Selago*, accompanying *C. fastigiata* on the Roof of the World, is a slenderer species of the same kind, more straggling and selaginelloid, and with blossoms that swing out on longer threads ; while in *C. Stelleriana*, from Sitka, the foliage is not scaly, but quite spreading and furry and dense on the shoots, with lobeless globes of blossom emerging from their tips.

Castilleia, a group of American Scrophularias, some of the most gorgeous beauty, with tall spikes of bracts and flowers all alike of the most flaming scarlet. Such is the Indian Paint-brush, *C. acuminata*, as you see it blazing in the coppices above Lake Louise, the most magnificent of all, among the many others being *C. miniata* and *C. pallida* and *C. indivisa*. There is, however, no need to particularise, alas ! for the whole race, like Bartsia, Euphrasia, Pedicularis, and so forth, has the fatal family tendency towards parasitism, and cannot, accordingly, be recommended for general culture — though indeed their clumps have a deceptively independent look, and *C. acuminata*, at least, has once been seen in glory in a damp corner of an Irish garden—but even so, in only a diminished and faded form ; for in conditions alien to its temper the colours of *Castilleia* no longer blaze with such passion as in its native hedgerows and copse-edges.

Catananche coerulea ; the noble blue Cupidone with a darker eye is very beautiful in wild rough places of the south of France, and no less splendid in any border or rock-work, with its wide and lovely blossoms waving on bare long stems of a foot or so, above the rosette of foliage all the summer through. It likes barren rough places of deep soil, and has a white variety only less attractive than its normal chaffy-cupped great Centaurea-hawkweeds of rich blue.

Cathcartia villosa is a small Himalayan Poppy, closely akin to Meconopsis, with heart-shaped foliage cut into three or five deep lobes, and then these lobed again, and all white with soft hair. The stems rise 18 inches or more, producing flowers of golden-yellow like those of *Papaver alpinum*. *C. lyrata* is of smaller habit, almost hairless, with the basal leaves soon dying away, and those on the stem spear-headed and sometimes repeatedly barbed; and slightly hairy on each side. The flowers are solitary or in loose racemes of a few only—rather small, blue or purple, with the four petals rather ragged at the ends and narrow. *C. polygonoeides* is in the same style, with oval heart-shaped leaves almost absolutely untoothed and clasping the stem, with small blossoms, and narrow petals of purplish-white perfectly intact at the tips. It sends up much taller bristly stems than the last, about some 3 feet in height. *C. betonicaefolia* should be the finest of all—an almost hairless plant, with long basal leaves ovate-oblong and blunt, the upper ones clasping the stem, wavy-edged and glaucous underneath, with a fringe of hair. The flowers spring from the embrace of such a leaf—numerous on very long foot-stalks, making a loose fountain as in *Meconopsis integrifolia*. They are large and well-built, with broad wavy-edged petals of bluish violet, with golden stamens. This species comes from Yunnan, and the rest are all of the same range, and should be grown in the rich moist ground, stony and perfectly well-drained, which offers the best chance with the alpine Meconopsids; *C. villosa*, the only one in general cultivation, is probably not the easiest, as it suffers the peril of its hairy foliage, beautiful as the rosette of this may be with rain-pearls lying gleaming in its loose pelt of tawny fur.

Caulophyllum thalictroides has no particular merit, though acceptable in the same conditions as Epimedium, with a thick root-stock, trefoils of lobed foliage, and showers of small greenish-purple flowers in April. There is also an Asiatic *C. robustum*, with less divided leaves, and blooming a few weeks later. They both attain some 18 inches (see also *Bongardia* and *Leontice*).

Celmisia, a huge race of large, stolid-stalked daisies entirely confined to New Zealand and the Antarctic Islands, where they abound in every size and shape, from minute high-alpines to fat and stalwart leafinesses, almost shrubs; but, with one glorious exception, never vary from the colour-rule of white. Only a few are in cultivation, and these seem to succeed in sunny positions in open well-drained soil, whether peaty or loamy, and may be seen in special force at Glasnevin. As, however, not all can be expected to be of equal hardiness, the following list merely selects from Cheeseman's *Flora of New Zealand* the mountaineering species likely to be of most profit to us, alike in vigour and in beauty.

C. coriacea is well known in cultivation ; it makes a tuft of very ample corrugated leaves, broadly oval and pointed, plated with a fine film of silver above, and woolly-white with down below. From this there emerge stolid stout stems, also densely woolly, about a foot or a yard in height, each carrying one big silvery daisy of shining white, that (as in nearly if not quite all Celmisias) is only just not quite large enough to balance the inordinate thickness of the stem. This species is general in the South Island, and the only one of the family that ever produces a branched scape ; and this only in cultivation. It sometimes seems to verge upon *C. Monroi*.

C. Dallii, much smaller, with flowers 3 inches across ; about a foot high or so, with leathery spreading foliage in a rosette, smooth above, and clothed in buff-coloured felt below. (Up to 5000 feet in South Island.)

C. Hectori is a branching and prostrate plant, often woody and with closely tufted leaves, narrow and about an inch long and rather blunt, packed into tightly serried rosettes, and beautifully silky-silver both above and below, curling down along their edges. The flower-stems are only some 2 or 4 inches high, stout, each carrying an inch-wide daisy. (Mount Cook, &c., 4500 to 6000 feet ; South Island.)

C. holosericea, rather larger, but with the same spreading leafage smooth above and white below ; the flowers are as big as in the last, carried on slender stems of a foot or two, these stems being glabrous, so that altogether why this species should be called *par excellence* the Wholly-silky does not clearly appear in its description. (Up to 4000 feet in South Island.)

C. laricifolia is a tiny prostrate thing, forming a carpet of very narrow-leaved stiff and prickly rosettes of silver spines, from which, on slender stalks of 2 or 4 inches, escape white stars of half an inch across. (*C. linifolia* is another charmer in the same line.)

C. Lindsayi, which is in general cultivation, has much more crowded leathery leaves to the tuft ; they are narrow-oblong and white beneath, while each carries a flower of about a couple of inches across, on a bending graceful scape some 2 to 8 inches high.

C. Lyallii makes a dense radiating star of quite narrow, sword-pointed foliage, stiff and tapering and fierce. The leaves are smooth above and hairless, while below they are corrugated, and either bald or felted with white. The blossoms are some couple of inches across. This is general in the Southern mountains up to about 4500 feet.

C. Mackaui, also in cultivation, has pointed entire leaves sometimes 20 inches long, conspicuous in the whole race for their simple greenness, neither downy nor woolly nor silvered, though there is a small fluff of white cotton at the base where they narrow to the trunk. The scapes are a foot or two in height, either cotton-clad or naked, and the flowers are some couple of inches across.

C. MacMahoni, from Mount Stokes in the South Island, at about 3800 feet, is a rare and lovely species, forming wide tufted patches of close ground-hugging rosettes, made up of narrow-oblong rather acute little leathery flat foliage, densely silked on both sides with a coat of either silver or tawny-gold. All over this carpet rise stout short stems clothed in long silk, and set with many bracts, each carrying a daisy an inch wide or so.

C. Monroi is an obscure difficult species, perilously close to *C. coriacea*, from which it should be distinguished by narrower and stiffer leaves, which are corrugated on both sides, instead of only on the upper as in *C. coriacea ;* while the flower-heads are rather smaller, and with shorter, broader rays. The distinctions, however, are not really solid, and these two Celmisias often seem to melt into one. (Alps of South Island.)

C. sessiliflora is another minute alpine carpet, common in the mountains of the South Island, from 2500 to 5500 feet. It makes a grey mat of very dense leafy rosettes, and the blooms do not emerge at all from it, but nestle into the ends of the shoots, starring the mass with white daisies.

C. spectabilis has flown too high in its ambitious name, which it is unable adequately to carry. It is a largish grower, and here the leafage is short and specially thick and stiff, matted or flocked (not closely felted), with buff-coloured wool on the lower surface. The scapes are several, towering high above the tuft, and each carrying a flower only some inch and a half across. (Mount Nelson, &c., to 4500 feet.)

C. Traversii has leaves from 6 to 16 inches long, and up to two and a half in breadth. They are oblong and either blunt or rather pointed, leathery in texture, and of a dark brownish green, with a silky midrib ; and their under-surface is clothed in soft fawn-coloured velvet, their leaf-stalk being half as long as themselves. The stalks rise to some 18 inches or less, rusty also in velvet ; while the marguerites have a certain loose white fluff, and are about 2 inches wide or rather less. (Alps of South Island, up to 4000 feet.)

CENTAUREA.

C. vernicosa breaks away from all the traditions of the family, and achieves the most sensational loveliness. Imagine a starry rosette outspread upon the ground, of long and narrow-pointed foliage, notched here and there into faint teeth, but so fat in texture that these teeth take on the look and feel of little knobs (especially at the tips of the young leaves), and of so profoundly glossy a green that each looks as if it had been overlaid with several thick coatings of the best varnish. Then from this rosette imagine countless stems radiating upwards all round to the height of some 5 or 6 inches, and each carrying an enormous single daisy, loose-rayed, opulent, and splendid, of pearly white, deepening to rosy flushes at the tips, and with an eye of brilliant violet. Such is *C. vernicosa*, which in future must not be allowed, any more than Jane Fairfax, to waste its sweetness on the desert air—a maid whom there are few to praise, and fewer still to love. For, alas! this treasure dwells very far away on the rocks and mountains of the Auckland Islands, up to about 400 to 1200 feet, and down to the sea again in the Campbells—a plant, therefore, of whose hardiness there can be no reasonable doubt, if only some prince of romance will adventure so far into the untrodden ways in search of a princess so beautiful. Not to mention the other fairies that haunt those islands, and pin one's eyes upon the uttermost Southern horizons of the world, in longings hitherto without fruit.

Celsia, not as a rule by any means an interesting or valuable group of erect, yellow-flowered biennials close to Verbascum; but better things might be hoped of *C. acaulis*, which is found by the sources of Eurotas close beside the melting snows of Taygetos at some 7000 feet. For this is a neat and tiny thing, alike in habit and in bloom, suggesting *Erodium cicutarium*, with small flowers.

Centaurea.—The Hardheads, as a rule, hover on the edge of being weeds, either gawky, leafy, or ineffective. However, there are some species admissible to the rock-garden, though none are indispensable. All can be raised from seed, all flower in the summer, and all are happy in any sunny place.

C. argentea is almost a one-headed *C. ragusina*.

C. axillaris only differs from *C. montana* in having a fringe of twice the length to the enfolding leaflets that enclose the flower-head.

C. babylonica, a vast and stately border-perennial with silver foliage and large knubbles of yellow prolonged up the five-foot trunk.

C. bella, from the rocks of Caucasus, is a tuft of green feathery leaves, hoary beneath, with starry pink flowers springing on stems of 9 inches or so, emerging from the outside of the rosette which forms at the ends of the old shoots.

CENTAUREA.

C. Bourgaei is acutely dwarf, woolly-hoary, with foliage very finely dissected, close to which, on stalks of 2 or 3 inches, are borne the wide and raying blossoms of pale yellow.

C. cadmea is especially pretty. The tufts of woolly closely-white hoary foliage emit a number of branching stems about 6 inches long, flopping or flaunting from the cliffs of Cadmus in Caria, and then break out in a diffuse shower of purple blooms.

C. dealbata, a well-known favourite stalwart of 2 feet or so, with feathery silver leafage and lonely stars of pink.

C. glastifolia is much taller, about twice the height, with smaller blossoms of bright yellow; not so worthy.

C. granatensis makes a white woolly clump of feathered leaves in the limestone cliffs of Granada, and sends up undivided stems of some 3 to 9 inches, carrying large golden-yellow fluffs.

C. lactucaefolia, in the same sheer rocks of Saint Elias that shelter *Campanula hagielia*, rises to a foot or 18 inches high, with foliage of a foot long; and carries on a stout and almost naked stalk four or five big rayless flowers of pale yellow, about 2 inches across, gathered at the top into an impressive solid head like a mace.

C. lanigera in the high places of Cappadocia sends up stems of 3 or 4 inches, above a tuft of rather woolly foliage, cut into remote scallops, and each stem ends in a large starry yellow bloom.

C. lycia is exactly as *C. cadmea*, but with basal leaves undivided.

C. macrocephala, a border giant of 5 feet, stout-stemmed and with green leaves, with fat round rayless heads of yellow.

C. macrorrhiza clings to the crevices of the Sierra de Maria in Almeria, and there forms perfectly tight mounds of pure snow-white rosettes packed into a dense hump, in which, hardly emerging from their wrapping of wool, sit orange-golden flowers, one or three to a shoot, never emerging upon any stalk unless they happen to be growing in a rather more shady exposure than the hot cliffs it usually affects. This, when obtained, should prove the pearl of the race.

C. montana is the universal leafy perennial cornflower of the alpine meadows,—type of all the Starry-blooms, with radiant long florets all round from the central head. It is common in borders, and fitted for grassy places in the wild garden, and has varied into countless colours all offered in catalogues.

C. Musarum pursues the Muses upon Parnassus. The Muses have long fled from their holy hill; but their Centaurea remains thriving on the upper slopes—a very hoary cushion, with many frail dwarf stems of 6 inches, each carrying some three or four rayless balls of gold.

C. napuligera is leafy and fluffy, about 9 inches high, each stem ending in a specially starry head of blue or red. (From Rhodope and Dalmatia.)

C. pindicola is the same as *C. Bourgaei, q.v.,* with the lower leaves undivided.

C. pulcherrima = *Aethiopappus pulcherrimus, q.v.*

C. ragusina, another vast border-plant of towering stature, set with stout globes of rayless yellow.

C. ruthenica rises to about a yard high, with feathered blue-grey smooth foliage, and light sulphur-yellow balls of blossom.

C. Tournefortii, about the same height, is bright-green, hairy, and has heads of deep golden-yellow.

Centranthus. — No attention need be paid to our own red Valerian. Let it be sown in any old wall, and there left to go on for ever. Yet finer, though, is *C. angustifolius,* from very hot and stony places of the Southern Alps, with showers of clean and ardent coral-rose.

Cephalaria, a race of most graceful perennials, close to Scabiosa, and of tall growth, producing countless large and long-stemmed flowers all through the summer, whose various shades of sulphur-yellow can make an entrancing effect amid the purples of certain Campanulas. All being 4- or 5-foot border-plants, here follow their names : *CC. alpina* (the least overwhelming in height, usually about 3 feet), *procera, ambrosioeides, dipsacoeides, leucantha, radiata, tatarica,* and *transylvanica*—*C. tatarica* being especially remarkable for the luxuriant splendour of its port.

Cerastium.—This unpromising race of weeds does, in point of fact, wander high and far into the stoniest places of the mountains, and there produces a number of species, most delicate and pure in beauty, as well as rather delicate in temper, too, asking for moraine-culture if they are truly to be happy. On the other hand, many of them are borderers and edgings of uncontrollable habits and excesses.

C. alpinum, which is found in the higher summits of Great Britain, is a very densely woolly species, paradoxically less easy of culture than many of its foreign cousins, as its excessive fluff gets soaked too often into rottenness in winter.

C. Biebersteinii, from the Alps of Taurus, is quite one of the best— all pure silver-white in leafage, slightly woollier than *C. tomentosum,* with leaves of narrower oblong form ; and, when the show of lovely pure-white flowers is done, the fruiting heads always stand erect, instead of turning earthwards.

C. Boissieri, from the south of Europe, is also closely akin to

CERASTIUM.

C. tomentosum, but so much less woolly that the woolliest forms of *C. Boissieri* only draw near to the baldest of *C. tomentosum*.

C. carinthiacum, a shingle-plant of the Eastern Alps, a fearsome ramper, running everywhere with masses of grey-green narrow foliage, concealed by drifts of white in summer.

C. glaciale is a form of *C. latifolium*, *q.v.*

C. gnaphalioeides is woollier yet than the woolliest varieties of typically woolly *C. alpinum*. This is a choice and densely-tufted species from the high Alps of Lycia, Cappadocia, and Cilicia, with narrow leaves on the stems, erect fruit-pedicels, and a short stem carrying from one to five flowers.

C. grandiflorum, another species of overwhelming habit but most beautiful and well known, with its rolling sheets of grey, very narrow leaves, thick and recurving often at the edge, snowed under by large white flakes of purity.

C. latifolium is the brilliant chickweed of the uppermost alpine stone-shingles, where it associates with *Viola cenisia* and *Campanula cenisia* ; it is a taprooted thing, matted and straying, with broadly ovate leaves, and delightful large bell-shaped blossoms of purest white. The species is said to divide into two main branches, of which *C. latifolium* prefers the highest limestone Alps, while the exactly similar, but rather hairier and smaller *C. uniflorum* (*C. glaciale*) prefers the granitic. In cultivation both of these are grateful for the moraine in which to do their best and make their loveliest show.

C. lithospermifolium is a loose velvety plant from the Altai, leafy and flopping, with showers of extremely large and notable flowers.

C. macranthum is the finest, however, of all. It forms a tuft of upstanding stems from 5 to 10 inches high, very thickly set, towards the base, with narrow grey-white leaves, which can be as much as 3 inches long towards the bottom of the flowering shoots, while on the barren shoots they are much narrower. The whole growth gives the effect of some erect wiry little Helianthemum ; until the wide loose heads of blossom are produced, large and snowy and splendid, the most impressive in the family. It comes from the high screes of Lycia, Isauria, &c., and should be treated as such, though it will also prove happy in more ordinary places.

C. maximum, also from the Altai, makes a display of similar refulgence, a hairy and almost glandular species, emitting runners, and throwing up magnificent pure flowers in a loose head or umbel. Neither of these last should be tried in the middle of a select plot, for fear that in time they might show the devouring proclivities of *C. grandiflorum* and *C. Biebersteinii*.

216

CERATOSTIGMA PLUMBAGINOEIDES.

C. ovatum, prostrate, tufted and creeping, has narrow leaves at the base, and broad or egg-shaped pointed ones on the stem. The blooms are few, with ample petals just notched and heart-shaped at the end, not cleft. It differs, among other points, from the rather viscid *C. latifolium*, to which it stands close, in carrying the fruiting heads spreading and erect, whereas *in all forms of C. latifolium they turn earthward*.

C. purpurascens comes from the Caucasus—a tufted species of variable height, with large flowers, and downy leaves with jointed hairs. (Its purpleness lies in general tone, not in any change from the white blossoms of the family.)

C. repens of our gardens is certainly not a synonym of *C. Biebersteinii*, which should be more or less woolly-white, whereas *C. repens* forms mats of fine narrow foliage which is perfectly green, sending up loose stems of blossom fine and white indeed, but of no remarkable brilliancy. The plant is, too, a weed of the most uncontrollable kind, and should never be admitted within sight of anything choice, or ever into valuable corners of the garden, any more than *C. grandiflorum*.

C. speciosum; a variety of *C. grandiflorum, q.v.* There are many other chickweeds rather more or less fitted for culture, but as a rule rather less than more ; all flower in summer, and all must be dealt with cautiously even among these quoted, lest you come bitterly to regret having admitted a voracious cuckoo into the midst of your neat nest and its delicate nurslings, whom soon the overgrown intruder will hustle into the outer darkness of death.

C. Thomasii (*C. Soleirolii*) forms a light lawn of dense ovate grey foliage, glandular and stickyish and downy, which throws up sprays of from one to three handsome white blooms. (From the high Alps of Corsica.)

C. tomentosum, the universal grey-white chickweed used for edging, is fitted for wild uses only in the garden, being of growth so irrepressible, and neither in colour nor in size of flower so brilliant as *C. Boissieri* and *C. Biebersteinii*.

Ceratostigma plumbaginoeides is that lovely plant of the Plumbaginous persuasion which fills some warm corner in light soil with a mass of leafy shoots, and in the early days of autumn breaks out into heads of large stars in the most dazzling deep azure blue. It used to be called *Plumbago Larpentae*, and as such has a place in every garden, or ought to, running about underground, and rapidly increasing if the soil and the situation are warm. It is a perfectly hardy Chinese species : the new *C. Willmottianum* is no improvement.

C. Griffithii, however, from 8000 feet in Bhotan, ought to give better results, and justify its claim to being a low and densely-branched shrubling, with red-edged leaves and flower-heads of a glorious blue.

C. Polhillii cannot be so praised ; though beautiful, it is best not to trust it in ordinary English climates.

Chaenorrhīnum glareosum is the only undisputed member of its family to deserve attention ; but this is a most choice and delicate little Toadflax of price, for a warm chink between rocks in a sheltered well-drained soil, or else in the moraine. It is a Spanish high-alpine, suggestive of a *Linaria origanifolia* that has got smashed down into a perfectly tight flat mass, where it has developed fatter, waxier, darker, smoother foliage, from which it throws out shoots of pinky-lilac small snapdragons from June to August, in a manner most neat and delightful. *Ch. glareosum* has also been held an alpine better-flowered form of *Ch. crassifolium ;* while there is no wonder that it is like the Linaria, for *Chaenorrhinum origanifolium is* actually the correct name of its other Spanish cousin, so much better known in gardens under the auguster style of *Linaria origanifolia*. *Ch. origani-folium*, then, is a variable species of the Pyrenees, generally a neat upstanding thing of some 6 inches, with fattish dark marjoram-like little leaves, and a profusion of rose-purple Linaria-blossoms all through the later summer months. It thrives quite easily, but is not always perennial in very damp, low, and stagnant soils. But then, what is ? The plant, in point of fact, is both perennial and hardy, but likes the sun, and light well-drained stony soil and moraine, to which it is no less entitled than the much minuter and neater *Ch. glareosum*, which is one of the choicest treasures there. Among the varieties of *Ch. origanifolium*, some of which might be offered as species, or under the name of Linaria, are *Ch. o. Bourgaei*, with a similar cousin *Ch. macropodum*, and *Ch. o. glabratum*, which should be particularly looked out for, as it is particularly beautiful, with larger flowers of richer blue-violet. As for *Ch. crassifolium*, this is intermediate be-tween *Ch. origanifolium* and the tiny *Ch. glareosum* that seems to have developed out of it—dwarfer, more intricate and mounded than the first, but not so minute and prostrate and neat as the second. *Ch. origanifolium* should always be guaranteed each year by seed or cuttings : and so should the others.

Chaenostŏma floribundum, an untrustworthy little rosy-flowered Scrophulariaceous sub-shrub from the Cape.

Chaerophyllum, a race of great Umbellifers to be avoided, unless for the wildest wildernesses of the wild garden.

Chaixia Myconi.—If this ever appears as an alluring name in a catalogue, depicted as a marvellous novelty, with rosettes of hairy mullein-like leaves, and a profusion of large violet flowers with a golden pointil, learn that this indeed is so, and the description true. But *Chaixia Myconi* has another name. It is *Ramondia pyrenaica.*

Chamaecytisus dalmaticus is an attractive low and creeping shrub from Dalmatia, not more than some 4 inches high, and spreading far and wide. The pea flowers are large, carried in pairs at the end of each little twig, while the leaves are in small trefoils, and the whole growth quite hairless.

Chamaelirion luteum is a small liliaceous species from America, whose name in lists is always *Ch. carolinianum.* It should be grown in dank cool places, such as suit *Allium ursinum.* Here it sends up in summer, to the height of a foot or more, its dense spikes of small white blossoms, which have no special charm, though quite admissible, if only for the sake of the green and shining foliage, broadly spoon-shaped and on stems.

Chamaemelon is a race almost interchangeable with Pyrethrum and Chrysanthemum, and indeed is frequently interchanged. All those here mentioned are mountain-plants of more or less value, for any light place and open soil, neat-growing Camomiles of ferny foliage and summer-flowering habits.

Ch. caucasicum is weak or prostrate, some 6 or 18 inches high, with one big daisy to a stem. And there is a stunted alpine form called *Ch. c. pumilum*, which lives at great altitudes in the Eastern Caucasus and only attains to some 3 inches.

Ch. daghestanicum, from some 11,500 feet in Daghestan, is a much more attractive thing altogether, having the large fine marguerites of the last, but produced on stems of only 3 inches or so, with a few leaves upon the brief stalk and the rest gathered below in a sweetly fragrant tuft—the whole growth rather recalling *Anthemis iberica.*

Ch. grandiflorum, from the grassy hills above Aleppo, has narrower, longer foliage than *Ch. caucasicum*, with longer, finer, and remoter strips and slashings. The stem is about 8 or 10 inches high, and the flower of enormous size for the plant, almost as big as in *Chrysanthemum maximum.*

Ch. Oreades, with a variety *Ch. O. Kotschyi*, and another species *Ch. monticola*, from Berytagh (which is very close to it), comes near to *Ch. caucasicum*, but differs in being downy, tufted, and with more stems. The blossoms are of medium size, and the type is found in damp stony alpine fields of all Asia Minor.

Ch. Pichleri is found in the damp woods about Brusa, and is closely akin to *Ch. Tchihatchewii, q.v.*

Ch. rosellum runs the risk of being pretty. For the rays of the flower, though so short as even to be less than its disk, are pale pink ; it forms a tuft at some 3000 feet on Malevo in Laconia, and only emits a couple of flower-stems or so from its neck.

Ch. Szowitsii is yet another species closely allied to *Ch. caucasicum.*

Ch. Tchihatchewii is the only species in common cultivation—a thing of much use and no contemptible degree of beauty, which makes the gardener less sceptic about the rest of the family. For *Ch. Tchihatchewii* forms, in the first place, never-ending, never-failing mats of bright dark-green glossy ferny leafage all over the ground, far and wide, no matter how hot and dry and worthless, no matter how cold and poor and helpless. It is perhaps one of the finest carpeting weeds we have, and is even used for forming lawns in places where grass proves impossible. But the blooms that so copiously come up from that lovely flooring on sturdy little stems of 6 or 8 inches, are hardly worthy of the plant's mellifluous name—they are little gleaming Camomiles of white with a dimmed eye of green and yellow. The species comes from the Maritime hills of Anatolia, and may now be seen growing on the French Riviera by hundreds of yards.

Chamaenerion is *Epilobium*—so sad a disappointment after a name so suggestive of loveliness : a Ground-Oleander would indeed be worth ensuing.

Chamaepeuce diacantha and *Ch. nivea* are glossy-leaved, spiny, white-veined thistles of South Europe, attaining some foot or more in height, which can be grown on any hot dry place if so desired.

Chartolepis Biebersteinii and *Ch. Tournefortii* are the respective Centaureas treated under these two names, *q.v.*

Cheiranthus.—This race has no certain borders, and many of its finest species have now strayed over the line, and will be found in the folds of Parrya and Erysimum, in which new species of Cheiranthus should always be looked up, lest the novelty prove only an old friend under a new family name.

Ch. Allionii is also Erysimum, *q.v.*

Ch. alpinus must certainly be looked for either under *Erysimum canescens, E. ochroleucum,* or *E. Cheiranthus.*

Ch. Cheiri, left almost alone in its glory, is enough to bear the name with dignity, and the dwarf horticultural forms of the Wallflower serve admirably for sowing on the austerer cliffs of the great rock-garden or wild precipice.

Ch. albiflorus is of another kidney, heading a section of unknown wallflowers from the Roof of the World, which should have the choicest position in the moraine, if they are to forget their own grisly moraines of Tibet. Here, in the stones between 12,000 and 16,000 feet, dwells *Ch. albiflorus*, a tuft of grey downy foliage with white blossoms in rather dense spikes.

Ch. himalaiensis (see *Parrya*) is a jewel of cold stone-slopes up to 17,000 feet in Western Tibet, where it forms many clumps, making a neat mass of foliage, from which are sent up 6-inch stems carrying rather close heads of deliciously-scented violet-purple flowers.

Ch. × *kewensis* is a garden hybrid, often appearing under the false name of *Ch. mutabilis*, but none the less a handsome if not certainly permanent acquisition—a wallflower of compact bushy habit and large growth (it attains 18 inches), with flowers varying through gold and bronze to violet. There is also another beautiful cross raised by Miss King, of subtle shades and neat habit and delicious fragrance and perpetual-blooming character. This, though no more surely perennial, and sterile, can be of course multiplied at will from cuttings. *Ch. Marshallii* is yet another garden-plant, of clear bright colour; and without doubt there are many others in existence or yet to come.

Ch. Menziesii=*Parrya Menziesii*, q.v.

Ch. mutabilis should be one of the parents responsible for *Ch. Kewensis*. It is a lower-growing species from the Canaries, not very hardy or long-lived as a rule, and hardly exceeding a foot in height, with flowers of a curiously sad and subtle violet, faded and wistful as the memory of an old maid's love-story. Distrust the name in lists.

Ch. parryoeides makes basal rosettes of narrow-rounded leaves, dense with a coat of grey wool to guarantee them against the winds that are born on the Roof of the World. And then appears a naked 9-inch scape carrying a spike of deep purple blossom.

Ch. Stuartii almost precisely repeats the beauty of *Ch. himaláiensis* in the highest screes of Ladak; but here the foliage is toothed at the tip, the pods are slender and bald, while the flowers open tawny and then develop into violet. Seed will be the only hope of these, and should always be collected yearly, for but few wallflowers have a long life, even if officially perennial—as may indeed be judged by the disproportion between their lush and stalwart development above ground, and the weak-looking ephemeral tap that supports their existence.

Chelidonium, the Great Celandine, that pretty weed, stands like *Meconopsis cambrica*, as the lonely outlying representative in Western Europe of an Asiatic mountain-clan, now divided up on small but significant botanical differences, though here, seeing their strong generic resemblances, it may not be amiss to treat them all under the heading of *Chelidonium*, all alike being Poppyworts of the same blood, and for the same uses in any cool and not too choice corner of the rock-work. *Hylomēcon (Stylophorum) japonicum* is lovely with its golden flowers in the woods above Nikko in March—a much more refined Celandine, of neater, dwarfer habit, and blooms much larger and more brilliant. *Dicranostigma* gathers into its uncouth embrace several former Celandines, of which the most famous is *D. Franchetianum*, with glaucous foliage and ample orange golden flowers ; the others are *D. lactucoeides* and *D. leptopodum*, both species of merit from the fields of China and Tibet. See Appendix.

Chelōnē.—These are rather dull-looking and unrefined Pentstemons, of which the 18-inch *Ch. obliqua* and the branching yard-high *Ch. Lyoni* are sometimes grown in borders, where they bloom from August to October. The pride of the family, however, has passed away into the rich house of Pentstemon, and must there be looked for as *P. barbatus*.

Chimaphila, a race of very lovely woodland fairies, closely allied to Pyrola, growing in the same light loose accumulation of vegetable rottenness, and therefore having developed the same frail and wandering root-habit that makes Pyrola also so difficult to collect satisfactorily, and re-establish with success. For this reason alone it is that, Chimaphilas (and one might add, coming nearer home, the Pyrolas also) are so rarely seen in gardens. There are not so many healthy and established stocks of either to draw upon. None the less, if well-rooted pieces are secured and planted in very rich, very light and spongy woodland soil (such as that recommended for the more difficult Columbines, but in a corner much more deeply ensconced under the shade of some little bush of fine Berberis or *Pinus montana*), there you should have no further difficulty with either Chimaphila or Pyrola.

Ch. japonica rambles throughout the mossy forests of Japan, a most delicate delicious thing. Suppose that *Pyrola uniflora* took to itself a habit of running about with long shoots trailing and shrubby (set with leathery sharply-pointed narrow-oval leaves, toothed at the edge), but then at the end sends up not only its ordinary flowers of waxy whiteness and celestial sweetness, but two of them into the bargain—thus you have a picture of *Ch. japonica* pervading the woods of Japan, with fine upstanding shoots, and blossoms daintily depending.

Ch. maculata is a more solid grower. It forms an upstanding tuft, almost a rosette, of oval-pointed broadish foliage, quite keenly and occasionally toothed, blotched with white markings on the upper face, and of reddish leather below ; then up are sent the flower-stems to the height of some 5 inches, unfolding into a loose radiating head of perhaps eight or ten white blossoms, waxy and sweet as in the last, but rather smaller, by virtue of being so much more numerous. (Woods of all North America.)

Ch. Menziesii repeats across the Pacific, in the woods of California, exactly the loveliness and grace of *Ch. japonica*, but here the habit is much more prostrate.

Ch. picta=*Pyrola picta*, q.v.

Ch. umbellata follows in the line of *Ch. maculata*, but surpasses it. The sturdy tufted habit is the same, but the dark and leathery leaves have no markings at all, and are yet more sharply and regularly toothed ; while the flowers, carried in the same way, and of the same size, are of delicate rose-pink, with purple anthers.

Chiogenes serpyllifolia and *Ch. hispidula* are small trailing Ericaceous plants from wet boggy places and cool woods, from Newfoundland through North America. They send out across the face of the earth a number of little stems, set with oval evergreen leaves, turning to russet ; and then emit small white bells. There are other species also, of which *C. japonica* differs in having the leaves tapering to the stem. All should be grown on the most shady side of the cool bog, or in gritty peat in the underground-watered moraine (with a specially large proportion of spongy soil).

Chionodoxa and **Chionoscilla.** See any catalogue of these joyous spring delights, where their names and relationships will be found set forth.

Chionophila Jamesii, a neat small alpine cousin of Pentstemon, from the alpine turf of Colorado, where it forms neat basal tufts of foliage, and sends up 6-inch spikes of dense creamy flowers in summer. As it calls itself a lover of the snow, it deserves a place in moist ground, or perhaps even in the well-watered gritty moraine.

Chrysanthemum.—Although such huge plants as *Ch. macrophyllum* (which suggests nothing so much as a gigantic and ugly flatheaded Achillea) are scarcely wanted in the garden, yet there is a choice alpine section especially suited to the moist moraine, and indeed occasionally demanding it. Almost all the following names are sometimes regarded as interchangeable with Pyrethrum and Chamaemelon ; which see when in doubt.

Chr. alpinum is that beautiful little high-alpine which is almost inevitable in the topmost moist shingles of certain ranges, with its fat fine foliage, and its golden-eyed single Marguerites of brilliant white on weak stalks of only a few inches. This should be grown under similar conditions at home ; it is by no means so easy and indestructible as it looks, but should have well-watered gritty moraine-mixture, and be carefully top-dressed in spring.

Chr. anomalum is almost a neat bush of 6 inches or a foot, in the high rocky places and muddy channels of the mountains of Northern and Eastern Spain ; it is clothed in close silk, and yet is bright green, with finely-divided foliage, and big white flowers whose eye fades from gold to red.

Chr. arundanum comes from about 6000 feet up in the Sierra de Ronda, where it forms a very dense mass indeed of closely hairy leafage, cut into threes and then again into threes. From this thrust up the naked stems of an inch or two, each carrying a Marguerite of pink or white.

Chr. atratum (*C. coronopifolium*) grows some 7 inches high, and its leaves are only toothed, not feathered.

Chr. flaveolum is a silky tuft from Leon, with smaller yellow daisies on 6-inch stems.

Chr. hispanicum is downy or silky, with jagged feathered foliage that does not follow far up the 2- to 10-inch stems. Each of these carries a single large flower varying from white through yellow and sulphur to purple, with the tips of each ray jagged into three teeth. A widely variable species from the high Alps of all the Spanish mountains up to 11,000 feet. Its named varieties are *Chr. h. radicans, versicolor, sulfureum*, and in all its forms it is a treasure to be much desired.

Chr. montanum is rather taller than *Chr. alpinum*, and here the fat green leaves are *not divided*, but merely sharply-toothed. It is general in the Alps. Other mountain Chrysanthemums after the same sort are : *Chr. arcticum* (pinkish), *Chr. argenteum, Chr. cerato-phyllum*, &c.

Chr. nipponicum is a tallish, leafy and not always permanent plant, attaining some 15 inches ; while the rock-garden has no room for gigantic *Ch. lacustre* and *Ch. latifolium. Chr. Zawadskyi*, though much smaller, is a rather leafy thing of about 9 inches or a foot, whose flowers it is flattery to describe as "rose clair," for they are in reality, as a rule, of a rather pallid dim tone.

Chr. tibeticum is a very handsome species, sticky and sweet-scented, and sub-shrubby, making tuffets of 6 inches high at some 9000 to 13,000 feet in Tibet, with delightful blooms of pink or white on long stems. Similar to this are *Chr. Griffithii* and *Chr. Stoliczai*, which have the same large flowers of snow-white, but are slenderer, with longer and less divided branches, and leaves more finely cut.

Chr. tomentosum, a most beautiful little development of *Chr. alpinum* from Corsica, which, like several other Corsican forms of high-alpines, has developed a coat of ash-grey down ; it is a neat low-growing gem of special charm, with the undiminished marguerite of *Chr. alpinum.*

Chrysobactron. See under **Bulbinella.**

Chrysogonum virginianum, a very popular and much-praised Composite of curious unattractiveness, though useful ; forming, under any treatment, masses of low foliage on which all the summer through appears a profusion of yellow flowers with rays so few and broad as to look like five-pointed stars not belonging to a Composite at all.

Chrysopsis villosa is an even more worthless American Composite, but its dwarf variety *C. v. Rutteri* has more use ; it only grows some 4 to 8 inches tall, in a loose massed habit of silky-grey foliage starred over with fine golden daisies all the summer through. Division at will.

Chrysosplenium forms a race of small Saxifrages, valueless unless in a mass, when, in wet and shady places, they form succulent carpets of foliage set with innumerable heads of innumerable minute golden blooms, effective by their force of numbers, that make a diffused effect of sunlight in the darkness.

Cimicifuga put fleas to flight; and, even if they did not,are worthy stalwart giants, like giant Actaeas, with spreading foliage, much divided and very handsome, like that of a shining Spiraea or Aralia ; and then, in late summer and autumn, long towering spikes of white fluff some 4 or 5 feet high. The tallest and most branching and decorative generally is *C. dahurica ; C. cordifolia* and *C. americana* are only about a yard high, and the former sometimes has pinkish flowers ; *C. japonica* (*Pityrospermum acerinum*) has particularly long spikes that endure till the frosts, and the plant is some 4 feet in itself, with a variety *C. j. acerinum* in which the leaves are of a special glossiness ; *C. racemosa,* or *Serpentaria,* is perhaps the finest of all, an Anak of 6 feet or so, inimitably graceful, with its sheaves of blossom towering far above the spreading, arching weight of lucent leaves ; and *C. simplex* (or *C. foetida × simplex*), has undivided spires of lesser altitude. All these thrive hugely in any rich deep soil, and are the glories of island, bog, or water-side in autumn. See Appendix.

Cineraria.—The grey-leaved Southern Senecios (*q.v.*) are sometimes removed into this name.

Cistus.—A race of Southern shrubs, of which the only certainly and invariably hardy ones are *C. laurifolius* (leather-leaved, with large white flowers, about 4 feet), and the hybrid *C. Loretii* of much the same stature. But all the following are valuable, to be let grow in light well-drained soil in a sunny position; and can easily be guaranteed by cuttings : *C. crispus,* with aromatic velvety foliage and flowers of crumpled pink, 18 inches ; *C. ladaniferus*, as tall and much finer than even *C. laurifolius*, the noble white blossoms having a basal blotch of purple ; *C. hirsutus*, a little sweet bush with the foliage as in *C. crispus* (only not velvety), and yellow flowers ; *C. monspeliensis*, with much narrower leaves, and attaining often to 4 or 6 feet, with smaller golden blossoms, often spotted with red, on long fine foot-stalks—a very attractive species ; *C. salvifolius*, a most fragrant bush with oblong leaves of velvet, and sulphurous flowers, going paler at the base, on long fine stems ; and *C. purpureus*, incomparably the best of all when the true species is obtained, having narrowish soft green leaves, and very large blossoms of a curiously brilliant colour in which the pale aniline tone of the family seems to be transfused with almost a note of true blood-crimson, so as to communicate an astonishing glow to the great bloom, each petal of which has a blotch of maroon at the base ; while other good species and hybrids are *C. lusitanicus*, the small yellow *C. algarvensis*, the white-flowered neat-habited *C.* × *florentinus*, and *C.* × *Corbariensis* (a hybrid of *salvifolius* and *C. populifolius*). *C. vaginatus*, from Teneriffe, with magnificent flowers of rich rose, is not safely hardy in most parts of England, and all the species, however willing, are creatures of the sun and drought, even though many of them will go on happily doing without either, with a far greater display of philosophy than human beings who have ever experienced those delights, and then been forced to return into rain and dark and cold.

Cladothamnus pyrolaefolius is a small Ericaceous bush from the Sitka Sound, producing small bells of reddish pink, and appropriate for any cool peaty corner.

Claytonias are pretty little weeds, but weeds no less ; from a single tuft in a garden almost any Claytonia will make itself an irrepressible pestilence in five years. There are various species : *C. caroliniana, sibirica, perfoliata*, and *virginica*—of which *C. perfoliata* has long been trying to thrust its name into the English Flora. These are all of much the same value for sowing, and sowing themselves, in any cool out-of-the-way place, either sunny or dank ; *C. caroliniana* may be taken as their type, making tufts a foot across of oval glossy fleshy leaves, from which all through the summer is jetted an insatiable shower of pearl-pink stars on graceful stems. But a more alpine species is noble *C. megarrhiza*, which makes a stout purple root-stock in the highest rocks of Wyoming, from which spray forth a profusion of big white flowers veined with violet ; while in *C. aurea* from Idaho the flowers are no less in size, but brilliantly golden.

Clintonia, American woodlanders of the Lily family ; *C.*

borealis and *C. umbellulata* are easy doers in cool soil, where they throw up oval, green, and glossy luxuriant foliage, in a tuft, far above which, on fine wiry stems, spring small and not particularly attractive huddles of green or greeny-white stars, like heads of garlic above the very leafage, but stiffened, of *Allium ursinum*. Rather more choice are *C. alpina* and *C. udensis*, perhaps ; but the one indispensable member of the family is lovely *C. Andrewsii* from the coasts of California, which has the same rosetted upstanding clumps of glossy foliage from the base, and then on a bare stem of about a foot carries a loose head of nodding rose-pink flowers, to be followed by berries of a brilliant blue on a heightened scape of nearly double its original stature.

Cnicus.—No rock-garden dares look at a thistle, whether it call itself Cnicus or Carduus or Cirsium or Alfredia ; but perhaps *Cnicus nivalis* may be for the moment beckoned. For this is a most rare and unproven high-alpine from the damp moraines of Mexico, and it is hoped that in similar treatment here it may repeat its original beauty of dense dwarf rosettes of thick leaves, from which emerge very leafy branching stalks with heads of snow-white woolly blossoms some 4 or 5 inches across, from June to October. Seed.

Cochlearia, a race of alpine or maritime Crucifers, forming attractive rosettes of spoon-shaped foliage, richly glossy and dark-green, with shorter or longer spikes of white flowers in spring. In damp rich places on the rock-work many are effective, *C. saxatilis* (*Kernera*) being the commonest, and of more airy grace ; the others are *C. Boissieri*, *C. alpina* (*Rhizobotrya*), *C. sempervirens*, *C. aphragmodes*, *C. groenlandica*, and *C. pyrenaica ;* and it may be doubted whether any are much finer than the high-alpine neat forms *C. danica* and *C. anglica* of the common *C. officinalis* as they may be seen in the high hills (as, for instance, under the Western face of Ingleborough), there achieving a dwarf stature which even in the garden they do not wholly lose, notwithstanding that the stems may eventually tend to elongate a little, and stretch themselves with fatness.

Codonopsis, which has also been **Campanumaea** and **Glossocomia,** is a race of twining, flopping Campanulads, greatly now in confusion ; to add to which, new species are perpetually coming in from the mountains of Central Asia, where the family has its home. They are all gracious laxities, and thrive perennially in good light soil, and are well placed on a high bank of the garden, where the leafiness of the foot-high straggling stems may not be so plainly seen, while all the summer through their pale pendent bells nod down at the passer-by, who can thus appreciate the full daintiness of their internal decorations, instead of merely being left cold by the chill blues of the bell's outside, which ranges from colours that may be called subtle to others that can only be called dowdy and indecisive. Among the species, all being of general similarity, and all being raised easily from seed, are :

C. affinis, with flowers of greenish tone and veined with purple; *C. Benthamii*, lurid purple-yellow, rather like a henbane; *C. clematidea*, reaching 3 or 4 feet in height, with flowers of white, stained with blue; *C. convolvulacea*, a most beautiful but almost unprocurable rarity, with bells of lovely clear blue, even outside; *C. Meleagris*, a novelty, rather leafy, and with fat-looking Campanulas hanging on very long erect pedicels of half a foot or more, so as to make a fine show of their beauty, for they are of the faintest shade of blue, each lobe with a backbone and radiating reticulations of chocolate; *C. ovata*, a name more frequently found than its rightful bearer, for which *C. clematidea* as a rule does duty; *C. ovata* has bells that widen inwards to their base, and the colour is of sky-blue or white, rather smaller than in *C. clematidea*, and the growth is clothed all over in fine down, whereas *C. clematidea* is more or less smooth; *C. purpurea*, which rambles and does not twine, with glaucous foliage and large bells of purple; *C. rotundifolia*, with scalloped foliage, and flowers of purple or greyish blue; *C. subsimplex*, resembling *C. Benthamii*, but with a wider bell of blue; *C. thalictrifolia*, whose blossoms are tubular and ill-smelling; *C. lanceolata*, attaining 2 or 3 feet, with bells of lilac, darker inside; together with other species a-many, and all much of a muchness—*C. tang-sheng*, *C. ussuriensis*, *C. viridiflora*, *C. viridis*, &c.

Colchicum has an evil colour but a valuable blooming season, even though the coarse handsomeness of the contemporaneous or subsequent leaves unfits them for the choicer associations that otherwise their cups of magenta-lilac would ask. Their best place, though they will thrive almost anywhere, is in deep and sunny soil, coming up in colonies and clusters, through a carpet of Acaena or Cotula, which will thus protect their blossoms from the mud splashed up by the autumn rains that wreck their effect in open ground (even if they are not destroyed by the slugs that nibble them into a disreputable damaged look). Though some of the species are choice, all are of facile culture—should be planted fairly deep, and may be multiplied in summer, when the leaves die down, by division of the clumps.

C. agrippinum (*not*, apparently, devoted to the wicked Augusta, as *C. Agrippinae*) is a rather stouter and erect-leaved form of *C. variegatum*, blooming in October and of unknown origin.

C. alpinum, a lovely and most rarely-seen little **Autumn Crocus** of the greatest delicacy, that breaks daily through the mown grass of the upper alps in the earliest days of August, with countless dainty chaliced stars of lilac about **3** inches high—the unintrusive foliage, of two narrow leaves, appearing in the following spring. It is always quite a local occurrence in the Alps, but leaps from the earth like a Jack-in-the-box the moment the hay is carried from the Mont Cenis or the upper valley of Macugnaga.

C. amabile, from the top of Delphi in Euboea, blooms also in the autumn, but with rather smaller goblets, most beautifully tessellated.

C. arenarium has much narrower leaves and smaller flowers than in *C. autumnale*.

C. autumnale is distinctly coarser and ranker, but its white form is pure, and even the double white, tinged with a faint warm flush of flesh-colour towards the centre, is by no means to be scorned ; but the leaves of all are so overweening and coarse that they must never be in a forward or choice place.

C. Bertolonii (or *C. pusillum*) blooms in autumn, with its foliage, in the low dry places of Syria, Attica, and the Argolid. The segments of the blossom are narrow and thin.

C. Bivonae is one of the very best, having flowers rather larger than *C. autumnale*, tessellated, and of the fullest segments, forming an incurving cup-design that might have served for Benvenuto Cellini. It is a species of obscure origin, probably from Crete.

C. Bornmuelleri is incomparably the grandest of all our Colchicums ; greater in size of bloom and height of stature than *C. speciosum*, with far more stately expanding chalices, large and sumptuous in the segments, and in colour of a tender rose-lilac, enhanced by the broad base of white. It also blooms earlier, and is in full beauty through August and September, in an endless succession of tall goblets from the huge and comfortable-looking corm. It is, however, rare and rather expensive at present.

C. bulbocodioeides. See *C. montanum.*

C. byzantinum, general in Southern Europe, may always be known by its knobbly irregular great corm, the size and shape of a closed fist. Its flowers are after the giant style of *C. Bornmülleri*, but rather smaller and paler, with the segments shorter, broader, and blunter than in *C. speciosum* and *C. latifolium*. The leaves are big and corrugated, following in spring after the blossoms, which have been abundantly and unanimously produced in autumn. Its only association with the Imperial City is probably as having been found there in gardens ; and it is brilliantly figured in the *Bot. Mag.*, t. 1122.

C. candidum, from Cilicia, is in the way of *C. autumnale*, but has poor pallid stars made up of long, narrow strip-like segments that produce a ragged effect, not atoned for by their palest feeblest whity-pink tone.

C. cilicicum, in reality, is a variety of *C. byzantinum*, but with flowers even larger and more splendid.

C. crocifolium usually appears, in such catalogues as offer it, as *C. " crociflorum,"* a name absurdly ill-fitting. And the figure representing it in the *Bot. Mag.* merely paints *C. autumnale*. *C. crocifolium* is a spring-blooming species, producing from the one corm a generous quantity of quite small and narrow-rayed lilac-pink blossoms simultaneously with the hairy-velvety leaves, extremely narrow, curving and spreading outwards. (South Persia, &c.)

C. Decaisnei, from Anti-Libanus and Baalbek, is an improved *C. autumnale*, with cups of twice the size, and paler in colour.

C. Haussknechtii is a beautiful autumn Crocus, found on the high limestones and schists of Elwend, with very long-rayed large pink flowers, opening widely out in a star.

C. hydrophilum loves damper places in Cilicia, and is profuse with its dainty pointed-lobed cups, all springing compactly in spring from the corm, with the foliage just appearing at the base.

C. Kochii has spreading grooved narrow-pointed leaves about 3 inches long, and rather narrow-rayed flowers in autumn of white or palest pink. (From Hymettus, &c.)

C. laetum, a synonym of *C. candidum, q.v.*

C. latifolium is the superb plant called *C. Sibthorbii* by Baker, and *C. Bivonae* (not of Gusson ; *q.v.*). It has very large lilac blossoms, with broad, incurving segments, and all beautifully chequered ; these are followed in spring by broad flattish oval or oblong foliage. It is found in the mountains of Greece, and there is a one-flowered variety, *C. l. euboeum.*

C. libanoticum blooms in spring by the melting snows of Lebanon. The anthers are yellow, and the leaves much more broad and short than even in *C. montanum*, which otherwise it exactly follows.

C. lingulatum may be recognised in spring by its wavy broad tongue-shaped foliage, tapering to the base ; the lilac flowers are three or four, narrow in the ray, appearing in autumn among the pines on Parnes.

C. luteum flowers in spring, when its three or four very narrow blunt leaves also appear. And its blossoms break far away from the traditions of all the rest in being small stars of gold about an inch and a half across, on a three-inch tube. They come by ones or twos from the corm, with styles protruding far out, and long spidery yellow anthers. (Alps of Afghanistan and Turkestan.)

C. montanum is a synonym, not of *C. Bertolonii* which blooms in autumn, but of the spring-beauty, and justly named, *C. bulboco-dioeides.* This, by whatever name called—and *C. montanum* has the weight of custom—sends up some three very broad, glossy, pointed little leaves in early spring, each leaf inclining to twist and curl to one side. From each cluster of these emerges a long lilac-mauve blossom, after the fashion of a glorified Bulbocodium. After a while the foliage curves inwards and tends to become concave. Alps of South Europe and the Levant—like a refined *C. autumnale,* but blooming by the snows with *Crocus albiflorus* and *Soldanella.*

C. Parkinsonii is often advertised, but the true plant hardly ever seen. It may, however, easily be recognised, for when, in spring, its leaves appear, they are but few in number, long and notably narrow, and *they lie quite flat on the ground, undulating and wavy at the edge.* Then, from the bare fields of Delos, Chios, and Naxos, there spring the flowers in early autumn, beautiful wide cups of deep lilac-rose vividly chess-boarded with squares of white. It may possibly only be a variety of *C. variegatum;* and in cultivation is nice, asking especially for hot soil in a warm and perfectly-drained exposure. There is now talk of a yellow Colchicum from Syria, which is attributed by some as a variety to *C. Parkinsonii.*

C. Parlatoris, from Taygetos, has leaves of excessive narrowness, and one or two little puny flowers in autumn.

C. parnassicum is an Autumnale with broader blunter foliage, and shorter segments to the cup, which is smooth inside instead of being velvety.

C. pusillum=C. Bertolonii.

C. Sibthorbii=C. latifolium.

C. speciosum, in which every autumn garden rejoices (if only the rain and the slugs will allow their full beauty to those stalwart vast upstanding goblets of claret-rose), has a range extending from Lazic Pontus into Persia. From which it may well be understood that one of the most beautiful and noble plants in the world, with its pure snow-white form, has sometimes been known to suffer damage in spring or winter by the nipping of its corm or foliage. None the less the white form is quite as safe and hardy as the type, planted deep in good soil, and left alone. But it must not be associated with smaller treasures, for, of all Colchicums, *C. speciosum* has perhaps the most tropically luxuriant foliage of all in spring and summer—huge high tufts and boskets of waving glossy splendour.

C. Stevenii, from the shores of Syria, is quite close to *C. Bertolonii,* but with more leaves, and the anthers yellow, not purple.

C. Szovitzii has not any special claims; it is allied to the equally unimportant *C. fasciculare* (*C. fasciculatum* of some catalogues), and *C. Ritchii*, these all having small stars emitted in spring with the leaves.

C. turcicum is exactly like *C. autumnale*, and a contemporary, but has borrowed its prostrate curling waving narrow foliage from *C. Parkinsonii*. (From Buyukdere in the suburbs of Byzantium.)

C. umbrosum produces small lilac flowers in the autumn, followed by unobtrusive leaves, and is possibly only a form of *C. arenarium* with strap-shaped foliage.

C. variegatum inhabits the stony fields of Crete. It is the parent species of *C. Parkinsonii*, having the same fantastic chequered blooms in autumn, but of a lighter pink, and rather larger ; while the narrow leaves are *held erect*. It is a variable species, of which forms sometimes appear as species—an instance being *C. chionense*. And there are other true species, but none as yet of conspicuously distinct merit from those quoted above.

C. veratrifolium is a close cousin to *C. speciosum*, but earlier, darker and larger in the goblet.

Colobanthus acicularis is an undistinguished curiosity from New Zealand, for a dry and sunny place. It suggests a patch of moss set with dullish greenish stars, like a Cherleria.

Colurea potentilloeides. See under *Waldsteinia*.

Coluteocarpus reticulatus (see under *Vesicaria*) ; an alpine Crucifer from the Levant, making clumps of rosettes, with little hairless toothed leaves, from which come heads of flowers like a Thlaspi's. Simple culture in light soil, as for Cochlearia or Draba.

Comarella multifoliata, or **Ivesia Purpusii,** is an interesting thing from Arizona, for dry stony places and the warmest exposures. It forms low masses, not more than seven or eight inches high, of beautiful foliage suggesting that of *Asplenium Trichomanes*, but very much stiffened and elongated ; the flowers are carried well above these, in a loose shower like that of some Hypericum's, at the top of a bare fine stem. They are small brownish stars of no startling charm, Comarella's chief value lying in its leafage. It can be propagated by cuttings or division.

Conandron ramondioeides ought most certainly to be hardy, and yet is not beyond suspicion in the matter. It is a most beautiful Japanese rock-plant, rambling over the face of the stone, and sheeting the cliffs (as behind the Kencho-ji at Kamakura, for instance) in a solid curtain of its ample glossy crinkled fleshy foliage, amid which spring so freely on stalks of a few inches those heads of lilac flowers with a bright golden eye, suggesting that a glorified

Potato has intermarried with *Ramondia Nataliae*. From such a station, indeed, hardiness need not be expected, but *Conandron* climbs high into the Alps, and up behind the great Regent's tomb at Nikko may be seen clothing the rocks (though in much finer dwarfer sturdier form) far up on the slopes of Nyo-ho-San and Nantai-San the Holy. Probably pieces from such elevations would prove more resistent than the fattened Sybarites of sea-level ; the tuber should anyhow be tucked into a cool, damp and lightless place on the rock-work—deep shade often being prescribed, while certainly the plant as often has no antipathy in nature to the fullest sun (and that the sun of Japan) —in such a position that it cannot be worried by drought in summer or wet in winter, or be too roughly visited, perhaps, by the perilous fingers of the frost. It is usually sent out in small divided fragments, but if larger pieces, less weakened by mutilation, could be obtained, probably there would be less trouble about re-establishing a thing so beautiful that no repetition of effort is too much. In face of such foliage it would be absurd to say that damp is the enemy ; yet it always has its centre of growth in a small tight crevice, and from thence sends out its fat brittle rhizomes up and down over the bare and sterile face of the rock. In Japan it is the Iwa-Tabako—the Rock Tobacco—on account of its leaves, which, though crisp and crinkly and very glossy, have some faint resemblance to the amplitude of a Nicotiana's.

Convallaria maialis.—The Lily of the valley is the worst of all delicious weeds where it thrives, and must never be admitted near a choice place. Fortin's variety preserves in the open garden much of its special size and nobility of bell ; while the rosy-lilac form is by no means to be despised when it has formed a wide and thick-set colony.

Convolvulus.—These are always plants of the South, in warm and rocky places, never straying into the cool alpine damps of the North. Therefore it is that we still lack some of the most ravishing delights our rock-gardens could have. And when at last they have successfully been wooed in our direction, let all such be planted in hot and well-drained chinks, or in sunny moraine, or in light and stony soil where drought can be their friend, and winter not so much their enemy. They are summer-bloomers all ; and their propagation is by seed or most careful cuttings inserted in sand in August. See Appendix.

C. althaeoeides is the only, or almost the only, trailer to admit—a pretty straggling thing, with finely-divided foliage, and flowers of more or less brilliant deep pink, sometimes amaranthine. It is not very hardy or satisfactory in the North, but is fitted for full sun and specially hot stony places in the South, even as you see it in full sun and the stoniest slopes, on railway cuttings and rough banks of the Riviera.

C. assyriacus, from elevations of 5000 feet in the cliffs of Argaeus, Aslandagh, &c., in Anatolia, forms a dense cushion in the rocks, acutely beautiful with shaggy fur of brightest silver. On this sit the long rosy-pink trumpets of blossom, peppered almost stemless over the tuffet.

C. cantabricus and *C. Dorycnium* are rosy-flowered species of South Europe, not tuffets, but attaining 6 inches in the first case, and 10 inches in the second.

C. Cneorum is a Spanish species, with which we do our best, and this in southerly cases is very good indeed ; the plant is of upstanding habit, attaining a foot or so, with large obovate leaves upstanding, too, and glistering with flat sheen of silver. The clustered flowers are fine and pink.

C. cochlearis is yet another cushion after the style of *C. assyriacus*, hard and fast in the stony pine-woods of Parnassus, Amanus, Berytagh, &c., always rather rare and eminently beautiful—a dense silver mass made up of microscopic ovate-pointed leaves, from which, sitting almost tight to the mass, come solitary flowers of rich purple, rather shorter in the tube than those of *C. assyriacus*, and with the argent sheen of the foliage more closely ironed down.

C. compactus may be seen in the dry sub-alpine regions at about 5000 feet, on Cadmus of Pisidia, Aslandagh, &c.—yet another cushion of silver-gleaming hoary leaves, very narrow indeed, and folded and pointed, with the glistering down smeared close and flat upon their surfaces ; and then the mass breaks out into the loveliest of pink cups, gathered in heads of from three to five, clustered stemless over the close delicious hassock.

C. cyprius, from the lower chinks of Cyprus, is a miniature of little *C. lineatus*, with markedly narrow glistering foliage.

C. incanus is our only American, but a gem of ray serene as any old-world species. It grows into a dense tuft of lovely narrow oval leafage of silver grey, on which appear big vases of blushing pearly white.

C. lanuginosus is sub-shrubby, with a branching stem from 4 inches to a foot in height, with leaves quite narrow, hairy and green, and less than an inch long. The blossoms are borne in dense heads at the ends of the branches (which are bare of foliage), and are pinkish or whitish and striped with purple, very hairy indeed outside, and enclosed in conspicuous bracts. From warm crevices, especially of limestone, in the lower regions of Eastern Spain and Central Spain. *C. sericeus* is a specially silky and silvered variety of this green hairy-leaved species.

C. libanoticus makes a low tuft of hoary grey, from which emerge flopping stems set with attenuated oblong leaves, and ending in large flesh-pink cups. (From Hermon and from Lebanon, in the dry alps above the Cedars.)

C. lineatus fills the hard clayey stony places, limy barrens, and dry screes throughout the Alps of Spain, and so, through all the Levant, away into the Altai. It makes a beautiful close mass of stalks, from 3 inches up to a foot, beset with oval foliage clad in a well-ironed pile of silver hair. The clustered flowers are white. Almost exactly similar to this is *C. holosericeus*, of the same habit and silvery glamour, but found in Asia Minor.

C. mauritanicus is a most useful trailer, especially in mild climates, where it runs freely about, throwing far over the rocks its long slender arms, set with dark kidney-shaped hairy foliage, and generous with large beautiful flowers of clear lilac-blue. A good cascade of this, in a sunny exposure and climate, is a thing of beauty all the summer through. Various improved forms are sometimes offered, of which *C. m. atrocoeruleus* is the best.

C. nitidus is one of the loveliest of all. Small mutilated fragments are now falling into our hands, and being sedulously nursed as they deserve. This treasure forms enormous, wide and perfectly tight masses in the dolomitic fissures, dry stony places, and barrens in the sub-alpine and alpine regions of the Sierra Nevada, between 6000 and 7000 feet (as on the summits of Dornajo, Trevenque, and Aquilones), but is nowhere common ; the cushion is built of ovate, blunt, folded little leaves, marked with nerves, and gleaming brilliantly with a plating of the finest silver sheen, soft and silky. Upon this spring stems so short as to be no stems at all, each carrying from one to four large and ravishing cups of rosy white, seeming to be scattered upon the surface of the mat ; and in their general effect giving the casual eye a notion that a clearly-blushing *Oxalis enneaphylla* (such as eye has never seen) must have stuck its blossoms over a dense high-alpine mat of *Potentilla nitida*. (It seems an awfully shy flowerer.)

C. oleaefolius is a more upstanding species, after the style of *C. cneorum*, and *C. lineatus*.

C. parnassicus=*C. cochlearis*, q.v.

C. radicans may possibly prove a variety of *C. cantabricus*. In the hard dry clay of the fields above Trikala, at some 5000 feet up on Kyllênê, it builds dense tufts rather like those of *C. cochlearis*, but that the foliage is smooth and silverless above, while below it is vested in rough whiteness. The flowers, on short stems, are reddish pink, with five blotches of dark purple at the base, about half an inch across.

C. sabatius is an extremely rare species, being confined entirely to that Capo di Noli so fertile in rarities. This, for the same uses and situations as *C. mauritanicus*, has the same large and lovely blue vases, but does not trail or wander, being content to sit at home in an ever-widening clump, from which are thrown out the 6- or 8-inch sprays of blossom. It is no less rare in cultivation than in nature.

C. Soldanella is the trailing Convolvulus of English shingle-banks by the sea, and not unworthy of a remote place upon the moraine, where its frail fat white shoots may wander about, with their fleshy glossy leaves like those of a Soldanella indeed, but three times the size. The trailing stems end in large open trumpets of pink and white.

C. stans is much more upward-growing, a typical silvery Bush-convolvulus from the South, set thickly with shimmering leafage and clustered heads of white. In the North it is hardy, but rarely thrives or blooms; in the South, however, and in the sun, it makes a fine effect.

Coprosma.—There are thirty-nine species of this unpleasantly named New Zealand race; the one in cultivation is *C. acerosa*, a low, wide, and prostrate shrubling, with its branches clothed in narrow leafage, and its valueless flower succeeded by a handsome bloomy blueberry of the sort that is officially styled a drupe. It is hardy, and thrives in light peaty or loamy soil.

Coptis, a race of small woodlanders of the utmost charm, easily to be cultivated in cool places in rich woodland soil. *C. asplenifolia* runs over the ground, carpeting the soil beneath Primulas and Meconopsis and Aquilegia with waving delicate fronds of fern-like foliage, from among which rise flowers like elfin white buttercups. *C. brachyphylla* repeats the charm of this, but is larger in all its parts. *C. anemonaefolia* has leaves so jagged and saw-edged as to look almost spiny, and the spike of flowers is smaller. But most attractive of all are *C. quinquefolia* and *C. trifolia*; the first has five-lobed leaves like those of some Potentilla, one or two from the tuft, about an inch and a half long in all, and between them, standing erect toward the daylight on an inch-tall stem, one single white star-cup like the daintiest of high-alpine buttercups. This same loveliness is repeated exactly by *C. trifolia*, but here the foliage has been stolen bodily from the Cardamine of that name.

CORONILLA.

Corema album, a white-fruited version of Empetrum, from Portugal.

Coreopsis.—The only member of the family for entrance here is *C. rosea,* a really beautiful little American species for the bog, or some cool place in moist and gritty soil, where it forms a small forest-like clump of aspiring fine stems some 6 or 8 inches high, filmy with the most delicate foliage, and tipped with a quantity of bright clear rose-pink Marguerites all through the later summer. (Seed and division.)

Coris monspeliensis is a very pretty but almost biennial and most improbable-looking cousin of Primula, much more like a Thyme in look and habit. It likes to grow in light well-drained soil, in a sunny position, where it forms a small bush of some 5 inches, its branches set with abundant narrow blunt leaves, and ending in summer with a fuzz of pinky-violet flowers with the lobes of the corollas so deeply cleft as to give quite a fluffy effect. The only other species, *C. hispanica,* differs in having the head elongated into a spike, and rather more regular, with flowers of paler pink, and whitish twigs.

Cornus.—The only dogwoods to be troubled with are *C. suecica,* a rather rare native, a rambling plant in heathy soil, sending up a 6-inch stem, set with veined oval-pointed leaves and ending in a cluster of flowers microscopically minute, but (for the delusion of insects) enclosed in four great spreading white bracts that look exactly like white petals, and give the whole the aspect of quite a striking pretty flower ; and the yet more valuable American *C. canadensis,* which is much larger and heartier and freer and more beautiful, forming wide mats and masses, awave in summer beneath their large and brilliant " blossoms," each open and erect at the top of a leafy 6-inch stalk. This likes a cooler place, and looks its best on the shadier side of the rock-work, where it forms ramping wide colonies quickly, and grows too heartily to admit of company.

Coronilla, a group of pea-flowered bushes or bushlings akin to Genista, and usually coming from regions of the South, too warm and dry to bear our climate well. Though many are offered, therefore, few should be chosen. Leaving out of count the larger shrubs, such as *C. Emerus,* the best species are : *C. glauca,* from limestone crevices of Spain, an 18-inch bush of very glaucous blue foliage, with packed rounded heads of large fragrant golden flowers on stems of 6 inches or a foot ; *C. cappadocica* (also wrongly called *C. iberica*), a fine sight all through the summer, of golden flower-heads on a glaucous plant of some 6 inches high ; *C. montana* (*C. coronata*), taller, with smaller blooms of feebler tone, but with a most attractive variety called *minor,* which forms neat round humps of not more than 10

237

inches high, especially profuse in flower ; *C. juncea*, fine and spindly of look, attaining to 2½ feet, and with smaller blossoms ; *C. minima*, with its two varieties, of which *genuina* is perfectly dwarf, and *australis* rather taller ; *C. globosa*, a handsome and strange species, after the manner of *C. varia*—an evergreen from the evergreen zone on the Cretan mountains, with persistent ascending herbaceous stems, each carrying a head of large white blossoms with a dark purple keel ; *C. valentina*, which is very like *C. glauca*, but less blue in tone of leaf, and with smaller flowers which are sweet at night—a frail lax thing. struggling up to a couple of feet or so, with packed heads of yellow ; and finally the totally different *C. varia*, a green lush weed that may be seen on any railway cutting of the Southern and Eastern Alps, throwing about its tall bare foot-stalks of some 8 inches, each carrying a coronal of blossoms in a rather washy and pallid pink (though better forms may no doubt be found). This, in the garden, becomes no less of a weed in any rough and stony warm place ; as for the others, all should be raised from seed, and then put out where they are to remain, in full sun and specially light and stony soil enriched with lime and rather on the thirsty side.

Cortusa Matthioli is a rare and precious cousin of Primula, occasionally but rarely found in some deep alpine coppice, wide sweeps of it unfolding among the alders which in their heyday will have completely hidden it from the sun. It is most like one of the new woodland Chinese Primulas, with soft crinkled foliage, lush and hairy and flimsy and lobed ; and taller stems carrying a loose shower, like the falling stars of a rocket, of pendent rosy-magenta bells. Some see more of the magenta, others more of the rose ; Cortusa will always remain a thing of more subtle and delicate charm than such flaunting Primulas as *P. lichiangensis* and *P. Veitchii*. There is a form called *C. M. grandiflora* ; and, though the copses of the Mont Cenis do not contain it, the wide woods of the world must surely somewhere have news of an albino which would be of inimitable beauty. *C. Matthioli*, indeed, occupies all those woods, occurring at intervals through Europe, and Northern Asia. There are many forms accordingly, some of which falsely claim specific rank ; such are *C. M. pubens* (with very deeply lobed leaves), *Protheri* with flowers of special magnitude from Himalaya, *villoso-hirsuta* (or *hirsuta*), and *pekinensis*. The only other true species in the group is the similar, similar-habited *C. Semenovii* from Alatau, with smooth leaves and yellow flowers, with the style protruding far out. All Cortusas are of the happiest temper in any cool woodland soil and position, where they have a rare appropriateness and grace of aspect, and soon form masses so handsome that they can be divided at will, or multiplied from fresh-ripened seed sown at the end of August. In the garden their favourite flowering moment seems to be July.

Corydalis.—A large race of rock or woodland plants, bulbous or tuberous, all for cultivation in half-sunny places in light, rich soil. There are countless species; all have beautiful foliage, ample and usually suggestive of blue-grey maiden-hair; and some have spikes of fine size or colour. See Appendix.

C. angustifolia, a frailer more delicate *C. solida*, with pink flowers, each about an inch long, with the lobes of the leaves much narrower. (Woods of South Russia.)

C. australis, clear pink, about 8 inches high.

C. bracteata, for sunny or half shady places; foliage glaucous, and flowers pale yellow, with touches of green in the spike. Six inches. (A plant of Altai.)

C. bulbosa, or *cava*, very near *C. solida*, but that the bulb is hollow. (European Alps.)

C. capnoeides from S. Europe, is an early bloomer, with yellow flowers on a 6-inch stem.

C. cashmiriana, about 6 inches, with the basal leaves soon dying. The flowers are half an inch long, rich blue with darker tips. (Sikkim-Kashmir, 9000 to 12,000 feet.)

C. caucasica.—Like a finer, larger, looser *C. solida*, with purple blossoms.

C. cheilanthifolia, a rather handsome plant, with long and very fernlike green foliage, and upstanding long spikes of yellow blossoms attaining 10 inches in height; a hardy Chinese species, but rare and choice, asking for a rich, well-drained, stony soil in the sunny and sheltered rockwork.

C. conorrhiza sends up many stems from 3 to 7 inches high, carrying purple flowers. (Armenia and Trans-caucasus.)

C. curviflora is a gloriously lovely species with loose showers of purest azure blossom, in all the scrubby places of the ranges up the Northern March of Tibet. I failed to introduce it, alas!

C. glauca, blue grey foliage and pink blooms from March to July. (America.)

C. Gortshakowii, woody and green-leaved (not glaucous), with big yellow blossoms; rather like *C. nobilis*, but the 18-inch stems are leafy all the way up. (From the woods of Alatau.)

C. Griffithii, a species from Afghanistan, recalling *C. persicum* but with flowers of half the size, and a much larger terminal lobe to the leaf.

C. juncea attains to 2 feet, with erect spikes of bright golden blooms and hardly any leaves at all, those few being more like bracts. (Nepal and Sikkim, 12,000 to 14,000 feet.)

C. Kolpakowskyana, from the Levant; about 8 inches high with yellow flowers.

C. latiflora has a spindle-shaped root, and is only 3 or 4 inches tall, with flowers three-quarters of an inch long and very wide, bright pale-blue, with darker tips, showing up well above the leaves, which are many and glaucous-grey.

C. Ledebouriana.—Quite like *C. rutaefolia*, but with a laxer shower of pink blooms, and fruiting capsules sticking out horizontal instead of turning down.

C. longiflora justifies itself by having blossoms of 1½ in. in length, and purple in colour. (Altai and Siberia.)

C. lutea, an ever-blooming, golden-flowered, ferny weed in every rock-garden, with a cream-white form which is equally pretty, and seeds true.

C. Marshalliana, from the shady places of Northern Persia, has ampler foliage than *C. cava*, and yellow blossoms.

C. melanochlora is another of my failures. Its deliciously haw-thorn-scented heads of black-eyed white-and-azure helmets nestle close upon the rich blue-grey foliage in all the bare high-alpine shingles of the Kansu-Tibetan March at 15,000 feet.

C. Moorcroftiana, a robust and spreading plant, rather like *C. conorrhiza* but much larger, spreading and branching, and the foliage hoar-frosted with roughness. (Tibet and Afghanistan.)

C. nobilis, one of the finest; a Siberian plant and rather leafy, in foliage suggesting *Callianthemum coriandrifolium*, akin to *C. lutea*, but magnificently larger in the leaf, and attaining 18 inches, with a per-petual profusion of fragrant yellow flowers with a dark tip.

C. ochroleuca blooms through the season, with pale blossoms on foot-high stems.

C. ophiocarpa, from moist places in Sikkim at about 9000 feet, throws up spikes of yellow on stems of 2 or 3 feet, and is distinct in the serpentine pods that follow its spires of blossom, above the very delicate and dainty fernlike foliage of opalescent blue tone and fleshy consistency.

C. parnassica is a small *C. cava* from Parnassus, lower, neater, glaucous-grey, with the leaves on the stem oblong and not rounded. Purple flowers.

C. pauciflora is a common plant all across Asia, glaucous-leaved, with dense and few-flowered heads of violet.

CORYDALIS.

C. persica, like a much more ferny-fronded *C. rutaefolium*, of ample leafage, the lobe at the end being bigger than the side ones. The clear pink blossoms are often more than an inch in length.

C. rosea is a lax spreading floppet of dank rocky places, with long spires of pale pink.

C. rutaefolia, from beside the melting snows of Asia Minor (as *C. cava* from those of our European Alps) is similar in habit—ferny fat-lobed leaves, one or two, springing from a bulb, which here is solid ; and the spike rises to some 6 inches, bearing large flowers of a pleasant pink. There is also, in the screes of Lassiti in Crete, a minor form, with only one or two blossoms, and those of deeper and more brilliant colour. This is *C. alpina*, Koch.

C. scaberula is a very handsome thriving Corydal of high stony places in the Da-Tung Alps, Kansu-Tibet, forming dense clumps of foliage, with many dense 6-inch spikes of dark-tipped claret-coloured bloom.

C. Semenowii, an oriental of some 8 inches in graceful sprays like a Thalictrum's, with little loose heads of bright yellow bloom on the laterals.

C. Sewerzowii grows a foot or more in height, and has fleshy, glaucous leaves with a scant and long-stemmed furnishing of yellow flowers tipped with brown.

C. solida, a beautiful species, forming wide massive tufts of ferny foliage from solid bulbs, and sending clear of them, to the height of some 16 inches or rather less, a profusion of flower-heads of purple from March to May : it prefers rather deep shade.

C. tenella is a little frailer, laxer, Caucasian form of *C. solida*.

C. thalictrifolia, new from China, is not quite so sound in temper as *C. cheilanthifolia*, though hardly less be-praised. In sheltered warm corners, kept sheltered and dry in winter, it forms a woody stock, which in summer becomes a mound of drooping leafage less like that of Thalictrum than that of the Great Celandine, and rather heavy in effect for the comparatively small spires of golden yellow blossom that continue to surmount it all the summer through.

C. tomentosa has specially glaucous, downy leaves and erect, foot-high spikes of green-tipped golden helmets in May and June.

C. verticillaris is a native of North Persia conspicuous in the special fineness of its foliage.

C. Wilsonii, a Chinese novelty, quite hardy, that should have the advantage of a sheltered sunny place in light and well-drained soil. It produces smooth grey-green leaves of extreme fineness and ferny delicacy, very feathery; and its stems of 8 inches or so carry blossoms of deep canary yellow touched with green, in April.

Cotoneaster.—For the rock-garden especially valuable are the neat little leaved bushes, *C. microphylla*, *C. thymifolia*, and the new spraying *C. perpusilla ;* but for hugging the rocks and robing them in a close-fitting coat of sprays and leaves and berries, especially admirable are the evergreens, *C. prostrata*, *C. humifusa*, *C. pyrenaica* (or *C. congesta*), *C. glacialis*, and the deciduous beautiful *C. adpressa*, all of them merely requiring to be stuck in and left alone. See Appendix.

Cotŭla.—The only Cotula which convenience may leave under this name (for they are all now *Leptinella*), is a most useful New Zealander, *C. squalida*, which has been unkindly named, for in fact it forms a peculiarly neat and beautiful carpet of minute, ferny, evergreen foliage, flat to the ground, and excellently adapted to carpet the ground for choice bulbs, or make a floor by the water-side ; it will grow with rampant ease in almost any conditions, and by the edge of the pond positively flops over and in, making masses of fine white rootage that go on waving in the water like the hair of an elderly mermaid. The flowers, it is true, might justly be called squalid ; but they are so utterly negligible—little heads of dinginess in summer, on stems of an inch or so, that really need not be considered one way or another, and in no way spoil the lawn one is treading, by calling any attention to themselves. (It soon becomes a wicked weed.)

Cotyledon (Echeveria).—The only generally and soundly hardy species is *C. Purpusii*, from the Californian Sierra Nevada. This should be planted in a tight, well-drained crevice, in a sunny, dry, and sheltered exposure, where it will be very pretty with its neat and succulent rosette of glaucous white-bloomed leaves, while its spikes of blossom recall those of a red-and-yellow Lachenalia.

Cousinia, weedy, coarse, thistlish, woolly-headed biennials from the Himalaya, of no attractiveness for us.

Cowania mexicana is a pinnate-leaved Rosaceous shrub or shrubling, from 4 inches high to as many feet, very branchy, set with those rose-like leaves, dark green, and hoary-white underneath, and then with large flowers of bright yellow. The bark has a way of shredding from the trunks, and the plant, being found in Utah and Colorado, should have a light, well-drained place in good soil.

Crambe cordifolia is a vast perennial cabbage about 5 feet high, but more across, that fills the air with a spray of small white blossom all the mid-summer, above that mound of enormous foliage. *C. orientalis* has the same habit, but larger blossoms, as also has *C. Kotschyana ; C. juncea* from Spain is smaller ; *C. tatarica* is notably handsome with blue-glaucous leafage, and *C. aspera*, rough with hairs, has also its place, like all these giant cabbages, in deep soil, on high exposures of the boldest rock-garden only. Sow seed as soon as ripe.

Crassula alpestris is a rather ugly-looking succulent of most doubtful hardiness, with narrow, fleshy foliage, leprous with dark blotches, and terminal heads of small, insignificant, pink flowers at the tips of the shoots. It seems only about 3 inches high, and might prosper permanently in a hot and stony place, though without contributing anything in the way of adornment.

Cremanthodium, a race of Asiatic Composites, of which some are greatly to be desired. They are close to Ligularia, but with nodding flowers. *C. pinnatum* is a lovely thing from the Kankola valley in Sikkim, between 12,000 and 13,000 feet. The leaves are at the base, kidney-shaped, and then deeply cut into five or ten lobes, almost to the stem; the stalks are from 4 to 7 inches high, slender and hairy, each carrying one very large flower of soft pink, the spokes being notched two or three times or more at the end, so as to give a fringy effect, while the blossom is held horizontally, the rays standing up and then opening out in bell-shaped design. *C. pinnatifidum* is much the same, but that here the leaves are almost all at the base, but with just a few on the scapes, whose flowers are yellow. This comes from the same valley at greater heights, and there are many more species yet to come, though hitherto *C. pinnatum* (with *C. rhodocephalum*) alone breaks the family record with pink blossoms. See Appendix.

Crenularia, a family of really beautiful cruciferous plants from the Levant, close to Aethionema, and asking the same treatment, which they repay with the same beauty. (Seed, and cuttings in August.)

C. eunomioeides, from alpine crevices in the Cilician Taurus, makes a woody, twisted little bush, standing erect, and with its twigs thickly set with fleshy rounded leaves in pairs, and ending in clusters of large pink blossoms.

C. glauca makes a mound not more than 3 or 4 inches high, of leafy blue-grey twigs, ending in a head of large rose-pink flowers. It much recalls *Iberis saxatilis* or *Aeth. schistosum*, and has itself been called *Aethionema Balansae*. (Cilician Taurus.)

C. orbiculata is half the size of this in all parts, except the flowers—emitting frail, densely leafy, short shoots from a fat and barky stock, with fleshy leaves in pairs, oval-rounded, and noble pink blossoms. (From the summits of Athos, Taygetos, &c). (Eunomia.)

Crepis.—No Crepis is worthy of admission to the rock-garden—or to any other but the wild-weed garden only—except the following: *C. incisa*, all cobwebby and fluffy, with a number of dwarf fat branching stems producing pink flowers in a powdery involucre; *C. rubra* from South Italy; and *C. lagoseris* with wide-expanded, silky, cobwebbed leaves, and tallish stems of large blue-purple blossom. Chalky cliffs of Taurus; while *C. incisa* is found at some 6000 feet in the Alps of Greece. These ought to have a place in the garden, if only for their summer flowering.

Cristaria coccinea=Malvastrum coccineum, *q.v.*

Crocus.—This precious race is still so unknown in the rock-garden that when the name is suggested for its glorification in autumn, nine people out of ten have never realised that there *are* any autumn Crocus, and think that Colchicum must be meant. Nor have even the vernal species come to their own in the rock-garden, perhaps because borders and grass-plots are so full of blowzy florists' Crocus (lovely in their place, indeed), that popular imagination cannot admit of any cousin of such being appropriate among the stones. Yet nothing in the world is better suited there, or looks so well, as these delicate fairies, whose grace makes impossible 'Arriets of even the most splendid garden forms. These indeed must never be admitted to the rock-garden, but all its high and low places, flat expanses, and open slopes cry aloud to be set thickly with Crocus species, little lovely things that do no harm, and never get in the way of even the choicest plants, and die away as soon as they possibly can after their hour of radiance so specially welcome, either in the wilderness of January or in that of October and November. The race is wholly Southern, and its blooming period goes the whole round of the year's clock. But many of the species accordingly are not fitted for culture out of doors in England, as the muds and floods of mid-winter wreck their delicate loveliness of blossom. And, indeed, all the species are best planted under a carpet of something else, not only for the protection of the Crocus bloom itself, but also that the something else may have its hour of glory when the Crocus is no more. *Arenaria balearica, Cotula*, the Acaenas, *Veronica repens, Hypericum reptans*, all leap to mind as being admirable carpets to associate with Crocus for the mutual benefit of both, and the gardener will easily think of a dozen more— to say nothing of prostrate shrubs like the precious Cotoneasters *glacialis, congesta, adpressa*, and *humifusa*. Or they may be set between choicer alpines, and their corms provide just the company enjoyed by *Potentilla nitida, Primula minima, Dianthus alpinus*, and *Gentiana verna;* nor do they ever look better than when they emerge from those glossy green mats and tuffets in autumn and early spring, even as does *C. albiflorus* on the Alps. And, yet again, the light cover of the Aethionemas, *Alsine, Linum tenuifolium*, the smaller bushy

CROCUS.

Pentstemons, *Erinacea, Genista horrida*, and many more of medium height and habit not too dense, take an added charm when their own flowers are over, if up amid their twigs come shooting the violet and lavender cups of Crocus, as *Crocus versicolor* peers amid the withered herbage and low tangles of lentisc and Smilax on the Cap d'Antibes down by the Mediterranean in mid-winter. In the way of soil, too, Crocus makes no demands ; their ground should be open and light, as that necessary to the best culture of all alpines ; nor are they less rigid than other plants in their insistence upon good drainage. But then this point is understood ; any book that talks nowadays of the culture of alpines takes it for granted that the whole construction is on sound lines from the beginning, with adequate foundation of drainage-blocks below, and the soil prepared throughout instead of merely being administered in those pernicious " pockets " that got alpines so miffy a name in days gone by, and slew their hundreds of thousands to the tens that fell victim to slug or mouse or climate. Mice, indeed, are vampires of Crocus, and the gardener troubled with such must let loose a leash of cats at once, if he does not wish to go round each morning and see a fresh little neat set of holes (exactly as if the ferule of an umbrella had been poked down), in every one of which lies the wreckage of some expensive Crocus, there discovered and devoured. No precaution otherwise appears to prevail ; if Crown Imperials are planted no good is done, though it was once hoped that the smell of their bulbs might drive away the mice from the Crocus corms ; which they pursue from above ground (without burrowing as they do for lilies), aided by some special sense like that of truffle-dogs pursuing their prey in the woods of France. Even red lead seems only to act as an appetiser ; often will you find the red-leaded latticed skeleton of the corm's tunic lying complete and perfectly empty, like the ghost of a Japanese lantern ; but of the lovely promise within no longer any trace. The remedy is only poison, or cats, or traps, baited with common Crocus-corms ; and the building of the rock-garden so soundly throughout that there are no hollows left for mice to make their homes. Here, then, is a complete list of all the Crocus species that are best suited for out-door culture in England, the arrangement being on the botanical principle, most simple in a race like this. Let these be planted at half again their own depth—or say some 2 or 3 inches, and the corms will give you news again of beauty when most you want it in the sere hours of the year, springing perhaps in the same sheet of Acaena, filled with *C. Imperati* for the dawn, and *C. speciosus* for the weeping sunset of the season.

CROCUS.

CLASS I.—FLOWER ENCLOSED IN A SHEATH SPRINGING FROM THE BASE OF THE SCAPE

SECTION I.—CORM ENCLOSED IN MEMBRANE, OR IN MEMBRANOUS COAT WITH PARALLEL LINES

AUTUMN FLOWERING

C. asturicus greatly resembles Nudiflorus, but has the leaves just showing as the flower comes up, and the throat is bearded. It is a beautiful species, and like so many, has an albino form, as well as various others—*lilacinus, atropurpureus, pallidus, azureus*, &c. (Northern Spain.)

C. byzantinus, Ker-Gawl., *C. iridiflorus*, Heuff., very beautiful indeed, with glossy pointed leaves much broader than usual, and the three inner segments of the lovely pure-violet flower remarkably smaller than the three outer ones—so as to give indeed almost the look of a minute *Iris unguicularis*. This does best in a rather shady position, and flowers about October. There is a fine white form, in which the stigmata are pale yellow instead of lilac as in the type.

C. Clusii from Portugal also blooms in October, and also sends up its leaves in advance of the lilac blossoms. But here the corm is clothed in a netted coat.

C. karduchorum, from Turkestan, differs chiefly from Zonatus in having the anthers yellow, and the segments of the cup feathered with dark lines.

C. nudiflorus, as usual in this group, has the leaves dormant at flowering time. It has notably large and nubbly corms, and increases freely when happy, by emitting runners from them. The throat is smooth at the base inside, and the inner segments have a purple rim, as they pass down towards the tube. Its native home is in the Pyrenees, but it has long established itself in England.

C. ochroleucus makes a flat corm, and sends up its narrow-rayed white cups with their white stigmata, together with the leaves, in October and November. (Palestine.)

C. Salzmannii, a very strong grower with a specially large corm, clothed in a specially coarse coat of membrane, with parallel fibres. It loves a sunny ledge, and heralds the approach of its delicate lilac flower in October by sending up its grassy tuft of leaves beforehand. It is a specially hearty grower, and mice accordingly feed upon it with a special heartiness. (Spain and Tangier.)

C. Scharojani requires care, and should be grown in a sandy moraine in a shady place, with water laid on underground. It is the earliest of all the autumn Crocus, or the latest of the spring ones; for its flowers, of the most brilliant gold, appear in August. It is always rare and expensive.

C. zonatus, on the contrary, is perfectly common and perfectly beautiful. It has a flattened, irregular corm, from which in September and October rise the buds, and open widely out into cups of a most diaphanous soft lavender. The anthers are white, and this delicate sweet beauty expands to her fullest happiness in a sunny exposure.

SPRING-BLOOMING SPECIES OF THE SAME GROUP

C. Imperati is indeed the ἔαρος ἀγγελος ἱμεροφωνος ἀηδων, the sweet-voiced nightingale of the spring, peering up into the sere dank world when all the ground is rotten with death, and January, like sad Barsanti, weeps across the scene. It is one of the very loveliest, emitting, first, its prostrate dark leaves, and then, wrapped in twin spathes, a chalice of blossom, opaque creamy buff outside, and feathered richly with lines of dark purple; then, when the rare sun calls, the goblet becomes a wide star of pure soft lavender-purple. Quickly it grows and quickly increases, but because of its loveliness and precocity, it should have a neat carpet to come through, and to keep the tears of winter from splashing its happy morning face. There is a white variety, too, and many others ; especially a second type, in which the leaves are erect instead of lying down, and the spathe is single. All these prizes are gathered in the neighbourhood of Naples.

C. Malyi from Dalmatia, blooms from February to March, and has white flowers with a golden throat both inside and out.

C. minimus is a wee jewel from Corsica, a cupling of purple in March and April, with broad and rounded segments. Here the bud-sheath sends up two spathes. For a very fine place and through a very fine carpet.

C. versicolor, a most variable beauty with the three inner segments feathered inside as well as out. A hundred forms may be found in the scrub and in the rough places down among the rocks by the sea, along the French Riviera, and up into the hills. (February.)

SECTION II.—WITH THE CORM IN NETTED TUNIC

SPRING FLOWERING

C. banaticus has lilac flowers, and a white hairless throat, with purple markings at the tip of the segments. (Hungary.)

C. corsicus, also in February and March, sends up only one spathe round each bud, and the stigmata of the purple blossoms are scarlet.

C. etruscus has very coarsely netted tunic-coats, but its blooms are of supreme elegance, the three outer segments being pale buff-coloured outside and feathered with purple, while the three inner ones are of soft blue-lavender inside and out. The flower is long and graceful, opening into a beautiful star of clear blue, looking its best and proving most permanent in rather rough grass, where it blooms in April. A most variable species in its featherings.

C. Tommasinianus comes into bloom in February and March, with beautiful long cups of lavender-blue that are often white on the outside and have a white beard to their throat inside. (Eastern Europe.) One of the hardiest.

C. vernus is a parent of the fat garden dummies that have no place in our territories, be they never so gorgeous and bloated (so obese, indeed, as to make one feel that there must be aesthetic feelings at work in the beaks of the sparrows that so assiduously pick them off or peck them to pieces). The true species has a delicate purple bloom, and is naturalised in several places in England. The variety *C. v. leucorrhyncus* is fat indeed, but redeemed by the white tip to its sheeny cup of satiny violet ; but far more beautiful is *C. albiflorus*, now raised to specific rank on the Continent—the dainty Snow-crocus of the Alps, that not only takes the place of the departing snow with its milky drifts, but is even in such a hurry to do so that it pushes its long, narrow cups (like old-fashioned fluted champagne glasses) of opalescent white or purple so sturdily through the hard-wrought whiteness itself, that over all its surface they stand expanded in the early days of June on the heights, long after they have become little more than the memory of lank grass down in the valleys below. But *C. albiflorus* is not quite so free or so ready to re-establish itself as less elevated and exalted forms of *C. vernus*.

AUTUMN-BLOOMING SPECIES

C. hadriaticus blooms in October among the miseries of Albania —a species very near *C. sativus*, but almost always white-chaliced, and sometimes with a yellow throat.

C. longiflorus sees the old year sad upon its way, at leaving in the garden a thing so beautiful and sweet at the merciless mercy of the elements. For in late November come the long violet-lavender tubes of *C. longiflorus*, opening to let loose on the world a flood of

PLATE 22.

CROCUS BIFLORUS.
(Photo. R. A. Malby.)

CROCUS SIEBERI.
(Photo. R. A. Malby.)

PLATE 23.

CYCLAMEN NEAPOLITANUM ALBUM.
(Photo. R. A. Malby.)

CROCUS VERNUS.
(Photo. R. A. Malby.)

VOL. L.

sweet fragrance and flaunting stigmata as scarlet as in the best, but not tasselled. The leaves come with the flowers. (Italy, with a variety *C. l. melitensis* from Malta, adorned yet further with violet featherings.) A princess among Autumn Crocus.

C. medius bears its fine lavender blossoms in October all along the rough places of the Riviera. It may be known by its wildly tasselled scarlet stigmata, as well as by the marked star of violet lines in its throat.

C. niveus, Bowles (*marathoniseus*, Held.), springs in the high places of Taygetos, and glorifies such gardens as can afford it, from October to December—the finest of all white Crocus known, with yellow anthers and stigmata of scarlet, the floral spathes just appearing above ground, the outer one having a greenish tip.

C. sativus is the true Saffron Crocus, but in the garden is chary of its purple flowers unless set high on a specially warm and well-drained ledge. The flaunting saffroned stigmata are undivided, and there is a star of purple in the throat of the purple flower; while the leaves appear before them, and are fringed with hairs at their edge. *C. s. Cartwrightianus* is a small variable form from Greece: while *C. s. Thomasii* is an Italian representative of the species.

SECTION III.—NAKED FLOWERERS, WITH NO BASAL SHEATH AT ALL

GROUP I.—NETTED CORMS

C. ancyrensis opens in February, a little golden star almost always undefiled with brown, and with scarlet stigmata.

C. cancellatus.—A beautiful early-flowering species of September, with white flowers appearing before the leaves, and stigmata slashed and fringy. It is striped in varying degrees of purple, and the form *C. c. cilicus* has a ground of delicate lavender blue. (E. Europe to Asia Minor, &c.)

C. dalmaticus comes very early in the year, with flowers which are buff or grey outside, opening into stars of rosy lilac.

C. gargaricus flowers before the leaves, with goblets of richest orange in the dawn of the Spring.

C. reticulatus from Eastern Europe has a separate basal tunic, unlike *dalmaticus*, which has none at all; and very various blossoms of mauve or white striped externally.

C. Sieberi breaks upon the world in January and February with flowers of soft purple, and a bright orange throat. It is a vigorous little loveliness from Greece, with a variety *C. S. versicolor*, diversified with white and violet, from Crete.

C. stellaris may possibly be the child of *C. susianus* and *C. aureus*. In the early year it makes a star of bright gold, and is finely feathered with brown on the outside.

C. susianus has cups of brilliant orange gold, heavily striped with dark-brown varnish outside, and opening into a wide star with so much heartiness that the segments often go too far and turn down the other way. It opens to the first call of the February sun, and belongs to the southerly parts of Russia.

GROUP II.—CORMS DRESSED IN FIBROUS MEMBRANE, NOT NETTED

C. Balansae now takes up the torch, coming into bloom with February and continuing onwards. It lives in Asia Minor, and has ragged stigmata, and golden flowers bronzed and browned outside. The best form of all wears the three outer segments entirely veneered with polished dark mahogany.

C. Boryi is the white of old ivory, but asks protection for the big blooms with their white anthers and much-cleft stigmata. (Greece.)

C. caspius dances by the shores of the Caspian Sea—one of the finest of its race, and one of the best to grow. The anthers are yellow, and the stigmata uncloven and unfringed, and the royal upstaring star is milky-white, in the cooling greyness of October, onwards into the darkness of December.

C. laevigatus may always be known by the eccentric fashion of its corm's overcoat, which is of very tough skin, breaking into van-dykes at the base in a manner unmistakable. The tough skin pervades the constitution of this lovely plant, too, for it sails unperturbed through October into January, never tiring in production of its varying white or lilac flowers, varyingly feathered and striped with violet.

C. Suterianus, however, has to be content with plain orange stars. *C. Olivieri* does the same, but makes up with broader foliage. Both flower in spring.

C. Tournefortii never learns wisdom. For lovely though it be in October and November with its wide stars of gentle lavender, white-anthered and with slashed stigmata—those tender stars, once they are opened, do not know how to shut again, any more than the heart of man. Accordingly they require the protection against storms which that other delicate flower requires also, but in vain.

CROCUS.

SECTION IV.—TUNIC OF STRONG PARALLEL FIBRES

C. aureus, with its flowers of gleaming metallic gold, opening in the dawn of spring, has the terrible responsibility of being parent to many Fat Boys of the garden and grass plots, no less than of many wild forms such as *C. lagenaeflorus*, *C. maesiacus*, the pale *C. sulphureus*, and the rare lovely *C. lacteus* of milky pallor. It is indeed a most gorgeous and delicate beauty, by no means to be excluded from the company of the choice, if only for the fact that this is the golden-rayed Crocus that shone upon way-worn Oedipus in Kolônos as heartily as to-day in our borders on us, though the Crocus and Oedipus and the nightingales and the Daphnes have all departed from Kolônos long ago.

C. candidus lives in Asia Minor. It has especially broad foliage, and the white cups are diversely feathered with lilac, but yellow and orange forms are known.

C. Korolkowii is golden as a Celandine, and browned on the outside. It has a very large flat corm, lives in Turkestan, and flowers from December to February.

SECTION V.—TUNIC SPLITTING INTO RINGS AT THE BASE

C. aërius, a rather delicate, lovely fairy, with a soft rind to its corm, and starry cups in a dozen different tones, with featherings of purple and crimson.

C. biflorus is called the Scotch Crocus because it belongs to the Mediterranean basin from Tuscany to Georgia, a neat and lovely small joy of extraordinary freedom and vigour in the garden, which is crammed in spring with colonies and clusters of neat clumped flowers feathered with purple on their buff-pale outsides, and within of the loveliest silver-lavender. The blooms are very variable, alike in colour and in feathering ; catalogues perpetually offer new named forms, for this Crocus, appearing in spring, has attained to public recognition as a decent, orderly-minded plant, with none of its cousins' ill-regulated habit of glorifying a time of year when no respectable Crocus can be expected to be up and out of bed, except on pain of being ignored ; and there are also many local varieties, forms or sub-species, such as *C. nubigenus*, *C. Weldeni*, *C. estriatus*, *C. Adami*, and *C. Alexandri*.

C. chrysanthus can be told from all other golden Crocus by the

black spot on the barb of the anthers, except in the variety *C. ch.*
fuscolineatus, in which the whole ground of the anthers is black. The
species is most variable, but invariably beautiful, the type being of
pure stainless yellow (with vermilion stigmata in the variety *C. ch.
superbus*), but the forms diverge on to sulphur-yellow and differing
shades of blue, with diversities of blue feathering. The finest form,
where all are good, is *C. ch. pallidus*, with specially large and ample cups
of pale soft citron. This noble creature, too, has given seedlings as fine
as itself, in the utmost degree of variation, the king of all being named
after the King of Crocus, *E. A. Bowles*, a familiarity towards the plant
that we deplore, while applauding the due honour paid to the man.
C. chrysanthus lives in Eastern Europe, and fills our spring with
loveliness from January to March.

   C. pulchellus, with an albino, and naked and leafless in flower,
comes into bloom in early autumn, one of the darlings of the
family, a neat and swelling little cup, expanding like a beautiful
wine-glass on its stem, and opening a broad-lobed goblet of the most
delicate lilac-lavender, exquisitely threaded with pale veins, drawing
down to the pale throat, where there is a ring of orange blots or blurs
at the base of each segment. *C. pulchellus* is neat and dainty enough
in habit for the choicest slopes and beds of the choicest plot.

   C. speciosus is the sovereign in size and splendour of all the *Autumn*
Crocus, and one of the most vigorous; and one of the very few, if not the
only one, that has forced itself upon popular recognition. It is the bluest
of them, too, with great upstanding goblets feathered and flaked and
blotched and blurred into the most lovely medley of rich blue-violet,
in the midst of which stand up the tasselled wild stigmata of intense
vermilion-orange. It always takes the breath with beauty, but never
more than when on some sad October day you see its noble, bare-
stemmed, delicate blue chalices swaying over the pale fading gold of
dead leaves from whose deathbed it is springing through a carpet of
prostrate ivy. There is a fine white form, which has lost too much to
be as good as the violet type, and there is the variety *Aitchisoni*, the
giant of the race—paler than the species, but of enormous size and
loveliness and stature, and no less vigour.

   Cyananthus.—There are many of these Campanulads in the high
Alps of India and China, but very few so far in general cultivation.
The chief is *C. lobatus*, which, from the central crown, makes a number
of prostrate shoots some 8 inches in length, set all along with small leaves
lobed into featherings at the tip, and clad in white hairs; and, at the
end, a single large and beautiful flower, in shape recalling a periwinkle,
of clear powder-blue, with a calyx very large and baggy, and vested

in very dark, stiff fur. In seed-time this bag proves a danger, holding water and rotting the capsule ; it is best to pull it away when the heads show signs of filling. This beautiful alpine blooms in August, and is of easy culture in deep, light and well-moistened stony soil, or in the underground-waterbed of gritty moraine mixture. Similar treatment will suit the similar species ; *C. incanus*, with flowers thinner in the star and longer and clearer and paler, with leaves almost entire at the edge, and tawny fur to the calyx ; *C. Forrestii*, a frail thing of lavender blossom ; *C. pedunculatus*, with the peduncle as well as the calyx dark and hairy as Esau, and with practically no white beard of fluff at the throat, as in *C. lobatus* ; *C. integer*, of the same habit, but with leaves less notched, narrow-oblong, toothed and scalloped, hairy-rough on both faces, but gradually becoming smooth ; *C. microphyllus*, very frail and small in the leaf, with a ring at the throat, from river shingles high up in Kumaon, and *C. leiocalyx* from Yunnan, which is a smooth-calyxed version of *C. incanus*, but with yellow flowers.

Cyclamen, though called the Bread of Sows, might more appropriately have been the Food of the Gods, even as *C. europaeum*, indeed, *is* called the *Patate della Madonna*. For their lovely charm is patent to all, and needs no bush except to grow in. All the species can be quite happily established in loose woody corners of half shade, where with the aid of plenty of lime they will be glad to make themselves comfortable, and the flower-heads of one year will roll up into tight corkscrews until the next, when they will suddenly uncoil to scatter their seed with such profusion and success that *C. europaeum* (at least) long claimed to be an English native on the strength of its abundance in certain woods of Kent. At the same time, the race is wholly Southern, and so far from being averse from sunshine that all the limestone screes of the Judicaria, in blazing daylight, are rubied over with the hovering butterflies of *C. europaeum*, while some of the finest clumps in these islands are growing in full sun in a gravel path where it is impossible to make out the shapes of the individual flowers, so dense is the congregation of rose-pink. All cyclamen can only be multiplied by seed, which germinates readily ; collected corms re-establish surely, but they also re-establish as a rule rather slowly, so that those gardeners who put in a thing on Monday and expect to have their eye filled with glory by Wednesday are sometimes apt to be disappointed.

C. africanum is a great-leaved plant also called *C. macrophyllum*. The big leaves appear in autumn, kidney-shaped, scalloped, and wavy at the edge. They are heralded by the yet earlier blossoms, with pointed petals of pink, marked by a mouth-ring of bright crimson. (Algiers, &c.) For a rather more sheltered place than the rest.

CYCLAMEN.

C. alpinum is found high up by the melting snow in the Cilician Taurus. It has the habit and inflorescence of *C. cilicicum,* emerging before the leaves, which are of kidney shape, rounded at the end, intensely green above, irregularly banded with a broken line of white, and carmine-purple underneath ; but the flowers are not pointed or elongate in the petal as in *C. cilicicum,* but fat and short and rounded as in *C. coum* and *C. ibericum,* from which they chiefly differ in not turning sharply up, but *spreading abroad.* In colour they are of a conspicuously fine bright rose, with a big and round (*never triangular*) blotch of dark purple at the base of each segment.

C. × *Atkinsii* is a garden hybrid between *C. coum* and *C. ibericum,* which has bred a good deal of confusion in its time. It has the leaves shaped as in *C. coum;* that is, of a fat kidney design, small, like a very big Soldanella's ; but here they are of a most brilliant green, and *blotched with silver white,* instead of wearing true Coum's unrelieved and sullen gloom ; the flowers are of palest pink or white, sometimes lined or flushed with crimson, and taking many named varieties in catalogues.

C. balearicum stands close to *C. repandum,* but has flowers of half the size, very sweet, on very long stems ; and the long-stalked leaves are merely heart-shaped—egg-shaped, dimly and remotely toothed here and there round their rim. They are purple underneath and dark-green above, marked with small white spots. The blossoms come up in spring, and are white with a throat of pink, but variable. (Stony places in the Balearics.)

C. cilicicum is perhaps only a variety of *C. coum.* It makes a large flattened corm in the Alps of Cilicia, and the leafage dies away in summer, to reappear in autumn after the first flowers have unfolded. These are softly pink, with very pointed petals, and a spot of intense crimson at the base ; and the style hardly if at all protrudes beyond the mouth.

C. coum is a small species. In autumn appear the small rounded leaves, of a sullen and leathery dark-green, black and leaden in effect, and *unrelieved by the smallest touch of white.* They are followed all the winter through by a profusion of little fat-looking flowers of a heavy magenta—though perhaps this judgment is not so harsh when they are seen bejewelling the January days with little glowing sparks of colour upon the dead earth. There is a much more attractive white form, but the shape of the small blossom always lacks the usual grace of the family. The true plant is not common, though its name is always to be found in the lists ; the sure absolute sign is the *unrelieved darkness* of the Soldanella-shaped foliage.

C. cyprium, an autumnal species, differing from *C. neapolitanum*

254

in the form of the foliage, which is excessively jagged and cut. The flowers are white, with narrow pointed petals twirled and tweaked fantastically.

C. europaeum is the best-beloved of all, and by far the most generally charming. It may be seen in the Swiss woods and coppices ; but in the Southern Alps it breaks into fullest profusion, filling the long limestone screes of Baldo or the Tombea with a crowd of dancing ruby flames, and ranging far into the East, in the rough low places of Obir or Jelenk. Its flowering time is from July on into the autumn, and its dainty carmine-magenta butterflies are of perfect proportion and delicious scent. It is of the easiest habit anywhere ; growing, as it does so often, in scree like that of the Long Scar under Ingleborough, it may be planted also in the coarsest moraine and gravel path in fullest sun. It may always be known by its *evergreen leaves*, which are rounded, *smooth at the edge*, dimly marbled, and with the rounded lobes almost touching on either side of their stems. There are various forms, of which the variety *C. e. ponticum* has broader petals, and leaves invariably and finely saw-edged. But the albino, though on record, is still to seek.

C. graecum, Link (*C. Poli*, Chiaje), sends up pink blossoms with a deeper base in autumn, on stems about equal to those of the leaves, which appear in full force a little later, and are heart-shaped and toothed regularly at the edge with horny teeth.

C. hiemale is perhaps one of the plants that passes for *C. coum* ; for its foliage is of the same size and shape, but blotted with white marblings instead of being uniformly dark. The stout dumpyish petals differ from those of *C. ibericum*, in having a rounded and not triangular blotch of colour at their base. It blooms through the winter unperturbed, the flower-segments each sending down into the throat a line of intense crimson.

C. ibericum has the same early habit, its carmine blooms emerging before the foliage in winter and earliest spring, each segment with a triangular blotch of crimson at the base. The leaves are heart-shaped or kidney-shaped, and only slightly wavy-edged, while the petals of both these last are in the fat style of *C. coum*.

C. libanoticum is the most beautiful of all the smaller-habited Cyclamens. It lives on Lebanon rather better than anywhere else, where its leaves shoot up in autumn ; they are roughly heart-shaped, with rare irregular toothings round their edge (but never deeply lobed or gashed), dark purple underneath, and on the upper side of deep grey-green with a continuous band of white marbling. In spring come the lovely and fragrant flowers, large and well-proportioned and well-liking, of a delicate and delicious warm rose-pink with a base of intense crimson. It is distinguished from *C. cyprium* by the leaves, which are never lobed and gashed ; from *C. graecum* and *C. persicum* by their lack of any horny margin. In cultivation it should have a warm place under the outskirts of some small fine bush such as Berberis Wilsonae, in full sun and with abundance of lime. It is not invariably easy to keep pleased.

C. neapolitanum flowers in autumn, and its leaves are very variable in size and shape ; typically they are exactly like some ivy-leaf, rather long from base to point ; they are dark and waved and marbled, while the beautiful flowers begin to appear before the hey-day of the foliage, and have the amplitude and grace of *C. persicum's*, in varying shades of pink to white, and with an intense, not quite bifurcating spot of crimson at the base of each segment. The plant is of delicate beauty, and extreme freedom in flower ; making solid clumps of soft flesh-colour or carmine in an open, sunny gravel path, no less than thriving as heartily, if not with such condensed ferocity of floriferousness, in places not so inhumane.

C. persicum can always be grown out of doors in a warm and sheltered spot, where, among bushes in tempered climates, it becomes more glorious than the rest in stature and size of bloom through late summer, winter, and spring. Old greenhouse corms can there be thrown away ; but they usually have the fat memories and the fat habit of their former home, and are neither graceful nor happy in wild corners. It is best then to get seed of some good simple strain —but not, at any cost, of the huge, highly trained, and comparatively coarse florist forms, which have wholly sold the birthright of grace for a mess of manure, and the stalled ox of hothouses. Let a plainer kind be sought and sown, and its young corms put out betimes in a cosy corner, and *C. persicum* will outdo nearly all its lesser kin. There are various wild varieties, including the smaller-flowered autumn-blooming *C. p. Mindleri* from the volcanic cliffs of Aegina, with different and altogether smaller habit. And *C. persicum* itself some-times takes refuge under the name of *C. macrophyllum*, Sieber.

C. pseud-ibericum is most obscure, and may possibly be but a synonym for the *ponticum* variety of *C. europaeum*. It has heart-shaped leaves rounded at the point and at the lobes, edged with horny membrane, intensely green on the upper surface, and marbled with blotches of silvery white. The flowers appear in spring, pale violet-pink to a paler base where there is a spot of black-violet to each seg-ment ; they vary, however, like all Cyclamen, in colour and depth of tone ; but excel the rest in their pre-eminent sweetness.

C. repandum has often wrongly been called *C. hederaefolium*, a name to be now dropped. It has thin-textured green leaves, of a broad, broad-pointed heart-shape, cut into shallow wide vandykes all round. The flowers also appear in spring, rather pinched and narrow, about the same height as the foliage, and of a most dazzling, malignant carmine, which looks its best and most effective when seen springing here and there in the young grass.

C. Rohlfsianum is near *C. africanum*, alike in home and habit. The leaves are kidney-shaped, irregularly cut, and toothed at the edge ; they appear in autumn, and close on their heels tread the fragrant blossoms of intense colour, paling to the tips.

The above list comprises, up to date, all the recognised species ; so that future names, unless described as new species (as, for instance, unproven *C. Jovis*), may be taken as synonyms or pseudonyms among the above, many of which, indeed, may be local developments one out of another ; as *CC. alpinum, hiemale* and *ibericum* from *C. coum*, and *C. balearicum* from *C. repandum* ; *CC. africanum* and *Rohlfsianum* from *C. neapolitanum*. Lonely in the race stands the isolated magnificence of *Cyclamen persicum*, distinct from all others of the family in carrying its fruit-heads *on erect stems*, instead of adopting the watch-spring fashion invariable in the rest.

Cynoglossum has lost almost all its gems. *C. longiflorum* must be found as **Lindelofia,** *C. Wallichii* under **Eritrichium,** *C. racemosum* under **Paracaryum,** *C. stylosum* under **Solenanthus,** and *C. umbellatum* under **Mattia.** Remain then, these :

C. furcatum, if ever offered true, is a worthless annual.

C. nervosum remains a beautiful thing of a foot high or so, from upper elevations in the Western Himalaya, taking kindly to culture in any sunny soil, throwing up sparsely hairy stems that end in showers of beautiful large flowers of deep azure like a neat Anchusa. Seed. But *C. sphacioticum*, which comes from the stony places high up on the Cretan mountains, and is some half a foot tall, is a perennial species, with goodly azure flowers even bigger than those of *Paracaryum myosotoeides*. Any other Cynoglossum advertised must be quested for in other races.

Cyphomattia lanata or **Cynoglossum lanatum** is a Borragineous species from high and rocky places of Lycaon, in Syria. Russian Armenia, &c., making a fat crown in the rocks, from which it sends up leafy stems, the whole growth being white with stiff hairs. These stems rise from 6 to 18 inches, and break at last into a woolly shower of very pretty flowers from red to blue. Sunny rocks.

Cypripedium.—The grandest and most august of Orchidaceae, the one great race which is supreme alike in the open and under cover, deserves full treatment to itself. The hardy Slippers are all lovers of copse-wood, forest, or rough open grassy places on the high hillsides of Asia and America. A glance at their root-masses should show the nature of the mistake that is often made in their culture, and has sometimes earned them a bad name. For it will at once be seen that the roots never descend, but spread in radiating masses in the superficial soil alone. That superficial soil is always of a light or close vegetable nature, and this supplies the plant with all the sustenance and anchorage it needs, while the vegetable decay of each season provides it with exactly the sheltering and stimulating top-dressing that it wants. Accordingly the hint should be taken in the garden ; no matter what the substratum of the bed, its surface should be filled with some 5 or 6 inches of rich loose soil-compost, including peat, leaf-mould, sand, loam and lime-chips ; and in these the clump should be planted so shallowly that next year's growth-buds appear above the ground. No winter will harm their tightly dormant innocence, while the plant itself will spread happily along the surface soil and soon form a handsome colony. One of my finest specimens of *C. hirsutum* flourished for long in a stiff and sunny bank of hard loam (where it had originally been "heeled in" and forgotten), but was killed at last one winter because soil fell upon it in the course of various earth-workings to the depth of some 3 or 4 extra inches, and was not removed. All Slippers bloom in early summer, and all can only be propagated by careful division of the clumps in early autumn, except in the case of the Japanese *C. speciosum*, which has the kindness to accept an English insect and form fat pods of seed. See Appendix.

C. acaule is a strange and notable American species, exceedingly abundant in coppices and open places of the woods. It sends up only a pair of thick soft leaves, nerved with some three or five veined lines ; up from this proceeds a naked stem of 6 or 8 inches, carrying a single large flower, with brownish-purple sepals and petals, and a huge shoe-shaped bag of soft rose, with a peculiar fold down the middle of the front. Very rarely a most beautiful pure albino is found, with the petals and sepals gone chrome yellow and the lip of snowy white ; less rarely, pallid and almost pure-white varieties. In cultivation with us this species is sometimes, for reasons known only to itself, not quite resistent to winter damps ; it should accordingly have sandy soil and a sheltered place, and be tucked under the filmy wing of *Pinus montana* or some such kindly evergreen growth, not too dense.

C. arietinum is hardly ever seen in gardens, and is not at all common even in the United States, except in Maine and Vermont, and the region of the Great Lakes, in damp low marls and the edge of peat-swamps, where it grows to a foot high, with leaves of 6 or 10 inches. It is usually a smaller jewel, sending up three or four dark apple-green leaves, ample and oval, with the fine bare length of the remaining foot-stalk ending in a single flower of extraordinary design. For the sepals and petals are of a brownish pink and all separate, while the lip is mottled white and dark purple, the usual little bag, but with a triangular mouth filled up with fluff, and tipping at the base to a blunt snout, which makes the sack look as if it were making a long nose at the earth. The effect, in profile, is rather that of the ram's head, which has earned the plant its name. (It has subsequently appeared in China as *C. " plectrochilum."*)

C. Calceolus still lingers in the upland rough woods of Craven here and there, nor has even been afraid to erect its head once more after many centuries, in the woods where Mrs. Thomasin Tunstall, that worthy gentlewoman and great—even excessive—lover of these de-lights, quarried it so pitilessly to send to Parkinson. Here the leafy stem ends most often in large twin flowers of twisting narrow chocolate segments, and a rounded lip of soft pale-yellow, deliciously sweet with the scent of roses.

C. californicum attains a far taller stature, growing to as much as 4 feet in the Californian woods on the Pacific Slope. It is a stout and leafy species, producing as many as a dozen flowers sometimes, in loose spikes, energing from leaf-like bracts. The blooms are small and neat in form, rather like those of a diminished *C. hirsutum*, alike in colour and design, softly pinkish and whitish and comely to see. In cultivation *C. californicum* is too seldom known.

C. candidum is a small plant from cold swampy lands, sending up a downy leafy stem, not unlike that of *C. Calceolus*, but only attaining some 6 inches or a foot, and ending always in one solitary flower, with chocolate-coloured segments, and a most attractive neat round lip of pure waxen white, striped with purple inside, and breathing sweet-ness like our own solitary Slipper, the last westward stray of its noble Asiatic-American family.

C. debile is a pallid, puny thing from the woods of Japan, so frail that though its little greenish-purply flowers are very small, and its stem only a few inches high, it cannot even bear so much of a burden, but declines and flops in a cowardly and disgraceful manner.

C. fasciculatum is found under young pine-trees along the Pacific slope of California, and is almost the smallest of the race, a minute thing of no merit for the garden.

C. fasciolatum, however, is a stalwart Asiatic, close in the kinship of *C. Franchetii*, but that the flowers are very much larger yet, with a round instead of an oval lip, of intense deep colour.

C. Franchetii takes us to the cradle of at least one branch of the race, to where, on the Tibetan borderland, in the rough grassy scrub of the mountains, is found a perplexing interfading group of Slippers. *C. Franchetii* is closely akin to *C. tibeticum* and the lovely Japanese *C. speciosum*, of which it has the big hooded flower, the swollen oval sack, the broad and drooping petals, all the parts being veined with rose-purple on a whitish ground, while the lip is of a richer flush all over. Its chief distinction from the confusing and obscure section of Slippers huddled into the name of *C. macranthon* will always lie in the fact that its stems are much more copiously woolly with a shaggy down. The height and habit of foliage in these do not greatly differ from those in *C. Calceolus*, though, as a rule, they are rather taller and stouter, and ampler in the leaf. See Appendix.

C. guttatum is a fairy among its kind, filling the dreary birch forests and lone pinewoods of the far North with beauty ; away over the dim expanses of the Siberian woodland dance those ample broad-hooded blossoms of pure-white, with their swelling lip that is blotched and marbled most fantastically with rose. If the plant be hard to grow (as hard it has always proved), this is probably only on account of its rooting habit, that makes it so specially difficult to collect. For *C. guttatum* sends fat rhizomes running and zigzagging here and there over the face of the ground, and so much resents being broken and torn that our chief hope must lie in collecting wide unbroken sods of it from its native forests, and bringing them into cultivation as they are. The whole growth is about 8 inches high, the stem being very fluffy at the base, and then set with a pair of oval leaves, grooved in regular parallel lines of nerves, and carrying one single bloom at the top of the long bare foot-stalk. It should have a damp level place in sandy peat, in close shade, and be kept as dry as possible in winter, to remind it of its Russian coverlid of snow.

C. himalaicum is another species of the mountains of Asia, closely allied to *C. Franchetii* and *C. tibeticum*.

*C. hirsutum.** —It is indeed a tragedy in the garden that names so apt and specially honourable as *C. Reginae* and *C. spectabile* should have had

---

* No: *C. hirsutum* of Miller, 1768 (which is the earliest name), though applied to the "Moccasin flower," is not sufficiently certainly attached by description to *the* rose-and-white Moccasin flower, to justify Robinson and Fernald in taking it as the first valid name of *C. spectabile*, Salisb. *C. spectabile*, Salisb., is, however, itself antedated by *C. Reginae*, Walt., 1788 ; so that we are left, after all, with the best and most adequate name for the Queen of Slippers, as the only valid one.

their precedence threatened by the prior claim of a title so undescriptive, dull, pallid, and general as that of *C. hirsutum*. Yet so it was; the royal Queen-slipper of rose and white, with her comfortable round-faced segments of snow, and her deeply-blushing swollen lip of pink, may originally have borne a name more applicable to some insignificant plant under the shadow of *C. parviflorum*. Her glory, none the less, continues; stout and leafy stems of 3 feet high in moist rich ground, earning our special gratitude, no less by their own tropical fullness, but also by producing their rotund Slippers, lonely or twin, later in midsummer, when the others of their race are nearly all gone. If only that lush folded foliage had not been hairy, so to enable the eyeless Miller of long ago to leap first into an empty field with so inadequate and unfeeling a description as "hirsute" for a beauty which subsequent authorities have ransacked the depths of their enthusiasm to crown with names sufficiently glorious!

C. hirsutum of catalogues comes under *C. parviflorum*.

C. japonicum is a curious species from the mountain woods, with stems of some 8 inches or more, and big solitary slippers of apple green with rosy lip, carried high above a single pair of corrugated leaves that are cut across their ends in a straight line (like 'Arriet's toes, as square as a nangkerchief), as if something had nibbled them off together when they were rolled up in bud.

C. Knightae grows only some 2 or 3 inches high, with one pair of oval leaves, and then a cluster of small dark brownish-purple flowers, their folded lips being varied with purple and green. (Medicine Bow Mountains of Wyoming.)

C. luteum, on the contrary, is a superb Asiatic splendour, from copses and wood-edges on the borders of China and Tibet, and also on the rims of the mountain streams in carbonate of lime. It is a newcomer in cultivation, and may best be described as a more fluffy-stemmed version of *C. hirsutum* with blossoms wholly of deep clear yellow, with a few spots on the lip. It is as yet unproven, except as to its absolute hardiness; but its stalwartness and stature and habit leave no reasonable room for doubt that under reasonable conditions of rich culture it will easily take its place beside *C. hirsutum* as soon as anybody is able to afford it. See Appendix.

C. macranthon is very difficult to decipher. It is a native of Mid-Russia, and has a leafy stem of 8 inches or more, and then one large, hooded flower after the description of *C. Franchetii*, all of rose and crimson veinings on a white ground, the lip being wholly of a carmine blush, pulled in at the mouth and *longer than the petals, which are oblong egg-shaped ending in a point*. It will, no doubt, be quite easy to grow, now that we have at last acquired the genuine species, after many seasons of confusion with its Japanese rival, which is neither *C. macranthon* nor *C. ventricosum*. There is also a not uncommon and hearty Albino of *C. macranthon*.

C. montanum is a leafy American species of 1 or 2 feet in height, most closely recalling *C. Calceolus* in habit, as in twisted fine chocolate-brown petal-segments, but that the flowers are two or three to a shoot, and their ample oval bags (like a bird's egg) are of a cool waxen white with veins of purple within, and a most delicious fragrance. From open low woods of California on the Pacific slope.

C. parviflorum.—This species is closely allied to the last, and even more closely with *C. Calceolus*, which it almost exactly repeats in America. The plant often offered as *C. hirsutum* is in reality only a larger-flowered form of this, which is general over North America and very variable; as is also another garden- and catalogue-species, *C. pubescens*, if it be not indeed a mere synonym of the last. These improved varieties are to be preferred to the species in the garden, not only because their blossoms are much finer and ampler, but because their sepals and petals are not dark but only streaked with darkness on a ground of yellowish green. In the garden they grow quite heartily with *C. Calceolus*, and exhale much the same delicate scent.

C. passerinum is peculiar to the Northern Pacific region. It grows about 8 or 10 inches high, with handsome yellow flowers, the segments being round and compact and straight, instead of twisting in the corkscrew curls affected by the last, which gives them such a saucily moustached and military air as they twirl their petals at all beholders. The lip too is large and round and paler at the edge, with deep spottings inside at the base.

C. Reginae is wrongly *C. spectabile*. See *C. hirsutum*.

C. speciosum is the beautiful Japanese treasure that for so long has been tangled up with *C. macranthon* and *C. ventricosum*. It is in the same style indeed; but with more the port and habit of *C. Calceolus*, carrying one magnificent hooded blossom, with petals and sepals veined with deep rose on a whitish ground, and the ample oval lip of a much richer tone. The sight of this, glowing with its noble baggy blossoms of pink and white among the rough grasses on the open downs above Ikao, or round the feet of Fuji-san, or peering here and there among the light bushes that they share at Shoji with *Paeonia japonica* waving its pearly cups above the Slippers, is enough to make any gardener resolve that no cost shall be too great for the procuring and success of *C. speciosum*. But fortunately the plant meets culture half-way in the most affable manner, and on any slope will soon, if let alone, spread into an ample clump; more than that, it exceeds the rest of the race in generosity by actually discovering a friendly insect and setting seed on its own account; and follows late, too, in the procession of Cypripedes, coming into blossom with *C. hirsutum* in the early weeks of June.

C. tibeticum cannot have the same praise, although it is found in the same reckless profusion in the same situations, in the rough grassy slopes, among countless other plants on the high open ridges of Tibet. It is a small squat thing, rather like a malignant Tibetan toad in appearance (no less than in character) when it produces its single stumpy stolid flower of immense size, on a stem of some 3 or 4 inches. For this is an evil-looking, hoody sullenness, with broad straight segments and bulging lip, the whole being of a whitish tone, but densely striped all over with lines of purple-black, while the bag is almost entirely of the same lurid tone. In cultivation, however, it avoids this condemnation by very rarely growing well enough to show those flowers at all. It has by no means answered the high expectations which its first appearance and the description of its habitat provoked—a mimpish misery, lingering on from year to year, and always sending up one barren shoot of foliage, but never mustering strength for anything more. It is quite likely, however, that it misses company; and that if, instead of setting it all by itself in special soil, as a precious treasure, we laid its roots in shallow light stuff, where they should have to battle their way about among other roots of fine Gentians and Dianthus and Arenaria and small Geranium, the plant would then begin to feel at home, and be stimulated into making an effort to thrive.

C. ventricosum comes from Mid-Russia and the Ural. It has nothing to do with the Japanese species sent out under this name, but should differ from *C. macranthon* chiefly, if not solely, in having *petals longer than the lip* instead of shorter, the lip itself being of the same shape and size, while those *petals themselves are yellow*. However, this entire group is difficult and doubtful, with shadowy definitions in what is perhaps merely one large and diverse aggregate.

C. Yatabeanum is a rare plant of Northern Japan, having affinities with *C. guttatum*. From the running rhizomes rise stems of 8 inches or less, with one pair of ample oval-pointed leaves, and then one baggy-lipped flower of marbled pink and white, with the two outstanding petals curiously clubbed at the end into a swollen round knob.

Cytisus.—The dwarfer Brooms have so much importance in the garden that they cannot be scanted of fair notice, shrubs though they be, sheeting the cliffs in flowers of white or pink or gold in early summer, and well adapted for any light soil and any sunny place.

C. acutangulus, a neat mound of 6 inches high, and silvery, very branching. White flowers before the tiny oval leaves. (Dalmatia.)

C. Ardoini, a quite low-growing treasure with flowers of brilliant golden yellow. Most fine and rare, from the downs above the Mediterranean, where the greedy goats prevent its seeding.

C. Beanii, a neat golden-flowering small bush ; with *C. Ardoini* the parent of *C. kewensis*.

C. diffusus is also *Genista humifusa*. A perfectly prostrate Dyer's Woad from Kynance Cove, and notably lovely, with its flat spread of branches set with pairs of little oval-pointed, dark-green eyelashed leaves, on which the golden spikes have an extra fine effect.

C. glabrescens, a charming Italian bushling, with pendulous branches hidden in golden bloom.

C. hirsutus, **L.**—This plant, very rarely met with, makes a widely spreading mass covered in a profuse eruption of gold.

C. ✕ kewensis, a garden hybrid of the greatest beauty, with prostrate long branches and hanging loose cluster-spikes of cream-white flower.

C. Kitaebelii=C. procumbens and *C. decumbens*.—It is found above Ragusa, and is almost exactly the same as *C. diffusus*, but that here the leaves are hairy all over and not only at the edge.

C. leucanthus, a neat bushling with clustered white flowers (*C. schipkaensis*).

C. pulchellus is a densely branchy stiff decumbent species, almost thorny, and with hanging yellow flowers, from the Adriatic Islands, rather suggesting a yet more compact *Genista aspalathoeides*.

C. purpureus ; very beautiful for high places, with its arching boughs of lilac, or white, or magenta-rose (in the form flattered by the name of *incarnatus*), and passing from cream to lilac in the specially free-flowering one called *C. versicolor*.

C. pygmaeus is found in shady stony places of Macedonia and the Levant. It is only some 4 or 6 inches high, the whole plant shimmering in a coat of golden silk with quite minute leaves and yellow blossoms gathered into heads at the end of the shoots.

C. sericeus is a silky low mat in the stony places of Vellebit, with yellow flowers.

C. smyrnaeus stands erect to the height of 6 inches, a grey mass of small ovate foliage, with the bloom in clusters at the ends of the shoots. There is a prostrate variety from Sipylus in Lydia, from the rocks where Niobe stands frozen into stone with sorrow against the face of the cliff.

C. tmoleus throws long prostrate branches along the highway sides of Tmolos, much more hairy, and with hairs much more closely ironed down than in the last.

C. Villarsii differs from *C. pulchellus* in being silky-downy, with no bracts to the pedicels of the flowers, and their keel as long as their wings.

This list draws the regretful line at anything exceeding a foot or 18 inches at the most ; above those heights there are many splendid brooms, but all alike, big or little, are so mixed up with Genista that the names are often interchanged, and a species not found under the one heading may well be appearing under the other.

D

Dalibarda repens or **Rubus Dalibarda**, though not always a quick grower, is a pretty little creeping plant with rounded scalloped leaves and white flowers like a strawberry, especially adapted for running over a cool slope or ledge in light loam or peaty soil.

Deciduous Daphnes

Daphne.—*Daphne alpina* is a low and neat alpine bushlet, twisted and branching, no more than a foot or 18 inches high, as a rule, and of grey charm, although it loses its leaves in winter, and is left naked but for the promise of buds at the ends of the boughs. In spring, however, or early summer, the small heads of a few rather small but very sweet white stars unfold, and after them the twigs each open out a tuft of blue-grey oval leaves amid which here and there gleam the scarlet berries. The plant is easy to raise from these seeds, and quite easy to grow anywhere ; it may be seen making neat tufts and bushes of mistiness among the coarse limestone blocks above the Lago di Loppio, and is, indeed, like nearly all Daphnes, a plant of the calcareous Southern ranges.

D. altaica has terminal heads of white flowers, and also loses its leaves, but does not, as a rule, attain even to the stature of *D. alpina*.

D. buxifolia is only some 10 inches high, and its heads of bloom are white ; and *C. caucasica* has the same, but attains a yard.

D. Genkwa is specially beautiful, a Japanese and Chinese species, of economic value in the making of paper—very frail and straggling in growth, a yard or two in height at the most, with a few weak branches, clad in a soft bark of brown velvet, and the few twigs ending loosely in a few large sweet flowers of clear lavender-purple, after which appear the leaves, only to fall again in autumn. Unfortunately this Daphne requires a rather warm and sheltered place, nor indeed does its gawky habit confer much grace on the garden.

D. kamtchatica is another tall-growing species with white flowers.

D. Mezereum has innumerable light, dark, white, and large-flowered and purple-leaved varieties—a most variable and variable-tempered species, thriving often in cottage gardens with no care at all, while often despising those of the rich and mighty, where it is civilly entreated and made much of. Fortunately there is no denying that the look of the shrub is leggy and stiff, and, while the crowded sweet flowers up the stems make a fine show, their colour is tainted with a heavy and poisonous tone that comes out also upon the heavy and acrid sweetness of the plant's breath. It has often established itself in English woods, coming freely from seed, but in one savage fold of the lonely hills under Ingleborough it has dwelt apparently from the beginning of things, as an alpine plant in an alpine situation, such as it chooses on the mountains of the Continent. The most interesting of its forms might also be a species; this is called *D. pseudo-mezereon*, and differs from the type in nothing but flowers of clear orange-yellow. There is a very fine white, and also poor ones.

D. Sophia is yet another indifferent species with white flowers in terminal heads, most closely allied to *D. altaica*.

EVERGREEN DAPHNES

D. acuminata, from Russian Armenia, is a small branchy bush, with velvety little red leafy twigs, the leaves being hairless, longish, and narrow. The velvety flowers are borne in dense heads of some five or seven, and the fruit is a gleaming orange berry.

D. arbuscula, Christ, is a Jurassic form of *D. Laureola*.

D. arbuscula of gardens, although in reality it is but a narrow-leaved and diminished Austrian form of *D. Cneorum* (and, though a pretty thing, indeed, hardly deserves the fuss that attends it or the prices demanded for it), falls between the two thrones of *D. petraea* and *D. Cneorum*, having something of beauty from both, and almost suggesting an enlarged version of *D. petraea*.

D. Blagayana is a noble creeping species that rambles about among stones occasionally, but not commonly, in the limestones of the Eastern Alps—a typical scree-plant, sending its long woody shoots here and there, and emerging between the blocks in a tuft of oval leaves and a large well-furnished cluster of creamy and deliciously sweet-scented flowers in the earliest morning of the year, and on into the spring. In cultivation here it merely requires a sunny warm corner (it does well in shade though, too), a rough soil of stones and peat and loam and sand ; and then to be treated like some independent-minded person in the palmy days of Hebrew priesthood, and stoned with stones until he—does not die—but lives the more gloriously, and makes of them a Bethel from which at every point peer forth his tufts of leaves and fragrant heads. Each passer-by, to be popular in the garden, should cast a limestone boulder (or any other sort of boulder) upon the Daphne, until its pile becomes a sort of Absalom's grave, perpetually getting higher and wider, and the Daphne therewith, until in the end you have a cairn of stones as at Glasnevin, half a dozen yards across, filled everywhere with the flower-heads of *Daphne Blagayana*.

D. Cneorum stands, of course, next to the unapproachable *D. petraea* in delicate loveliness, and stands even above that rare wonderful jewel in garden value and show. Not that even this is a plant of easy temper. Daphnes are born democrats, and *D. Cneorum* shows neither fear nor favour. You may court it in vain, as you may court a cat, with cossetings and comforts uncounted—but with no result to show but the sickliness of a dying plant ; yet in some neighbour's garden, where it was ignorantly shovelled into hard common earth to act as an edging like Arabis, it will have run far and wide, with masses of neat well-furnished shoots each ending in those ample heads of waxy, brilliant, rosy trumpets that fill the air of June with fragrance. Or, having had the plant in glory for many seasons and filling wide beds, you may see it one day departing from you firmly, and never be able to establish it again. Some of the trouble arises, perhaps, from the soil in which it is so elaborately grown, for, though the turf in which *D. Cneorum* is found consists of peat, the rock is always limestone, and lime is what all these Daphnes crave, in spite of legends and ancient superstitions to the contrary. So, let their soil be a mixture of peat and loam and lime, and there should be no trouble with any of them ; they will even thrive magnificently in a mixture of half mortar-rubble and half leaf-mould. It is specially interesting to see, and try to collect, *D. Cneorum* in the light woodland by Schluderbach, for there it has woodland compost of some 3 or 4 inches depth, but after that the immense yellow rat-tail of the root goes plunging for a foot or so into the subsoil, which is absolutely nothing but pure limestone silt, undefiled with soil or apparent nourishment of any shape or kind. The species is found in the Jura, and then not again until you reach the Southern ranges, where it abounds far into the

DAPHNE.

Eastern limestones and far West into the Pyrenees. An eye should always be kept open for forms—there are better and worse. The form called in gardens *major* is incomparably superior to most wild types, though it makes a neat small bush, instead of letting a few frail stems lie about in the hillside and glow among the grasses with rare heads of waxy pink like sweet Bouvardias, as does the type, in such lovely form and circumstances, on the last high slopes of Monte Baldo. (And there is also a pure white variety which will certainly be called *D. C. album* unless betimes we avoid the insidious trap and insist on *alba*.) It is in sun indeed that the Daphne habitually makes its frailest growth, but its finest flower; in light woodland waxing into more of a bush, but tending to produce heads of smaller trumpets; it is also curiously local—will abound for miles and then abruptly cease, as it haunts all the Ampezzo valley, but will not stir a step to the left up that appalling hill to Misurina—reluctant perhaps to intrude on the territory of *D. striata* (which there begins on the other side of the river), or disdaining such inefficient rivalry.

D. collina is a plant close to the true *D. sericea* that so often bears the name in gardens (for *D. sericea* is *D. collina* of Smith and *D. neapolitana* of Loddiges), but the genuine *D. collina* has fatter downier stems than *D. sericea*, with longer, larger, hairier leaves, and a special profusion of flowers: it forms the same neat pudding-bowl bush, all covered with sweet heads of lilac-pink in summer. It grows readily in any fair place, and is also *D. Fioniana* of catalogues, besides having a yet downier variety called *D. c. Vahlii*.

D. × *Dauphini* or *D. hybrida* is a perpetual-blooming and tall-growing shrub of glossy foliage with frequent heads of purple-lilac; it is born of *D. indica* and is no less valuable.

D. glomerata makes a dwarf neat bush, almost wholly glabrous, and about a foot high at the most, its branches radiating out neatly to form a mound, with rosettes of leathery leaves at the tips, and flowers pale pink outside and whitish within, that not only emerge in heads from their tips but sometimes also from the axils of the upper leaves. (Alps of Lazic Pontus, Caucasus, &c.)

D. Gnidium, pontica, Laureola, Philippi are dowdy greeny-flowered shrubs of which no note need here be taken.

D. indica, odora, japonica, Mazelii are all forms or sub-species of the indoor Daphne, which, in point of fact, is perfectly hardy out of doors in sheltered positions, though too large in the development of its great glossy bushes for the rock-garden, and shy of producing its fragrant heads unless well-ripened by a hot summer in the previous year.

DAPHNE.

D. jasminea, in the rocks of Parnassus and Euboea, claims twin-ship with *D. petraea*. For it makes the same minute and prostrate mat of twisting brittle branches, set with very tiny, oval spoon-shaped leaves, sitting tight to the depressed compacted shoots, and of a blue-grey tone that beautifully enhances the beauty of the two or three waxen trumpets in which each of those shoots terminates—delicate sweet tubes of pink outside, and four-pointed stars of white as they open. So dense and complicated is the habit of *D. jasminea* that it ends by being almost spiky, spreading out exactly like a mass of *Salix herbacea* among the stones, and blossoming with equal zeal in spring and autumn. At present we hold out our hands for it in vain.

D. petraea dwells high and far in the Southern Alps, confined to one small district, and there haunting hot and terrible cliff-faces of rose-grey limestone fronting the full radiance of the Italian sun. In the tightest crevices of the rock it grows, in chinks so close that the point of a pin will hardly enter; yet there the Daphne roots deep down into nothing, sending its fat masses of yellow rootage browsing far in, with only the lime of the rock to feed them; but so the neck grows thick and stout, emitting a mass of tiny branches, clothed in tiny oval leaves, grooved and dark green and glossy. Thus the plant develops, and its twigs lie close and flat against the sheer cliff which, as far up as you can see, is plastered with those mats of lucent green darkness, until at last they turn to mats and splashes of even more lucent rose, when every one of those shoots is ablaze with a head of three or four big waxy pink tubes of the most crystalline pure texture, the most brilliant clear colour, and the most intoxicating fragrance. The flowers begin in June and continue through August; the sight of those sheer awful faces blotted with scabs of living pink flat to the cliff and unbroken by any touch of green is one that amply repays the distance, difficulties, dangers, and despairs that sometimes wait on the worshipper of *D. petraea*. For the Daphne grows only in the most adamantine faces, and only long sedulous search (by very superior persons) may produce here and there a tuft from milder places; while in the rock it is brittle at the neck, and snaps sharp off at an irreverent touch. Seedlings indeed do occur, but seem of the utmost rarity; I have never yet seen sign of berry on the plants. Yet seed they do and must, for reasons to be more fully stated below, but in the cliff their increase is chiefly by a thready runner breaking along the crevice and erupting out of the blank wall again into what soon proves another tight flat huddle of sweetness and light. In cultivation *D. petraea* has no unwillingness either about growing or flowering. Collected pieces, however, usually having lost some of their substance, need time to form fresh rootage and get re-established. Patience, therefore, is called for, but will surely be repaid, especially as it is not possible by any other means to possess the wild Daphne. It is possible and pleasant and profitable indeed to graft its shoots in summer on to seedlings of *D. Mezereum ;* the loveliest little neat bushes result, round and wide and concise, and covered with flowers to the astonishment of all beholders. Is there not here in happy existence the specimen of the world, a grafted bush that has never failed to blossom exactly in time for the first summer show of the R.H.S., with such uncanny regularity, whatever the alterations of date, that I suspect the plant of thoroughly realising its fame, and enjoying the popular applause that has greeted its unfailing appearance for the last twelve years. No sacrifice is too great for it ; the flowers open the day before the show, and the nervous tension is such that they all drop off the day after it is over ; it has refused the most tempting offers to go to America, and in its passion for publicity does not even shrink from the peril of the assassin's knife, which one year surreptitiously tried to cut it in two. But this is a glory special and apart ; it often happens that grafted pieces in the open miff suddenly away, nor do they ever have quite the charm, as erect trunked bushes, that is so entrancing in the typical tight flat mass of the wild plant, beset with living jewels of blossom so absurdly disproportionate to the packed minuteness of twig and leaf—a compactness which wholly vanishes in the grafted specimen. Let, then, your carefully collected tufts of the wild Daphne be carefully re-established for a year or two in small pots and in fullest sun ; then let just such another situation in full sun be chosen (among rocks to give the fullest character)—and there let the clump be planted in a deep mixture of lime-rubble, leaf-mould, good loam, sand and peat, all mixed up with almost an equal part of limestone chips ; there the treasure will be happy and increase far more certainly and unfailingly than *D. Cneorum,* and, in a season or two more, have grown so strong as to make up its mind for that annual display of blossom in June It even seems to appreciate the administration of those fertilising pilules called Plantoids.

D. retusa is a valuable new introduction. It is a small and very slow-growing bush, of extreme stolidity and sturdiness, with stiff boughs, clad in foliage exactly like that of *Polygala chamaebuxus,* but much thicker, stiffer, and of a more sombre leaden greenish-black. The flowers come at the ends of the shoots—delicious fragrant heads of large pink and lilac stars, rather like those of *Daphne indica,* produced in the later summer. It is quite hardy and happy in any peaty mixture, a solid and sombre little uncompromising dome of great attraction, for, even though it ultimately attains 2 feet or so, its owner will probably be a great-grandfather before it does so.

D. rupestris=*D. petraea*.

D. sericea (*D. collina*, Smith ; *D. neapolitana*, Loddiges), our well-known round bush, covered in summer with heads of lilac fragrance silky outside. It differs from *D. collina* in having thinner and less downy stems, while the grey-green leaves that tend to roll down at the edge are smaller and not so hairy. *D. sericea* is of perfectly easy culture, forming comfortable-looking round puddings often 2 or 3 feet high ; but it has a way of dying off suddenly in parts, —a trick which sadly damages the symmetry of its growth.

D. striata is the commonest and the least attractive of the European alpine Daphnes, being of the same growth and habit as *C. Cneorum*, but with flowers of half the size, and no brilliancy at all by comparison, either in shape or colour—sad and dingy tubes of lilac, more pallid within. Unlike the rest it is indifferent to its rock, and is as abundant on the granites of the Engadine as on the slopes of the Pordoi or the Tombea. At the same time this must not be taken as meaning that *D. striata* has no beauty ; only that *D. Cneorum* and *D. petraea* have so completely spoiled the market for any competitor in the same line that one can hardly have eyes afterwards for even the neatest mass of *D. striata* condensed over the face of a rock, and half-hiding it with its delicious flowers of fragrant lilac-pinkness. The plant, in point of fact, has indeed been crowded out of catalogues by its rivals, and is very rarely grown, but chiefly requires sandy and thoroughly stony peat in full sun and air to do nearly as well as the rest ; though, like all the rest, it resents disturbance, and its fat yellow roots have no friendly feeling for the collector. This species, however, sets seed ; and in the Heuthal or on the South side of the Bernina its orange berries may be gathered in quantity, and should then be sown as soon as possible. Sharp and skilful eyes have lately discovered a white form of remarkable beauty on the Grigna, and no doubt it may well also be found elsewhere.

D. tangutica is a species from the East, evergreen, and attaining a height of some 24 inches. And that seems about all there is on record of *Daphne tangutica*. But see Appendix.

D. × *Thauma*, Farrer, has the romance of high parentage. For it is the result of *D. striata* by *D. petraea*, found in a lonely colony on one precipitous pinnacle of the Cima Tombea in company with a few dying tufts of *Saxifraga tombeanensis*. It has the whole habit of *D. striata*, but is much neater and more compact, and the smaller neater foliage has the bright glossiness inherited from *D. petraea*. The flowers, though finer, longer, and larger than those of *D. striata*, yet have not inherited the full rosy glow of petraea's; but they have added size, and they also have petraea's throat, dark purplish-rose and velvety outside. In constitution this admirable and most precious find proves to have more than the vigour and temper of either parent, and is likely to prove a treasure in the garden.

D. Verloti is frequently praised and advertised at high prices. It is nothing more than a reasonably attractive local form of *D. Cneorum*, —quite as pretty, perhaps, but certainly no better.

Deinanthê bifida, for cool, choice, and rich, well-drained peaty places, under the lee of rocks, and not suffered to thirst, is a strange and noble species of creeping root-stock, and nearly related to Saxifraga. Its crinkly great leaves stand up to about 8 inches high on their stems, and have the fatness, the crumpliness, the brittle gloss and roughness of a Begonia's; the flowers are at the ends of the stems between the divided leaves, inhuman orbs of waxy white in clusters, in the latter days of summer. Contemporary, but even more enthralling, is *D. coerulea*, which, with the same habit, the same needs, and the same crisp fleshiness of more divided handsomer leaves, has larger hanging flowers in a curious and lovely tone of sad pale violet, clear yet rich as white marble in shadow at sundown, most harmonious to the subtlety of modern taste, and specially attractive in so weird a blossom as this, like that of some monstrous waxier Pyrola that has known sorrow both wisely and well.

Delphinium (this list being merely a selection among some of the best species for the rock-garden, giants being usually avoided). All will come profuse and true from seed; all will thrive in any deep rich loam, in full exposure, though not parched or ungenerously treated.

D. alpestre, 4 to 8 inches, a downy plant with fingered foliage, and a few large and stocky blue blossoms. (Alpine rocks of Colorado, rare.)

D. azureum, from the North American Rockies. Formerly taken as a variety of *D. carolinianum*. One to two feet high with simple or branching stems and sky-coloured flowers from April to June.

D. Belladonna. See under *D. elatum*.

D. bicolor.—Not more than 12 inches high, stout and sturdy, with a lax spike of blooms about half an inch across or more, the upper part being yellowish and veined with blue, while the rest is blue.

D. brachycentron attains some 18 inches, a downy species near *D. cheilanthifolium*, with large wide blue flowers. (Siberia.)

D. brunonianum is a curiosity from the high Alps of Tibet, not

PLATE 24.

CYPRIPEDIUM MONTANUM.
(Photo. R. A. Malby.)

CYPRIPEDIUM LUTEUM.
(Photo. W. Purdom.)

VOL. I.

PLATE 25.

DELPHINIUM PYLZOWII.
(Photo. W. Purdom.)

DELPHINIUM CASHMIRIANUM.
(Photo. R.B.G. Kew.)

VOL. I.

DELPHINIUM.

more than a foot at the most in height, with large and rounded hairy flowers of pale blue in a loose and long-peduncled corymb. The *D. brunonianum* of gardens is usually of a deep and very sombre purplish black.

D. carolinianum is a beautiful American species from which *D. azureum* has been separated. It grows about a foot and a half, and has big flowers of blue. *D. Penhardii*, being its counterpart in pure white, was long regarded as a variety, but now is raised to specific rank.

D. carporum, a most beautiful and strange rare prize from the Pacific Rockies. Its hairy many-cleft leaves are all huddled at the base, and then arises a foot-high velvety stem, undivided, carrying a rather close spike of more or less densely hairy-petalled flowers of white and pink, with the spur sticking straight up behind at right angles to each.

D. cardinale is a giant in stature and a freak in colour. It is usually about a yard high, but can be more than twice as much, with noble helmets of glowing metallic scarlet that open widely out, unlike the pinched nightcaps of the frailer and smaller *D. nudicaule*. This should have a specially hot and well-drained place in light rich soil, being a Californian; and seed should always be watched for.

D. caucasicum is only some 4 or 5 inches in height, with hairy, leathery leaves cloven in threes, and then, on long footstalks, the most lovely large clear-blue flowers with purple outside and white eyes, almost nestling above the tuft of foliage. Altogether beautiful in port and colour. From the highest slopes of Kasbek, &c., 14,000 to 15,000 feet. See Appendix for its cousin, *D. tanguticum*.

D. Cockerellii is a fine handsome species from South Colorado, from 2 to 4 feet high, tawny with sticky fulvous down, and making a big bush of leafage above which go towering the spreading graceful pyramids of scantly furnished sprays, the blooms being large and ample of outline, very veiny and of a brilliant purple.

D. coelestinum, from Eastern Szechuan, is one of the queens of the race. It stands near *D. coeruleum*, and has very finely-divided leaves, and spires, simple or branching, of especially grand and lovely flowers of dazzling azure, loosely arranged upon the boughs so that all their beauty can be seen.

D. coeruleum is found up to some 17,000 feet in Tibet and Sikkim, —a glory for the garden, freely branching, and yet not more than a foot high at the outside measurement, with leaves slashed into strip-like thongs, and splendid blossoms of pale clear blue seeming almost to be carried solitary in that pyramid of beauty.

DELPHINIUM.

D. Penhardii. See under *C. carolinianum.*

D. Pylzowii from Kansu, is only about 6 or 10 inches high, yet has violet-blue flowers about twice the size of *D. coeruleum's,* and carried in sprays almost like umbels. See Appendix.

D. scopulorum lives by the stream-sides in the mountains of California, and can be some 4 feet high with slender unbranching spires of indigo above the rather glaucous foliage, very finely divided.

D. Souliei has lucid perfectly smooth green leaves, cut and cut again, from which issues a hairy, downy spike of 6 inches, carrying a dense array of blossoms with the upper petals pale and the lower ones dark. (From dry places in Szechuan.)

D. suave is blandly beautiful. The leaves are much gashed, and a great number of stems are sent up, about half a foot or a foot in height, undivided, and carrying a generous number of large pale-blue flowers with the two lower petals creamy white. (Kurrum valley in Afghanistan, 7500 to 10,500.)

D. sulfureum, Bois. and Hausskn., is not *D. Zalil,* as pretended, but an annual or nearly annual species, or subspecies, to *D. ochroleucum, q.v.* —handsome pale-yellow things both, to decorate the late summer border for a year; but by no means deserving the name they usurp, or any other comparison with *D. Zalil.*

D. tanguticum has all the neat lovely habit of *D. caucasicum,* not exceeding some 4 inches or so, but the flowers are even larger and finer. See Appendix.

D. tatsiense (*sic.,* for surely it should be always Tatsienense and Sutchuenense, the forms to which the termination -ensis is affixed being Sutchuen and Tatsien, not Tats and Sutch) is a tall, branching, hispid, and airily elegant species, producing in summer the most noble pure azure flowers with specially long spurs on finely loosely-branching spikes of some 12 or 18 inches. Its nearest cousin is *D. grandiflorum,* of which, however, it does not seem to possess either the hardiness or permanence. At least in the North it has a way of sometimes vanishing softly and silently away like a snark, from even the best drained of beds.

D. trolliifolium is of a different kidney altogether. This appears very early in the year, for about the end of March the specially green, hearty, fleshy foliage begins to sprout, and in April are shooting the spikes of a foot or so, set with large helmets of a luscious and velvety dark sky-blue with an eye of white. This is of quite easy culture and much more trustworthy.

D. vestitum is a superb species from the Himalaya at considerable elevations, making in the garden a fine mound of handsome hairy foliage, high above which shoot the abundant flower-spikes in July, August, and September, when almost all Delphiniums are done. They are some 3 to 5 feet in height, set thickly with flowers of a rich deep violet with a white eye. A perfectly easy, useful, and beautiful species by no means properly appreciated.

D. Zalil differs from the impostors that fare forth and do ill under its name, in being a perennial plant of strong constitution; and its flowers are not pale, but of brilliant yellow—so brilliant, indeed, that all the rolling meadows and downs about Gilran are an undulating sea of gold when it is in bloom. It is exported thence for dyeing silk— a beauty whose clump of tubers cannot be too much cherished if we want to adorn our gardens in late summer with its fine ferny foliage and 3-foot spikes of rich pure colour.

Dentaria, a woodland or marshland race of tallish Crucifers, much entangled and interchanged with *Cardamine, q.v.* All are for cool places, on shady banks and damp exposures, in heavy garden loam. Our own *D. bulbifera* is a rare native about a foot or two in height, with fine much-divided foliage, graceful stems, and heads of pale purple flowers, rather large. It might easily be ousted from some woodland corner by a worse thing. But far finer is the similar ample-leaved *D. digitata* from mid-Europe, with larger blossoms of a fine lavender rose, with the foliage gashed into threes and fives. Another charming plant is the rare *D. enneaphylla* as it may be seen in the woods of the Eastern Alps—as above the Brenner, coming early out of the ground with a glossy stem ending in an opening cluster of pointed, folded, shining folioles looking rather like the frill of some monstrous nemorosa-Anemone, and with flowers emerging, in a bunch of creamy white, that looks not unlike the cluster such an Anemone might emit, if cluster it could. Then by degrees the growth unfurls into a tall and stately Dentaria of nearly a foot, with three whorled leaves on the stem, cut into three, slashed into sharp lobed lobes now like Anemone trifolia, but with hanging sprays of large cream-white flowers; even finer is its twin, *D. glandulosa*, with flowers of purple; *D. intermedia* from Switzerland is a bigger thing than *C. digitata*, and *D. pinnata* is like a few-flowered light-lilac *D. bulbifera*, but lacks the bulbils in the axils of the leaves. And yet other species are *D. diphylla*, white; *D. maxima*, very large, whitish lilac; *D. incisa* is of the same colour; *D. heterophylla* is purplish; and yet others are *D. incisifolia* and *D. anomala*, and *D. Kiliasii*, a stately species with blossoms of purple rose from the Eastern Alps. The smaller species are most neat and pretty: such are *D. quinquefolia*, from damp orchards of Russian Armenia, which is only some 10 inches high, but with larger flowers than

DIANTHUS.

Bulbifera's on a smaller plant ; *D. microphylla*, much smaller yet, only about 6 inches, yet with undiminished blooms, and *D. bipinnata*, which runs about in the high-alpine screes of Western Caucasus with creeping rhizome thick with little oval bulbils, and leaves not an inch tall, and flowers just as in the last. There is also a pretty little *D. trifolia* of 6 inches, smaller even than *Cardamine trifolia*, and with blossoms of lilac; *D. polyphylla* attains 10 inches, with handsome foliage again and blossoms of cream white from the Eastern Alps (very near *D. enneaphylla*, but its leaves have seven long pointed lobes); *D. savensis*, lilac, rises to 8 inches ; *D. pinnata*, and *D. pentaphylla*, are both mauve, and both about a foot high. These all bloom about April, with *D. polyphylla* continuing into May ; all can be raised from seed, or divided quite easily at pleasure at any time.

Dianthus.—In no race is there more confusion, and in no race is there a larger proportion of second- or third-rate species. Catalogues abound in wrongly-named Dianthus, in undescribed or indescribable or merely mongrel Dianthus ; and to adventure into the maze in search of a good new species is a hopeless task unless some kind Ariadne has provided you with a clue. To play such a part shall be the effort of this list. And all that now remains to be said is that almost all Dianthus are of the very easiest culture in any light soil and any sunny place (especially rejoicing in the moraine), while all of them can be profusely raised from seed, or propagated by cuttings like Carnations. The race is essentially Old World, southern, heat-loving, drought-loving, lime-loving, but there are exceptions to these last rules, for certain species climb high upon the mountains, while others have developed a distaste for lime. Their blooming-time covers practically all the season, opening with the blaze of *D. alpinus*, and filling June with the Fringy-flowers ; while later summer is more barren, but has the larger species, such as *D. arenarius*, and *D. superbus*, and *D. atrorubens*, going gaily forward to the point at which *D. Seguieri* takes up the tale in the latest days of autumn.

D. acaulis is also *D. frigidus*, and *D. frigidus* belongs to *D. silvestris*, q.v., which ought only to be called *D. inodorus*.

D. acicularis from the Ural is quite near to *D. squarrosus*, but with especially narrow leaves and flexuous stems.

D. actinopetalus.—From 12 to 18 inches, many sterile boughs, but also many flowers, two or three, as a rule, to the stem. Petals obovate, pale and sharply toothed. (Rocks of Cos, Lycia, &c.) *D. a. elegans* is a small compact form of only some 3 to 8 inches in height.

D. alpester or *D. alpestris* is a difficult name, always appearing vaguely in catalogues. The first *D. alpester* (Sternb.) is a name for *D.*

DIANTHUS.

Sternbergii, q.v., a variety of *D. monspessulanus,* which in itself is a sub-species or form of *D. fimbriatus.* Look up *D. Sternbergii.*

   D. alpester, Balb., is also *D. strictus* (S. and S.), and *D. integer* (Balb.), *D. integer* (Vis.), this last also being known as *D. brachyanthus.* The group, cruelly variable and widespread, is also made by Paoli and Fioretti (whose methods never err on the side of mildness), to include the wholly dissimilar *D. neglectus*; this, however, if only for gardening purposes, may well be kept apart. The aggregate of *D. alpester* has high value in the garden, being a set of close green tuffets of small fine leaves, spraying out a great quantity of fine stems some 8 inches long, and waving pink stars at the end, in a vast profusion of small rosy blossoms, scentless, and either smooth at the edge or toothed, but never fringed. Their general resemblance is rather to some specially free-flowering and much smaller *D. inodorus,* but here the calyx is larger in proportion to the smallish flowers, whose effect lies in their mass and their graceful port, as they sway and spray in a loose spouting shower from some dark hot rock in the Cottian Alps. Here occurring, it is a typical form of the group, *D. pedemontanus.* Yet another development that often figures in gardens and lists is *D. Lereschei,* a thing of denser habit than the type, with petals deeply toothed.

   D. alpestris, Uecht = *D. speciosus, q.v.*

   D. alpinus is perhaps the most precious of the race, sheeting the high grassy moors of the Styrian limestones with miles of bright foliage, distinct in its breadth, bluntness, and gloss of clear dark-green from any other's; and then turning the whole hill to a blush of rose-crimson through July and August and September, with those full bearded cartwheels of brilliant colour on stems of 3 or 4 inches. It varies, though not very widely, and it is possible to collect some lovely forms peacock-eyed with purple, or smooth-edged, or larger, or dwarfer, or ampler than the others. There is a rather dirty pinched-looking white form, and a slightly better one from the Hochschneeberg; while there I found the finest development known, *D. a. Adonis,* with abundant, large, and solid flowers, which open of a perfectly pure salmon-pink untouched with impurity, and so pass on in nature to a pure and delicate pearl-white. This proves no less vigorous than the type, which in our gardens ought always to be irrepressible, and may be seen, as at Ribston, forming a mat of glossy foliage several yards across from one plant. And yet the species often fails and gives trouble; in all cases that I have seen, from soil too heavy and ill-drained. *D. alpinus* requires perfect drainage, but will grow robustly in either peat or loam, so long as plenty of lime is administered. In the moraine it makes a glorious mat, and sometimes blossoms again later in summer with the small Campanulas. Its normal hour is the first or second week in June. It seeds freely, and comes well from cuttings or divided pieces, but in districts where such pests prevail should carefully be guarded from wireworm.

D. anatolicus forms a dense mat of shoots half shrubby from a woody stock, and sends up foot-high stems that sometimes even attain three. These carry pale-pink flowers at the end, yellowish beneath, and with the petals bluntly scalloped. The secondary flowers are borne on very short foot-stalks, and so seem to sit quite close to the stem. From Sipylus, with a variety *D. a. Kotschyanus*, smaller in the flower.

D. angulatus, an Indian species, is close cousin to *D. Liboschitzianus* and *D. Jacquemontii*, *q.v.*, with petals deeply toothed.

D. anticarius; from 2 to 3 feet high, with glaucous blue leaves and fairly large blooms, solitary at the ends of the stems, purple-red with toothed petals. (Rocks of South Spain.)

D. arboreus is a strange distinct Southern species, forming stout bushes about 3 feet high and 5 feet through, of handsome green foliage broad and lush of effect, all over which shoot out long stems bearing noble flowers of bright pink, several in a head, but not all trying to open at once, so that the effect is unspoiled by overcrowding. It blossoms all the summer and is quite hardy, but, as it comes from far down on the Mediterranean coasts, it should have a very warm sheltered corner in very deep light soil or moraine, as well as ample room to develop its full magnificence.

D. arenarius, related to *D. squarrosus*, is much laxer in the habit, with fewer flower-stems, taller and frailer and larger, with very fringy whirligigs of white or pale pink. It does not dislike a cool and shady position so much as the rest, and blooms through late summer and autumn.

D. aridus, a species akin to *D. Friwaldskianus*, erect-growing to about 9 inches, with two or three rather small pale yellow blossoms.

D. aristatus is a native of dry rocks in Armenia, where it forms a close hoar-frosted grey mass, with 8-inch stems and pink flowers, yellowish underneath, and deeply toothed at the edge.

D. Armeria is the Deptford Pink, a feeblish annual of no worth.

D. Arrostii.—A plant of no merit near *D. pallens.*

D. arvernensis. See under *D. caesius.*

D. asperulus, a 6- or 12-inch Cluster-head from the cliffs of Armenia.

D. atrorubens is a Cluster-head common in the Alps, with stems about 6 or 9 inches high, and flowers of comparatively large size for the section, and of the most gorgeous velvety scarlet-crimson. More

DIANTHUS.

splendid yet, however, is the form or hybrid of this called the *Carton Park* or *Glasnevin* variety. This is a very big thing with long grass of greyish green, and very long stems spraying out this way and that, and loosely branching. Each stem ends in a head of two or three large flowers opening in succession, and of the most perfect and undefiled crimson-scarlet velvet that the garden holds. It is a pity of course that the plant should be so high and loose in habit, for its 2- or 3-foot sprays are rather overpowering even for those glaring blossoms ; yet, on a bold shelf it makes a noble show in late summer and autumn, and should be kept going by means of cuttings in case that show should prove to have been too generous. But the permanence of the clump itself can be guaranteed by cutting the whole thing down at the end of September, to within 3 inches or so of the stock.

D. attenuatus is a worthless weed.

D. Balansae is almost woody in habit, a low dense mat of twisted twigs, with dwarf delicate stems, and pink flowers with ten or eleven teeth to each petal. (Cappadocia.)

D. Balbisii, a species incessantly advertised in the same lists with *D. liburnicus*, is simply a synonym, or at best a sub-species in a large and crowded group, including *D. pruinosus, D. giganteus, D. bannaticus;* all of these being more or less tall and gawky 2- to 3-foot Clusterheads, with bunched little flowers of magenta-crimson, looking rather ineffective at the top of their naked lanky legs. In *D. bannaticus*, however (*D. giganteus*, Urv.), the hairy heads reveal flowers of bloodscarlet, less impure and unpleasing than in the others, though small and without dash.

D. barbatus ; the Sweet-William has little place in the garden ; nor should it admit, *me judice*, any terrible podgy double dwarf forms of repulsive aniline crimson, such as those called *Napoleon III*, *D. barbatus compactus grandiflorus plenus*, and so forth ; their chief merit is that of generally flowering themselves to death, and of showing still further consideration in not making any grass by which they may be propagated. *D. Atkinsoni*, however, redeems this ephemeral habit by the almost overdone gorgeousness of its pure scarlet-crimson flowers of rich velvet, and *D. striatiflorus* has usually unstriped blooms in a lovely soft shade of pink.

D. biflorus, lately raised to specific rank, is the high-alpine development, rare in the stony regions of Euboea and Parnassus, of the glorious *D. cinnabarinus*, which has now been divorced into two halves, as *D. biflorus* and *D. Sammartanii*. This is a green and smooth-leaved species compact in habit, sending up 6-inch stems, each carrying perhaps two large flowers of an écru-copper colour, most strange and beautiful. The plant is at times shy of making grass for cuttings, and in seed is by no means always faithful to itself ; it should for choice be grown in a sunny stony place or in the moraine.

D. Boissieri, from the limestones of lower Spain, is a diminished *D. caryophyllus.*

D. brachyanthus. See under *D. alpester*, Balb., being a synonym of *D. integer* (Vis.). In the high limestone Alps of the Sierra Nevada it develops, however, a specially beautiful form called *D. nivalis*, which makes wee tight tufts of very blue stiff little recurving leaves with rose-pink flowers larger than in the type, and on stems of only about half an inch. The blueness of the foliage varies, and the effect of the neat mass is that of an unrecognisably glorified *Silene acaulis*. Some authorities and all catalogues raise the type of this species out of the ruck of *D. integer*, and give it specific rank as *D. subacaulis, q.v.*, the chief difference (and one of great importance to the gardener) being the dwarfer habit in all these forms, differentiating them efficiently in the garden from *D. integer, D. strictus, D. pedemontanus*, and *D. Lereschei.*

D. brevicaulis is near *D. haematocalyx*, forming the same close tight mat on which the rose-mauve flowers with their toothed petals (which are yellowish underneath) seem almost to sit close, each lonely on its stem. Only here the leaves are shorter, blunt, and soft, while the calyx is not so big and baggy. (High Alps of Taurus.)

D. Broteri makes a neat half-shrubby bush of some 8 inches to 2 feet high. The flowers are large and pink, with a dark spot at the base of the petals, while the leaves are stiff and three-nerved. (Portugal.)

D. cachemiricus is like a slenderer *D. Falconeri*, erect, with channelled foliage and delicate, much branching stems, attaining 2 feet or so, with large blossoms like those of *D. caryophyllus*, not fimbriate.

D. caesius (properly *D. glaucus*, Huds.) ; the lovely Cheddar Pink with its sheets of blue leafage overshadowed in June by fragrant flights of fringed rose-pink flowers, in number as the stars of the sky but far exceeding them in homely charm, is the stay and stand-by of every sunny rock-garden. It is sub-alpine in dry places through the main ranges, and includes at least two other first-class garden-plants in its embrace. The first is *D. suavis*, which, except that it is larger in bloom and habit, seems in gardens indistinguishable from *D. caesius* either in beauty or value. And the other is that most delightful miniature, called *D. c. arvernensis*, perfectly minute and compact, with the same lovely dainty flowers on much shorter stalks of 2 or 3 inches. (*D. furcatus* may, perhaps, owe something to *D. caesius*.)

D. caespitosus makes very dense rosettes, and throws up a number of stems with big white flowers, much cut at the edge and often purple-eyed. It is a variety of *D. arenarius*, either undivided or with sparing branches. (Podolia and Taurus.)

D. caespitosus in gardens is sometimes *D. caesius*.

D. × *calalpinus* is the hybrid occurring freely in every garden where *D. alpinus* and *D. callizonus* are happy. It is a fine dwarf plant of rather glossy leaves and large brilliant flowers, but it does not surpass either of its parents, and is so dutiful as hardly to compete with them.

D. callizonus itself is indeed far beyond all competition, incomparably the loveliest of Alpine pinks, running freely underground and forming cushions of rich foliage, glaucous, broad, and stiff, from which proceed stems of a few inches—in the finest forms only about 2 inches —each carrying an even larger, rounder, ampler flower than in the type of *D. alpinus*, in a lighter shade of pink, with a deep band or belt of darkness, peppered with minute points of white light. Many superstitions attend the cultivation of *D. callizonus;* it is said to prefer shade and to abhor lime—strange quirks, indeed, for a species that is only found in hot, sunny, rough places on the limestone Alps of Transylvania. But this is not so ; division is the chief enemy of this Pink ; get well-rooted tufts and let them be put out in light rich limy loam in sun or shade, but efficiently watered, and there is no more reason to fear trouble with this than with *D. alpinus*, even if the plant be perhaps rather less inclined to be a centenarian, and, in proportion to its especial beauty, ask for a little special observance and protection from the roaring slug that goeth about seeking whom he may devour. *D. callizonus*, too, often continues sporadically to bloom into autumn, long after the first flush of the year is over.

D. campestris; a thing of little worth, in the way of *D. deltoeides*, but no improvement.

D. carpaticus. See under *D. Carthusianorum.*

D. Carthusianorum is the type of the Cluster-heads. Its lank ugliness is notorious, of tall naked stem, topped by a tight brown-calyxed head, from which spasmodically peep small spotty stars of magenta-rose or crimson. Varieties of this are *D. C. congestus* and *D. C. uniflorus*, *D. C. carpaticus*, and *D. C. vaginatus*, often put forward with praise as a species. Others in the same undesirable persuasion are *D. cruentus*, taller and looser and paler ; *D. Carmelitarum*, with shorter leaves and cinnamon-coloured flowers ; *D. atrorubens*, already treated ; *D. stenopetalus*, about a foot high, with a head like a nut ; *D. viscidus*, with many stems of the same stature ; *D. tymphresteus*, with fewer blossoms than the last, and a black spot at their base ; *D. Hymenolepis*, a most variable species, of some 10 inches as a rule ; *D. Lydis*, about a foot and a half, with pale green leafage ; *D. cibrarius*, rather dwarfer, with leaves three-nerved instead of five-nerved ; *D. pinifolius*, half a foot high, from a dense mat, with pale purple flowers ; *D. lilacinus*, with the same height and habit, but of a pale lilac ; *D. capitatus* (also *D. glaucophyllus* and *D. calocephalus*) a yard high, with minute stars of bricky-scarlet ; *D. bannaticus*, or *D. giganteus*, or *D. Balbisii ; D. Haynaldianus* (*D. intermedius*, Boiss.), square-stemmed, like Liburnicus, 2 or 3 feet high, with leafy wrappings to the head ; *D. lateritius*, like *D. pinifolius*, but with shorter, bluer leaves and square stems ; *D. trifasciculatus*, *D. heptaneurus*, *D. quadrangulus*,*D. Formanekii*, and *D.Holzmannianus* (round-stemmed and close to *D. cibrarius*, but with longer scales and flowers of dark blood-colour).

D. Caryophyllus.—The parent of the Carnations, and a fine ornament of rough rocks, with sheets of blue-grey foliage, and large pink flowers, to be known, among other points, by their *smooth-edged petals*, from *D. plumarius*, the parent of the Pinks, which is also not near so tall in the stem,nor branching. It has also many named varieties,including *D. C. virgineus* (*D. longicaulis*), *D. C. coronarius* (intensely sweet), *D. C. siculus*, rather sweet, and *D. C. corsicus*. By some botanists it is even made to include *D. inodorus* (*D. silvestris*).

D. cibrarius. See under *D. Carthusianorum*.

D. ciliatus is nothing special—a small erect-stemmed branching plant of half-woody nature, and with rough saw-edged leaves, from dry places of the South ; up the stems here and there, on short foot-stalks, it stiffly carries several smallish pink flowers more or less smooth at the edge, in a sort of lax spire. It is very close to *D. cinnamomeus*, which chiefly differs in having bluntish leaves and notched petals.

D. cinnabarinus. See at one end *D. biflorus*, and at the other *D. Sammartanii*.

D. cinnamomeus. See under *D. ciliatus*.

D. collinus, an ugly fat-headed form of pleasant *D. Seguieri*.

D. confertus. See under *D. Carthusianorum*.

D. coronarius. See under *D. Caryophyllus*.

D. crinitus=*D. hungaricus* (Clem.).—This has stiff pointed spiky leaves, and its uncomfortable thorny wide mats send up stems from 4 to 12 inches high, carrying either one flower, or some three or four on erect branches. These flowers are white, and slit to the very base into a fringe as fine as hair, differing from *D. fimbriatus* in this exaggerated fringiness, no less than in the greater length of the blossom. It occupies Asia Minor, and has two varieties, *D. c. tomentosus* and *D. c. crossopetalus*.

D. cruentus. See under *D. Carthusianorum*.

D. Cyri, a worthless annual.

D. deltoeides, a native species, and always pretty, with flopping masses of bright-green, and incessant abundance of small brilliant pink blossoms freckled with crimson. There are still brighter forms, and a good albino.

D. dentosus is an obscure and difficult name. Robinson, of old, used to wax quite eloquent over the charms of the Amoor Pink, which was said to form a neat glaucous tuffet, with lilac-purple, dark-eyed blooms on 6-inch stems. This sounded acutely desirable, and it is perhaps only on the principle of demand creating supply that Russian botanists do now send out seed whose results hitherto suggest the old description, so far as the broad, rather glaucous, slightly wavy leafage of the tufts is concerned. But in the meantime the "Index Kewensis" declines to recognise *D. dentosus* at all, and makes the name a synonym of *D. sinensis*, which (even if it resembled the description in any other point) is not perennial. And it must be confessed that such a supply has demand already created, that from Russia, before this, there have often emanated so-called *D. dentosus* that have proved only the most pale, ragged and dingy weeds. Therefore the question hangs in suspense until the latest batches have bloomed.

D. dissimilis may be separated, by those who please, from *D. neglectus*, in being rather taller, in having rather more flowers to the stem, and in being more or less bald at the throat. But this is all a matter of "rather."

D. dumulosus, a variety of *D. fimbriatus*.

D. elatus is like a much improved form of *D. deltoeides*, with larger flowers of pale purple, cut deeply into elongated teeth. (Siberia.)

D. elongatus, no use; fifteen inches of unbranching stem, and then narrow petals of yellowish white. *D. leptopetalus* is exactly the same, but that the stem branches and the petals are blue underneath. They do not open till the evening. (Thrace and Macedonia.)

D. erinaceus makes a dense, tight and prickly mound, on Sipylus and Ida. The blossoms are carried solitary on stems of 6 or 9 inches, and are toothy-petalled and pink, with a beard at the throat. There is a yet dwarfer closer form called *D. e. alpinus* or *Webbianus*.

D. erythocoleus.—It is a pretty compressed tuffet of half an inch, with short narrow blunt leaves, on which sit singly rose-coloured flowers after the style of *D. plumarius* and *D. serotinus*, very ragged and fringy, on stems of about a couple of inches. (High Alps of Kurdistan and Armenia.)

D. Falconeri sends up stout stalks of 5 feet or so that divide into equal branches, each carrying blossoms rather smaller than those of *D. Caryophyllus.*

D. fallens, from the Pyrenees, recalls *D. monspessulanus*, but that it is sturdier and stands erect, and is smaller in all parts.

D. fimbriatus (*D. orientalis*) has a reddish calyx, and the stems rise from half a foot to a foot above the neat cushiony mass, each ending in a single large pink flower—the type of the Fringed Section, being slashed and gashed into the wildest lace-work. The species is wildly variable, and includes the varieties *D. f. obtusisquameus, brachyodontus* (*dumulosus*), and *brevifolius.*

D. floribundus is near to *D. anatolicus*, but has blossoms so deeply cut as almost to approach the Fringed Section in appearance, with a variety *D. f. pruinosus* which is the *D. noëanus* of Boissier.

D. Freynii can hardly be separated from *D. microlepis*, of which it has all the neat exquisiteness and lovely charm, alike in tight bluish cushion, and dainty little stemless Pinks of white or rose that look especially happy and pretty against the grey stones of the moraine.

D. frigidus. See under *D. silvestris.*

D. Friwaldskyanus (*D. rupestris*, Friv.) also forms a tuft, and sends up smooth roundish stems of some 9 inches or less, each producing two or three pink blooms of no great size with notched petals.

D. fruticosus is a noble bush after the style of *D. arboreus*, but rather less loose and with leaves flatter and broader; the trunk is also thicker, and the flowers larger and of more brilliant pink. But there is some obscurity in the relations of the two plants and their respective beauties and values. (Rocks of Crete.)

D. furcatus (see under *D. caesius*) is in the same line as *D. alpester*, Balb.—a small species, making cushions of dark-green leaves, soft, blunt, and narrow, in the hot black rocks of the Southern ranges, from which spray forth an unimaginable profusion of 9-inch stems, branching at the ends, so as to carry some two or three rather small flowers, pink or white, smooth-edged or toothed, whose especial value lies in their profusion and the grace of the countless stems that carry them so delicately in a wavering unanimous shower of bright stars against the darkness of the cliff behind. The *branching habit*, among other points, distinguishes it from the other small species of the same region.

D. gallicus is a pretty thing, suggesting a very much glorified *D. deltoeides.* Here the ample foliage is clear-green or bluish, short

DIANTHUS.

and narrow and not pointed, with the leaves at the base so rough with a fringe of hair as almost to seem toothed. The flowers are borne solitary at the ends of the flopping or ascending 12-inch shoots, which vary between 6 and 9 inches or more, and are large, rosy, fringy, and specially fragrant. (From the dunes of Northern France, &c.)

D. gelidus belongs to *D. glacialis*.

D. glacialis has a name beyond its merits, and a reputation alike for difficulty and for beauty that it does little to earn. For it avoids glaciers and their neighbourhood with great heartiness, and is a plant of the alpine turf, which it abundantly occupies at the high levels of the Engadine, or on the Pasterze moor above Heiligenblut, there even descending into the gutters by the highway side. Nor is its beauty so rich, though sufficient enough : a taprooted species, forming a single clump of bright-green leaves rather long, broad and blunt, and producing among them, each on its stem, flowers of bright pink indeed, but hardly of an amplitude to elicit cries. In fact, though the clump be only a couple of inches high, it has not the look of breeding and charm that one expected of a Dianthus called Glacialis. As for its reputation in the garden, this dates from those pernicious days of pockets, when it was indeed looked upon and found (like almost everything else) a miff and a mimp, no matter what elaborate pains were taken with stone and aspect and shade and special mixtures of soil—on a rock-work essentially undrained and ill-constructed and ill-soiled, with just a small pecked hollow here and there which you filled with made compost for the imagined behoof of some special treasure. No wonder, then, that in those days alpines as a class were regarded with awe, and approached with genuflexions of terror. Now, however, we have learned that the only right course is to build the rock-work properly throughout, from base to top, in the beginning of things, and that then there is hardly a child of the hills that will not prove naturally at home, or can ere long be made to. We have no more pockets, but our gardens are made and mounded with light and well-mixed soils, with the result that all the glamour has gone from *D. glacialis*, and all the glory of growing it successfully ; seeing that in any open situation, well-watered in summer (and for preference from underground), and in any sound and stony mixture of peat and leaf-mould and rough sand, this Dianthus at once makes a fat little clump of green foliage, and covers itself with rosy cartwheels all the summer through. In decline it should be kept drier ; and the plant, it must be remembered, has the lushness of its look—a soft thing strayed un-advisedly upon the mountains—and may, if too generous in flower, damp off in the ensuing winter, supposing that a slug has not saved it from such a fate by eating the whole tuft flat in autumn. The species varies in the course of its distribution; there is a specially large-flowered form in the Alps round the Pflerscher Tribulaun, and in Transylvania lives that variety which catalogues offer as a species under the name of *D. gelidus*.

D. glaucus, Huds., is the correcter name of *D. caesius*.

D. gracilis is allied to *D. Seguieri*. The stems are square, and rise to some 10 or 12 inches, ending in two or three fairly large pink flowers with sharp-toothed petals, gathered together at the top, or often solitary. There are two more attractive forms of this from high-alpine stations on Athos and in Macedonia—*D. g. pumilus*, with short stems of 2 or 3 inches; and *D. g. armerioeides*, which is quite a close and densely clustered clump.

D. graniticus forms one member of that vague aggregate known as *D. hirtus*, a pervasive type in the Pyrenees and Southern France, of which this development haunts the granite, and the other, *D. Requienii*, the limestone. Neither of these is very attractive; they are prostrate flopping species, in the way of *D. deltoeides*, with abundance of small leaves and small starry pink flowers gathered two or three in a head, the shoots being from 6 inches to a foot long, and the petals notched. *D. graniticus* is the best of the forms, and sometimes its blossoms make a fine effect like those of *D. deltoeides*, by virtue of their mass in summer.

D. gratianopolitanus is a pleasant synonym for *D. caesius*.

D. Grisebachii, a foot-high cluster-head from Bulgaria with flowers of bright magenta.

D. haematocalyx; a flat close cushion of flat, stiff, sharp and fierce leaves, from which rise stems of 6 or 9 inches, carrying from three to five blossoms in an erect corymb or very loose spike. The calyx is baggy and big, blood-red and hoar-frosted, and enclosed in four red scales as long as itself; while the large flowers are purple, with sharp-toothed petals, yellow underneath and bearded at the throat. A handsome species from the stony wood-regions of the Thessalian Olympus, with two marked varieties—the one *D. h. pruinosus* (*D. pruinosus*, Boiss.), laxer in habit, more bloomy, and with one flower only to the stem; the other, *D. h. alpinus*, a lovely tight footstool from the summit of Parnassus, with undiminished Pinks sitting tight in a mass—a rare delight of concise magnificence.

D. Haussknechtii is a little Cappadocian cushion, with many stems of 4 or 6 inches, each carrying a whitish flower whose petals are toothed at the edge and rosy underneath.

D. Haynaldianus. See under *D. Carthusianorum*.

D. heptaneurus. See under *D. Carthusianorum*.

PLATE 26.

DAPHNE PETRAEA.
(Photo. R. A. Malby.)

DIANTHUS ALPINUS.
(Photo. R. A. Malby.)

PLATE 29.

DIANTHUS INODORUS [D. SILVESTRIS].

DIANTHUS ARENARIUS.

VOL. I.

DIANTHUS.

D. hirtus. See *D. graniticus.*

D. hispanicus might possibly be *D. pungens,* L. It is a tuffet with narrow blunt glaucous leaves, erect or curling aside on the shoots, which are from 6 inches to a foot high, carrying each a lonely pink blossom with the edges almost smooth. From rocky barrens in the lower region of Eastern and Central Spain, &c. Widely variable.

D. Hoelzeri is said to be a fine thing, of some 18 inches high, with pink flowers. It comes from Turkey and seems suspiciously rare.

D. Holzmannianus. See under *D. Carthusianorum.*

D. humilis, a most neat small mass with a multitude of finely delicate little one-flowered stems of 6 inches or so, each ending in a pink bearded bloom. Different from *D. pallidiflorus* and *C. campestris* in its much shorter leaves and tuft of unbranched short stems.

D. hungaricus (Clem.), a synonym of *D. crinitus, q.v.*

D. hungaricus (Griseb.), a synonym of *D. petraeus, q.v.*

D. hymenolepis. See under *D. Carthusianorum.*

D. hypochloros is a beautiful little dwarfed alpine species almost identical otherwise with *D. zonatus,* growing only some 3 inches or half a foot in the high dry alps of Isauria.

D. inodorus (L., 1753) is the only correct and valid name for the species universally beloved as *D. silvestris* (Wulf., 1786), *q.v.*

D. integer (Vis., and also Balb.) is, strictly, the variety *D. brachyanthus* of *D. strictus, q.v.* See the welter of rival names under *D. alpester,* Balb. It is common in gardens, under a general confusion of names at which no one can wonder. The form it takes with us is that of a neat dark-green tuft of fine leaves, with fine upspringing stems of 6 inches or so, each ending in a white flower not quite big enough for the calyx. Sometimes the edges of the petals are smooth, and at others more or less scalloped. They are never fringed or sharply toothed ; and may be pink, but are most usually white : in no Dianthus can the colour be held a diagnostic, and this group is even more variable in all respects than the rest.

D. intermedius. See under *D. Carthusianorum.*

D. Jacquemontii is quite close to *D. Liboschitzianus,* but the petals are more deeply toothed.

D. judaicus = *D. oxylepis,* a useless weed.

D. juniperinus makes a neat hard blue bush of about a foot, with stiff and almost prickly foliage ; and has several pale-pink flowers gathered together on each shoot. There is a larger and more graceful variety *D. j. Sieberi,* also called *D. aciphyllus,* which may possibly prove the original *D. arboreus.*

DIANTHUS.

D. Knappii, a weakly little plant of miffy temper, wanting a situation specially well-drained, where it produces hardly any grass for cuttings, and usually dies after flowering without setting seed. The blooms, however, have the rare recommendation of being clear yellow (though not large, and gathered in a head at the top of one or two straggling stems of 5 or 6 inches).

D. laetiflorus has no reason whatever for having glad flowers, unless it be because they stand erect—when in point of fact they would do more decently to depend, if only in shame for their smallness. It is an inferior species closely allied to *D. pallens.*

D. Langeanus is a lankier looser-jointed *D. hispanicus* with much poorer flowers.

D. laricifolius is a graceful thing from the fields of Spain, with cushions of furry-fine bright-green foliage, almost prickly, and delicate stems of between 5 and 14 inches in height, each bearing one or two pink blossoms with scalloped edges to the petals.

D. lateritius. See under *D. Carthusianorum.*

D. leptopetalus is anathematised under the heading of *D. elongatus, q.v.*

D. Lereschei, a form of *D. alpester*, Balb., *q.v.*

D. leucophaeus has a hard rhizome, emitting prostrate shoots, and forming (after the fashion of so many) a mass of foliage, from which emerge stalks of 6 inches or so, ending in a dusky dark calyx which emits a white flower, with petals almost entirely smooth at the edge and dusky-brown underneath.

D. libanotis throws up a loose shower of very ragged lilac-white Pinks, hairy inside and spotted at the base, two or three to a spray, on stems of about a foot, above the glaucous-grey narrow tufts of leaves. (Alpine region of Lebanon, &c.) *D. atomarius* is almost the same, but much more feeble and flopping.

D. Liboschitzianus, from the stony places of Ararat and the Levant, also makes a mass of narrow flaccid leaves, from which come stems of some 4 to 8 inches, bearing each one bloom of white or pallidest pink, either perfectly smooth at the edge, or else faintly and widely scalloped. *D. l. integerrimus* is one variety, with quite smooth-edged petals ; and *D. l. multicaulis* another (*D. petraeus*, MB., not WK.).

D. liburnicus. See under *D. Balbisii.*

D. lilacinus. See under *D. Carthusianorum.* This dwarf Cluster-head sounds as if it might perhaps be admissible.

D. liliodorus has white flowers with the special recommendation of smelling like Lilies of the valley.

D. longicaulis, a form of *D. caryophyllus, q.v.*

DIANTHUS.

D. Lumnitzeri is a laxer-habited reproduction of *D. serotinus*, with flowers smaller and less violently fringed.

D. macranthus, from South Persia, has white blossoms, solitary on 12-inch stems.

D. masmenaeus is not unlike *D. hypochloros*, but the leaves are shorter and broader, and hardly prickly, while the whole mass is clothed in white down. With a variety *D. m. glabrescens* (*D. mutabilis*).

D. Mercurii makes a mass of smooth and blue-grey foliage, from which come 9-inch stems carrying two or three flowers, or perhaps only one ; these are pale pink, and yellow underneath, with the petals sharply vandyked. (Achaea.)

D. micranthos may perhaps be a high-alpine development of *D. anatolicus* which it closely resembles, though only some 6 inches or a foot high. But the petals are quite smooth at the edge, whitish pink, and deeper underneath. (Alps of Taurus.)

D. microlepis (*D. pumilus*), is a most lovely tiny plant for the moraine, differing principally from *D. Freynii* in being rather green than blue-grey in the leaf, but varying greatly in this point, as in many others, but never in being a most charming neat mat of softish broadish little leaves, on which sit almost close the delicate stars of pink or white blossom. It is of the easiest culture, but so dainty and choice that no place is too prominent for it, and its tidy round pin-cushions rarely exceed 5 or 6 inches in diameter. This, with *D. Freynii*, may be said botanically to come near *D. glacialis ;* in every detail they are as far removed from it as possible in the gardener's eye — incomparably more exquisite, permanent, neat, minute, and delightful.

D. minutiflorus=*D. strictus brachyanthus* (*D. alpester*, Balb. ; *D. integer*, Vis.).

D. monspessulanus (a variety of *D. fimbriatus*) must not be neglected ; this is a ragged rascal running among rugged rocks with frail growths and grassy foliage ; and then emitting stems of 9 inches or more, zigzagging and stiff, with large and very sweet and very fringy pink flowers in the later summer. For the rock-garden, however, it exists more in the background than its variety *D. m. Sternbergii*. (Also called *D. alpester*, Sternb. See under *D. Sternbergii*.)

D. multipunctatus is worthless.

D. musschianus is a tight compact Cluster-head from the Armenian Alps, growing in dense mats, and sending up stems of only 2 or 3 inches, with bunches of purple stars enclosed in purple calyces.

D. myrtinervius is another lovely jewel from the alpine fields of

Scardus, after the habit of *D. microlepis*, forming a dense floor of flopping stems, 2 or 3 inches long, densely set with overlapping blunt little narrow short leaves to the very tip, each leaf having three fat nerves, of which the two outer ones run along the rims, so as to make them seem especially thick. The flowers are pink, with obovate scalloped petals. And there is a form *D. m. oxylepis*, in which they are narrower and more star-like.

D. nazaraeus, from Gargaros, is not unlike a branching *D. silvestris*, with solitary pink blossoms, and six teeth to each petal.

D. neglectus, however ill-fitting its name, cannot be merged into the dim title of *D. alpester* by any gardener who rightly values those round great concise tufts of grass that it makes, beset all over with those enormous cheery round faces of the most brilliant cherry-rose, with a blue eye and a buff reverse. It is a treasure, too, of the most indestructible vigour and permanence, taproot and tufted habit and all. Get it into poorish deep soil in full sun, and its massive circles will yearly increase, and with them will increase the profusion of its blossom, not only in the heyday of June, just after those of *D. alpinus*, but again (and hardly less splendidly) in autumn, glorifying late August and September. It is a plant, in nature, obviously lime hating, but not so completely so as *D. glacialis*. Even in nature, however, it may be found (though less violently happy) on more calcareous soils, as for instance, *but rarely*, on the gypsum downs of the Mont Cenis; while on the granites and schists above it runs riot even in the rough grass (though not in the roughest)—a species of the coarse alpine turf, and, on the Mont Cenis in August, attempting a race of prodigality in rose and violet with the clumped purple suns of *Aster alpinus*, in colonies and sheets of interwoven colour among the fading wreckage of *Orchis sambucina* and *Anemone Halleri*; or else, a little higher, all by itself in finer grass, fringing the Vaccinium bushes with blots of rose, and erupting on the embankments of the track itself, or close beside the age-trodden windings of the great highroad. A little further, though, towards the alpine heights, and it takes the most beautiful alpine developments, both on the Mont Cenis, for instance, and high on the Cottians, growing into neat tiny tufts of finest lawn-grass, as close as those of *D. microlepis*, but that the stemless flowers are typically ample and brilliant, never growing up on taller stalks; not even in seed, for the pods of the past may be found sitting as tight to the tuft as the flowers of the present. These beautiful dazzling dwarfs remain constant, too, in cultivation, though asking for moraine that their fullest beauty may be enhanced. In the Southern ranges the species tends to become a trifle more leggy, and on the Col de Pesio may be found straggling among the bushes on stems almost as long as in *D. inodorus*, though stiffer and less graceful. It is here, accordingly, that we can, if we wish, differentiate a second species, *D. dissimilis*, taller in habit, with two or four flowers to the stem of 8 inches or so, instead of the shorter stalk, and the solitary (*rarely* two, but *never* more) flowers of typical *D. neglectus*, but with a throat more or less hairless, as against the invariable fluff in which the throat of characteristic *D. neglectus* is clothed. But these are rather idle subtleties for the gardener, to whom *D. neglectus* will always remain one, glorious and indivisible. The plant has a limited range, only being found in Dauphiné, the Graians, Cottians, and Maritimes, in the upper alps, and so to the uppermost (though never to the highest alpine elevations); *D. glacialis* has a wider range, from the Engadine away over all the granitic chains to Transylvania; *D. alpinus* only begins in the Salzkammergut, on the high limestones, where it is local if not rare, and thence stretches away eastward over the calcareous ranges of Styria, and down to the Semmering; last of all comes *D. callizonus*, dwelling alone among the vampires in the remote seclusion of Transylvania. *D. neglectus*, however, varies in its forms far more than *D. alpinus* or *D. callizonus* (though this also has worse and better forms, while hardly any flower of *D. alpinus* is surpassable, except by its next-door neighbour). Many are the thin stars, many the ragged and ruptured wheels of rose that you will find, and many the lanky and untidy growers. It is not safe (if you want that very best which alone is good enough for good gardeners) to procure *D. neglectus* at haphazard, out of flower. It should either be picked out at a show, or selected amid the far more enormous display on its own hills. (And this truth *applies to all the race*.) But the colour hardly ever alters by a shade, nor the delicate nankeen reverse that so enhances it. In nature *D. neglectus* runs riot with runners from its central tap, often wandering threadily here and there through the grasses, and coming up in tufts that are almost indistinguishable; but in the garden its tendency is to sit tight in its place, and there make a tuffet the size of a dinner-plate, hidden from sight in June by its round patines of pink on 6-inch stems springing all in a mass of glory together.

D. nitidus, in another style, is well worthy of praise—a neat cushion of prostrate shoots, forming a mat with weakish bluntish little narrow leaves, one-nerved, and of very brightly-shining green, with a suspicion of hairy fringe at their base; and then short stems of one inch only, perhaps (or as many as four) each carrying one or two buds, with short calyces of dark purple or black, from which issue blossoms of a clear rich pink, bearded inside and more or less toothed at the edge, and with three characteristic deep crimson lines down the throat of each petal. (Alps of Macedonia.)

D. nivalis. See under *D. brachyanthus* and *D. subacaulis.*

D. noëanus makes a dense mass of wide-spreading stiff three-nerved foliage, narrow and prickly-pointed. The flowers are white, carried *in a loose bunch* of from three to five at the top of 9-inch stems —this habit being quite special and distinct and recognisable. The blooms are white, and not fringy, indeed, but cut into narrow fine strips for about half their length. It abounds, rightly or wrongly, in catalogues, but as there represented, rather questionably, is not a species of outstanding merit.

D. × *oenipontanus* is the correct name of a most beautiful plant that surely deserves to be known by some more distinctive tile, than a mere repetition of its parental names. For this is *D. alpinus* × *superbus* of catalogues—a magnificent and thrifty hybrid, with the tight habit of *D. alpinus*, but with broader glaucous leaves, pressed down in neat clumps, and as handsome as in *D. callizonus*, though larger; and then, on stems of 3 inches or so, really enormous flowers that have borrowed triumphantly from both parents, having the ample cart-wheel of *D. alpinus* (but twice the size), of soft rose with a broad eye of dark crimson-purple; while from *D. superbus* it has drawn a decent and modified version of the fringe, so that the general effect is that of some extraordinarily handsome Chinese Pink, sitting close upon the otherwise naked clumps of a giant *D. callizonus.*

D. pallens (*D. cinnamomeus*, Fl. Gr.; *D. emarginatus*, DC., Prodr.) really does not deserve such a rivalry of authorities for the honour of naming such a weedy mass of flabby glaucous rough-edged foliage, strongly nervy too, with notch-petalled stars of white, dirty greenish beneath, and opening in the evening like a Melandryum.

D. pallidiflorus is of equally little use—stems of 1 or 2 feet, with loose sprays of pale pink bloom all one colour throughout. This is *D. pallens*, MB.; *D. ramosissimus*, Pall.; but equally unprofitable, no matter under what name purchased.

D. pedemontanus. See under *D. alpester*, Balb.

D. pendulus acquires its name in the cliffs of Lebanon, looking down on Sidon, where it makes a bush from the rocks of prickless foliage, and sends out stalks of 18 inches, carrying one pale pink flower, or two or three pink flowers in a bunch, their petals being deeply toothed in finger-like strips.

D. petraeus is the right name of the plant called *D. hungaricus*, Griseb., and therefore the father of pardonable confusion in catalogues, seeing that there is no real *D. hungaricus* at all; but yet another species, *D. crinitus*, has been called *D. hungaricus* by a different authority ; so, on the principle of things that are equal to the same thing being equal to each other, there may well arise muddles between *D. petraeus* and *D. crinitus*, the two Pinks so anxious to avoid the name of Hungary that they have been made to share. *Dianthus petraeus*, then, makes a flopping mat, as usual, of specially narrow, short, stiff, prickly leaves, each of them with *three specially conspicuous nerves*, roughish at the tip, and edged with hairs at the base. The stems are very numerous and bare, rising up in a crowd to some 6 inches, each carrying a fine flower of white or pale pink, with the edges regularly *deeply notched* into oval scallops or lobes. (Stony places of Croatia, Bosnia, &c.) *D. crinitus* (*q.v.*) is *wildly fringy*.

D. *pindicola* is probably identical with *D. haematocalyx alpinus*, a beautiful form, *q.v.*

D. *Planellae*, on the other hand, is valueless.

D. *plumarius*, the father of all the Pinks, neat of habit and blue of leaf and strong in growth to the point of rankness, and profuse in his delicately toothed sweet flowers of pink, is well worthy of admission from the walls of some old abbey, where he has ensconced himself, to some high place in the rock-garden, where his masses can fall over, and decorate winter with the blueness of his leafage, as summer with the pinkness of his blossom.

D. *polyclados*. See under *D. Carthusianorum*.

D. *pruinosus* (Boiss.) is the variety *pruinosus* of *D. haematocalyx*, *q.v.*—a lovely alpine, but laxer in mat than *D. h. alpinus*.

D. *pruinosus* can also stand for a variety of *D. floribundus*, *q.v.*, a plant of little value, also called *D. noëanus*, Boiss. (not the above).

D. *pubescens* is found on Hymettus, Pentelicus, &c. It forms a mass of decumbent shoots, making a cushion of very narrow pointed leaves, with three conspicuous nervy ribs. The stock is hard and the trunks clothed in glandular down ; from the mass arises, or rather declines, a great number of almost always unbranched stems, some 6 or 9 inches long. The flowers appear on these, either lonely or in pairs, and are purple, with yellow underneath, and with the petals coarsely and irregularly toothed here and there. *D. p. glabratus* and *D. p. cylleneus* are varieties with rather smaller blooms.

D. *pungens* is a Pyrenean species, suggesting a diminutive *D. silvestris* of about 9 inches high. It multiplies rapidly by running about, and earns its name by means of long, hard, prickly-pointed leaves.

D. *pyridicola* is a most charming small species, having the shoots leafy as in *D. deltoeides*, but the whole tuft quite tidy and compact, only 3 inches high or so, in a little greyish-green leafy clump, from which emerge pink blossoms larger and brighter and altogether more attractive. (Greece; as easy as the prototype on which it so vastly improves.)

D. quadrangulus. See under *D. Carthusianorum.*

D. repens forms a mass of quite smooth pointed narrow leaves, and the 6- to 9-inch stems divide at their very base into two ascending branches that split no more, and each produce one flower, this having long petals equal to the calyx and scalloped almost into teeth at the edge. (East Siberia.)

D. Requienii. See under *D. graniticus.*

D. rigidus is a dim Russian species, notably branchy and woody-trunked.

D. robustus (*D. superbiens*) hangs from the cliffs of Armenia—a noble giant, in the way of *D. fragrans*, with stems about 2 feet long, half-woody and breaking into two- to three-flowered sprays of fine large saucer-shaped blossoms of pink with shallow toothing to the petals.

D. rupestris, Friv. = *D. Friwaldskianus.*

D. Sammartanii, the other extreme of what used to be *D. cinnabarinus*. It has the few copper flowers of *D. biflorus*, yellow beneath, very large and splendid, as big as those of *silvestris*. But here the growth is taller, and up to 18 inches or so, and the blooms are gathered closely in heads of three or four, at the tops of the many stems that spring from the stock. (From the stony region of Parnassus, &c.)

D. scaber. See under *D. Seguieri.*

D. scoparius, a close mound of shoots, and then 6-inch stems, each with one great ragged Pink, after the fashion of *D. fimbriatus*, but that it has a shorter calyx. (South Persia.)

D. Seguieri has the best of its value from blooming long after nearly all the rest are gone. In rough woods and coppices and shady banks about Saint Martin Vésubie, for instance, as everywhere throughout all the seaward ranges of the South, you may find its single lank branchy stems of 9 inches or so in the herbage, ending in the single large toothed flower of amaranthine magenta, with purple eye (perhaps two or three to a stem). The herbage of the tuft at the base is scanty, long, and quite grass-like; a few pairs of the same long narrow-pointed leaves are set at rare intervals by the joints of the stem. The plant has the greatest value for bloom in autumn, and in cultivation proves extremely enduring and desirable in stony places, whether they be in sun or shade, the brilliance of its tone redeeming it from reproach. It has two varieties in its wide range, but neither *D. S. scaber*, nor *D. S. collinus*, is nearly so well worth collecting as the type.

D. Seidlitzii is another stemless minute jewel, forming dense wee tuffets in the high Alps of Persia in the way of *D. microlepis*, but that the little narrow leaves are gentler to the touch, and much more highly nervous, while the stars that come to hide them have more of a beard at their throat.

D. serotinus makes specially neat tight rosettes at the base of each 6-inch shoot ; these come up late in the season, tall and bare, all in a crowd, to the height of 6 or 9 inches, bearing each a deliciously fragrant flower, large and white and wildly fringy, darkening towards lilac purple at the base. The rosettes that make up the mat are, indeed, almost as tidy as a Draba's, and the stalks occasionally emit a branch. (Austria, Croatia, &c.)

D. serratifolius is another species of no worthiness.

D. serratus=*D. pungens*, *q.v.*

D. serrulatus=*D. pungens*, *q.v.*

D. serrulatus is but an inferior version of *D. petraeus*.

D. siculus. See under *D. caryophyllus*.

D. silvestris, Wulf., 1786, must be known in future by its prior name of *D. inodorus*, L., 1753. It is the joy of all who behold it in the Alps, on every hot bank, in rough open places, forming concise tufts of long grass, from which spray out and about the most delicate bending sheaves of delicate arching stems, dividing into long-stemmed branches, and carrying big flowers of the clearest pink, oftenest smooth at the edge but sometimes toothed. It varies, though, greatly, and care should be taken to choose only the best, largest, and amplest in size, the softest, purest, and brightest in colour. For on the sunny slopes where it waves among Paradiseas and rich Asters and *Campanula spicata*, it will be flourishing broadcast a thousand blossoms of glowing round face, but also a certain number of feeble and squinny stars. There can also be found, too, white forms of a dainty purity unsurpassable. And all these will thrive in the moraine, or anywhere else, in light stony soil in full sun, as heartily as in their own rough places, and, even in the moraine, sow themselves. This Pink was called Silvestris because it is never found in woods. A beautiful and dwarf treasure has lately been going about and earning rich laurels under the name of *D. frigidus ;* this is nothing but a fine-flowered close-habited form of *D. inodorus* from some high station— a form of special preciousness, and not less so in that it keeps constant and comes true from seed.

DIANTHUS.

D. speciosus is also *D. grandiflorus*, *D. alpestris* (Uecht), and *D. Wimmeri* (Wichura): it is none the less a beautiful thing—a higher alpine development, standing towards *D. superbus* as does *D. Sternbergii* (*alpester*) to *D. monspessulanus*, or *Campanula Scheuchzeri* to *C. rotundifolia*. It has handsome glaucous-blue foliage, and the erect stems carry one or two noble pink or deep rose flowers, intensely sweet, and very fringy, but not so much so as in *D. superbus*. (South Switzerland and Tyrol, in damp meadows between 5000 to 7500 feet ; rare.)

D. sphacioticus is a small loose mat from Crete with pale pink blooms on stems of 2 or 3 inches.

D. spiculifolius of catalogues is but a development of *D. petraeus*, not by any eyes to be distinguished, unless the flowers be perhaps a trifle larger, and perhaps more deeply fringed.

D. squarrosus, from the sandy places of South Russia, is a general favourite in the garden. It makes mats of green rosettes, the leaves being narrow, stiff, grooved, pointed, and the outer ones recurving ; while the stems rise up about 9 or 12 inches, to carry some two or three, or only one, large white or pink blossom of an *excessive fringiness*, like a whirlwind of lace. There are other forms of this, including a *D. s. nanus*, of more compact habit, and more copious production of stems about 6 inches high.

D. stenocephalus carries one or three whitish-grey blossoms in a cluster, and has little worth accordingly.

D. Sternbergii should stand for the right name of the Alpester variety of *D. monspessulanus*—a most lovely delight, which may, for instance, be seen and smelt from afar in at least one fold of the long limestone screes that descend the pitiless flanks of Monte Baldo. For its fine growths run grass-like about among the stones, just as in *D. monspessulanus*, but the stems are only about 6 inches high, appearing here and there in the scant green of the stone-slide ; and each only carries one single flower, and that, by comparison, of larger size, and, out of all comparison, of deeper, livelier colour—fringy great moths of vivid rose hovering airily over the greyness of the scree, and haunting the wide world with the deliciousness of its scent—so that if your fate leads you to descend the mountain in a mist, you know where you are at once upon its pathless slope by meeting the breath of the Dianthus rising up towards you like a helpful incense from far down below in the gully by which your way should lead.

D. stramineus is, in its habit and flower, like a small *D. fimbriatus*, but that its whirligigs sit stemless to their loose spike, and should be of pale straw-yellow.

DIANTHUS.

D. striatiflorus. See under *D. barbatus.*

D. strictus is the *D. integer* of gardens (this also, with its variety, *D. s. brachyanthus*, being now swept with *D. integer* (Vis.), and *D. integer* (Balb.), into the rather too catholic net of *D. alpester*, Balb. *D. strictus*, then, though generously advertised, is not a Pink of prime rank. Its neat mats, its crowd of 6-inch stems, its cloud of small white blossom, smooth-edged or toothed, will all be found described, for the sake of convenience, under the false and confusing botanical name of *D. integer.* The whole group, however, varies chaotically in size and also sometimes in colour. There is certainly a form going about, called *D. strictus* (*integer*), *grandiflorus*, which remedies the defects of the type by having white stars more adequate in size to the calyx and the stem. It should be noted that in all this race the petals may be either smooth or nicked, but they are *never ragged or fringed.*

D. suavis, a beautiful rock-garden Pink, exactly midway between *D. plumarius* and *D. caesius*, but very much nearer to the latter (*q.v.*) in general effect and beauty, though more deeply jagged at the edge of the petals. It is, perhaps, a hybrid.

D. subacaulis of catalogues can be nothing more than Boissier's variety *brachyanthus* of *D. strictus*, reappearing under another form. In other words, it is a variety of *D. alpester*, Balb., and will be found under *D. brachyanthus.* It is also listed as *D. " nivalis."*

D. superbiens = *D. robustus, q.v.*

D. superbus.—The stalwart but lanky giant Fringy-pink, with wild pale Ragged-Robin flowers of lilac or white, so often to be seen in hayfields and bushy places of the lower alpine region towards the Southern and Eastern ranges, is too soft a thing (as any one can tell from its rare tufts of broad green leaves) to prove a firm perennial ; nevertheless in cool remote corners its beauty makes an effect in summer, and the few-stemmed gawkiness of its habit is not seen. (Its variety from Japan, *D. s. monticola*, is also a fine thing.)

D. Szowitsianus.—A sub-shrubby woody-stocked mass, otherwise like *D. Seguieri*, with stems of 9 inches, and the same blossoms, sharply toothed and densely bearded. But here the trunk and boughs are thick and woody, while the leaves are stiff, and the habit of the plant a dense mound of sprouts and foliage, with shoots as thick as a goose-quill.

D. tabrisianus is a twin to *D. fimbriatus*, from which it differs chiefly in the longer, freer fringe to the petals.

D. talyschensis is an 18-inch version of *D. monspessulanus.*

D. tergestinus, a lax long-leaved, loose-flowered species after the style of *D. silvestris*, but with smaller flowers. It has also a short-leaved form, by the name of *D. Marchesettii*.

D. toletanus makes 8-inch stems and bears two or three blooms to a head—intensely purple, with toothed petals and blue-grey leaves. (Castile.)

D. trifasciculatus. See under *D. Carthusianorum.*

D. tripunctatus, a worthless weed.

D. tymphresteus. See under *D. Carthusianorum.*

D. uniflorus. See under *D. Carthusianorum.*

D. vaginatus. See under *D. Carthusianorum.*

D. virgineus. See under *D. Caryophyllus* (*D. longicaulis*, Godr.).

D. viridescens, an undeserving plant, akin to *D. strictus.*

D. viscidus. See under *D. Carthusianorum.*

D. Wimmeri=*D. speciosus*, q.v.

D. xylorrhizos makes its woody roots in the rocks of Paleokastro in Crete ; a stout and handsome species with tortuous trunks, and many stems flopping and hanging. The leaves are smooth and long and weak, the flowers large and whitish.

D. zonatus (*D. oculatus*) ends the list condignly, a beautiful matted Pink of glaucous foliage, with countless erect and often shortly branching stems carrying abundance of magnificent rosy flowers, of full outline and sharp toothing to the petals, which are bearded at the throat, and marked with a deep zone of crimson velvet. The calyx is striped and usually toothed with purple, and the colour, of course, varies to white. All single Pinks have a way, in catalogues, of abusing the specific name of *D. zonatus.*

HYBRID PINKS

Of these there is now no end. *D.×Pritchardii* is a " novelty " for which large sums are asked, but on which no excessive regard need be lavished, for it is no such remarkable improvement on *D. deltoeides*. *D. Spencer Bickham*, however, is a most startling tufted thing with abundance of stiff little 6-inch stems, that have big blossoms sharply, deeply toothed, and in colour are of virulent magenta rose. *D.×Coedcoch* (named after the place, presumably, where it first saw the light, rather than according to the noise made by him who himself first sees it), is not what such a jargon would announce, but reported a neat thing, of well-orbed and of especial beauty. *D. oenipontanus* and *D. calalpinus* have both had their share of notice, but *D. caesius×squarrosus* is a good if not immortal hybrid, making a bush of neat broad green foliage, set all over, all the summer through, with flowers

300

brightly rosy and of Caesian size, but edged with something of the Squarrosan fringe. And of natural hybrids, the following are suggested (among many, and for the present) as being of good blood :—

D. × Duftii	*= Carthusianorum × deltoeides.*
D. × Laucheanus	*= barbatus × deltoeides.*
D. × Seehausianus	*= arenarius × deltoeides.*
D. × Jaczonis	*= deltoeides × superbus,* peach - coloured, intensely sweet.
D. × oenipontanus	*= alpinus × superbus.*
D. × fallax	*= alpinus × deltoeides.*
D. × callizonioeides	*= callizonus × inodorus.*
D. × Dominii	*= plumarius × caesius.*
D. × varians	*= Seguieri × monspessulanus.*
D. × Mammingorum	*= Seguieri × inodorus.*
D. × Woodfordii	*= alpinus × deltoeides.*

To which list it is only necessary to add that anyone who possesses any of the better species, can make himself, any day, the possessor of hopes more beautiful yet than any of these realities. For the possibilities of loveliness that lie in front of the alpine Pinks have not yet begun to dawn on minds too closely preoccupied with carnations to have as yet much foresight of the glory and the value that will attend successful races of huge-flowered dwarf mats and edgings and tuffets, bred out of *DD. alpinus, superbus, Sternbergii, neglectus, caesius, callizonus,* and *inodorus.* As the crossing of these is easy, and their raising easier still, gold and glory are here unusually ready to hand.

Diapensia, a race of shrubs so minute as to be smaller than almost the smallest plants. All the species are miffy delicate subjects, though one is often exhibited under the name of *Pyxidanthera barbulata,* to the general applause and the seduction of many, in the most beautiful imported sods that are one sheet of wee russet foliage quite hidden by the profuse pearl-white rounded stars that sit almost close all over it. *D. barbulata* comes from the pine-barrens of New Jersey ; but the others, *D. lapponica* (with a variety *D. l. asiatica*), and *himalaica,* are very high-alpine or Arctic species, or both, forming close grey-green scabs like domes of hard lichen on the rocks, and then, from the pressed mat of their microscopic rosettes, sending up stems of an inch or two, each with a rather large and lovely white flower : the whole plant having but a remote—or very remote—resemblance to the Saxifrage that says it is like them. All the three species should be grown in specially gritty, stony, chippy ground, in a soil compounded of roughest sand, to a third part of blended peat and leaf-mould—the whole to be kept constantly moist from underneath (in which case sunshine is not contra-indicated).

Dicentra.—The Bleeding Hearts are often hearts of gold, as in the case of *D. chrysantha,* a rare loveliness for dryish rocky places, from California, rather larger in habit than the North Californian *D. formosa,* with its ample Herb-Robertish foliage, and clear rosy hanging hearts in little clusters like a hyacinth's. Yet ampler in the leaf, and more hyacinthine in the head, is the 10- or 12-inch *D. eximia,* with blossoms of deeper pink ; *D. cucullaria* is a finer, frailer thing in the way of *D. formosa,* but only 4 inches high or so, with flowers of pale pearly white, most delicate ; as is also the similar *D. cambensis,* which to blossoms of whitish-pink unites the ravishing fragrance of the Hyacinth. And every garden knows the most bleeding of all hearts, the towering and regal *D. spectabilis* of spring, so much more rudely if aptly styled when liberal gardeners give the grosser name of Dutchman's Breeches. All these are easy and appropriate for sheltered corners, higher or lower, in the larger rock-garden.

Dichondra repens is an ugly little green creeping Convolvulad with microscopic axillary flowers of yellowy-white. It runs along over a cool level with rooting stems and kidney-shaped leaves ; but is not worthy of such a place, not long retains it, for it is not soundly hardy.

Dictamnus Fraxinella, with its major-form, *D. purpureus,* and its greatest of all developments, *D. giganteus,* also called *D. caucasicus,* are superb Burning-bushes, with ashlike foliage and portly airy spikes of 18 inches or 2 feet in early summer of white or mauvish flowers, which, on a hot still evening, will blaze unconsumed in a supernatural glow, if a match be applied to kindle the volatile essences that hover in a halo round the petals that distil them. These are best grown from seed or bought clumps, and put out into rich and very deep double-trenched soil in a warm exposure, where they must remain thenceforth undisturbed for ever.

Didymophysa Aucheri is a differently lovely thing, a dwarf spreading mat of small shoots, clad in little leaves, gashed into some three or five strips, and clustered at the tips of the shoots, which then emit close clusters of a dozen or so of pink Crucifers like those of *Petrocallis pyrenaica,* which the whole tuffet mimics ; only that here the seed-pods are twins, and their valves the shape and size of a pea. From the same sort of rocky places in the Alps of Persia, Elburs and Demavend, &c.

Dielytra, an early name of **Dicentra,** drawn from the likeness of the flower to the wing-cases (*Elytrae*), of an insect. But the name was misprinted, and turned out of the printer's hands as Diclytra, an error which for long kept hold of the popular mind.

Dierama is always in catalogues accorded a feminine adjective, although their compilers do not fall into the same trap of the Greek neuter termination in -ma, when dealing with Aethionema (they are a little wobbly about Onosma). This plant, therefore, is *D. pendulum* and, in forms that evoke special enthusiasm, *D. pulcherrimum*. It has a grace and glory all its own, a long tuft of upstanding narrow foliage rather suggesting that of a stiffened, elongated *Iris unguicularis*, and then, in late summer, tall, thin, but toughly wiry stems of 4 feet or so, wavering and swaying this way and that beneath a long dropping shower of chaffy-cupped rose-purple bells on pedicels so fine that they hardly seem to be attached at all to the stems. There are white forms as well as the clearer pink ones called *D. pulcherrimum;* all should be planted very deep, about 7 inches down, in warm soil of sandy peat in a situation sheltered from excessive wet in winter. For Dierama, though South African, is perfectly hardy, yet requires so much respect for its memories of home, at least in colder and wetter parts of the country.

Digitalis.—Of the many Foxgloves obtainable, the rock-garden may perhaps be glad to use, for adornment in dull moments : *D. lutea*, with close spikes of rather small yellow tubes ; *D. ambigua*, with looser spikes of much larger finer yellow bells ; *D. minor*, not much more than 6 inches high, with a quite lax and leafless stem of a few quite large pink flowers, with only a central basal rosette of leaves ; *D. Thapsi*, rising from half a foot to 18 inches, vested all over in tawny-pale wool, with large and rather pendulous pink flowers, and the leaves all dead when they unfold ; *D. lanata* and *D. leucophylla*, more or less whitely-woolly, and with blossoms of yellowish tone, veined with violet. There are many others of tall habit, *D. aurea*, *D. grandiflora* (also yellow), &c. ; all are profuse from seed, and like almost any situation and soil ; as a rule, in nature, non-calcareous (not that they really mind !), and inclining, as a rule, in nature, to prefer half-shady places.

Dionysia, a race never found in either list or garden, but well deserving to be cherished in both if it would accept of such observance. For this is a race entirely confined to the highest Alps of Persia, where it so entirely and deliberately replaces *Androsace* as to be (like the marmalades) a precise and absolute substitute—neat cushions in the rocks, studded with blossoms which differ from those of the Aretian and all other Androsaces in having a notably long flower-tube, curiously bulged and swelling in the middle. Of these unacquired treasures the most tantalising to hear of are *D. oreodoxa*, yellow ; *D. heterochroa*, golden, in dense grey cushions, and from altitudes so high as to leave no fear of its temper ; *D. tapetodes*, yellow, and as close as the closest *A. helvetica* ; *D. Michauxii*, a specially tight hard dome of grey velvet ; *D. ianthina*, most beautiful indeed in its form of tight silky-grey cushions of violet blossoms ; *D. bryoeides*, of the same habit and colour, but clothed in glistering crystalline glands instead of silky hairs ; *D. aretioeides*, with the habit and foliage rather of a narrow-leaved *Eritrichium nanum*, with long-tubed stars of yellow ; *D. hissarica*, hanging out of the cliffs in huge tight masses, with toothed leaves, and citron-coloured blossoms of nearly an inch across, distinct from all the rest in its general amplitude. These, then, among some twenty species, will suffice to feed our vain ambitions yet awhile ; if ever acquired, they should have the care and cherishing deployed upon their cousins the Aretian Androsaces, in similar conditions, but even warmer, dryer, and more sheltered corners.

Dioscorea caucasica is a climbing Yam, a rampant sprawling Liane of 2 yards and more ; *D. pyrenaica*, on the contrary, is a neat wee thing, extremely rare and of interesting history. But it is more properly *Borderea pyrenaica*, and, as such, will be found treated in the note to *Androsace hirtella*.

Diotis maritima, a white and intensely woolly-fluffy Everlasting, branched and with soft bunched heads ; but, though a rare native of English sea-shores, it is essentially a Southern and Mediterranean species, and too soft and enwoolled to be really hardy in a damp inland garden, unless in fullest sun and an especially dry stony hot place.

Diphylleia cymosa, a tall and ample Berberid, for a shady place in woodland, about 8 inches high, with umbrella-shaped leafage gashed and lobed ; then topped by a shower of small white flowers in May and June, succeeded by blue berries.

Disporon Hookeri, a dingy American liliaceous species of small merit, with rough oval leaves and spikes of greeny flowers. See Appendix for *D. pullum*.

Dodartia orientalis grows in the salty fields of Northern Caucasus, a pretty little Scrophulariad, with erect stems from an almost leafless and rush-like stock, carrying some three to seven five-lobed flowers of purple in a terminal raceme in summer.

Dodĕcătheōn, the Shooting Stars, or Flowers of the Twelve Gods (whoever these may have been), are all American Primulads for the decoration of deep moist ground, where they make tufts of large rather lax oval pale-green leaves, from which shoot stalwart naked

PLATE 30.

DODECATHEON MEADIA (var. HENDERSONI).
(Photo. R. A. Malby.)

DIANTHUS × WOODFORDENSIS [D. ALPINUS × D. DELTOEIDES].
(Photo. R. A. Malby.)

VOL. I.

stems carrying what can only be called a bunch of hanging narrow Cyclamens, with mouth of gold and protruded style. *D. Meadia,* so much grown in gardens, is so big and stout as almost to be coarse and overweening; it has white varieties and pale varieties, and *splendens* varieties a trifle more malignant in colour than the magenta-rose or lilac of the type. This species, broadly oval in the leaf, varies greatly, and America contains many others closely allied and minutely differentiated. *D. conjugens* is a smaller, neater plant of not more than a foot high at the most, but usually some 8 or 10 inches, with fewer but larger and finer flowers; the leaves are always smooth at the edges instead of being more or less scalloped, as almost always is the case in *D. Meadia; D. Clevelandii* has them nibbled at the rim, and the base of the blossom yellow and not white. *D. Jeffreyi* may easily be recognised by its especially long and narrow foliage standing rather erect, and with the leaves always running to a point. The scape is tall and stout, the flowers many and sometimes sweet-scented. *D. integrifolium* is told from *D. Meadia* by the possession of specially fleshy bracts beneath the flower-head; but the rock-garden, now that the bog and water-edge are well-furnished (without further wading into the subtleties that differentiate the many tall American Dodecatheons, and are often based on isolated and perhaps uncertain specimens), has its own primary concern with the delicate and lovely species of the high Alps. Delicate and lovely these are indeed, small frail stems of 6 inches or so above the clump, and carrying few flowers, and those large and brilliant and exquisite. These lovelinesses, however, are too rarely seen; they are not very long-lived, and for their happiness demand a specially gritty compost almost amounting to moraine, of the most perfect drainage, but watered subterraneously all through the summer. Of such are *D. pauciflorum,* most elegant and fine, about 6 inches high, from the upmost slopes towards the snows, as it may be seen sparsely glowing here and there on the highest banks of the Lakes in the Clouds, among the stones, with the grey striped squirrels chittering around it; *D. frigidum,* from still further North, towards the Behring Straits; *D. acuminatum,* often with white flowers, from Missouri River; *D. cylindrocarpum,* near *D. pauciflorum,* but with broader, fatter foliage, and the filament much shorter; *S. pubescens,* a delicate dainty thing of 4 inches, with blossoms of a fine "blue-purple," from Missoura mountain in Montana; *D. pulchrum,* 8 inches, with a tight head of rosy-violet, and a very dark wavy line round the mouths of the flowers, from the Yellowstone Park; *D. puberulentum,* always downy-stemmed, about 8 inches or less, with rosy-mauve flowers and a broad band of yellow round the mouth;

D. radicatum, beautiful and hearty, and profuse in shoots ; *D. cruciatum* (*D. speciosum* of gardens), eminently handsome, about 8 or 10 inches high, with very short and broad rhomboidal leaves, and flowers of great amplitude and brilliant red-purple, deepening to the base and there ringed with yellow ; *D. Hendersonii,* intensely green leaves and larger bracts under the head of the blossoms, which are as those of *D. frigidum* on stems of about a foot ; *D. patulum,* pale-green, and with stems of only about 8 inches, clothed in minute glands, and with white flowers, with a yellow ring at the base and then a purple mouth (there is a dwarfer alpine form of this called *D. p. bernalinum,* with rosy flowers and with a broad white or creamy band at the mouth ; it blooms in March on the summit of Bernal, by San Francisco). All these should be raised from seed, and can also be sometimes procured from their native places. The smaller species are here all on record ; of the larger, the garden could well content itself with those previously named. They are all summer and early summer bloomers. (The race supplements the poverty of Primula in America.)

Doronicum has not, like **Aronicum,** the recommendation of being at least a high alpine race (even if its members may not look it). Moreover, if any of them are to adorn the remoter wilder higher parts of the rock-garden in spring, the species are all much of a muchness in their leafy, rank, rampageous habit, stout stature, and coarse yellow suns of blossom.

Dorycnium, not a valuable race of tufty Pea-flowers from the South, herbaceous or sub-shrubby, shrouded in grey leafage, with heads of smallish pinkish flowers not large enough to make any worthy effect. The neatest is *D. herbaceum,* about 10 inches high, the two others most often offered are *D. latifolium,* and *D. suffruticosum,* both rather rank and insignificant things of a foot or more, not of any fine show, though the stems are not ungraceful.

Douglasia, a group closely akin to Androsace, entirely confined to America, with one beautiful strayed reveller over the high Alps of South Europe. They should have choice positions in the grittiest and stoniest underground-watered bed of sandy, peaty leaf-mould, for they do not always take to the Spartan régime of the moraine.

D. arctica is a tight and tiny species very close to *D. montana,* of which it is only probably a form, with flowers lonely over the clump, on stems about twice the length of the small, blunt, compacted leaves.

D. "cinerea" of a recent plant-list might be *D. dentata,* but that the blooms are *said* to be white. It is most probably only a form of *D. Vitaliana.*

D. dentata.—This plant (being taken as identical with *D. Dickieana*), is not the most attractive species, having narrow leaves irregularly toothed into a little trifurcation at the point, and gathered into lax clusters. From the rather loose mass, all dusty-ashen with stellar hairs, rise downy stems of some 3 inches or so, carrying a tight head of some half a dozen violet flowers rather shut up and pinched, instead of amply open like the Sarmentose Androsace that the tuft's whole habit recalls.

D. *laevigata* has come into cultivation, and is a beautiful species indeed, forming a wide tufty cushion of broad, pointed leaves, smooth and brilliantly glossy-green, above which abundantly rise stems of an inch more or less, clothed in close stellar hairs and carrying a neat head of some two or four charming wide-open flowers of rich rosy pink with a yellow eye, the whole mass faithfully recalling a clump of *Androsace Charpentieri*, but that, apart from other differences, the flowers here are gathered in a head, while the leaves have no hairs upon them anywhere. This comes from the Cascade Mountains, &c., and thrives best in the conditions indicated above.

D. *montana* is a variable type, of which the best picture may be gained by saying that its one-flowered variety from Montana is almost mistakable for *Androsace Wulfeniana*, with rose-pink flowers sitting close and single to a tuft of shining rosettes. Usually, however, the stems rise higher above the cushion, and carry one, two, or even three blossoms. It is a specially neat lovely thing.

D. *nivalis*, a softly downy plant, more or less closely tufted, with rosettes on almost woody bare little prostrate branches (as in *Androsace villosa*). The leaves are blunt, in lax clumps, and the stems are hardly as tall, each carrying some three to seven flesh-pink flowers with rounded lobes on unequal foot-stalks. From about 10,000 feet in the Cascade Mountains.

The only other recognised species in the race is *D. Vitaliana*, so completely distinct alike in habit and in distribution as indeed to deserve the distinct name of *Gregoria*, by which it has sometimes been known (as well as standing immortal in the affections of most people as *Androsace Vitaliana*). It might just as well box the compass and be *Dionysia* too, for it has many more obvious resemblances to these than to either *Douglasia* or *Androsace*, though for its beauty's sake alone it deserves admission into the august dominant race of the group, with which it has definitely cast in its lot, rather than with either *Dionysia* or *Douglasia*. For *D. Vitaliana* abhors America where all the remaining Douglasias live, and, like so many other Americans, leaves its relations behind and makes its home entirely in the Old World—a plant of alpine elevations, abundant in the Southern Alps,

and especially on the non-calcareous ranges (though by no means exclusively so), as anyone can bear witness who has seen it sheeting the flawed boulders of the Mont Cenis in such floods of citron-gold, so cunningly applied in all the right fissures and ledges, that the gardener yearns to dig up the whole complete and compendious rock-garden at once, and bring it home as it is. This is a local species, only occurring on the Southern rims of Switzerland, but spasmodically ranging through all the Eastern and Western Alps, to the Pyrenees on the one hand and Venetia on the other, but becoming, as a rule, less frequent or happy as it descends into the South on the Cottians and Maritimes. Where, however, it is found at all, it is found, like most local plants, in the most prodigal abundance, clothing the rocks and stony patches and the very path-sides in loose flat spreading masses of rambling greenish-grey shoots, finely narrow and juniperine and delicate, but wholly hidden from view by the profusion of its long-throated wide-trumpeted flowers of pure citron, looking exactly like dropped carpets of some smaller yellow jasmine, its colour having so special a clarity and lucence that you can recognise it from far away on the mountain side, among all the other conflicting commoner, cruder yellows in which the flanks of the great alps are clad in June. It varies but little; the Mont Cenis yielded once a lovely form with flowers of palest lemon, but the " novelties " offered in catalogues of specialities as *A. praetutiana* and *A. cinerea* are merely forms of *D. Vitaliana*, varying in the amount of greyness in which the foliage is invested. In cultivation the plant takes a little time to recover the annoyance of being removed from its native turf or gravel-slide ; its hard rat-tail roots, dark-brown and woody, make no hurry in seeking new sustenance, and patience has to be exercised with collected pieces, which, however, offer the only original means of securing the Douglasia. But if the clump be left alone accordingly to sulk awhile in the sand-bed, fresh tufts of evergreen foliage will ere long come pushing from below, and, in a season's time the restored specimen can be put out into any open wholesome slope, in very deep and light and well-drained stony ground, either of ordinary loam relieved by sand, or with an admixture of peat and leaf-mould to enrich it. Once there, the plant must be left alone for ever and ever to get bigger and bigger each year, forming a wider and wider carpet of neat green-grey shoots, upon which the favour of spring will produce you the golden flowers in numbers so tactful as never by any means to debar you from contemplation of the foliage.

Draba, a family of the first rank for decorating even the choicest and most prominent places in the choicest rock-garden ledge or

moraine. Yet somehow a race that never attracts the full notice
that it ought, and in catalogues is represented by a longish string of
bare names with little or nothing to enlighten them. So that but
few species are ever recognised or grown, where there are many more
well worth the very slight attention they require. For almost all
Drabas grow with the utmost ease and readiness in any light open soil
and place, can be raised abundantly from seed, and (in the section
Aeizopsis and *Chrysodraba* at least), are easily propagated by removal
of shoots or rosette about August. The race is alpine and high-alpine,
very freely spread in the loftiest and sternest rocky places of both
the Old and the New World, extending in a wide range, right down
the Andes; and it is divided into three groups, so clearly marked
and notable that it will be convenient to make use of them here.
The first section then, *Aeizopsis*, consists of species never forming into
a carpet, but growing in a cushion, large or small, of tightly-clumped
rosettes; and the leaves of these rosettes are always edged with so
regularly-placed a chevaux de frise of spiny teeth or bristles as to
have quite a toothed effect. The flowers in this group are, with one
conspicuous exception, invariably yellow, and the tuft of fringed-
looking rosettes has the aspect of some microscopic green Aloe, thanks
to the finely thorny look of the foliage. In the second section,
Chrysodraba, there is *none of this clumping, none of this thorny look.*
All the species form smooth and loose mats of rosettes extending often
widely, and the leaves are of soft texture, downy or hairy, but *never
with any bristle-points at the edge or anywhere* else. Here again the
flowers are *invariably yellow.* The last section is called *Leucodraba*;
the species in this are of much less importance, soft-leaved, and
invariably with white flowers.

SECTION I.—AEIZOPSIS. SPINY-LOOKING CLUMPLINGS, AND YELLOW FLOWERS

D. aeizoeides.—This is one of the best known and most useful, a
species of specially wide range, occurring principally in the limestones at
alpine elevations, throughout the Alps (and always on the rock itself,
or stony scree), through Sicily, Greece, and Asia Minor. Coming
northward, it is very rare in Belgium, and its last outpost is on the
walls of Penard Castle by Swansea. It forms a most neat and hearty
tuft of bright-green, thorny-looking rosettes, rather large and ample
for the race, being often nearly an inch and a half across, upstanding,
incurving and aloe-like; each one of these in spring sends up a head of
golden-yellow flowers on a *hairless* stem of 2 or 3 inches, and succeeded

by oval-pointed, veinous bald pods. The plant varies considerably in size and stature, and some of its more marked forms are occasionally offered as species. These are *DD. Bertoloni, affinis, elongata, bosniaca, montana, Beckeri, alpina,* and *scardica.* With no doubt as many more as you could choose to differentiate, each range that possesses the species probably possessing some special local form of it, and that again varying into different developments of which you well might name the extremer versions. None will be found much finer, however, than some that may be collected no further away than the Alps of Switzerland. One of the most marked named off-shoots, however, is also a Swiss plant—this is the minute stunted species almost universal at great elevations in the granitic Alps, and sometimes sent out as *D. Zahlbrückneri,* being in reality *D. Hoppeana, q.v.*

D. aeizöon (*D. lasiocarpa,* Koch.) is also a plant of the limestones, but only from the Carpathians through Transylvania, to Dalmatia, with one outlying station in South Austria. It is much larger in the clump than *D. aeizoeides,* and of these larger rosettes there are fewer, only two or three, while from them rises a taller stem, carrying a larger head of smaller, paler flowers, and elongating into quite an impressive spike of flat *downy* pods. Its varieties are *D. a. compacta,* and *D. a. Haynaldii,* this last appearing often as a species, and being a small compact and very narrow-leaved development of the type, with stems of only an inch or so, and only a few flowers to the head.

D. armata is a sub-species of *D. longirostra, q.v.,* almost neater and smaller and yet more charming in its reduced, concise, minute habit, and the fine golden blooms that seem even finer for the dainty scale of the massed rosettlings above which they stand. This plant continues the distribution of rare *D. longirostra* on into Croatia, where it is yet rarer.

D. Athoa occurs only on a few mountain tops of Greece, and is a handsome species making a dense and rather wide mass of specially spine-edged, broadish foliage, with the foot-stalks of the flowers longer and more spreading at the top of the bare little stout 3-inch stems, so that the bright yellow crosses, with their tall anthers, look specially wide in the cluster. A form of this is *D. A. Lacaita,* a smaller, compacter, tighter tuffet still, with short anthers and short petals. Possibly this may be a true species.

D. aurea is the type of *D. cuspidata, q.v.*

D. Bertoloni. See under *D. aeizoeides.*

D. bruniaefolia. See under *D. olympica.*

D. bryoeides. See under *D. rigida.*

DRABA.

D. cantabrica, W. K., from limestone crevices in Navarre, &c., may be known from *D. aeizoeides* in having *downy, not hairless, stems*, paler flowers, broader petals, and leaves longer and more drawn out (nothing could vary more in all these respects than *D. aeizoeides* itself, but the *bald stem* is an essential diagnostic in all forms of *D. aeizoeides*).

D. compacta. See under *D. aeizoon.*

D. cretica is entirely confined to one or two mountain tops of Crete. This is a little spine-edged, broadish-leaved mass almost as close and wee as an Aretian Androsace, with yellow blossoms that hardly rise above the clump, until their starry-haired stems have towered to the height of perhaps half an inch (in the case of a giant), to carry the four or five fat oval-pointed pods, downy and comfortable-looking in a coat of starry hairs.

D. cuspidata may always be known from *D. aeizoeides* by the downy stems, by the tight and never relaxing clumps of its rosettes, by a toothing at the point of its beard-tipped leaves, by its wider flowerhead, and by its bigger pod, not veined, but a-bristle with stiff hairs, instead of being smooth and bald as in every form of *D. aeizoeides.* (Eastern Alps, &c.)

D. Dedeana is a most important Spanish species with two varieties even more remarkable than itself. It is a dense massed tuft of rosettes at the end of bare branches on the ground, these rosettes being made up of very lightly overlapping little leaves, oblong-blunt and narrow, clothed at the end in the characteristic stiff white bristles of the group. But the flowers break clean away from it, for they are of pure snowy or creamy whiteness, instead of the otherwise unvarying yellow of this section, rising up in heads, at the top of the 3-inch stems, and fine and large and beautiful into the bargain. *D. Mawii*, of gardens, is merely a form of this, and a form with smaller, fewer blossoms and narrower foliage, though endowed with green sepals. And yet more important is the second variety, *D. D. Zapateri.* This is a delightful thing from shady places in the Jurassic rocks of Aragon, and abundant on the hills of Albarracin. It forms the typical dense matting mass, with leaves of brilliant green, very close-set in the packed columnar rosettes; and the inner ones curve inwards, while the outer ones tend to spread or reflex. The stems are half an inch or even an inch and a half high, and the flowers in their loose dome are always pure *bright white* with a golden set of anthers, and often a purple calyx, the whole plant being clothed in a soft down.

D. dicranoeides (Boiss. and Huet.)=*D. rigida, q.v.*

D. glacialis almost approaches the next section, and is a copy of *D. alpina* in general appearance—a neat mass, emitting a number of short golden-headed stems; but the broad leaves have that edging of stiff white bristles which assigns it at once to the section *Aeizopsis*.

D. globifera, from the rocks of Ararat, makes a quite dense tuft, composed of rosettes like little balls of wool, with the leaves bristled at their edges and a trifle bearded at their points. The golden-yellow flowers are as in *D. olympica*, but slightly smaller.

D. Haynaldii. See under *D. aeizoon*.

D. hispanica has its name under false pretences, for Spain is not its centre, but merely its one *pied à terre* in Europe. The species ranges from Atlas and all along North Africa, at last effecting a lodgement on the hills of Southern Spain, where, however, it is abundant both on calcareous and non-calcareous formations. It is a magnificent species, the type out of which *D. Dedeana* has evolved an independent existence. But *D. hispanica* is much larger—a woody-rooted mass of rosettes, stout and shining, pale bright-green with long-pointed fringed leaves, the inner ones standing up and the outer spreading upon the column of bygone relics. The stems are stout and many, about 2 inches high, or less at the time they are carrying their golden flowers on pedicels of which the lower are so long that the blossoms seem to be borne in an almost flat head or umbel.

D. Hoppeana, Reish. (*D. Zahlbrückneri*, Sauter) of the high Alps, is like a minute form of *D. aeizoeides*. But it may be known by its preference for *non-calcareous soils*, and most especially for not confining itself to rock, as *D. aeizoeides* almost invariably does, but always occupying the *bare places* and open earth-pans of the heights, in which situations it is a most familiar foe to all who have ever been there. For it is not a species of any charm, minute and tight in its tuft, rather minute and greenish-lemony in the effect of its little flowers on their scantily-furnished head.

D. hystrix is an obscure swollen-podded plant from Afghanistan, horrid with the spiny remnant of its dead leaves, while the living ones, besides the bristle-teeth at their edge, are all clothed in spreading white hairs.

D. imbricata is a tight mass quite like an Aretian Androsace, to be met with in stony places high in the Western Caucasus. It is very dense and very very wee; the very wee leaves being very tightly packed into very wee rosettes, on which, almost stemless—(but what stem there is being quite hairless)—appear heads of some five blossoms, intensely golden-yellow, succeeded by bulging fat pods. It is rather like *D. rigida* var. *bryoeides*, but still more minute, and of the most especial charm.

DRABA.

D. Lacaita. See under *D. Athoa ;* though perhaps it has a right to stand alone.

D. Loiseleurii comes not far away from *D. hispanica*, but differs in its larger, shorter leaves, while its rosettes and masses are looser and bigger-leaved, and more open than in *D. Dedeana ;* from *D. olympica* it emerges distinct in its broader foliage and flowers of paler yellow ; in short, the picture presents a really fine and stalwart lemon-yellow-flowered cushion after the fashion of *D. aeizoeides*, but with swollen pods and wide masses, which are confined entirely to the high places of Cinto, Rotondo, and others of the Corsican mountains (*D. corsica*, Jord., *D. cuspidata*, Arc.).

D. longirostra is equally restricted, occupying rock-crevices in the mountains of Dalmatia and Montenegro. This is a small neat species, making a clump suggestive of Petrocallis, with few-flowered heads of yellow, on stems perhaps an inch and a half above the cushion of tidy little green and spinous-looking rosettes.

D. Mawii. See under *D. Dedeana.*

D. natolica has blooms of intense golden-yellow, and the thorny-looking clumps are all clad in soft-spreading down, while on the pods also there are starry hairs. (Alps of Cappadocia, Anatolia, &c.)

D. olympica is a very variable species and very valuable in all its forms. It makes wide mats and masses, but is otherwise nearest to *D. cuspidata*, yet with narrower foliage and flowers of perhaps an intenser golden-yellow. The swollen pods are notably small for the mass, which hangs in the rocks all over Asia Minor, Syria, &c. Its varieties are of the most diverse ; *D. o. bruniaefolia* is well known in gardens, a plant of looser habit, and, like *D. Hoppeana*, preferring the open ground on the mountains, as *D. olympica* and *D. aeizoeides* cling to the rocks ; *D. o. hetericoma* is a smaller neat thing, with most brilliant blossoms and great attractiveness ; and yet others are *D. o. ericaefolia* and *D. o. diversifolia.*

D. oxycarpa makes little dense masses, with hardly any stems, and pointed pods, in the cliffs of Hermon, and on Lebanon above the Cedars.

D. parnassica, a rare species from the upper rocks of Parnassus, is suggestive of a much smaller and tighter *D. hispanica*, but so much smaller as to be only a tiny tuft or dense cushion, from which spring stems of 1 or 2 inches, carrying four or five golden flowers in a loose radiating head, to be followed by a little less radiating head of flattened pods (not rounded and swelling) beset with spreading hairs.

D. rigida is *D. dicranoeides* (Boiss. and Huet.), a tidy treasure of special beauty and brilliance, with minute spinous-edged leaves packed into vivid shining rosettes at the top of columns of dead ones, the leaves being short and keeled as in a Hypnum, and the whole forming into a neat cushion of an inch high or so, and 4 or 5 inches across. The blossoms are vivid, too, in their display of intense pure golden-yellow; the variety *D. r. pulvinaris* is tighter still, while *D. r. bryoeides* even outdoes it in the minute compactness of its huddled foliage, making globular rosettes like some miniature of *Saxifraga bryoeides*. (All these come from the rocks of Caucasus and Armenia.)

D. Sauteri is a lime-loving species confined to rock-crevices in the Alps of Salzburg, whence it radiates into the outskirts of the Bavarian mountains on the one hand and into those of upper Styria on the other (Watzmann, Tannengebirge, &c.). It is a most strange alien to find in this group, being perfectly slackened and loose in habit, with short, loose, narrow, oval-pointed leaves, arranged in the feeblest apology for a rosette, rather suggesting tufts and small clusters ramifying here and there, and densely fringed at the edge. The few flowers are yellow, with oval petals, not making any fine effect above the mass of leafage on their stems of an inch or less.

D. scabra also stands apart from the group to which it belongs. For it is *perfectly hairless all over*, and has not even any of the section's bristly spines up the edges of the leaves. However, to make up, they are very *rough along the edge*, alike to the eye and to the touch. Otherwise the plant is like a larger and rather looser *D. o. bruniaefolia*.

D. Zahlbrückneri = *D. Hoppeana*, *q.v.*

D. Zapateri. See under *D. Dedeana*.

SECTION II.—CHRYSODRABA. LOOSER, SOFTER HABIT AND NO SPINY TEETH AT ALL TO THE LEAVES. FLOWERS INVARIABLY YELLOW

D. acaulis.—A most lovely little fluffet, of minute close habit, like an *Androsace helvetica* with the leaves of Eritrichium, reduced indeed in size, but clothed in the same glistering soft silver coat. The beauty of the tiny silken cushion is such that it can hardly be added to even by the almost stemless heads of two or three golden flowers appearing in spring all over the wee mass, which is never more than 3 or 4 inches across at the outside, so that its preciousness may be appreciated; and that appreciation should be shown in the nice choice of a specially precious place, and protection in winter, perhaps, against incessant wet. (From high rocky places of the Cilician Taurus.)

D. Adami is hispid-hairy all over, and has smaller yellow flowers.

DRABA.

D. algida, from the tops of Altai, has hairy stems and leaves that are oval-oblong and smooth above, but hairy below and fringed.

D. alpina ranges all round the Arctic Circle, and then, by way of Korea, down through the mountains of China into the Himalaya, which it densely occupies, a neat and useful mass of soft oval-pointed rather large leaves, from which rise many stems of 4 inches or less, carrying heads of yellow blossom hardly big enough to justify the lax look of the leafage below—at least not after the brilliant and concise beauties that we inspected in the more noble earlier section.

D. calycosa makes a dense clump in the crevices of Argaeus in Cappadocia. It is remarkable for keeping its calyx even after the valves have fallen from the pod (*D. rosularis*, Boiss.). There is a variety, *D. c. Aucheri*, of larger size.

D. cappadocica has much the charm and the habit of *D. acaulis*, but the stems are taller, and the hairs that clothe the plant are split.

D. elegans is an obscure name, representing a species with golden-orange blooms, that makes small mats of rather stiffish foliage, arranged scantily in rosettes, and rough to the touch. (Cilician Taurus, &c.)

D. incompta, from Western Tibet, &c., is a minute downy tuffet with shoots of about half an inch, and naked little stems ending in a bunch of leaves, and composing a rather loose mat. The variety *D. i. persica* is larger.

D. mollissima and all its beauty may be imagined when we hear that it is like a silky-velvety version of *Androsace cylindrica*, with golden flowers in heads at the top of minute stems. (Western Caucasus, &c.)

D. ochroleuum has leaves hairy all over. The stems are huddled and low, with pale-yellow flowers, lengthening afterwards. (Summits of the Altai.)

D. polytricha is *D. Reuteri* (Boiss. and Huet.), and a little treasurable mass of 3 inches wide, in the manner of *D. acaulis*, forming neat dense clumps in columns on the piles of dead leaves that never fall. The leaves are minute, very narrow-oblong, and the whole growth is clothed in simple white hairs; the ample yellow petals are much blunted at their end. (From alpine rocks of Turkish Armenia, &c.)

D. repens, a quite green species emitting leafy runners long and lax. The foliage is narrow-oblong and pointed, untoothed, and decked with a little close sparse down. (From the grassy alps of Caucasus, &c.)

D. rosularis. See under *D. calycosa*.

D. tridentata is loose and rambling as *D. repens*, with the scanty leafage of the rosettes cut in two or three teeth on either side. The leaves are also obovate, roughish, and shortly downy.

D. velutina is a beautiful species from Techdagh in Armenia, after the whole style of *D. mollissima*, but with larger leaves, not packed and compiled on columns of dead, while the flowers are larger too, and of intense golden-yellow.

D. vesicaria, in the clefts of the summit of Lebanon, is a compact tuffet with the foliage overlapping all the way up the stems. When the yellow flowers are gone the pod swells into a great puffed hairy bladder.

SECTION III.—LEUCODRABA. FLOWERS INVARIABLY WHITE

This group consists of small alpine plants, for the most part quite worthless, and only to be rehearsed lest their undescribed names should some day lead the innocent into temptation (as, for instance, with *D. gigas* and *Arabis karduchorum*). Of such condemnation, then, are *D. carinthiaca*, with the closely allied *D. Wahlenbergii* and *D. incana*, *D. carinthiaca* sometimes appearing also as *D. nivalis*, and also as *D. Johannis*, in honour of some bygone Archduke of Austria, insufficiently honoured, indeed, in a weed so dowdy and insignificant. *D. tomentosa*, however, is rather prettier, forming tufts as whitely woolly as those of *Androsace imbricata*, and often accompanying them in the high hot granite chinks of the South. The white flowers, too, on their 2- to 3-inch stems, are quite visible to the naked eye, but the plant has an impermanent difficult look, promising exactions in the way of cultural care far beyond any merit of its face-value. *D. stellata*, from the limestone regions, is frailer, not woolly, with shorter stems, and therefore rather larger-seeming blossom ; this might be worth the trouble of admitting. In the high granites, too, lives *D. flatnitzensis*, making woody trunks, crowned with tufts of almost smooth little leaves, fringed at the edge, with many little stems carrying a certain number of little white flowers, of no gay brilliance, indeed, but neat and dwarf and profuse. But *DD. frigida, confusa tibetica, helvetica, lapponica, androsacea* (forms, probably of *D. flatnitzensis*, if not mere synonyms), *lasiophylla, siliquosa* (a species that most likely includes *D. carinthiaca* and all its large misty following, unnecessarily and minutely differentiated), *ambigua, hirta, subamplexicaulis, stylosa, ramosissima, arabisans*, &c., all these indeed are a long way past praying for, and would be better by the prudent prayed against.

Doubt, however, hangs round the name of *D. ciliata*, which has been much praised. Yet the *D. ciliata* of gardens is always either *Arabis Scopoliana*, or some other equally valueless Cruciferous weed, whereas the description of the genuine *Draba* sounds as if the result should be more pleasing. For it ought to be a running plant with rather pointed leathery leaves, of which the lower ones make rosettes on the ground, and are obovate, and with horny toothings, bristlish and fringed with hairs, while those on the stems are oblong and smoother. The flowers are large, white, and handsome, with notched petals, carried in heads at the top of leafy stems of a few inches. This species (if species it is) comes from sunny stone-slopes of Dalmatia, and perhaps is but an old and improved rendering of *A. Scopoliana* after all.

SOME NEW-WORLD DRABAS, WITHOUT RESPECT TO GROUPING

D. alyssoeides.—Quite a small bush with big white flowers. (Chimborazo.)

D. andina, from the high barrens. Very dense, the little trunks being huddled with the dead leaves of many years. The stiff pointed fringed leaves of the season overlap, and are clothed in stellar down, but the stems are smooth and about 3 inches or so in height, carrying a great number of blossoms passing from pale yellow to white.

D. aretioeides, a minute dense tuffet from the Colombian Andes, as is also *D. obovata*.

D. cheiranthoeides has the same flower as *Cheiranthus ochroleucus*, with very long narrow leaves at the base, irregularly toothed. (Sierra Nevada.)

D. chrysantha, from New Mexico, is a fine half-prostrate thing, with narrow leaves more or less toothed, and more or less fringed. The stems are some 2 to 6 inches high, bearing big golden blooms in open loose spikes.

D. densifolia makes a neat close tuft, and sends up rather woolly stems of some two and a half inches, carrying smallish yellow stars.

D. depressa has much the same ways as *D. aretioeides*. It makes a depressed mat of prostrate shoots, clothed closely in little oval spoon-shaped leaves, rounded at the tip, all forming a tight mass and all clothed in a hoary-grey coat. This mat is produced at 17,000 feet on Chimborazo, and the flowers are pale yellow in heads (*D. cryptantha* has flowers a third of these in size).

D. grandiflora has a promising name, the excuse for which may at present be best ascertained about 17,000 feet up on Chimborazo.

D. Helleriana; rather firm small leaves and stout erect branches with more leaves sitting close to them. Pods twisted.

D. luteola has convex downy pods, twisted in fruit; the whole plant is grey, some 6 to 12 inches high, with yellow flowers of bright clear colour set on a number of short spikes (it is also *D. lutea, D. subalpina*).

D. oligosperma is probably worthless, having leaves rosetted at the base of the 3-inch stems, which end in white flowers. And all white-flowering Drabas (except *D. Dedeana* and its forms) are to be severely distrusted. In white, *Draba*, like most Cruciferae, is inexhaustibly prolific of obscure and worthless weeds.

D. radicata is hoary and woody, with diffuse shoots that end in graceful stems of large pale-yellow blooms carried above the huddled rosettes of narrowly spoon-shaped leaves. (Quito Andes, 12,000 feet.)

D. saximontana is very near *D. andina*, but has quite narrow leaves, instead of rather broad ones. It is possibly nothing more than our old friend *D. alpina* in a new form, or perhaps a similar old friend, *D. glacialis*.

D. spectabilis, from the Alps of Southern Colorado and New Mexico, is also *D. oxyloba*. It has quite green but rather downy leaves, narrowly obovate, set on woody trunks; and branches reaching from 4 to 16 inches, carrying showers of large yellow blossom.

D. streptocarpa is about 2 inches to half a foot high, clothed in grey down, and sending up many stems of white flowers. (Alps of New Mexico, &c.)

D. surculifera dwells on cliff-sides in Wyoming. It has large thin leaves and spikes of white often more than a foot high, and often much less.

D. violacea is a foot-high bushling from some 14,000 feet in the Colombian Andes (Assuay), with large flowers that break the family record by being of a fine violet.

Dracocephalum.—In this race there are many border plants, not here to be noticed. The rock-garden admits, however, *D. nutans*, a leafy species, rather inclined to creep and form masses, with 9-inch stems in June crowded with leaves, and rather nodding flowers of blue-violet. *D. austriacum* has finer foliage, neat and narrow, with large Snapdragons of blue, on stems of often more than a foot, while yet finer in the blossom and with undivided leaves, is *D. Ruyschianum*, with a white flowering variety, *D. japonicum*. Neither the names, however, nor the descriptions are quite solid; possibly to this, and possibly to *D. austriacum*, pertains a singularly beautiful species of fine frail wiry habit with stems of 6 or 9 inches and very large flowers, in scattered whorls, of the most soft and lucent lavender-blue, which may be seen here and there gleaming at sundown like a cold flame in open places of the high moors going up to Ikao in the mountains of

DRACOCEPHALUM.

Japan. The name *D. japonicum* is, moreover, often used to cover that of *D. altaiense*, a wholly different species round whose synonyms so much confusion ranges that, as among them lurks at least one species of extreme beauty for the rock-garden (if of no less difficulty), it will be best to give the synonymy and diagnoses of *D. imberbe*, *D. altaiense*, and *D. grandiflorum* in fuller measure.

D. altaiense, Laxmann, is an erect grower of 6 or 9 inches, hairless below, and then downy-hairy above. The leaves are kidney-shaped, oblong-elliptic rounded, with heart-shaped lobes at the base, scalloped and toothed at their edge, the lower ones being on long footstalks, and all of them clothed in spreading hairs. The whorls of big blue flowers are gathered at the top into a *tight head*, which afterwards draws up to an *oblong spike*, and under each there is a *very conspicuous rounded leaf or bract*, wedge-shaped to the stem and cut into *sharp saw-like teeth*. And this plant is also *D. altaiense*, of Willdenow, as well as being *D. altaicum* (Schangin), and *D. grandiflorum* (Bentham)—here being the source of primal error.

D. grandiflorum of Linnaeus has the sole right to this name for which they are all battling. It is *less erect* than the others, rather weak at first, and then rising; with the stem clothed in downy pubescence, and the leaves oval-oblong, scalloped or saw-edged, *not heart-lobed*, but *wedge-shaped to the base*, and grey with spreading hairs; the flowers are narrower than in the others, less divided, and their whorls *not crowded* into a head or spike at the top, but perfectly distinct, and with oblong bracts, almost *uncut at the edge*, and ending in a protracted point as fine as a tip of hair. Whichever plant of these three is got hold of, under whichever name, will prove a beauty none the less, and should be grown with special care in a very gritty morainish bed, or in the moraine itself, with water flowing below, perhaps, in summer, but as perfect drought as possible in winter. For these have not the robustness that their robust and squatting look appears to promise. They all bloom in high and late summer like almost all their family, and it is no wonder if, amid such rivalry for the same names, confusion should be rife among them.

D. imberbe is *D. grandiflorum* of Willdenow, and *D. altaiense*, Hiltebr. This is, as its name tells us, an imberb thing, not hairy but only downy, and with the kidney-shaped, almost rounded leaves *quite smooth on both surfaces* as a rule (but perhaps hoary underneath), and always very deeply scalloped. The habit is much the same as in the last, but here there are not the long bracts, and the whorls of blue blossom are in spiked heads.

Of other meritorious Dragon-heads are *D. argunense*, of 10 inches and blue flowers; *D. botryoeides*, of 4 inches and pink; *D. hetero-phyllum*, of 6 inches and yellow; *D. thymiflorum*, of 10 inches and violet-blue; and *D. peregrinum*, also violet-blue, but a foot high. These are of easy culture in light open places. Seed. *D. fragile* is a dainty thing from Davuria, with the flower-whorls in a cylindric spike, and two new species have lately come in from China, *D. bullatum* and *D. tanguticum*, neither of them in the front rank; *D. bullatum* being after the fashion of the Grandiflorum group, but soft and lax, with luscious foliage to the luscious and pleasant blue Dragon-heads, while *D. tanguticum* is no improvement in this, forming a bush of narrow-leaved densely leafy shoots of some 8 inches or so, closely set in late summer with such a profusion of blossom that, though the individual flowers are rather small and wizen and of no great show, their abundance results in a pleasant fuzzy-looking cat's-tail or thin plume of violet all through late summer till far into autumn. It grows and establishes quite readily, and has almost the look of a large-flowered, erect rosemary-bushling, while *D. bullatum*, so it is hopefully said, will show yet finer character if allowed to occupy for some years some sunny place, where it may form a wide mat, each shoot being headed by those meek dragons that may perhaps be more effective in a mass. And much finer is my *D. Purdomii*.

The New Zealand Dragon-heads, however, also are of a distinguished note. Of these are fitted for our hopes *D. Menziesii*, a little shrub of a foot or two high, with concave sharp stiff leaves clustered at the tips of the naked shoots, and then beautiful great helmets of waxy-white, wide and ample. This, in its dwarfer states, is an alpine of the South Island up to 4500 feet. *D. muscoeides*, according to Kew = *D. minimum* of Tasmania, also a treasure, but this has stiffer, shorter, less acute, more overlapping foliage; it forms into a dense, minute, moss-like mass, with white flowers either solitary upon it, or in rounded clumps of a few. (From the Alps of the Southern Island, 4000 to 6000 feet.)

Dryas octopetala is the sovereign of all shrubs for the rock-garden, with its hearty flat evergreen carpets of little oak-like leaves, grey beneath, and snowed over in June with immense flowers like creamy and glorified versions of *Anemone baldensis*, on stalks of 2 inches or so, that afterwards draw up to 4 or 5 inches, to bear the hardly less beautiful silver fluff-whirls of the seed. The plant can be grown in any reasonable soil, and in any sunny place, requiring nothing but to be well planted and then left alone (with a top dressing at times) to get larger and wider for ever. It often wrestles in the Alps with *Gentiana verna*, and perhaps might be so far from " throwing " it in the

PLATE 31.

DOUGLASIA LAEVIGATA.
(Photo. R. A. Malby.)

DRABA AEIZOEIDES.
(Photo. R.B.G., Kew.)

PLATE 32.

DRABA DEDEANA.
(Photo. R. A. Malby.)

DRABA BRUNIAEFOLIA.
(Photo. W. Irving, Kew.)

garden also as to provide just that company and stimulating rivalry
which the capricious beauty so misses when planted in splendid chilly
isolation. But in the garden it might be feared the Dryas may prove
a rather overpowering neighbour. This may easily be raised from
fresh-sown seed, but takes two or three years to reach any fair flowering
size, and yet more to make a mat of any amplitude. So that it is well
to remember that August cuttings stuck in sand, root with the most
perfect promptitude and ease ; while in the Alps, if found growing on
sandy or limy hummocks in loose soil, mats of the Dryas may be torn
without damage from their thick wooden trunk, for all along their
arm's length they will have been stimulated by the sand into rooting
with fine new fibres, so that the whole may be sent home as it stands,
and as it stands put straight into more sand, and then into the garden,
or else divided at pleasure into many comfortable rooting fragments
and grown on for next season. On the other hand, little but failure
ever results from the laborious collection of young seedlings in the
Alps, for these have only the one seedling root, already growing woody,
for their subsistence ; they bitterly resent the disturbance of this, and
very rarely re-establish. The type is of enormous range over all the
alpine chains, but varies to a certain extent in its forms—that of the
Mont Cenis being as conspicuously large and glorious and free as almost
everything else that hails from that marvellous if non-existent mountain ; while in the Dolomites, as a rule, *Dryas octopetala* is so squinny
and poor as hardly to be recognisable. Forms have been found, too,
with flowers double or semi-double, or with a second row of petals recurving, so as to give a cup-and-saucer effect ; while both the Engadine
and Monte Baldo have yielded a variety whose blossoms as they open
are of a very soft and shell-pink flush, which tends, however, to fade,
like other roseate hues of early dawn, under the fierce white light that
beats upon the garden. And hardly more than local developments
again are the other Dryads, *D. integrifolia*, which often appears under
its secondary name as *D. tenella*, Pursh—a pretty miniature of the
Royal Oak, with tiny leaves curling over at the edges, so as to lose
their scalloped effect, and with the delicate flowers on a scale to match
the plant ; and also *D. lanata* (sometimes *D. vestita*), another little
variety, differing not only in lessened habit, but in a coating all over
of *fine greyish down*. These are both as easy as the type, though much
smaller and neater, for a choicer place—*D. lanata* being rather the
more spreading of the two ; and much the same may be said in praise
of our own delightful form, *D. octopetala minor*, from Arncliffe Clouder,
a dainty Octopetala divided by half in all its parts. *D. Drummondii*,
however, is a disappointment, from the stony places of the Canadian

Rockies, where it forms mats and masses in the shingle, exactly like those of *D. octopetala*, except perhaps that the leaves are greener, and stand more erect. The most delirious expectations are roused by its habit, no less than by the knowledge that it has flowers of golden yellow; and are not damped by the profusion with which their hanging buds appear over the carpet. And then—nothing more ever happens; those flowers never open, never rise up to take the daylight on their golden faces. *D. Drummondii* is therefore a plant of no value in the garden; but Sündermann has lately sent out *D.* × *Suendermannii*, a hybrid of the most cheerful and vigorous habit, which ought to combine the vigour and rich wide saucers of its one parent, *D. octopetala*, with something of the golden colouring of its too coy and unmanly father, *D. Drummondii*. The whole family is of a pedigree and antiquity so dizzying that *D. octopetala* is even found as a fossil in the frozen heart of the world.

Drypis spinosa is a little branching, thorny-leaved bushling of vivid glossy-green leafage, for the hottest of dry places, where it covers itself in summer with small white flowers after the fashion of microscopic pinks.

E

Ebenus Montbretii is a woody-rooted Steppe-species, for a warm and stony corner, forming neat low masses of foliage (that endures for three or four years), and emitting in summer a profusion of round heads of purple pea-blossoms, richly clothed in longish hair. Not unlike an Astragalus, its cousin, either in look or needs.

Echeveria. See under **Cotyledon Purpusii.**

Echinocereus. See under **Opuntia,** for all the hardier Cactaceous possibilities.

Echium.—The giant Echiums of Teneriffe are gorgeous and tropical-looking splendours, usually monocarpous; but, though some of them prove hardy, they hardly come within the scope of the rock-garden, unless upon the boldest and highest ledges of the biggest, in warm and sunny parts of England. Such are *E. simplex*, *E. fastuosum*, and many more. But *E. albicans* from Spain is a hardy perennial from half a foot to 18 inches high, with handsome stars of rosy-pink that pass to a rich violet. For the one true rock-garden treasure that has ever borne this name, see **Lithospermum petraeum.**

Edraianthus has only minute barriers to separate it from Campanula and Wahlenbergia; for the sake of convenience we will here retain the name for the cluster-headed race that stands so close to **Campanula** in the Balkan region, leaving the single-flowered members of this group in the new name of **Wahlenbergia.** In this Adriatic range the Cluster-heads vary greatly, and there are probably not more than some three species in the whole list of names so copiously quoted by catalogues, synonyms having been recklessly multiplied, and a brief variation often promoted to specific rank. For these plants are, indeed, very much alike and very subtly to be differentiated; often, in lists for instance, four names appear, all separately described and priced, yet all in reality no more than vague varieties or synonyms of one species, *E. graminifolius.* One general picture paints the race— they all make rosettes of narrow leaves, from which radiate flopping stems bearing up bunches of purple Campanulas at the end; and all, though rather rank in look, somehow, are bright and useful and quite easy in any deep light loam and a sunny position. Seed.

E. caricinus, Schott, is a form lurking close to *E. tenuifolius*, DC., and *E. croaticus*, if not actually undecipherable. In any case it is a mere variety of *E. graminifolius.*

E. caudatus, Vis.=*E. dalmaticus*, DC. It has rather *broader leaves* than most, and the stems that lie about among them are *more or less bald*, only having a little down near the top. The leaflets or bracts under the flower-clusters are broadly egg-shaped and very much shorter—some three or four times—than the tubes of the purple bells themselves. (From sunny hilly places about Clissa, Salona, &c.)

E. croaticus may be doubtfully known by having its foliage only fringed with hairs at the base. This also belongs to *E. gramini-folius.*

E. dalmaticus (DC.)=*E. caudatus.*

E. dinaricus. See under *Wahlenbergia.*

E. graminifolius, L., is perhaps the best. Its leaves are all downy or even hairy, either smooth at the edge or sometimes with small glandular toothings, hairy underneath and bristly above. The bracts under the flower-heads are egg-shaped, but taper outward in quite a tail. The flowers themselves are of special brilliancy and opulence. This species occupies all the Dalmatian coasts, and takes a large number of variations, so that in the end it includes *E. caricinus*, *E. croaticus*, *E. tenuifolius*, &c., as mere varieties, though catalogues often treat them as species, whereas they are not even permanently definite varieties among themselves, but shading into each other in their several stations, and usually coarser in habit, smaller and dowdier in flower than the best form of the species (with other varieties, *australis*, *siculus*, *pusillus*, *elatus*).

323

E. Kitaebeli may be recognised on close inspection. For it is the only member of the family that in the bay of the calyx-lobes has, between each, a *little reflexing tooth of green*. The whole plant is itself of *bright-green colouring*, not greyish like the last, of which it otherwise looks like a larger and robuster form. (Hills of Croatia.)

E. niveus stands brilliantly out in the group as the most beautiful of all—though quite unknown in cultivation. Here and there on the ranges of Bosnia, limestone crops out among the granite : and there at once, upon the highest sunny peaks, appears a pure-white *Edraianthus*, with clusters of great velvety bells, smooth on the outside, flopping in their snowy bunches on violet stems, from the clumps of long narrow leaves most hairy at their ends. It is a very lovely thing, and perfectly distinct. Albinoes, apart from this—a true unvarying species —are extraordinarily rare, if not unknown, in the race.

E. Parnassi is an ugly Cluster-head, hovering between *Edraianthus* and *Campanula*, with rosettes of fringed leaves and a foot-high stem bearing a bunch of small purple bells in long calyces.

E. serbicus is a true species, growing *upright* about 7 or 8 inches —a *hairless* plant too, with clusters of purple bells about an inch long.

E. tenuifolius, DC, is probably no more than *E. caricinus*, Schott, and they are both certainly no more than poorer developments of *E. graminifolius*.

Eomēcon chionantha, the Poppy of the Dawn, is a beautiful Chinese Poppy-wort from Kwangsi, northwards from Hong-Kong, which is none the less quite hardy, and in any moist warm corner at the foot of the rock-work ramps prodigiously and even becomes excessive with its runners; the rather heart-shaped scalloped fleshy leaves of whitish-glaucous tone are very beautiful on their stems of some 6 or 8 inches; unfortunately these are usually the only stems the plant produces—being painfully chary, as a rule, unless specially well ripened, of its foot-high divided stems emerging from the sheathing leaf-stalks to carry four-petalled milky-white poppies of full rotundity and charm, like small versions of the white *P. alpinum*, in full summer.

Epigaea is almost a monotypic race, though with an Asiatic development. *E. repens* is the American Ground-ivy, quite common there, and often gathered up in its mats, and stored "down cellar" in trays of leaf-mould so as to be brought up at Christmas to delight the house with its creeping masses of rather ample oval roughish green leaves, amid which in clusters shine the waxy stars of pearl-pale blossom, exhaling a steady breath of the most delicious fragrance. It is not easy to get good specimens of *Epigaea* in England. For, like all of its kind and habit, it resents the mutilation of its woody roots, and is usually sent out from nurseries in small over-divided pieces, with no possibility of staying power. If, however, good sods of it are got from America the plant is still not always easy to make happy in England, requiring a light and leafy soil (which is easy enough), but being also so devoted to shade that nothing can well be too dense for it ; and in the end, the best chance of making it produce its flowers is to grow it in a place where there will be no possibility of your ever seeing them. However, in April and May, if not earlier, you will suddenly be made aware of them by their scent as you pass by. It is not easy of propagation either, coming grudgingly from seed, resenting division, and chiefly capable of multiplication by cuttings carefully struck in sand about the end of the summer.

Epilobium.—A most fearsome race of rampant weeds, usually either 5 feet high or perfectly flat upon the floor, but in all cases weeds of the worst, even when pretty. The Alps, however, give us two charming species for a stony place where they will be in no one's way. Of these *E. Fleischeri*, Hochst (*E. dodonaei*, Vill.), is very familiar in all the shingles of the alpine river-beds, which it fills with a haze of rose in August. This is a delicate branching plant, about half a foot or 9 inches high, set with fine dainty narrow leaves of glossy green, and bearing loose clouds of large pink crosses, between the petals of which appear the reddish vandyke-brown sepals, thus giving the star a special richness. This can only be acquired in its home by seed, as its root, woody, dark and devious, wanders so insatiably far down among the barren round boulders. Less commonly seen is taller, airily graceful *E. rosmarinifolium*, whose sheaves may be seen waving, for instance, among the red porphyry rocks in the bed of the Eisak, going up from Waidbruck towards the close-impending Schlern, and the rolling fields of villas at its feet. *E. rosmarinifolium* has tall plumes of narrow foliage topped with loose spires of blossom as brilliant as in the last. But here the roll-call of admissible European Epilobiums ends ; for no one is so temerarious as to admit *E. hirsutum* or *E. angustifolium*, in any of their forms of pink or white—at least if they have any wish or hope for future peace in the garden.

Of Dwarf Willow-herbs it is New Zealand that is especially prolific, our own not being worth the trouble of getting into the garden, though well worth the far greater trouble of getting them out of it again. The New Zealanders are prostrate rambling small plants, with flat and often glossy leaves, and sometimes rather pretty flowers of pink or white, uprising from the carpet. They thrive in any cool shady corner especially well, and seed themselves everywhere, but are not so impossible (being small and frail in habit) to tear away when doing harm. Perhaps the best is *E. vernicosum,* which runs along with shoots of specially leathery glossy little leaves, and then rears up at the tips to carry some three or five large flowers of nearly an inch across, almost sitting on the ends of the sprays, and of a soft pale pink. *E. crassum* also has large blooms, with leaves remarkably crowded, fat, thick, glossy, and fleshy ; *E. glabellum* is a copiously variable type, allied to *E. vernicosum,* but tending to have longer runners; *E. Macropus* creeps, and is wholly of a purplish colour, with slender stems, and pairs of rather distant leaves, while *E. purpureum* is wholly of a blackish purple, except for its flowers ; *E. pallidiflorum,* however, is a much taller species, growing erect, and with large white blossoms ; *E. Hectori* has a still more erect habit, but is only some 6 inches high, with narrower leaves, hardly toothed at all, and purple capsules ; *E. alsinoeides* creeps, with pale flowers near the end of the shoots, from the axils of the almost untoothed leaves, and followed by capsules clothed in greyish down ; *E. rotundifolium* creeps for a foot or so, with opposite sharp-toothed leaves that become alternate towards the end of the runners ; *E. linnaeoeides* is a miniature of this, quite prostrate, with all the leaves opposite and only one blossom to a stem ; while *E. gracilipes* is quite pretty, perhaps half a foot tall at the most, graceful in habit and nearly related to *E. Macropus.* And, finally, *E. flavum* is a North American species, not unworthy of admission, because, though tall and rather leafy, in the way of a smooth and much smaller *E. hirsutum,* its flowers, much the same in character, are of pale lemon-yellow. But the rock-garden establishes its claim to one species especially, and this is the really beautiful and gorgeous little *E. obcordatum* from the Sierras of California in Tulare County. This, from its high ledges, flounders forth in a mass of leafy shoots clothed in green rounded leaves, and ending in clusters of very large and very brilliant full-petalled flowers of glowing rosy-pink, in that tone which compilers of Rose-catalogues describe with such elegant tact as "satiny cerise." This rare choice treasure should have its birthplace remembered, and find itself accommodated accordingly with a sunny ledge in perfectly light deep stony soil, or moraine. It can readily be multiplied by August cuttings, and is itself at its best in July and August, forming a decumbent mass of shoots, 6 inches long at the most, concealed from view by the riot of those large and well-liking blossoms. It is quite hardy if not kept stagnant in winter, but is too soft and generous in nature to be of very long life, so that it is best to keep a stock perpetually going.

Epimedium.—The Barren-worts are all much of a muchness,

except in the colour of their flower-flights—plants of extreme but un-appreciated value for quiet shady corners of the rock-garden, where they will form wide masses in time, and send up in spring and early summer 10-inch showers, most graceful and lovely, of flowers that suggest a flight of wee and monstrous Columbines of waxy texture, and in any colour, from white, through gold, to rose and violet. Then, beginning later than these, appear the leaves, hardly less beautiful an adornment to summer than the blossoms to spring. For these are of a delicious green, much divided into pointed leaflets, and borne on airy wiry stems. Among the best of these delightful things—for our own *E. alpinum*, a stray in some of our North-country woods, is not eminent in the matter of its rather small dark-red stars of bloom, though the leafage is as beautiful as in all—are *E. pubigerum*, which replaces it precisely in the woods of Byzantium, but that the red flowers are large and evident and fine; *E. niveum* from Japan, very near the next (for all the Japanese species are at present in a dire tangle, which has led to a most unprofitable multiplication of synonyms in catalogues), but smaller, with waxy flowers of white; *E. macranthum*, notably handsome and tall and splendid, with large, long-spurred Orchideous-looking blossoms of creamy tone, with a variety, *E. lilacinum* or *E. violaceum*, of lavender tinge; *E. pinnatum* (or *colchicum*) from the Caucasus, with particularly handsome short-spurred flowers of bright yellow, dividing into two forms or sub-species—*E. p. elegans*, with straight, stiffer, tall spires of bloom; and *E. ochroleucum*, with stars of sulphur yellow. *E. diphyllum* from Japan is *Aceranthus diphyllus* (*q.v.*), a lovely little thing, while *E. hexandra* is **Vancouveria** (*q.v.*). *E. musschianum* and *E. musschianum album* had better be at present referred back to *E. niveum* and *E. macranthum*—*E. Youngianum* being also one of their synonyms; while not much more can be said as yet of beautiful waxy lilac *E. Ikariso*—a silly specific name indeed, being merely Japanese for the whole family. However, under whatever name you acquire an Epimedium, you may rely upon its always being of the easiest and most indestructible temper in any cool place; and also, except in the case of *E. coccineum* and *E. alpinum*, of the most astonishing and delicate loveliness alike in form and in colour of its dainty crystalline flowers in spring.

Ereica (in order, by keeping the right spelling, to get the pronunciation right—in place of the excruciating Erïca, that one so often hears). Of heaths for the rock-garden there are not many that need be troubled with, *EE. carnea, tetralix, cinerea, ciliaris*, and *Mackaiana* being those of prime importance. Among these the winter-blooming tendencies of *E. carnea* give it a quite peculiar value, to reinforce the already sufficient value of its fine foliage and brilliant flowers. There are white forms and better forms, and better forms even of the white (to say nothing of the fact that it grows in any soil and enjoys lime). The others, with their bells of amaranth, rose, or waxy flesh-colour, are chiefly asked for in low sunny stretches of sand or peat, where they may, when not busied with their own beauties, make themselves useful by acting as cover to lilies, daffodils, and other bulbs of medium growth whose loveliness never looks so serene or proves more impregnable to the changes and chances of the weather than when they are sprouting from some lax fine mat of the dwarfer heaths.

Erigĕron.—This Aster-like race (and, like Aster, attaining large sizes as well as small) can easily be known from the rival family. Look more closely at any purple Aster-flower—if the purple rays are in *one row only*, no matter how crowded, then the plant is a *true Aster ;* if those crowded rays are in several or many rows, then it is a *true Erigeron*, and as such a thing of general garden value quite equal to Aster, similar in habits and needs, and similar in times of blooming, except that Erigeron is usually rather earlier than Aster, and certainly leaves off sooner.

E. argentatus is by some authorities now called *Wyomingia*. It is, in point of fact, a beautiful Erigeron from the deserts of Colorado, Utah, and Nevada, forming densely clustered tufts of narrow spoon-shaped leaves all silver with a close coating of down, and then from these tufts arise many stems of some 4 inches or a foot high, each carrying one large broad-rayed violet Aster about an inch and a half wide. This should have a warm, well-drained, dryish place.

E. aurantiacus, a very well-known and handsome garden plant with orange flowers, which need not be at all out of place in the rock-garden.

E. compositus, sometimes also called *E. multifidus*, is a lovely little species of neat small habit, making a flattened tuft of tidy hand-shaped leaves, which are then slashed and cut into three lobes, and these again divided into more. The whole clump is inclined to be sticky, and is usually hairy, though sometimes almost smooth when older. The delicate daisies of palest lavender are carried solitary in summer on quite short stems of 2 inches or so. (For moraine or choice corner.)

E. concinnus is a rare plant of the Pacific Slope, with tufts of very narrow leaves clothed in long white hairs, and branching stems of some 4 to 8 inches, set with leaves, and carrying blue flowers about an inch and a half across.

E. Coulteri is like a leafy-stemmed great white- or mauve-tinged daisy, of about a foot high, in the damp mountain meadows of California, with blossoms lonely on their stalks, and narrow in the rays.

E. elatior may be only a variety of *E. grandiflorus*, a tall leafy affair with purple flowers, of some 2 feet high, from mountain stream sides in the Central Rockies.

E. flagellaris is quite charming, but spreads at a devastating rate, running about everywhere, and perpetually increasing its mats of downy grey leaves, from which spring the single-stemmed daisies of whitish purple on stems of 5 inches or so throughout the summer.

E. glabellus grows from 4 inches high to nearly 18 inches. The lower leaves are spoon-shaped, with foot-stalks, while the upper ones embrace the stems but leave off before they get to where it branches into a head of some half a dozen large lilac-purple Asters. All the leaves are untoothed at the edge, and all pretty nearly smooth, except for a fringe of hair at the edge. The flowers are very thick set with rays, having about a hundred, more or less.

E. glandulosus is found in the mid-alpine region of Wyoming, where, from a stout stock, tufted with thick hairy leaves, oblong spoon-shaped, it sends up a number of stiff leafy stems of some 6 inches or so, with flowers of reddish lilac as large as in the last (there is also a *major* form).

E. glaucus is possibly a synonym of *E. asper*, which, like the beautiful sounding *E. formosissimus*, is but annual or biennial. It is none the less a handsome plant, like a Samphire in leaf and habit, growing in the sea-rocks of California, which it adorns with its display of big starry violet daisies.

E. hybridus, Asa Gray, is a hybrid of *E. aurantiacus*, with flowers in varying shades of apricot.

E. intermedius is a fine species, emitting runners, and profuse with its noble large suns of clear lilac.

E. leiomĕris (sometimes called *E. spathulaefolius*), is one of the very loveliest, a neat and exquisite thing for the choicest of spots. For it forms a tidy tuft of bright-green spoon-shaped foliage, which is perfectly smooth except for a certain amount of hair, perhaps, on the stems; and then, among these, alone on stalks of 3 or 4 inches, spring the most beautiful daisies of a curiously delicate and translucent lavender-blue, wanly pale indeed, and yet pure and clear and radiant. (From the Alps of Utah to those of Wyoming, and in the choice bed or moraine a treasure of especial charm.)

E. luteus lives in the sandy banks of the Yellowstone, there forming matted clumps of very narrow ash-grey foliage, which send up a great number of stems not more than 2 or 3 inches high, each one of them carrying a single fine flower of pure pale-yellow, broad and short in the ray.

E. macranthus is a leafy thing from 2 to 3 feet high, with heads of blossoms not so large as its boastful name would import, but remarkably abounding in the number of their lilac rays. This is also known as *E. salicinus* and *E. platyphyllus*, an *embarras du choix* for a plant so little pre-eminent in beauty.

E. melanocephalus may be found in moist places and parks of Colorado and Wyoming—sending up from its clumped clusters of elliptic-oblong narrow leaves several stems of some 2 to 6 inches in height, each terminated by one large and ample violet blossom about an inch and a half wide. The plant may always be known by the dense black wool in which the cup of the flower-head is wrapped.

E. " mesa grande speciosus " is usually advertised as an Aster; under this congeries of names lurks a very obscure but handsome Erigeron, with leafy stems of 3 feet high, and abundant sprays of large violet Asters from June to August—a beauty of much brilliancy and value for bed or border.

E. mucronatus= Vittadenia triloba, q.v.

E. philadelphicus has no value—a running species with the usual leafy stems that so often spoil the effect of the bloom in Erigeron; and here the pinkish flowers are smallish into the bargain, and poor-rayed as so many of the European Erigerons.

E. pinnatisectus, however, is a beautiful high-alpine. The leaves of the basal tuft are slashed into nine or ten lobes, which in turn are sometimes themselves more or less cloven again into quite a ferny and plumed effect. These tufts are grey, downy at first, tending to grow more smooth; and the stems are few, 4 to 8 inches high, each stem carrying a single large violet-purple Marguerite about an inch and a half across.

E. poliospermum forms a crowded matted tuft of hairy fringed leaves about 2 inches long (especially hairy on their stalks), crowded upon the crowns, from which are sent up a large number of practically leafless stems of 2 inches or half a foot, each carrying a single portly purple flower.

E. pulchellus has the whole aspect and habit and flower of *Aster alpinus*, but here the flower-stems are not bare, but set with a few leaves that do not however continue near the flower-head. Moreover, the stems, though usually one-flowered, can enlarge their capacities to the production of three, or even as many as nine—wide suns of pale purple, with about fifteen rays to the bloom. The plant throws offsets, and its hairy (sometimes stickyish) leaves are spoon-shaped. This is also called *E. bellidifolius*, the leaves being obviously suggestive of a common Daisy's. In the descriptions of *E. pulchellus*, however, from the Alps of Asia Minor, the stature seems to be smaller, the number of flowers less, and their colour pinkish.

E. pulcherrimus (*Wyomingia*), a leafy tuft marked with yellowish lines, from which ascend stems of some four and a half inches, carrying large goodly Asters in a range of colour from white, through pink, to violet, the whole plant being clad in a down of close-pressed white hairs. (Sandy places of New Mexico, &c.)

E. radicatus, from the highest alpine regions of the Central Rockies, follows exactly after the lovely habit of *E. leiomeris*, making a little tuft of narrow spoon-shaped hairy foliage, from which springs a quantity of delicate lavender-blue daisies, alone on stems of 2 inches or rather more. This might also, with luck, be met with under the disguise of *E. Parryi*, *E. Scribneri*, or *E. vetensis*.

E. salsuginosus is a handsome rank species, almost best fitted for the border, growing about 2 feet high, and crowded with sprays of big narrow-rayed flowers rather fine and ragged in outline, of lilac-pink or white. The leaves are smooth and thick and perfectly untoothed, and the plant is found in the damp mountain region of the Central Rockies, &c., taking a specially beautiful high-alpine form called *E. s. glacialis*, and sometimes recognised as a species—quite dwarf, and with only one bloom to the stem. *E. angustifolius* is also very near this.

E. speciosus is smooth also, except sometimes for a few white hairs. It makes a woody base, from which arise a number of stiff straight stems of some 12 to 20 inches, set more or less in the embrace of narrow leaves, with leaf-like continuations down their stalk; the flowers are fine and large, about two and a half inches across, and lilac-blue. This has also been called *E. conspicuus* (Rydb.).

E. subtrinervis is much the same, but finely downy, with blossoms of blue or pink.

E. superbus.—A rather vague species, fading away into *E. salsuginosus* and *E. macranthus*, to both of which, in any case, it stands very near; its principal official differences lying in the usually undividing upright stems, the fewer, larger, more distant leaves (more or less fringed with hair), and the fewer but larger flowers in loose heads.

E. trifidus (*E. flabellifolius*, Rydb.) is a close cousin to dainty *E compositus*, of which it has the same foliage, habit, and flowers, but that here the leaves are rather fleshy and the whole growth hairy.

E. Tweedyanus (*Wyomingia*) is about 4 to 8 inches high, and white with wool when young, with narrow leaves and naked stems, each ending in a single broad white blossom. (From dry arid places in Wyoming.)

Other names of Erigeron there are, in strings; but almost always, unless certainly described to the contrary, it can be taken that most of them are leafy and undistinguished weeds of rank growth, or else, if matted and alpine, have but the dingy stodgy little flowers of our own *E. alpinus*, with the densely-crowded rays of dullish pinky tone, quite inadequate in length for the fat yellow disk, from which they do not even try to open out into a star, but remain huddled and close and bunched up. The race, it will have been seen, is a very large one, alike in the Old World and the New; but, while many of the New World species are big and leafy things, either dowdy or splendid in flower, it is from the New World also that the more precious alpines come, almost without exception, the Alps of Europe and Asia having wholly refused to let Erigeron anywhere come into rivalry with Asters of the alpine group, and so have restricted the race to the decent poor-cousin dowdiness of *E. alpinus* (as you will often see it on the highest slopes standing duskily in the background of Aster Alpinus, and by its own dinginess supplying the most dutiful of foils), whereas in America, Aster is already so dominant and diverse and overwhelming that the hills no longer consider it unbecoming for Erigeron to make some show on its own.

Erinacea pungens is so beautiful a little bush that no garden can lack it—a dense hedgehog of very long silver-green spines, about 5 inches high and perhaps a foot across. From this, in due time, emerge a few inconspicuous leaves, and then in early summer a cluster of large pea-flowers of the most entrancing clear lavender-blue, proceeding out of big baggy calyces all shaggy with silver fluff. This beautiful wee shrub, whose unfriendliness to the touch reserves such an amiable surprise for the eyes, is abundant on warm slopes and open earthy places, especially on the limestone, throughout the hills of Granada, Valencia, and South Catalonia, where it is known as the Piorno d'Azul or the Erizo. And notwithstanding its birthplace, Erinacea is perfectly hardy and happy into the farthest North in deep light soil, and in a hot exposure. It grows with decent slowness, but rooted fragments can occasionally be removed; and cuttings struck about midsummer and kept close for a while, develop readily into plants. Seed can, as a rule, only be got from its native land.

Ērinus, the Spring-flower; who does not grow *E. alpinus*, with its rosy forms, and its lovely albino that comes true from seed and sows itself with all the profusion of the type? The only other species is *E. hispanicus*, sometimes called *E. hirsutus*; this is a softer, laxer, hairier thing altogether, in a much lighter and more delicate tone of pink, with lines of brilliant crimson in the throat. This may be seen all over the South of Europe, and has established itself on the Roman Wall at Hexham.

Eriogonum, a strange race of most improbable-looking Rocky Mountain Umbellifers—woody and prostrate small bushes, with heads of flower in a large cup, often shaggy. There are a bewildering number of these, but the only one in general cultivation is *E. subumbellatum,* with heads of yellow; this thrives in the open in light peaty soil, and it is probable that many others of its fellow-countrymen will do the same, and should be introduced, if only for the neatness of their habit and carpeting tufts of oval downy leathery leaves gathered into rosettes or clusters at the base of the shoots. Among the others may be mentioned : *E. subalpinum,* near *E. subumbellatum,* with flowers and heads varying from white to deep purple, borne in lavish numbers on a mass of special density ; *E. flavum, E. niveum* (yellow-gold and snow-white heads respectively), *E. campanulatum, E. arborescens* (pink), and many another, idle at present to name, seeing that few are within reach, and still fewer deserving to be clutched at with any violent zeal, for after all they are an "interesting" rather than a brilliant race, suggesting clustered Everlastings more than Umbellifers.

Eriogyna pectinata is more properly known as *Spiraea, q.v.*

Eriophyllum, a race of American Composites of which *E. confertiflorum* and *E. caespitosum* are both worth growing in light soil and a sunny place. This latter makes large dense masses of low growth, with divided foliage, greyish-white with down, and then emits in June a profusion of flower-heads on shoots of about 6 or 8 inches, these flowers being big disks of rich yellow, surrounded at intervals by some eight broad and very short rays of much lighter tone, giving almost the effect of blobs round the circumference of the orbicular bloom.

Eritrichium.—In a race of dowdy and impermanent weeds lies lurking, like the precious jewel in the head of the toad, the Crowned King of the Alps, the Herald of Heaven, Woolly-hair the Dwarf. But in the vast family of Eritrichium we may first deal with the few other species that ask admission, before we go on to the huge aggregate gathering round that *E. nanum* of many years' devotion, which ought now to be called by its prior ridiculous name of *E. tergloviense.* The first of these is a really pretty little Himalayan species, *E. strictum,* which is none other than the plant now sometimes offered by catalogues as *Cynoglossum Wallichii.* This is, or should be, a sound perennial, with a woody base, that sends up many stiff straight 8-inch stems in summer with branching sprays, near the top, of lovely flowers, purely celestial, and making a fine effect against the close-ironed silver down in which the clump is vested.   It has a yet more lovely form than itself, *E. s. Thompsoni*, which is larger in growth and larger in flower, and silverier in complexion.   Then comes *E. Guglielmi* from Japan, charming in a daintier way, having a tuft of small upstanding oval leaves, from amid which rises a loose erect spike of blue stars about 6 inches high or more, the whole plant suggesting rather an Omphalodes (and, indeed, as in many Borragineous families, the separations of kinship are obscure, and Eritrichium, Omphalodes, Cynoglossum, and Paracaryum are all names that fade so subtly into each other as sometimes to be interchangeable and interchanged). *E. basifixum* is yet another high Indian alpine, making very dense clumps with one, or a few, erect shoots of some half a foot, dividing at the tip, and carrying blossoms of blue-violet.

Eritrichium tergloviense.—It is quite impossible, priority or no priority, that a name so limited and restrictive should apply to a species so vast and catholic as **E. nanum** that was.   The type is one of enormous range, not only high-alpine but Arctic, all along the great mountain ranges and frozen islands alike of the Old World and the New.   Almost every chain and every country has its Eritrichium, on the lonely and fearsome crests of the rocks, or lining the seashore of the Arctic Circle with its silver velvet cushions.   And all are offshoots or contemporary developments with the King of the Alps.   Of larger plants, however, less closely connected, Himalaya offers us *E. villosum, E. latifolium, E. sericeum,* all silver-silky high-alpine tufts of azure blossom, but less tight and close than *E. nanum,* suggesting rather *Myosotis rupicola.*   But of pure Nanum-cousins a representative will surely be found on every mountain system and on every island of the far North.   *E. persicum* hugs the topmost rocks of Elburs—a diminished *E. nanum* in its flower; in the Eastern Alps of Europe dwells *E. Jankae;* but the Roof of the World seems bare of true *E. nanum,* nor do we hear of it from its eaves, descending in range over range down into China ; but all are possessed by the larger forms and species already quoted.   In fact *E. nanum* is rather Arctic than alpine in its range, a strayed visitor in the high central chains of Europe and Asia, from the focus of its distribution along the fringes of the Arctic Circle. On Spitzbergen it carpets the low lands by the sea, and across Russia and Siberia go various forms.   *E. Chamissonis,* with broader, stouter leaves *never pointed,* hairier with whiter hairs, and overlapping on the stems, pervades the whole of Northern Asia, and crosses by the Aleutian Islands into America.   *E. aretioeides* has the same range but does not travel so far—a smaller, much tighter-tufted form, with narrower foliage and fewer flowers to the spray; but the American distribution is prolonged by *E. Howardii* in the high Alps of Colorado and Wyoming. This is a beautiful dense tuft with narrow spoon-shaped leaves clothed in short silver fur, and with larger brilliant blossoms. Rather smaller in the star, and much narrower in the foliage, and clad in long white hair, is *E. argenteum* from the same ranges, while *E. rupestre* in the Altai has specially narrow leaves in a close clump, and vested in a velvet hoar of tight-pressed silver hairs. And it is not easy to doubt, indeed, that one might almost as readily differentiate a fresh named species on each district of the Alps where *E. nanum* occurs.

Of this there is no need to speak, to those who have seen it; no profit, but vain temptation only, in speaking of it to those who have not. For no eye of faith is quite keen enough to gulp the whole glory of the King of the Alps, as you see those irresistible wads of silky silver nestling into the highest darkest ridges of the granite, and almost hidden from view by the mass of rounded yellow-eyed little faces of a blue so pure and clear and placidly celestial that the richest Forget-me-not by their side takes on a shrill and vulgar note. The blue of Eritrichium is absolute; lacking the tinny violence of *Gentiana verna's* sapphire satin, and the almost vicious intensity of *Scilla bifolia*, it has a quality of bland and assured perfection impossible to describe as to imagine. And still more impossible to believe by those who have only seen the comparatively rare and squalid stars of faded turquoise which are all that Eritrichium usually condescends to show in cultivation—if it ever condescend to reach that pitch of ostentatiousness at all. Eritrichium is *the* typical high-alpine, only to be seen with climbing and effort; it is the motto of the mountaineer, and the crown of achievement for the walker in the Alps, who will have trudged over leagues of Flannel-flower before once he catches sight of the King of the Alps, set in blobs of sky across the face of some dark cliff, or on some sunny slope of the highest ridges making blots of fallen heaven among the scanty herbage of the hill. Unlike another Arctic species of high-alpine distribution, *Ranunculus glacialis*, Eritrichium is comparatively rare in the central ranges of Switzerland—always a local plant, indeed, but almost always of the most generous abundance wherever it occurs. Only on the Southern borders of Switzerland will you begin to see its full beauty, and after that it grows steadily commoner and commoner as you go South and East, until in Tyrol you may almost always count on finding it wherever volcanic or granitic rock breaks up through the Dolomite. And, whereas in the main chains it is rarely found below

ERITRICHIUM TERGLOVIENSE.

9000 or 10,000 feet—as, for instance, in the Engadine, where the high granites of the Languard, Piz Ot, and the Rosegg are full of it—in the Southern ranges it will be met with at much lower elevations of seven or eight. Its Central European form is invariably calcifuge to the intensest degree, but there *are*, or have been, a few suspicious records of it on the dolomite of the Rosengarten, Pala, and Brenta groups; yet so violent is the plant's evident preference for granite or volcanic crag, so invariable one's own experience that on limestone it is perfectly useless to look for it, even in its own districts, where its occurrence on the granite close by may be taken for granted, that one had better verify such records of it on limestone for oneself before putting any confidence in them. I have been told, indeed, that in the Karawanken it is never found anywhere *but* on the limestone—a statement which gave me many a gulp before I could get it down, the more so as my informant had just pointed out to me *Campanula Bellardii* as *C. Scheuchzeri*, and had offered me plants of *C. pulla* under the name of *C. Morettiana*. Yet, with regard to the far Eastern Alps, the Balkans and Transylvania, judgment may be held in arrest; it is rather probable than otherwise that Eritrichium, in its determination to haunt the highest crests everywhere, must sometimes find itself obliged to put up with limestone. In the well-trodden ranges, however, it may be taken as *absolutely calcifuge*, all rumours notwithstanding.

In form I do not know that much variation can be established. It is peculiarly magnificent on the Angstbord Pass, and plants from thence appeared to possess a stronger habit than most. The beauty of it on the Col de Clapier, again, is such as to stimulate tired hearts far more than whole meals of alpine wormwood, but its results in cultivation have not been good. The most glorious of the stations known to me is also the most accessible—all along the ridge of Padon, above the level Bindelweg, from the motor-reached level of the Pordoi Pass, where it is in profusion so prodigal as even to make blue jewel-work in blots on the stone-heaps by the track side, while the unscaleable black cliffs overhead are filmed in August with a dim suggestion from far away, which when you draw nearer to their feet, may be seen to consist in myriad tufts of Eritrichium, blotches and splashes of sky adhering all up and down those dark and immune precipices. Here there was a white form of special size, with golden margins to the leaves; and yet another on the Passo delle Selle, where suddenly to your surprise, as you come up over the cold moor veiled violet with *Primula glutinosa*, you find the shallow summit-ridge ablaze with Eritrichium. From both these stations specimens have proved to have a fair resisting power—in some cases a quite remarkable resisting power.

PLATE 33.

ERYTHRONIUM REVOLUTUM ("PINK BEAUTY").
(Photo. R. A. Malby.)

VOL. I.   EDRAIANTHUS DALMATICUS.
(Photo. R. A. Malby.)

PLATE 34.

ERODIUM MACRADENUM.
(Photo. R. A. Malby.)

ERODIUM TRICHOMANEFOLIUM
(Photo. R. A. Malby.)

ERITRICHIUM TERGLOVIENSE.

Of verified records I can give (and give without scruple, seeing that the heights are so daunting, the distances so remote, and the abundance of Eritrichium when found so inexhaustible)—Piz Ot, Piz Languard, the rocks at the base of the Piz Rosegg (and general throughout the high granites of the Engadine); in Switzerland it is rare and local, chiefly confined to the Southern border, in the heights of the Valais, Angstbord Pass; Graian Alps—Col de Clapier, Malamott; Maritime Alps—Col de l'Arpetto (not apparently in quantities so great as usual); Dolomites—very abundant on all the high volcanic outcrops round the Marmolata, and more sparingly on the granites of the Rolle Pass; Bergamask Alps—quite sporadically on the Cima Torsoleto (the adverbs referring only to what my own eyes may have noted; possibly a quarter of a mile further along the same ridge the plant might cease altogether, or become profuse). Let no one blame me for not grudging to anyone capable of getting there, the sight of the most marvellous beauty that the Alps have to offer; it were better that all the ranges should become destitute of flowers (that at present, after all, unvisited by man, have to sit content in the admiration of marmots), than that one earnest seeker after a joy so pure should go hungry. Indeed, the cant on such matters is a little sickening; of what value to the world is a beauty's existence, if the world be not allowed to see it? And what is the point, and where the sanity or sentiment, in leaving the last three bulbs of a Tulip to moulder on some Macedonian mountain, where no one will ever have any satisfaction in their existence, rather than in bringing them home to rejoice everybody, including themselves, with a new lease of their life? This tiresome nonsense, indeed, is largely talked by those who never have seen such joys, and have a sentimental notion that some mysterious sacrosanctity attaches to the fact that no one else is ever to see them either. Humanity's ingrained snobbishness has an incurable passion for the arcane. Nor in any case need we fear that anyone will ever succeed in devastating the remote, high and difficult places where alone the King of the Alps holds his court. Even at the most hardened collector His Majesty laughs out with undaunted blue eye from his unassailable fastnesses, secure in his impregnability no less than in his astounding abundance. There is enough Eritrichium in one range of the Southern Alps for all the men and all the marmots ever made—and with plenty more left over for the gods to delight in for ever.

But the King of the Alps, when all is said and done, should be adored, not touched. He is so impossible of cultivation that to take him from his native crevices seems murder as clear as to bruise a butterfly in our hands—an act more certain to put the blue heavens (whence the plant has surely descended straight and undefiled upon our dusty earth) in a rage, than any number of robin red-breasts in cages. Impossible? yes, not impossible, with great pains and fusses, to keep alive, alone and palely loitering, in his pot or pre-pared nook; but impossible, indeed, to make anything but a homesick exile, impossible to inspire with the air of his lost hills amid our pallid temperatures, or fill his veins with the blood of blueness that he draws from the blasts of the wind-swept arêtes where he has his home. And yet, and yet—what gardener worth his salt will ever give up hope of a happy and hearty Eritrichium? Somewhere, somewhere in the world, on some strange mountain or penguin-haunted Arctic isle, there must surely be an Eritrichium, form or species, that shall prove of happier temper, and gratify the lucky gardener with the garter of his highest ambition. Indeed Eritrichium is more to blame than the collector, for it looks so happy, so indestructible and cosy in its crevice or sandy slope, that it does not seem possible for a mass so compact of blossom, so tidily rooted in a ball of fibre, to prove anything but as robust as it looks. The plant provokes the trowel. In cultivation, then, let us do the best we can, seeing that no amount of wise words will ever induce us to come empty-handed off a mile-long ridge, turquoised with round slabs of blue; let Eritrichium be *bone-dry* in light sandy gritty mould all the winter through, from September to March, and from that time onward let it be in a sunny moraine, or very morainy chipful mixture, with water flowing underneath. For it is not perhaps always realised how much water the root will not only take but actually demand throughout its growing period—so long as that water is not administered over the soft and silver-silky coat. Another point that is not realised is one that too much escapes the notice of those who cope not only with this but with other presumably difficult alpine species. Our natural first inclination is to put something rare and difficult into a rare choice place all by itself, where it cannot be invaded or worried by rivals. But this is precisely what the poor thing does not want; it misses in its loneliness the cheery society of the little grasses and weeds of the hills, that made company for it at home, gave its roots something to fight, something to carry off superfluous moisture and fatness, kept it going, in fact, with the interest and keenness of life which is always sure to flag, alike in plants and humans, under the system of too elaborate shelter and seclusion. So Erit-richium rarely if ever grows alone, and is always happiest and at his widest tuffets and broadest expanses of blue smile, if he is wrestling it out with the smallest and finest of herbage, Arenarias, Sedums, minute high-alpine Gentians, and all the little lovely fry that fill the upmost gaunt ridges with life. Never shall I forget the beauty and the luxuriance of Eritrichium on Malamott, for instance, where it not only had all this society to cheer it, but was threaded in and out everywhere in a wide carpet by the runners of *Phyteuma pauciflorum*, sending up its rich tufts of glossy green even through the silver of Eritrichium's cushions, and with its myriad fluffed heads of deep translucent violet making among the turquoise slabs of Eritrichium a colour-effect of such audacity as only nature could have conceived or carried out with success. But I fear it is long before we shall have that carpet in our gardens. None the less, let it be remembered that Eritrichium is not really by any means of desperate difficulty to keep alive and growing, if the various precautions here indicated are faithfully ensued; the real trouble with the plant is that, even if it lives, it can never be made really to seem happily at home, can never—like many another high-alpine—be induced to show anything to suggest the size, brilliance, and prodigality of blossom with which it delights the unobservant heavens on its own inhospitable ridges.

Erodium, a precious race very close to Geranium and Pelargonium, and of the highest importance in the rock-garden, where all its members require much the same sunny position and light deep calcareous loam, and all repay it by thriving on into fine clumps, and blooming right away through summer into autumn. The race is large, comprising many worthless plants, and many annuals or biennials; only one of these do I here mention. The entire family belongs to the South and its sunniest hills; it can not only be raised easily from seed, and propagated by cuttings, but can also be hybridised. *The hybrid Erodiums all follow at the end*, after the descriptions of their parents; for these, being divided into definite and marked botanical groups, may so most conveniently be taken in their order.

GROUP I.

All the species large-leaved *like indoor Pelargoniums*, and silky.

E. Gussonei, from South Italy, is a lush and leafy thing, with woolly ample foliage lobed irregularly in scalloped lobes, but roughly heart-shaped in outline. The flowers are rather numerous in a head on the top of a stout stalk, all the petals being equal, and the whole blossom of deep unspotted pink with darker stripes, very handsome. For all this group, keep in mind the fleshy stock, the stout habit, and leafage of a tender, sweet-scented Pelargonium, whose whole habit and head of flower its members recall.

ERODIUM.

E. guttatum is sub-shrubby, with stems simple or branching, and more or less leafy all the way up. The leaves are silky-downy, grey-green, oval heart-shaped, with rather faint fat lobes scalloped at the edge. The flower-stalks are some 3 inches long, carrying two or three blossoms equal to the last, pink but spotted. This is found all over the South Mediterranean range, with varieties *E. g. Malopo* and *E. g. subacaule*.

E. pachyrrhizon comes from Algiers and is therefore probably not of much use : it is like a taller *E. Gussonei*, but with few basal leaves and these soon dying.

GROUP II.

Same habit : leaves never silky.

E. asplenioeides has a fat stock, and all its leaves are huddled at the base, being of a long heart-shape, deeply lobed and scallopy-toothed, clothed in short pressed down with short woolly hairs on both surfaces, and with the two basal lobes often cut to the very stem. Up from among these rise the bare flower-scapes, from 2 to 7 inches in height, carrying some half a dozen blossoms or less, with the petals all equal in size, and their colour of violet-pink. (From Tunis to the Sierra Nevada.)

E. atlanticum, from Atlas, is much the same, but a good deal larger.

E. Gaillardotii, a very humble and quite dwarf flexuous weakling, with the stems dividing into two, and at times branching. The lower leaves are on long stems, oblong heart-shaped, and scalloped, but unlobed, while some of them are just cut into three lobes (of which the end one is much the largest and sometimes seems to have a foot-stalk of its own), and these lobed again into threes. The whole growth is hoary-grey, with heads of pale-pink blossoms (in the sunny rocks above Damascus).

E. montanum is yet more like a velvet-leaved Pelargonium, about half a foot or a foot high, and branching, clothed in glistering bristles, and with a great number of leaves at the base, fattish and heart-shaped. The flowers are purple-violet, with all the petals equal, and are carried in heads of six or eight. (West Algiers.)

E. pelargoniifolium, another leafy species, woody, and with many trunks and shoots. The leaves are long, heart-shaped, but pointed, and not deeply lobed, scalloped at the edge, and, like the whole plant, more or less clothed all over in glandular hairs. (From the lower mountain regions of Cilicia, with flowers as in *E. Gussonei*.) (*Bot. Mag.*, 5206.)

ERODIUM.

E. hymenodes is not very pretty, being yet more in the way of a scented-leaved Pelargonium with fat undivided leaves.

E. chamaedryoeides, however, leaps to quite the other end of the scale. For this is that lovely tiny species from the lower limestones of the Balearic Islands and Corsica which used to be called *E. Reichardi*, forming a neat mass, not an inch high, of minute dark scalloped foliage, in tufts and rosettes on its stalks, amid which rise up all the summer through innumerable pretty little white stars, each by itself on a stem of about half an inch or rather more. This treasure has a stout stock and a deep root ; as a rule, moraine proves too jejune, and it should be planted in a choice sunny ledge in generous depth of good light soil.

E. corsicum is not by any means so small, but forms mats and wide carpets of silver-downy, crumpled, scalloped leaves, among which sit the rose-pink flowers with all the petals of equal size, and veined delightfully with a deeper colour. The plant really makes a branching mass of stems, but its habit is so dense that nothing is seen of this but the close carpet of soft grey-velvet foliage, studded and jewelled with the numberless glowing blooms. This should also have a sunny, if lower and less choice place, and its running arms can easily be taken off in summer and struck as cuttings. Its only homes are in Corsica and Sardinia.

E. gruinum is the one annual or biennial species that shall here find a place, and this on account of its especial and remarkable beauty. For it is a frail tuft, with a few soft leaves, of heart-shaped general outline, but then very deeply lobed into fives or threes, the lower lobes often cutting nearly to the base, and all of them scalloped all round. From this slight tuft spring a few naked stems of 8 or 10 (or sometimes 20) inches, each bearing a single nobly large flower of violet, and not unlike a big Czar-violet in shape, but with an eye of darker colour. It may be seen throughout the whole Eastern circuit of the Mediterranean.

GROUP III.—ABSINTHOEIDEA

All the leaves slashed on each side to the leaf-stalk and then slashed again : all with true stems, branching and set with foliage (except one).

E. absinthoeides must, for its beauty's sake, be forgiven the perplexities that it has occasioned, alike to those who compile catalogues and to those who con them. For it is also *E. anthemifolium* (Marsh), *E. petraeum* (Sibth. and Sm.), *E. olympicum* (Clem.), *E. Sibthorbianum*

(Kotschy.), and *E. armenum* (Woronow)—any or all of these names appearing very often in the same list that has already described *E. absinthoeides*. Here the leaves usually form a smaller neat tuffet, their stems being about as long as they are, while they themselves are grey with glandless close-pressed downy hairs, and slashed and slashed again into a plume of rather narrow-pointed jags. The flowers, in loose heads on shortish foot-stalks, are notably large and handsome (the finest of the family), and notably variable in their range from white to pink and violet. The following varieties are all most beautiful, and all are apt to be treated as species in catalogues, to the confusion of the collector (*E. absinthoeides*, Sibth., and Sm., is *E. chrysanthum*, *q.v.*).

E. abs. amanum, very delicate and lovely indeed, much dwarfer and slenderer than the type, hoary with dense short white hairs, with a number of basal leaves, stems of 6 inches or so, and the most ample flowers of pure and brilliantly lucent white in a lax spray. (Akma Dagh in Northern Syria.)

E. abs. cinereum, taller, with stiffer stems to the flower-heads; greyer, and with the strips of the leaves *long-pointed* and *very narrow*. (Turkish Armenia, &c.)

E. abs. Sibthorbianum (*E. olympicum*, Boiss.), with the leaves almost silky, and then turning smooth, growing in a dense tuft, and in outline oval-triangular, but feathered into finer narrower strips than in *E. amanum;* but here again the stem is only about 6 inches high. Blossoms large as before, but rosy-lilac. (From Pontus, the Bithynian Olympus, &c.)

E. alpinum is the only plant in this group where there is *no true stem*, but the scape of the flowers springs directly from the stock. By this it may *always be known* in this section; and, from the next, by the *lack of any little lobule* between the feathering along the leaves. Very often it is not an inch high, this stem, and never exceeds half a foot or so, rising up amid a copious mass of leafage, and carrying heads of some two to nine violet butterflies more than half an inch across, with petals unspotted and of equal size. The leaves are narrow-oblong in outline, scantily clad in short hairs, and cut and cut again into rather broad acute jagged strips, sharply toothed along each jag, and with their foot-stalks densely woolly. (High Alps of the Abruzzi and the Roman Apennines.)

E. cedrorum (*E. Kotschyanum*, Boiss.) makes a many-headed trunk, sending up short and often branching stems of some 7 or 10 inches, set here and there with foliage, and dense with glands. From the stock itself springs a great number of basal leaves, hairy and egg-shaped in outline, feathered and re-feathered into jags more or less untoothed at the edge, and rather broad and bluntish. The blossoms in their loose heads are nearly an inch wide, white or purple, with the two upper petals *smaller than the rest*, and with a deep blotch of colour at their base. (Alps of the Cilician Taurus, &c.) *E. c. micropetalum* is a smaller-flowered white form.

E. chrysanthum is a very famous and coveted species, one of the finest and most distinct, rejoicing also in the synonym of *E. absinthoeides* (Sibth. and Sm.). It makes a specially beautiful wide tuft of feathered silver-gleaming leaves, gathered and crumpled most daintily, soft and velvety to the touch as to the eye; it then sends up the branching stems with here and there a small leaf, carrying heads of large blossoms in the most delicate *sulphur-yellow*, shining clear and pale above the spraying tuffets of that plumy silver foliage. It belongs only to the high mountain region of Parnassus, Kyllene, Taygetos, &c., and is the only one of its race to be a trifle capricious in some gardens, though really trustworthy and safe enough if only its corner be sufficiently sunny and its deep light soil perfectly drained, so that the trunk is secure against excessive wet in winter. It also varies in the amount of silver on the leaves, and a batch of seedlings will yield many degrees of beauty in this respect, and will also yield varieties of sex that help to explain the comparative rarity of the plant in cultivation. For it believes fatally in the separation of the sexes. One tuft bears only male flowers, another only female; unless you can have two such masses growing and flowering side by side, you will never get pregnant seed of the Erodium. On the other hand, if you do, such seed will germinate readily, and make good progress. Of the two sexes it is murmured that while the male probably is pre-eminent in the manly qualities of sober solidity, the female has the advantage in outward glitter and size and show.

E. Guicciardi; almost shrubby, with stems dividing into two equal branches and usually almost hidden among the basal leaves. These spring in lavish numbers from the stock, on stems as long as themselves; they are clothed in fine silky wool, and the strips into which they are feathered are narrow and rather pointed. It is a plant all gleaming with flat silver, about 6 or 8 inches high, with pink flowers of equal petals, and in size like those of *E. chrysanthum*, carried in loose heads of from four to seven, rather lost amid the excessive masses of the foliage. (Northern Greece.)

E. leucanthum is only about 6 inches high in all, with leaves cut into the *very finest* and most delicate of strips, and entirely clothed in short glandular hairs. The blossoms in their heads have equal petals and are white—but smaller than in *E. chrysanthum*, and smaller still than in *E. absinthoeides*. (From the Alps of Cilicia and Caria.)

GROUP IV.—PETRAEA

Flower-scape always springing straight from the stock : *no true or branching stem at all ; leaves gashed to the base on each side as in the last group, but always with a* secondary little lobe between the main strips. A group of small dainty treasures.

E. cheilanthifolium (*E. trichomanefolium*, Boiss.), which is found in the mountains of Southern Spain and Morocco, is the same in habit as these last four, but may be known by being *densely wrapped in hoary-grey down*. (*E. trichomanefolium* is evidently what usually passes for this in cultivation.) There is also a precious dwarf variety, *E. ch. valentinum*, which forms into perfectly tight mounded tufts barely half an inch high, of compressed leaves especially velvety with thick grey down. (High Alps of Valentia, Pico de Penagolosa, Sierra de Javalambre, &c.)

E. Choulletianum is a more remote and doubtful species from Oum Settasini, Algiers—the same in habit as *E. macradenum*, but with the finely-feathered foliage vested on both surfaces in dense pressed-down short hairs. The flowers are reported violet and equal-petalled.

E. macradenum differs in the first place in being *wholly green* and *smooth, glandless and bald*—except sometimes for a few spreading hairs. The leaves have the same finely ferny design, but here the pink blossoms with their pointed-oval petals have the two upper ones *smaller than the rest*, and freaked with a most dainty black blotch of radiating darkness which gives each delicate-veined pale flower a most ingenious and fascinating expression of innocent worldliness. (From the high limestones of the Pyrenees.)

E. petraeum.—Two- to six-inch stems, weakly ascending, and carrying, on fairy-fine foot-stalks, two or four spotless pale flowers with equal petals veined with deeper pink. The leaves spring only from the base and are very numerous, with stalks about half again as long as themselves, softly hairy. They themselves are more or less hairy and downy on each face, with a toothed lobule between each of the main lobes, which are narrow-oblong and lobed again. (From the high limestone rocks of the Upper Pyrenees, Narbonne, Montpelier, &c.) **This whole Section, in fact, stands throughout as the upper-alpine development of the last, dwarfer accordingly, and without true stem.**

344

ERODIUM.

E. pet. viscidum is a sticky variant of this. *E. pet. lucidum* is a smoother bluey-grey one. *E. pet. crispum* is a specially curly-hairy one.

E. supracanum is a species of the rarest loveliness, having flat foliage, rather like those of the last, not crimped and feathered so much as in some, and all overlaid with a plating of the most delicate silver. They are very nearly hairless too ; and above them come 4- to 6-inch flower-heads on bending stalks, in the most delicately contrasting beauty of bright unspotted equal-petalled pink butterflies, fine and round. This is only found on the Montserrat and neighbouring hills.

E. trichomanefolium is all densely clothed in glands, *green and downy*, otherwise with the fine foliage much as in the last. The flowers, in heads of some three or seven on stems of about 8 inches, are likewise equal-petalled, spotless and pink ; but they do not quite so far exceed the calyx, and they are veined with deeper colour. (High places of Hermon and Lebanon—with an albino form.)

GROUP V.

Same habits, but no lobules *between the featherings of the leaves.*

E. astragalocides, *E. daucoeides*, and *E. carvifolium* are species of no worth as compared with the rest, their pink blooms having a tendency to remain shut up in a closed cup-form, instead of opening out.

E. Manescavi is a large coarse rankness universally known in gardens and rather showy, though of small attraction, with jungles of aromatic stickyish green ferny foliage, long and large, and large flowers of a heavy flaring magenta-rose. It is a comfort to learn, then, that this is not typical *E. Manescavi*, but its variety justly named *luxurians*. The true or type-plant sounds much more to be desired. For *E. Manescavi genuinum* or *supinum* is quite a neat dwarf thing, not more than some 6 inches high or less. Nor should this be unattainable, as all the forms of this species are native to the Pyrenees.

E. romanum (*Bot. Mag.*, 377) ; stemless, with the stalk of the flower-heads rising some 6 inches or so, carrying a head of half a dozen blossoms of fine bright pink on delicate foot-stalks. The whole clump is hoary to the point of silveriness, and the leaves are cut to the base in simple fat undivided lobes. There is a yet hoarier variety, *E. r. canescens*, with longer foot-stalks, and foliage more deeply lobed. (All round the Mediterranean basin.)

E. rupicola, very near the last indeed, but with rather larger blossoms, and all the plant downy-glandular, but rather green than grey, and the leaves not only cut into lobes, but those lobes cut again into more. (Sierra Nevada.)

E. tataricum is exactly like beautiful *E. supracanum* (allowing for the essential difference between the groups), but the leaf-stalks of the dead leaves remain attached to the stock, and form, in the end, a sort of chevaux-de-frise all round its base. The flower-stem is 3 or 4 inches high, carrying from two to four blooms in a head, and these have the petals *unequal*, instead of equal as in *E. supracanum*. (Dahuria and temperate Asia.)

HYBRIDS OF ERODIUM

E. absinthoeides × *E. macradenum* is a common garden hybrid, rather taller than its parents, and with flowers of paler pink. Nor is it to be doubted that each year will bring us more and more named mules in this race, such as painfully soon to put our tale of them out of date. Few, however, if any, will beat their best originals.

E. "Crispii" appears on a list as being a hybrid of *E. absinthoeides* and *E. chrysanthum*; but, as the Crispine *E. absinthoeides* is simply *E. chrysanthum* under its secondary and invalid name, the result should merely be *E. chrysanthum* again, perhaps improved.

E. × *hybridum* = *E. Manescavi* × *E. daucoeides*, and comes near to *E. Manescavi*, but that the flowers are smaller, and fainter in colour, while the leaves are finer and fernier.

E. × *Kolbianum* (Sünd.) = *E. supracanum* × *E. macradenum*. It is a most beautiful plant with ash-grey laxer leaflets than in *E. supracanum*, and the flowers not pale-pink but varying from white to the softest shell-colour, veined with lines hardly deeper than their ground.

E. × *lindavicum* (Sünd.) = *E. chrysanthum* × *E. absinth. amanum*, and has kept the broader leafage of *E. chrysanthum* and turned *chrysanthum's* yellow to an obscurer note.

E. Willkommianum (Sünd.) = *E. cheilanthifolium* × *E. macradenum*, and has yielded an intermediate result, with the leaflets larger and hairier than in *E. cheilanthifolium*, but not quite downy.

Erpetion reniforme has gone back to *Viola reniformis, q.v.*

Ervum gracile = Vicia unijuga, *q.v.*

Eryngium.—Setting aside the giant species, best fitted for the border, and adequately described in any catalogue of such things; setting aside also the terrible species from America which are best fitted for the hot and stony wild garden (where their tropical-looking foliage, like the tusk of a sword-fish, may have its splendours, and not be disgraced by the ensuing dingy heads of blossom enclosed in a cup of pointed bracts like some Protea or an Artichoke gone mad)—it is important for the rock-garden to know which species will best suit its style, and, more important still in one case, which is which. For beautiful *E. amethystinum* is often sent out under the name of the much more beautiful and much rarer *E. alpinum*. But the two are very easily known apart. Look down from above upon the hard sugar-loaf of blossom enclosed in its wide-spreading frill of steely blue : if that cup be handsomely but thinly starry, with long spiny bracts rather broad and stiff and solid, and owning a toothing here and there, then the species is *E. amethystinum*. But now what a change. Look down upon the next : here the frill is double, treble, quadruple, and each bract is toothed again and again into long thorny-looking spines of its own, until the whole effect is that of a blue lacy collar of richness unparalleled. This is the only, the unsurpassable *E. alpinum*, a plant of the mid-alpine limestones, scattered locally here and there along the mountain chains, nowhere in any great quantity, though common enough in the small limited stations where it occurs. But in nature, accordingly, it is a prize of such preciousness that it should neither be dug nor picked—even if its root did not forbid the one crime, and the hope of seed dehort from the other. It is indeed a superb and uncanny splendour of some foot or 18 inches high, blooming through the later fullness of summer, and, like all its kind, perfectly happy in the rock-garden in any very deep loam. No other, following, can compete with this, except its peer, *E. giganteum*, of nearly a yard high, from the Caucasus, with much the same frill, but here of an ivory-white so ghostly-clear that the plant is called Elves' Bones. For the rock-garden, too, is fitted rare and lovely *E. Spinalba* from the Southern European ranges, about 18 inches high, firmly spinous, with stems and frill of a silvery pale grey-blue fading into white. But for places of choice, even in the very foreground of the rock-work, there are two species of front rank to match. Of these *E. prostratum*, in our gardens, forms a quite small central rosette of thin oblong green leaves, sparingly toothed and wholly unarmed, from which lie out upon the earth in a star all round short prostrate stems of 3 or 4 inches, with flowers and frills of a beautiful blue. This is sometimes treated with tenderness, and felt to be impermanent, if not a biennial, even when grown in good rich ground on sunny exposures. In point of fact, this is a bog plant from Texas, and in *damp places* should make a running carpet, rooting as it goes, along all its ground-hugging branches. Quite different from this is the last Eryngium with which it is at present necessary for the rock-garden to concern itself (though there are many others to supply a full collection).   For in the high dry open places, between 8000 and 11,000 feet up in the Sierra Nevada of the Old World, dwells *E. glaciale*, the neatest, finest, and most unfriendly of little thorny tuffets, armed in copious spikes of silvery grey, deepening towards shades of blue, with fish-bone spines of ivory glinting as its stems of 3 or 4 inches unfold towards the frill and the flower.   This, indeed, is thankful for open very deep soil in the fullest sun and with perfect drainage, where it grows on happily into a clump, and may be raised from seed, having, like all its kind, a root so heroic and profound as utterly to discourage division or removal.   It blooms in summer.

Erysimum, a most valuable race of Cruciferous beauties from the Old and the New World alike, which have by now absorbed almost all the more worthy species that used to shelter under *Cheiranthus*.   In constitution these are all quite good, but sometimes have the impermanence with which pious Cruciferae (if beautiful) have a special way of reminding us that the good things of the world are specially transitory.   (Bad Cruciferae, on the contrary, make a pride of being as eternal as sin or folly.)   They should all, then, have a perfectly well-drained crevice or comfortable moraine, in full sun ; and all, to make sure of them, should annually be multiplied, either by their abundant seed or by cuttings.   Their blooming time is early summer.

E. aciphyllum makes a tuft of long, stiff, almost pungent grey leaves in a dense clustered tuft, sticking up and out on all sides like those of some miniature Agave.   Up rises then in the midst an almost bare stem, carrying yellow flowers of medium size.   (Cadmus in Caria, Tmolos, &c.)   *E. leptophyllum* differs only in its hairs, which are simple, and not, as here, split each into four.

E. Allionii= *E. Perowskianum.*

E. alpestre has also medium-sized flowers, and is a densely leafy tuft of 4 or 5 inches.

E. amoenum.   See under *E. Wheeleri.*

E. Aucheri (*E. pulvinatum*, Gay), creeps about among the high-alpine screes of Northern Persia, there forming neat mats of hoary cushions with the grey rosettes that emerge from the end of each sublapidary runner.   The flowers are in heads of three or six, of medium size.

E. australe (Gay)= *E. longifolium, q.v.*

E. Bocconii grows from 8 inches to 2 feet high on the hills of Portugal, and has large yellow flowers.

E. boryanum is also *Cheiranthus Parnassi*, a grey-hoary tuft from which spring a number of gracious almost undividing stems, with loose spires of pale-yellow blossom, variable in colour and size.

ERYSIMUM.

E. caespitosum comes from Northern Persia, and forms most fascinating dense grey cushions, almost shrubby, with stems of some 4 to 6 inches carrying heads of immense lemon-gold flowers as in *E. helveticum.* There is also a variety of this called *E. c. brachycarpum.*

E. canescens, from Southern Europe, is only about 2 inches taller, with stars of similar colour.

E. comatum has very long and very narrow greyish leaves, splayed out in a wide and most elegant rosette ; the 10-inch spike comes up in the middle, and does not do it so much honour, for the flowers, though large, are thin and floppety, alike in texture and arrangement ; while their tone is rather a starved-looking lemon-yellow than the fervent orange that pictures sometimes present. (Balkan States.)

E. deflexum is a most tiny plant from the Kongra Lama Pass, some 15,000 feet up on the Roof of the World. Its hoary little leaves are only about half an inch long, and its twigs bend down to hug the inhospitable ground, and there end in smallish blossoms of ochreyellow.

E. dubium, Suter, is the valid name of *E. ochroleucum.*

E. elbrusense, on its eponymous mountain, mimics *Alyssum montanum* in golden heads, from a densely hoary tuft of quite narrow foliage.

[*E. filiforme.* See under *E. linifolium.*]

E. gelidum is like the last in habit and blossom and stems of only an inch or two in stature, with flowers of the same orange-gold. But here the hoary leaves are oblong spoon-shaped, and the lower ones have longish footstalks of their own. There is a variety, *E. g. Kotschyi*, which is even more minute and close and dwarf and delightful.

E. helveticum is usually taken as a mere stunted variety of *E. longifolium.* It occurs on the warm slopes in open places here and there, in tufts of narrow grey-green leaves, and then heads of large clear-yellow blossom on stems of some 8 inches or so, beset with foliage.

E. Hookeri will be found treated under its less correct name of *Cheiranthus Griffithii.*

E. Kotschyanum has huddled dense tufts of especially narrow palegreen leaves running to a point, and toothed or often rolled over at the edge ; from this rise stems of a few inches, carrying a few splendid blooms of orange-yellow in a loose head. From the high screes of Asia Minor in Lycia, Caria, Pisidia, &c. There is a tighter-tufted alpine form still, *E. K. rupicola*, not more than 2 or 3 inches in the stem, from the Cilician Taurus; and yet another, *E. k. Jacomellii*, from the Bithynian Olympus.

E. Kotschyi. See under *E. gelidum.*

E. linifolium grows into a branching bush often of 2 feet high in the dry cliffs of the Serra de Estrella in Portugal, where it makes a noble sight with its big purple blooms. But its usual habit is rather to be creeping and procumbent, with most graceful stems of 5 inches or so, delicately ascending from the mat, well above the narrow green leaves. And there is also a variety yet more especially to be craved for the rock-garden; being *E. l. filifolium*, a minutely-tufted dense alpine form, with undiminished lovely flowers. The type itself, however, is sufficient of a delight, requiring the very hottest, poorest ground on pain of proving itself less than a perennial, but there developing promptly into a wiry little mass about a foot across, which never ceases producing its flowers of strong cold lilac from spring right on into the winter, unperturbed by frost or snow or rain.

E. longifolium (*E. australe*, Gay) has something of the habit of *E. linifolium*, but is rather more erect, and with flowers smaller than in *E. dubium*, but of much brighter yellow. It is the larger type of which *E. helveticum* is the more mountainy development. General in the Alps; note that in this the narrow, grey-green leaves continue up the stems, which will usually be about a foot high.

E. mutabile is an attractive beauty, forming into grey cushions of oblong spoon-shaped stalked leaves with very fine and frail flopping stems set with foliage, and not more than 2 or 3 inches long, ending in a head of some two to five good-sized blossoms, which vary from citron to violet. (From the high screes of Lassiti in Crete.)

E. nivale (*E. radicatum*, Rydb.) grows only about 3 inches or half a foot, sending up many stems from a centralt uft of green and narrow foliage. The flowers are handsome, nearly an inch across. (Lower alpine regions of Colorado.)

E. ochroleucum is the younger and less correct name of *E. dubium*, Suter. This is a quite well-known, useful thing, forming large low loose cushions of grey-green narrowish-leaved rosettes and shoots, sending up spikes of pale lemon-yellow almost all through the summer, sweet-scented, and passing into straw-colour as they fade. The species is not uncommon throughout the Alps, and, though not choice, is useful for a rough sunny place where big procumbent masses of leaf and flowers are wanted.

E. odoratum (*E. carniolicum*) is a fragrant biennial, with large golden blossoms on erect stems above a rosette of toothed green leaves.

ERYSIMUM.

E. pachycarpum makes a stout growth at high elevations in Sikkim and Tibet, branching, erect, and 18 inches or 2 feet high, with spikes of orange-yellow.

E. pallidum, in the alpine rocks of Lycia, has the habit of *E. alpestre*, growing about half a foot or less, with medium-sized flowers of pale yellow.

E. × *Perowskianum* is the garden hybrid usually known as *Cheiranthus Allionii*, a beautiful but almost biennial impermanence in many places, with loose spikes of very dazzling orange-fiery flowers—though not, in habit of 9-inch or foot-high stems, particularly well suited to the standards of the rock-garden.

E. pseudocheiri is an obscure species, with big yellow blossoms, a dwarf close habit, and grey leaves crisp with curly fine down.

E. pulchellum can grow from 1 to 2 feet high, and it can also earn its name for daintiness by not exceeding 2 inches. It makes a tuft or mat of oblong spoon-shaped leaves, deeply toothed, with the end lobe the largest, while the narrower stem-leaves are also sharply toothed. The flowers are brilliant, of an intense and flaming orange-gold. The variety *E. p. microphylla* of this species, an alpine form from the Bithynian Olympus, is dwarf, and has *untoothed oval* foliage : it has also been called *Cheiranthus rupestris*. There is yet another dwarf toothless form, *E. p. Calverti ;* and *E. pectinatum* from Taygetos, &c., differs chiefly from the species in being hairy and carrying its pod perfectly erect instead of in a rather spreading fashion.

E. pumilum is one of the most beautiful of all. It may be seen in sunny dry slopes of the Alps (but not in Switzerland), as for instance on the gypsum dunes of the Mont Cenis, making quite frail tufts of narrow green foliage, and then sending up inconspicuous stems almost entirely bare of leaves, and only 2 or 3 inches high, which carry a wide head of bright pale refulgent-yellow blossoms so enormous for the plant as wholly to conceal the stem that carries them, and the clump of leaves from which they spring. All over the flowery ups and downs its wide domes of clear living light stand definitely out among the commoner yellows, like patches of living moonlight in the broad day. Nor does it fail of similar loveliness in the garden, but should be kept starved in the moraine, lest its stature exceed the alpine limit. It may always be known, if there were any doubt, from *E. helveticum ;* in the first place it is *never found in Switzerland ;* in the second it hardly ever has any, and then only a few, *leaves on the stem*, whereas *E. helveticum* always has a good many ; in the third, that stem is far shorter, the whole plant dwarfer, and the flowers of incomparably fuller size and splendour and refulgence of calm colour.

ERYTHRAEA.

E. purpureum, however, far away on Lebanon and Hermon, runs it close in the race of charm, and bids high for the prize, with its blossoms of sad and lovely purple. It is quite a low species, often rather procumbent, and making an almost shrubby growth, with shoots from 3 to 6 inches long, and the lower leaves feathered almost to the base in backward-pointing barbs.

E. rupicola. See under *E. Kotschyanum.*

E. strophades is an obscure but much-desired Mesopotamian, shining silvery, and with many stems of rather more than half a foot, carrying flowers that vary from pink to white.

E. thyrsoeides unfortunately has biennial habits, but is worthy of praise for its especially dense rosette of long narrow silver leaves, from which arises a pyramid of golden flowers as large as Wallflowers, clothed in blossom to the very base. (Dry alpine regions of Asia Minor.)

E. Wheeleri carries our hopes to Utah, where it makes masses of rough and narrow grey foliage, clumped in a cluster of clumps or in a single one, according as the stock itself is simple or branched into many crowns. These all, then, send up stems of 6 inches or rather more, or a little less, and the large blossoms in which they terminate are unable to make up their minds which colour they are going to prefer. For they begin with brilliant orange, and then, getting bored with this, turn from brown into bright rose, and so on into rich purple, ending up, like so many varied careers, with a pallid return to their first choice, in the form of soft pale yellow as they fade.

Erythraea, a lovely race of small Gentians, neat in habit, about 6 inches high or less, in tidy clumps, with small glossy leaves hidden by a profusion of bright waxy rose-pink stars in later summer. They are all, however, of either rather tender or biennial temper or both: and should occupy cool peaty soil or light loam, not droughty, but in full sun. There are many species, all very much alike: such as *EE. chlöodes, pulchella, spicata, grandiflora,* &c.; but perhaps the best, where all are good, is *E. Massonii*, which passes always in catalogues under the name of *E. diffusa*, a specially neat, brilliant, massive, and free-flowering little beauty from Corsica.

Erythrochaete palmatifida=Senecio japonicus.

Erythronium.—The Dog's Tooth Violets are among the most precious and exquisite things for spring flowering—not by any means duly realised in gardens, where *E. dens-canis*, very pretty, but the least striking perhaps of all, is often the only one to be seen, and that only because it survives from the enthusiasm of Parkinson's day. But there are many more species and garden seedlings, all of the most invaluable grace for cool choice corners of the rock-work. America too has sent us a number of species that not only have flowers in shades of cream and white and gold, but also carry two or three of them at rare distances on a stem of perhaps 8 inches or more, and contrive to look as if they had seen the unknown Queen of all Martagon lilies passing by, and had faithfully remembered her beauty. These should be planted in autumn, about 5 or 6 inches deep, and then left alone for ever. Catalogues deal copiously and faithfully with the species and their varieties and hybrids in cultivation ; those of *EE. revolutum, Howellii, Johnstoni, californicum,* and *grandiflorum* being perhaps the best, yielding delicate wide Turk's-caps in the loveliest soft shades of pink and cream. *E. montanum,* a rare and not so easy Californian species, should have flowers of pure white : the common golden *E. americanum* rejoices more than the rest in full sunlight ; while of especial beauty is the specially tall and uncommon *E. Stuartii,* a hybrid of graceful stature about a foot high, with spreading and revolving pendent flowers of cream and sulphur hanging high over the glossy marbled foliage of silver and brown.

Euphorbia fills corners ; not a race of any lovableness, though it has its uses. But the place of this vast and poisonous family is rather in the hideous deserts of the world, which they make more hideous and unhomely yet by pretending to be Cacti—as if anybody, anyhow, no matter what the stress of sand, would want to eat their venomous flesh, or drink the deathly white milk of their envenomed blood. However, enthusiasts and catalogues sometimes tell us of Euphorbias, big and little, that lend value to high hot places or low worthless ones. Magnificent is huge and tropical-looking *E. Wulfeni,* indeed, and many others that follow in its train, and so often bear its name, that it is not always easy to procure the true species. Milder, in the same style, is *E. polychroma,* with conspicuous heads of yellow : our own rare native *E. pilosa* might well be included ; and there is no lack of other large bushy species. Of smaller ones, another native, or semi-native, *E. Cyparissias,* rambling about everywhere and a most voracious weed, is yet not valueless for the roughest and remotest gravelly places, which it occupies with its fine 10-inch sprays of dainty narrow foliage, even as it occupies the stony banks at mid-regions on the Alps. But much more choice and even precious is *E. Myrsinites* from Corsica, creeping along with stems of 6 inches, set with thick blue-grey foliage and heads of yellow; *E. capitulata* from Dalmatia is another dwarf running plant, and can be multiplied by cuttings ; *E. epithy-moeides* recalls *E. polychroma,* but is very much smaller, dwarfer, and neater, with golden heads ; it is not a synonym of *E. polychroma,* but quite distinct. And there are others still smaller and tidier : but all of them are poisonous, alike to eye and taste.

Eustoma Andrewsii is the one (by courtesy, and the benefit of the doubt) hardy species in that noble Gentian-group which yields our hothouses Exacum and Lisianthus (*E. Andrewsii* has sometimes borne the name of Lisianthus). This glory is found in Colorado, sending up a crown of smooth glaucous blue-grey oval leaves from the rather fleshy roots ; and then, from these, a number of stems from 4 inches to about a foot high, simple below but sometimes branched above, and bearing sprays of the most gorgeous violet flowers, starry cups of nearly 2 inches across, each on a long stem of its own. And meanwhile the provident plant has also prepared its clump for next year, which lurks at the base all through the winter as an evergreen rosette. So far this species has hardly if ever been successfully grown here ; it should probably have a peaty gritty mixture, very loose and deep and strong, with abundant moisture in summer, and perfect drought in winter, in a warm and sheltered corner.

Exarrhena. See **Myosotis.**

F

Falkia repens is a tender and useless little plant from the Cape which has been most rashly proclaimed a treasure.

Farsetia.—*FF. clypeolata, eriocarpa, lunarioeides* are large yellow-flowered Crucifers, with velvety white leaves and fine flat fruits, for walls and hot worthless places ; the best of the Europeans, perhaps, is *F. triquetra* from Dalmatia. But *F. suffruticosa* carries us to different realms and merits ; for this is a high-alpine of extreme beauty, from Elburs and Russian Armenia, forming a clump of narrow foliage, from which rise many stems, simple or sparingly branching, with spires of very large and brilliant violet flowers. And another species that may have charm is *F. pendula*, which seems to make a specially dense silver-hoary tufted bush of 3 inches high or so, somewhere, probably, in Persia. The big species are rather weeds.

Felicia petiolata is a lush and worthless weed, flopping rankly about, and set with insignificant minute and pinkish daisies. But *F. abyssinica*, if it can only be prevailed on to prove hardy, is a most lovely small bush of a foot or so in height, like a miniature and wire-drawn Rosemary, stiff and dainty and fine, emitting all the season innumerable delicious little daisies of softest lilac-lavender, as it were blossoms of *Bellium rotundifolium*, powdered over the mass. At first its seedlings seem resistent and hearty : in any case it should have a specially warm sheltered place in light well-drained soil.

Ficaria.—There is a finer Celandine than our own in Spain, *F. grandiflora*, sometimes called *Ranunculus ficarioeides ;* there are also double forms and rather presumptuously named white forms (that have really only lost the gilding and gone pallid) of our ordinary plant ; and there are a few other species too, all of the same kidney, and all neat bright things for admittance to a cool corner, where nothing better is wanted, and where their metallic glitter may cheer the dawn of the year.

Fragaria.—There are countless strawberries, ramping running weeds in every degree of merit ; but by no means the worst, when all is said and done, is *F. vesca* in its varieties, if any waste corner is to be carpeted. Exactly similar is *F. indica*, but that this has yellow flowers and its luscious-looking crimson strawberries are a delusion and a fraud. The handsomest, however, is the wildly rampant *F. Daltoniana*, with glossy dark foliage and fine white blooms—a valuable cumberer of the ground, so long as it does not cumber it too much, and become as pervasive a pest as *Potentilla reptans*.

Francoa.—The Bridal Wreaths verge upon being hardy in a sheltered warm corner, but are best, and best-suited, in the greenhouse, where their towering tails of pinky-white seem most in character, and are most tranquilly displayed.

Frankenia laevis, our own common Sea-heath, is the best of its race for the garden—a useful little plant to carpet the ground, with its minute neat foliage and pretty pink stars, in any place that asks for covering by something not of great importance. On sunny banks in goodish soil it should serve admirably as a cover for Crocus and other bulbs.

Frasera speciosa lies in so calling itself. For in reality it is an ugly thing, rather like a Swertia with greeny-white flowers. It comes from North America, loves shade, hates lime, and grows a yard high.

Fritillaria.—A lovely race, but adequately coped with by catalogues of such delights, except that they always follow the mistake of the *Bot. Mag.*, Plate 6365, in giving the name of *F. armena* to a charming cone-belled yellow Fritillary, whose real name is *F. Sibthorbiana*, whereas the true *F. armena* is a dingy and lurid purple-flowered plant of lower stature. Many of the race are very miffy or very mimpish or both, and the family all round has a bad character. Among those members of it, however, who have earned a better, comes first our own *F. Meleagris* in its many forms and seedlings, standing high among the best of all; *F. pallidiflora* is of more stalwart stature, with beautiful solid white bells, freely produced from a bulb of good sound perennial temper; *F. lutea*, of half a foot, has single golden flowers; *F. aurea*, of half the size, has half-sized golden bells; and catalogues will be your sufficient guide to such of the rest as may be for the moment available—so long as it is remembered that catalogues do not always emphasize the miffy temper of the prizes they proclaim; and that a nod ought to be as good as a wink to a blind gardener, accordingly, in the way of "should have sand" or "is best if planted early." Not to mention—a fact which catalogues rarely do—that an enormous number of Fritillarias have more or less stinking bells of dingy chocolate and greenish tones, which often appear transfigured by the enthusiasm of those who desire to get rid of them, as "rich purple" or "amaranthine violet."

Fuchsia gracilis and *F. pumila*, to say nothing of *F. Riccartonii* and several more, are quite hardy and most decorative for the rock-garden in warm soils and countries, the two first named being the best in dwarf size and dainty habit. And there are various garden forms and hybrids specially adapted to the rock-garden, and specially quoted for the purpose by catalogues.

Funkia tardiflora is the only species we have at present fitted in stature for our realm, where its delicate foot-high spires of lavender-pale lilylings in autumn have a fine effect; while all the summer through the huge foliage and the fine spikes of its larger cousins may well have been glorifying the edges of the pond in rich damp soil.

G

Galanthus.—Every beautiful Snowdrop—under which head we will not count the double ones—has its place on the outskirts and high ledges of the rock-garden, where their decorative values and their cultural needs are all so very much of a muchness that anyone, not a special specialist, can cater for his desires in catalogues.

Galatella is so near Aster that the glorious *Aster acris* has sometimes borne the name. But even more profuse in flower than this is *G. davurica*, bending beneath the weight of nearly a hundred ragged blue-violet stars, whose rays turn backwards in a manner most elegant and refined. It may be known, apart from these points, from the Aster by the fact that here the cup that holds the blossoms is *hemi-*

spherical, while in the Aster it is *conical*. And there is yet another *Galatella*, the very variable *G. Hauptii* from the Ural, with many rays to the star. And see Appendix, under **Aster.**

Galax aphylla.—The Wandflower of America makes a beautiful tuft of leathery shining leaves that go to russet and brown in autumn, and send up from their midst in summer long fluffy tails of white blossom on stems about a foot high at the most. It is a precious evergreen for cool vegetable soil, not parched, and, for preference, in half shade. It also has the advantage of making runners underground.

Galium.—Among the many weedy and unbecoming Bedstraws, the rocks of various warm mountain ranges offer us a selection of tight and tidy little tuffets set with white or creamy (as a rule) flowers often as attractive as in their near allies the Asperulas. Like these indeed they are children of the South, and enjoy a sunny ledge with us in light soil. They are best propagated as a rule from pieces taken carefully off in summer; and summer is also the season that sees their fullness of bloom. Among the best are :

C. caespitosum, which makes especially graceful neat cushions, fine and soft and dense, with delicate frail square stems of an inch or two, set with whorls of six or eight green little leaflets, and ending in a bunch of a few flowers that barely emerge from the shoot. (Limestone and schistose rocks of the Pyrenees.)

G. cyllenium, finest tufts of green moss, from which the flowers scarcely win free.

G. delicatulum and *G. kurdicum* are masses of green, with flowers on heads of 5 or 6 inches or less. (From Northern Persia, Demavend, &c.)

G. ephedrioeides is stiff and smooth, with stems of half an inch or an inch, forming intricate masses in and out of each other ; their rush-like sprays being set with tiny obovate leaves in whorls of four. The flowers are in loose clusters at the tips of the shoots, fat-lobed, and of creamy whiteness. (Crevices in the hot regions of Granada.)

G. hypnoeides and *G. pusillum* are minute alpine tufts, occurring along the European ranges, and valuable rather for their green cushions—though in *G. pusillum*, indeed, this is ashy grey—rather than for their inconspicuous little flowers, which are much of the same worth in the silvered hairless mound of *G. pyrenaicum*, though laxer in the rosier-flushed *G. cometerrhizon* which only occurs in the schistose screes of the Pyrenees, and then again in Corsica.

G. jungermannoeides, on the other hand, is in every way the most valuable hitherto of the race. For high on the cliffs of Lebanon, it forms very dense close masses of interlacing fine stems, often half a foot across, starred over with large fine purple flowers not emerging from the ball, but appearing all over its surface, produced not only from the tips of the shoots but also from the axils of the upper leaves, in clusters of two or three. For this, as yet, we still vainly crave.

G. olympicum, from the Mediterranean region to the Bithynian Olympus, is one of the most delightful. For it makes a neat, quite small turf of soft brilliant green, in fine delicate shoots not an inch high, and as thick as fur, covered over in summer with loose heads of really charming waxy-white flowers—the plant being in the same tufty nature as *G. baldense*, *G. helveticum*, *G. majellense*, &c., but far superior in the beauty of its blossoms, that fully equal in charm the tidy pleasant-ness of its emerald cushionlet. There is an even tighter form with larger white stars—*G. aretioeides*, from Tolos, Cadmus, &c.

G. Pestalozzae is nothing better than a Woodruff; but not more than 6 inches high, in a concise clump, from the sub-alpine regions of Lebanon.

C. pruinosum has stems of nearly 2 inches at the most, and is all bluish grey with natural rime, while the flowers are gathered into bundles of three or six. (Moist rocks of Granada up to about 5000 feet.)

G. purpureum is a fine fuzzy upstanding bush of some 10 inches, set with loose showers of dull minute flowers that are not purple but of a brownish red. It is a distinct elegant inconspicuous plant, and may be seen in the limestone cliffs, for instance, along the lake-side road from Varenna towards Colico. Very similar in deceptiveness is *G. rubrum*, which is dismal in colour as the dregs of wine.

G. pyrenaicum not only makes a tight tufted cushion, but a fairy cushion of gleaming silver with stems of an inch or two and dense overlapping leaflets in whorls of six, tight-pressed together; while the white flowers are borne by themselves from the upper axils of the shoots. (High crevices up to 10,000 feet on the Pyrenees.)

G. tolosanum is a little taller, for its stiff stems attain a height of 2 or 3 inches, standing erect in a crowd, finely delicate, and set with minute fleshy roundish leaflets in whorls, the whole forming a solid mass starred with white flowers, on the shady porphyry rocks of Amanus on the passes of Tolos.

Genista.—Of Genistas there seem no end. But, without dealing even with such charming medium-sized bushes as spidery *G. radiata* of the Southern Alps, our feet must surely be held back a moment from the field of Gentiana to notice such smaller Brooms as may benefit the rock-garden. Of these the best of all, *G. humifusa*, has already been treated under CYTISUS; but there still remain, of minute bushes, or creepers, some special little species for hot open slopes.

GENTIANA.

All of these can well be raised from seed or propagated by cuttings, and grown in warm poor soil.

G. albida is a densely branching prostrate plant, of as many varieties as merits ; for it contains *GG. Pestalozzae, armena, Montbretii, Goldettii.*

G. aspalathoeides is often sent out from Spain, in which as a point of fact it does not at all occur. For the true *G. aspalathoeides* lives only in Algiers and Tunis, venturing just at one point into Europe, where it effects foothold midway between Africa and Italy, on the island of Pantellaria. It is in any case a most neat and hostile little porcupine of a bush about 6 inches high, and a worthy golden-flowered peer to Erinacea.

G. Boissieri is the Piorno Fino of the mid-alpine region of the Sierra Nevada, a neat tight thorny mass ; exactly the same description serving also for *G. horrida*, which is the common Erizones, from the dry places and fields, especially on limestone, in the mountain region of the Eastern and French Pyrenees. But in *G. Boissieri* the calyx of the no less golden flower is shaggy with silver fluff.

G. libanotica makes a creeping very branchy mat and sends up stiff erect shoots with leaflets clad in white hairs. It grows among the Cedars on the mountain, and extends higher up into the stony places.

G. Loebelii is the pretender almost invariably sent out as *G. aspalathoeides*, which it precisely repeats, except that the lower lip of the calyx is larger and *deeply cut into three lobes.* This species occupies all the Northern half of the Mediterranean region.

G. micrantha is a tufted bushling from 4 inches to a foot high, with pointed shining leathery little leaves, quite narrow and quite hairless, with thickish racemes of some five to twenty yellow flowers. (Woods and downs almost all over Spain, except in the West.)

G. murcica is, like *G. Loebelii*, a twin to Erinacea—or rather an elder brother ; for, while *G. Loebelii* matches it at 4 or 6 inches, *G. murcica* develops to the greater stature of 6 or 9.

G. sagittalis is common and coarse, but most useful for a hot and worthless place, with floundering long masses of dark-green cactoid foliage, not like leaves at all, and abundant spikes of gold in early summer, that flow across the shingles in a bright flood.

G. teretifolia is bigger, but graceful and pretty, with foot-high stems, fine and dainty, silver-hoary and specially free with golden blossoms. It grows with *G. (Cytisus) tinctoria* in the fields of Pampeluna.

Gentiana.—Take it all in all, perhaps Gentiana offers the rock-garden more glory than any other race, and more persistently denies it. To please Primula is possible, to cope with Campanula is even comfortable; but there is no jesting with a Gentian, except, indeed, when the Gentian does the jesting—grows ample and splendid and hearty, only to gratify you at the end with dingy little flowers amid a mass of foliage so ill-pleasing that you feel indeed more mocked by such a success than if the plant has followed the example of its beautiful cousins and wholly refused to grow. All the more noble Gentians, indeed, may be said to be a kittle cattle, and hard to please; but when pleased, with what pleasure do they not repay the pleaser! Those all are children of pure mountain air and moisture, Oreads beyond all others impatient of the plain-lands; they have no down like Androsace to threaten danger and show dislike of wet; they are not living limpets of the rock, like the saxatile Campanulas and Primulas. But their hunger is always for the air of the hills, and, even more, for that persistent aura of moisture in the clear atmosphere which the sunlight draws from the steaming flanks of the mountains when the high snows are gone or going, throughout the growing period of the Gentians on their slopes. Therefore, while all the taller species in the lovely leafy sections of Asclepiadea are easy to deal with in any cool moist soil, and many of the Lutea group will grow colossal in field or border (to say nothing of the family weeds that will grow too well anywhere), the alpine section, where all the Queens of the family are gathered together, require undoubtedly the most especial conditions. But these granted, the difficulties fade as the silver clouds of morning fade from the Tombea in sunrise, leaving the blue and violet masses of *Gentiana verna* jewelled with fine dew-drops in the early freshness of day. Let a bed be made of ample depth; let it be deep enough to bury despair so soundly that he can never rise up again; at the bottom, some 3 feet down, cast a foot or 9 inches of coarsest rough drainage of clinker-burrs and sharp-edged broken stone (and the bed should be at a slight slope into the bargain, open to all the air and sunshine that there is). On this then set a layer of reversed turves, and begin filling with a mixture variable to taste and place, but approximately consisting of two-thirds canary-cage grocer's-sand to the other third of leaf-mould, with a *very little* peat shredded in perhaps, but *the merest pinch*, as the object is to get a compound that shall be always loose and never cake, as peat so soon imparts to all its mixtures a tendency to do. To this compound add chips to pleasure, the more the merrier, almost to the point, if you like, of half and half, but varying the proportions as you please, and, in different ends of the bed, if only for the sake of experiment, using chips of lime or sandstone. *Half fill* your grave with this, till its surface is not more than a foot below the level of the ground, or a little more. Then lay a pipe throughout, connected with a tap; let the pipe be pierced on either side (or perhaps, better still, along the under-side only) with a few *very* small holes (through the merest pin-prick water escapes in fountains unbelievable, and, if your holes are too large and frequent, all your garden will be a bubbling swamp). We now put in all the rest of the mixture, flush with the ground; and when it has settled we respectfully insert our Gentians, the last step being to turn on the tap so that water flows beneath their feet all through the summer. So they will immediately be appeased, and go ahead through the season, even the most difficult, until with the approach of autumn they begin to ask for rest. And now the treatment must be quite reversed; off goes the water, and not only that, but if you want thoroughly to please the Gentians, and invest a little extra trouble in the certainty of their cent. per cent. return next season in the way of flower, the whole bed should be roofed over with glass *or gorse,* and kept safe for the winter, ridiculous as such a precaution may seem, in plants that look so glossily winter-proof, and devoid of perilous fluffs. Yet it is not to be told how even one pane of glass over one clump will gratify *G. verna* or *G. bavarica;* the sufficiently enthusiastic have been known to subsist entirely through the summer on glass-potted tongues and shrimps, in order that the receptacles of these delicacies should afford a sufficient number of roofs to shelter all their Gentians in winter. Nor must more precautions be neglected : in the first place, top-dress them all in spring with coarse sand well silted down between the shoots : and in the second, more important still, do not forget, in the beginning, to give your Gentians company; do not plant them tuft by tuft, neatly, at respectable distances from each other, as if you were bedding out stocks, and leaving them room to develop. Gentians, if they hate being crowded, also hate being left alone with their roots waving through the wide earth in unrelieved solitude.* *G. verna,* indeed, affects the roughest of the alpine turf in nature, and the splendid clumps that are imported from Ireland bear painful witness to its unrefined fondness for company; for every kind of ram-pageous grass and willow and Ladies-finger and Ladies-bedstraw develops in no time from the heart of the Gentian, and the bed is filled in a week with weeds. But even if so coarse and dangerous a taste as this be not indulged, yet company the plant must have, for even the high-alpine species, sitting lonely in round tufts among the barren stones, are grateful in the garden for a little fine society to

---

* Gentians are also more or less inclined to associate, for mutual benefit, with a microscopic root-fungus; but really, in our present state of knowledge, few gardeners can be expected to fuss profitably with fungi.

distract them from their thoughts of home. Among such company may be *Phyteuma pauciflorum, Saxifraga retusa, S. Rudolphiana, Soldanella pusilla, S. minima, Primula minima, Veronica canescens, Arenaria ciliata, Eritrichium, Douglasia laevigata,* and *Vitaliana,* the Androsaces *Charpentieri, carnea Laggeri,* and *Wulfeniana, Myosotis rupicola,* and many another choice fine thing to be thought of with care ; while 2 inches underground are bulbs of *Crocus vernus, minimus, Scharojani,* &c., with all the choicest wee Daffodils and bulbous Irids for the early year. For *G. verna* that likes coarser fare, such fine grass as *Festuca ovina tenuifolia, Dianthus alpinus, Primula farinosa,* and perhaps, if you are rash and an able weeder, the silver mats of *Antennaria dioica.* In any case, with such comforts your most difficult Gentians should be at home ; though this is not to say that here is the only means of making them so, but merely a suggestion of one that may prove to be among the best. As for *G. verna,* luck and temper play pranks with the plant, and it succeeds paradoxically every now and then in the oddest places, and under the weirdest conditions ; one of the finest masses I ever knew was growing in pure hot sand in which it had been ignorantly put by somebody who apparently mixed up Gentiana with Abronia, and on the same bank, in full sun and the same dry ground, was growing *Nymphaea odorata.* So that there is always hope, and never any hard rule : but only good-fortune assisting experience.

Gentiana is a race of extraordinary diffusion and diversity, alike in habit and colour. The Gentians of the New World are hardly less abundant than those of the Old ; and on the Arctic rims of the North, their fame is hardly less widespread than on the Antarctic of the South. Nor is the race less various in size and colour, ranging from the statuesque proportions of *G. venosa* to the minute charm of *G. imbricata.* In colour, too, it contains every note of the prism, from the dazzling azure of *G. verna,* the sombre browns of *G. purpurea,* the clear lovely purple of *G. pyrenaica,* and on, through the yellows of *G. lutea* towards the delicate waxy pinks and whites of *G. concinna* and *G. cerina* (none of the New Zealanders being blue, and none of the Himalayans anything else). All of these can be raised from seed, but with care and slowly ; all the alpine tufts can be propagated by cuttings, but with equal care ; but established tufts of Gentian should always be left alone, lest a worse thing befall. Their blooming season fills the summer ; the high-alpines usually take up the fading mantle of *G. verna* in July, and continue on through the glories of the Asclepiadea group, with *G. verna* very often reappearing in September and October to finish the round that it began in May ; while *G. Gentianella,* the old

G. acaulis, is nearly always finely in bloom at Christmas and throughout the earlier part of the winter. All the species in the following list (which ought to prove helpful up to date for the best), are perennials, with a very few stated exceptions. And see Appendix.

G. acaulis, L.—This august name has at last burst asunder with the number of definite species that it has been called upon to contain. No one who has ever met Gentians on the Alps can have failed to see that the name "acaulis" was made to cover so much that it ultimately came to mean nothing at all. And, as for the *Gentiana "acaulis"* of gardens, this, it is clear, has nothing to do with any form of any species at present known on any of the hills of the world. Therefore the old name of *Gentiana acaulis* had better be now finally dropped ; for the garden plant we have a common name, which, though absurd, has the advantage of being euphonious, so that it may stand distinct as *Gentiana Gentianella,* to keep its position plain and definite ; *G. excisa,* Presl., shall still hold its own, though placed in this group ; but *Gentiana acaulis* of Linnæus is a dead name, concealing five definite species, which, however, with their cousins, shall here be treated together under the heading of *G. acaulis,* in order that their relationship and distinctions may be kept clear. They are usually inferior in flamboyancy of beauty to *G. Gentianella,* but are most lovely and interesting alpines, growing with perfect readiness in conditions much less elaborate than those indicated for the smaller species.

G. ACAULIS, L., with all it connotes and has ever included :—

G. alpina has a limited distribution, and is rare in that, being only found at *great elevations,* first of all in the far South of Spain, on the Sierra Nevada, then along the Pyrenees into the Graian, Cottian, and Maritime Alps, and on into the south-western fringe of Switzerland. It is remarkably distinct, *much smaller* than the others, and so *minutely dwarf* as to be actually *stemless.* The leaves are like those of *G. latifolia,* but *very little* and *very broad,* and, though not pointed, more rhomboidal and less round. In colour they are like those of *G. latifolia,* greyish green. Then, straight upon the rosette of these, staring stemless up to the day, appear fine and perfectly straight-sided trumpets of pure blue, more or less flecked inside with emerald, the calyx-lobes being full and swelling and tapering like the outlines of a dome from the Brighton Pavilion, but *bluntish* instead of running to a point. This tight dwarf Gentian is no stunted form, but a true species, remaining constant under cultivation ; in nature it is supposed to prefer non-calcareous conditions.

G. angustifolia, again, has a smallish range. It occupies the

GENTIANA.

Dauphiné, just to the west of *G. vulgaris* in its lowest range, and topping off the long enclave of *G. latifolia*. Here the leaves are *very long indeed*, of a *very protracted squeezed narrow paddle-shape*, rounded at the tips, more or less, but *never pointed*. It may easily and always be known at a glance by the characteristic *narrow* leaves, quite different from those of all the others, and tapering at long length towards the base; they are *bright-green*, and the whole plant is taller and slenderer than the rest, with flowers of good clear blue (but not specially large, and without any frecklings), each on a delicate stem of 2 or 3 inches or more, the segments of the calyx being much as in *G. occidentalis*, but smaller in proportion to the bell and not so sharp or long.

G. dinarica is a rare species, only possessing one small district in Bosnia, with a patch in the South Carpathians, from which it leaps across into Italy like Attila, and occupies the ridges of the Majella in the Abruzzi. It is exceedingly distinct at first sight, by its leaves, which are *small*, and *broad*, and *pointed*, and *bright-green*, almost *diamond-shaped*, with the two lateral angles of the rhomb just blunted. It is nearest to *G. latifolia*, of which there is a stretch close adjoining it in Bosnia, but the segments of the calyx, though in the same swelling design as all these, are very *much longer* and rather *narrower*, and drawing to a *longer sharper point*. The unspotted bright-blue flower-trumpet is of good size on a definite good stem, though not so tall and slender as in *G. angustifolia*—indeed, not slender at all, but rather stout.

G. excisa, Presl., is by far the grandest in the group, though too rarely seen or offered. It has the lobes of the calyx-segments *very full and fat and sharp*, like the Pavilion-bulb with the apex left on. The leaves are *longer, larger, broader, stiffer, darker, greener, glossier* than in all the foregoing—elongated ovals in design, tapering, though gradually, to a *definite point*. The flower-stems, too, are stouter and much *taller*, with a pair or more of ample oval-pointed leaves or bracts opposite to each other about half way up; then come the great flowers, with the bulbous-pointed segments of the calyx *spreading widely out*, yet infinitesimal in proportion to that huge trumpet of rich sapphire silk, so much more wide-throated and gaping-mouthed than in the rest, with the flapping lobes of the corolla *cut and jagged* and standing agape as widely as they can, to show the full intense beauty of the bell. There is no mistaking this species, which is usually found on non-calcareous alps; but it never seems common, or prevalent, like the others, but merely an occurrence every now and then, conspicuous for its size and deep pure blueness of flower, and deep dark greenness of

364

glossy leaf, *stiff*, and broad, and ample; conspicuous too, in often forming tight tufts, with half a dozen of those immense flowers glaring about at once on their tall and stalwart stems of 4 or 5 inches. Its place in the family is between *G. latifolia* and *G. vulgaris*, with both of which it probably produces intermediates, as it is not restricted to any range of its own, but occurs in both of theirs. It is even quite probable that *G. Gentianella*, so old in gardens that all trace of its origin is lost, is a hybrid, originally, between *G. excisa* and *G. vulgaris*.

G. Gentianella needs no advertisement nor description, for before the face of the border Gentian all others of its race must hide their heads and flee back again to the wild hills where they are so much happier. For *G. Gentianella* is the dog who has accepted the collar and comforts of civilisation; while its cousins are still the untamed wolves of the mountain, descending to ravage our purses, against all the defences of our home-dog, which declares to us anew every spring that we need go no further than our own familiar friend if we want to see the beauty of the hills. Yet this is not quite so; *G. Gentianella*, for vigour and homeliness and glory and popularity, has made a certain sale of its primitive simplicity; and there will always be a delicious stimulating tang about the caprices of a wild species, that there can never quite be about the complacence of a garden plant, however ample and well-liking it may be. *G. Gentianella* has taken to lining borders, and acting as an edging: that says all. No one will ever tame *G. verna* or *G. excisa* into making edgings; nor would it be right that they should. None the less, in deep rich soil, how unutterable a glory is this ancient development of our gardens, so far leaving behind in display the wonders of its probable parents, *G. excisa* and *G. vulgaris!* No richness is too great for it; feed it upon the blood of kings and it would but grow the stouter and bloom the bluer; if the best is to be desired of it in the way of unbroken sheets of midnight sky in May, some part of its beds and borders should always be remade every five years, a trench being dug some 2 feet deep, and filled up for a foot or so with every kind of pig-trough garbage you can think of, and mown lawn-grass and old boots and every possible enrichment: then, on the top of that, the fattest of loam with abundance of lime, and then the Gentians planted firmly and always kept well watered in the earlier year. (And even here, in hot dry climates, the underground pipe would work wonders.) So, always in fullest sun and openness of site, the plants will take hold; the year after planting they will do something; the year after that they will do more, and cause you to caress the hand of your wife with sighs; but the third year heaven will have fallen solid upon your earth, and nothing short of a garden-party will meet the case ; in the fourth year heaven will be broken by rare clouds of green ; and in the fifth you will feel, if massive shows are your aim, that the process must be begun anew. Therefore it is as well to keep your beds of *G. Gentianella* in rotation, so as always to have some in perfection ; so that you may be in the end like a friend of mine, of whom I had heard that he grew *G. Gentianella* to some purpose, and wrote accordingly to inquire what sort of extent he had in display. To which inquiry came back the stunning answer that he did not think he had much more than five miles of it. And so indeed the matter proved. At the same time, may we not urge upon all true lovers of the plant, not to take too much advantage of its wonderful good nature and robin-like attachment to the gardener, by growing it in tight hard lines as edgings and borders ; be it never so splendid, it is not thus it looks its best. For the scent of the hills is too strong upon it still, though it may pretend to have forgotten them, or even think it has. But, if it can achieve such miracles of beauty in the dry wood of the border, what could it not achieve in the green, of proper rock-garden treatment, planted in rich wide sweeps and banks and stretches of fallen sky, with *Crocus aureus* here and there among it for spring, and *C. zonatus* among it here and there for autumn ? And, for a closing recommendation, remember yet again that the plant is a child of lime, and a glutton for full doses of mortar-rubble and bone-meal. It is well worth raising, too, from seed, as several glorious pale blues have so arrived ; but the white form is but a poor thing of thin colour, like inferior sermon-paper soaked in water ; its only chance of effect is to be planted here and there among the azure masses of the type, instead of being stuck away by itself as a precious jewel, where its full inferiority shows unrelieved by contrast. As for the so-called rosea-form, this belongs to the wild species ; to which, after this parenthesis, we return.

G. latifolia.—This name covers the common alpine Gentian of the upper turf that always has had before to put up with a chief share in the huge word *G. acaulis.* It swallows up for ever, too, these three confusing names of lists and catalogues : *G. excisa, G. grandiflora, G. Kochiana.* This plant may easily be recognised by the disappointment it usually occasions in one who has met *G. " acaulis "* of popular usage in the garden, and had thought that *G. acaulis* of the Alps would at least bear it some small resemblance. But this is a sad inferior thing, and its spotted trumpets are almost always of a dead indigo tone, light or dark, sometimes even muddy and slate-coloured, but hardly ever tinged with the skyey note that one demands of a Gentian. However, in this matter it varies, as indeed do many ; and on the Rolle Pass, for instance, there is a type of *G. latifolia* (on the limestone) which is smaller in the flower but of quite a true clear blue, not violent indeed, but clean and pure (yielding good white forms, also). The species may be known at once, too, by its ample foliage ; for this is large, but lax and limp in texture, lying rather flaccid on the ground (as the flowers usually tend to do also, instead of standing bravely up like those of *G. vulgaris* or that noble giant *G. excisa*), and in colour *of a pale and washed-out yellowish green without any gloss*. The shape of the ample leaves, too, is most distinctive, for they are perfectly paddle-shaped, and, like a paddle, oval-rounded at the end, and *never at all pointed*. The plant is almost always non-calcareous, standing nearest in the race to *G. alpina ;* and the segments of the calyx, very much longer in proportion to the bell than in that of *G. excisa*, are more pavilion-like than ever, short and fat and swelling, and then passing into a brief point. The species is general over all the chain of the Central Alps, on granite, schist or volcanic rock, stretching into the Western Pyrenees, but in the Eastern ranges of Tyrol occurring in more sporadic outbreaks. It is the tourist's typical *G. " acaulis."*

G. occidentalis (including *G. sabauda*, Kusn.) is *only to be found in the Western Pyrenees*. It is near to *G. excisa* in general shape of leaf, but the leaf is of less than half the size, and rather broader and more swollen in the middle in proportion to its point. The stem is quite short, and the trumpet blue ; and the lobes of the calyx are long, bulging and pointed as in *G. dinarica*, but not so extreme in their pointedness and length. There is, however, an obscure Savoyard plant, *G. sabauda*, Kusn., which is not far away from this, though much more acute in the segments.

G. vulgaris is the last, and perhaps the greatest, species under this heading. This rather ugly name is now to swallow up *G. Clusii, G. excisa, G. Rochellii, G. grandiflora*, and *G. firma*—all species recognised by former authorities, each one of whom it will be seen has created a *G. excisa*, Presl's alone being now allowed to stand. The name in any case would have been singularly ill-applied to this species, which stands quite alone in the group by having the calyx-segments *perfectly triangular and straight-sided*, with *no bulge or swelling at all*, mere very long, pointed, and quite straightforward narrow deep vandykes. The leaves, too, are narrow and perfectly acute, dark and glossy-green, rather smaller than in the last, as a rule, but much more crowded and stiffer in their rosette than the pallid lustreless grey-green leafage of *G. latifolia*. The stems are taller and sturdier than those of the last, and the flower, if not quite so big as *G. excisa's*, is perhaps the most beautiful and satisfying in the whole group, being an upstanding wide-awake trumpet of the most lovely azure-blue. It is predominantly if not exclusively a limestone plant, and may be seen very abundant and in great beauty in the Dolomites, always at higher levels than those which produce *G. latifolia,* until at last indeed one gets to associate it with the summit ridges of the high calcareous ranges where, even in the topmost inhospitable white rocks of Monte Baldo, it makes glossy tufts carrying half a dozen celestial goblets ; this tuft-forming tendency combining, with the gloss of its stiff dark leaves, the pure tone of its flowers, and the plant's leanings toward lime, to make one suspect that here is one of the parents responsible long ago, perhaps through Clusius or Aicholtz, for the generation in our gardens of *G. Gentianella.* Its range overlaps that of *G. latifolia* all round, except at the extreme south-western corner below Geneva where the species come into contact for once, but there produce no intermediates ; again, in the Eastern ranges, the two occur together, but at different heights (*G.* × *digenea* is their result, *q.v.*). As, for instance, on the way up to the Forcella Lungieres under the Drei Zinnen you will cross lawns all tufted with indigo masses of *G. latifolia* at the upper alpine level, but it will not be till you have reached the ridge itself, and left *G. latifolia* a couple of hundred feet or more below, that you will begin to come on clumps of *G. vulgaris,* so undescribably brave and heartening in the cheery stiff gloss of its dark-green pointed clustered foliage, no less than in the sturdy magnificence of its broad-lobed sapphire bells, which are no less brilliant in the garden, and even in the moraine.—*Here ends the group once covered by* **G. acaulis, L**.

G. aestiva may be held to have attained specific rank. It is the plant like a very much glorified *G. verna* that may be found here and there on the Alps in company with *G. verna,* and often so fading into it by degrees as to be at last suspected of being merely a large variety. The type is, however, so definite that it seems easier to suppose it a true species interbreeding with *G. verna,* and so producing many shades between the two closely-allied parents. There is no doubt as to the distinctness of *G. aestiva* as a garden species. It is, briefly, *G. verna* with twice the size of flower, twice the solidity and brilliance, twice the length of stem, and more than twice the vigour of habit. It does not, moreover, run about so much as sit still, in large and tidy widening clumps of foliage much ampler and glossier than that of *G. verna,* from which it sends up stalwart blossoms all the spring, summer, and autumn through. In the garden it has the further merit of being by far the easiest of all the alpine Gentians ; indeed, so hearty, and of temper so good, that no soil or situation seems to

PLATE 35.

GENTIANA HEXAPHYLLA.
(Photo. W. Purdom.)

GENTIANA ASCLEPIADEA.
(Photo. R.B.G., Edinburgh.)

VOL. I.

PLATE 36.

GENTIANA DETONSA.
(Photo. R.B.G., Edinburgh.)

GENTIANA FARRERI.
(Photo. R.B.G., Edinburgh.)

come amiss to it. It is a treasure of local occurrence only, and its neighbourhood may always be guessed from the superiority of the typical Vernas in those parts ; so that, if the normal *G. verna* of an alp is good, you may usually reckon on soon finding *G. aestiva*, which may always be known at a glance, not only by its special amplitude and clumpiness, but by the folds of the baggier calyx, of which all five are exaggerated into *deep flaps or wings of green*, a symptom never found in the neatly folded five-angled flower-cup of *G. verna*.

G. affinis is a narrow-leaved Cluster-gentian from moist places in Minnesota, &c. It grows from 4 to 16 inches high, and has its blossoms in a thyrse-like spire, these being blue, with the folds between the lobes of the corolla almost as large as the lobes themselves and fringed into a ragged crest. (Summer.)

G. algida, of Siberia and Central Japan, comes near to *G. septemfida*, but is not quite so good, sending up erect stems clad in pairs of large oval-pointed leaves with a bunch of blue trumpets at the top in summer.

G. alpina. See under *G. " acaulis."*

G. altaica is a magnificent little species, after the habit of *G. pyrenaica*, making a dense minute tuft of oblong pointed leaves, from which are sent up countless stems of half an inch or so, each carrying a single great violet-blue bell, much larger than *G. pyrenaica's* in proportion to the calyx. The folds between the lobes are rounded and scalloped. This beautiful Unknown should have the consideration of all the choice jewels when we get it ; at present, when the name appears, it is found by sad experience to cover a huge and hideous leafy species of the *decumbens* persuasion.

G. amoena dwells high in Sikkim, at some 17,000 feet—a glistering tuffet often of no inches at all, and never of more than 2 inches. The flowerless shoots are leafy and succulent ; the flowering ones contrive to branch, and are densely wrapped in overlapping little blunt obovate leaves with a glistening edge. The lobes of the big blue bell stand erect.

G. Andrewsii is the Gentian that never wakes up. It has a slender stem of some 9 inches, at the top of which in summer appear two or three long bulging bags of dull dark-blue, tipped with white. These give high hope of glory ; unfortunately they never do any more. In America, where it lives, the disappointing plant is known as Dumb Foxglove, and, as it never opens or has any charm, there seems no reason, except its indestructible easiness, why it should so often find a place in catalogues.

G. angulosa=*G. aestiva, q.v.*

GENTIANA.

G. angustifolia, Vill. See under *G.* " *acaulis.*"

G. angustifolia (Mich.) is an American late-summer species, of 18 inches high, leafy stems, and clustered blue flowers.

G. arvernensis. See under *G. Pneumonanthe.*

G. asclepiadea is the glory of the sub-alpine woods in moist coppice and open damp fields, where its long bending sheaves of graceful blossom make a famous loveliness in late summer and autumn. The Willow-gentian is of the same amiability in the garden, and soon, if planted in a deep cool bed or border, will be showing swathes of flower 3 feet high and more in August, inclining this way and that beneath the burden of its beautiful sapphire trumpets, tucked all along the upper half of the boughs in the axils of the dark oval-pointed leaves in their flattened arch of pairs. Care should be taken to get good forms, however ; the Alps have produced plants of dingy and slaty colouring, though such a degradation is rare. They have also produced a white of much charm, though less than that of the type—as is almost always the case in Gentiana—and rich forms harlequined with snow ; and, beside many paler tones, they have once produced, and may again, the now almost vanished *G. a. phaeina*, with flowers of dazzling Cambridge-blue like a summer sky at dawn. Many are the pretenders to this name and claimants to this praise, but among many beautiful light-blue and pale forms there has only once been a Phaeina. Seed of the species germinates like cress, and makes good flowering plants in some three seasons. Where the plant occurs at all in the Alps, it occurs with lavish profusion, wholly indifferent, it seems, as to whether there be lime in the soil or not.

G. barbata should be disregarded. It is a fringed biennial or parasitic Gentian after the style, beauty, and impossibility of *G. ciliata.*

G. barbellata (*G. Moseleyi*), though a Fringe-flower, is truly perennial, from a slender fleshy stock. It is a delicate beauty, some 4 inches high, with about four pairs of broadish oblong leaves on the stems, and then an inch-long bloom of dark blue, wildly fringy at the edge and filled with wool inside. A rare species of Colorado for a choice place in the choice bed.

G. bavarica is the grief and the glory of the gardener in wet meadows of the alpine level, where its satiny stars of dark sapphire appear like splashes of midnight among the turf in August. Often a difficulty is found by travellers in differentiating this from *G. verna*—a difficulty quite incomprehensible indeed, but still requiring to be smoothed away. In the first place, the flowers in *G. bavarica* are of a characteristic *velvety intense darkness*, unlike those of *G. verna* in any form, and they are carried on taller slighter stems of 3 inches or so. In the second, the foliage of *G. bavarica* is of a *bright yellow-green note*, quite distinct from the duller grey-green of *G. verna ;* the leaves are *glossy* and *brilliant*, much smaller, much more numerous and *never pointed* at all, but little ovals packed upon the barren shoots, with the exact look of a small sprig of Box—*G. verna's* being much fewer, paler, flatter, larger, broader, and always grooved and pointed. And for a last detail, as you follow down the shoot of *G. verna* the leaves get *larger and larger*, till the basal foliage of the rosette is much the biggest of all, spreading wide out upon the ground ; if you follow down the serried leafy little shoots of *G. bavarica,* you find the cupped yellow-green ovals *diminishing towards the base* until the lowest are much the *smallest of all*, hugging the stem at its birth. So much for the differences between these two very different plants which, for the rest, are not often to be found in the same situations—*G. verna* not liking wet places, and *G. bavarica* insisting on them (and flowering, besides, much later in the season, when the main show of *G. verna* is well over). However, towards the upper-alpine levels they do some-times meet, or are found close at hand, a juxtaposition from which intermediates have resulted. In the garden *G. bavarica* wants thoroughly-wetted soil in summer, and should be planted in the water-bed close to the influence of the pipe ; it can also be quite happy in pure flooded silver sand ; and in districts where the rainfall is up to the average of Noah it will even thrive in silver-sanded peat in the open border. Get it to grow, and there will be no chariness of flower ; and this, too, in full and later summer, long after *G. verna* is only a memory. The species is local, but where found is usually abundant, always in damp places of the upper alpine turf, shores of lakes or marshes, sides of rivulets or water-cuttings, all along the central, Eastern, and Western ranges, never descending so low as *G. verna*, nor mounting so high. It is a plant indifferent to lime or granite, and is as glorious in dark-blue velvet patches among the fallen limestone blocks on the way up to the Forcella Lungieres as on the high damp meadows of the granite above the Glocknerhaus. A violet form has been reported from the Mont Blanc range, and also an albino.

G. bellidifolia, a most lovely stranger from the Alps of the North and South Islands of New Zealand up to 5500 feet. The spoon-shaped leaves, thick and fleshy, form a rosette clinging to the ground, and the noble white flowers are either alone on a stem of from 1 to 6 inches, or else borne in loose clusters, there being so many of these stems emerging from the crown that the clump becomes a dense dome of blossom.

GENTIANA.

G. Bigelovii is very leafy and very near *G. affinis*, with the leaves thicker and often exceeding the flower-clusters. It is 4 inches to a foot in height and of no especial value.

G. Boissieri awaits us in the high-alpine region of the Cilician Taurus on Aslandagh, Gisyl Tepe, &c.—a most beautiful small plant, exactly like a tight and tiny *G. Pneumonanthe* but for the oval-pointed leaves which bring it nearer to a minute compacted form of *G. septemfida.* It is only about 3 inches high, with flowers as large and blue and splendid in late summer, for the same cool treatment.

G. Boryi may commonly be found at great elevations in the Sierra Nevada, on the southern face of Mulaha鮭en, in wet turfy places just below the summit, &c. It makes a dwarf tight tuft of leafy stems, each stem carrying a single flower, not very large, of whitish colour, deepening to pale blue in the lobes and folds, which are almost as long as lobes themselves, the flower sitting at the end of the shoot, enfolded in four leaves, and the same leaves, little, oval, fat, and shining, clothing the stem all the way down.

G. brachyphylla is the high-alpine glory that takes the place of *G. verna* on the uppermost stone-slides, as does *G. imbricata* that of *G. bavarica.* It may quite easily be known, not only by the height at which it is found, but by the look of its neat tight tuffets, often nearly a foot wide, but usually concise round tartlets of pale glaucous-green, about 3 or 4 inches across, sitting close among the stones of the summit ridges and topmost shingles, and built of very many packed rosettes of rather incurving leaves, very broad and very pointed, in all respects like condensed, more numerous, fatter, stiffer leaves of a diminished *G. verna*, but specially distinct in the *clear bluish-grey, yellowish-green tone of the tufts.* The stemless or almost stemless flowers, too, cover the mass in a profusion so brilliant that to see a slope of hill occupied by *G. brachyphylla* in August is like looking down from heaven upon fallen slabs of sky. They are rather smaller than those of *G. verna*, of a blue more clear and light, thinner in the star, and with much *longer thinner tubes to the corolla.* It is generally distributed through the main alpine chains in the high shingles, and in the garden is curiously easy and satisfactory to cultivate under the common conditions of care required by all the small alpine Gentians. The flowering-time, alike in the hills and here, is in July and August, after *G. verna*, and with *G. bavarica* and *G. imbricata.*

G. bracteosa blooms in May—an American species of some 4 inches, with flowers of lilac-blue. For the special bed. It is a narrow-leaved version of *G. Parryi, q.v.*

G. brevidens is a floppet of the worst—a vast leafy great weakly rubbish with tight heads of little and insignificant bluish stars in August, ridiculous at the end of those stalwart stem and wide wrappings of oval slack-textured foliage. (Siberia.)

G. Burseri is a leafy tall yellowy-brown ugliness in the way of *G. punctata.*

G. cachemirica may be found between 9000 and 13,000 feet in Kashmir and Kumaon. It is a neat tuft not unlike that of *G. bavarica,* but laxer, longer, leafier, with the flowers sitting at the tops of the 2- or 3-inch shoots, and wearing their lobes erect, as is so often the fashion among the high Indian Gentians, and almost unknown among their alpine cousins of Europe.

G. calycosa belongs to the highest levels of the Central Rockies and California, and is a striking beautiful species, growing from 4 inches to a foot high, with stems clad in pairs of oval leaves about an inch in length, of which the upper ones enclose the solitary baggy bluebell of a flower that unfolds in later summer. There is a variety *G. c. xantha,* with yellowish blossoms, and sometimes those of the type are not solitary but two or three.

G. cephalantha comes from China, and should go into the special bed if enthusiasts care to risk its threatening height of a foot and the ominous cluster-headed description offered by its name. The flowers, however, in their heads, are described as being of a brilliant blue.

G. cerina.—It is a yet further cry to *G. cerina,* whose long branches, clothed in long narrow leafage, very fat and fleshy, and of the richest and deepest varnished polish, lie out and about on the lonely sea-rocks of the Aucklands, and up to 1000 feet in the hills, and end amid their leafage in clusters of wide ravishing flowers, shallower-belled than in our species, and more deeply divided into rounded lobes, but of glistering waxy whiteness, streaked with delicacies of pink or purple. For years the longing of the world has leapt across the distances to *G. cerina,* secure in those unvisited islands of the remotest South. Yet no one ever goes there, not even for *Celmisia vernicosa, Pleurophyllum speciosum, Bulbinella Rossii,* or *Gentiana cerina.*

G. ciliata is the type of the impossibles. It is a very common species in all the alpine chains, flowering so late in the summer as to be the hateful harbinger of autumn ; and belongs especially to the lower levels (though it can also ascend to some 6000 feet), and always chooses rough plebeian places in the soil, by path-sides and so forth. It is particularly fine, for instance, along the first part of the zigzag that climbs from Misurina to the Popena Ridge, where its frail leafy stems spring up in mushroom-like abundance and rapidity as soon as the plant smells autumn. The big *four-lobed* blooms are of rare and sinister loveliness ("soft lashes hide thine azure eye which gleamest "), for the lobes are fringed into a fine long fluff of hair-like strips; though Mrs. Fitzroy Timmins's colour-epithet will not fit, for the flower is of a clear and stone-cold electric blue, luminous and mute. But in cultivation *G. ciliata* is hopeless, for all that rough-cast heartiness of apparent habit. It is either biennial or parasitic or both; the knobbed frailness of its white root-threads gives away the secret. It may be coaxed in special conditions into coming up the second season, but it rarely does more, and soon fades dreamlike away. And seed of such species offers little better hope.

G. Clusii is *G. vulgaris.* See under *G. " acaulis."*

G. coerulescens is a Siberian species of small merit and nearly a foot's stature, with blue flowers in late summer. It is quite easy to grow, which is too often the makeweight of an immeritorious Gentian.

G. cordifolia. See under *G. septemfida.*

G. coronata, a very dwarf high Himalayan, but not among the best, unless we are to trust Royle's amazingly beautiful figure of it.

G. corymbiflora is a New-Zealander either perennial or monocarpic, but nobody yet seems sufficiently intimate with it to know which. It may possibly be only a variety of *G. saxosa*, and is abundant in the Alps of the South Island up to 5000 feet, there making rosettes of fat obovate leaves, leathery and fleshy, about 3 inches long, with just a pair or two upon the stems, that rise from 6 to 20 inches at times, forming a dense wide pyramid of large white shallow bells in large compact clusters. Though possibly a variety of *G. saxosa*, it is interesting to note that the Antarctic Gentians do not develop an alpine race like their cousins of the Northern world, alike in the Old and the New, although they themselves may ascend to considerable elevations in the mountains.

G. crinita is another annual or biennial species after the style of *G. ciliata*, being often much taller, up to a yard in height, but having the same four lobes, the same fringes, the same beauty, and the same tantalising intractability of temper. (Low levels of North America.)

G. cruciata is quite common every now and then in low hot places in the Alps, usually growing in very hard turfy loam. It is perfectly easy and vigorous in any sunny garden and deep soil, but is not particularly attractive, although its clustered heads of four-lobed little bright-blue blossoms have a cheerful effect in August and September; but the plant is leafy, a foot high or more, and with excessively broad dark foliage outweighing the merit of the flowers.

G. dahurica is a coarse and worthless leafy cluster-head, of dowdy bloom and overwhelming leafage, only differing, if at all, from the similarly undesirable *G. decumbens*, in having the lobes of the calyx even instead of markedly uneven.

G. davurica is the same thing.

G. decumbens, again, is the same in ugly rankness; but here the calyx-lobes are of *quite irregular size*. But it is a variable weed, and probably the last two no more deserve specific rank than they do admission into any but the coarsest parts of the garden. There is also another variety that sometimes is offered as *G. mongolica*, and is in reality only a Mongolian form, unimproved, of *G. decumbens*.

G. depressa, however, gives us back the beloved habit of *G. bavarica*. For this, on the Roof of the World, has exactly the same dense tight tufts of small packed leaves, but a trifle larger. The blue flowers are erect-lobed cups, however, sitting solitary all over the cushion.

G. detonsa is very near to *G. crinita*, and is best, therefore, not bothered with, any more than *G. serrata* and *G. contorta*, all from Himalaya and western China.

G. × digenea is the natural hybrid occurring between *G. latifolia* and *G. vulgaris*—see the description of these under *G. "acaulis"*—the occurrence of such intermediates of course blurring the distinctness of the species, and making them more difficult of determination on the hills.

G. dinarica. See under *G. "acaulis."*

G. divisa occurs, but not very commonly, in the mountains of the South Island of New Zealand at about 5000 feet—a species of peculiar magnificence whose leaves are rather thin and membranous, lying on the ground, but wholly hidden from sight by the broad mass, some 3 or 9 inches high, of big white flowers on many branching stems. At 4500 feet on Mount Nelson lives the even more superb variety *G. d. magnifica*, which makes domes of sheer blossom like huge snowballs, nearly a foot round, up and down the slopes of the mountain.

G. × Doefleri, an uglyish hybrid between *G. × superlutea × G. punctata*. (The prefix "super" to a hybrid's name merely means that that particular parent is dominant in that particular cross: this to distinguish it from Superman, the name not suggesting a specially extra-luteous *lutea* as the original parent.)

G. Douglasii is a not very valuable species from the Sitka Sound.

G. elegans = *G. serrata*—an annual after the way of *G. ciliata*, about a foot high, with fringy blue flowers.

G. Elwesii, on the high lands of Sikkim, recalls our own *G. Pneumonanthe*, having erect stems, with flower-heads of two to ten blue bells, swollen in the middle of the tube in the same way. It is about half a foot or more in height, the basal leaves being rather pointed.

G. excisa, Presl., is the only plant now subsisting under a name which in time past has been used for *G. latifolia* no less than for the quite unexcised *G. vulgaris*. It will be found described under *G.* "*acaulis*," so as to make our Alpine Trumpet-group complete.

G. Farreri is the marvel described under *G. ornata*, *q.v.*

G. Favrati leads us again upon the alpine mountains cold. It is a rare species, occasionally to be met with in the limestone Alps. It is, in habit and everything else, a yet dwarfer and more beautiful *G. verna*, but its flowers are of a much lighter and more brilliant soft azure, and so much broader in the segments than most forms of *G. verna* that the lobes are often wider than their length ; above all, the plant may instantly be recognised by the leaves of its pleasant clumps. For these, arranged more in rosettes, are not only more numerous, but *round or oval*, instead of having any trace of the point which is *invariable* in *G. verna*. It is almost stemless at time of flowering, and is altogether a most beautiful jewel, and not of any difficult temper, though usually sent out, unfortunately, in little wizzly thready pieces, so rootless and minute as to have no reasonable chance of reestablishing themselves.

G. Fetisowii is another rather profitless coarse weed of pallid flower and leafy habit from Siberia, blooming in late summer, for what its anaemic heads of insignificant blossom may be worth.

G. firma = *G. vulgaris*. See under *G.* "*acaulis*."

G. flavida (*G. alba*, Man. not Muhl.) is another ugly thing—tall and stout, and wrapped in ample leafage with whitish flowers packed into clusters. Sandy places of North America are responsible for this.

G. Forwoodii follows the fashion of *G. affinis*, but is smaller.

G. Freyniana clings close under the shadow of *G. septemfida*, and its claims to specific rank are not universally acknowledged. For the garden, however, it is a plant distinct and precious, in any cool rich soil making tufts of shoots, clad in pairs of dark glossy leaves, oval and pointed, and then in late summer, when they are some 6 inches high, unfolding a head of one, two, or three large and brilliant bells of bright blue, after the habit of *G. septemfida's*, with the same wide lobes, and the same interlobar folds, conspicuous and crested.

G. frigida belongs to the highest granite ridges of the Alps, where it is rather rare and (like many special plants of the high granites) rather ugly. It has narrow fleshy leaves at the base, long and few ; then arise one or two stems about 3 inches high, more or less, set with another similar pair or so ; bearing at the top, from a cup of two or three leaves (very often) a single flower or a pair of flowers, rather fat and baggy in outline, not opening out at the mouth, of a rather pallid creamy-white, with five stains of palest blue, and various greenish or blackish frecklings in the throat, with more of them outside. In cultivation it soon seems to die ; and is little mourned.

G. Froelichii is a charming little species far too rarely seen, especially as it combines beauty with ease of character. In point of fact it lies beyond the beaten track of tourists, living far away in the highest turf of the Eastern and Styrian limestones, where, in combination with *Primula Wulfeniana*, it fires even German botanists to speak of the lordly carpets there unfolded. In this carpet indeed *G. Froelichii* makes blots rather than patches ; forming quite small clumps, of two or three crowns, in a tuft of very narrow grooved leaves, the whole plant rather suggesting one or two stray rosettes of an exaggerated *Dianthus alpinus*, though of a paler yellower green and a dulled gloss. From this come up one or two stems of 1 or 2 inches, each usually carrying only one single flower, which is long and in shape a swollen tube, with lobes erect and not opening out ; yet very attractive in its size and in the clear pale-blue colouring of it, fading to yellow at the base, and spotted with dark at the throat—altogether suggesting blooms of a soft-blue *G. Pneumonanthe* poising singly over a grassy tuffet like that of a big *Phyteuma pauciflorum*. In cultivation *G. Froelichii* proves perfectly easy and happy in the choicer part of the bed—if only you can succeed in starting with reasonably rooted pieces. For, in common with all alpine Gentians, it loathes root-disturbance ; and, like all that make but few fibres and do not form wads, it loathes root-disturbance to such a point that the few lonely odds and ends that are usually sent out by collectors stand little chance of re-establishment under several seasons' cure. Let but the plant, however, be collected reverently and with pains, and the next spring will see it as healthy a tuft as ever, quite ready to go out, and prosper more heartily than many of its kind in the Gentian bed, whether sandy or lime-fraught—flowering there with no less heartiness, too, in August, than it shows upon its native high downs.

G. × Gaudiniana.—An ugly hybrid of *G. punctata* and *G. purpurea*, big and dingy.

G. gelida lives on the Alps of Anatolia. It is quite near to *G. septemfida* in all its wants and ways, but the leaves are narrower, there are no fringes to the folds between the lobes of the corolla, and the corollas themselves are *pale yellow*.

G. glauca is a small Pneumonanthe of only 2 or 3 inches in height, with weak little stems set in pairs of elliptic leaves, and ending in a single bloom at the tip, or a cluster of several, with others springing from the axils of the upper foliage. The flowers are bells of green and blue, while the leaves are greyish-green in tone. (Northern Asia, Arctic America.)

G. grandiflora=G. vulgaris. See under *G. " acaulis."*

G. hexaphylla, a very lovely species from the high Alps up the Szechwan-Kansu march of Tibet, for which see Appendix.

G. imbricata, Schleich, is the beautiful tiny development of *G. bavarica* which replaces its larger original in the topmost granite shingles, as *G. brachyphylla* replaces *G. verna;* not always, however, so common, as *G. bavarica* is on the whole itself less universal than *G. verna. G. imbricata* repeats all its parent's effect in a tight dense tuft of wee glossy yellow-green foliage like the smallest box-tuffets that were ever squashed together and then re-varnished. The flowers are no less darkly deeply beautifully blue ; while in the garden, as *G. brachyphylla* follows the comparatively unexacting nature of *G. verna,* so does *G. imbricata* pursue the uncertain courses of *G. bavarica,* and must be very courteously entreated in the damper choice spots of the special bed : with a good top-dressing of sand in spring.

G. imbricata (Froel), rather unfortunately promoted by Mr. Stuart Thompson in his admirable book, is in reality only an invalid later synonym for *G. tergloviensis, q.v.*

G. Kesselringii.—Yet another Siberian leafage with bluey white poor blossom in late summer, on stems of some 10 inches.

G. Kochiana=G. latifolia, for which see under *G. " acaulis."*

G. Kurroo came down from the Roof of the World by happy chance, some unsuspecting passer-by in those parts having a friend at home who pestered him persistently for seeds. Accordingly, remembering this, and desiring peace, he clutched the nearest pod he could perceive and despatched it to England : where, in due course, it revealed a Gentian beautiful among all other beautiful Gentians. *G. Kurroo* forms a single and unmultiplying tuft of a few very long, very narrow, grooved and glossy leaves of dark-green. From this, in late summer, proceed one or two smooth mahogany stems, set here and there with a pair of leaves, and once or twice (or yet again) emitting a separate flower-stalk. These dark and shining stems, although so solid, do not stand erect, but lie along the ground for 4 or 5 inches and then rise up with the grace of a swan's neck, to show off at respectful distances from each other, those three or four magnificent great flowers, widely gaping cups of pure rich blue, with folded lobes, and flecked with interior pallors, and altogether lovely. The only reason why a good connotation was ever attached to the name of *G. brevidens* was because it was once applied to *G. Kurroo*, as a varietal name of the frightful *G. decumbens*—both *G. decumbens* and *G. brevidens* being, in point of fact, mere versions of type *decumbens*, and not by any means the originals of *G. Kurroo*. In cultivation *G. Kurroo* has its caprices; its raiser grows it in rows like potatoes in rich kitchen-garden soil, under a hot wall in a hot exposure of a hot county. None the less the plant is perfectly hardy, and has weathered many Northern winters unhurt, on open sunny banks of the rock-work. But it is as well to remember that it seems to crave heat and damp and perfect drainage. It should be at the foot of a rock in the sunniest and hottest exposure of the garden, in a soil that should be a deep, rich, and heavyish stony loam ; and there be kept well watered from underground in spring and summer.

G. × *Laengstii* is a natural hybrid between *G. pannonica* and *G. lutea*.

G. Lagodechiana. See *G. septemfida.*

G. latifolia. See under *G. " acaulis."*

G. Lawrencei is a slighter, paler, frailer *G. Farreri*.

G. linearis is an American species of some worth, blooming in late summer, and for the treatment of all the Septemfidas and Pneumonanthes. It is slender and erect in habit, some half a foot or 18 inches or more, with slender bluish-white funnels, erect-lobed, gathered at the tops of the shoots into heads of about five. The leaves are narrow (there is a broader-foliaged variety called *G. l. latifolia*), and the plant is a lover of bogs.

G. lineata belongs to regions untrodden of the far South, where, in the Stewart Islands, as also in the Southern Alps of New Zealand, it makes tufts so dense that they form into a turf of basal foliage emitting erect densely-leaved little shoots. From these mats arise naked wiry stems of 3 inches or so, carrying each a single flower about half an inch across.

G. lutea.—The huge and stalwart yellow Gentian of the Alps has not always been duly appreciated. There is no doubt that at its best it is a truly glorious object, with its vast corrugated leafage, and towering spires of fine-rayed golden stars in dense whorled clusters to the top of the 3- or 4-foot stem. It may be seen especially magnificent on the banks between Susa and Bardonecchia ; while the slopes at the upper end of the Mont Cenis Lake are aglow in August with the countless multitudes of its golden campanili. The plant's medicinal root, however, is huge and wholly unnegotiable, nor does its stature admit it to the rock-garden : but in open sunny places of the wild, in hayfields like those of the Alps where it shines so richly above the field-geranium and the Paradise Lilies, it would have all the value of its amplitude and tremendous port, if planted in very deep rich open soil in colonies and stately groups, and there left alone for ever to glorify the whole season with its *formes architecturales*, and then, in full summer, become a stalwart torch crowded with radiating sparks of sunlight in successive tiers.

G. macrophylla is a species of quite singular worthlessness even among the large and leafy flopping Cluster-heads. It blooms in late summer with packed heads of little pale flowers enveloped in leafage at the top of stems that are rank without even the power of standing erect. There is also a variety, temptingly named *G. m. cyanea*, which may perhaps be a trifle bluer in blossom than the other, but is in no other way an improvement. China is fertile of these frights.

G. Makinoi in the shrubby and boggy mid-regions of Japan makes tufts of foliage recalling some very thin long-leaved plantain, and then sends up foot-high stems set here and there with pairs of leaves, and carrying at the top a head of two or three white trumpet-shaped blossoms.

G. montana belongs to the mountains of the South Island of New Zealand—a stalwart species of some 2 feet high or less, with a large rosette of broad flat leathery fleshy leaves at the base, and then one or more unbranching stems, carrying wide heads of specially large white flowers not crowded on the sprays.

G. nikoensis is a Japanese species like a rather taller *G. Pneumonanthe* with fewer, much larger, baggier blooms, inclined to be pulled in at the mouth, and only two or three at the top of an erect 9-inch stem towards the end of summer.

G. nipponica is a dwarf plant, blooming in June, with smallish flowers of bright blue on stems of some 2 inches, weak and leafy.

G. nivalis.—The little annual Gentian of the high Alps which tingles out at you from the upmost fine herbage in tiny sparks of living turquoise is of none avail in the garden, sow you it never so wisely nor so often. There is something evil in its nature ; to the wickedness of being an annual—a crime of exceeding rarity in the high Alps, it adds the still worse blackness of being probably a parasite into the bargain. The best chance would be to sow seed broadcast on a prepared ground, mixed up with other seed of the Alpenwiesen, in hopes that one among them might offer food for its roots. But the Alpenwiesen, though alluring in idea, are not always profitable in practice, unless you have collected the various seeds yourself: the finest I ever saw in an English garden had yielded noble crops of chickweed fit to take the prize at any show ; but nothing else. And yet another Alpine

Meadow of precious mountain seeds, bestowed by the most evident of female zealots, had produced an unrivalled show of Escholtzias and cornflower and common annual poppies. Therefore unless the seed be wholly trustworthy and alpine, it is too sanguine to hope that you will possess *G. nivalis*, even as some of the high Scotch Alps possess it, glinting here and there with its eyes of a blue so violent that they even atone for the minuteness of the eyes themselves.

G. nubigena is born of clouds on the Roof of the World; it is some 6 inches high at the most, but usually much less, with weak stems set with pairs of oblong narrow leaves about a couple of inches long, and ending in one or two fine trumpet flowers of an inch and a half, emerging from a calyx which is very much shorter than they. The blossoms are sometimes even three to a stem, being set on little footstalks, so as to give the effect almost of a spire.

G. occidentalis. See under *G. "acaulis."*

G. Olivieri is a poor thing in the same way as *G. cruciata.*

G. ornata very doubtfully exists at all as a species, and the Veitchian plant sent out at first under the name has been promoted to *G. Veitchiorum.* Yet more superb is *G. Farreri*, which sends out many flopping slender shoots from the stock, clad in very narrow foliage, and ending each in a single huge up-turned trumpet wide-mouthed, and of an indescribably fierce luminous Cambridge blue within (with a clear white throat), while, without, long vandykes of periwinkle-purple alternate with swelling panels of nankeen, outlined in violet, and with a violet median line. As you see *G. Farreri* coming into bloom in mid-September in all the high-alpine sward of the Da-Tung chain (Northern Kansu-Tibet) it is by far the most astoundingly beautiful of its race, reducing *G. verna* and *G. Gentianella* to the dimmest acolytes. It thrives also with singular vigour in a cool rich soil, forming masses a yard across, whose glare of splendour is almost painful to the eye in August and September.

G. pannonica is rather handsome in its coarse way; being a tall leafy upstanding thing about 18 inches or 2 feet high, with large enveloping corrugated leaves in pairs, after the style of *G. punctata*, and then a series of axillary plump bells in the same style, with a big bunch at the top. But the spike is better furnished, and the ample flowers are of a dingy reddish-purple, with the lobes of the calyx *turning downwards* instead of sticking to the corolla. *G. pannonica* scarcely occurs in Switzerland at all, but is not uncommon in the high pastures of the Eastern ranges, especially on limestone. In the garden all this section responds readily to treatment in free sunny loam, not parched, and kept open with chips and perhaps enriched with peat. The value of all these, however, is special and sentimental, rather than owing any of its force to the beauty of the species themselves.

G. Parryi sends out many stems from a woody root. The egg-shaped leaves are thick and of a glaucous blue-grey tone, set in pairs up the foot-high stems, and at last almost embracing the head of some one to five bright-blue blossoms. *G. bracteosa*, of catalogues, is a form of this with narrower foliage: the type is found in the alpine regions of the Rockies, and Cascade Mountains. It should be given the same conditions as suit all these leafy species, that is, the rich and cool soil which agrees with *G. septemfida* and *G. asclepiadea;* like all the rest it blossoms in later and latest summer.

G. patula is a New Zealander, quite common in the Alps of the South Island, and standing near to *G. bellidifolia*, but taller and much more doubtfully perennial; and, in short, of doubtfully specific rank altogether.

G. phlogifolia needs and deserves no special care. It comes from the Eastern Alps, is about 10 inches high, and has clustered blue flowers in June.

G. phyllocalyx stands near *G. amoena*, but sends up only one stem, and that stem only has one blossom; but, to make up, that one is very much larger, in the shape of a stout swollen tube, pulled in below the lips. It grows about 5 inches tall, and lives in Sikkim, between 13,000 and 15,000 feet.

G. platypetala is either weak or strong in stem, clad in pairs of elliptic three-nerved blunt leaves, roughened at the edge, and ending almost always in a single squatting bell of blue, with the calyx lobes outlined in white, and cut into two or three teeth, the lobes themselves being broader than they are long. (Sitka.)

G. Pneumonanthe, our own by no means uncommon heath-Gentian, with its slender stems beset with pairs of dark and narrow leaves (variable in this respect, however), and ending in a bunch of long dark trumpets, greenish-blue outside, but of rich sapphire and emerald within, is very well worth establishing in a cool and peaty corner. There is also a striking form with pure-white flowers flecked with gold and green. But even more striking is the foreign form; for, where *G. Pneumonanthe* occurs in the low levels of the Alps, in heathy marshy places, it is in a variety twice the size of ours, a plant of special splendour sometimes distinguished as *G. P. arvernensis*, of similar habits and needs to the type, and flowering also in August.

G. Porphyrio (*G. angustifolia*, Michx.) makes slender and usually unbranched stems of some 4 to 16 inches in height, amid the moister pine-barrens of Florida and New Jersey. The leaves are very narrow and stiff, in pairs up the stem, and the azure flowers are gaping funnels of 2 inches or so, with their fine lobes twice as long as the cut-edged interlobar folds. (These North Americans all bloom in later summer.)

G. procēra is a Fringe-flower, except that it is not fringed. For, while it resembles *G. crinita* in all else, the rounded lobes of the petals are merely toothed at the edge instead of cut into fine eyelashes.

G. prostrata, however pretty, is only an annual and therefore of no use.

G. Przewalskyi goes through life unfairly hampered by its truly un-propitious name, and is a species whose very existence is doubtful; the lowlands of Koko-nor, Tibet, yield abundantly a smallish plant of slender and flopping growth in the cousinship of *G. Kurroo*, with narrow pairs of dark leaves, and gaping bells of violet or blue in summer, quite happily displayed in any deep rich soil, not shaded, in a sunny exposure. For a surer treasure, see *G. Purdomii*.

G. puberula is found in the dry prairies of North America from Georgia to Minnesota; where, in October, it sends up slender stems set with minutely downy rough narrow-oblong leaves, and ending usually in one large widely-open flower of bright blue, whose corolla-lobes are twice if not three times the length of the toothed folds between.

G. pumīla makes a mat of very narrow-leaved and small rosettes, that send up each a slender flower-stem of an inch or two, and carry each a single wide and starry blossom of a sapphire-blue velvet rich and deep and round as that of the midnight sky. The species is too rarely seen, for in gardens it merely asks the special bed into which all the special species are to be put; it is not familiar to the popular mind, for, though found not uncommonly in certain ranges, it is unknown in the hills that are beaten nearly flat with the feet of tourists, and may be hoped for only in the highest finest turf of the Eastern ranges, in Dauphiné, here and there in the Pyrenees of Aragon, in the Apennines on Monte Corno; and then far away in the mountains where no one goes, in Styria, Carinthia, and Carniola. It may, however, be quite easily known, if not by its darkly passionate blue flower, then by its tufts, like those of a most minute lax *G. verna*, but with the leaves as perfectly straight and narrow and pointed as those of some tiny Dianthus stiffened and dulled. It is a plant of the rarest charm, no less in its delicate habit than in the soft and sombre profundity of its habitual colour.

G. punctata, unlike *G. pannonica*, prefers the non-calcareous Alps, where it is abundantly found in the higher alpine pastures, bringing reproach on *G. lutea* by the faithful way it imitates the habit of its superior in stout stem, clad in stout pairs of corrugated light green leaves, but only about a foot high, and ending in a head of flowers (with one or two axillary in the last of the leaves, but not nearly so well furnished as in *G. punctata*), which, instead of being gay and numerous, smallish, starry, and brilliant yellow, are few and very large—deeply baggy six-lobed bells, of the dingiest and sickliest greenish pallor that it would be possible for even the grossest flatterer to call yellow ; and, even so, they are speckled with darkness inside till you feel you are looking into the throat of a sick frog for whom you have been called in to prescribe against the jaundice. No difficulty attends the culture of this treasure in cool peaty soil, and in full sun.

G. Purdomii (F., 303) is near *G. Przewalsky*, but much better, with white-speckled flowers of intense sapphire blue.

G. purpurea follows in the footsteps of the last ; it is of the same height, rather fatter and coarser in the stem : but has more numerous limper narrower foliage, highly grooved with nerves, and of a glossy dark-green ; the flowers are of the same size and shape, with six rounded lobes, and a long calyx gashed to a third of its total length (instead of the *short calyx of the last,* which is hardly cut into lobes at all, having only its six irregular teeth). As for the blossoms, they earn their name for purpleness by being of a rich vandyke-brown, with pallors and mottlings unnameable. An evil weird thing is *G. purpurea*, but handsome to find upon the hills (which it occupies at intervals through the Alps away to Kamchatka, often found in single clumps or specimens or colonies), but not deserving the fusses that sometimes seem necessary to win its approval in the garden—where, like the rest of the group, it should flower late in the summer.

G. pyrenaica makes a break in the family tradition. This, though small and precious in the highest degree, has neither the high-alpine habit nor the high-alpine temper ; but, even without the special bed, will sometimes thrive and make wide mats in rich deep sandy peat kept reasonably moist in summer and open to the sun. This lovely and rare species has many points of interest ; in the first place it does not, as I say, climb high into the hills, but forms sound masses in heathy and turfy places, damp or dry, on lime or granite, between 4000 and 5500 feet. And, in the second, it has a most curious distribution ; it wins its name in the Pyrenees, where it abounds in the Eastern side of the range, alike on the French and on the Spanish frontier ; but it then ceases abruptly and is no more heard of throughout all the main chains of the Alps, until we come to the Carpathians, where it suddenly breaks out again, and then again completely ceases till it has girdled the earth and once more leaps to view in Western Asia. It makes

PLATE 37.

GENTIANA TRIFLORA.
(Photo. W. Purdom.)

GENTIANA LUTEA.
(Photo. R. A. Malby.)

VOL. I.

PLATE 38.

GENTIANA VERNA.
(Photo. R. A. Malby.)

GERANIUM LANCASTRIENSE.
(Photo. R. A. Malby.)

mats and carpets of little dwarf shoots, all densely clad in small pointed glossy leaves, rough at the edges, and of a bright shining green that gives the turf of them a comfortable and well-furnished look. Then from the densely leafy shoots of 2 or 3 inches protrude the flowers in May and June, each by itself, emerging from a longish narrow calyx (whose lobes do not stand out or spread) and then unfolding into a star of bright violet, the long tube expanding in five rounded lobes, with between them the toothed or crested interlobar folds so well developed also that the flower has the effect of having ten segments instead of five; which gives it a richness of outline to match the richness of its clear and astonishing colour, which it should not be possible to call *bleu d'azur* (in Correlonian phrase), as it is of the brightest, softest, and most decided pure violet.

G. quinquefolia has a silly name which ought of course to be *quinqueflora*. Not that even its terminal clusters of five or three wide lilac-purple flowers in October can give it any special claims upon the garden, seeing that it attains a foot and a half, and that its pyramids of blossom, however comely upon the stem and branchlets, are hardly likely to show full value with us, unless it be in a specially warm and sheltered place in sandy rich mixture of peat and loam.

G. Rochellii = *G. vulgaris*, for which see under *G. "acaulis."*

G. Romanzoffii is the American *G. frigida, q.v.*

G. Rostani is a most interesting species, akin to *G. bavarica* in habits, but in nothing else. It is very rare, confined to a few points at high elevations in the Cottian Alps on the French as on the Italian side, being found here and there in wet places among the grasses and stone-slides under Mansoul and Paravas and Monte Viso, where it may be seen in spring growing happily beneath a sheet of running water an inch deep. It forms tuffets as in *G. bavarica*, but the leaves are entirely personal, and distinct at a glance from all others. For they are notably thick, almost fleshy, oval, and very pointed, incurving upon the shoots, and giving the clump a special look of its own, quite unmistakable. From this tuft of leafy short shoots spring the flower-stems, which are slender and rather tall, about 3 inches high, with one or more pairs of those narrow, incurving, pointed leaves set on them at rare intervals, and then ending in a single wide flower-star of the most brilliant light velvety azure. If the mind of man can picture an intermediate between *G. brachyphylla* and *G. pumila*, it might not make so bad a picture by which to recognise true *G. Rostani* if ever the feet that that mind owns are fortunate enough to stray across *Rostani's* marshes high up on the desolate granitic necks of the Cottians. In cultivation the plant does not always seem complacent, but resents disturbance and needs time and care for its re-establishment. There are two magnificent specimens of *G. Rostani*, however, in England; their only drawback being that they are not *Gentiana Rostani* at all.

G. Saponaria makes a handsome spectacle in moist places of American woods from Connecticut to Ontario, &c.; a smooth species of uprising habit and stems of about 9 inches or a foot high, set with pairs of narrowish oval-pointed leaves, and ending in late summer in a cluster of flowers, with others appearing in the axils of the upper leaves. These flowers are wide-mouthed, and of brilliant blue, the lobes of the corolla being very little longer than the lobed fold between each, which is gashed into two conspicuous teeth, so as to give special richness to the contour of the blossom's fringy-looking lip.

G. saxosa lives rather below the level of one's reasonable hopes, on the shore-rocks in the South Island of New Zealand, not ascending more than some 800 feet into the hills. Yet such are the surprises of horticulture that we may well continue longing to give a chance to this superb Gentian. It makes a number of branching stems that first decline and then ascend, being some 6 inches or so in length, set with a crowd of fleshy nerveless leaves on footstalks as long as themselves, and so concluding with nobly large and sumptuous white cups like those of a gigantic Linum, either solitary or in clusters of some three or four, or even half a dozen.

G. scabra is a handsome species, erect in habit, with narrowish oval dark leaves and loosely branching pyramids about 9 inches high, or more, of ample blue-purple bells. It is an Asiatic plant, and its Japanese form, *J. scabra Buergeri*, is perhaps even handsomer, but blooms even later (though quite as easy of culture), so as hardly to have attained its fullest beauty in most English gardens by the time the frosts and rain are beginning to descend in their final violence. It should be given the treatment of *G. septemfida* in full sun to hurry it.

G. Sceptrum is a fine large species from 2 to 4 feet high, with fleshy stems set in oblong-narrow pairs of leaves, and ending in a cluster of big deep blue blossoms about 2 inches long. (North America.)

G. septemfida with its various varieties is indeed a friend of man. No Gentian is more amenable, and hardly any more beautiful. It occupies all the alpine fields of the Caucasus up to about 9000 feet —a species after the heart and habit of *G. asclepiadea*, which it there accompanies. And none the less easy of culture; for, if a good sound piece be planted in good sound soil of peat and loam, in a comfortable place not parched or stagnant, it will yearly go ahead for ever with ever-increasing multitudes of its rather weak 9-inch stems, set with pairs of oval-pointed leaves, and ending, in August, with heads of the most beautiful ample open flowers, large and splendid, of clear soft blue, with the lobes of the corolla almost equalled by those of the folds, which are cut and jagged so that the wide bell has a rich look of ten segments, especially fringy and decorative and luxuriant. *G. septemfida* varies greatly, and many forms are often put upon the market as species. Such is *G. s. cordifolia*, from Turkish Armenia, a form differing only in the extra broadness and heart-shapedness of the leaves, which are also less pointed than in the type. *G. s. latifolia* likewise explains itself, and *G. s. procumbens* is a minuter delicacy or high-alpine development, from greater elevations in Caucasus and the Siberian Altai, with shorter prostrate stems, set with much smaller more broadly egg-shaped leaves, and ending usually in only one flower to a stem-shoot, or at most only a very few. The name *G. gelida*, sometimes given as a synonym for *G. septemfida*, belongs in reality, as we have seen, to an allied but wholly different species. *G. Lagodechiana*, however, is a dwarf *G. septemfida*.

G. sikkimensis is a common cousin of *G. Pneumonanthe* from the high Alps of Sikkim, where it sends out a large number of flopping stems about half a foot long, each ending in heads of blue bells nearly an inch in length, framed in a frill of the uppermost stem-leaves, while the blunted round ones at the base still persist.

G. sino-ornata forms vast hassocks of erect azure trumpets (in September) in any low rich cool level of the garden.

G. siphonantha; a blue August-blooming Cluster-head from China about 8 inches in height.

G. × spuria is a hybrid of *G. punctata × G. purpurea.*

G. straminea comes from Siberia, with flowers of palest yellow.

G. symphyandra is a rare species found on Oeta, and like a magnified *G. lutea*, with blossoms on longer footstalks in their bunches.

G. tergestina is the Dalmatian equivalent of *G. verna.*

G. tergloviensis must be carefully guarded against confusion with *G. imbricata* (Schleich.), the same name having been imposed on this species by Froelich. *G. tergloviensis* is an obscure little plant, which may occasionally be seen at considerable elevations on the granite of the Eastern ranges, but will usually be passed over as being *G. brachyphylla* in a loose condition. It is a lax and rather weak tuft, with oval-pointed small leaves overlapping thickly *even on the elongating flower-shoots*. They are truly like those of a small *G. verna*, but their density differentiates them, and they are also *rough at the edges*. The flowers are, as in the others of the high-alpine group, long-tubed stars of brilliant blue standing up almost stemless from the tuft. It should go into the special bed and there be faithfully cherished.

G. thianschanica is of large and leafy persuasion, though not quite so tall as the next, and with blue flowers.

G. tibetica attains the distinction of being ugly among the ugliest, a coarse weedy weed, inordinately leafy, with the packed clusters of blossom inordinately small and poor, of a dingy whitish-yellow in late summer. It will be found in every catalogue.

G. × Tommassii is a hybrid of *G. punctata × G. × superlutea*, the reverse cross to that which has produced *G. × Doerfleri*.

G. Townsoni is a most beautiful New Zealander from the Alps of the South Island, with quite small trowel-shaped leaves huddled at the base, and only a few ascending the slender stems of some 12 or 20 inches (or less), which are crowned with a large dense head of large white blossoms.

G. triflora comes from the mountains of Central Asia, and is very handsome, with narrow, glossy, dark foliage along the erect foot-high stems that carry a cluster of three or five blue trumpets at their ends, with perhaps one or two in the axils of the uppermost leaves. The plants should be grown in the conditions that suit *G. Pneumonanthe*, of which it gives a highly glorified picture—blooming, however, later in the summer, and indeed, even into late autumn. (R. F. 1915.)

G. tubiflora belongs to the high Alps of Kashmir and Kumaon, and is a minute dense tuft, about an inch or so in height, densely leafy, with small pointed leaves up the shoots of the season, which each end in a fine blue flower about an inch long, and half an inch across its face.

G. utriculosa is a pretty annual often seen in the Alps, with bright blossoms almost as large and bright as *G. verna's*, several in a loose spire up erect stems of 4 inches or so, and emerging from a remarkably baggy calyx.

G. Veitchiorum was originally shown as *G. ornata*. It is a beautiful species, making a clump rather like that of a narrow, longish-leaved *G. Gentianella*, and blooming generously in August, with long trumpets of gorgeous sapphire, opening widely with five ample lobes (and between them the fold-lobes of little less size) carried singly on rather weak and flopping stems of 2 inches or so, the whole plant tending to have an untidy look, thanks to the length and unevenness of the shoots. It should have the culture of *G. verna;* and has the glory of *G. excisa*.

G. venosa is only a name. It is a noble Chinese giant of several feet, with enormous white flowers veined with green, and almost suggesting a lily's.

G. venusta makes the same lovely tuffet, and has the same big blooms and the same prostrate stems as *G. tubiflora*, but the densely packed little leaves are oval, and the teeth of the calyx not pointed.

G. verna, though, is the Gentian of gentians, engraven sadly on the conscience of every gardener. How then shall the glory of the upper alps be made to repeat itself in sheets of heaven fallen over our gardens in June ? *Quot gentianae, tot sententiae :* give them masses of lime, says one ; give them no lime at all, says another ; a third recommends full sun ; and yet a fourth's Aunt Emily grew it for years in shade ; and while some prepare it a soil loose and spongy as possible, others ram down the loam with hammers to make it as hard as a threshing floor ; and many put it in sand, and many in peat, and many in loam ; and all sooner or later have plants that succeed ; and all, much sooner than later, have many more plants that don't. The fact is, that after the first essential of perfect drainage is attained, the treatment of *G. verna* may reasonably vary within very wide ranges in different gardens and conditions. It is a species of remarkably accommodating temper at home, and flourishes in soils and circumstances most diverse, so that there need never be any dogmatic prophesying that *G. verna* will wholly refuse to tolerate such and such an apparently preposterous treatment. There are, however, three points to which the hitherto unsuccessful cultivator would always do well to address himself : in the first place, let the soil of your Gentians consist of one part fine leaf mould, to two or three times as much of the coarsest Red Hill sand (for countless other mixtures do well, but this excelleth them all) ; in the second, let their bed be on a sunny slope, and their soil lightened with chips, and the bed itself be resting on a firm bottom of the roughest drainage ; in the third, let it be copiously watered by underground pipes all through the summer ; and in the fourth, and most important perhaps of all, be sure that the clumps are not solitary, but with plenty of company. It is the most sociable of species, and in the Alps and in Ireland it makes tussocks of unbroken glory in turf where, a month later, it is wholly hidden by the rankest jungle of grass, dock and Astrantia and all the overweening herbs of the pastures, grown up over its head in a tall impenetrable tangle ; nor is it ever found—or very rarely—even at higher elevations, sitting solid and solitary in a tuft like *G. aestiva*, but always forming tissues in the dazzling carpet of the alpine herbage. This, then, is no recluse to set in melancholy if honourable isolation in the garden ; it is too vigorous in growth, indeed, and likes neighbours too vigorous, to suit the choicest bed where the choicer smaller species live ; but in its own place it should have such company as *Saxifraga oppositifolia, Antennaria dioica, Festuca ovina tenuifolia,* thymes *Alyssum Wulfenianum,* and other lightly spreading species with which it can cope on equal terms and be the better for doing so. Furthermore, it will be greatly helped if, like the rest, it be kept dry with panes of glass or boughs of gorse in winter—these Gentians always want a good winter's rest, quite as much as do such obvious fluffets as Eritrichium ; and, indeed, at all times, despite their incessant thirst while growing, much prefer to have that thirst gratified from underground, and are by no means fond of having it administered overhead.

G. verna is a remarkably variable species in the Alps, and it is most dangerous to buy collected plants unless you are sure of the collector's eye and care and taste. For there are many small, thin, squinny-starred developments, not to be borne with when once you have seen the best forms doing their best, and with ample broad-lobed galaxies running *G. aestiva* close in the race of beauty. Whole districts of the Alps produce only worthless types of *G. verna* ; on the Grigna, for instance, it is not worth the trampling ; but where you get *G. aestiva*, there *G. verna* is always nettled into showing what it, too, can achieve. On the Mont Cenis, on the Schlern, it is more magnificent than tongue of man can tell, tangled up in a riotous carpet of Violas, Globularias, Potentillas, Erysimum, and Forget-me-not, till the gardener's soul falls fainting upon that floor of colour in helpless and hopeless ecstasy at sight of a reality so dispiritingly far ahead of his most radiant dreams. There are colour-forms, too, offered for large prices, and some of them worth having : *G. verna chionodoxa* is not at all infrequent— a pure albino, looking like a little white periwinkle ; the *rosea* variety, however, flatters itself, and is not so much pink as of a dingy mauve ; of which there is also another, of a curious dead-amethyst colour, rather subtle and attractive in its flat lifelessness ; Grandifloras and Atrocoeruleas are, of course, merely pre-eminent flowers in the type ; but *G. verna coelestina* is one of the very loveliest of plants, and as rare as *G. asclepiadea phaeina*, though forms of pale Cambridge-blue are not uncommon, and extremely beautiful. But they do not catch the keen and sharp-edged note of *coelestina's* vivid young azure, fresh as dawn and visible from far away on the hill ; and on some of the limestone alps of Lombardy the prevailing form, in great patches up and down the fine turf of the upper slopes, is of rich and velvety violet purple, lighter or darker in tone, but always opulent and splendid. Finally, let no one be unhappy for the white eye of *G. verna* gone blue ; that white eye merely marks the advertising stage of the flowers ; they all have that moment, and it is after fertilisation that they all economically shut it up again, and seem wholly blue. The plant may be propagated by cuttings struck in sand, or raised from seed ; it is exceedingly unsatisfactory and odious to collect in the Alps, as a rule, owing to its habit of running threadily about in the grass ; unless, indeed, a favoured spot can be found, where it tends more to form clumps, as it does indeed, by the million, in the West of Ireland, among the rank herbage of Ladies' Tresses, Ladies' Bedstraw, Ladies' Fingers, and the whole botanical department of a lady's plenishing. But in the alps of Teesdale it is usually thin and weazen in habit, with singleton rosettes. This species is the most widespread of the mountain-section, stretching from England and Ireland, through all the alpine chains of Europe, far away into the North and West of Asia, hybridising here and there with others of the group, as with *G. bavarica* below the Col de Clapier, but never, apparently, contracting, any more than any other of the star-gentians, any alliance with the trumpeters. Like *G. bavarica* and *G. Gentianella*, too, it has a pleasant habit in the Alps, as in the garden, of sending up a lovely bloom or two in the autumn.

G. villosa (*G. ochroleuca*, Froel.) is of no such value, being a stout and leafy American plant, with open flowers of greenish white, veined with green, and striped with lilac.

G. vulgaris. See under *G. "acaulis."*

G. Walujewi is lumping and gollopshious as its name—a leafy coarse Siberian of 10 inches, with clustered small stars of pallid bluish tone in late summer.

G. Weschniakowii, again, dispenses us from calling upon its name in loving tones. For who will coo upon *G. Weschniakowii*, and murmur the music of its syllables to the moon, when they learn that it is even larger and leafier than the last, with flowers of a similar unattractiveness, produced in autumn ?

Geranium.—It is not possible here to enter the vast tangle of the bigger Geraniums ; the race is one of bewildering magnitude in the North and the South, and the East and the West, climbing often from the lower to the upper alpine regions, and continuing down the long line of the Andes along the crests, in a race of minute and lovely dwarfs. Of larger species, valuable in border and wild garden, there is no end, either in the Old World or the New ; and, heavy though be the need of guidance among the false names and synonyms of these in catalogues, they are not so germane to our rock-garden as to leave us time (as I had hoped) to linger with them, but we must at once pass on to the smaller and more appropriate species, all of which bloom through summer into autumn, can easily be raised from seed, and are of the easiest cultivation in full sun and light open soil.

G. aconitifolium is the correct name of *G. rivulare.*

G. alpicola beckons our hopes to the high alps of Guatemala, where it nestles in neat mats of very finely-divided foliage (all except the upper surface of the leaves being shimmering silver), set with staring wide flowers of soft lilac-blue, that sit in stemless loveliness close upon the cushion.

G. argenteum is one of the loveliest things in nature, as you see the long grassy lawns along the crests of Monte Baldo all shimmering with the sheeted hoar-frost of its packed and glistering silver foliage, scattered over, up and down the green expanses, with great diaphanous dog-rose blossoms densely peppered over the ridges as if someone indeed had strewed pale little wild-roses across the lawn, for the passing of some heavenly bride. In gardens, however, this rare and most choice treasure (only to be met with here and there in the high warm turf of the Lombard limestones, Tyrol, Carinthia, the Apennines, and very rarely indeed in Dauphiné) grows with such an excessive willingness as to forget the hills and become fat, waxing into a tuft a foot across, and 6 inches high, instead of keeping the packed dwarfness of its mountain stature. In any case it is always of the rarest loveliness, and if it be specially desired to keep it dwarf, the plant can be restricted to meagre diet, in specially poor and stony soil. It may be propagated by seed and by fragments pulled off the crowns and struck as cuttings ; it usually sows itself freely in the garden.

G. caespitosum makes many crowns, forming into clumps of fine leaves, and then emitting a number of stems about 5 inches high, carrying big flowers that vary in different shades of intense purple. (Wyoming, &c.)

G. cinereum replaces *G. argenteum* in the Pyrenees, where the more beautiful species is not found. For *G. cinereum* has not the neatness of habit, nor the argent foliage, nor the sweet pinky pallor of blossom, but is a little ampler, a little duller, a little larger and less fine in the foliage (which is ash-grey rather than silvery), a little taller in the 5-inch stems, and blunted in the tone of its big flowers, whose ground is of washed-out white, lined and flushed with dim claret-rose. A handsome, recommendable, and pleasant little Geranium, yet unwise in thus presuming to challenge comparison with the incomparable *argenteum.* There is, however, a white form, of a purity and brilliance and charm beyond all others, and, until *G. argenteum* has gone and done likewise, the honours almost remain with the white *cinereum*, which, however, does not breed true from seed, but produces all gradations of flush in its children, and hybridises with its fellow-type, *G. argenteum*, of the same blood, but different Alps.

G. Fremontii.—This, as sent out, is a gawky and odious weed. But the true species should surely not be thus. It has many rounded, regularly incised leaves in a tuft, each on a foot-stalk from **3** to **8** inches long. The leafy branching stems are about 6 inches high, set with leaves, and bearing big flowers of pale rose-purple. (From the Central Rockies, as far as the coast of California.)

G. grandiflorum slinks into this category by missing the full stature of *G. pratense*, being a weakly or decumbent plant with clear-blue, white-eyed flowers of enormous size, more or less in clusters at the end of 10-inch stems, and twice the size of *G. pratense's*. (It has a specially lovely dwarfed form, *G. g. alpinum*, from the upper alps of Turkestan.)

G. Kotschyi.—Though *G. tuberosum* has little charm, better things may be said of its alpine sub-species, which, high on Elburs, sprouts from a round dark bulb like a cyclamen's, and sends up a twisting stem of only 4 inches, carrying a close spike or pyramid of large rose-purple blossoms, which, like those of *G. tuberosum*, have the lobes so deeply cleft that they look as if the flowers had ten petals.

G. Lozanii, in the bushy places of the high Mexican Alps, has the whole habit of *G. caespitosum*, but the enormous flowers are golden.

G. minimum is the smallest of all, a lichen-like scab of smooth, unsilvered, hairless foliage, jewelled with white cups of large size for a plant so microscopic. A high-alpine from the Andes, with other kindred, of which the best are *GG. cucullatum, stramineum, sericeum, Lechleri*, and *Ruizii*.

G. moupinense is precisely like our own neat glossy *G. lucidum* in leaves and habit, but the flowers are of twice the size, pale purple, and like those of *G. pratense*, borne on twin pedicels of which one, however, outgrows the other. (From the same sort of situation that *G. lucidum* affects, in the shady mountain rocks of Szechuan.)

G. muscoideum is like nothing so much as a dome of *Androsace helvetica* studded with the white stars of a Potentilla ; a minute and lovely tuft of silver silk, shining on the mountains of Peru.

G. nanum is a quite tiny dwarfed version of *G. cinereum* from Djebel Ghat in Morocco.

G. napuligerum is a fine species, with a sort of bulb for a root. In habit it often suggests *G. cinereum*, but with larger, brighter pinkish flowers on weakly flopping or ascending stems of 8 or 10 inches.

G. nivale is, however, the last word that this race has to speak in the way of beauty, and that word unfortunately is spoken to the deaf winds high on the limestone crests of La Oroya in the Peruvian Andes, 12,000 feet above the steamers passing far away at sea. Figure a very dense sheet of minute silver-sheening, fleshy foliage, like that of some *G. argenteum* fed for many years on gin, and reduced to the most Lilliputian proportions ; then, into that sheet and all over it, among the upstanding finely-clawed and fingered foliage, stick flowers like those of an *Oxalis enneaphylla*, larger and whiter and wider and more delicately vase-shaped than any ever seen by man. Thus you will have some faint notion of *G. nivale*, and its triumphant loveliness.

G. Pylzowianum stands eminent among the most precious of my introductions. In the alpine hay throughout the Northern Marches of Tibet, it runs very frailly about, ejecting on twinned thread-fine pedicels larger flowers than those of *G. sanguineum*, and of a purer, clearer rose ; while the gaunt, barren shingles above, at 13,000–14,000 feet, are filled with tufted masses of what is at present declared, but certainly mistakenly, to be only a high-alpine form of this, but making such clumpy cushions of gleaming silver foliage, so over-borne by flights of palest pearl-pink blossom, that *G. argenteum* itself is beaten out of the field.

G. Renardii hardly reaches a foot, so that its beauty may make a successful claim upon our notice. Its five-lobed rounded leaves are all clad in silk on both sides, and shimmering with silver beneath. The blooms stand up in a loose pyramid, and are of clear white delicately veined. This lovely thing belongs to the fields of Ossetian Caucasus.

G. sanguineum is too large and coarse, and of too fiery a terribleness of colour for any choice spot in the rock-garden, but its albino is so dainty and graceful as to be worthy of admittance anywhere, while its variety, or sub-species *G. lancastriense*, is, in present default of *G. nivale*, the jewel of the race, making flat cushions of fine green, set all the summer through with the most beautiful wide ample flowers of the tenderest and truest rose-pink, veined with deeper lines, and each dancing in delight at its own loveliness, on a delicate fine stem. From spring to winter this never ceases to be in bloom, and from seed comes copiously and true. Even as one of the sights of the world is that of *G. argenteum* sheeting upmost Baldo in silver, and starring its lawns with wavering rose-pale bells, so another parallel wonder is to see the fine lawn of Lancashire, at the one classical place, all set with the similar dancing, blushing blossoms of *G. lancastriense*, flat upon their mass, and starring the long levels of seaward turf with galaxies of pink. And here, too, though it remains constant to itself, yet it also seems to breed back towards *G. sanguineum*, and the most magnificent forms may be seen, together with every degree of inter-mediacy, with *lancastriense's* close-matted prostrate habit, and the large, uniformly crimson-red blossoms of *G. sanguineum*, yet richer and truer in tone, and with that opulent veining ; but always keeping flat, whatever be the colour of the flower. And always keeping flat, no less, in the garden, though they do not there have quite the neat, ground-hugging tendencies of *G. lancastriense,* for which one of the loveliest of associations on rock-work is to get it in drifts, with *Potentilla nepalensis Willmottiae* in deeper shades of hot rose, and cool clouds of china blue among them from *Campanula Bellardii,* or, even better, *Campanula haylodgensis.*

G. sessiliflorum says that it is in cultivation, but the ugly little prostrate weed we have by no means answers to the description of *G. sessiliflorum* in the Alps of South America and Tasmania. For our treasure merely forms a mat of dowdy leafage, close beneath which sit huddling still dowdier little white flowers; whereas in its proper form the plant makes a great woody trunk, at the end of which it breaks into an immense rounded head of countless small white blossoms, with leaves suggesting those of *Saxifraga granulata,* standing out all round on long stems with the oddest hen-and-chickens effect.

G. soboliferum belongs to the bogs of North China and Korea, and is a handsome species with very finely-divided leaves, and violet flowers more than an inch across. Its rhizome often emits runners.

G. subargenteum is recorded by Willkomm from the Pyrenees, and declared to be nearer to *argenteum* (which does not there occur) than to *G. cinereum* (which does); from which it differs in its neater habit and leaves clothed with silver on the under surface.

G. Traversii stands alone in its section, a really beautiful and dwarf silver-leaved thing from New Zealand, which proves hardy, and spreads heartily, and is most attractive with its tidy habit, all shimmering with silk, and its multitudes of pretty rose-pink flowers on stems of a few inches. At least it is thus they are worn with us; there are other descriptions, and fancy names, such as *G. Traversii elegans,* &c., which seem to mask a certain doubt of the plant's true standing, a doubt which is not annihilated by the official description, which records the flowers of *G. Traversii* to be large and white, whereas in general experience, and in the words of catalogues, they are bright pink, and also (not in the words of catalogues), a trifle small for the foliage-masses —which rather suggest, as a rough parallel, a trebled and silvery version of *Erodium corsicum.* It is a species, in short, of cosy look and the most endearing rosy charm, to be treated with due regard to its provenance, and given a good warm slope to fill with its runners, of which some may be taken off and potted in autumn, lest winter wreak some harm to their parent with its wet.

G. Wallichianum.—This name is the father of perplexity. There are so many usurpers of it that each catalogue usually contains two. The true species may, however, be known at a glance. If you look at the stems you will see that where the leaves and sprays break out from them, there will always be, at that dividing point, *a pair of very large and broadly-oval reddish bracts or leaflets,* fusing together at their meeting-point on the stalk, to which they then form a sort of short sheath. And these are to be seen *in no other Geranium.* The species comes from bushy places on the Himalaya, and in cultivation the one form or sub-species to be reckoned with is that gem called *Buxton's variety,* which is a Geranium of extreme charm and value, decumbent and almost a match in habit for *G. lancastriense,* but with larger, thicker foliage, not unlike that of a condensed and diminished *G. pratense,* with a white mark between their lobes, and often white marblings on their surface ; while the flowers, which appear through late summer far on into autumn towards winter, are of the most imperial size, and in the best forms (for it varies a little from seed) of glorious violet-blue with a clear, broad eye of white. This should be grown from cuttings, as well as from seed, and it should have a choice and sheltered corner in good soil, for it is well worthy of the highest favour, and is not always perfectly resistent if the winter be specially raw, or the plant's position too exposed.

G. Weberbauerianum is a dainty little Peruvian species, with tufts of small, scalloped, rounded leaves, standing up on thread-fine stems of about 3 inches, among which, and surpassing them, appear other fine stems carrying delicate veined flowers of white. This also should have a choice and forward place, being a plant that does not run, but remains a neat and concise mass from the woody root. (This description also roughly fits *G. Webbianum* of gardens—a variety of an Indian species.)

G. Weddellii takes us back to the high land of longing where *G. nivale* also dwells. For it is on Sorata in the Bolivian Andes, at 12,500 feet, that will be found this gleaming beauty, being the perfect twin of *G. nivale,* but that the great white cups inserted all over the silken-silver cushions are rayed with colour instead of being purely snowy, while the packed leaves are slightly smaller, only about three-quarters of an inch across. So here most worthily ends the complete list, to date, of the best among the small-growing Geraniums, of which indeed, as well as of the big ones, there are hundreds more in every country, climate, and situation—the foregoing choice having shown that in their race we have indeed all the world to pick from, and that if Observation with extended view surveys mankind from China to Peru, she will also incidentally be embracing in her gaze an almost equal diversity of Geraniums, and an almost equal diversity of merit in them also, from the weeds and glories of the tropics to the weeds and glories of the Alps.

GEUM.

Gerbera Jamesonii is not in place among alpines, nor hardly, unless with precautionary fusses which its spidery and artificial beauty does not entitle it to receive, in the garden at all. As for the Asiatic Gerberas, *GG. piloselloeides, nivea, lanuginosa, Anandria*, and *Kunzeana*, these indeed are hardy, but instead of an artificial beauty have a wholly natural ugliness that disqualifies them no less for the garden, being dowdy little weeds after the style of *Homogyne alpina*, with nothing that even enthusiasm can say for them, except that the cottony reverse that some of them have to their dark and shining leafage has a certain value. And we do not possess any other of the South Africans, some of which, such as the purple-flowered *G. asplenifolia* and *G. Elsae*, might well be beautiful, if one had any hope that they would not prove tender as well.

Geum.—Many and bad are the bad Geums, and very good the good. In almost all cases any quite ordinary soil and sunny situation suits them ; and they flower freely through the summer, and can readily be raised from seed.

G. Borisii, from Bulgaria, has merit in the rock-garden, producing flowers of brilliant yellow on stems of only 6 inches.

G. bulgaricum is a worthless plant when true, forming tufts of immense leaves like washed-out green flannel, among which appear clusters of bloodless little pale-yellow flowers. But there is a false plant under this name newly come into cultivation, which promises to be magnificent, having fine foliage, not unlike that of *G. reptans*, but neater, and fine glowing flowers of flame.

G. coccineum, a much confused species from Asia Minor, which has yielded many varieties, especially Mrs. Bradshaw, a double form about a foot high with fiery scarlet blossoms of special size ; like all the red Geums it does best in a rather cool place, and like the rest, it is spoiled for the rock-garden by its height, and the legginess of its look. The same applies to the quite different *G. chiloense*, which is often confused with *G. coccineum*, being a distinct and much taller species from Chili. *G. Eweni* and *G. Heldreichii* are forms of garden origin arising out of *G. coccineum*, with big flowers of orange red, more or less double, and varying into other developments, perpetually appearing as " magnificum," " splendens," and so forth, but all inclined to look gawky in the rock-garden, with no mass of uprising stalks, but three or four sticking out this way and that.

G. dryadoeides, from Northern Japan, strikes out a wholly new line of attractiveness, however, for it makes running masses, closely clustered, of toothed, leafleted foliage, like that of a Rose or a Sanguisorba, and well above these, alone on perfectly bare stems of 3 or 4 inches, stand sturdily erect the ample-petalled staring blossoms of pure white.

G. elatum, from the high woods of Himalaya, is disqualified by its height of some 2 feet and more, though individually the big golden blooms have merit, if only they would not so stand on stilts.

G. magellanicum can reach 2 feet, or stay at 2 inches. Its nearest neighbour in the race is *G. pyrenaicum,* and it is often confused with *G. coccineum* and *G. chiloense.* The flowers range from yellow to red.

G. miniatum is *G. chiloense.* See under *G. coccineum.*

G. montanum, when all is said and done, is almost the most precious of the family in the rock-garden. It is the golden Geum that creeps so close to the ground with its puckered green leaves and their large, rounded lobe at the end, and then those fat suns of bright gold that sit almost stemless on the Alps, and even in the garden do not exceed a quite modest stature of some 3 inches or so, as a rule. It is by far the most lovable of its race, and in the garden blooms early, and combines most especially with *Anemone Robinsoniana* and the double *A. nemorosa,* thriving so heartily almost anywhere that it soon forms into ample mats, whose fluffy roseate whirls of seed in autumn are only less notable than the ample yellow orbs of spring.

G. pyrenaicum is very much the same, though taller in habit, even if rather larger also in the blossom. The leaves, too, are much longer, with the rounded lobe at the end especially big, and the little feathering leaflets up the blade more distant, and reduced to almost nothing. There are, however, dwarf high-alpine forms of this that approach the neat golden charm of *G. montanum.*

G. radiatum (*Sieversia Peckii*) is a North American species of some value, varying between 4 inches high and 16 inches, and with from one to five large yellow flowers.

G. reptans is the special glory of the highest moraines and shingles on non-calcareous Alps, where it makes vast woody rootstocks running down for yards among the blocks in the most coarse and barren tumbled ruins of those grim places, forming wide jungles of ferny foliage, with the leaves much more evenly feathered, and longer and finer and taller and more upstanding than in the tight and compacted stout-looking foliage of *G. montanum* (which is about a third of the size in all parts), and making mounds and green colonies that look singularly unnatural up there, where nothing, one feels, ought to have a stem at all; and yet here are boskets of this great thing among the boulders in plumy masses of 9 inches high and several feet across, often spreading into colonies many yards wide, or else in single clumps, from which long red strawberry-runners are emerging, to

convey the youngling tuft at the tip to a new habitation of its own, and
so establish the group in spreading force. The flowers, too, are of a
magnificence to match the clump, for they are borne singly on stems
that may be as much as 6 inches high, and are enormous golden suns
that would make two of *montanum's*, to be succeeded by a similarly
reduplicated splendour of silkier, fluffier, more wild and catherine-
wheelish whirls of silver. *G. reptans* is never found except at these
gaunt grey heights and never found except on the primary formations,
where, however, in the last and most terrible barrens of stone, you may
pretty confidently reckon upon seeing its luminous faces glowing at
you from afar like flecks of fallen sunlight there among the débris.
It is undoubtedly the noblest and most gorgeous of high-alpines, alike
in growth and in flower, and there is nothing in the world for which
it can be mistaken. In cultivation, however, its heart fails and it
often proves a mimp, though sometimes thriving massively for a year
or two in the kitchen-garden border, abundantly blooming and seeding, indeed, but never abiding long in one stay. For on its subterranean water-supply I think the plant depends far more than even its
other neighbours up there—as any one may understand who has seen
to what a depth those woody trunks have to plunge for food, through
what a sahara of stony sterility, where none of its neighbours usually
dare to intrude on ground in which only the Geum could find support.
Yet there, and there alone, will the Geum live, and in such places
accordingly, for the sake of its permanence at least, should it be tried
in the garden, though here it may be very happy for awhile in fatter
circumstances, and often, in cultivation, seems thus to be more profuse
in the production of its huge and brilliant flowers from August through
September. It is always free with its seed, but this is curiously reluctant to germinate, and perhaps should be sown on the most arid
parts of the ashpit instead of cosily in pots, so as to make it feel more
at home and prompt in springing : the plant, however, should be
multiplied by its copious runners, each one of which will root like
that of a strawberry whether you look after it or no. Finally, a bird
in the hand is worth two in the bush ; and rich, very deep soil, full
and fat, will give you a greater certainty of joy in its flowers than
will, so far as my experience goes, the more austere circumstances of
the ordinary moraine, in which the Geum goes on living from year to
year indeed, but is chary of its glory. A moraine, in fact, ought to be
built specially for it—a special moraine, 3 or 4 feet deep or more, with
a stream running below all the summer, and a mixture composed of
practically nothing but granitic grit, and powdered old manure, silted
among the largest and coarsest granite or sandstone blocks in

brutal assortment, from the size of a child's head to that of a man's coffin.

G. × rhaeticum is the result of one of the rare meetings between *G. reptans* and *G. montanum*. For it is only in the high places of the Engadine that, as you are walking across a stone patch, you are suddenly struck with a monstrous *G. montanum* at your feet—a mass of the ordinary dense creeping habit, but with leaves that somehow look different, even if the flowers were not so much larger, and had not that especially short-petalled, fat look, and cool clear glamour of electric gold that one is so familiar with in the more noble *reptans* : and, true enough, though one takes the high road and the other the low road, the two species have met at last here beside the waters of the upmost rivers of the Engadine, *G. reptans* descending from their austere source, with the stones that are their cradle, while *G. montanum* mounts with the Primulas, in the comfortable fine turf to which the stone-slides fall. And here, accordingly, *G. rhaeticum* is born, and a most beautiful and valuable child, of a glory rare among Geums, having the beauty of one parent and the heartiness of another ; the general neat charm of *montanum* coupled with something of the immense and irradiating flowers of *G. reptans*, whose alloy of gold-and-silver light makes so much sharper and keener a pale flame than the more ordinary robust yellow of *G. montanum*.

G. rivale is our own Water-Avens, and a common species in the sub-alpine meadows of the North, though a rare one in the South. It is, however subtle in its charm of nodding terra-cotta-coloured flowers in purple calyces, too unsubtle in its manners for admittance to the garden, for it soon proves as much a weed as ugly little *G. urbanum*, and has to be as laboriously got rid of. But there are finer forms advertised in catalogues : Leonard's variety is good, and so is the natural hybrid, *G. × intermedium*, between *G. rivale × G. urbanum*, which results in large, wide, rosy-salmon blossoms of the utmost beauty and too rarely seen. It is, alas ! many years now since, in an open place of the woods here, I came upon my first and unrepeated sight of *G. intermedium*.

G. Rossii should now, according to some, change its name to *Sieversia turbinata*. But the old classification will serve for English gardens which are not often troubled with the American Geums, handsome though this particular species be, dwarf after the style of *G. montanum*, only about 3 inches high or half a foot at most, with fine flowers of bright yellow, showing up well above the dark green and purple of the foliage.

G. triflorum (*Sieversia ciliata*) is a tallish, reddish North American

PLATE 39.

GERANIUM PYLZOWIANUM.
(Photo. W. Purdom.)

PLATE 40.

INULA ACAULIS.
(Photo. R. A. Malby.)

ISOPYRUM FARRERI.
(Photo. W. Purdom.)

plant, not as attractive as our own *G. rivale*, though rather in the same line.

G. uniflorum is the only good Geum for our purpose from New Zealand, and a really valuable species, for it has the neat dwarf habit of *G. montanum*, with no leaves except at the base, creeping along the ground ; and these densely eyelashed leaves are after the ferny style of *G. reptans*, but the flowers on their slender stems of 3 inches or a little more are large and fine indeed, as in the rest, but of a pure white.

Not here, however, ends the tale of Geum, but so many are the dowdy and unprofitable species alike from the Old World and from the New, from the North and the South, that collectors will be well advised to look with doubt on any species not engraved upon this list, unless it have a full and alluring description of its own.

Gilia.—This race of flimsy but astonishingly brilliant and lovely plants from California and the warm States of the New World (standing between Phlox and Polemonium) offers our gardens, indeed, delicious dainty annuals or biennials of rare charm, if such things be permitted there, in a warm, worthless, sandy place, as *GG. Parryae, aurea, aurea decora, dianthoeides, androsacea, dichotoma*, but it also gives us a few good perennials for the same situations (if in rather better though still light soil) in that *G. pungens* which is now being sent out with the most " bragian boldness " as *Phlox Hoodii*, being a spiculous-looking, erect bushling, of pinky-white stars (with a variety *G. p. caespitosa*, which helps to excuse its false pretences by being a fair copy of *Phlox Douglasii*, very densely matted, and densely covered with *four-lobed* pale-white flowers). And there are many others that might be tried in the South : *G. californica*, so lovely with its solid white-eyed blooms of silky rose and lilac ; *lilacina, Veitchii, Watsonii*, the variety *Bridgesii* of *G. aggregata* (which is only about a foot high, sweet, and with trumpets of the most flaming rose-scarlet). And then there is still the little prostrate creeping perennial with violet flowers, *G. Larseni* from Lars' volcanic peak in California ; and *G. Nuttallii*, about a foot high, with divided leaves and many dense clusters of white stars with a yellow throat. No others clamour to be catalogued.

Gillenia trifoliata and *G. stipulacea* are two gracious plants for cool, moist ground, making bushes of some 2 feet high and more, with leaves divided into three lobes, and erect, leafy stems that end in a loose, wide shower of a few pinky-white stars, very delicate and well-bred in effect, if of no dazzling show, suggesting some dim and starved Spiraea of scanty bloom. They blossom in full and late summer too, so have their especial value in the bog garden or moist corner, being ample in their dainty development, but not rampers or runners.

Gladĭŏlus sĕgĕtum and *G. illyricus* may be poked in anywhere on the upper slopes, but *G. paluster* and *G. imbricatus* are smaller and more jewel-like easy species that may have a more prominent place : the latter may be seen glowing among the orchises and milkwort and rough glorified herbage of every kind of lovely flower that fills the open slopes of coppice on the climb from Varenna to Esino on the Grigna, being only about 6 or 8 inches high, with beautiful flowers of an amaranth that glows like carbuncles amid the grass in the sunshine, but might be rather trying in more sophisticated places or less fierce illumination. It prolongs the season of the race by blooming into August, and does not hate damper places. As for the many that remain, they may be found in catalogues, and these will not easily produce a beauty to conquer *G. primulinus*, which in nature loves the drenching incessant spray of the Victoria Falls, but in the garden seems to put up with almost anything, yielding, too, a lovely race of hybrids as hearty and as happy as itself, and flowering likewise in latest summer.

Glaucidium palmatum is a stout imperial Ranunculad from the woods of Japan, about 2 feet high or more, with ample and splendid foliage like that of a maple, at the top of which hang solitary flowers of satiny rich violet (and there is also *G. violaceum*).

Glaucium.—Among the countless numbers of Horned Poppies, one is pre-eminently perennial and useful. This is *G. grandiflorum* from Eastern Europe and the Levant, which has silky very finely divided and beautiful lyrate leaves, with big blossoms in April, of a fulvous orange with violet blotches at the base. Hot sandy places.

Globularia.—A group of useful if not brilliant little shrubby plants carrying larger or smaller balls of pale grey-blue fluff. They are all Southerners, and should have light soil on a warm slope. Rather large and coarse are *G. trichosantha* and *G. nudicaulis*, both of which send up 6-inch stems ending in a steely mop, but in the one case the stem is naked, while in the other it is set with leaves. These are not high-alpines, and thrive well in any sheltered and not too torrid place, being plants of the upper coppice, usually in the limestone ranges. Of the two, *G. nudicaulis* has the greater preference for half-shade, this being the plant that one so invariably passes through on one's way to the alps, occupying the uppermost woodland zone in the coarse grass and sedge. *G. Willkommii* differs chiefly from *G. trichosantha* in having but one nerve to its 10-inch leaves instead of five. The most generally useful, however, is the much smaller and neater

G. cordifolia, which makes flat lawns and carpets of neat, dark, ever-green rosettes, almost concealed in June by the number of its nearly stemless fluffets. It is especially beautiful as a harmonising mist in that tissued carpet of the higher alps, where it supplies a neutral ground of softest blue-grey haze, for the golden crashes of Erysimum and Potentilla, the restless universal dance of the mountain-pansies in every shade from creamy-white to purple, and the flaring blues here and there of *Gentiana verna*, with the dropped indigo trumpets of *G. latifolia* among them in tones of sudden darkness. These are the uses of the plant in the garden—to accompany others, and supply an obbligato to Gentians and Erysimum on light and sunny slopes. Its twin beauty, however, *G. stygia* (which differs from it in having larger leaves, yet shorter stems, and branches very frail indeed and not woody), is far too rare at present, even in its own home on Chelmos, to be thus easily prescribed for in the garden, and used as a nurse ; nor must we so outrage the equally rare *G. spinosa* from the limestone crevices of Spain, which is smooth and prostrate and spiny, with rosettes of toothed, oblong, hairless leaves. There are many depths of colour among the different forms and species, and of all Globularias albinoes also. Even smaller and neater than these last are the livelier-beautied *G. bellidifolia* and *G. incanescens*, of which this latter has especially charming grey-blue foliage, while *G. nana* is the smallest of all, hardly more than an inch high at the most. These three, being so minute and lovely, will be welcome in much choicer places than those of *G. cordifolia*, and it must be remembered that all are lovers of sun and drought and light limy soil in a specially intense degree, so that ill-drained richness and damps make them as tender as Perilla.

Gnaphalium.—Hardly any of these are worth trying, but *G. Traversii*, from the Alps in the South Island of New Zealand, is a dwarf neat thing, white with wool and about 3 or 4 inches high.

Goebeimia alopecuroeides (Sophora Jauberti) is a feather-leaved pea-flower of some 2 feet high or less, for a hot, dry place, with heads of white blossom in summer.

Goodenia (Sellera) repens is a rare little Tasmanian for a very sheltered warm spot in cool moist soil, where it runs along with ground-hugging narrow foliage, and lonely short-spurred white flowers that go blue at the tips.

Grindelia.—No species of this Composite family is valuable : its members are like coarse and inferior small Inulas.

Gunnera.—While the great Gunneras have their places beside the water, there are a number of small Gunneras that are as tiny and neat as their brothers are vast and tropical. Of such are *GG. monoica*, *magellanica, prorepens, microcarpa, flavida, densiflora, dentata, arenaria,* and *Hamiltoni*—tidy ramping carpets for a rather moist sheltered level. They have, however, no attraction apart from the covering of foliage with which they deck bare ground in summer, but which they put away in winter, leaving it barer then ever.

Gutierrezia Euthamiae is a small North-American bush of some 10 inches or so, beset with small Composite yellow flowers in late summer. It makes no powerful appeal.

Gymnolomia multiflora, a Mexican immeritorious Composite of tender and almost annual habit.

Gypsophĭla, a race of greatest value for the rocks, where its members heartily thrive in any open and sunny place in very deep soil (for they have enormous roots), gratifying the whole summer with a never-ceasing shower of pink or white stars. Many, too, are the taller, stouter sorts, after the fashion of *G. paniculata;* but these are best avoided, with that one exception, for many of them are coarse and leafy things of no charm, such as ugly *G. Rokejeka.* All of them seed freely, and all may be multiplied by cuttings, either of shoots or of roots. The following list contains such of the species as are best fitted in habit for the rock-garden :

G. alpigena declares with truth that it is born on the Alps, where it attains a stature of 4 inches or so, delicately spraying this way and that with blossoms of rose and white.

G. aretioeides is most especially to be desired. In the high Alps of Persia, as for instance in the cliffs of Demavend, it forms masses flat and hard and dense, resembling those of *Silene exscapa,* but infinitely more beautiful when the whole cushion is closely starred with pearl-pale flowers.

G. cerastioeides is creeping, dwarf, and hairy, forming into cosy neat tufts, unlike one's ideas of the race, however, in the green fatness of the foliage, no less than in the size and amplitude of its solid, stolid white blossoms, with veins of purple, that appear in profusion over the clump of 2 or 3 inches (or less)—a charming easy-going species from the mid-alpine regions of Kashmir and Sikkim.

G. erinacea makes a tight twisted woody bush of five inches or so, very grey, with sharp fine leaves like fat needles, and then loose erupting sprays of white flowers. (Alps of Cabul.) (*G. acerosa* has the same habit, but differs for the worse in having tight-headed flower-clusters.)

G. frankenioeides may perhaps be a variety or sub-species of *G. libanotica,* but is especially neat and dwarf upon the ground, with rosy blossom.

GYPSOPHILA.

G. glauca is found in the screes of Kasbek, and is like *G. repens* but that the whole blue-grey little plant is clothed in glands.

G. libanotica is rather larger, attaining even to a foot, but none the less attractive, with small stiff fleshy leaves of blue-grey, set on the countless stems of 6 or 12 inches, burdened with their spattering showers of large pink stars that may be seen in the highest cliffs of Lebanon and Cappadocia. (*G. curvifolia* is near this, but a foot and a half high, with purple blossom.)

G. microphylla is a yet minuter flat sheet than *G. frankenioeides*, still more like a Frankenia. (Alps of Alatau.)

G. nana forms close cushions in the high rocks of Greece, and is then set with pink flowers as big as those of *G. repens*, often sitting singly on stems that hardly emerge at all from the cushion of colour.

G. ortegioeides is also *Tunica xylorrhiza;* no bad companion for *T. Saxifraga,* which it exactly recalls in habit and spraying fine grace, and copiousness of pretty blossom ; but the plant is hairy, it has a woodyish stock, and the flowers are white with veins of red. (Cappadocia.)

G. petraea is a creeping running species from Alatau, very branching and leafy, with many very narrow leaves ; and then terminal sprays of blossom, whose fruiting heads ultimately turn downwards on their stems. The flowers are described by authority as varying from pink to blue. "Credat Judaeus Apella" for the present ; blue is a colour hardly treated by authorities, who seem to think it a kind of charity-word to cover many sins. When in doubt, say blue, seems their motto ; I have known *Saxifraga florulenta* described as blue, to say nothing of *Androsace alpina,* that pinkest of all pinks that blush on the cheek of the world.

G. repens is the universal beautiful Gypsophila of all the stony open places and banks in the Alps, and a species of no less beauty and value in the garden as well, making mounds and long dense curtains of foliage from a ledge, surfy with sprays of rosy or pearly white all through the summer. There are forms to be found on the hills : whites and pinks of exceptional brilliance or size of blossom ; the variety *G. monstrosa* is a hybrid with *G. Steveni*—a thing of amazing floriferousness and beauty, but in habit of flower more branching, and more Tunica-like in the profusion of its 6-inch fine sprays of flower that make a mass a yard across ; whereas typical *G. repens* continues steadily on its forward downward way, throwing up its not-quite-so-abundant showers of bloom on stems that are not so freely branchy as those of the hybrid—which it was indeed unfair to label with a name so ominous and so suggestive of duplicity. Both are indestructible.

405

G. serpylloeides has all the neat perfectly prostrate habit of a little Thyme, but the flowers with which it is jewelled are large and pink as those of *G. repens*, making a rare carpet of beauty.

G. Steveni has no great merit, for it is in the same line as *G. repens*: from the screes of Georgia, but with smaller stars of about half the size, and a taller habit that can attain to a foot or more.

G. × Suendermannii is a hybrid between *G. repens* and *G. cerastioeides* —a really valuable addition to our gardens, being a stronger, lower-growing plant than *G. monstrosa*, and conspicuously free of large ample white flowers even among the rest of its prodigally-blooming kin.

G. tenuifolia lives in the upper alpine rocks of Caucasus, where it makes a stout thick branching rhizome, emitting tufts of smooth rosetted foliage, and then stems of 3 or 4 inches waving sprays of rose-pink blossoms larger than those of *G. repens*.

G. transylvanica is the plant often offered as *Banffya petraea*. Under either name it has no particular or special merit, being a rock Gypsophila with loose and airy galaxies of white stars.

G. venusta fills the vineyards of Syria with profusion of extra-large pink flowers with purple at their base. In growth, however, it is of rather taller habit than these last.

G. violacea belongs to Eastern Siberia, where it makes cushions of hairless foliage which emit a number of branching leafy stems carrying each a scanty burden of violet stars.

G. Wiedemannii is a diminished version of *G. venusta*.

H

Haastia is the Vegetable Sheep of New Zealand, forming humped rolling masses of minute foliage so closely packed as to seem one solid dome or mound, like dotted sleeping sheep up and down the hills. As it ascends to alpine elevations it might be made to prove hardy, if worth the trouble.

Haberlea rhodopensis is twin-sister of Ramondia, for any shady cool nook or crevice in well-drained rich leafy soil—there forming annually increasing rosettes of hairy toothed leaves, dark and soft and comfortable, of stiffest dusky flannel, which profusely emit in early summer their sprays of small lilac-lavender Streptocarpus or Gloxinia-flowers. There is a most beautiful albino, too, *H. rh. virginalis*; and *H. Ferdinandi-Coburgi* seems no more (? *H. Austinii*) than a specially fine form of the type, which varies greatly in size of blossom and width of mouth and speckling of gold in a throat of lighter or darker tone, so that out of an imported batch you are sure of several equally nameable beauties. The plants can be in due course divided, and seed can readily be raised, with care. For it is very minute, and must have the constant moisture and the constant attention that one gives to that of Rhododendron, the seed-pot standing in a saucer of water, and having brown paper and then glass over the top, which every day is to be removed, while with the point of the tie-pin you gently as possible keep open the fine sandy peat on which the seed is sown, and remove the slightest sign of stagnation—Marchantia or any other of the noxious and cloying green growths that closeness so soon engenders.

Hablitzia tamnoeides.—We will not worry about weeds.

Habranthus pratensis, a brilliant fire-scarlet Amaryllis, of doubtful use except for a tropically torrid sandy corner.

Hacquetia Epipactis (formerly **Dondia**) is a pretty little curiosity, suggestive of a wee glossy-leaved Astrantia, some 2 or 3 inches high, with many-rayed heads of minute golden flowers enclosed in a frill of clear-green leaves. This will grow in any decent corner, and has its special place among the spring Anemones with whom it blooms.

Halenia, a little race nearly allied to Swertia, and of no great importance. Under the conditions, however, that suit Swertia they may be grown, and have the attraction of their odd flowers, suggesting sometimes those of an Epimedium strayed on to the leafy spire of a Swertia. *H. elliptica* is from Himalaya, with tufts of fine green, and large flowers ; *H. Perrottetii*, from the Nilgherries, might perhaps be only biennial, but has tight spikes of large and handsome clear-blue blossom. And there are others whose biennialness is beyond doubt.

Hamadryas magellanica and *H. argentea* are strange plants from the remotest islands toward the Antarctic Pole. They have silky foliage like that of some Buttercup, and then, on upstanding stems of 4 inches or so, a single erect bloom of white or pale-yellow, with the segments spun out into a long wispy point, so that the flower looks like some absurd hybrid between an Anemone and a starfish.

Harbourea trachypleura is an Umbellifer of no value.

Hastingsia alba, an unpleasing American Liliaceous species near Camassia, with spikes of whitish-green flowers.

Hedysarum.—Many of these are tallish shrubby plants, unfit for our present purpose, unless we include the yard-high *H. multijugum*, beautiful in summer with its many long and erect spikes of rose-purple Pea-flowers. Of the lower-growing species there are many, all plants of enormous wandering deep roots, requiring to be established in deep and stony ground, there to be left roaming among the blocks, where they blossom from the middle of summer. They are almost all about 10 inches or a foot tall, sub-shrubs of some choiceness; such are *H. altaicum,* red; *H. boreale,* deeper carmine-red (claret is the tone infused in all these reds); *H. caucasicum* and *H. elongatum,* carmine; *H. flavescens* and *H. splendens* (why "splendens"?), both creamish white; *H. microcalyx, H. neglectum,* and *H. sibiricum,* in varying shades of carmine-purple. On the Alps, however, there is one quite familiar Hedysarum deserving fuller notice. This is *H. obscurum,* which there often rouses wonder by its unalpine habit and look, as it runs about in the high turf of the hills, making tangles of large leaves, dark and thin and green, made up of leaflets in uneven number; and then among these, sends up a foot-high stem with a loose spire of hanging pea-flowers, large and brilliant, of rich reddish-violet, by no means deserving the plant's unfair name (which perhaps accounts for its rarity in gardens— unless indeed that interminable and unnegotiable root be cause sufficient). It must be raised, like all, from seed. Of smaller species, however, there are several that promise especial charm for the rock garden. *H. capitatum* is a prostrate species of the Mediterranean region, ultimately almost hairless, and with big flower-heads of the strongest purple; *H. erythroleucum* goes so far to please us as to form a dense cushiony mass, which, by a further stretch of kindness, is silvery with a dense ironed pile of silk. The flowers stand out from this on stems of 2 or 3 inches, and even now the plant does not relax its generous effort to delight us completely, for they are of intense purple. This beautiful thing haunts the precipices of Asia Minor, in Cilicia and Cataonia, &c.; while of the same kidney is *H. brahuicum,* from some 11,000 feet in the Alps of Afghanistan. And other species of charm are *H. sericeum, H. elegans,* and *H. argenteum,* these being of neat habit and vested in shining silk. See Appendix.

Heeria elegans is now being proclaimed without shame as a hardy plant. It is no such thing. It is rather more tender than Odontoglossum, being a loose, thin-textured, prostrate delicacy from Mexico, with many large flowers suggesting those of *Epilobium obcordatum,* but wider, singly borne, and of an even more vehement magenta-crimson. It should be grown, at need, in light soil on a warm shoulder, and treated as an annual of which cuttings must each year be taken to keep up the stock.

Helianthemum.—Of garden Rock-roses there are now so many, and those so incomparably more precious than any others, that the wild types tend to sink out of cultivation. *H. umbellatum,* however, is a species of special charm, forming a fine-leaved upstanding bush of

10 inches or so, each shoot ending in early summer with a loose head of rather large white flowers (a red-blossomed one has been found at Fontainebleau). It likes a warm situation, and in nature is not fond of lime. In spite of the cold that it is frequently called on to endure, the common *H. Tuberaria* of the Riviera is not always safely resistent to our damper conditions; it makes mats on the ground, of corrugated broad glossy leaves, from which rise up short spikes of large yellow blossoms. *H. obtusum* is a yet neater small plant—a hoary tuft some 2 or 3 inches high, set with big white cups; and *H. lunulatum* makes especially delightful little bushes some 6 or 9 inches tall, the branches thick with oval-pointed grey leaves, and ending in a quantity of small clear-yellow flowers, which can always be told from usurpers of the name by a *crescent-shaped blotch of deep gold at the base of each petal*. This species belongs to the Mediterranean coast, and is extremely rare on the Col de Tenda, where it sometimes takes on almost a spiny look with the abundance of its older dead twigs. Of the garden developments achieved by *H. roseum, H. grandiflorum, H. mutabile, H. apenninum, H. sanguineum, H. vulgare, H. rhodanthum, H. purpureum, H. coccineum, H. croceum*, and a long line of etceteras, are not these faithfully and flamingly dealt with in all catalogues? There is no end to the variety of them, no end to their names, neither Alpha nor Omega to the dazzling and diverse beauty of their profuse flowers, scattered over the low masses all the summer through, and filling even the worst places of the sunny garden with a glory not to be equalled by the best. They can be multiplied to any extent by cuttings, and seed also should be raised in the best strains, in the hope of even finer varieties yet to arise. Helianthemum does not seem to have the secret of ugliness, and even the double forms, *H. Balgreen, H. coccineum, H. plenum*, &c., have their place, though they cannot cope in beauty with such grey-leaved and be-rosed lovelinesses as *H. roseum*, or the even neater tuffets of *H. amabile*, perhaps the most dainty and brilliant of all, alike in its concise hoary bushes of 6 inches high, and in the prodigal show of its especially flaming rose-pink flowers. Many of the larger forms, it should be noted, have a tendency to get leggy (like Lavender) if left too long alone; and should therefore, by those who value tidiness, be cut back as far as you please in spring, when they will accordingly bush forth again in green, and form masses as tight or loose as your pruning has desired, quite restored to their pristine prodigality of blossom.

Helichrysum.—The Sungolds, or Everlastings, offer us various low-growing beauties for the garden, but all are more or less woolly, and all are more or less tender or miffy. They should be grown in particularly light open soil, with the most perfect drainage and in full sun ; and then they should also, in August, be freely struck from cuttings, that the parent plant may not depart from you in winter and leave you wholly desolate. These are the best of the smaller species :

H. bellidioeides is perhaps the best of all, and a treasure not only of singular beauty but also of a far happier temper than most. For it lacks the dense and dangerous ermine in which the rest go garbed, and in any warm sandy soil grows at such a pace as in a summer to be a flat carpet a yard wide, the long shoots being set with oval-pointed leaves, white-grey below but on the upper surface dark and smooth and shining. Then, all over the mass, on stems of 3 or 4 inches, come the most delicate wide Everlastings, snowy and gleaming and scaly. The plant is not only easy, it is also quite surely hardy in all fair conditions, and comes from the Southern Alps of New Zealand and the Antarctic Islands beyond. (*H. bellidifolium* of lists.)

H. Billiardieri; very small woolly-white leaves along the shoots that form into dense cushioned masses, and then send up 6-inch stems, carrying each a single pure-white Everlasting, specially wide and ample and shining, with the silvery scales of the flower-frill of unequal length. (From the cliffs of Lebanon.)

H. compositum lives in the highest rocks of Cadmus in Caria, and elsewhere in Lycia—making most dense and wide cushions of pure white wool, with flower-stems of nearly a foot.

H. frigidum gives more trouble than all the money it costs. For it is a daintily lovely species from high warm places of Corsica, minute, mosslike in growth, with tiny shoots of close-packed bluish-white foliage, and then the most beautiful Everlastings of snowy silver-whiteness, on stems of 2 inches or so. This miffy beauty exacts the most profound regard. There is little use in sending for it to dwell beneath cool and weeping skies of grey ; even in hot and sunny gardens it should have a place of special choiceness, full in the foreground, on a warm slope, in soil that is light, yet nourishing as the diet of such an invalid should be, and filled with stones to promote digestion and avert dropsy. And then, when the plant has lived through the summer, and made a rather less minute tuft than before, hostages should be taken off it in August and struck in sand, while the clump itself, no later than September, should go to rest beneath a large and wide-spread roof of glass or bough of fir or gorse.

H. grandiceps is truly magnificent. It plays at being a Flannel-flower, and on the Edelweiss greatly improves in having remarkably broad and short woolly-grey bracts (not leaves transmogrified) frilling out round the flower-head, which is borne on a stem of half a foot or more. *H. pauciflorum* is in the same line, and both are to be got in the Southern Alps of New Zealand.

H. Leontopodium is that notably beautiful New Zealand alpine which utterly wipes the Flannel-flower out of reckoning, so much whiter is it, and so much wider, woollier, and more silvery the heads of Edelweiss that it carries on the same stems (but clad in oblong overlapping leaves), and from much the same tufts as its crushed rival or feeble imitator or dethroned original. It has also been known as *Gnaphalium Colensoi*, and is desperately to be desired.

H. niveum hugs the hot rocks of the Pamphylian Taurus, whence it sends up stems of a foot or 18 inches, carrying flowers whose blossom-bracts are of an especially firm and gleaming opacity of solid silver-white, though its height is a trifle excessive for our needs.

H. virgineum is yet more lovely. For it is a very neat close tuft of snowy wool in the sheer summit-walls of Athos, making quite a woody trunk to bear its packed masses of whiteness, from which emerge stems of 2 or 3 inches, each, as a rule, carrying but one large and pure star-head, with its gleaming glossy bracts of silver broad and spreading. They call it Amarantos there, the " everlasting "—by so cruel a fate has so beautiful a name (for a thing so beautiful) become transferred to the ugliest colour in the garden. There is a kindred species to this, *H. amorginum*, rather larger in the habit, with stems of half a foot and more, and rather smaller in the flower, from the rocks and barren places of Amorgos.

Heliosperma, a sub-division of *Silene*, *q.v.*

Hellébŏrus.—In ample room and in deep rich soil at the foot of the rock-garden, or in broad sunny (or cool) slopes together with Colchicums, all the Christmas Roses and Lent Roses are in place, ample in their splendid foliage, and in their blossom either weird and sumptuous, or pure with a dazzling chastity that seems inappropriate and hypocritical in plants so poisonous and sophisticated. Yet *Helleborus niger* is one of the candours of the world, in all its forms of a white and unchallengeable flawlessness. Many forms it has indeed, and one day in winter or earliest spring in the sub-alpine woods of Garda or Como—even within a quarter of an hour of Menaggio and all its hotels and old maids—will yield you half a dozen extra-special Christmas Roses pre-eminent in size or precocity, or lateness, or whiteness, or breadth of petal—all being true prizes each in its own way, advancing the hour of the bloom or protracting it. So now we have a period from October to the end of April that is never without *H. niger*, so called because its heart, or root, is black, while its face shines with a blazing white innocence unknown among the truly pure of heart.

Catalogues offer many forms, and all are most lovely, while the best of acknowledged ones is *H. maximus* (or *altifolius*); but the woods of Italy are full of its peers and masters, and imported plants will in due course yield a harvest of wonder. "In due course," because it is of no avail to put in Hellebores one day and expect them to have filled the garden with their silver glare in a week. They take time, and even a long time, to get established; collected crowns must have two years to show much leafage, and three, probably, before they really flower in character, but after that will grow increasingly glorious every year, and should never again be moved or touched, as they passionately resent disturbance and division. Nor should they ever be allowed to starve, but their soil must perennially be enriched with abundance of every coarse fatness, for their greedy appetites are of the grossest, and, like Mrs. Norris, nobody more hates pitiful doings. Their finest association is in clusters and drifts over a broad bank in the sun, with Cyclamen and Colchicums to accompany them in autumn, smaller ferns and lilies for the summer, and for spring common bluebells, Hepaticas, and Wood-anemones.

The other Hellebores are more frank in revelation of their inner natures, and all their flowers, livid, speckled, or bronzed, are eloquent warnings of an evil principle. Most splendid is *H. orientalis*, with flowers of pinkish white, several to the taller stem, and leaves downy beneath; there are countless garden hybrids between this, *H. lividus*, *H. colchicus*, &c. This last has solitary flowers of deep purple, with broad oval sepals and a solitary basal leaf to each stem; *H. guttatus* has stems of some 18 inches to 2 feet high, carrying a loose group of blooms on branching sprays, each star being nearly 3 inches across and of clear white, heavily freckled with purple. Very large flowers are produced, before any leaf appears, by the pearl-pale and pinkish-flushed *H. antiquorum*, which has broad-pointed sepals, and two basal leaves ultimately to each stem; *H. hybridus* is the vast name of the garden-bred races, which, like the last (and indeed all the taller and branched Hellebores), come into blossom about March and April, and are fertile of the most sumptuous and beautiful colours in glowing claret-reds, sombre metallic purples, and so forth—all the best to be found described in such catalogues as offer them; *H. giganteus*, *H. purpurascens*, and *H. atrorubens* have flowers in shades of deep rose or claret, very handsome; *H. guttatus* is a rarity, with blossoms of yellowish white; and one of the strangest and rarest of all is *H. torquatus*, not a large grower, with noble flowers of a bloomy powdered-looking steely slate-blue. Of the green-blossomed species, none have so much importance, though *H. odoratus* has the charm of its sweetness, and

H. lividus makes a superb spouting fountain of hyaline bells in spring ; and *H. caucasicus*, though only a foot high, and a mere dwarf by comparison with the last, with only one basal leaf to each stem, has flowers, one, two, or three, large and starry, with the sepals diminishing to the base, and their green enriched with purple ; while *H. cyclophyllus* is but a bigger version of our own *H. viridis*, which with *H. foetidus* and many kindred forms from abroad of magnificent dark foliage are hardly choice enough for admission to the rock-garden, unless it be built on a scale vast enough to admit of wild and out-of-the-way corners in shade and woodland.

Helonias bullata is a tall Liliaceous plant for the bog, which can easily be grown and easily divided, and from its basal rosette of thick green leaves sends up a naked stem of 18 inches or so in April or May, on which unfolds a thick spire of smallish pink flowers rather starry and pretty in effect.

Heloniopsis japonica requires rather more choice positions than the last, being a smaller copy of it, with larger bell-shaped pink nodding blossoms clustered upon leafy stems of some 6 or 9 inches in spring, standing sturdily up from the basal rosettes of evergreen shining leaves ; we also have in cultivation *H. breviscapa*, also from Japan, in which the flowers are white or whitish, and the spike condensed into a tight head. An alternative name for the family is *Sukerokia*, under which euphonious title *H. japonica* is figured in the So-moku-sousets', with all the exquisite beauty and accuracy of Japanese drawing, so different from the stiff and leaden style of Europe, where all the character of the plant is lost without any compensating enhancement of correctness.

Helxine Soleirolii exists for other purposes than that of breaking jaws. The race-name is drawn from εἱλισσω, "I cling and twine," which has also given us Helix the Ivy, and Helix the curled formation of the snail and the human ear. And the plant that here bears it is a minute Corsican carpeter with small rounded crinkly-looking leaves of bright emerald sheen, especially delightful for rambling about in a cool and shady rock ; which it does, indeed, with the devastating vigour of *Arenaria balearica*, which it so much resembles in habit but that the leaves are larger and flatter and glossy-green, while the flowers that appear upon them are of no effect in themselves, but merely look as if the carpet had been expensively powdered with gold-dust. Helxine, for the uses indicated, has high value and charm ; pieces taken off will root, of course, immediately, and though the carpet does not always or everywhere resist a specially odious winter, there will always be a resurrection here and there in spring, from different parts of the blackened mass.

HENNINGIA ANISOPTERA.

Henningia anisoptera is a rather pretty Liliaceous species from sandy wastes of the Altai, suggesting *Narthecium ossifragum* but that the leaves are toothed and fleshy and spotted with black, while the flowers are white with a black spot at the base of each segment.

Hepatica. See under **Anemone.**

Heracleum, a race of vast and statuesque Umbellifers that have no place in the rock-garden, but are of noble effect in the wild.

Herpolīrion Novae Zelandiae is in the same race as Henningia—an interesting tiny species forming large mats and masses in the sub-alpine swamps, with glaucous crowded rolled-in leaves about 2 inches long at the most (and the inner ones much shorter), while among them, almost stemless, sit largish stars of blue or lilac nearly an inch across.

Hespĕris.—Among the large and inelegant race of the Rockets lurk two small treasures greatly to be craved for the rock-garden, where they should be grown in light soil or moraine in full sun, and have their seed sedulously collected, lest they should prove impermanent in proportion to their prettiness. (The remainder, however, are professedly perennial, and should gladden us in early summer :)

H. breviscapa is only 2 or 3 inches high ; there are rosettes of minute rounded scalloped leaves, and then, from the very base, a flower-spike of large bright-pink blossoms. The whole plant is softly downy, and dwells in the Alps of Armenia and on Olympus.

H. humilis (*H. Kotschyi*—not *H. Kotschyana*, a taller thing) is in the same way of charm, but here there is more hoary-greyness and the leaves are hardly scalloped at all, and narrower, and drawn more gradually to more of a leaf-stalk ; but the 3-inch spike is still here, and the large flowers ; but this time they are purple. (From the limestone cliffs of Pisidia, and on Gisyl Tepe of the Cilician Taurus.)

Taller kinds are *H. violacea, H. Kotschyana,* and *H. bicuspidata;* and beautiful, but biennial, is *H. thyrsoidea,* which from the base becomes a wide pyramid of blossom like that of the common Dame's Violet ; and also there is *H. secundiflora* with elegant long one-sided sprays of flowers, sad in a tender sadness of muffled violet which mourns in gentle fragrance for the departed day. This is from the shady ghylls of Hymettus, Parnes, Sipylus, &c.—perhaps a Niobid transformed long since into a dim regretful flower.

Hesperochīron pumilus is a delicate treasure, cousin of the Hydrophyllums, of very dwarf habit, making a tuft of slender stalked foliage, and then emitting white bells about half an inch across and tinged with purple. This will thrive in any light and well-drained loam. As also will *H. californicus,* in which the flowers are not tinged, but definitely striped with dark purple. (Idaho, Oregon, and California.)

Heteranthĕra limosa is a pretty little marsh-plant of the American mountains. Its kinship is with the Pontederias, and its small blossoms are of brilliant blue.

Heterotŏma lobelioeides is a handsome Lobeliad with red and golden flowers, from the high Alps of Mexico ; on this at present all judgment must be suspended until it can be better based.

Heuchera.—Since this race fell into the fingers of the florist it has ceased to be in place in the rock-garden, even if it ever was, indeed ; for the family in all its species has the perfect air of having been born for the border, and for a hundred thousand years to have been a sleeping beauty, waiting for the florist to come along and wake it to its own possibilities. One little plant, however, that bears the name is welcome in the rock-garden, though indeed it bears the name unjustly, being not a Heuchera by birth but by (or in spite of) marriage. For it is a hybrid between *Heuchera* and *Tiarella*, so that there is a double injustice in labelling it *Heuchera tiarelloeides*. It is, none the less, of placid pleasantness in a quiet woodland corner, where room will not be grudged to its prettiness. Here it will sit in a clump of leaves like those of some small Heuchera, but soon begins to run about and form a patch. In summer rise up the delicate straight stems of some 4 or 6 inches, at the top of which unfolds a loose spike of pink flowers that at first seem rather insignificant, but go on developing until they have quite conquered one with the expanded charm of their vase-shaped rosy little cups.

Hieracium.—The name of Hawkweed fills the botanist with despair or with gruesome glee, according to his temper and passion for the minute and merciless multiplication of insecure species ; and upon the gardener's heart it blows chill. Out of all the race there are none that the rock-garden really wants ; and the two that may be admitted are such weeds that the garden which has been foolish enough to admit them will soon be in a position to admit nothing else. These are *H. aurantiacum,* and its lighter orange hybrid *H. rubrum* (of which the other parent is *H. Pilosella*), and which has so much more mercy than its mother that it bears no seed. Few others are of distinct value even in the roughest place, though on the wild limestone cliffs of the North few things can look handsomer in their place than the big golden suns and black-blotched toothed broad leaves of the best forms that develop in that all-embracing name of *H. murorum.*

Hippocrepis comosa, one of our prettiest natives, like a refined, neater Lady's-fingers, with a better-furnished head of golden pea-flowers flopping from the neat mass of leaves in June, is an admirable plant for a sunny bank in any ordinary light soil, and by nature a lover of lime. Smaller than this is *H. glauca* from the alps of Greece, which forms a close tuft of hoary grey instead of a radiating cushion or long curtain of clear green, and has woodier trunks and slenderer stems to the flower-heads, of which the golden peas are smaller. (Seed.)

Homogȳnē, a dingy little family from the alpine woods, whose neat rounded kidney-shaped leaves of glossiest veined green give promises of beauty that are not borne out by the squalid tassel of a flower, alone and sad upon a naked stalk of some 6 inches. The species at the disposal of specialists (and in damp shady woodland corners the foliage is not without attraction) are *H. alpina, H. discolor,* and *H. silvestris,* of which the last alone has lobes to the leaves, the kidney outline of the others remaining unviolated. *H. discolor* is known by the silver-haired reverse to the foliage, which in *H. alpina* is merely set with scanty hairs.

Horminum pyrenaicum.—The time is gone by now for *Horminum pyrenaicum.* In former days it was the one thing over which books of gardening and catalogues alike waxed really lyrical ; and in catalogues, indeed, the name endures to this hour, in spite of the fact that the poor gardener, that patient worm, has long since turned, and declared that if ever there were an undistinguished dowdy weed it is this—a coarse and rampant thing, forming large rosetted tufts of dark sullen-looking scalloped oval foliage, leaden and dull, from which rise spikes of some 8 inches with dull and leaden little flowers of an uninspired purple like those of some very indifferent Salvia. It is predominantly a plant of the Pyrenees and then of the Eastern ranges ; it is interesting to note that even Mr. Stuart Thompson has only met it on the Stelvio, whereas in the Dolomites, that paradise to which the Stelvio is the dreary gate, you cannot take a walk in any direction without trampling leagues of Horminum, a typical limestone species, indeed, that fills the upper alpine turf with its wads and masses of vulgar leafage. In cultivation the plant is worth the trouble it gives, which is none. It likes lime, and there is no more to be said for it. Occasionally rather more ample forms are to be found, and once I got a white one that was really pretty, with a fine hem of purple round its lip, but on the whole this dowdy thing is best left to catalogues, which never fail to include it, and proclaim its charms vociferously—perhaps, as Mr. Stuart Thompson rather cruelly but justly suggests, because it is almost the only large alpine Labiate that could possibly, by the utmost stretch of even a catalogue's courtesy,

PLATE 41.

HABERLEA RHODOPENSIS.
(Photo. R.B.G., Kew.)

LEONTOPODIUM ALPINUM.
(Photo. R. A. Malby.)

PLATE 42.

JANKAEA HELDREICHII.

HYPERICUM POLYPHYLLUM.

Vol. I.

be said to have any charms to proclaim. In this case it is indeed a one-eyed king in a blind kingdom.

Hottonia palustris, the Water-violet, so called because it grows in the water and has a distinct resemblance to a Stock, may often be seen in still pools and backwaters of England ; it is a valuable weed for the pond, which it fills with its foliage, fine as fern, from which rise clear of the water, in July and August, its spires of large lilac-pale flowers, that might indeed be those of a big Cardamine had they not five segments and other details that assign them so improbably to the august family of Primula.

Houstonia, a family of American Rubiads, of charm and daintiness inestimable, of which the oldest and still the favourite in cultivation is *H. coerulea*—a creeping treasure with spreading tufts that emits all the summer through (but especially in May) an incredible and plant-hiding profusion of exquisite little pale-blue four-rayed stars borne singly on fine stems of 3 or 4 inches. Rather larger than this, and taller and more spreading, running and rooting, but no less lovely and profuse in the blossom, is *H. serpyllifolia,* with the same flowers suggesting a heaven of blue china, but here a more violet heaven of powder-blue ; and there are other species still with broader leaves, of which one is called *H. purpurea* because its flowers are white and its buds pink (in heads like those of a Bouvardia). The culture of all these fairy things (for which in America they have the rarely felicitous name of Bluets, or Innocence) is special. In fullest heat of the sun they soon lose the nitor of their leaves and bloom ; so that their site should be a shaded one, and in rich loose sandy free soil, kept quite moist from below. Thus treated the Houstonias (except frail and purple *H. tenuifolia,* which likes dry rock) will make no bones about delighting their planter, and in the garden will themselves make old ones ; the finest masses I ever saw were growing under dense hazel-covert, in wet and heavy calcareous loam. There are various colour-varieties, purples and albinos (*H. faxoriorum*) and so forth, in this race, but nothing could equal, much less surpass, the special loveliness of the types themselves.

Houttuynia, the correct name of the small race which has already been treated, for the sake of convenience, under its catalogue description of *Anemiopsis*—usually, too, "*Anemonopsis*."

Hudsonia.—These, of which there are two species, are very pretty bushlings about 9 inches or a foot high, with fine foliage, and altogether like Hypericums in look and in profusion of golden stars, which are produced in summer. *H. ericoeides* is indeed a heathlike little plant of much charm, from the sandy hills of the American coast ;

while *H. tomentosum* has flowers more sessile, and hoary foliage closely packed in overlapping rows. Their needs are an open, light and peaty soil, most perfectly drained and in full sun.

Hugueninia tanacetifolia (or **Sisymbrium pinnatifidum**) is a really beautiful great Crucifer, of very rare occurrence in the Swiss Alps (and only on their fringe in the Valais), but, like nearly everything else of charm, becoming less unusual as soon as you have come South and East of that country of hotels. On the Mont Cenis, for instance, it fills many of those curious pot-holes among the gypsum dunes with the fine and stalwart elegance of its truly Tansy-like leafage, from which the summer calls up a stem of 3 feet or so, lacy with the same fine ample foliage, and ending in flattened wide showers of blossom, which, though each flower by itself is small, are borne in such a mass of golden-yellow that their volume produces a rare effect of graceful magnificence. In the garden this splendid plant is never seen ; where its beauty deserves to be inevitable and where, well planted in some shady corner out of the way in cool and rather damp well-drained soil, it will also prove immortal ; not to mention that the seed is abundant every season.

Hulsea algida, a 4-inch hairy Composite of aromatic fragrance, from California, with compressed feathered leaves at the base and lonely little yellow flower-heads on stems of 6 or 7 inches ; not startlingly attractive, but adapted at will to warm dry corners.

Hutchinsia alpina may be very common, but it is none the less precious, filling any cool bank with its mats of feathered dark small foliage, animated in May, and for some months onward, with little spikes of brilliantly pure-white cruciferous flowers, for that race astonishingly refined and bright and charming—besides being of the highest value as cover for Crocus or fine Daffodil. It is an abundant species in the high Alps, but on the primary formations its place is taken by *H. brevicaulis*, which may always be known, not only by the rock it grows on, but also because the plant itself is so much smaller and tighter, with a shorter, denser, and flattened spike of flower. *H. Auerswaldii*, from Spain, has none but small botanical differences, and all are sometimes found lurking under the disguise of *Noccaea*.

Hyacinthus, the name of the beautiful boy long since immortally dead in the love of a god, has gone to crown a race no less beloved by Apollo than once was Hyacinth the Beautiful. Let all of this race then, for the sake of that memory, have a place full forward in his beams, set in soil both deep and rich and light enough for the soul of Hyacinth each year to rise again untrammelled from the safe coffin of his bulb. Of this race there are many children, but the head

of all is *H. orientalis*, the delicate and lovely Lear of all the terrible
mondaine (or elderly demi-mondaine) Hyacinths, immense frizzed
women of the world, scented and unctuous and rather stolidly complacent, that decorate every home in spring. Yet even these, in time,
like Hall Caine's heroines who wax fat on urban vice for a while and
then remember the parental farm, and go back there to recover virtue
on a diet of milk, will eventually, after a year or two of prostitution in
pots, remember Hyacinth and the favour of the sun, and will even
grow worthy of the rock-garden if put in some deep warm corner,
where their stems will become slender with repentance every season and
their blossoms renew the untarnished purity of their innocence. As
for their father, *H. orientalis*, there is no bulb in the garden more
absolutely a gentleman, and the darling of a god in all except that he
does not die young, but continues for many a summer, never greatly
increasing indeed, but yearly reappearing to greet his master with a
delicate peal of pale-blue bells with which returning Hyacinth rings out .
in spring the doom of hated winter. And other Hyacinths there are :
there is fat *H. campanulatus*, which in all catalogues is made to offer
itself for planting broadcast in place of the dainty natural Bluebell of
which it is so vulgarised a fattened caricature ; and there is *H. cernuus*,
less known, but also less unworthy to understudy the Bluebell ; and
then there is *H. amethystinus*, which without legend, or rivalry, or
comparison stands high among the loveliest bulbs we have, and yet is
one of those most rarely seen, although it lives as long, and multiplies
as readily, as *Narcissus poeticus* itself—the most exquisite of all bulbous
delights for early summer, with colonies of decumbent grooved leaves,
and 8-inch stems crowned with a spike of the most glorious and clear
china-blue bells with a paler streak, and that wide mouth which is the
one, the final differentiation between Hyacinth the open-lipped and
smiling and Muscari of the dark face and the puckered lips and
constricted pinched expression of bell. Of similar but not greater
charm is lovely *H. azureus*, which ought more properly to be known as
H. ciliatus, a very beautiful thing from Asia Minor, with the lower
bells deeply drooping and of deep blue, with their colour overflowing
at the top into the tip of the densened spike of wide-open azure flowers
almost sitting close to the blue stalk in a tight cone of blueness, on a
stem some five inches high (or less) in February or March, rising up
amid the grooved erect leaves of bluish-green. There are other species
too, though many have betrayed their parentage and passed over
into *Scilla* and *Bellevalia ;* of which *H. lineatus*, only some 4 inches high
at the most, is the very companion asked by the choicest Daffodillings,
in a carpet of *Helichrysum bellidioeides*.

Hydraspis canadensis is not interesting, but will therefore prosper easily in a cool shady place, where its creeping yellow rhizome sends up a single kidney-shaped glossy leaf at a time, divided into some five or seven lobes; and then upright stems of 6 or 10 inches, carrying each a single little greenish-white flower in April.

Hydrochăris Morsus-ranae.—The Frog-bit is a pretty native water-plant, with floating clumps of kidney-shaped dark leaves, and three-petalled white flowers all through the summer, floating on the surface of the shallow pool.

Hydrocotўlē.—These will only grow in damp places, and no one who values his garden or his peace will admit them there.

Hydrophyllum canadense and its relations, again, are capable of success in a damp place, but more valuable, in that their lobed palmate leaves suggest a tiny lotus's with the pearl-drop rolling in their cup, although their spires of purplish bloom be insignificant, as is often the way with the outward charms of those who hold the jewel of the world in their hearts.

Hylomēcon japonicum, the correct name of *Stylophorum japonicum, q.v.* (See also **Chelidonium.**)

Hypericum.—The St. John's-worts are a puzzle, not in their multiplicity only, but in the pronunciation of their race-name. Under neither of the two possible derivations can any sense be made out of it, and, therefore, as Hyperïcum has the weight of custom, there seems no strong reason for replacing it by Hypereicon, the correctness of which, though plausible, is only problematic. In their needs the plants are not thus obscure, but all are of the most perfect ease, in light and open soil, submitting to be multiplied by cuttings or by the abundant seed that they yearly set. The race is of enormous range and size, occupying mountain districts, in woods and alps and fields, across the Northern temperate zone of the New World as of the Old, and ranging in stature from a flat carpet to a towering shrub of 6 feet high and more. With these last, however, we cannot here cope, but in the ensuing list will deal only with those that are fitted by their growth and habit for admission to the rock-garden, where among their conspicuous merits they have that of flowering, like Campanula, in the later days of summer and far on into autumn.

H. adēnoclădon stands only some 4 or 5 inches high, with panicles of golden bloom, and huddled finest foliage on the shoots, the leaves being very dense with glands, and narrower than those of *H. repens*, to which otherwise the plant has affinities. (North Syria.)

H. adēnótrĭchum belongs to the shady mountain woods of Anatolia, and reaches some 6 inches or so, with slender almost unbranching shoots that die down in winter, and are studded with narrow densely-fringed leaves (there is a yet hairier-foliaged variety, *H. a. myriotrichum*).

H. adpressum is a taller species, of a foot or more, making runners in the marshes of Massachusetts.

H. amanum is also some 2 feet high or so, with ample foliage, and then a big stiff pyramid of blossom shining above the smooth and blue-grey foliage. (Northern Syria.)

H. Apollinis breathes to the world in its name the enthusiasm with which it was able to animate the botanist who thought it worthy of no lesser owner than a god. It is a very beautiful plant, faithful to Apollo on the slopes of his mountains of Helikon and Parnassus, in the stony limestone region of the upper alps, where it repeats *H. olympicum*, but is half the size in all its parts, making a blue-grey mass of stems some 6 inches high at the most, often weak and declining, and often carrying only one lovely golden flower to each.

H. "argenteum." See *H. tomentosum.*

H. armenum comes quite near to *H. repens*, but is woody at the base, more erect in the branch, with leaves *not curled down* along their edges, and with fewer flowers, or only one to the shoot. (From the high mountain regions of Armenia at about 8800 feet.)

H. asperulum is a Persian, about 12 inches high, with black-spotted uncurled foliage, nibbled-looking at the edge, and roughish. Otherwise it is close to *H. callianthum* in habit and beauty of blossom.

H. Athoum may be called to mind by a picture of *H. fragile*, from which however it differs in being wholly *hairy*—a twisting mass of fine unbranching stems, with rather larger and more scattered leaves. Its home is in the high clefts of Athos.

H. atomarium is densely woolly-downy, with leaves about an inch and a half in length, and panicles of blossom some 3 or 4 inches or even a foot in height, the leaves being pointed-oblong, heart-shaped, and stem-embracing at the base.

H. Aucheri stands near *H. armenum*, but is finer and frailer, only 3 or 4 inches in stature, and very slender in the shoot, the bracts and the sepals being fringed. The sprays carry few flowers, or only one or two. (Mysia.)

H. australe stands related to *H. hyssopifolium*, but more suggests a glorified and especially handsome version of *H. humifusum*, with longer, blunter, unpitted stem-embracing leaves. The flowers, rich and ample and often carried in similar sprays, have veins or flushings of red in their gold. (Algiers, North Africa, South France.)

H. bithynicum is a copy of *H. Richeri*, but the leaves are blunter, and not pitted with pellucid dots, while the flower-cluster is closer. (Olympus of Bithynia and the neighbourhood of Byzantium.)

H. Burseri makes yet another imitation of *H. Richeri*. But here the leaves are set with glands, and green below, while there are no longitudinal stripes on the seed-capsule. It comes from the Pyrenees and has also the name of *H. pyrenaicum*. The group is interesting rather than of special grace or charm, being inclined to stolidity of port.

H. callianthum, however, brings us more beauty from the sub-alpine slopes of Kurdistan. It is about a foot high, rich in narrow blue-grey foliage with black dottings and no inclination to curl down at the rims, while no branchlings proceed from their axils. The stem concludes in a graceful pyramidal shower of yellow stars, and the plant has had the alternative name of *H. lysimachioeides*.

H. cardiophyllum is a small-flowered poor bush, of 4 feet, from Syria.

H. cassium stands near *H. bithynicum*, but is taller and coarser.

H. concinnum, from California, is a neat thing, standing erect to some 12 or 18 inches, the stems being set with pairs of sword-blade leaves, each nursing a bud in the axil, and ending in two or three flowers, rather large, erect and brilliant, on a stem set with a degree of leafage not by any means enough to dull the edge of their delight.

H. confertum, from the shady mountain regions of Cappadocia, Anatolia, &c., has much the look and habit of *H. repens*, but is covered with warty down all over, with triangular narrow leaves curled back along the edge, sitting tight to the shoots, which emit buds from the axils as well as barren branches. The other name of the plant has been *H. satureiaefolium*, and there is a variety with closer spires of blossom called *H. stenobotrys*.

H. Coris brings us back to find one of the best-beloved jewels in the whole race, abounding at our own very doors in the limy way-side gutters of the Maritime Alps, where it forms spreading clouds of finest little stems set in finest blue-grey foliage, narrow as a heath's, but expanded and delicate and cloudlike in effect, from which rise up and spray abroad, like shot stars of a rocket, sparkling ample flowers of pale clear gold, whose petals never fall from the perfectly unbranched spires on which their wide galaxy is displayed. This lovely thing makes even richer yet no less dainty masses in the rock-garden, and always gives pleasure whether in flower or not; but never more than when its elfin flames float glittering over the limestone road-rims by St. Martin Vésubie, amid the pearly orbs of *Linum tenuifolium* that once was *L. salsoloeides*. This species is a child of the warm Southern limestones, coming most shyly northward, though on the hot and non-calcareous rocks above Susa it may be seen. But in the main chain of the Alps it is exceedingly rare, preferring only two valleys which are specially open to the Föhnwind, a taste in which the Hypericum stands alone. It may be seen about Stans, and here and there round the shores of Lucerne, by Weggis, and by the Mythen. If its aesthetic value is not sufficient, it will also serve you as a diuretic.

H. crenulatum haunts the alpine rocks of the Cilician Taurus—a frail exquisite species with shoots of some 3 or 4 inches, thready and fine, studded with short-stemmed tiny blunt leaves, green and smooth and wavy at their edge, making an effect not unlike that of the more erect and more pointed-leaved *H. nummularium*, with the same large lovely flowers of clear gold. There is also a form with larger flowers still.

H. cuneatum is yet another seductive rock-plant, but this belongs to warm crevices of the alpine region in Syria and Cilicia, and should not yet be looked on as beyond reach of a specially evil winter. It is, however, so beautiful that not the choicest corner in the garden need be grudged it. *H. cuneatum* forms a tiny branching bushlet of very dainty weak stems, some half a foot in length, and adorned with small leaves, wedge-shaped to their base (where they draw to a little foot-stalk), glaucous-blue beneath, and either smooth at the edge or a trifle crinkled. The golden orbs of blossom are carried in a loose spire on leafy reddish-stemmed sprays. This has also been *H. myrtilloeides*.

H. decussatum, likewise out of the East, is a 6-inch form, or species, of the usual refulgence.

H. delphicum is all green and laxly softly hairy. Its height varies between 5 inches and a foot, and it belongs to the leafy section, with markedly blunt foliage about an inch long or more, heart-shaped at the base.

H. elongatum only just escapes being swept into the crowd of varieties that cower beneath the name of *H. hyssopifolium*. It has the same qualities as those, but its stem is *always undivided*, and its pyramid of blossom is narrower and longer. (Anatolia, &c.)

H. empetrifolium makes a pair with *H. Coris*, but the stems are branching (*which those of Coris never are*), and the petals fall when they are finished (*which those of Coris never do*). It may be seen on the warm hills of Athens, and over Asia Minor, &c.

H. erectum is the Japanese plant now being sent out under the name of *H. japonicum* which, in reality, belongs to a worthless little annual weed (*q.v.*). *H. erectum* is a stalwart species of some foot or more in height, with ample pairs of leaves, and large flowers in a cluster at the top ; by no means an unpleasing thing, though lacking the refinement of its smaller cousins.

HYPERICUM.

H. ericoeides, again, from the limestone or gypsum cliffs of Southern Spain, is a tighter version of *H. Coris*, making a closer tuft with twisting ascendent stems that are bare below but higher up quite densely packed with whorls of four needle-narrow leaves, minute and hoary, with curled-down edges—the whole neat tuft of 6-inch stems having thus the look of a heath's packed shoots, but that they end in an oval loose head of golden stars.

H. fragile provokes high praise from many, but by me is not held to compete at all with *H. reptans* and *H. Coris*. It is, none the less, a beautiful species, lax and flopping, with very leafy branches crowded with little overlapping grey-green foliage of four-ranked effect all along the multitude of stems of some 5 inches or so, emitted by the fat woody root-stock ; and each ending in two or three ample and fluffy flowers of clear pale gold, that suffer in effect (though so much larger) from not having the specially fine filmy leafage of *H. Coris* to set them off. *H. fragile* comes from the high rocks of Euboea, and in cultivation is as easily grown and multiplied as the rest.

H. galioeides is a slender taller branching plant of America, with quite fine foliage, and quite small flowers in abundant racemes from the axils as well as the tips of the shoots.

H. gramineum grows wirily erect, sometimes to rather more than a foot in height, with heart-based curled-edged leaves, and blooms carried on erect stems in a loose wide head. (North America.)

H. Grisebachii is very near *H. Richeri*, about half a foot high, and densely leafy with *little* huddled leaves, in which it differs from the ampler-leaved species in the group—*HH. Richeri, bithynicum, cassium, Montbretii, Nordmannii, barbatum, fimbriatum*, &c. ; while from *H. Richeri* it specially differs in having shorter sepals with much shorter fringes. (Scardus.)

H. Helianthemum adorns the desert places of Syria with no great éclat, being about 6 inches high, with narrow foliage and small stars.

H. heterophyllum is an obscure Persian species akin to *H. linarifolium*, and about a foot high, with fat, sharp, and very narrow leaves, and petals not equalling the sepals.

H. hirtellum also inhabits Persia and Babylonia. It is rough with short hairs, and has dense tight spikes of blossom.

H. humifusum is a pretty native, like a frail Creeping-jenny, and superior, as it grows perennially, to the true *H. japonicum*, of which it is a much finer version, while *H. australe* in turn is a glorified form of this.

H. hyssopifolium is a precious plant of wide range and variation.

HYPERICUM.

Its erect and typically *unbranched* stems of some 8 inches are grooved in two lines, and set with smooth small leathery leafage, blunted and narrowish, rolled over at the edge ; the shoots end in a long narrow spire of bright blossoms. It also, in the axils of the stem, produces fluffy-looking little tufts that seem like bundles of leaves, but are in reality branchlings minutely condensed into a ball of foliage. Its range is from the far West to the far East of the Mediterranean region; so that in this distribution it varies widely, and many of the forms are often offered as species. Among these are *H. h. lydium*, which is paler-green, sometimes branching, and with the sterile shoots more laxly set with leaves, and its flower-sprays bearing some seven blooms or so. This occupies dry mountain-copses from Antilibanus away into Russian Armenia, and its taller forms approach that of the European typical *H. hyssopifolium*. *H. h. latifolium* suggests *H. elongatum*, but here the leaves are rather broader, and *not curled at the edge*. (Cilicia.) Especially fine is *H. h. lythrifolium*, which is a condensed alpine form from the Cilician Taurus, &c., with short stout stems very densely furnished with overlapping little leaves, and flowers larger and finer than even in the type— a glory which does not belong to *H. h. microcalycinum* from Lycaonia. But Spain produces one variety of special merit in the ample-sheaved *H. h. callithyrsum*.

H. japonicum, an inferior-flowered *H. humifusum, cleaving to the ground*, poor in blossom, and annual or biennial in character. (Quite a different species is sold falsely under this name. See *H. erectum*.)

H. kamtchaticum, an erect leafy weed of no value.

H. Kotschyanum grows about 6 or 8 inches high, and the whole mass is velvety with a short hoar of hair ; the round stem is set with flat little oblong blunt leaves, which are most densely rolled together on the axillary sprays. The flowers are borne in short oblong panicles, two or three to a shoot, and with the petals markedly narrowing to the base. (Alpine limestones of Syria and the Cilician Taurus.)

H. lanuginosum comes from damp and shady places on the coasts of Syria, and may be known by the densely woolly coat in which its inch-long stem-embracing leaves are clad. The stems are half a foot to a foot high, with panicles of blossom, and there is a variety *H. l. gracile*.

H. latifolium. See under *H. hyssopifolium*.

H. leprosum makes fine delicate stems of 3 or 4 inches, and earns its displeasing epithet by being leprous with tubercular warts. The flowers are rather smaller than in *H. origanifolium*, and the plant comes from the rocky places of Caria, where it develops into two varieties, *H. l. Bourgaei* and *H. l. rigidulum*.

H. linarifolium is a handsome plant of very rare occurrence in the south-west of England, lax in habit, and throwing up a few slender wiry stalks of some 8 inches, set at intervals with upstanding pairs of stiff and very narrow leaves, and ending in a wide head of particularly bright handsome flowers, rather like those of some glorified *H. humifusum*, arranged in a cluster at the top of some narrow-leaved spray of *H. perforatum*, especially fine and slender.

H. lydium. See under *H. hyssopifolium.*

H. lysimachioeides=*H. callianthum*, q.v.

H. lythrifolium. See under *H. hyssopifolium.*

H. Montbretii. See under *H. Grisebachii.*

H. myrtilloeides=*H. cuneatum*, q.v.

H. nanum hardly justifies its name, for it forms a round and tight little bush a foot high, its branches set with minute rounded leaves, and ending in close spires of nine or ten flowers. This is found in the sub-alpine cliffs of Lebanon, &c.; and there is a most lovely form called *H. n. prostratum*, on Hermon, which closely hugs the ground, as if it were *Rhamnus pumilus* or *Prunus prostrata*.

H. neurocalycinum is a downy thing, but otherwise faithfully recalls *H. confertum* but that its leaves are tinier, and curled over at the edge, while the blossoms, in their clusters, are borne in a long broken sheaf. (Stony bushy places in the Alps of Lycaonia, &c.)

H. Nordmannii. See under *H. Grisebachii.*

H. nummularium is a most beautiful little species that may be met with (but rarely) in stony damp places of the limestone ranges throughout the Pyrenees to the Maritime and Graian Alps. It is not a strong-stemmed grower, but inclined to be tired and lie down; its shoots are from 4 to 12 inches long, and the shorter they are the more erect. They are set at intervals with pairs of small *round* fattish-looking leaves, pale underneath (and of a leathery russet later on), and marked all along their upper surface with a regular line of little dots, following that of the margin; these and their frail stems have a singular elegance and daintiness of their own already. But they are worthily crowned and completed in loveliness by the loose and radiant head of pure golden flower-stars. The species is one that can never be confounded with others, and should always be looked out for, alike in cliffs and in catalogues.

H. olympicum is an erect or flopping treasure of rare beauty, its fine wiry stems being set with very fine narrow blue-grey leafage of oblong blunt dotted leaves, heart-shaped at the base, and varying in width. The woody root is generous with these stems, that are some 6 or 8 inches high, and end in a bunch of four or five notably large and brilliant suns of spraying gold. The plant is not uncommon in the warm sub-alpine stony places of Greece, and away into Asia Minor and Russia. It should have a warm and sheltered corner in rather specially light poor soil, and care should be taken, if possible, to get the narrower-leaved form which gives even more grace than the others to the great glowing blossoms that sometimes look almost too excessive and bunchy for the plant's fine habit, and in summers of Noachian weather cake into a wad of soaked and brown decay.

H. orientale has the same height or less, with rather broader foliage that sometimes embraces the stem. By so much it is a trifle less attractive, though the flowers are fine and large, borne on herbaceous stalks that are usually *quite simple and unbranched*. There are several varieties, for *H. orientale* has a wide range in the Levant.

H. origanifolium (with a variety *H. o. pulverulentum*), from the rocky places of Asia Minor, is a pretty thing, not more than 6 inches high, all clothed in short grey down, and set with blunt little oval leaves, and carrying blossoms of good size and brilliancy. Quite close to this is *H. ghewense*, from Northern Anatolia, which however has broader leaves, almost heart-shaped at the base, and is clad altogether in much longer softer fur.

H. Pestalozzae is a graceful weakly grower with very fine stems of some half a foot or more, and showers of yellow blooms that are smaller than in *H. tomentosum*, while the leafage is veiled in the same soft grey velvet. (Pamphylia.)

H. polyphyllum stands in the foreground. It has much the same habits as *H. olympicum*, but is smaller in all its parts, and is a much bushier grower, about 6 inches or a foot high, in a mass of leafy shoots, bluish-grey, and set more densely with smaller and more upstanding pairs of little leaves, each of the stems bearing a head of some half a dozen wide golden stars (only a trifle smaller than in *H. olympicum*, and with a much smaller calyx) in such abundance as to make the whole bushling a dense constellation of light, with the fine fluff of the stamens adding that extra touch of fantastic elegance in which all the St. John's-worts are thus pre-eminent. *H. polyphyllum* comes from the warm limestone rocks by Mersina in Asia Minor, and in cultivation has a temper of perfect adaptability to any decently light and sunny situation: of which there is nothing more brilliantly worthy.

H. repens is so called because it has no tendency to creep (or "repe"), but, on the contrary, makes low masses of narrow foliage, growing in a dense and flat mass about 6 or 8 inches high—the whole effect closely resembling a very tight-packed stout *H. Coris*, or a very much dwarfer *H. hyssopifolium*, from all of whose forms indeed it can quite easily be told by its lower stature, flattened habit, and by the flowers which are carried in *long racemes* that look like remarkably drawn-out loose spikes. It is a good and useful species, but in no way a peer to either of the plants it follows in example, nor to the one that follows it in the alphabet. It comes from sunny hills all over Asia Minor, and is common in gardens and catalogues.

H. reptans is a wonder in the race—a beauty absolutely prostrate and of growth almost excessive in its vigour, forming such streaming curtains of its shoots over any high rock that in time the sheet may spread wide enough to be a nuisance to choicer but no more beautiful neighbours. The whole mat is of bright light green, the oval leaves that clothe the stems being of thin texture, smooth, and of the heartiest emerald, so densely developed that the plant is a verdant carpet, which, however, takes tones of yellow and red in spring and autumn. The flowers flop or lie upon the mass, from late summer until winter says "no more." They are of enormous size and amplitude, like dog-roses of electric gold, and on the outside their buds are varnished with a burnished mahogany-crimson, most strange and brilliant among the unfolded pale gleam of the flowers. This most lovely of its race should be set, like a city, upon an hill, so that the faces of its flowers may not be hid, but stare forth at the passer-by from their sheeted background of green, cascading from a sheer rock. It may readily be raised too from seed, its capsules often standing unscattered through the winter; and may no less readily be raised from cuttings too. Though perfectly hardy and of almost terrible vigour, it should be remembered that this precious evergreen comes to us from the temperate region of Sikkim, and is not always patient if set in situations *too* bleak and exposed to the rigours of cold and wind. But in more decent places there is no doing anything but brilliantly with it.

H. retusum is a twin to *H. hyssopifolium* but that the leaves are specially blunted or notched at the end. (Syria.)

H. rhodopeum (*H. origanifolium*, Urv.) is a prostrate grey-hoary tuffet from sun-trodden slopes of Thrace and Macedonia, with blunt oblong little leaves, and the flowers, one, two, or three, at the ends of the shoots.

H. Richeri has been used as the type of so many of its kin that it must now be described with a minuteness that its beauty does not deserve, though its rarity may. For it is rather a stiff stout thing, with a roundish stem about a foot high, ending in a cluster of large and brilliant flowers. This stem is set with, and almost embraced by, a certain number of oval leaves in pairs, marked with a line of black dots round by their rim, such dots of darkness also to be detected on the sunshine of the flower. It is a species of the South, and may be found occasionally in the higher alpine turf, most rare of all in Switzerland, but not strange to the Col de Lautaret.

H. rubrum is the variety *rubrum* of *H. laeve*, and a strange beautiful break in the family, springing from soil of blood and iron in Syria, where empires have bled to produce this fine head of crimsoned flowers in place of the Hypericum's otherwise unvarying gold.

H. rumelicum is in the same line, but only about 6 inches high, with stiffly-fringed calyx and narrow leaves rolled down along the edges. (From the Macedonian mountains.)

H. rupestre has none of the merit that the name ought to confer. It is an overweening bush near *H. cardiophyllum,* but with looser heads of flower. (From the cliffs of Cilicia.)

H. satureiaefolium = H. confertum, q.v.

H. scabrellum springs by the source of Cydnus, and in many another damp mountainy place of Asia Minor—a much more graceful species than *H. atomarium,* with fine stems of 10 inches or so, having blunted rough leaves almost heart-shaped at their base, and open loose spikes of blossom. The stem below the leaves is roughish too.

H. scabrum has no particular merit, being an unpolished erect herb of the Levant.

H. serpyllifolium is a bush of some 3 to 6 feet, with the branches packed with whorls of little narrow foliage like that of a Thyme, &c., and ending in dense spikes of blossom. (From the ruins of Seleucia.)

H. sinaicum, on the damp rocks of Arabia the stony, is a more graceful and unbranching counterpart of *H. tomentosum,* which goes no further East than Sardinia.

H. Spruneri. Comes under *H. Grisebachii.*

H. stenobotrys. See under *H. confertum.*

H. thymbraefolium is a *tiny-flowered* species which is otherwise in the way of *H. hyssopifolium.* It is found about Kharput in the subalpine regions of Anatolia, and has unbranching little stems of 6 inches set with red glands.

H. thymopsis is still smaller, being only 3 or 4 inches high, with a great number of fine stems set with narrow cylindric leaves, rolled over at the edges, and with buds in their axils. (Higher slopes of Antitaurus.)

H. tomentosum is a woody plant with many flopping stalks clothed in oval foliage that in its turn is clothed with fluffy down or wool. It is not a common species, being found here and there in the warmer parts of South and Central Spain ; with two varieties, *H. t. dissiti-*

florum and *H. t. intermedium.* A thing is now being sent out under the name of *H. "argenteum"* which is, in truth, no more than this. It is not a very good thing, though a most expensive one, such sums being asked for it that in return one hopes for at least a good quality of Sheffield plate on the foliage, instead of so thin a coat of Britannia ware that in a week or two all the leaves, large and oval and too big either for the flower or the floundering 6-inch branches, are gone of a dull and leaden bald green, revealing the inferior metal on which the brief plating was applied in order to elicit gold. Far finer is *H. pubescens*, from damp places down in Granada, which is an erect twin to *H. tomentosum*, but with flowers of twice the size and show.

H. trichocaulon may only be seen in the rocks on the south side of Cretan Ida. It is a lovely little jewel with blossoms as large as in our own *H. perforatum*, but carried lonely and erect (sometimes in a head) on many dainty stems of only 4 or 5 inches, set with pairs of oblong leaves, perfectly smooth and green, sitting close upon the stalks.

H. tymphresteum is a good species, quite near *H. hyssopifolium callithyrsum*—a bushy tuft of branches with fine blue-grey foliage of which the lower leaves hardly roll at all at the edge, while the upper ones are specially huddled and involved on the barren shoots, and the flowers are of special brilliance in their loose spires on the 9-inch sprays. (Suspiciously close, indeed, to *H. hyssopifolium.*)

H. uniflorum makes a minute prostrate tuft in the way of a miniature *H. Apollinis* or *H. rhodopeum.* Its little fine shoots are not more than 2 or 3 inches long, set with tiny blunt leaves, and each producing one solitary golden star at the tip. (From the schistose region of Anemas in Lycaonia.)

There are, of course, numberless more St. John's-worts, and many more of merit, most especially in the larger and shrubbier sections of the race, which have not here been touched at all. But with regard to the smaller and choicer species, Europe, America, and the Levant have here not grudged us of their best.

I

Iberidella. See *Thlaspi rotundifolium.*

Ibēris.—In no race does worse confusion rage than among the Iberids, the muddle here being as much the fault of the Iberids themselves as of anyone else; for they are not content with growing far and wide, and seeding copiously in any sunny slope of well-drained

deep soil, but they must needs interbreed with each other, till there is
now a number of garden-species with which there is no possibility of
coping. Enough, then, if a little clearance can be made among the
more or less perennial species, and some of them restored to the right
names they have too long exchanged with others. Such, then, will
be the Iberids here unravelled; all of which, in soil that is light, and
a situation that is sunny and well-drained, will continue easily thriving
for many years—flowering as a rule in early summer, but in many cases
spasmodically on through the year, and especially in winter. Almost
all the species seed with infidelity and profusion, and all root so readily
that almost any shoot broken off and stuck into almost any ground
will make a plant within the month.

I. Bernardiana is a pink annual, confined to the Pyrenees, and often
known by the alternative name of *I. Bubanii.*

I. cappadocica. See under *Ptilotrichum cappadocicum,* or when
sated with the music of this name, under *Schivereckia iberidea.*

I. conferta is a very dense tuft of 3 inches high, woody at the base,
and with rosettes of smooth narrow leaves, and naked flower-stems
carrying heads of white blossom. (A lovely rarity from great elevations in the Serra da Estrella of Portugal.)

I. contracta makes a prostrate weakling mass of shoots, clad in
short and narrow foliage (the lowest rather inclined to have teeth)
and ending in widely-radiating starry heads of pink or purple blossom.
It is a species nearly related to *I. gibraltarica,* and seeks the low dry
places of Algarve in Portugal.

I. corifolia, with which it is often confused, is quite a different
thing—a small and precious jewel standing close to *I. saxatilis;*
not the false "*I. saxatilis*" of gardens, but the true *I. saxatilis,*
L.—that minute and prostrate plant with yew-like fleshy dark
leaves which a few fortunate owners still know as *I. "petraea."* In
all these points, habit, density, prostration, and fine narrowness of
night-dark little leaf, *I. corifolia* follows its model closely, but with
the one difference that the *leaves are fringed with hairs.*

I. correaefolia, on the contrary, is the species that makes such enormous masses in all our gardens, dense with long glossy dark-green leaves
clustering towards the ends of the long fleshy branches that are more
bare below, and form into a spreading flopping bush a couple of yards
or more across, and some 8 inches high or less, with the sombre beautiful leafage hidden from sight in May by the great innumerable heads
of large snow-white flowers. This beauty is too often spoken of as *I.
sempervirens* or as *I. corifolia,* Iberids with which it has no relationship
whatever, these being smaller and choicer, but this by far the most

sumptuous and precious garden-plant for general effect that the whole race produces—a huge mass to sprawl over any unsightliness and shroud it in glory both by summer and winter.

I. Garrexiana. See under *I. sempervirens.*

I. gibraltarica usually daunts the timid with its name and its reputation for delicacy, and yet, in a dry warm bank of a South-country garden (or North-country one for that matter), why should one be afraid to grow this glorious alien, seeing that, although it is chary of seed in our climate, it can be struck like any Pelargonium from cuttings ? It makes a rather straggling bush, a foot more or less in height, set with leathery spoon-shaped or wedge-shaped dark-green leaves that are cut into teeth at their tip. The flowers are borne from the end of every shoot in June, and are large rounded heads of big pink or lilac. By judicious cuttings-in to taste the growth could of course be cured of its one fault, and taught no more to rove but to remain a neat dome of leafage and blossom. It is very rarely seen in cultivation, every other kind of inferior thing being sent out under the name.

I. Jordani, from the mountains of Anatolia, emits many branches from its fat neck, and these are not strong enough to stand up, but flop round in a star, rising up at the tip to bear their white heads of bloom, larger than those of the Candytuft, though smaller than those of *I. Pruiti.* The branches are not more than some 3 or 6 inches long, and the plant a brilliant one.

I. jucunda = Aethionema coridifolium.

I. odorata is probably only annual. It stands close to *I. pectinata,* but is much smaller, and with radiating heads of white fragrant blossom borne on hairy-white dwarf tufts, with the leaves cut at the tip into several short lobes. (Greece.)

I. pectinata is a flopping large-leaved thing whose foliage is cut into deep sharp teeth ; big whitish flower-heads. (Southern Spain, &c.)

I. petraea, of gardens, belongs to that good and gifted woman Mrs. Harris. See *I. saxatilis,* L.

I. petraea (Jord.)=*I. Tenoreana,* DC., which is too often also the *I. saxatilis* of gardens.

I. pinnata is a matter of much confusion in nurseries. Countless very charming plants are sent out under this name, which all prove to be round perennial bushlings with dark fine narrow foliage ; whereas the one and only *I. pinnata* is an *annual or biennial species,* with all the *leaves feathered into lobes.* There can hardly be any doubt that the pretenders to this undesirable name are in reality all developments and seedlings of *I. sempervirens, q.v.*

IBERIS.

I. procumbens is a large lax Iberid with radiating flower-heads from the coasts of Portugal; it is perhaps the same as *I. pectinata*.

I. Pruiti belongs to Sicily, Naples, Aragon, &c.—a low species forming a central rosette and then sending out below it, all round, stems of some 6 inches that rise up to make almost a little bush with their close *non-radiating* heads of rather small white blooms. The leaves are fat and oval spoon-shaped, *perfectly uncut* at the edge, and *perfectly hairless*, like the whole robust and half-shrubby plant; and they draw gradually down into a foot-stalk.

I. saxatilis, L. (*I. petraea* of gardens) is a well-known, dark, minute jewel with prostrate fleshy twigs of Yew, which are terminated by close sugar-loaves of white blossom often tinged with purple, especially as they fade. It varies to larger and smaller forms, but the best known is the old tiny prostrate type with its shoots so hearty and well-furnished-looking in their furry vesture of succulent midnight-green foliage so fat and narrow as to be cylindric. This likes to be planted in sunny moraine or on a good open bank in light and very well-drained soil, where it will ere long make mats of flat and fine obscurity of a foot across, each radiating shoot uprising in spring at the tip to show its long heads of blossom. It sets fertile seed, but is quickly multiplied by cuttings. This species, quite unmistakable (once its name is grasped), will be found in the high and stony lime-stone places of the Southern hills from the Pyrenees to Sicily. In gardens it has had its name mixed up with that myth, *I. petraea*, so that now a chassé-croisé has to be made: what we have long grown as *I. petraea* becomes *I. saxatilis*, while our former *I. saxatilis* becomes *I. petraea* (Jord.) on its way to final rest under the prior name of *I. Tenoreana*, DC.—by which, and no other, it is to be henceforth known.

I. sempervirens suffers more than even the rest from false and over-crowded names in the garden, this being the parent of many valuable forms—Snow Queens, Little Gems, Grandifloras, Superbas, Plenas, Perfections, and various other most delightful and free-flowering little neat bushes table-clothed with white in due season, that all derive from the beautiful *I. sempervirens*, which in its type may best be thought of as great *I. correaefolia* divided by half, with stiffer, darker, narrower foliage, fringed more or less with hair at the edge, and often with a margin of cartilage. It is always a most lovely and lovable plant, of the easiest and most imperturbable nature so long as it has the sun to dazzle with its sheets of white. And no less beautiful are the various forms, that usually are compacter in habit, tighter domes or round masses, no less profuse in blossom. In *I. sempervirens*, also, which is found all along the Alps from the Pyrenees to Asia Minor,

IBERIS.

must be included various local forms often acknowledged as species, such as rare *I. s. Garrexiana*, a little earlier in bloom and a trifle floppier in habit, with fewer laxer branches, which may here and there be seen in the high and stony fine turf about the Col de Tenda.

I. serrulata, a perfectly smooth and hairless bushling from the Levant, with small oval leaves, daintily *saw-toothed along the cartilaginous margin*, and very pretty heads of white blossom at the tips of the shoots.

I. Spruneri is like a more erect *I. Jordani*, with closer heads, and stems more slender. It lies under suspicion of being an annual.

I. stylosa = *Thlaspi stylosum*.

I. subvelutina makes a dense grey-velvet mound of 6 inches or so, on the dry hills of Aranjuez, thick with erect shoots clothed in small needle-narrow leaves, and ending in loose-spiked heads of pink or white blossom.

I. Tenoreana, DC., is *I. petraea* (Jord.), and sometimes *I. " saxatilis "* of gardens, its own name being usually borne by some form of *I. sempervirens*, while the true *I. Tenoreana* is more often heard of than beheld. It is a low-growing tortuous woody-based species in the way of *I. Pruiti*, with thick oval dark leaves tapering to the base, clothing weak and rather downy branches of some 5 or 6 inches. The flowers are pink or white, borne in *very radiating* heads. It may at once be known among all others of its habit by the fact that the leaves are *fringed with hairs*, and *more or less toothed at the tip*. All forms of *I. sempervirens* have leaves *perfectly entire*, and it should be easy to detect thus, in any garden-plant labelled *I. saxatilis* or *I. petraea*, whether the pretender be a form of *I. sempervirens* or whether it really does belong to the much smaller, weaklier, declining *I. Tenoreana*, under one of its invalid names. As for confusion between this and the true *I. saxatilis*, L., there can be no possibility of such a thing, *I. saxatilis* being about a quarter of its size in all parts, to say nothing of its *perfectly narrow keenly-pointed toothless little dark leaves, cylindric in section and fleshy*. *I. Tenoreana* is not common, but ranges from the Pyrenees to Sicily; and should have light sunny soil or good moraine, as otherwise it sometimes proves impermanent, and, indeed, should always be kept going with cuttings.

I. Zanardani is a most rare and attractive downy bushling about 3 or 4 inches high, and leafy *all over* (instead of, as in *I. saxatilis*, most especially so towards the tips of the shoots). The leaves are notably narrow, pointed and fleshy, huddled alternately in a spiral up the shoots to the very base of the flower-heads, which are white or whitish. (From the island of Lesina off the coast of Dalmatia.)

INULA.

Incarvillea.—Even if *I. Delavayi* be now too large and common for the rock-garden, there still remains its beautiful dwarf version *I. grandiflora*, a treasure of only 4 or 5 inches high, and twice as rich in brilliancy and beauty ; this need only have its great stout carrot established in deep, rich, light, and well-drained loam, there to go on for ever, blooming most gloriously in June with its wide golden-throated Allamandas of flaming rose borne singly on stems of 6 inches or so. Other species are incessantly being offered at advanced prices, with shrieks of proclamation, as *I. brevipes* and *I. Bonvaloti*, being in reality mere forms, and not improved forms, of *I. grandiflora*—not that in themselves they lack merit, but that on *I. grandiflora* nothing could improve, unless the seed (in which all of the race are profuse) should some day yield a snowy albino. Of other species, we have *I. variabilis* and *I. Olgae ;* but these though pretty in ways wholly different from those of the Delavayi group—being feathery-leaved small bushes with clusters of diminished rosy trumpets—are both uncommon, and hardly ever satisfactory in England, dreading wet above all things, and craving for any amount of ripening sun. (*I. Olgae* is also *I. Koopmannii.*) As for *I. lutea*, this is a Delavayi of 6 feet high, but with the same acanthoid splendour of leafage, darker, and magnified, and ample Allamandas that are more allamandic than ever, in being of clear pure yellow. However, it saves our nerves from the shock of such splendour by never revealing it, and has not once been known to flower in cultivation, though it grows like any cabbage.

Inula.—Magnificent as the large Inulas may be, they are matter fitter for the wild garden or the border than for the select kingdom of the hill-children. Even of the big species, however, a word may be put in for the superb and not overweening *I. Roylei*, with its huge basal leaves, oval and crinkly and green, with stems of 2 feet or less, carrying flower-heads enormous even in proportion to the foliage—vast spider-rayed fringy golden suns in August and September. Then there is *I. acaulis*, truly appropriate for choicer foreground places, with blossoms like those of *I. salicina*, sitting single and close all over a mat of oblong-leaved tuffets. This is a true alpine from the high places of Berytagh and the Cilician Taurus. And no less alpine is *I. Montbretii* from the same mountain of Berytagh (and others), with huge golden flowers as before, and stems of 4 inches or half a foot. Of similar stature is *I. Aschersoni*, half bushy at the base, but no less clothed in close-pressed silk ; and *I. fragilis* from Berytagh, with many almost stemless stems covered deep in fluff, each carrying from three to five noble blossoms nearly sitting on the tuft, from which they just emerge on the delicate stalk that the stout undelicate root-stock emits. All these have the merit of the easiest possible temper, and may be divided at pleasure in autumn or raised from seed. And the last comment that the dwarfer members of the family afford is that they give a brilliant warning to the cultivator never to be daunted by a plant's habitat. For round the torrid coasts of Egypt and all the Levant there lives in the very sea-rocks themselves a dwarf and fleshy-leaved Inula with golden flowers, of which well indeed might the cultivator despair, and this book tell no tales ; yet *Inula crithmoeides* is quite as happy playing at samphire on half the headlands of England and Ireland as ever in the more classic rocks that look out over the waters of the Mediterranean and the bird-haunted hot lagoons of Egypt.

Ionactis. See under **Aster.**

Ipomoea stans.—For a hot deep and sandy corner in a hot garden this beautiful weak-stemmed hairy-leaved Convolvulus may be of value, with its 10-inch stem, erect or flopping, and its large cups of pure blue with a sheen of violet, through the later summer. In winter, however, its roots might well be taken up and stored like those of a Dahlia.

Iris.—None has a right to lay his word at the foot of this august race unless he is prepared to say nothing about any lesser matter. Rock-gardeners will find all they need to know of Iris in the exhaustive and final works of Mr. Dykes—the little one-and-ninepenny book is recommended to the rich : for only the really poor will be able to afford the six-guinea tome. Here, accordingly, there is no need for us to linger paddling in the fringes of the vast ocean that is Iris ; enough to realise that for sheltered banks, and more especially under the glass that shelters the choice Gentian bed, we shall be very happy in spring with the violet jewellery of *I. reticulata* (good and kind enough, indeed, to gratify open ground and border) ; the blue-and-gold beauty of *I. Vartani ;* tiny yellow *I. Danfordiae ;* violet-velvet little *I. Bakeriana ;* the splashed sapphire-and-turquoise of the Van Tubergen *I. histrioeides* (do not be deluded into accepting substitutes) ; and the crimson-velvet of the best *I. Krelagei* (the poorer ones are cotton-backed, and the aniline colour has run at that) ; and then the unimaginable flowers of *I. persica*, pearly pallors splashed with kingfisher-wing blue and the green of young grass, with a blotch of purple brown and a central streak of gold. Pale-grey and indigo is its close cousin or child, *I. Heldreichii* (*I. stenophylla*) ; and in deep contrast stands its twin, *I. Tauri*, with imperial purples threaded by fine gold. These all are bulbous Irids, and in many cases had best be treated as annuals in England, or else taken yearly up and stored as Tulips are, planting them again soon, however, that they may get betimes to their work of growth, and break stemless into living explosions and ragged bombs of pure bursting colour in the first dawn of the year, when the raw earth is far too dead and bare, it seems, to be pregnant of such outbreaks without a miracle—and when, therefore, they stand no chance at the hands of wind and worms and slugs and birds and weather, unless they have the kindly shelter of a glass to reward them for their excessive promptitude in glorifying a world not yet sufficiently awake and comfortable to gratify them with a welcome warm and dry ; though it seems hard, indeed, that the muddy tears of dying winter should wreck the first babies of spring, Caesarian-born from earth in its darkest dankest hour. Therefore, even if bulbs have to be bought every year, their beauty and opportuneness is such, and the expense so small, that indeed it need not be grudged ; while *I. reticulata*—which has the most beautiful varieties, including one rather restrictively called *Cambridge*, whose colour is not that of Cambridge alone but that of the finest pale summer-dawn of gold and turquoise that the world ever saw—*I. reticulata*, I say, will continue to live and prosper and multiply in the open like a Squill if suited ; and is even the better for being relieved in autumn, every two or three years, from the overcrowding mass of its own bulbs. Alas, that so much cannot be said for *I. persica ;* it is older in England than the Divine Right of Kings, but in three centuries has almost grown as weakly and ragged and rare as that other alien importation, so much less perdurable and precious.

These are all bulbs ; of tubers let the rock-garden have (if it can get it) the true *I. pumila*, as rare as the Dodo, in despite of catalogues unanimous in offering it. Of this, too, let it have the best coerulean blue form, not the grey one ; let it avoid the soaked old-blotting-paper-coloured *I. p. gracilis*, in spite of its sweet scent ; let it seek out golden little *I. minuta* from the Far East, and blue-and-white dainty *I. ruthenica* (some of whose varieties, however, do not seem to flower at all). Then there are *I. cristata* and its variety from the Great Lake-shores of America, *I. lacustris*, both of quickly-creeping habit and the rarest crimpled powder-blue-and-golden beauty of blossom—*I. lacustris* being the bluer and deeper, but also the more minute and precious. And yet another North-American is *I. verna*, with wide clumps of sword-shaped tiny leaves, and exquisite fragrant and abundant starry Irises of blue and violet and gold in early summer. This, as sent out, is usually so divided as to have no root or vigour left, but solid unhewn clumps of a foot across have only to be planted in cool rich soil in a moist and shady aspect to go ahead with all the vigour of *I. pseuda-corus*. The Californian Irises have a different temper, and a sunset

loveliness of rose and cream : *II. tenax, Douglasiana, bracteata*, in varying subtle flamboyancies of claret and silver, apricot and rose, are
much larger than all these last, hate lime, and enjoy a deep sunny
place in sandy peat where they can wax for ever. Then there is creeping wee delicious *I. arenaria*, with its golden flowers and their orange
beards, so freely produced that often the plant dies of its own beauty ;
this should have a surface depth of sand, but richer matter some four
inches underground to root in ; it should also at need be top-dressed
and divided. Only a little larger is *I. cretensis*, the small form of
I. unguicularis (*I. stylosa*), with peacock-eyed cups of powder-blue and
gold in winter, filled with scent, and like gigantic goblets of *Crocus
byzantinus ;* and there are also rare and lovely *I. kumaonenis* and
I. Hookeriana, of mottled red and purple, hungry both for sun and fullness of moisture while in growth. While of the small Flag-Irises
no rock-garden will be without commoner things such as *II. chamaeiris,
bosniaca, rubro-marginata, balkana*, subtle sad *mellita*, and *olbiensis* that
has lost its home. And last of the list, and for the moment the most
exquisite of all, the filmy grace of *I. gracilipes*, from the cleared upland
coppices of Japan, where it grows as primroses grow in a Kentish
clearing, all the hillside covered with its dancing 5-inch sprays of wide-
winged delicate butterflies in the tenderest crumpled silk of pale-blue,
with beard and enrichments of gold, and a pale veined eye—the most
perfectly fairylike of its race, so that one feels that it is indeed a-flutter
for its final flight. Yet in the garden in light woodland soil, not overhung,
but sheltered from the excess of sun and rain and wind, *I. gracilipes*,
at the fringe of small low shrubs, remembers the Thousand Islands of
Matsushima, and flutters gaily in a garden many thousands of miles
away. And we now have *I. Potaninii*, and lovely *I. goniocarpa*.

For the bog garden there is no place here to speak of *II. sibirica,
versicolor, virginica, Delavayi, Forrestii*, gorgeous golden-veined and
imperial *II. chrysographes, setosa, laevigata*, and all the huge clan that
is Kaempferi (to be kept wet while growing, and dry while resting),
II. aurea, Monnieri, delicate *cuprea*, and a hundred others. But of the
Oncocyclus Irids, none. They are a doomed and lonely race of irreconcilable Troades in weeds of silken crape, sullenly and grandly un-
resigned to exile and captivity, passing out of their captor's hands
in a last defiant blaze of dark and tragic magnificence. They are
chief mourners in their own funeral-pomps, wistful and sombre and
royal in an unearthly beauty of their own, native to the Syrian hills
that have seen the birth of gods, but strange and hostile to the cruder
colder lands. They are the maidens that went down into hell with
Persephone, and yearly in her train they return to make a carpet for

her feet across the limestones of the Levant. But not for ours—their loyalty to their mistress holds only good in Syria ; they do not recognise her in the rain-cloaks that she wears in the West, and lands of younger divinities shall never twice re-greet such children of mystery as these. And their offspring, the less impossible *Regelio-Cyclus* group, have somehow sold the honour of those silken sad uncertain queens, their mothers, for a mess of comfort in the garden. One is glad they are such comparatively willing captives, yet even their purchased affability one regrets as a betrayal. Nor is it, even in itself, so much to boast of ; let them be in deep beds of cow-manure with a foot of hot sand on top : so they will thrive and bloom, but will not for long continue, unless glass and bells be put over them in winter, a set of precautions that turn the garden from a paradise into a kindergarten or re-formatory ; and are only permissible when employed to help, as with the rare Gentians, but not as the only hopes of prolonging an artificial existence, as with the more fractious Irids of the East.

Isātis.—Despite clamours in catalogues no Isatis ever fails to be too large and coarse for the rock-garden ; *II. glauca, glastifolia, alpina,* &c., are sometimes advertised, but are not of value, except perhaps in the weed border, where they are tall and stately, with big hardy showers of minute golden or white blossom in summer.

Ischārum, with *Biarum,* makes up a race of evil Aroids whose ominous goblets break through the bare earth of Syria in spring, but will not go on doing as much for us unless our gardens and our soil and our site be specially hot and dry.

Isopyrum.—In the woods of Switzerland and Central Europe dwells pretty little *I. thalictroeides,* with dainty bright-green thalictroid foliage, a few inches high in early spring, and pearly stars of blossom— a delightful plant for any light woodland corner, where it rejoices March and then gets promptly out of the way again until next year. Not of much merit is *I. adiantifolium,* but *I. anemonoeides* is a charm-ing thing like a diminished *I. thalictroeides,* from the rocky woods of Afghanistan. *II. caespitosum* and *uniflorum* are choicer yet—tuffets of the rock, with flowers of blue. But the grandest of all is *I. Farreri,* from the cool and danker limestone precipices over the Alps of Koko-Nor, Tibet, where in the fast crevices it forms cushions of dainty leafage of greyish-blue, more than a foot across, covered in due time with a profusion of gold-fluffed flowers like miniature Meconopsids of lavender, or purple tinge, balancing on single fine stems of 2 or 3 inches, in such profusion as to hide the mass from which they spring. This most beautiful rarity is by no means difficult to rear from its abundant seed ; it germinates with readiness, and the seedlings advance in the world with almost equal celerity, whether much care be deployed upon them or none at all. (*Root disturbance is best avoided.*) When raised to months of discretion, too, there is every reason for us to rejoice in the prosperity of this unique loveliness, under the same conditions of careful culture that make the happiness of choice Saxatile treasures, so long as it has a well-drained depth.

Isotŏma fluviatĭle is a little New Zealand Campanula of the bogs with small pale-blue flowers.

Ivesia Purpusii. See under **Comarella.**

J

Jaborosa integrifolia is a dwarfish, creeping-stemmed Solanoid from the Andes, with large foliage and fragrant long-tubed starry flowers of greenish white. It wants deep warm rooting room, and is not very hardy or trustworthy or lovely.

Jankaea Heldreichii, on the contrary, deserves all the care it exacts. For this lovely thing makes rosettes like those of Ramondia, but silvery with a dense pelt of white down, so that it is obvious that no place will suit it where water falls or lodges. Let it then be planted in rough, coarse, sandy peat with plenty of grit, in such a hollow of the overhung rockwork or hole of a stone as can never be visited or corroded by rain, and there its silver flat rosette will take no hurt and continue to shine untarnished, till one day in June or July you will see the stems spring up some 2 or 3 inches and unfold their spray of ample little Gloxinia flowers, which are of palest clearest lavender, and of a texture so thick and crystalline that they seem to have been carved from tinted snow, glistering all over their substance with minute sparkles of light. This can be raised with care like Haberlea from seed, and, like Haberlea, Ramondia, or Begonia, it can also be made to root from the leaves struck in sand, with the greatest care, about July, and nurtured up in heat. It is the pride of Thessaly and its shady mountain walls.

Janthe (Ianthe) bugulifolia.—This is a Celsia or Mullein of a weird attractiveness, about a foot high and closely suggestive of *Verbascum phlomoeides* in habit of loose basal rosette, but with spires of blossom in the strangest tones of greenish blue and metallic bronze, evilly spotted with black or purple, from June to September, opening in succession round the spike.

Jasione, a race of meadow Campanulads that try to be Globularias, failing in their efforts to be accepted as Phyteumas. One, *J. perennis*, may often be seen in England in summer, with heads of small azure fluff on slender stems that suggest a delicate and bright-blue Scabious. Others of similar stature, and all of the easiest culture, are *JJ. Jankae, montana*, and *amethystina ;* smaller and more choice is *J. humilis*, only some 4 inches high, and *J. supina*, of the same size, easily to be raised from seed, and grown in any open soil, probably good company-plants for Gentians, though not in themselves either desiring or deserving such refinements or society.

Jasonia tuberosa, a yellow-spiked, stiff-leaved Composite of 15 inches high, flowering in July and August, and admissible to a specially barren, dry, hot place, but valuable nowhere.

Jeffersonia diphylla (*J. binata*) is a small North American Berberid, very like Epimedium, with divided, shield-shaped leaves, blue grey beneath, and little white flowers lonely on a naked stem of about a foot high in May ; this thrives in woodland culture. But far more precious is *J. dubia*, from the forests of Manchuria, which must be grown in light forest-mould in a sheltered place, where it will freely throw up its rounded, scalloped, glaucous leaves of metallic dim-violet tone and thinnish texture, each on its fine frail stem of 3 inches or so : and, not by any means so freely, its flowers like those of a pallid large Hepatica of lovely blue, on similar stems in May or June. Careful division.

Jovellana.—This is a sectional name in the vast race of *Calceolaria*, and has now been revived, for the undoing of the uninstructed, as a race-name for the particular group of CALCEOLARIAS that have a gaping twi-cleft lip, instead of the usual rounded bag. In any case it will be understood that the name means no more than *Calceolaria*.

Jurinea alata is but a biennial Composite, but perennials of much more worth are *J. depressa* and *J. humilis*. They both make dense tufts of foliage in the high stony places of the Alps, the one in Spain and the former in the Levant. In the case of *J. humilis* the blue heads of blossom sit tight to the tuffet and are about half an inch across ; yet more attractive is *J. depressa*, the only one of this big plain Levantine family to call for commendation. For this makes a rosette of lyrate leaves, green above and all hoary-cobwebby, lying outstretched in their tufts on the ground ; upon the mass appear large hemispherical thistles of white or pink, smelling sweetly of vanilla. The whole plant indeed, especially the root, is strongly aromatic, and makes a popular medicine in the Alps of Anatolia where it lives, and where the peasants call it the Musk-rose. These should both be raised from seed, and grown in the sunny moraine.

K

Kaufmannia Semenowii. See *Cortusa Semenowii.*

Kelloggia galioeides has no value except for being lost in damp woodlands, being a climbing Rubiaceous plant with greenish-yellow little flowers like an Asperula, on stems of 10 inches, in thick masses.

Kernera. See under Cochlearia, but it is hardly worth while.

Kirengeshōma palmata, a most curious and magnificent Japanese oddity for rich soil in a cool, damp place. The black-dark, shining stems rise to some 3 or 4 feet, and are set with nobly handsome foliage like that of some Spiraea, green and palmate ; then, in late August, or later still, until sometimes the frost blackens them untimely, noble waxy-yellow flowers, very conspicuous and large, hover in large, loose clusters at the tops of the stems, and are like nothing in the world, except that their weirdness of shape suggests dimly some magnified and monstrous Impatiens. This splendid thing should be well planted and left alone : ultimately, when the clump is too big, it can be multiplied by division.

Knautia.—None of the large Scabious are demanded by the rock-garden, but in its wildest outskirts room might be made for *KK. longifolia, magnifica,* and *macedonica,* all blooming through the summer, and all being tallish, thrifty plants, the first lilac-flowered, the second rose-mauve, and the third brilliant carmine-purple. (Seed.)

Kniphofia, the correct name of **Tritoma,** where all Kniphofias will be found.

Kohlrauschia, a set of annual Tunicas, so far as known.

Krynitzkia Jamesii (Eritrichium Jamesii) should be grown in a warm, sandy place. It is a half-shrubby, silky-leaved plant, with spikes of blossoms like white forget-me-nots in summer.

Kuhnia eupatorioeides.—Narrow leaves with white hair, and stems of a foot or two, carrying Ageratums of cream-white fluffs.

L

Lactuca. For all these see under **Mulgedium.**

Lagēnóphŏra, a small family of pretty little stars, replacing the Daisy in the temperate Antarctic regions, and making no bad substitutes. They are not specially showy, and their flowers have no golden eye, and consist only of a fuzz of white rays. None the less they have their value for covering any sunny open slopes in light soil. They are hardy, and can be divided at will: a bank dotted with the countless blind Daisies of *L. Forsteri* is notably charming in late summer. *L. Barkeri* has leafy stems; slighter, smaller-headed, narrower-rayed are *LL. lanata, petiolata,* and *pinnatafida,* while *L. Commersoni* is a neat thing from Chili and the Falklands: all are free growers when established, and run about, and freely cover the ground, from which they copiously send up their dainty stems of 3 inches or so.

Lancea thibetica is a small creeping Scrophulariaceous species forming a close tuft with rosettes of leathery toothed leaves, and violet-blue flowers on leafy stems of 3 or 4 inches, and themselves nearly an inch in length.

Lathȳrus, a race intermixed with *Orobus* until each species of the one race had better first be looked out in the other. As a rule *Lathyrus* may be held to imply chiefly large and rampant climbers, such as *L. latifolius,* the Everlasting Pea, with its beautiful white form, and the gorgeous Californian *L. splendens* of the same size and flowers of dazzling crimson, very large and numerous—this latter for a warm, sheltered bank where its 10-foot stems may have room. Of others, to pursue the big climbers no further, *L. pannonicus* must be looked for under *Orobus Smithii; L. ornatus,* from the Rockies, grows some 4 to 8 inches high, often has blue-grey leaves, and carries three or four large, fine, purple flowers an inch wide on its footstalks; *L. incanus* is the same thing, but with a vesture of down; *L. decaphyllus* is smaller, woodier, and more branched, with stiff, veined foliage and heads of some three to five big purple blossoms. *L. roseus* comes better under *Orobus; L. grandiflorus* climbs amid the mountain-woods of Greece and Macedonia, Sicily, and Naples, with one to three enormous flowers to a stem, the keel being crimson and the wide wings purple; less than this in all parts is *L. undulatus;* and *L. rotundifolius* is a smaller *L. latifolius* from mid-Russia. *L. filiformis* makes fine, erect, wiry growths, with finely divided, almost grassy-looking leaflets, and the whole plant in June becomes a waving mass a foot high, of delicate loose heads of large blossom in the most beautiful violet-blue. This, though erect and not a climber, has the family passion for spreading, and in any light soil and open situation offers you the risk of no less inexorable a weed than our own *L. pratensis* of the golden flowers. Of the remaining names, most of those that belong to species valuable in our domain will be found, like *Lathyrus cyaneus,* under *Orobus; L. inermis* is *O. hirsutus; L. Linnaei, O. luteus; L. venetus, O. variegatus; L. vernus, O. vernus.* In fact, under *Orobus* now go all the non-scandent un-tendrilled species—all, that is, with which we are immediately concerned. Those that here remain may copiously be raised from seed, and grown with almost excessive ease. It must be remembered that they are usually either big or vast, ill fitted by stature and invasive habit for any choice place or usurpation of the foreground.

Laurentia, a race of small Lobelias, all of paludose proclivities and much charm. America sends us *L. eximia*, and Spain, *L. Michelii*, which grow in the wet places of their respective countries, sending up, in summer, leafy stems of some 2 to 6 inches, bearing little Lobelias, which are pale-blue in *L. Michelii*, and dark-blue with a golden fold in *L. eximia*. The most beautiful of them, however, is the even daintier *L. tenella*, of damp places and sphagnum beds in Southern Europe, which grows quite happily with us in any cool (and sometimes even in any hot and dry) place, often seeding itself into chosen corners, and making neat, tiny rosettes of foliage, from which spring, all the summer through, a profusion of naked fine stems some 2 inches or more in height, each one carrying the most delicious and fairy-like Lobelia of soft china-blue, outlining the star of its clear, pale eye, most dainty and elfin to behold. Seed. The life of Laurentia, though truly hardy, is probably not long.

Lavandŭla.—The large common Lavender is hardly, perhaps, well placed in the rock-garden, but the dwarf form, sometimes called *compacta nana*, is very neat and tidy in growth, with a lovely unanimous outbreak of 9-inch spikes in summer, emitting much larger flowers than the type, in a tone of much more brilliant purple. It should be grown in full sun, kept cut into shape, and propagated by cuttings. Even sweeter and more delicious in its intense fragrance is *L. lanata* from the Sierra Nevada, where it is abundant in the crevices, especially on limestone, with masses of woolly snow, and long broken spires of violet ; and there are many other minor Lavenders, all of the south.

Ledum.—The Labrador Teas are neat little shrubs with neat evergreen foliage, and neat heads of white flower in early summer. Their place is in limeless soil with Heath and Rhododendron ; in the solfataras of Noboribets in the Hokkaido, *L. labradoricum* is so far from being attached to *terra firma* that it grows on the volcanic crust that is hopping all the time beneath it like the lid of a kettle. Other species are *LL. glandulosum* and *palustre*, but though useful and pretty, they all have a smug and stolid look, suggesting the kind of person who is always described as " a thoroughly nice girl, and such a help to her mother."

Leiophyllum buxifolium is a pretty comely American shrublet of 8 inches or so, for the same treatment as these last, but with rather less of a boarding-house look, with glossy small foliage and looser heads of pink-budded white stars, much more pleasant and emancipated.

Leontĭcē.—For treatment and general description, see under *Bongardia*, with which the race may almost be joined. Species that may be grown—all being yellow-flowered—are *LL. Alberti, altaica, chrysogonum*, and *leontopetalum*. (Often **Caulophyllum**.)

Leontopodium alpinum.—The Flannel-flower is of the easiest cultivation in any open place in light soil. It dreads wet and stagnation in winter, as becomes a desert plant ; and lime in abundance helps to keep white the whitened sepulchre of its sham flower. It can be grown admirably in window-boxes in London, where the smuts enhance its colour. Were it not for the idiotic superstitions and persistent rubbish of romance that have gathered round this species, no one would refuse credit and even affection to its wide woolly stars of silver, which, in the garden as on the wild hills, take special value if grown in the moraine among clumps of violet-and-gold *Aster alpinus*. It is often a really beautiful sight, covering the highest lawns of the Alps with tufts of grey, and galaxies of pale flannel starfishes, as common Daisies cover an English tennis-court. But to call this plant an alpine, to imagine it rare and precious and difficult of attainment, this is to provoke the meekest into exposure of a fraud so impudent and foolish that thereby the merits of Edelweiss itself are unduly shamed and darkened. It is not an alpine at all ; it belongs to the great central European and Asiatic deserts, but, being a very profuse seeder, has established itself on every mountain range of the Northern hemisphere in the Old World. It is not a rarity, but so universally common that you may rely on tramping acres of it on almost any alpine range above the altitude of 5500 feet ; but it is so far from being a typical and representative high-alpine that it never ascends beyond the fine mountain turf of some 7000 feet, more or less ; and it is so far from being difficult of attainment that on every such slope or final valley under the peaks, or ridge between them, one is treading dense flat lawns of it, in places where a dozen prams could race abreast without imperilling themselves, their conductors, or their inmates. Yet every season the misguided go dropping off precipices on which a few stray tufts have seeded down ; not knowing that 200 feet higher, in the soft alpine grass, they could be picking basins-full of blossoms in half an hour's gentle and octogenarian stroll before dinner. So the insane legend still continues, fostered by guides who make a practice, in front of the hotels, of seeming to quest Edelweiss along the face of pathless precipices, where eyelash-hold is of the slightest ; and sustained by pompous measures of protection in favour of the commonest and most reproductive and most massively colonising of all mountain plants. Still the reverent inquiry is made in hushed tones, "And have you ever seen the Edelweiss ? " Still maidens grow misty-eyed at the thought of it, and after having tramped the Alps from end to end declare that they would die happy if only they could see the Edelweiss ; an aspiration which proves their pedestrianism never to have progressed beyond the highroads of the passes, for, had they anywhere there diverged a hundred yards to right or left it would have been hard luck indeed had they not found themselves upon level lawns of their heart's desire. It is necessary, indeed, to repeat, that in almost every range, be it of lime or granite, you have only to get to the open downs about 2000 feet above your hotel, to find matted wide carpets everywhere of Flannel-flower, sharing the scant and stony herbage with *Aster alpinus* and *Anemone vernalis.* Go higher, into the grim and stony places where the true high-alpines have their home ; Flannel-flower has ceased completely, a species belonging exclusively to the levels of stone and fine poor grass at mid elevations on all the ridges of the world. It varies greatly in form ; some districts in which it abounds produce only dumpy stems and stars of miserable size and scanty rays ; on others it grows fine and fat, till certain valleys produce Edelweiss so noble that, as I was once told, for encouragement, "All men look your hat, if you have such an it "— the "it " not being the hat (which is hardly hypothetical) but the ample bloom of Flannel-flower with which Teutonic fashion adorns it. Garden forms of special amplitude have been raised from the seed which it so copiously produces, such as *L. a. lindavicum,* together, always, with "*majors*" and "*grandiflorums*" and so forth, being selections from the type ; the other sub-species are more distinct, each range, almost, producing its own. *L. sibiricum* is in all parts taller, with a variety of its own, *L. s. altaicum ; L. transylvanicum* comes under the heading of *L. a. lindavicum* : *L. himalaicum,* with its under-form *sikkimensis,* has smaller stars and bears them later in the season ; and the most remote of all, deserving perhaps to be raised to specific rank of its own as *Gnaphalium Sieboldii,* is *L. japonicum,* being almost a tiny bush with very many more rays to the star, and the leaves only white beneath, but on the upper surface of a deep and glossy dark green. All these come as readily from seed as the type-species, and may be grown with as little difficulty. And see Appendix.

Lepidium nebrodense, the only admissible species of its

race, is an 8-inch Crucifer, with spikes of white blossom in spring, adapted for special enthusiasts in sunny places. Seed.

Leptarrhenas are worthless dowds.

Leptinella (or **Cotula**) has already given us one devastating carpet-plant in *C. squalida*. There remain, however, many other species, all of the same countries, charms, and uses; *L. coronopifolia* being, however, taller and therefore less admissible, seeing that all the species are valued for dwarf habit and leaves alone, the flowers being either feeble or frightful; *L. atrata*, of greyish-green; *L. millefolium*, very feathery-fine, pale-green and aromatic, with lax leathery leaves, some-times as silvery as Yarrow or Gooseweed; *L. Mamatoto*, quite minute, a mat of soft silk; *L. scariosa* and *L. lanata*, like thickly woolly carpets of *Chrysanthemum alpinum*, but with hideous, fat, rayless flower-heads; and *L. propinqua*, standing between *L. scariosa* and *L. plumosa*.

Leptocōdon gracilis is a climbing plant of Lachen, close akin to Codonopsis, with tubular curved bells of blue, swollen at the top.

Lesquerella is almost the same thing as *Vesicaria*, which is almost the same thing as *Alyssum*. All the species make very neat tuffets of very neat rosettes, may be raised from seed, grow readily in any light, open ground, and have spikes of yellow flowers in spring. *L. condensata* is a mass of peculiar density, the stems being no longer than the leaves; *L. alpina* is a trifle more lax, and the stems emerge further from the tuft; *L. Engelmannii* (*L. pruinosa*, Greene, *ovata*, *ovalifolia*) is together bigger, with oval silvered foliage, stems of 6 inches or a foot, and flowers about an inch across. *L. Kingii* is pros-trate, with hairy rosettes of oval leaves. (All these from the North-Western States of America.)

Leucanthĕmum always hovers on the verge of being *Chrysan-themum*, so that any described species not found under the one heading stands an excellent chance of being discovered under the other, unless it has succeeded in escaping into the shelter of *Pyrethrum*. *L. Gmelini* and *sibiricum* are species quite close to each other—Chrysanthemums of branching habit, the latter lying down and only rising up at the ends of the shoots, while the former is fluffy-woolly at first, and then becomes smooth. *L. arcticum*, on the other hand, is wholly smooth, and, as sent out, has large fat foliage like that of some mossy Saxifrage; it is the duty of this to carry one ox-eye to each stem of some 5 inches. Culture, &c., as for the alpine Chrysanthemums. *L. montanum* is indeed now reckoned *C. montanum, q.v.*

Leucelēnē ericoeides is **Aster ericaefolius,** a dry-ground American of some 3 to 7 inches, hoary and soft and branching bushily, and fine of leaf, with flowers of white or pink on branchlets delicate as threads.

Leucocrīnum montanum (the White Lily of the Mountains) is a common beauty in the Central Rockies, but not by any means frequent with us. It makes a tuft of soft, narrow leaves, and then in early summer prepares an umbel underground in such a way that each large, spreading, narrow-tubed star, sweetly scented and in whites that vary to blue, seems springing by itself from amid the tuft on a stem of 3 or 4 inches. It is a most entrancing species, worth any comfort that its fleshy roots exact. It should be grown in fullest sun, in a sheltered and specially well-drained bank, in light, rich, and especially sandy warm soil of ample depth; and the apple of the eye should not be more cherished.

Leucocyclus formosus (or **Anacyclus**: but these are valueless little annuals) is a pretty woolly-white Composite for a warm, dry bank in poorish soil; with foliage so finely feathered and hoary and curled as to suggest a Santolina; the single handsome white Marguerites are borne freely on stems of some 8 inches or more throughout the later summer. (Cilician Taurus, especially above the lead-mines.)

Leucoïon.—Too delicate for most gardens is exquisite thread-frail *L. autumnale* (*Acis autumnalis*) from Gibraltar, with dainty roseate bells in autumn on stems of 2 or 3 inches. It may, however, be grown well in warm, sandy soil in the south. But by far the best of all is *L. carpaticum*, which sends up ample, cosy, wide cups of pure white, tipped with gold in earliest spring, hanging from stout stems of 3 or 4 inches, and incomparably more cheerful than those chilly Snowdrops, more warm and brilliant in its white, set off by that golden tip to each segment, more hearty in the shape of its flower, and more luxuriant in the bright-green gloss of its broad foliage. It may be a form of *L. vernum*, but is far superior, if the true plant can be got; and others in the same line of charm and dwarf stature are *L. trichophyllum*, *L. hiemale*, and the very rare *L. nicaeense* from Eza.

Leuzea conifera is not a thing of high charm. It is like an untidy Centaurea from 2 inches to a foot high, with feathered foliage, silvery below, and almost unbranched stems that bear big, egg-shaped flower-heads, in summer, of a purplish-lilac tone. Seed. (From West Europe, and fitted for a dry, rocky, poor place in the sun.)

L. rhaponticoeides is much handsomer, taking the Artichoke for its model, and growing some 3 or 5 feet high, with ample purpled heads, and splendid, ample feathered foliage of brilliant green, with white on the reverse.

Lewisia, a race of quite hardy plants, some of them coming from the far North, and all American. In family they are nearly related to *Calandrinia*, but have much greater beauty, and are well worth a sunny place in deep and rather rich soil, lightened with abundance of chips. *L. rediviva* is the best known, a hot-land species, whose narrow, Mesembryanthemum-like leaves accordingly die away, to your despair, in wisps of dead string, and then miraculously revive, while the tuft emits satiny pink cups of blossom on stems of an inch or two. *L. Tweedyi* is the most beautiful of all, and may sometimes be seen happy in low and damp places; it has ample broad leaves, less stiffly and fleshily rosetted than the rest, but more upstanding; while the similar flowers, but larger still, arise on stems of 3 inches or so, suggestive of idealised single tea-roses in the most melting tones of apricot, salmon, cream and milk. *L. pygmaea* is *Calandrinia pygmaea*, with very narrow foliage and small alpine tufts, and silky pink flowers of six or eight petals; *L. columbiana*, *L. brachycalyx*, *L. Purdyi*, and *L. oppositifolia* have beauty, the latter being notably profuse with its cups of white in summer; *L. Howellii* (in the Moony Mountains of Josephine co., Oregon), has wide rosettes of quite narrow fleshy foliage greyish-green and elegantly crimpled at the edge, with radiating heads on 3-inch stems, of softly apricot flowers, narrow-lobed, and flamed and streaked with rose; while one of the queens of the race is *L. Cotyledon*, in the same line as this last, but with broad plain leaves lying down in a neat flat rosette, from which rise rather shorter stems that ray out into heads of fewer larger flowers, flesh-pale, with a central band of deep rose to each petal. The Lewisias can hardly, as a rule, be propagated, unless by division, for which a well-established old clump is by far too lovely and precious.

Liatris, the Gay Feathers of America, may all be planted in light open soil, where their tall spikes, set with regular little round fluffs of bright-purple blossom all the way up their 2- or 3-foot stems in late summer and autumn, make a fine effect as they rise in noble spires of passionate magenta from the handsome masses of long narrow foliage. There are many species, unnecessary to name, as all have the same needs, seasons, and habits, while in none is the colour more friendly; the least in height is *L. spicata* of only a foot, or a foot and a half, small and sturdy, suggesting some strange autumnal Orchis.

Libertia grandiflora is a most stately New Zealand Irid, quite happy here, but at its best in deep rich soil in a warm garden, where it makes enormous clumps of sword-like foliage, like a massed Phormium in miniature, from among which proceed, in late summer, long broken spikes of three-petalled-looking flowers of clean ivory-white, free and beautiful and steadily succeeding each other through the season.

Kindred species are *L. formosa* and *L. ixioeides*, of the same habits and temperament.

Ligularia, huge and statuesque Senecios for the wild garden or the bog, all the species there having their value, either in spiked yellow spire of 5 feet high, or in tropical amplitude of foliage; but having little anywhere else, owing to their overweening habit.

Ligusticum, another huge-growing group, this time of Umbellifers, whose name makes us long only for the two superb species of the race that have their sole refuge in the uttermost parts of the sea, where, even up to the mountains of the Aucklands, towers great *L. speciosum*, like a 6-foot Angelica, with heads, wide and spreading, of the richest rosy-mauve or purple, all exhaling aromatic sweetness on the desert air; while nearer to the sea in moist places lives the looser-headed but still bright-purpled *L. antipodum*, with foliage no less splendid, but this time more finely divided so as more to suggest a gigantic Fennel gone to glory.

Lilium.—We will not turn our overburdened eyes in this direction, lest we should never be able to turn them away again, for thinking of the hot limestone rocks in the far South where *L. pomponium* hangs among the brushwood in balls of scarlet fire, above the dancing clear-blue flames of *Aquilegia Reuteri;* or the alpine meadows filled with the stark and stalwart chimes of *L. Martagon;* or the dark sombre cliffs of the Cottians where *L. croceum* finds root-home where none can be, in the smallest ledges of the cliff, till up and down the sheer and terrible walls twinkle at you from afar a thousand little sparks of flame that are the golden goblets of the lily, held up to catch the daylight in the darkness of the precipice, and radiate it forth again in living fire. But are there not books of such matters, to be bought for 1s. 9d.? Let these then be purchased; for indeed Lilium is no special race for the rock-garden, and, though all its members are always and everywhere to be desired and worshipped, they are not so special for the rock-garden as for beds especially made on their behalf, where their cult may be unstinted and unchallenged.

Linaria.—Catalogues and lists are filled with names of Linaria. Many of the Toad-flaxes offered, however, are more toad than flax—weeds irrepressible, or annuals, or dowdinesses. Let the wise rock-garden avoid such; let it even in prudence avoid the magnificent ramping species, such as *L. purpurea* or *L. repens*, that tall invasive beautiful pest with its dwarfer and rather less violent albino variety.

L. aequitriloba is a Tiny Tim of extraordinary charm. It is the miniature of the common Toad-flax, looked at through the wrong end of a telescope—a minutely wee thing from Corsica, that fits into the minutest sunny crannies, and runs along them and outlines them in a delicate thread of green, on which sit violet-pale Toad-flax faces, hardly smaller than those of our own, and also persisting through the season.

L. alpina may always be counted on to accompany you up into the high and stony places, though not always into the highest, preferring, as a rule, the rougher open stony earth-pans and shingles at mid-elevations, from which it often descends far in the river-beds and stone-slides, making mats of imperial violet blossom lipped with orange flame, crowding out of sight the weak shoots and blue-grey delicate fleshy foliage. There are pale forms, too, and one called *L. a. rosea*, which in reality is like bad lobster-sauce seen by candle-light ; and then there is *L. a. concolor*, which has lost the consecrating spot of orange fire, and is all of a lovely but unenlightened lavender ; and another form, more beautiful, where the lost flame is replaced by a blur of pallor ; and finally a white variety tipped with golden-orange on a flower of radiant and breath-taking purity of tone—a most precious rarity, and one to be most ardently ensued. All these are for the moraine, or light stony bank, where they will be happy, and freely seed. The species is not long-lived, but is certainly not annual ; nor does it in the garden seem to trouble about lime or granite, though in my alpine experiences, while it does not actually avoid the limestone ranges, it is far finer and freer and more fiery on the volcanic and granitic. No one who has ever descended from the Antermoja Pass or ascended the Monzoni Thal can fail to have been struck with the sudden eruption of *Linaria alpina* in a perfect fury of violet and flame, the very instant you arrive on the dark volcanic slopes, after traversing pale acres of Linaria-less limestones. In cultivation the plant, like several of those heights, wants a renewal of soil if it is not to lose something in size and vital violence of colouring.

L. Cymbalaria, our own Toad-flax, while an admissible lovely weed for clothing rough cold walls, especially in its albino form, is the type of several other species that must for the same reasons either be avoided or most carefully used. Of such is *L. hepaticaefolia*, a really beautiful creeper from South Europe, with fleshy marbled leaves of kidney design, and abundant toad-flaxes of lilac ; but it sends the white macaroni of its runners so far, and they grow so robustly from the least fragment left remaining in the ground, that the plant should only be allowed in far exile from anything at all precious. And of the same nature, but yet more beautiful, is *L. pallida*, unkindly named, because its flowers, the largest and the most generously borne in this group, are not pale but of a clear lovely lavender and sweet scent, sitting close in profusion all the summer over the foliage, which here is hairy, and disposed to gather into tufts and wide clumps, the plant running underground indeed, but not with the ferocity of the last.

L. dalmatica, with its form *L. macedonica,* is the type of the tall upstanding Linarias, admirable for any place with their glaucous foliage, and their long perennial pyramids of noble golden blossoms, but not special for the rock-garden, and to be found in all catalogues.

L. glacialis magnifies *L. alpina,* from the highest damp shingles in the snow regions of the Sierra Nevada. It is a humble, frail and blue-grey plantling, with stems of 3 inches or half a foot, set with fleshy leaves in whorls of four, and ending in loose spikes of very large lilac flowers as big as those of *L. vulgaris,* striped with gold and with a Hapsburg lip of tawny orange. Seed ; for the underground-watered moraine.

L. glauca is probably the beautiful species that is sometimes seen in the high stone-slides of the Cottians and Maritimes—a frail thing of many graceful stems, with the habits almost of *L. alpina,* but having the spikes and the ample blossoms of *L. vulgaris,* our own common field Toad-flax or Butter and Eggs,—citron yellow, with an orange lip.

L. nivea, despite the seductiveness of its name, had best be treated with caution, lest it reward unwary hospitality in the cuckoo-like manner of *L. repens,* to which it stands so closely allied.

L. origanifolia. See under *Chaenorrhinum origanifolium.*

L. petraea comes quite close to *L. alpina,* but is a much less common species of looser habit and rather paler flower, usually devoid of the orange lip. Its centre is in the Jura, and it may also be found above Lanslebourg at some 6500 feet.

L. pilosa, from the Abruzzi, has much the same stature and blooms as *L. petraea,* but the foliage is hairy.

L. satureioeides has stems 2 or 3 inches in length with fleshy blue-grey leaves arranged in whorls, and loose spikes of pale violet flowers with lips of golden velvet. (From the Spanish Alps, &c.)

L. triornithophora does indeed seem to carry three birds in each blossom—three birds, too, of the most vivid rich purple—so strangely are its flowers beaked and winged and hooked. It is a very pretty erect-growing perennial from Spain and Portugal, about 4 or 5 inches in height.

L. villosa is a downy-hairy species from Spain, with flowers of pale violet and stems of some 2 or 3 inches.

Lindelofia spectabilis is a most beautiful Borragineous plant with croziers of large deep-sapphire anchusa-flowers uncurling all the summer through on stems and sprays of some 12 or 18 inches. The plant is easily to be raised from seed, and of very easy permanent nature in rich, deep, and open soil. There is a still nobler variety in cultivation, *L. s. afghanica;* and yet another, of special beauty, called *L. s. Levingii,* from some 11,500 feet about Pir Pangul in Kashmir.

Linnaea borealis is not an easy treasure. Cool wood banks and moist rich places often suit the Twin-flower, which is, however, sometimes seen quite happy in sunnier ones, when once it has been got to start ; running about over the rocks, it forms a perfect curtain with long prostrate trailers, set with pairs of small rounded shining leaves of bronze and green, while along their lines stand up at intervals the finest dainty stems imaginable, each hanging out a pair of almond-scented little pendulous Gloxinias freaked and lined inside the bell with pink. Much easier, however, than *L. borealis* is *L. americana* (*L. canadensis*), which is larger in all its parts, freer in its habit, and of brighter crimson in the delicate cut-velvet freakings of its bell. It occupies the woods of the Canadian Rockies, even as *L. borealis* those of Norway or Scotland or the deep mossy darknesses of the upper Engadine (a rare plant otherwise, so far south in Europe, but also found in some of the woods in the Valais, as, for instance, on the way up to Meiden). Cuttings can be struck of these, but sometimes take a little while to get ahead ; layering is more useful, for both will root readily along the shoots, and will also come freely from seed. Summer.

Linum.—A notable race for the sunny dry banks of the garden ; all the Flaxes that we have are children of the hot South, and rejoice in warmth and sunlight and open deep soil, rather poor and exhaustively drained. All of them fill the whole summer with their waving galaxies of blossom, and all will come readily from seed.

L. alpinum is the only species of the central European ranges, where it may locally be seen in the southerly chains making its mild contribution of pale china-blue to the almost chaotic chorus of glory with which the high-alpine turf is then clamorous. It is a weakly prostrate thing, bowing out this way and that with its frail greyish fine-leaved shoots, beneath the burden of the big gentle flowers at their end, in loose showers, one after another throughout the summer. It is usually a rarity except in the districts where it abounds, as, for instance, in Dauphiné and the Western Graians. It is very near *L. perenne,* and has varieties of its own, *L. a. obtusatum, pycnophyllum, glaucum.*

L. arboreum makes a stout tree a yard high in the rocks of Crete, with leaves clustered at the ends of the naked boughs, scarred where the old foliage has fallen. The flowers are of brilliant gold in rich clusters. Gardeners usually regard *L. flavum* as a synonym of this, than which nothing could be more unjust, the one being a plant of ordinary herbaceous tendencies, and the other a definite shrub of about three times the size. There is also a beautiful alpine form of *L. arboreum*, most charmingly neat and dwarf and compact.

L. aretioeides is perhaps the most to be desired of all. It makes a quite tight small mass of leafage, narrow, fine, frail, and huddled so that the whole looks exactly like a cushion of *Douglasia Vitaliana;* in which, however, sit stemless the flaming cups of gold, each by itself, as the similar cushion of *Geranium nivale* is set with open white goblets of the same shape, and those of *Convolvulus nitidus* with pink. This lovely jewel belongs to the high mountain region of Cadmus in Caria, and Tmolus in Lydia.

L. arkansanum is about 8 inches high, with sprays of large yellow flowers with a pink base.

L. austriacum replaces *L. alpinum* in the Southern ranges, and may be seen in the upper turf of Baldo or the Cima Tombea. It is near *L. perenne*, and generally like the other, but a far more beautiful thing, less despondent in its habit, with fine stems that stand up about 6 inches or less (much more in the garden) and proudly wave their blossoms of a blue rich and clear as a Gentian's, softer in note and yet with something not unlike that peculiar coerulean effulgence. Its colour and charm set it supreme over the other well-known blue Linums, and in cultivation it does as well as the best.

L. Balansae lives in the wild hills of Cappadocia, and is 6 inches or a foot tall, with blooms as in *L. flavum*, but that here they are of rich orange with a dark eye, while the leaves on the stems are rather shorter and broader.

L. campanulatum belongs to *L. flavum (q.v.)*.

L. capitatum, from Southern Europe and the Levant, is akin to *L. flavum*, but with the flowers in a closer head.

L. carnosulum may be pictured in all its loveliness by saying that it is a tight cushion 2 inches high, with azure flowers like those of *L. austriacum*, of which the plant is a close and compacted miniature (thus giving a blue companion to the picture of *L. aretioeides* and its yellow tussocks), but that the foliage is fleshy and not pointed, and densely huddled, while the fruiting capsule is not round nor borne upright. From the stony places of Lebanon, above the Cedars; among the dioritic screes and sandy shingles of the Cilician Taurus, high up, there is a form of this, *L. c. empetrifolium*, which is a tighter cushion still, with leaves yet more densely overlapping and serried.

L. compactum is a densely crowded American cushion-species, with yellowish creamy flowers, the whole being about 2 inches high.

L. elegans is quite near *L. arboreum*, but differs in having narrower, more pointed sepals, though similar in all else, but only about a foot in height at the most, and usually much less. (From the high rocks of Parnassus, &c.)

L. empetrifolium. See under *L. carnosulum.*

L. flavum is a herbaceous plant ranging from Germany to Russia, well known in all gardens, making a bush of 10 inches or so, with many shoots well clad in ample oval leaves of leathery dark-green, and generous at their tips with loose heads of large and brilliant golden flowers, that often come a deeper orange from seed. *L. campanulatum* is not to be separated from this ; and very close to it come *L. orientale,* almost shrubby at the base, instead of herbaceous ; *L. cariense ; L. tauricum,* with smaller inferior flowers ; and many another variety : while near Sebastopol is found the finest of all, *L. Pallasianum,* a neat tuffet, close and dense, and not 2 inches high, with an undiminished glory of golden cups.

L. hirsutum is a more or less downy, tall, fine Flax from all Southern Europe and away to the Levant, on dry grassy hills—a graceful plant with large blue flowers, white-eyed. There is a compressed alpine form, *L. h. olympicum.*

L. humile is like a dwarf but more branchy variety of our own common Linseed or Flax of commerce, but with glandless sepals. (It is found in the fields of the Levant.)

L. Kingii follows the habit and the flower, of *L. arkansanum.*

L. leucanthum inhabits the most torrid and arid rocks of limestone on the holy headland of Sunium, and is a lovely thing with many stems of about 6 inches, carrying very large pure-white blossoms.

L. Lewisii is a fine blue-flowered Flax with specially graceful sprays of long-stemmed blue stars, on stalks of a foot or a yard, but it cannot claim to be more than a variety of *L. perenne,* or *L. sibiricum.* (North America.)

L. maritimum, from the coasts of Southern Europe, is dwarf in habit, only attaining to some 6 or 9 inches, with blossoms of yellow ; it is probably not to be separated from *L. flavum.*

L. monogÿnum is a stately and beautiful species from New Zealand, with many fine stems about a foot or more high, set with filmy-fine foliage, and forming a neat jungly bush which is covered with large and noble white flowers all the summer, most graciously and freely borne. In comfortable sheltered sunny corners, in light well-drained deep soil, there is no doubt about the hardiness of *L. monogynum.*

L. Muelleri is an extremely rare suffrutescent species with yellow flowers from Corsica and Sardinia.

L. narbonnense, from all the Mediterranean region, is about half a yard high, specially profuse in flower and specially rich in their blues—quite the best of the taller blue-flowering Flaxes.

L. olympicum is yet another beauty in a new note of colour, from the high stony places of the Bithynian Olympus, where it forms a shrubby mass some 4 or 6 inches high, with shoots set in elliptic narrow leaves, and then emitting few-flowered sprays of large violet blossoms.

L. perenne is the wild English perennial Flax. There are many forms of it, including pinks and white ; nor is it easy to separate some so-called species from this ; especially the gardener's *L. " sibiricum,"* which has just the same showers of blue stars, varying also to white (like all blue Flaxes), and to pink also, which is less common. These are both large, 18 inches or 2 feet high, but of the usual airy grace, though their flowers are surpassed by those of *L. austriacum* and *L. narbonnense.*

L. puberulum is a glaucous blue-grey plant of some 8 inches from North America.

L. rigidum is a taller, stiffer American species of some 18 inches.

L. salsoloeides. See under *L. tenuifolium.*

L. sibiricum. See under *L. perenne.*

L. Stocksianum is another variety of *L. perenne.*

L. sulfureum inhabits the most calcareous cliffs and slopes of Antilebanon, where it makes an almost bushy mass of 12-inch shoots, set with leaves that differentiate it from the rest of the Flavum-group, and especially its nearest relative, *L. orientale,* by being markedly minute and narrow and pointed. The flowers, too, are of soft pale yellow.

L. tenuifolium is a furry fine-leaved species of Southern Europe, with rather the habit of *L. austriacum,* but scantier, and with rose-lilac or pink flowers. The species is universal all over the warm banks of the South even into the mountain ranges, where, for instance, it may be seen above Bormio at the foot of the Stelvio. Unfortunately we now are bidden to include under the name of this polymorphic species one of the loveliest and most distinct of Flaxes, *L. salsoloeides,* which fills the field-sides by Saint Martin Vésubie with mats and masses of pale pure colour, visible as a solid sheet from afar ; and wanders thence down into the roadside gutters, to toss its wide great open cups of pearly pallor among the golden star-showers of *Hypericum Coris.* *L. salsoloeides* is anyhow a most outstanding plant, neater and lower in growth, forming, from one crown, a forest of uniform stems some 6 or 8 inches high, ascending from a mass of low-lying shoots like miniature sprigs of larch, and unflinching beneath the weight of their erect and splendid soft flowers, shell-pale, with a melting flush

PLATE 43.

LEWISIA TWEEDYI.
(Photo. R. A. Malby.)

LINUM TENUIFOLIUM (SALSOLOEIDES NANUM.)
(Photo. R. A. Malby.)

PLATE 44.

LITHOSPERMUM INTERMEDIUM.
(Photo. R. A. Malby.)

　　　LYCHNIS ALPINA.
(Photo. R. A. Malby.)

of darkness towards their heart, of a sheen and delicate lustre and lucence irresistible. Better forms than others, however, may easily be found in its favoured districts; whereas in some it is so poor as to sink back into *L. tenuifolium*—scraggy in the stem, gawky and lank of limb, with small starved stars of a paleness that is sickly, instead of being the palpitating clear loveliness of a pearl in perfect health. Let us then pick our plants of this Flax with pains; acquiring those of neat and tufted habit, especially hearty in the outline of their cups. But, with luck, we may even find a treasure greater yet: this is *L. sals. nanum* or *prostratum*, which hardly aspires to any stem at all, but forms a dense close mat of fur, like that of some Arenaria, over the face of the rock or bank, hidden from view in summer by an unending succession of almost stemless vases, fine and rounded as in the best forms of the type, and suggesting that someone has densely stuck a cushion of *Alsine laricifolia* with hundreds of flowers from *Oxalis enneaphylla*, having first squashed the oxalis-blossoms wider with his thumb. *L. tenuifolium*, though it mounts up, also descends low, and is found on the hottest banks of the Mediterranean; which means that the choicest warmest banks of the garden are none too good for *L. " salso-loeides."* This, indeed, is perfectly hardy, so long as the deep light soil be perfectly drained, and the situation sunny. Seed can be collected from abroad, but in cultivation the plant is chary of them, and the dwarf form can only be propagated by cuttings taken off about midsummer and struck with care. Like the rest, it is a sound if not very long-lived perennial, if its feet are kept free from persistent wet in winter; and, like the rest, it cannot be divided nor even moved with propriety when well established, for they all make one frail crown, with one main root, deep and woody and slender; they greatly, therefore, resent disturbance, and *L. salsoloeides* from its hot banks, with its few thirsty wiry fibres, is one of the hardest trophies to persuade into re-establishing itself when collected and sent home, with care no matter how courteous and complete.

L. toxicum has the merit of being odious to goats. It lives high up on Hermon, and makes hard stiff-boughed little clumps of some half a foot high or less, with sepals likewise stiff and broad and short, revealing the golden flowers of all the Flavum-group.

L. velutinum haunts the upper limestone chinks of Kurdistan, where it forms a tight bushy mass of shoots some 2 or 4 inches tall, dense with very short spoon-shaped leaves, till the whole plant is a cushion of grey velvet, from which emerge rather close clusters of white bloom.

L. viscosum is quite unlike these others. It is a stalwart few-stemmed or single-stemmed species, set with broad oval leaves at intervals, and slightly branching at the top to carry several specially large upstaring flowers of soft lilac-rose. The stems, one or two to a crown, are some 12 or 18 inches high, and the entire growth is sticky ; it has a stalwart and quite unflax-like effectiveness—a rather rare species of the South which may, for instance, be seen on the rough slopes above San Dalmazzo de Tenda, in company with *Lilium pomponium* and *Aquilegia Reuteri*. Into cultivation it is difficult to bring, on account of its characteristically, but especially, lignescent unfibred root ; but, once obtained, it continues to thrive perpetually, being, of the family, the least avid of sunshine, avoiding the hotter slopes where *L. tenuifolium* is thinly and in poor form there luxuriating, to inhabit the folded copsy gullies under the cliffs, where things more precious still than itself are to be seen. There are variants on the not specially alluring vinous mauves of the huge soft flower ; once I found a form of really lovely lavender-blue, and there is no doubt a white.

Lippia repens is a rather tender little summer-blooming Andine, like a trailing small pinkish Verbena, for warm and sandy places, if you please.

Liriope spicata, a Liliaceous plant from Japan, with tufts of dark grass-like foliage, and spikes of small white flowers, for use in the South as an edging.

Lithophragma affinis is a delicate and pretty Saxifrage-cousin from damp and mossy woods of California, with stems of some 9 inches, set at intervals with large white five-pointed stars, whose five rays are gashed again, so as to give a look of specially whirligig daintiness, as in *Mitella*.

Lithospermum (including **Moltkia**).—Worthless plants in this race, annuals or weeds or both, are *LL. angustifolium, tenuifolium, Sibthorbianum, apulum, hispidulum, callosum, incrassatum, pilosum, tuberosum.*

L. aureum (*Moltkia*), a sub-shrub from the hills of Caria, bristly with short hairs, and with stiffly ascending short stems with golden flowers, and a very short corolla-tube.

L. canescens is a pretty American species from the sandy woods between New Mexico and Saskatchewan. It makes a tuft of narrow leaves, hoary when young and silky later on, and gradually growing greener but *never rough ;* the stems rise up some 6 inches or more, carrying sessile heads of bright orange-yellow flowers, with a prominent crest in their throat. The plant can be raised from seed and multiplied by careful division in spring ; it grows with reasonable readiness in warm sandy and stony peat very well drained and in a sheltered warm exposure, but is, as a rule, no centenarian.

LITHOSPERMUM.

L. coeruleum (*Moltkia*) is a blue-flowering sub-shrub from Lycia and Caria, &c.

L. erythrorrhizon is a meibuts', or special sight, of various plains and moors in Japan; it is the Ko-murasaki, the Little Forget-me-not, from whom one of the saddest of Japanese heroines has her ill-starred name; and is a centre of lovers' meetings and old romance, since the days of the *Sumiyoshi monogatari* of a thousand years ago, when the prince-lover had his sight of his long-lost Little Princess, on the moor of the *Lithospermum* that they had both gone out, like all the world, to see—just, for all our world, as nowadays they would have met at the Kinematograph, or outside the windows of Harrods. But *L. erythrorrhizon* does not quite deserve in our eyes all this celebrity, despite its blue flowers and its red root. For the red root is difficult to import and hard to re-establish, while the blue flowers are small enough on stems sufficiently leafy to dull the edge of our regret for the fact. (My original *L. "erythrorrhizon"* is *L. japonicum.*)

L. ✕ Froebeli is a garden hybrid of great beauty, akin to *L. intermedium*, with the blood of *L. graminifolium* in its veins, conjoined probably with that of *L. petraeum*, resulting in a tidy mass of long and narrow-leaved dark rosettes on erect shrubby stems of a few inches, and divided branching sprays of beautiful deep azure of early summer.

L. fruticosum is a branchy woody bush about 6 or 12 inches high, set with narrow foliage rolled over at the rims, and with each twisting peeling trunk ending in many clusters of large blooms of brilliant purple-azure. From the dry stony places of Eastern and Southern Spain, but most especially in the limestone. For the same fate seems to have overtaken *Lithospermum* that so long lay heavy on Daphne; being always found actually growing, like all hill-children, in the peat of the hills (which are naturally composed of little else, by the decay of a thousand centuries), their unobservant recorders failed to notice that the subsoil of their happiness was almost invariably lime; so that they have been treated ever since as plants resolutely calcifuge, with the worst results to their own reputation, as to every gardener's purse and reputation.

L. Gastoni is a distinct and rare species from the Pyrenees, with dependent shoots well furnished with rather broader laxer foliage than in most, with nestling heads of noble large wide flowers of a glorious clear blue-and-white, seeming to stare out from the sheet that the shoots form in the shadow of a rock. Much has been talked and written of its culture, many men prescribing many treatments. Probably the trouble is that, like so many Lithospermums, it is really a passionately lime-craving plant, but is always denied its right food by the decrees of fashionable horticulture. One of the finest specimens in England is giving daily thanks by its fineness for a soil composed of one half leaf-mould and the rest old mortar rubble. Other soils, however, in other places have brought success, and the treasure has thriven ill and well, alike in sun and in shade; though its look makes a distinct appeal, it would seem, for mercy against the full weight of the sun—at least in hot gardens. When well-established it will run about and make itself a nuisance—a nuisance for which many gardeners would gladly compound.

L. graminifolium makes the chief of the herbage in some of the higher hills that fringe the Plain of Lombardy; there its huge masses, 2 or 3 yards wide, of very long and very narrow dark grass-like foliage fill the upper grass of the whole mountain; and its cushions flop over the track and sheet the slopes in pure colour at the end of May, with their branching heads on 6- or 9-inch stems of the most lovely swinging tubes of soft pale blue. In the garden it is almost the best of its race, having always, alone of its race, been allowed the lime it wants. So here it forms masses hardly less wide than at home, no less profuse in June with its spreading rockets of delicate sky-pale bugles—at least when you can get the true plant, which is now grown rare, although it multiplies not only by seed and by cuttings, but also by layers managed like a carnation's, with sandy soil worked down among the rosettes of the mass.

L. Hancockianum is talked of with bated breath as being about to come out of China and make the dawn ashamed with the magnitude of its pure celestial blossoms. I know no more of *L. Hancockianum*.

L. hirtum is another American species, of the same needs and brief prosperity as *L. canescens*. This comes from the pine-barrens, from Minnesota to Colorado, making the same tuft of foliage, which here is bristlish to start with, and ends by being rough. The stems are 1 or 2 feet high, carrying heads of fine ample-orbed flowers of bright orange, deeply cleft into five lobes with prominent arching crests and ten hairy flaps round the ring of its throat.

L. intermedium stands, in habit if not in birth, between *L. graminifolium* and *L. petraeum*, making sub-shrubby masses of long-leaved dark rosettes, from which arise 8-inch stems with spreading heads of brilliant deep-blue blossom in June or late in May. This is of untroubled comfort in even ordinary loam.

L. japonicum must have blossomed unseen, for the Japanese to have turned their eyes on *L. erythrorrhizon*. For *L. japonicum* turns the upland woods and open coppices to wide unbroken sheets of pure fallen sky in its time, with profusion of great shilling-wide planets of the most dazzling clear pale azure, all over the leafy mass of trailing shoots, which in a way, though greener, recall those of *L. purpureo-coeruleum* in loose procumbent habit ; but the flowers are not borne in heads, and are much larger, lighter, lonelier, and more lovely. English gardens will have a surprise when *L. japonicum* is at last introduced—if only it will behave here as in the woods below Nikko, or even as it gleamed in long dropped strings of turquoise among the grasses of the high downs at the foot of Fuji, or amid the strange orchids that gloomed upon the islands of Matsushima, between the sundown fires of *Azalea mollis,* and the cool lilac-purple smoke-wreaths of Wistaria, reflected in the ripples of that dreaming sea.

L. Kotschyi belongs to the rocks of South Persia—a very dwarf tight hoary bush of 6 inches, with bright blue flowers.

L. multiflorum and *L. longiflorum* (if true difference indeed there be), are two more Americans from Colorado and the lower Rockies. *L. multiflorum* is about a foot high, often *coarsely bristly,* and carrying its blossoms in wide branching showers, these being bright clear yellow and with short round lobes. Culture, &c., as for the other yellow Americans, of which this is the most obscure and difficult species to decipher, if not to grow. (*L. californicum* is of the same stature, but *softly* hairy and not bristled.)

L. oleaefolium is a most precious and not particularly easy Lithospermum of extreme beauty that is but rarely seen. It is rare in the cliffs of the Catalonian Pyrenees on both sides of the frontier (La Muga, S. Amio), and makes a dwarf diffuse mass of shoots, not more than 6 inches high, with the leaves especially bundled at the tips of the branches ; they are narrow-oval, green and shining, and with white silk below. The flowers are few and rather large, in a cluster at the ends of the shoots, of a specially lovely opalescent violet, with shifting lights of blue and pink to deep and pale. Those who have grown it well shall advise upon its culture. It is not a thing as easy to meet with as dullness or folly, nor as easy to keep as a plain daughter.

L. parviflorum (*Moltkia*).—This is exactly like our cherished *Mertensia echioeides,* but that the spikes are denser and the corolla-tube shorter with the filaments protruding. (Kashmir, 6000 to 8000 feet.)

L. petraeum (*Moltkia*).—It might be hazarded that this plant is commoner in gardens than at home, where it is of most rare occurrence, in the Alps of Greece (as on the face of Oeta looking eternally down upon Thermopylæ). Well worthy is the *Lithospermum,* " so to name her what she lawful is," of such a spectacle, being a neat woody bush of a foot or more, with pale leathery narrow leaves to the tips of the shoots, and abundant heads of beautiful pale-blue and purple flowers.

LITHOSPERMUM.

This is of quite easy culture, too, in any decent loam, but specially repays a choice crevice on the sunny side of the rockwork, where the tidy bush may develop its full fecundity. Cuttings or seed (freely produced by all our species, in those tiny grey pebbles, polished and hard, that have earned the race its generic name of Stony-seed).

L. prostratum has the flowers of *L. fruticosum*, but a prostrate habit that we all know well. The plant occupies Northern, Central, and South-eastern Spain, indifferent, it would seem, to lime or granite, but in the garden occasionally giving trouble in the matter, though while its best masses are usually associated with sandy and non-calcareous beds and gardens, some others, not inferior, have their soil so filled with chalk that its chunks have to be picked off the mats so as not to damage their effect. And yet other prolific patches are growing in pure leaf-mould and mortar rubble, even as the wild types, so it is said, grow with the passionately lime-loving *Daphne Cneorum* among the limestone blocks about Biarritz. In any case, wherever the plant may do well, it is a point to remember that legginess is best controlled (alike for the clump's happiness as for the gardener's) by a drastic cutting-back, such as is applied to the Rock-roses. There are varying forms of *L. prostratum*, such as the glorious Heavenly Blue, which gives a just, if minimised, foretaste or sample of *L. japonicum ;* and there either is, or soon will be, a white, for which we shall all tumble over each other to pay vast sums, but which will inevitably prove inferior to the coerulean loveliness of the type.

L. purpureo-coeruleum blushes deeply blue in some rare copses of the West of England, a notable treasure, though often to be seen glowing like sapphires in the shady river-gullies of the Riviera, among dark brushwood and lushness of the ravine. In the garden this lovely thing is a ramper, and must only be put where it can do no harm ; for the long willowy sprays bend out, and take root at their tip, and so *da capo* all over the place—jump and sprawl, jump and sprawl, till nothing is left but the *Lithospermum*, and between the arches of the running sprays rise up on 6-inch stems the heads of large deep blossoms, purely sapphire in their true-blue splendour.

L. rosmarinifolium is, in brief, a bright-green bush of Rosemary, which persists in putting forth clusters of azure stars in mid-winter, a trick it learned on its native rocks of Naples and Capri, and which it has never been able to unlearn under the different conditions of an English climate ; so that, for an English garden, *L. rosmarinifolium*, though in itself quite reasonably hardy, must be pronounced to be valueless except in so far as a stray bloom here and there, managing to slip out into beauty between two snowstorms and two deluges at the

New Year, may have value as a suggestion, tantalising us with such brief hints of what splendours it was, more rich than all Rome's purples, that the sad and lonely old Emperor went away to contemplate in his rock-bound seclusion of Capri.

L. Zahni may not, however, prove so hopeless, though in the same style of charm. For this makes just the same bushes of Rosemary as the last, in the highest rocks of Laconia, which should surely guarantee a Spartan temperament. It is a perfectly dense branching little bush, with the narrow leaves bright and smooth above, but felted with a grey coat beneath. Stemless at the end of the shoots sit clusters of large blossoms in the most brilliant and celestial blue.

L. Zollingeri, from the nearer East, has the habit of *L. purpureo-coeruleum*, rampant with long radicant sprays, but the 9-inch stems that arise from the crown carry starrier wide blooms of a much lighter blue and inferior merit.

Lloydia serotina is a small and most dainty little bulb, with thread-like stems and leaves, of 2 or 3 inches, and a dim paper-white cup streaked outside with darkness, which may be seen here and there abundant in the alpine turf, and here and there also not less abundant in the high grass of certain Welsh mountains. In culture it is not very easy, and must have soil of peaty grit in a cool corner, damp but well-drained. It would be well to use it in the choice gentian-bed. See Appendix for *Lloydia alpina*.

Lobelia is often confused with Pratia, a confusion that need never recur when it is remembered that Pratia has a capsule, while Lobelia has a berry. Of the larger sorts the garden in August and September is grateful to the vehement scarlet of *L. cardinalis*, the clear rich blues and purples of *LL. syphilitica, Kalmii, kamtchatica*, and specially beautiful *L. amoena* (specially hardy too) with one-sided spires of long and lovely blue flowers on stems of a foot or two ; to say nothing of the many new intermediates raised in gardens, in the most satisfying shades of rose and violet, all to be made happy in the bog garden or at the water's edge, in soil that is very rich and deep and damp. Damp, indeed, seems the prescription for all Lobelias, and our own china-blue *L. Dortmanna* keeps its fat fleshy tufts actually below the water, and raises its head clear through a foot or more. But more ordinary conditions of open soil mixed with peat will suit the new *L. taliensis*, a beautiful blue-flowered dwarf species, no less than the most valuable of all (at present) for the rock-garden, lovely *L. linnaeoeides*, which indeed is like a *Linnaea*, or some New Zealand *Epilobium*, sheeting the bank in wandering prostrate shoots beset with small round pairs of leaves, metallically dark in tone, from which in August spring countless fine naked stems of 3 inches or less, each carrying the most dainty pale butterfly of a Lobelia blossom, in shades of gentle blue and white. Though this be from New Zealand it is of perfect hardiness, even proving a nuisance if too happily established in the neighbourhood of something small and choice, but itself the best possible of carpets for choice small bulbs. It has a rare cousin, *L. Roughii*, of much the same habits and beauty, filled with bitter milk of unkindness, and creeping among the shingles of the South Island up to 6000 feet. It may be known by the two dorsal petals (the upper lip) being divided to the base. Both species have a fancy for a pinch of peat.

Loiseleuria procumbens is a little alpine Azalea, trailing tiny flat masses, like a small glossy leathery thyme, in close carpets over the high alpine turf, and starring them with clusters of natty waxen cups of soft pink and rose. Though it holds the same eminences on the Scotch Alps it is by no means an easy plant to acclimatise in the garden, requiring specially careful collecting, careful re-establishment of its woody root, and then a sunny position in light and elastic stony peat, well-watered in spring, but absolutely sharp and perfect in drainage.

Lotus.—The common Ladies' Fingers will not need an introduction to your garden, being usually more in need of a chucker-out, but *L. Gebelia*, with pea-flowers of pink, may have its uses for a warm dry slope, while to wander about in a damper lower one is predestined the lonely-blossomed Lotus with large flowers of peculiarly moonlit clear yellow, which you may sometimes see in the grass by the roadsides in the Alps, and which is *L. siliquosus*, when not rejoicing in its more stately title of *Tetragonolobus siliquosus*. *LL. creticus*, *montanus*, and *cytisoeides*, are taller things of no value.

Lubinia lubinioeides (so happy a thought of some fertile mind to call a plant the Lubinia like a Lubinia—what else, then, should it be like, pray ?) is also *Lysimachia maurantiana*, an African species of no possibilities in English gardens.

Lupinus.—The tall herbaceous and shrubby Lupines have their place, but America breeds a vast race of decumbent Lupines often excelling in beauty of flower or leaf, and easy of cultivation in very light soil on a warm and well-drained bank. They are not always easy to raise from seed, having a tendency to miff off ; nor is their span of life always as handsome or long as their span of spike. *L. decumbens* and *L. argenteus* have for a time rejoiced us with their spires of lavender blue, in summer rising 6 inches or so from the sheeted mass of foliage, often beautifully silvered ; and yet others among the many that we do not yet possess are *L. caespitosus*, a dense cushion of silver-

PLATE 45.

VOL. I.   LLOYDIA   ALPINA.
(Photo. W. Purdom.)

PLATE 46.

MACROTOMIA ECHIOEIDES.
(Photo. R.B.G., Edinburgh.)

MECONOPSIS LATIFOLIA.
(Photo. R.B.G., Edinburgh.)

silky leafage 3 or 6 inches high, in which peer forth spikes of pale-blue blossom ; *L. Kingii*, of the same comfortable habit, but with flowers more purple, and further advancing out of the tuft ; *L. monticola*, a beautiful plant from alpine elevations in Wyoming, branched and bristled and grey, with silver-silky leaflets, and fine blossoms with broad wings of dark blue to a paler keel, the spike being some 2 inches long, to the plant's branches of four or eight ; *L. humicola*, a spring flower from the undershrubby slopes of Wyoming, with many crowns from the branching root-stocks, and those crowded with the stalks of dead and gone leaves ; and then fresh branches of a foot or so in length, ending in a dense spike of blue, 4 to 8 inches long, with the flowers arranged in whorls ; together with others yet a-many, beyond all hope of more than naming a few—*LL. laxiflorus, Bakeri, ammophilus, barbiger, Wyethii, Burkei, ornatus, leucophyllus, ramosus, flexuosus, Greeni*, among which will no doubt be found in time many beauties equal or superior to those already recounted.

Lychnis.—Let the border be concerned with great *LL. bungeana, Coronaria*, and *chalcedonica*, though even the mention of the two names side by side sickens the mind's eye with the suggestion of Coronaria's wide cups of claret-crimson velvet side by side with the huddled, shallow, and spiteful scarlets of *L. chalcedonica*. But *L. Flos-Jovis* is a gentler plant, with comfortable mild leafage of loose and ample silvered flannel, that may be seen here and there abundant in stony places of Cottian and Maritime granites, &c. ; adorning them with a few clustered large flowers of clear carmine pink on wool white stems of a foot or 18 inches in summer. Next, for the bog garden and water-side, in warm sheltered exposures, and soil of perfect drainage, yet always rich and damp in summer, Japan has been inordinately generous with big Lychnids in the way of *L. Haageana* (itself a hybrid between *L. fulgens* and *L. Coronaria*), with its blazing royal blossoms of scarlet and vermilion in August on lax leafy stems of a foot or two. Even more superb is *L. grandiflora*, and the cry of magnificence goes still crescendo with *L. Miqueliana, L. Senno*, and *L. laciniata*, with its long long scarlet petals cut into long long radiating strips, stiff and narrow, of the most spidery effect, like the flowers of some colossal Ragged-Robin that have stiffened themselves up with a tonic, and then dipped themselves in fresh blood of a slaughtered Sun-god. *L. fulgens* and *L. striata* are in the same line of splendour, and none of these (except *L. Haageana*) have yet proved quite satisfactory or permanent in our general conditions, and evidently have yet to be further experimented with and satisfied before they become, as their beauty is bound to make them if revealed, the inevitable darlings of every fat-soiled dampness of every warm and sheltered garden. And we now come to the alpine group.

L. alpina is a neat little tuffet with a neat little head of magenta-pink stars in summer on stems of some 2 or 3 inches. It may be seen at Flannel-flower levels in the alpine turf, and on one or two mountains of Cumberland and Scotland. It is easy of culture in moist cool soil, and easily raised from seed, from all of which facilities the cultivator will justly augur that it is not specially fascinating, the Lychnids running unanimously to pinks of unpleasing chalky tone, light or dark, until, in the lands of the Rising Sun, they at last catch his fire and break into the magnificent and resounding vermilions of the East. There is a pretty white form of *L. alpina*, however ; nor can *L. lapponica* be by any means dissevered from the type, unless it be by a slight addition of cubits to its stature.

L. Lagascae is a plant of cliff-chinks in Spain, and a recognised object of cultivation and commendation in England, often because it is supposed to be difficult, and sometimes because it is supposed to be beautiful. In neither quality is it really pre-eminent ; it can easily be cultivated in rich and *well-drained* soil—that vain desideratum by which so many easy doers in old days acquired an undeserved prestige for being difficult—and it comes profusely from the seed it profusely sets ; but in the effect, somehow, of its straggling leafy masses of blue-grey stems and foliage there is a curious lack of breeding and mountain brilliance ; the plant looks like some common little edging species of the *Saponaria calabrica* persuasion, and the effect is not lessened by the chalky carmine stars of blossom that appear in profusion all the summer, and always seem, nevertheless, alike in general show and individual size, rather small and mean for the lush loose floppiness of the general 6- or 8-inch mess, branching and diffuse, with no touch of alpine concision or look of refinement.

L. nivalis is a plant from Transylvania, very much in the same line and with the same needs, though choicer, perhaps, and certainly rarer. Even as *L. Lagascae* appears often under Willkomm's acknowledged name of *Petrocoptis*, so does *L. nivalis* often make our mouths unnecessarily water by appearing undescribed (except by its price) as *Polyschĕmŏnē ;* while yet others, alike of Lychnis and Silene, have flown away into the new fold of *Melandryum*, where those in vain desiderated under their ancient names will surely be found.

L. Preslii is a tall Andine, with flowers of magenta pink or purple.

L. pyrenaica is a marked improvement on *L. Lagascae*, having the same habit, the same flopping stems, and the same glaucous foliage, but broader in the basal leaves than *L. Lagascae*. Its flowers, however, have just precisely that added degree of size and amplitude required to carry off the foliage and habit of the plant, and give it a well-furnished appearance no less than a rich elegance of habit and blossom. If colour is in dispute, it may either be white or pink. There is in cultivation a treasure rejoicing in the name of *L. pyrenaica grandiflora rosea,* which may be nothing but a type of the species ; and, under any name, is by far the most beautiful of all, bearing throughout the summer a profusion of generously-rounded stars in the most delicious shade of pure pale pink, absolutely clean and sweet and delicate—with their tone (no less than with their size, shape and abundance on the less lush mass), driving *L. Lagascae* dishonoured down into the lowest steps of the garden. All these should be raised annually from seed ; they are easy and hardy, but are apt to resent winter-wet if their soil be not drained to perfection. *L. pyrenaica* belongs to the walls and shady cliffs of the Western Pyrenees, as in the crevices of the old monastery at Casa Baja, at some 3300 feet.

L. Viscaria is a much magnified *L. alpina,* of a foot or two in height, with clustered bunches of bright magenta-pink flowers. It is of the easiest culture, and blooms in early summer. Some gardens rejoice in the double form, which has heads of yet fiercer colour, and is called *splendens Fl. Pl.,* being a development from a type-*splendens,* of special size and virulence of blossom ; there is also an albino (as of all the pink ones, whether known or unknown), called *alba grandiflora,* no less than a much superior one for our purpose, *L. V. alba nana,* being only some 4 to 6 inches high, and sometimes going disguised under the name of *Silene tatarica* ; while *L. yunnanensis* holds a median station between *L. Viscaria* and *L. alpina,* having clearer pink flowers on stems of half a foot or so in May and June.

Lysichiton kamtschatkense is a sumptuous Aroid well worthy of its sumptuous name. It is a plant of the very deep and very rich bog, where, in the early year, it throws up stemless great yellow Callas after the fashion of Symplocarpus, to be followed by the unfolding of vast glaucous-green tropical foliage like that of some banana. So it is always said to be, so it always proves, and so it may be seen in the wild marshes of Japan, and all across the Rockies. Yet when first I saw it, in a stinking deep slough of the Hokkaido, in the last chill clarity of sundown, one early April of that frozen far island, the huge cups were not only as large as those of *Calla aethiopica,* but also as white ; and their beauty and impressiveness, shining among the pools of still pale water at twilight, was far, far in excess of anything ever attained by the common yellow-blossomed form, magnificent though this may be, and identical in size and development.

Lysimachia.—Almost all of this huge race escape our province by their stature, being tempestuous big weeds for the wild garden. Among the rocks our most useful friend in the race is still the old Creeping Jenny in its grandiflora-form, a useful ramping carpet for worthless cool corners. *L. secunda* or *lobelioeides*, which has similar weak stems and large white flowers, might also be tried ; but *L. Henryi*, often passionately proclaimed, is neither hardy nor choice—a lush leafy little thing with yellow flowers. There is, however, so vast a choice remaining in the hills of China that possibly in time more worthy candidates may present themselves for admission to the rock-garden. *L. violascens*, for instance, is a tall purple beauty, much to be desired. Seed will stock you with these, and they all bloom from midsummer.

Lythrum.—The sham Loose-strifes, like their predecessors in this alphabet, the true ones (but why or how they soften strife, who is there that can tell ? in the garden they bring not so much peace but renewed war, of battling horrible colours ; and in the end an Armageddon of the spade in the effort to be finally quit of them) are too big for our subject. The handsomest is *L. alatum*, a fine spreading plant, with long sprays of large magenta-purple blossom. Especially branching is also the neater and clearer pink *L. virgatum* ; while our own *L. Salicaria*, besides hybrids with the last, has yielded various named catalogue-forms in which the colour claims to be sensibly mitigated.

M

Machaeranthera.—A race now vanished into Aster, with two beautiful species, *M. latifolia* and *M. canescens*, both having big purple flowers in late summer, on stems of 9 inches or so ; but both having a desire for warm sandy soils, and a biennial temper into the bargain. *M. Pattersoni*, on the other hand, has a quite different character, and has already appeared as *Aster Pattersonii*.

Macrotomia, including **Arnebia.**—A family of Borragineae, containing some plants of rare beauty, and at least one that is easy to grow, though all are grateful for light rich soil in full sun. They are to be raised from seed, or divided in spring, and bloom from early summer onward.

M. Cephalotes has begun to be advertised at prices too terrible for temptation, especially as it is confessedly coy and hard to please. And yet it has a wide range, being described even by the prudent tongue of botanists as making the glory of the alpine rocks on Chelmos, the Bithynian Olympus, Aslandagh, Berytagh, and many another favoured mountain in Transcaucasia and the Cilician Taurus. Here it hangs, in fat scaly stocks that emit a quantity of very long narrow leaves, dense and hoary-grey with pressed-down bristles, among which appear a number of leafy stems 6 inches or a foot high, bearing at their end a stout head as large as an egg, of nobly frank wide flowers of golden yellow. There are few specimens of this as yet in England, and fewer yet successful ones; it must have a hot place jammed between firm rocks, with a rooting medium behind down into a perfectly-drained depth of poor gritty pebbly stuff with a little enrichment of loam and leaf-mould.

M. cyanochroa, in the cliffs of Southern Persia, makes tufts of narrow foliage 2 or 3 inches long and harshly bristly; among these, and hardly any longer, appear a number of stems with short heads of bright-blue blossom.

M. densiflora stands very close indeed to *M. Cephalotes* in its whole habit and beauty and needs, coming even from the same region of Transcaucasia. It differs, however, in being much more silky, and with silk, too, that becomes tawny toward the upper parts of the stems; it also has clusters of wide bowl-shaped yellow flowers in the upper axils of the leaves, no less than in the main bunch at the top.

M. echioeides.—This is the well-known Prophet-flower, the one member of its family to be popular in gardens (and even in borders), forming masses of green narrow rough foliage, and abundant in 9-inch stems in June, carrying bunches of blossoms like glorified cowslip-heads of yellow, with a black spot at the base of all five lobes, which spots, however unlike black marks in other walks of life, fade away as the flower grows older and wiser, till at last it reaches a reverend old age of unsullied lemon-colour.

M. guttata, from the Siberian Altai, has dense one-sided spikes about 9 inches high, and yellow blooms very widely expanded and spotted with black at the base of each lobe as in *M. echioides*.

M. perennis has smaller flowers than these last, and blue-purple in colour.

Maianthemum bifolium is that specially beloved little fairy of the alpine woods, with two glossy heart-shaped leaves on fine stems of 3 inches or so, and between them an upstanding fluffy plume of pure-white in May or June. Even so may it be seen in one or more woods in the North of England, and in the garden is an invaluable delight for any cool soil or place, running about and forming wide glossy carpets that look especially well if they be threaded through also with the fine fronds of *Cystopteris montana*. *Maianthemum canadense* is our old friend multiplied in all its parts by two or three, with the same needs and habits and values.

Malvastrum, a race now often included under *Sphaeralcea*, contains one good thing for the rock-garden in *M. coccineum* (*Cristaria*). This is an almost prostrate little Mallow (seed or cuttings), its shoots clothed in fine bluish-grey, much-divided leaves (as has also *M. campanulatum* with clustered heads of large gay saucers through the season), and producing from their axils throughout late summer stalked Mallow-flowers of the most intense scarlet. This is to be recommended only for very warm well-drained banks in very light and pebbly soil of peat and much sand. *M. elatum* is a tall version of this, and no other is of much use or beauty. (Southern States.)

Mandrágŏra.—Those who yearn for the strange may grow this dingy innocent plant of awful reputation in any cool deep warm place in bed or border, at such a distance from the house, though, that you may sleep undisturbed at night by the screaming of its roots, supposing a cat should take a fancy to dig it up. *M. officinarum* has greenish yellow flowers in spring, but there is another, *M. autumnalis*, which blooms at the later end of the year and has purple ones.

Margyricarpus setosus (with other species) is a little weakly bush of 9 or 10 inches, with very finely-divided greyish leaves, and insignificant flowers that are followed in later summer by large berries of waxy white. It will grow in open sunny loam, and may be struck from cuttings. From South America, and, being evergreen, specially suited to flop over a sunny rock, upon which also its pearl-berries take their fullest value.

Marrubium.—No one wants to grow the common Horehound, but this is often sent out under the name of *M. sericeum* (*M. supinum*), a dwarf decumbent mass from Spain, for a sunny shelf, all clad in white silk, with whorls of small lilac Labiate flowers in late summer. This can be as much as 2 feet high in the mass ; much neater is *M. libanoticum*, of a bare 10 inches or so, equally silky-white, with flesh-pink flowers ; and there are various other species, but none of special charm or value.

Marsdenia erecta.—A Levantine of 2 feet recalling the Dog's Banes (*Vincetoxicum*), and thus not ardently to be ensued.

Marshallia caespitosa.—A rather tender small trailing Composite from the Rockies, with oval leaves and flowers of bluish pink.

Matthiola, a race of wild stocks to which belongs our own lovely *M. incana*, that makes such huge grey bushes in the Southern cliffs of the Isle of Wight, and, on its way to being the Garden Stock, bears profuse spires of warm carmine through winter far on into the summer, so as hardly ever to be out of flower ; and will do as much from a warm dry crevice of the large rock-garden, but is far too big for the small. Ill-suited also is *M. sinuata*, but a different tale may be told of the smaller members of the family that have exactly the uses, needs, habit, and character of *Erysimum*, but bloom later, as a rule, offering full joy of their display in summer.

M. fenestralis is an erect sturdy thing from Crete, beginning with one stiff stout stem of 6 inches or 9 in height, with broadish grey leaves that twiddle and quirl and quirk themselves this way and that upon it, till the whole mass has the oddest crumpled effect ; at the top of this appear the loose spikes of brilliant carmine-crimson flowers. *M. fenestralis* is perfectly hardy in warm well-drained places, but, from the look of it, no less than from the fact that it comes from Crete, admirers will be well advised to collect its seed after flowering, lest the parent vanish.

Similar 8-inch wild Stocklings with flowers of rust-colour, lavender-grey, mauve and brown, often intensely fragrant, are *MM. montana, odoratissima, oyensis, tristis*, and *thessala* ; it is quite probable that many of these names, however, and the geographical names more especially, are reducible to that most wide and variant species, *M. varia* (*Cheiranthus varius*), which already contains, as varieties confessed, two of the best plants of all, but is itself only found typically true in Spain and in Greece, the easterly and westerly extremities of its range. It is never a really common species, but occurs in stony sunny places, which it occupies with underground runners that throw up fresh tufts here and there, and will root from the smallest fragment in the garden. *M. v. pedemontana* is the first and the more precious of the named varieties. This forms a small neat tuffet of the customary leaves, long and narrow and softly hoary-grey ; and then in summer, and up all over the tuft, from July onwards, abundance of loose 6- or 8-inch spires of blossoms which are as large as those of the type, but of a rich rosy-purple more brilliant, though no more attractive, than the wistfully appealing lavender and phillimot tones worn by the other smaller Matthiolas, as by so many other plants that do not love the garish day, but mean only to exhale their full sweetness into the quiet evening air, for the benefit of such fly-by-nights as share these views, and on whom, accordingly, bright colours would be love's labour lost, seeing that all Matthiolas will share the common greyness of all cats by night.

M. vallesiaca is a rarer and less attractive variety than the last, of *M. varia.* For the stems are fewer, more stiffly erect, and often as

471

much as a foot high, densely leafy at the base ; while the flowers are smaller than in the others, of a sad violet, tinging towards a mauve exceedingly subtle and modern. This sadness may be seen on the Simplon Road, about Binn, in the Cogne Valley, as well as round Susa and Termignon, to north and south of the Mont Cenis.

Mattia (sometimes **Cynoglossum** and sometimes **Rindera**).— A valuable but hardly ever seen group of Borragineae, precious, like so many of their family, for hot dry places in hot dry soil, where they will rejoice the garden more or less perennially with bloom in later summer ; and may anyhow be kept re-stocked from seed.

M. caespitosa makes a close and silvered tuft, high in the Alps of Armenia, as on Aslandagh at some 9000 to 10,000 feet. Then, from the cushion of narrow foliage, start the unbranched stems of a few inches, breaking in loose showers of starry blossom, pink and blue.

M. graeca, from the highest rocks of all the Greek mountains, is just as silver-silky, but the stems attain 6 inches or so, and the flowers (ampler in outline and not so starry) are of rich purple.

M. Schlumbergei is perhaps the finest, where all are brilliant promises. It is, however, of the most grievous rarity, based on hardly more than the one specimen collected on the upper alps of Lebanon in 1872. It is a close tuffet as before, but the leaves are much broader, oblong-spoon-shaped, while the flowers are carried in a loose shower on stems of 4 inches—brilliant purple bugles, opening into five wide deep lobes. *M. Bungei* is yet another of these tufts, from North-East Persia, with shallow-lobed blooms of red, and far protruded style ; in the granites of Turkestan lives *M. cyclodonta* (*Rindera*), hairless, and 6 inches in the stem.

M. umbellata, however, strikes out a line completely new. For this, from its tufts of abundant big long leaves, narrow and pointed and clad (like all the plant) in silky-greyness, sends up a number of tall leafy stems, 18 inches or 2 feet high, each of which bears a wide branching head of many blossom-sprays curling outwards at the tips, and loaded with brown-crimson flowers in calyces of white wool. This it does from May to June, and is a plant of Southern Hungary, asking for a dry hot place with plenty of stone, and that (for a natural preference) non-calcareous.

Mazus.—A race of small prostrate or quite low-growing Scrophulariads standing very close indeed to Mimulus, about some of which there has lately been some rather unnecessary confusion. All the species are tolerably hardy and easy of cultivation in a moist, warm, and sheltered place, not parched by the sun ; all can be raised from seed, but even more copiously multiplied by division, in the case of the perennial species, if the winter be feared or an increase of stock be desired. The species all flower through the summer, and the usual effect is then like large rather pointy blossoms of lavender-and-gold Linarias lying scattered on flat carpets of verdure.

M. dentatus is the largest-flowered of the group. At the base of each stem it has some three or four leaves (sometimes less), and these are rounded and pointed, heart-lobed at the base, rather oval and irregularly toothed and waved. The flowers are nearly an inch across, distant from each other, and either smooth or sparingly hairy. This plant *is a perennial* and throws out *no runners*, and comes from Sikkim.

M. pumilio is a species from both Islands of New Zealand. It sends up short leafy branches, and the stems carry from one to six blossoms of lilac-violet, or blue and white, or whitish, of which the lobes are notably narrow and pointed, so as to make the flowers look specially starry on their footstalks that spring free of the leafage. The plant is *perennial*, forming a *dense running carpet* of clear green foliage ; and it is, in any case, much smaller in its parts than the *annual M. rugosus* from India.

M. radicans (*Mimulus radicans*), has the metallic-purple leaves stalked and huddled and spread out, rather obovate, and more or less smooth at the edge, unless with a quite dim waving. The foot-stalks spring from the ends of the shoots, carrying from one to three large white flowers, of which the lower lip is the largest part, and has a yellow centre and a violet blotch. This is a *perennial,* throwing out *rooting runners*, from the mountain marshes in both Islands of New Zealand, and very handsome in the level damp stretches of the sheltered garden, with the delicate gaiety of its flowers in fine contrast with the sombre tone of the dense carpet on which they are scattered.

M. rugosus, Lour., about which obscurity has raged, is confined entirely to India and Asia. It is a *smooth hairless plant* (as a rule), or *very* sparingly hairy ; it throws up numerous flowering stems from round its neck, and these carry several blue flowers of some quarter of an inch or half an inch long. The basal leaves are stalked, obovate-spoon-shaped and scallop-edged ; as you see the plant, a single tuft, or clump of tufts, with flower-stems springing round the central axis, so it stays and does no more. For it throws out *no runners*, and is *an annual*.

M. surculosus, Don., stands very near to *M. rugosus*, but the leaves at the base are often almost cut and feathered into lobes. This plant *is a perennial* (probably), *and throws out runners*. (From rather lower elevations than the last, in the mountains of Khunawar and Bhotan.)

Meconopsis.*—The best thing for all parties concerned will be to give a compendium of all the twenty-eight possible species at present on record, almost all of which are ardently to be desired, and most especially cosseted when caught. Many different species will develop many differences of taste and temper ; meanwhile, for the more difficult ones, the bed should be made in a sheltered place in a bay of shrubs, and after the prescriptions laid down at the beginning of Gentiana ; but it should have a soil-depth of at least 2 feet. The drainage-depth below should be another 15 inches, the water-pipe should be about 2 feet below the surface, and the soil should consist of two-thirds very coarse grit, and the rest a half-and-half mixture of peat and leaf-mould, plenty of rough sandstone being also dug in. They should share their ground happily with the more nervous Columbines, and will admit of much smaller beautiful fry in the way of the newest and rarest Asiatic Primulas, to say nothing of ground-fry, such as *Linnaea* and *Mitchella*.

M. aculeata can be perennial or biennial or monocarpic. But, whatever its powers of endurance may be, its powers of beauty take the breath. It stands about a foot or 16 inches high at the most, and the whole plant is of blue-grey tone, horrid everywhere with bristling hairs and spininesses. The leaves are irregularly feathered into notably *deep rounded or pointed lobes* (note this), and are on long footstalks, and bristle almost invariably on both sides. The flowers are borne on long footstalks, also, in a most graceful, loose spike ; and they are of noble size, *four-petalled,* of a crumpled pale-blue silk, filmed with a diaphanous iridescence of violet—against their golden spray of stamens a colour indescribable in its pure beauty, like a sky of dawn remembering very faintly the first touch of amethyst in which it died the night before. Nor do they seem to vary into worse tones with the copiousness of other blue Meconopsids. It is specifically quite close to *M. horridula* and *M. rudis,* wholly replacing the first in the North-western Himalaya. It differs from them in its leaves feathered *into deep lobes,* and from *M. sinuata* in its shorter pod. (See note to *M. sinuata.*) And *M. latifolia* beats it, both for beauty and constitution.

M. bella makes a different departure ; this is a neat small tuft of fine foliage, which, fine ferny foliage and all, precisely suggests a small tuft of *Papaver alpinum.* Even so are the flowers borne, each on a footstalk springing straight from the stock (which grows so old and large and stout in the cliff that the root must clearly be perennial). There are four petals to each, and the delicate blooms are of delicate lovely blue. The plant, however perennial, yet needs the most careful care ;

* For later information and the newer Meconopsids, see Appendix.

its home is at some 12,000 to 14,000 feet in the Eastern Himalaya, where, unlike its larger kindred, it grows only in the hardest crevices of the rock, and never in the loose soil of the slopes below.

M. cambrica.—The Welsh Poppy is a sad exile from all the rest of its family. Many thousand miles now lie dividing it from the nearest Meconopsis in Asia. However, it must have taken the step long since, and the sadness of separation has evidently been wiped out by having everything its own way here without any rivalry by relations, until late years. There is an enriched orange-coloured single form of this lemon-coloured weed, and a double yellow, and another double of a vermilion-orange, so intense as to be quite beautiful. Even the duplicity becomes bearable, and the plant is true from seed in a strangely large percentage of cases. Of the rock-garden, however, the Welsh Poppy is so appreciative that it very soon becomes a pest there. Its admission is almost tantamount to a confession of weakness on the gardener's part, or, at best, of a catholic charity so complete as to verge upon the maudlin. And yet, and yet—*M. cambrica* is always so charming!

M. chelidonifolia; a stately 4-foot perennial for peaty ground, very freely branching, and hanging out delicate egg-shaped buds that expand into flat four-petalled flowers of crimpled pale-yellow silk on stems as fine as wire, spraying from stems and branches that turn dark-brown and almost black. The foliage is tri-lobed, and the pods almost hairless. It grows easily, and may be divided in spring; blooms in July, and develops young plants from bulbils formed on the pegged-down stems.

M. crassifolia.—An American annual, about 10 inches high, and properly profuse with orange flowers, having a purple eye at the base of each petal. This, with *M. heterophylla,* may be sown broadcast in light soil in full sun.

M. Delavayi first appeared in public at the Chelsea Show of 1913. It is a most exquisite creature, though almost certainly only biennial or monocarpic. All its leaves are at the base, narrow, rather glaucous-green, and smooth on the upper surface, long-stalked and rather rhomboidal in outline. Up come the firm little stems of some 6 or 8 inches, almost wholly smooth, each carrying one large half-nodding flower of the most glorious shimmering imperial violet, with a central tassel of brilliant golden anthers. It sometimes has some *six or eight petals*, and more usually the fashionable four. This jewel is native to the stony turf in and out among scant small bushes at the foot of the limestone precipices in Yunnan, and up to the snowy passes of Likiang.

MECONOPSIS.

M. discigera grows in the high meadows of Western Sikkim. Its habit is that of a rather close spike about a foot high, with big weary-looking flowers in flushed unhealthy combinations of blue and crimson: and the leaves are specially numerous, in dense upstanding star-fishes of grey-green with glaucous-grey reverse, long-stalked, hairy, oblong and lobed, or coarsely toothed at the tips. As with *M. bella* and *M. quintuplinervia*, the abundance of dead leaves and stout old stocks gives hope of permanence for the plant.

M. grandis; a yard-high perennial, with a basal rosette of narrow oval leaves roughly toothed and downy like the whole growth. Similar leaves clothe the stems, almost forming into whorls as they go higher, and in these whorls the stem produces auxiliary buds. Finally, from the crowded leaves of the upmost whorl escape the several long bare flower-stems, each carrying a stately cup-shaped bloom of handsome size—about 4 or 5 inches across—and varying in colour from rich violet and clear-blue to duller slatier tones, as is too often the way of the blue Meconopsids (so that it is wisest to get seed from a pure colour among the monocarpics, and with a perennial to pick out your plant in blossom). It is a common beauty in the high meadows of Western Sikkim. Picture this as a big *blue*-flowered and *perennial* replica of *M. integrifolia.*

M. Henrici. See under *M. lancifolia.*

M. heterophylla is another annual of Pacific North America. It is nearly allied to *M. crassifolia*, but taller, more drawn out, and rather less free in the flowers, which are of scarlet-orange with a black blotch at the base of each petal, and a most delicious scent of Lily of the valley.

M. horridula stands very close to *M. aculeata*, but differs finally and absolutely from Aculeata, Racemosa, and all others of its cloudy group, by having no uprising trunk at all, but single ample blue flowers, almost pendulous, with some *five-eight petals*, borne *each by itself on a bare stalk of some 8 inches.* In other respects the habit is as in *M. aculeata*, but there is a most important difference, in that the leaves, instead of being feathered into lobes, are *nearly, if not quite, entire, in their rather narrow outline.* The number of petals, too, separates it from the invariably *four-petalled M. aculeata*, which it replaces in the highlands of Central Asia, Sikkim, and Tibet, being best taken in reality as a form of *M. racemosa*, in which the central stem does not develop. The character seems fluctuating and insecure.

M. integrifolia differs from *M. grandis* only in having yellow flowers and the leaves always perfectly *untoothed and uncut at the edge,* and very hairy underneath ; this glorious plant, with its huge lemon-pale globes, will therefore give us our best imagination of *M.*

grandis, much taller, with rather smaller violet-blue globes of the same build and poise. But *M. integrifolia* is, alas! not (like *M. grandis*) a perennial. However, it seeds freely in England, even without the aid of man—a plant amenable to any fair cultivation in deep rich soil, not parched. In nature it abounds most especially where the turf is thinnest on the upper meadows of Yunnan, Szechuan, and the Tibetan border ; luxuriating, for instance, in light stony soil, gripped in the bitter cold of the Mekong-Salwen Divide, in hollows of melted snow and ground that is as mere snow-bog at flowering time as the hollows of Mont Cenis when the buds of *Anemone Alpina* come pushing. There is a variety of this, too, *M. i. Souliei*, which may perhaps prove a separate species ; it is in all parts less hairy, smaller and more graceful (for the habit of *M. integrifolia* is rather stumpy, and its stalks too fat) while the petals are less broad. See Appendix.

M. lancifolia.—A lower-habited plant in the group of *M. Delavayi*, with tufts of very numerous radical leaves very much drawn out to a point at each end, hispidulous, and almost always wholly untoothed at the edge, about 3 to 6 inches long in all. The stem is some 8 inches high, bearing a loose pyramid of *four-petalled* ample flowers, nodding modestly in youth, and of a gorgeous satiny-violet with golden stamens. From the highlands of Central Asia—a most lovely but monocarpic species, to which it may be more convenient here to reduce two other Meconopsids that seem so closely related as not to be more than local forms. The first of these is *M. Henrici*, which stands to this very much as *M. horridula* to *M. racemosa*. That is to say, instead of a stem branching into a fountain of flowers, it has practically no stem at all, but each bloom seems to spring straight from the base on a stalk of its own. They are about twice the size of *M. lancifolia's*, but of the same intense and lucent violet, nearly 4 inches across, and built not of four but of some *six or eight widespread goodly petals*, distinctly clawed at the base. In conjunction with the larger flowers, it has much smaller foliage, only some 2 inches long or a little more, while the stems of the blossoms are about 6 inches. Occasionally there is a secondary bloom to a stem, thus suggesting more than ever the plant's relationship with *M. lancifolia ;* its degree of hairiness differs greatly, and sometimes it is even as horrid as *M. horridula* itself ; but the bristles are never hard or hostile. From the dry high lawns of Szechuan, and sometimes from between the rocks ; it has its name from Prince Henri d'Orléans, who collected it by Tatsienlu, and is indeed responsible for all the recent Asiatics attributed to " Henry." The second sub-species of *M. lancifolia* is *M. primulina*. This differs for the worse from its predecessors as far as the gardener is concerned, having smaller flowers of duller colour, carried as in the last, but one to a central scape, and with a few more on shorter lateral ones of some 4 or 5 inches. There is nothing primuline, as might have been hoped, in the colour of the diminished nodding flowers, which are of dim violet-purple. The essential quality of the plant, however, is that its stigma is bi-lobed, with two epaulette-like warts suggesting the rudiments of a disk. But between *M. Henrici* and *M. lancifolia* the habit (central-stemmed or with many solitary scapes from the base) fluctuates exactly as in *M. racemosa*.

M. napaulensis, D.C., 1824, cannot definitely be separated from *M. Wallichii*, except by the colour of its flowers, which are of sad and dusky purple. But, as every gardener knows to his cost, it is precisely to such dim and dusky purples that *M. Wallichii* itself too frequently varies, so that the conclusion must be that *M. napaulensis* is not a species that can definitely and soundly be separated, but had better return to the former status awarded it by Hooker in the *Bot. Mag.*, T. 6760, as *M. Wallichii fusco-purpurea*—a plant we need have no place for, then, in the garden : though all this group has its value in that their magnificent rosette of foliage lasts immortal through the winter. All other forms of this name are later and invalid, applying to *M. paniculata*, *q.v.*, while this *M. napaulensis* of the *Pflanzenreich* is now to be transferred to *M. robusta*.

M. Olivieri can only be distinguished by its capsule from *M. chelidonifolia*. For in the present species the stigma sits tight on the ripened pod, whereas in *M. chelidonifolia* the pod is more high-shouldered, and the stigma, after the usual fashion of the race, retains its position on a little column atop. Both species present a close resemblance to some glorified magnified version of the Great Celandine, though it is possible that the flowers of *M. Olivieri* may prove purple.

M. paniculata is also *M.* " *nepalensis*," as well as itself, in gardens and catalogues, besides often covering the true *M. robusta*, *q.v.* The confusion arose originally through the reduction, by Don, of some extreme forms of this plant, to the wholly different *M. napaulensis*, DC., *q.v.* It is a species of bitterly poisonous nature, and has the stature, needs and splendour of *M. Wallichii*, lacking, however, the long russet fur, and with the leaves not feathered into such picturesque deep lobes, but merely, as a rule, *rounded into a few bays*. As soon as it has sent up its towering spire of pendent *yellow* flowers in August (to match with the blue ones of *M. Wallichii*), the whole plant dies, and the seeding stem develops into a sere rocket-stick, wrapped about in the wisps of dead leaves. It inhabits Sikkim,

Garhwal, Bhotan, and Nepal, where its common name is Espoo swa'. It has a variety, *M. p. elata*, passing by many intermediates back into the type, but sufficiently distinct in its extremer forms, by the much less well-furnished spires of blossom, the flowers being borne usually on single pedicels in simple unbranched sprays, arranged in tight spires. It is this form that has especially bred trouble; for it was figured in *Flora and Sylva* (1905) as *M. "nipalensis,"* following Lemaire's *Ill. Hort.*, iii. (1856), through *M. nipalensis*, Hooker, fil., and Thomp., dating back to Wall., *Cat.* (1828). *M. "nepalensis"* of gardens accordingly has no real existence at all.

M. petiolata (DC.) = *Stylophorum diphyllum* (*q.v.*).

M. primulina. See under *M. lancifolia.*

M. pseudintegrifolia stands to *M. integrifolia* as does *M. simplicifolia* to *M. grandis.* That is, though identical in almost every other respect, it has no stout stem branching into two or three foot-stalks to its great sulphur-yellow globes, as in *M. integrifolia*; but the same *flowers spring straight from the stock*, each lonely on a stalk of 6 or 8 inches. This superb species, equal in flower to *M. integrifolia*, but so much dwarfer and more elegant in habit, is found in the high alpine turf about the source of the Mekong, &c.

M. punicea is well known by now, with its thick tufts of loose long oval-pointed hairy green leaves, and its abundant uprising single stems, at the top of each of which comes a single large flower of a royal crimson, so floppy and tired in texture that each blossom hangs on its stem like a blood-stained flag hoisted to its pole on a windless dull day in late autumn. This plant gives no problem of culture in the Meconopsis bed, but is, of course, monocarpic like all the rest (except where honourable exception is made, as for *M. bella* and *M. grandis*). See also Appendix for a better account.

M. quintuplinervia now hovers on the fringe of cultivation, and is most eagerly looked for, like the Maestro Jimson's Opera. For it is certain that despite its place in the group, *M. quintuplinervia* is going to prove the soundest perennial of the family; and so beautiful that the senses ache at the multitudinous loveliness of its myriad dancing lavender butterflies over the rolling upper Alps of the Da-Tung chain (Northern Kansu-Tibet). In fact, in well-bred exquisiteness of charm, it stands, in my eyes, supreme over its race. It forms a dense carpet of clumps, all clothed in stiff russet hairs, and with numbers of basal leaves, elliptic and acute, about 3 or 4 inches long. Above these spring up the bare foot-stalks of some 10 inches or a foot, each bearing a single nodding bell-shaped flower of pale purple, each with *four petals*. The number of these, the scantier tassel of stamens, the violet colouring, the hairier capsules, *and* the perennial habit—all help to differentiate it from *M. simplicifolia*. (See Appendix : by now the Harebell Poppy is well established in cultivation.)

M. racemosa stands to *M. horridula* as *M. integrifolia* to *M. pseudintegrifolia*, that is, with the same leaves (but almost entire and *not feathered deeply into lobes* as with *M. aculeata*), and similarly glaucous-grey and horrid with stiff yellowish bristles ; its flowers do not spring straight and lonely from the stock, but the plant throws up a definite spike, and this in turn throws off foot-stalks so long that the spike becomes a loose elongated pyramid or rhomb of blossoms about 18 inches high, the flowers being large, in variable shades of rich blue or violet, with *never* less than five petals, but almost invariably with six. The blossoms open irregularly, and when the lower stems are expanding their blooms, the upper ones have long since elongated stiffly and stalwartly to carry each its erect short-haired swollen pods. This species, a delight of Szechuan and Eastern Tibet, is more conveniently reduced to a local development, with *M. rudis*, of *M. horridula* (see the note under *M. sinuata*), from which it only differs in forming an emergent stem for its flower-stalks to spring from, instead of letting them rise straight from the stock. That is, the stock in *M. racemosa* behaves like a telescope, and elongates above ground ; in the type it is a telescope compressed, and the stems have to spring, as it were, from its outside rim. The plant, however, passing under this name in gardens, is often *M. sinuata ;* true *M. racemosa* will be known by its petals never being *less than five and usually more ;* in this bristled group only *M. aculeata* and *M. sinuata* have four petals ; the plate of Graf Silva Tarouca's book, for instance, refers rather to *M. sinuata* than to *M. racemosa*. It is probable, though, that the plant from near Chebson Abbey, on which Maximowicz based his *M. racemosa*, was the species now known as *M. Prattii* which there exclusively abounds, true *racemosa* occurring (with its form *M. horridula*), only in the Alps south-west of Si-ning. The whole question is obscure.

M. robusta.—This is a fine giant, figured in *Flora and Sylva* as *M. paniculata*, a species which it replaces in the high alps of Garhwal and Kumaon, and from which it finally differs in lacking the stellar hairs, and also in having its leaves very deeply lobed after the fashion of *M. napaulensis* and *M. Wallichii*, which they closely resemble, but have only a few scanty hairs, long and soft and spreading. It is, of course, the *M. " paniculata "* of catalogues, thus leaving the true *M. paniculata* free to bear the false name of " *nepalensis* " in those fallacious pages. Between the two, however, there is little for the gardener to choose, both having ample and stalwart spires of yellow flowers,

PLATE 47.

MECONOPSIS GRANDIS.
(Photo. R.B.G., Edinburgh.)

MECONOPSIS DELAVAYI.
(Photo. R.B.G., Edinburgh.)

PLATE 48.

MECONOPSIS HETEROPHYLLA.

MECONOPSIS HENRICI.

Vol. I.

PLATE 49.

MECONOPSIS QUINTUPLINERVIA.
(Photo. W. Purdom.)

VOL. I.

MECONOPSIS PRATTII.
(Photo. W. Purdom.)

PLATE 50.

MECONOPSIS RUDIS.

Vol. I.   MECONOPSIS RACEMOSA HORRIDULA.
(Photo. W. Purdom.)

and both dying after they have produced them. Even this plant has been *M. nipalensis*, Hooker, fil. (in *Bot. Mag.*, T. 5585), as well as the *M. paniculata* of *Flora and Sylva*. By any name it may smell as little ; but there seems no reason why it should not wear the right one.

M. rudis (*M. racemosa*, Franchet, 1886 ; *sinuata Prattii*, Prain.)— This, like *M. racemosa*, must be shut into the fold of *M. horridula*. It replaces this last in Yunnan and Szechuan, and differs first of all from *MM. sinuata* and *aculeata* in having its pointed green leaves beset with straw-coloured bristles. These leaves soon wither away at the base of the plant ; their under surface is pale, and at their edge they are *almost entire, instead of being feathered* into deep lobes. Up rises from the rosette a fat cylindric stalk, of 18 inches or more, leafy two-thirds of the way up and then bare, and breaking into a loose spire of smooth clear-blue flowers, with a generous fluff of golden anthers at their heart, and built of some five to eight petals. Its much longer style separates *M. rudis* from *M. horridula*, and its rich yellow anthers from *M. Prattii*. See Appendix for *M. Prattii*.

M. simplicifolia is to *M. grandis* as *M. horridula* to *M. racemosa*. That is to say, that here again there *is no stalk and no spike*, but the large (but rather smaller) purple or blue blossoms spring straight from the neck of the stock, each on their own stems of about a foot high (though sometimes twice as much in fruit) and three or four in number. The plant, apart from the colour of the flowers, has a general resemblance to *M. pseudintegrifolia*, but wears the big *Cambrica-like capsule* of *M. grandis*. And *M. simplicifolia Baileyi* is quite the most gorgeous of the single-bloomed Meconopsids, with big flowers of dazzling azure.

M. sinuata replaces *M. horridula* in the Eastern Himalaya. It differs from *M. aculeata*, of which it is a very close relative, in nothing but in having its leaves *irregularly and much less deeply lobed*, and also a *narrowly obconical capsule* instead of a nearly round one. Otherwise, stature, spike, four-petalled flowers, coerulean tone of crumpled silk, all are the same, as are also the needs and the character. And here, in a clouded and complicated group of Meconopsids, where all the species are armed with stiff bristles, it may help the seekers after clear thought if I recapitulate. There are probably *only two main species* or aggregates instead of five : (*a*) *M. aculeata*, loose-spiked, with *leaves feathered into very deep lobes* on either side, and four-petalled flowers and a nearly *round capsule ;* with a sub-species, *M. sinuata*, whose leaves are not nearly so deeply lobed, but rather *merely waved into bays*, with the same four-petalled flowers and a *narrow obconical capsule ;* (*b*) *M. racemosa*, with *many-petalled* flowers and *no stems at all*, but the blossoms springing each on its long foot-stalk from the base, and the leaves narrow and *almost entirely uncut or toothed at the edge*; with other sub-species :—*M. horridula*, a fluctuating development with only solitary basal scapes developed instead of a central stem, a condition not found in the other two Meconopsids of this kinship ; *M. rudis* and *M. Prattii*, differentiated at a glance by the rich yellow anthers of the former and the cream-white ones of the latter. As for *M. sinuata* "*latifolia*" of catalogues, this proves in reality a quite distinct and very magnificent true species, *M. latifolia;* for which see Appendix. The whole group is still obscure.

M. Souliei. See *M. integrifolia.*

M. superba.—This poor thing, again, was *M. "nepalensis"* of *Flora and Sylva,* iii., whereas it really deserves a name of its own, and this particular name too, being a most stately species of 2 yards high, in the line of *M. Wallichii,* and clothed all over in a dense soft coat of grey down, as well as a vesture of soft spreading hairs. It is in all respects like *M. paniculata,* but is taller and larger in every part, and has much larger flowers too, which break away from the family traditions in being *pure white* instead of yellow, while the leaves would also serve to differentiate it from the rest, for they are only lobed into bays with definite teeth at the edge. It is on the high alpine meadows of Bhotan that it makes its superb spouting spire of snowy blossom.

M. torquata differs in little from *M. discigera,* except in having closer-set spikes of flowers, and these upheld on shorter foot-stalks. This spike is some 12 inches high, dense with blooms in shades of pale scarlet. The foliage in this curious group is much the same as that of *M. grandis* on a smaller scale, while their inflorescence is rather that of *M. aculeata,* but more crowded and compressed, so as to make a spike and not a spray, not loose and tall and stately as in the group of *M. Wallichii,* but sturdy and close-set and impressive. Add to this, that the remains of much old foliage about the thickened root-stocks gives good hope that these Meconopsids may prove sound perennials when they have at last been introduced from the heights of Western Sikkim and Southern Tibet and the Alps that look down on Lhasa the Holy.

M. Wallichii closes the list—a plant superb among the best, whether you have its noble rosettes of feather-lobed leaves all russet in their tawny fur, and nursing glistering globules of rain on an autumn morning ; or, in July next year, a forest of its gracious 4-foot spires of ample blossom in the clearest dawn-tones of azure. At least, if you be lucky; if you are not, *M. Wallichii* has the horrible habit of varying from seed into a hundred dismal and dirt-coloured tones of slate or claret, till many are the hapless gardeners who look at the plant they have cosseted so long, and say piteously that it never can be *Wallichii* after all. Yet it is—or rather, that terrible disappointment, *M. napaulensis* (of the *Pflanzenreich* : really *M. Wallichii fusco-purpurea*, Hooker, fil.). But no disappointments will cure the courageous of continuing to raise *M. Wallichii*, and planting it out in the damp rich ground where this and the others of the Robusta group so richly thrive and flourish for their too brief span of splendour.

The hand of the hybridist should fall of course upon Meconopsis ; so far, however, one hybrid only has to be recorded. This is a plant raised in Ireland, between *M. sinuata "latifolia"* and *M. grandis*. Unfortunately, though the plant inherited the perennial habit of *M. grandis*, the colour got mixed between the two blue-flowering species, or perhaps an inferior form was used, for the result was no improvement on *M. grandis*.

Medeola virginica is a Liliaceous plant whose sole merit is that its root smells of Cucumber, while its flowers and growth imitate an Asparagus. Such a lack of originality is not to be encouraged.

Megacarpaea, a race of rare Crucifers, with very large arching feathered foliage, and thickish spikes of reddish purple or yellowish flowers in the early year. Of *M. armena* it is said by some that it comes from the Himalaya, which must surely be a libel ; but in any case it has a creeping stock and fat basal leaves, and produces the flowers of its kind on the rims of the glaciers. And from Kumaon comes *M. polyandra*, with white blossoms, a plant of the easiest culture, and with magnificent foliage suggesting rare and refined leaves of an Artichoke, but not always duly generous in the matter of its blossoms in spring.

Melandryum is a name now embracing many good friends in the house of *Silene*, all of them but one of little worth, but that one of more worth than all the Silenes ever seen. We need not linger over our common *Lychnis vespertina* and *L. dioica*, both of which offer themselves for the garden in double forms under the name of *Melandryum* (though the double *Melandryum album* is a handsome plant and rare in gardens, because not easy of propagation). Then there are Arctic and Himalayan species of a singular worthlessness, *M. apetalum (Wahlbergella)*, and the almost equally petalless *M. nigrescens*. But next comes a rare and beautiful thing in *M. dicline*, from the lower limestone slopes of Valentia, but even there uncommon—a bright-green hairy, many-stemmed plant of some 3 to 6 inches, with spoon-shaped basal leaves on long stems, and flowers solitary at the end of the flopping shoots, or in sprays at the tops of twin-branched divergencies. They are large and pink, with the lobes of the corolla bi-lobed ; and the plant indulges in both sexes on the same tuft, with the usual result that here again the females have the advantage in mere size and show. And finally comes the Queen of the family :—

M. Elizabethae.—Dead long since is the Archduke Rainer of Austria, and long since dead the Archduchess Elizabeth his wife ; yet most worthily do they both live on, the one in pink and the other in blue, by means of the two most permanent and illustrious inhabitants of his province of Venetia. High upon the limestone cliffs lives *Campanula Raineri,* and high upon other limestone cliffs *Melandryum Elizabethae,* a jewel to be long sought afar, and sometimes seen nestling upon the cooler side of limestone ranges in among the stones and moss of the track-side amid little Tofieldias and *Ranunculus bilobus,* or sometimes seeding down into the shingles of the becks, and there occurring in a profusion unknown above, where its tufts of narrow glossy foliage sit here and there among the stones and scantier grasses, but need a practised eye to spy them out—here a one and there a one, but never a mass or colony. Not difficult, though, is it to tell them in late July, when forth from under each rosette stray the stems of downy claret-coloured velvet, wandering along the ground for a few inches and then rising up like the neck of a serpent, to unfold one or two of those enormous ragged flowers of flaming magenta-rose that look like some monstrous Godetia gone lost among the alpine herbage. But in the river beds are its roots best studied, for it makes fat and solid yellow rat-tails of a yard or so ; and, since it will readily root again in sand from almost the smallest fragment, it is more profitable to study and collect the thing at its best, than to quarry it from amid the limestone cliffs above, prising away the slabs in vain, and tearing wide the fissures, without ever seeming to near the end of the Melandryum's root. In cultivation this beautiful rare treasure, so much more tropical in the look than alpine, is of the easiest culture, in moraine, or in light rich soil, cool, full of stones and as deep as possible. It must never be forgotten that the plant is not a peat-lover, nor an inhabitant of hot shales, as has been in old days declared, but on the contrary a most local species of the Lombard limestones, where it always prefers the less sun-flogged aspects of the mountain. Get it, however, established in the garden, and it will give no trouble, but continue forming yearly, for some half a dozen seasons, more and more of its wide shining Dianthoid tufts of emerald-green ; and, in the meantime, if the gardener be provident, he will yearly save his seed and keep a stock in progress.

M. Zawadskyi is the correct name of *Silene Zawadskyi* (*q.v.*).

Melittis Melissophyllum, the Balm, is a really and rarely beautiful Labiate, uncommon in England, but by no means so in the foothills of the Southern Alps, where, however, it varies in forms, some of which are not worth the wear of looking at, by comparison with the best. In these the plant sends up a single stem, set with pairs of ample leaves, and then, near the top, few-flowered whorls of very large blossoms of the most vivid white and pink, with ample lip and showy helmet, the whole being like a sainted Dead-nettle of inordinate magnificence. In some ranges, *e.g.* the Dolomites, the prevalent form is pure-white. This can be raised from seed, or in due course divided, and succeeds excellently in any light cool loam, where it grows a foot high or less, and flowers in full summer.

Mentha.—The Mints are of no value, but *Menthella Requieni* is a microscopic jewel from Corsica, which you put in a cool, damp level place and then wholly forget about, but that you think the spot is covered with some minute and bright-green lichen ; till some day you tread that carpet, and are assaulted by the delicious pungency of mint. The plant needs no attention, for, if killed in a hard winter by chance, it will assuredly have sown itself ; the little violet mint-flowers appear in August, and the whole carpet has an air of some exceedingly wee Mazus, foreshadowing the same needs and treatment.

Menyanthes trifoliata, the Common Buckbean, is admirable for pervading shallow waters with its branches of handsome trefoil leaves, and then in early summer sends up its heads of open waxy pearly cups filled with white surf. In Sitka there lives another species (sometimes called *Villarsia*), *M. Crista-galli*, which has greater leaves, as it were those of Nymphaea, and spikes of fluffed cups as close as in Aponogeton. This will also want the same watery life as its common cousin.

Menziesia, however you may elect to pronounce it, means a race of little fir-foliaged heaths, from the tips of whose shoots proceed large bells of pink or mauve on delicate foot-stalks. One of the most celebrated is now lost to the name, in the person of the former *M. coerulea,* now become *Phyllodoke taxifolia,* though none the less still a precious treasure of the Sow of Atholl in Perthshire ; and, as the generic names vacillate in this group between *Phyllodoke, Bryanthus,* and *Menziesia,* this last shall here be made to cover a multitude of sins. All the species then in this kind are of fairly easy culture in peaty stony ground open to the sun and kept well watered ; their height is measured in inches, and their blossoming season is through the summer. Most delightful of all, perhaps, is the commonest, *M. empetriformis,* which may be seen as happy in gardens as in the stony places of the Rockies, forming neat bushes a foot across and 9 inches high, of fine shoots, ejecting showers of delicate rose-pink bells in summer. *M. Breweri*, close beside the lake-edges and by the cool snow-drips from overhanging banks in the Sierras of California, makes dense masses of small upright packed shoots like erect yew-twigs, ending in lovely clusters, round and close, of dainty rosy globules; while *M. Gmelini* in the wilds of Siberia and Kamchatka follows a different principle, and is like a prostrate Heath with the leaves of a thyme, with its sprays ending in loose showers of pink bells. As to the propagation of these last, the famous recipe for hare-cooking applies; for *M. empetriformis*, this may be multiplied by careful division in the later summer, if the plants be large enough.

Mertensia.—A good deal of confusion has at times prevailed among the members of this glorious race, almost all of which are choice delights, wanting well-drained ground, moist beneath; they flower, for the most part, in early summer, are generous in setting seed and in germinating. The family is entirely a mountaineering one, across the high ranges and polar fringes of the Old World and the New.

M. alpina has lent its name to many species that wrongly bear it. The true plant belongs to high altitudes in the Colorado Rockies; it is some 6 inches in stature or less, *almost hairless*, and *bluish-grey in tone*, with radical *leaves unstalked* and about an inch or two in length. All the leaves are oblong or almost paddle-shaped. The flowers are at first in a close head, but afterwards shake themselves free to show their wonderful beauty of brilliant soft azure-blue.

M. amoena is a variety of *M. Bakeri*, q.v.

M. Bakeri also belongs to the mountains of Colorado. It stands about half a foot or a foot high, the flowers are borne in crowded clusters, the stalks of the basal leaves are longer than the leaves themselves, and the whole plant is vested in fluffy fine down.

M. brachyloba stands very close to *M. lanceolata*, from which it differs chiefly in having broader lobes to the beautiful blue stars.

M. brevistyla grows some 4 to 8 inches high; it is all downy with short pressed hairs, and the blossoms are of a gorgeous deep blue, borne in loose sprays.

M. ciliata is none other than the species we often grow as *M. sibirica*. It has the quality of being as easy to grow as a Dandelion, of sowing itself about the garden, and of blooming all through the later summer. For these qualities, however, it has sold much of the charm that is the birthright of the race. For it is a leafy lavish blue-green mass of a couple of feet high or 18 inches, and though the flowers are borne in the uttermost profusion on the branches and shoots, so as to form a loose airy fountain, and though in themselves they are beautiful opalescent bugles of pink and blue, yet they are not large enough quite to redeem the leafiness of the plant, which accordingly has a lush rankness that banishes it from beds where *M. pulmonarioeides* would be an eagerly-pressed visitor. And see *M. Drummondii.*

M. coriacea (*M. perplexa*) has a stature not exceeding a foot, and the stems are set with crowded leathery leaves, and arise from tufts of the same, all smooth and with their blades longer than their stalks. The flowers are blue tubules and are borne in dense heads. There is also a more widespread variety, *M. c. dilatata.* (Alpine region of the Rockies.)

M. coronata has large roots that justify themselves by emitting large tufts of many large leaves, finely roughish on the upper surface ; amid these proceed stalwart shining stalks of some 14 inches, more or less, carrying loose open showers of ample blue blossoms.

M. cynoglossoeides is a depressed plant, with stems of some foot or 18 inches, that can only rise to a few flowers, broad in the tube.

M. davurica has passed into a noble and regretted memory, and not even in botany books can any gleam of its blue beauty be re-captured. It is one of the loveliest of all, bald below, but almost hoary with close-pressed down above, with the same coating on the upper side of the stalked basal leaves, which are usually smooth beneath. The flowers are borne almost in showers on stems of 9 inches or so— nodding lovelinesses of azure whose sprays ultimately elongate till they stand erect. It dwells in the sub-alpine fields of **Davuria** and **Baikal**, and once was known in English gardens too.

M. denticulata is smooth and blue-grey, with an almost unbranching stem.

M. Drummondii is a dwarf and very beautiful form of *M. ciliata,* redeeming all the faults of its parent by being itself an alpine treasure, neat and stunted and large-flowered, revealing its charms along the frozen coasts of Arctic seas. This too has borne the name of *M. alpina.*

M. echioeides is by now well known and dearly prized. It is *a green and softly-hairy plant,* with stems of 6 or 9 inches that continue unfolding their croziers of rich pure-sapphire flowers through the later summer, and may be relied on unfailingly to decorate and occupy any decent corner in deep rich soil not parched or burnt. It may be known in any case of doubt by the corolla-lobes, that are *erect and not reflexed ;* with the anthers, too, protruding. (High Himalaya.) It has nothing at all to do with *M. lanceolata,* sometimes sent out as if it were a synonym or variety.

M. elliptica comes from Kamchatka, and of this it may be said that it is a sturdy thing with a few hairs below, but bristlish higher up, and ample-stalked elliptic leaves drawn to a point at either end and smooth on the upper surface; the stems of blue blossoms stand stout and erect.

M. elongata belongs to the high places of Kashmir, but goes no higher than some 8000 feet, to match the 8 inches of its own stem. The plant is *clad in short, close-pressed hairs,* and the oblong basal leaves are 2 or 3 inches long, by an inch or so in breadth, and borne on long foot-stalks. The shower of blossom is handsomely furnished, and the flowers are tubes of deep china-blue of the most brilliant and delicate beauty. In the garden it thrives especially well with moisture; and pot plants, after flowering, often droop and deposit seeds in the bosom of a neighbour, where they promptly germinate.

M. foliosa is of deep dark-green, with thick ample foliage roughened at the edge, and the root-leaves often on stalks of twice their own length; up among these rise many stems of about a foot, carrying a crowded oval cluster-shower of blue. (Moister places of Wyoming, &c.)

M. kamtschatica is dwarf and barely erect, rough all over, with long-tubed flowers.

M. lanceolata (M. alpina, Gray) lives on the plains and open places of Colorado and Wyoming. It has narrow paddle-shaped leaves, with a very minute down on their upper surface; and *the whole growth, leaves and all, is rather fleshy, almost smooth, and glaucous-blue in tone.* The stems are either unbranched or spray into wide rocketing heads of lovely clear-blue flowers. No difficulty attends its culture except that of slugs, from which all valuable Mertensias have to be guarded as a young baby from a gorilla. It is often wrongly mixed up in lists with *M. elongata* from far away in India, and sent out misleadingly as *M. echioides lanceolata*—a preposterous attribution.

M. lateriflora is a lesser-flowered variety of *M. Bakeri, q.v.*

M. longistyla allows little more to be said of it than that the long styles do indeed protrude far out of the blue tube. And it is at least something to know that the name is justified.

M. maritĭma is our own Oyster-plant, found here and there in the seashore on the fringe, just out of reach of ordinary tides. None the less, and in spite of the elaborate pits of sea-sand that worshippers accordingly consider must be necessary for its salvation in the garden, it yet thrives much more happily and robustly in ordinary rich loam than ever it did in the sterile sands of the sea. At the same time, it is never a species of very long life, as an eye to its habit and way of living in nature will reveal; plants should be kept coming on from seed or cuttings if the garden wishes to continue enjoying its trails of foliage, luscious in tones of pure bloomy pale-blue, with lights of shimmering bronze and violet—the whole effect completed in summer by its heads and clusters of white-eyed blossom in melting tendernesses of china-blue and pink and turquoise and lilac.

M. moltkioeides takes us back again high upon Himachal to contemplate once more the beauties of *M. elongata*, of which this is a plagiarist but that the whole growth is much more softly hairy. And there is a superb variety of this haunting the heights of Kashmir at some 11,000 feet, *M. m. Thomsoni*, with flowers so ample as to be half an inch across, and of the usual softly celestial tone.

M. nivalis is in reality a high-alpine development of *M. paniculata*. It is found at great elevations in Utah, and the leaves are barely an inch long, with all the little tuft to match, except for the beauty of its porcelain flowers. It stands in fact to *M. paniculata* as does *M. Drummondii* to *M. ciliata* ; and, in its general effect, oscillates between *M. lanceolata* and *M. oblongifolia*.

M. oblongifolia has leaves of narrow oblong outline, and the whole clump *is fat and fleshy and bluish-grey and smooth*. The stems are about 6 inches high, carrying *close clusters* of lovely blue flowers, with their styles sticking out, and the little threads in their throat as long and broad as the anthers. Moist alpine slopes, from Montana to British Columbia, coming early into flower at home and in the garden.

M. ovata may be found in the sub-alpine rocks of Colorado. From tufts of broad egg-shaped leaves, minutely roughened above, it sends up a number of stems some 8 inches high, carrying heads of blossoms crowded upon their quite short foot-stalks.

M. paniculata is a big stout border-species, in the same line as *M. ciliata*.

M. papillosa needs little love. It is about a foot high, with roughly warted leaves curled over at the edge, and small tubular flowers.

M. pilosa is only some half a foot tall or less, hairy all over, and with erect stems that are usually undivided, but sometimes branch at the top to carry ample blue blossoms, whose lobe is as broad as their tube is long. It is found in Arctic America and the Kuriles, &c.

M. pratensis, from South Colorado and New Mexico, is a good deal more than a foot high, with thin-textured, pointed leaves of bright-green, and showers of pinky-blue blossoms each about two-thirds of an inch across. There is an albino of this (as, indeed, of all; for whether they have been seen or not, they assuredly exist in the "inexhaustible self-inexhausting Possible ").

M. primuloeides is one of the most beautiful and choice of all, and a special delight of the moraine, especially if watered from beneath.

MERTENSIA.

The clumped masses are only some 3 inches high, built of *oval-pointed roughish grey leaves* from which there arise in summer a number of fine 6-inch croziers that gradually uncurl large blossoms, golden-eyed, which range, according to age, through varying shades of pink and turquoise and sapphire to the most gorgeous velvety-violet, which is the prevailing note, being struck by the flowers about the third day after their opening. There is now news of a yet finer form of this lovely plant, *M. p. chitralensis*, with taller stature and larger bloom. And also we know of *M. p. Tanneri*, with leaves much narrower, and flowers of unvaried violet—all these being native to the highest Alps of the Western Himalaya, and in the garden of astonishing ease, readily to be multiplied by division or cuttings, and enjoying moraine.

M. pulmonarioeides is the old and glorious *M. virginica*, with its ample metallic foliage of bronze and blue and grey and violet in early spring, followed by its generous tall and spraying heads of ample flowers in tones of clear china-blue and pink and lavender and turquoise, waving and shining on the spreading handsome stems of half a yard or more in height. No difficulty at all lies in wait for the Virginian Cowslip ; let but good root-stocks be obtained, not cut and split up for propagation beyond any hope of recuperation, but large and hearty ; let these then be planted in deep and very rich open soil, well drained, but in a sheltered position, where that lovely leafage shall take no hurt at the heartless hand of spring ; and then for many years to come the Mertensia will yield you, undisturbed, an ever-increasing harvest of pleasure in its flowers and leaves alike.

M. racemosa is a weak high-alpine from India, almost hairless, and with feeble stems of some 3 to 8 inches at home. The basal leaves are stalked and very nearly round, and the stem-leaves too are almost all stalked. The flowers are borne in loose sprays, and are large and beautifully blue, the tube being twice the length of the calyx, and the face of the flower not far short of an inch across.

M. rivularis is an inferior *L. pilosa*, with heart-lobed leaves and shorter calyx-lobes.

M. serrulata, from Baikal, stands too close to *M. sibirica* to have any separate value.

M. sibirica. See *M. ciliata.*

M. simplicissima is simply *M. maritima* arisen from its bed of sand, and standing bolt upright without any branches.

M. stylosa has leaves more definitely opposite each other than in *M. longistyla*, and the spike of blossom breaks into two divergent branches.

MICHAUXIA.

M. tibetica shrinks before the blasts and snows of the Karakorum, at some 14,000 to 16,000 feet. It is a little species, 2 or 3 inches high, with quite minute stalked leaves almost all at the base, and roughish ; the clumps then send up stems of 2 or 3 inches that unfold into sprays of funnel-shaped flowers.

M. Tweedyi is only about half a foot in stem at the most, and the stems are rather weak at their base, emerging from a loose tuft of oblong elliptic leaves, dark-green and microscopically rough with warts on the upper surface, carried each on a long fine foot-stalk; the blossoms are borne in delicate wire-strung showers, and are of deep sapphire-blue. (From the high alps of Wyoming, &c.)

M. viridis comes also from the high alps of Wyoming, where amid the stones and screes its large woody stock goes plunging, and sends up weak flopping stems, a foot or 18 inches long, from tufts of bristlish and bright-green leaves, with flowers very much as in the last.

Michauxia.—These are gorgeous monocarpic Campanulads from the Levant, that hate excessive damp and should be cultivated in rich but very stony soil, with perfect drainage and plenty of limestone in a sunny place, sheltered from behind by shrubs, and for preference on a slope that will facilitate the departure of unnecessary water. They bloom in high summer of their second or third year, set abundant seed, and die.

M. campanuloeides, from the dry rocky places in the lower mountain region of Cappadocia, makes first a great rosette of hairy deep-lobed foliage outstretched upon the ground, and then in time sends up a stem of more than a yard high, gracefully branching towards the top, and along each branch hanging most delicately out a peal of white flowers like small Martagon lilies. The species figured in the *Bot. Mag.*, t. 3128, under this name is *M. laevigata*, from the hills of Armenia and Kurdistan, which differs in having broader leaves, a *smooth stem*, and flowers *carried in a spike*, not in an airy pyramid.

M. Tchihatchewii is worth the pains of pronouncing its name to procure, for it is a most noble species, wholly different from *M. campanuloeides*. It branches only at the very base, sending out a few stiff arms, but the central stem shoots starkly upward for a couple of yards or so, and this (and all the branches down below) blazes solidly out into one dense column of wide blue flowers, like an eight-lobed *Campanula pyramidalis* of far ampler stature and finer blossom, that has learned the trick of opening them all at once, packed into an unbroken yet not squashed or crowded mass along the stalwart upstanding spire, and no less stalwart branches far below, that curve stiffly outward and upward from the base.

MICROMERIA.

M. thyrsoidea is of more modest stature, hardly achieving more than half a yard, with a rosette of some three to six irregularly toothed leaves, oblong in outline, the whole plant being hoary with grey velvet. The stem is perfectly unbranched, and rises stiffly up for a foot or 18 inches, set closely all the way from the base with wide velvety bells of blossoms. (Hot cliffs and crevices of Cilicia.) And yet other species are *M. stenophylla* and *M. nuda*, but these have inferior blossom, and do not therefore so clamour for our notice.

Micromeria; a charming race of wee labiate bushlings from the South, of fine habit, aromatic sweetness, and daintily pretty pink blossoms. They stand so close between Thymus and Satureia that nowadays the whole family is swept into the fold of Satureia, and there will be found in more learned catalogues. Here, for the sake of those less learned, we retain the old distinction without prejudice. All the species can be multiplied by seed, division, or cuttings, and all appreciate the hottest aspect of the rock-work in warm light soil. They are very close to Thymus and Satureia, and when an idea is conceived of them as having most delicate stems of fine wire, upstanding wirily, and delicately set with small fine leaves, and sprinkled in late summer with lively little flowers, there is hardly need minutely to differentiate between the many species that have been invented. *M. juliana* is taller than most, but variable, a giant of 8 inches, with varieties of condensed alpine port ; and a species or sub-species quite near it is *M. myrtifolia*. These both have long loose spikes of pink. *M. cristata* has especially many stems of 1 to 3 inches, beset with purple flowerets ; so has the precipice-lover, *M. cremnophila*, from the sheer walls of Parnassus. *M. graeca* is downy and bears pink blossoms in clusters from the upper axils ; notably exquisite and intricate and tortuous is *M. microphylla*, of 3 or 4 inches, and usually rather flopping, pale in the flower ; *M. nummulariaefolia* is bright-green in the leaf and almost as decumbent as a creeping thyme, with uprising fine leafy stems of 2 or 3 inches, set with purple thyme-blossoms ; *M. libanotica* is silver-hoary and erect and unbranching, about 5 inches high, with pink flowers in sprays of a few ; *M. mollis* is conspicuously graceful and devious with intertwining hoary little erect shoots, and loose spires of blossom. *M. serpyllifolia* and *M. marifolia* are much alike, with upright elongated sprays of flower, and stems clothed in pressed fine hairs ; *M. congesta* belies its name by attaining 10 inches, and is hoary, with terminal flower-spikes of about an inch ; *M. Douglasii* is rampant and repent, and very sweet, and rather tender in raw climates ; *M. filiformis* and *M. Piperella* may both be seen in the rocks of the Mediterranean Alps, inimitably delicate bushes of 4 or 5 inches, dainty with little leaves on wiry little unbranched stems, each standing up distinct and by itself from the root-stock, and so making a notably graceful and lacy effect— *M. filiformis* having pale-pink flowers and being altogether like an erect version of *M. microphylla*, while charming *M. Piperella* is bright with blossoms of clearer rose. As for *M. pamphylica*, this is a plant of some 3 to 6 inches, with *M. Haussknechtii*, a little taller, from the limy crevices of the Persian Alps. The whole family has a brisk refined charm that is too often overlooked, dowdiness and coarse dullness being too universally postulated in Labiatae, with the result that a group like this has never yet come to its own, though nothing can well be prettier than the tufts of *M. Piperella*, for instance, sprouting in stiff little threadlike erect stems, from the hot boulders of San Dalmazzo de Tenda, supra-trichomanoid in fine elegance, even without the dainty grace of the bright thyme-flowers with which the aspiring stems conclude in summer and autumn.

Microulia is a small race of Borragineae, of which *M. sikkimensis* has lately come into cultivation, while *M. Benthami* is a very high-alpine from Parang, forming close tufts of leaves longer than the flower-spikes of 2 inches or so, that carry blossoms large and beautiful for so minute a plant.

Mimulus.—The Monkey-flowers, or Musks, are often coarse and rampant ; they may be trusted to make themselves at home—if not, indeed, excessively—and fill the summer with show. Among the best, however, are some of the garden hybrids now being raised from *M. alpinus*, which they exceed in size of blossom, but not in stature, making glossy mats of foliage which they decorate in early summer with stems of not more than 6 inches, deploying enormous flowers of crimson-velvet or salmon-scarlet, together with many other forms mottled and blotched, and splendid in a morbid and perverse flimsiness of pardlike spottings, rather suggestive of monstrous paper flowers in a pantomime, out of which are to issue toads or goblins. The pure-coloured forms are *M. Brilliant* and *M. Model ;* they are the most beautiful of all, rosy or vermilion, but should be looked after and propagated yearly lest they suddenly die out. Less beautiful by a great deal are the larger hybrids and species, and often too coarse for admittance even to the bog. On the other hand, some of them are low and useful, all seeding readily, and almost too readily to be multiplied by cuttings taken off at any time. The race often merges into **Mazus**, *q.v.*

M. alpinus is only about 4 inches high, with flowers of coppery-yellow.

MIMULUS.

M. Burnettii is more than twice as high, and brownish-red.

M. caespitosus, from California, is more in the line of the rock-garden, being neat in the tuft and with stems of some 4 inches, with flowers of brilliant yellow.

M. cardinalis and *M. glutinosus*, the first with scarlet dragons and the second with golden ones, are both too coarse and lush in the habit for the size of their blossoms, or for any use except in the wildest of wild or bog gardens, where *M. cupreus*, rank and flopping in growth, has unsurpassed value at the edge of a pond, for the protracted profusion of its copper-orange bloom, in size and in weakly stems like those of the wild Monkey-flower, but borne on denser masses.

M. Douglasii gives better hope still, being often only half an inch high, and never more than six. The flowers are maroon-red, with a yellow lip, erect lobes, and very long tubes. (California.)

M. Geyeri (*M. Jamesii*) and *M. Langsdorffii* are rather weak in the ascendent stems, with yellow flowers of ample size and effect. They are both spreading plants, as is also *M. glabratus var. Jamesii*, with rounded leaves that lack the longish foot-stalks of the other two.

M. Lewisii unfortunately attains a foot in height, or even a couple ; but has narrow snapdragons of fiery scarlet.

M. luteus.—The race will travel far before it beats, alike for convenience of habit and brilliancy of great yellow flimsy flower, our own half-native Monkey-wort, by now established in half the stream-beds and river-shingles of England. By the water's edge it vies with *M. cupreus* in producing a solid and sheeting mass of colour.

M. moschatus.—Nor need the common Musk be disdained ; it can, however, be trusted to look after itself, whether or no it lose its sweetness when the air is no longer desert for it to be wasted on.

M. nanus is a really beautiful species from the gravel hills of California—a sticky stout thing, with stems of half an inch perhaps, or as much as 4 inches, and then comfortable flowers of rose-purple half an inch across, and freaked with gold and dark violet. (*M. Tolmiaei*, Benth., Rydb.)

M. primuloeides and *M. alsinoeides* are miniatures, of which the former is a specially dainty charmer, making mats of stems not 2 inches high, with flowers of brilliant yellow. It is accustomed to grow in damp corners often submerged, and has provided itself with precautionary swollen life-bladders that detach themselves and float away and form new plants on the subsidence of the waters. In cultivation it should have a choice, level, cool corner, rather damp, and with a careful eye kept upon its moods.

M. radĭcans = Mazus radicans, q.v.

M. repens is a glabrous succulent little densely-creeping species, rare in the salt marshes of both Islands of New Zealand, with smooth oblong *toothless* leaves in pairs opposite to each other, emitting from their axils in succession single stems of half an inch or so, each carrying a single funnel-shaped blossom of white and lilac with a golden throat, in lovely contrast to the leaves on which they lie. It is a capital carpet for sheltered and moist levels.

M. ringens has square stems of 2 or 3 feet, embraced by oblong leaves, and bearing very large violet flowers of an inch and a half. (From the bogs of Manhattan, &c.) Closely similar to this is *M. alatus*, from the bogs of Kentucky, Connecticut, &c., only differing in that the leaves do not embrace the stems, but thin out to a leaf-stalk, continuing down it in a leafy flap or wing.

M. rubellus is some 2 to 8 inches high, with rather small pink blooms that greatly vary.

Mirabilis multiflora.—The many-flowered Jalap is a quite hardy species from the Rockies, making a lushy leafy bush about a foot high, and more across, filled, all through the summer, with trumpets of shining rosy-red. It should have a specially sunny place, however, in soil especially light and deep and well-drained.

Mitchella repens.—The Partridge-berry of Northern America is a neat charming Rubiad, well repaying the careful culture that it asks in a cool peaty stony place in shade (especially, in nature, of Conifers), where it will branch freely and run over the place, with dainty flat sprays of dark-green glossy evergreen leaves, small and oval and opposite each other in pairs, ejaculating pairs also of sweet little white flowers like long-tubed four-lobed jasmine-stars, from April to June. No less charming is the similar-habited *M. undulata* from the forests of Japan, with big boat-shaped bracts or cups cut into a few wide, deep, and sharp bays, from which issue the exaggeratedly long white tubes of the twinned flowers, opening at the end into four white lobes, fantastically fringed in white fluff. The flowers are followed in Mitchella by scarlet berries; but the plant then considers it has done enough for man, and the fruits, though possibly dear to the partridge, are savourless to human beings.

Mitella.—This is a woodland American family, like very small and dainty Tiarellas in the leaf and habit, and suited to the same culture in cool mossy corners of the garden. Their beauties are of the modest and evasive persuasion, the flowers being merely small greenish disks up a naked stem of some 6 to 10 inches in June; but closer inspection will show their extreme delicate loveliness, for each of the five points of the star is lacerated into the finest possible of stiff outstanding fringe-work, giving the flower the effect of a whirling little five-pointed catherine-wheel. Of such are *M. pentandra* and *M. nuda*; but *M. diphylla* has twin leaves dainty and scalloped, with 6-inch spikes of white; white, too, are the flowers of *M. violacea*, but on stems of some 18 inches—fifteen or twenty to the well-furnished spire; similar in height is *M. stauropetala*, but here the flowers are white with fringes often coming violet; while *M. Parryi* is altogether of more modest scale than these last—all of which may readily be divided, or raised from seed.

Modiola geranioeides, a frail 5-inch Malvad, with slender stems, divided leaves, and larger flowers of carmine cherry-colour through the later summer. It comes from North America, and should have a warm sunny place in light soil. (Seed.)

Moehringia, a queer race of rock-plants, dwarf and cloudy in effect, erupting into a profusion of four-petalled little white stars in summer. The commonest is *M. muscosa*, truly moss-like, and abundant in all the alpine woods; the Southern ranges yield more essentially saxatile species, and all may at pleasure be cultivated in the chinks of the rock-work, for preference on the cooler exposures. Besides *M. muscosa*, there are *M. ciliata* and *M. alpestris*; *M. sedoeides* (*dasyphylla*) hangs in masses from the grottoes of San Dalmazzo de Tenda; respectively smaller and taller are *M. glauca* and *M. diversifolia*; *M. glauco-virens* is a specially neat tiny tuft that shares the impenetrable precipices of *Daphne petraea*; and there are many other species, interesting and dainty, but quite without show: *MM. Grisebachii, Jankae, papulosa, pendula, polygonoeides, Ponae,* and *villosa*—not all of them easy to come by, but all equally admissible to chinks and corners, where they will behave like the small and fairy-like four-petalled Arenarias that they are.

Moltkia. See under **Lithospermum.**

Molucella spinosa is **Ballota spinosa,** a small rare nuisance of the Southern ranges, and tender and frightful and thorny.

Moricandia arvensis is an unrecommendable cruciferous weed, from the walls and fields of the South, tall and straggling, with glaucous foliage and purple flowers. There are other, but no better, species.

Morina, a race of valuable herbaceous plants, to be discovered in catalogues accordingly. Several species are in cultivation, and more are yet to come; all spring freely from seed, all thrive in deep light soil, all bloom in late summer, and all suggest a strangely handsome dead-nettle that has married a thistle—with a result of

PLATE 51.

VOL. I.   MICHAUXIA TCHIHATCHEWII.
(Photo. R. A. Malby.)

PLATE 52.

MORISIA MONANTHOS.
(Photo. R. A. Malby.)

glossy spiny foliage and tall spikes of labiate or acanthoid flowers in lively tones of pink, pink and white, or yellow.

Morisia monanthos (formerly *M. hypogaea*, but the older name takes precedence) is a most interesting little endemic Crucifer from Northern Corsica and Sardinia, where in sandy rocks and wastes at quite low elevations by the sea it makes wide tufts of brilliant and glossy-green foliage, suggesting an *Asplenium viride* with more pointed triangular leaflets; from which, nearly all the year, proceed almost stemless flowers of bright golden-yellow, each by itself on a stem of an inch or two. After flowering these reveal the curious idiosyncrasy of the plant, for they at once turn earthwards and bury their capsule underground, to incubate in earth. In cultivation *Morisia* grows easily and is quite hardy, but with an inclination to grow coarse and blowzy in good soil, developing its foliage until the effect of the continuous flowers is lost, and the whole clump takes on a vulgar parvenu look which is not belied by its tendency, in such circumstances, to show its spoiled sybarised temperament and swelled head, by sulking unexpectedly off in the damps of winter. To prevent all these misfortunes, therefore, alike to cultivator and cultivated, it is best to treat *Morisia* sternly, sticking it into barren moraine in the sun, where it will not, indeed, grow so large, but will keep much flatter and neater and more refined in the rosette, while the erupting golden flowers have thus the full value of their brilliance, and hardly ever cease wholly to appear from the beginning of October till the end of May, and sometimes longer. The plant will come from seed, but even more profusely and promptly from root-cuttings laid in sand. It was introduced to us by seed from the Botanical Garden of Turin, and has held its own over here ever since; originally quoted from the Bonifacio district, where it is comparatively poor, the treasure was for a time clean lost, and omitted from the local Floras, until its abundant centres of distribution were discovered about Cap Corse, Stello, Arponi, &c., in the Northern part of the island, where it abounds in the plebeian low-lying sands that it affects.

Mulgedium includes **Lactuca**, for the races are so closely allied as to be inseparably mixed. One of the most valuable is the smooth-leaved little *Lactuca perennis* of the Alps, where it may be found in dry hot places, sending up, from tufts of foliage rather like that of some large glaucous-grey Dandelion, a stem of a foot or two, branching into a loose head of pale china-blue Dandelions (in one very pretty form pure-white ones). This may be profusely raised from seed, and luxuriates perennially in a dry, hot, and worthless stony place. Closely similar is *L. tenerrima*, differing for the better in forming a thick bushy clump of many stems, quite bare, and daintily branching from the very base into looser sprays of blue. It extends from rocky and muddy places of the Southern and central Spanish mountains into Piedmont and the South of France. The true *Mulgediums* are plants of vast foliage and vast stature, most suitable for filling the wild garden (where they ramp amazingly), but far too large and invasive for the rock-garden. Among such—and all are very handsome, with great heads or spikes or showers of big blue-purple, porcelain, or lavender flowers in summer, on stems of architectural proportion above foliage that leaves the Acanthus humbled though horny—are *MM. alpinum*, *Plumieri* (quite succulent, hairless, and hollow), *giganteum*, *Bourgaei* (especially pretty and rather neat, not ramping, but sending up 3-foot stems, set loosely all up with lovely blossoms of soft pearly blue), *tataricum*, *macrophyllum* (*M. grande* of gardens). And, of *Lactuca*, *LL. adenophora*, *Morsii* (of enormous height as a rule, from rich ground in Massachusetts), *Steeli*, *pulchella*; of Indian species, *LL. graciliflora* (specially ample and beautiful), *rapunculiflora*, *decipiens*, *bracteata*, *hastata* (purple or dark red), *macrorrhiza* (very big, blue-purple), *Lessertiana* (almost the same but of neat 12-inch habit, freely branching), *pulchella* (of a foot or more, with violet flowers, from the Rockies), *macrantha* (magnificent in blossom, yet only about 2 feet high); all of these last being now to be included in Mulgedium, but even more to be desired than such as we possess, being evidently neater as a rule in their habit, but no less sumptuous in their flower. Some of our well-known species, such as *M. giganteum* (often wrongly sent out as the *smooth, succulent, and hollow-stemmed M. Plumieri*), are growers so dense and rank that in the garden they burn away all the herbage beneath, and nothing is left in winter but a sere black patch like the remains of a bonfire. Accordingly they are of the greatest value as cover for snowdrops, which come up in the bare ground and then are admirably dried off as the jungle develops—a hint which ought to be a pointer to the possible use of the big Mulgediums as nurses for rare and mimpish small Narcissi, such as *N. Bulbocodium monophyllus* and *N. viridiflorus*.

Muscäri.—The Grape-hyacinths need no commendation, and uncommonly little cultivation. Nor are they infrequent in catalogues. At the same time a brief note of their differences among themselves may help enthusiasts in knowing what they are trying to get, and whether they have got it. In the first place, *Muscari* may always be known from Hyacinth and Bellevalia by the constricted mouth that gives them their characteristic Rugby-football shape of flower; and after that (in botanical, not alphabetical, order):—

MUSCARI.

All in this following group have *oblong bells:*

M. racemosum has grooved rushlike leaves lying on the ground, and a dense egg-shaped spike; it has a variety *M. r. brachyanthum* which is *M. Szovitzianum,* Rupr., of catalogues, and stands apart in being shorter in the bell and different in the leaf, though with the same rounded capsule.

M. latifolium has one broad leaf embracing the 12-inch stem; the sterile flowers sit close to the spike and are tubular, while the fertile ones depend and are urn-shaped (*M. paradoxum,* Tchihat.).

M. pendulum stands near to *M. racemosum,* but the *pods are long and pendulous,* instead of being erect and round.

M. pulchellum differs from *M. racemosum* in having a long loose spike instead of a dense egg-shaped one; and the blossoms hang from longer pedicels on the stem, and their little turned-back teeth are larger, longer, and whiter. The leaves are threadlike and floppety.

M. neglectum is in all its parts a larger *M. racemosum,* with leaves that are not narrowly grooved, but with a *broad ample furrow.*

M. commutatum, again, is near *M. racemosum,* but has broader leaves, a shorter denser spike still, and no sterile flowers. Its bells are dark violet-blue, and the little teeth do not turn back much, and are the same colour as the rest of the flower.

M. mordoanum, from Corcyra, has longer and less open bells, with whitish teeth; and the bells are of bright amethyst.

M. Bourgaei is near *M. commutatum,* but both the leaves and the stem are much shorter, with the flowers on longer pedicels, in a looser spike. It is an alpine from beside the snows of Cadmus, &c.

M. polyanthum has much the same ample leafage of *M. commutatum* and *M. neglectum,* but the foot-stalks of the bells are longer, and the spike consequently looser, while the pod is conspicuously much smaller.

All in this following group have *rounded or oval bells:*

M. botryoeides has long thin very narrow grooved leaves, pointed at the tip, with a short oblong or cylindric spike of many flowers; these being violet-blue and *globular,* with *short whitish teeth* a little re-curved—the whole plant so familiar and well-beloved in all its forms as hardly to need this police-court description, unless to tell it from its cousins. The form Heavenly Blue is of a rare exquisiteness, and there are paler and far more lovely beauties yet, to say nothing of white forms and roseate forms, all rare and expensive.

M. Heldreichii is an alpine kinsman of the last, from the stony places and snowfields of Chelmos and Parnassus, differing in having larger flowers that do not hang, but stand out *horizontal from the spike*, and have much *broader* whitish teeth, *much more recurving*.

M. Aucheri is very near, but dwarfer, only 2 or 3 inches high, but with shorter leaves too, and hardly any foot-stalks, so that the balls sit tight in a dense round head.

M. pallens has quite thready leaves and is especially dwarf; with pendulous blooms of white or pale-blue in close heads.

M. parviflorum, from the Balearics, &c., has especial importance, and may be known at once. For it is the only one of the race to display its pale-blue bells in *autumn*.

The following group approaches *Bellevalia* in having the bells less pulled in at the mouth than usual:

M. pycnanthum is merely a *M. neglectum* with more gaping-lipped blossoms.

M. discolor has heads like a nut, of violet flowers, white-edged and almost bell-shaped at the mouth.

M. acutifolium has leaves of 5 inches long or so, narrowing to their base instead of embracing the stem; the flowers are intense violet, not urn-shaped, but deeply cloven, and with the teeth not recurving.

The above list will guide collectors among the best-known species. There remain other good kinds, of course, such as the vivid blue *M. atlanticum*, not to mention the monsters and livid towzle-spikes and the sad straw-yellows, all of which, as specialities, will be described in the lists that offer them; but they by no means compete in beauty with the ordinary Grape-hyacinths, nor are everywhere so to be relied on for permanence as the ordinary species, which cannot be outraged, but are lovely through the early year (*M. botryoeides* rises at dawn) in bed or grass or border, and intoxicating in the cool vinous sweetness of their dark and heady scent. Then, after flowering, they die down harmless long before their decadence runs any risk of being a nuisance. All increase freely and can be raised from seed like cress.

Myosotidium nobile is the county-flower of Cornwall, a most respectable plant that occupies the thoughts of the county to the exclusion of everything but Daffodil and tender Rhododendron.

M. nobile dwells in the far sands of the Chatham Islands, which have long since gladly abandoned it to Cornwall; it is like a vast and glossy gross Funkia in the corrugated bright-green foliage, with fat stalks of 2 feet high among it in May and June, opening bunches of blossoms suggesting those of some gigantic Forget-me-not that has not made up its mind what colour to be, so compromises on a velvety ring of blue, outside another of blurred white, the whole effect being strangely muddle-headed and indeterminate, by no means redeeming the plump little flowers from their look of stolidity, as well as meanness, in the midst of the tropical leafage from which their congregations feebly peer. It is a tender thing, too, and has to be cosseted with sand and seaweed. In other parts of England it will usually have to be taken indoors and cherished through the winter. In Cornwall you grow it in solid rows under the wall of the kitchen garden, like artichokes. You then measure the flowers with a piece of cotton and compare them with your neighbour's. And if his are larger, you throw away *Myosotidium*, and concentrate on *Embothrium* or any other exotic to which some quirk of climate, soil, or situation forbids him to aspire so successfully. At least, so say the envious and wicked.

Myosōtis.—The distribution of this family seems even odder than that of Gentian. For while overflowing freely into the Antarctic Alps, the Forget-me-nots do not seem to effect any lodgment in America; and even as Gentianeæ, in their New Zealand range have odd fantasies of colour. No Himalayan Gentian, for instance, is anything but blue; no New Zealander is ever blue at all (and never anything but white or pink). Similarly with Myosotis; no New Zealand Mouse-ear is ever anything but white or yellow. The race is a large one, prolific of annuals and worthlessnesses. Of such the following list shall take no note; the remaining kinds at their choicest only ask for light open places (or moraine) on the rock-work; and are of every degree in beauty, flowering in summer, and easily to be multiplied either by division or seed. The New Zealanders especially have long been clamouring for a fair trial. Some of the species have been lately set apart as a new race under the name of *Exarrhena*, but it seems more convenient from every point of view here to retain them all under the good old name of *Myosotis*. And see Appendix.

M. albo-sericea is about 6 inches high or less, clothed in bright silver-silk, with one or more naked flower-stems, expanding large ample stars of bright sulphur-yellow. It is very rare, unfortunately, in the South Island, above Otago.

M. alpestris has by now yielded so many varieties that its name is almost swamped. Such can always be found in catalogues, and the best of all is a most curious form or hybrid by the name of *Ruth Fischer*, tight and dwarf in growth, with specially large fat leafage, strangely crimped and curled upon itself; and then, in the second year, its full display of enormous soft-azure flowers on quite short and branching stems. Only by the utmost botanical niceties, if at all, can *M. pyren-*

aica and *M. olympica* be separated from *M. alpestris;* these occupy the high damp alps and stream-sides, the one on Olympus and the other in the Pyrenees ; just so does *M. alpestris* ascend the alps of Central Europe to the point at which it is succeeded by *M. rupicola,* which, with all its affinities, still deserves to retain specific rank, at least in the garden, and for the rock-work has value so great that it almost excludes even beautiful but taller *M. alpestris* from our realm.

M. amabilis is no less dense with white hair than *M. albo-sericea,* but its stems of 6 or 9 inches are weakly, and only rise up at the end to show a lengthening head of large white blossoms.

M. azorica has a sound habit, and a singular beauty of large flowers in the most intense rich violet-purple. Unfortunately it is not safely hardy, but should be raised annually from seed (though quite perennial), and put out in sunny and rather light soil. The garden plant, Impératrice Elisabeth, is a development of this.

M. Cheesemannii makes a hairy white tuft about 3 inches wide, with sweet-scented white flowers sitting solitary in the upper axils of the shoots. A very pretty neat dense little alpine from some 6000 feet up on Mount Pisa in the South Island.

M. concinna is also a New Zealander, but much larger, often over a foot in height, emitting from its clumps of silky foliage a number of stems either simple or forking, that unfurl lengthening sprays set closely with large fragrant flowers of yellow, or of white with a golden eye, deeply lobed, and short in the tube. From the limestone rocks of Mount Owen in the South Island.

M. decora is a white-flowering hoary tuffet with the anthers far protruding from the blossoms. Limestone rocks of Broken River Basin, South Island.

M. explanata is the plant that sweeps out of notice *MM. australis, Forsteri,* and *capitata.* For it is a far finer and neater species from the high passes of the South Island, about half a foot or a foot tall, all white with short and silky hairs, and specially profuse in its very large white blossoms.

M. Goyeni is a grey, magnified, and taller version of *M. albo-sericea,* with larger flowers to make up.

M. Hectori will be pictured under *M. pulvinaris.*

M. Hookeri makes wee cushions on the Roof of the World, like a tufted alpine Cerastium, and rejoices our eyes at last with a return to Forget-me-not blue. Its little stems branch again and again in the mass, densely clothed in whorled-looking leaves, venerable in long white hairs, and altogether having not at all an unsuccessful game of making believe to be the King of the Alps himself, with fur-clad foliage, and ample, generous sprays of big flowers, brilliantly blue, which, despite the branching of the stems, seem always to be sitting tight upon the tiny cushion, so close and small is the habit of the plant.

M. lithospermifolia has no merits that call for comment, any more than *M. caespitosa* or *M. sylvatica*, of which, however, the former has the charm of tight clumps, beset with azure stars. But have we not Abana and Pharpar of our own, rivers of Damascus, in the sufficing and swamping personality of *M. rupicola?*

M. macrantha has the same habit as *M. concinna*, but the lobes are shallow and the flower-tube long, while the whole plant is less silky. It justifies its name by being large-flowered indeed, and its wide-eyed stars of tawny orange have their mouths filled with the most delicious sweetness. It is a not uncommon sub-alpine species of the South Island, and there is a variety *M. m. pulchra* that is more diffuse and less bristly-haired.

M. palustris, the Water Forget-me-not of our ditches, would have a place in all our swamps were it not itself outswamped by its larger *semperflorens* form, which in its turn is pushed aside by its own various varieties—a very proper reward for its undutiful behaviour to its own parent-type. These are *Fairy's Eye* (*Nixenauge*), with particularly large blossoms; the terribly named *Graf Waldersee*, early and dark; and *stabiana*, the darkest blue of all. These with their parents are glories of the whole season, beside the pond or stream, especially admirable for helping Mimulus to hide the borders of the pool.

M. pulchra. See under *M. macrantha*.

M. pulvinaris, with *M. uniflora* and *M. Hectori*, has the high honour of bearing up the mantle of Eritrichium in the Alps of New Zealand, which they discreetly and reverently do by forming neat and woolly cushions, which they then make no attempt to decorate with the King's royal blue, but stud them instead with many pretty stars of yellow or white, sitting, unlike Eritrichium's, lonely over the tufts, as in Androsace, each at the end of a shoot of its own. Try moraine.

M. Rehsteineri has no certain claim to more than varietal rank. It is, in any case, a charmingly neat little smooth-leaved prostrate and creeping species, near *M. palustris*, but forming dainty carpets of very bright green foliage in level damp places, which it copiously bejewels with clear-blue stars in summer. In cultivation it should be looked to, and divided from time to time, lest the wide mat grow too big for itself and miff suddenly away in winter. It has its home by the shores of some Swiss lakes, but may also be seen from time to time in the Southern ranges, as amid the black and blasted rocks of Bobbio.

M. repens need not be bothered with.

MYRRHIACTIS.

M. rupicola is the Queen of all alpine Forget-me-nots, making tidy cushions over the upper alpine turf, hidden by domed and crowded heads of large flowers of the most exquisite dawn-blue. Nor does it ever even in cultivation show any relationship to *M. alpestris*, but preserves its own tight habit, and comes easily profusely and honourably identical from seed, though on the Alps, as it descends, the form begins often to fade into the taller fashions of the *M. alpestris* from which it no doubt derives, and which in turn derives from the common *M. sylvatica* down below. But what a pedigree of rapid advancement ; not the three Dudley generations, from the condemned scrivener to the Duke of Northumberland with a sham Sovereign in his pocket, could make such a boast, of ascent so high and rapid, from beginnings so base. In the garden *M. rupicola* delights especially in the moraine, and there loses a certain tendency to miff away in winter, from which it occasionally suffers in fatter ground. But it is no unfriend nor stranger to our climate ; its close patches of heaven may be seen nestling into the topmost crags in certain corries of Ben Lawers and Micklefell.

M. Traversii has leathery leaves in pleasant tufts, from which issue many much-branched stems of 3 inches or half a foot, each unfurling a bristly crozier, thickly-studded with large sweet-scented blossoms of lemon yellow, the whole growth being in many ways like a larger and looser development of *M. Cheesemannii*. It is common in the high screes of the South Island up to 6000 feet, and should rush into our moraines accordingly with open roots.

M. Welwitschii is not perennial and should be ignored, though vivid in the blue of its flowers and fairly modest in its 6-inch stature.

Myrrhiactis, a race of small alpine Composites, pre-eminent in worthlessness.

Myrtus offers us nothing legitimate for the garden (unless we include neat-leaved little *M. tarentina*), except the great beauty of *M. nummularia* from New Zealand, which is perfectly hardy, and covers any open peaty level with prostrate flat masses of neat-leaved shining shoots, and emitting in due course little white fluffs of flower, to be followed by scarlet berries, from which, no doubt, the plant could be raised anew, were not all Myrtles so generous about striking from cuttings.

END OF VOL. I.

Printed in Great Britain by
Thomas Nelson and Sons Ltd, Edinburgh